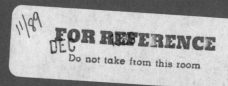

GREAT LIVES
FROM
HISTORY

GREAT LIVES FROM HISTORY

Renaissance to 1900 Series

Volume 2
Cra-Huy

Edited by
FRANK N. MAGILL

SALEM PRESS

Pasadena, California   Englewood Cliffs, New Jersey

Library of Congress Cataloging-in-Publication Data
Great lives from history. Renaissance to 1900 series /
edited by Frank N. Magill.
    p.   cm.
  Includes bibliographical references.
  Summary: This five-volume work examines the lives
of 495 individuals whose contributions greatly influenced the world's cultures that flourished from the Renaissance through 1900. An annotated bibliography accompanies each entry.
  1. Biography. 2. World history [1. Biography. 2. World
history.] I. Magill, Frank Northen, 1907-
CT104.G68   1989
920'.009'03—dc20
[B]
[920]   89-24039
ISBN 0-89356-551-2 (set)   CIP
ISBN 0-89356-553-9 (volume 2)   AC

LIST OF BIOGRAPHIES IN VOLUME TWO

LIST OF BIOGRAPHIES IN VOLUME TWO

GREAT LIVES
FROM
HISTORY

LUCAS CRANACH, THE ELDER
Lucas Müller

Born: 1472; Kronach, Upper Franconia
Died: October 16, 1553; Weimar, Saxony
Area of Achievement: Art
Contribution: Cranach established an individual decorative style of paintings, drawings, and prints during his fifty-year career at the court of Wittenberg. A personal friend of Martin Luther, Cranach was one of the first German artists to incorporate elements of early Reformation theology into his pictures. His numerous examples of mythological subjects and portraits can be related to Humanist scholars at the University of Wittenberg and to erudite tastes of the Saxon court.

Early Life

Lucas Cranach, the Elder, probably received his first training as an artist from his father, Hans Müller, in Kronach. Cranach later changed his name to reflect the town of his birth. Older accounts of Lucas' life suggest that he might have accompanied Frederick III, Elector of Saxony, on a trip to the Holy Land in 1493. He is mentioned in Kronach documents between 1495 and 1498 and in Coburg in 1501.

Between this time and 1504, Cranach settled in Vienna, where he produced a series of distinctively dramatic paintings and woodcuts. The most notable of the Vienna paintings include the double betrothal portraits of the university rector Johannes Cuspinian and his wife, Anna (1502-1503), a *Saint Jerome in Penitence* (1502), and an asymmetrically composed *Crucifixion* (1503). Along with woodcuts, such as the *Agony in the Garden* (1502), these works show Cranach's flair for exaggerated gestures, emotive facial expressions, and bold draftsmanship. His interest in placing his figures in the ambient space of primordial Alpine landscape settings credits him with being an early founder of the "Danube style" of landscape painting. Some compositional elements in these early works show that Cranach was familiar with the art of his famous Nürnberg contemporary, Albrecht Dürer. Cranach's works up to 1504, however, show a conscious decision on his part to reject the studied geometry and classic proportions of Dürer's figures. Instead, Cranach's pictures seem more spontaneous and free, rendered in an almost nervous drawing style.

Life's Work

Cranach may have joined the court at Wittenberg as early as 1504, but he was definitely in Frederick's employ in April, 1505, at which time he was paid for making decorations at the elector's castle in Lochau. Cranach worked, uninterruptedly, for the court until his death in 1553, serving three successive heads of the Saxon court: Frederick III, John the Steadfast, and John Frederick the Magnanimous. In 1508, Frederick held him in high enough regard to grant him a coat of arms of a winged serpent, a device Cranach used to sign his pictures throughout his life.

In the same year, Frederick entrusted him with a diplomatic mission to the Lowlands. Cranach's biographer and friend, Christoph Scheurl, related the attention Cranach received from Netherlandish artists with his lifelike portrait of the youthful Charles V (which he supposedly painted on an Antwerp tavern wall). Cranach's familiarity with Netherlandish art is documented in his monumental *Holy Kinship Altarpiece* of 1509, which is clearly derived from Quenten Massys' triptych, now in Brussels.

After his return from the Lowlands, Lucas settled into a prominent and extremely comfortable life in Wittenberg. His wife, Barbara Brengbier, bore him two sons, Hans and Lucas the Younger, and three daughters. He was so successful in his business affairs that in 1528 he was listed as the second wealthiest burgher in Wittenberg. He owned an apothecary (which has functioned to modern times in the town), a winery, several houses, and a publishing house. He served on the city council between 1519 and 1549, and he was elected to three consecutive terms as burgomaster, 1537-1543.

Cranach's busy life and the vast number of pictures he produced have led most historians to believe that he was aided by a large and well-ordered shop of assistants. Certainly his two sons were central to his production. Little is known of Hans, but two dated paintings of 1534 and 1537 by him survive, along with an interesting sketchbook in Hannover; he died in Italy in 1537. It seems clear that Lucas the Younger was the inheritor of his father's workshop, and he no doubt played an increasingly important part in the workshop, especially in Lucas the Elder's later years. The role of the Cranach shop makes definite attributions of individual works to Cranach himself difficult to establish, even when they are signed and dated.

The terms of his court appointment were apparently never written down, but his position did entitle him to a yearly stipend and to a rather pampered life; moreover, there were seemingly no restrictions on commissions he could accept from outside the court. Court documents show that his clothing and that of his assistants, feed for his horse, kitchen provisions, and various household services were all provided to him on request. Except for the trip to the Lowlands in 1508 and local visits to the elector's castle in Lochau and his hunting lodge in Torgau to supervise decorations, Cranach rarely traveled. He was extremely reluctant late in his career to follow the court of John Frederick and consequently was dismissed from service temporarily between 1547 and 1550. He ultimately did obey John Frederick's request to move to Augsburg in 1550 and subsequently to Weimar in 1552, where he died the following year.

Between 1505 and 1510, Cranach's style manifests an interest in solid, three-dimensional figures, including a series of drawings on tinted paper, two-color chiaroscuro woodcuts, and large-scale altarpieces, particularly the Saint Anne Altar. By 1515, however, Cranach's style shifted to emphasize silhouetted shapes, strongly patterned compositions, and images with flatter, less insistent volume. Excellent examples of this stylistic change are two nearly life-size, full-length marriage portraits of Duke Henry the Pious and his wife, Duchess Catherine, of 1514. Accompanied by their pet dogs, the figures are spotlighted against plain dark backgrounds and dressed in splendrous, colorful costumes. The jaunty attitude of the two and the decorous surfaces of the panels communicate a statement of class rank that is unmistakably present in any number of other court portraits, including that of John Frederick of 1532-1535. The finery and aloofness of his court portraits contrast with another class of portraits of wealthy burghers of Wittenberg (such as *Dr. Johannes Scheyring*, 1529), in which Lucas presents a more straightforward and even plain characterization of his sitters.

There is a clear change in Cranach's art from his Vienna days. The boldness and expressiveness of his early works give way to works designed to cater to the effete tastes of a court hungry for decorative surfaces, erotic subjects, rich colors, and elaborately designed brocades. As a component of his "court style," Cranach developed a distinctive type of female figure, more Gothic than Renaissance. In his early engravings of *The Judgment of Paris* of 1508 or his *Venus and Cupid* woodcut of 1509, his nudes followed the Vitruvian proportions of Jacopo de' Barbari and Dürer. Barbari had preceded Cranach at the Wittenberg court, and the two may have known each other. In these early works, Cranach's figures are full-bodied, with insistent three-dimensional modeling; they are faithful in spirit to the classical sources of Italian art. From the 1520's on, Cranach's nudes change dramatically from the geometric proportions and the volume influenced by Italian art. He preferred instead female nudes who are adolescentlike, with large abdomens, small buttocks, and tiny breasts. They are willowy and lithe but ungainly and self-conscious. They assume choreographed poses that conform totally to the decorative surface rhythms of his later pictures.

Among the many mythological subjects produced by his shop, three themes recur frequently: the judgment of Paris, the sleeping water nymph, and the Venus with Cupid. These subjects are preserved in a number of versions dating in the 1520's and 1530's. In the 1530 version of the *Judgment of Paris* in Karlsruhe, Cranach transforms the mythological narrative into a courtly event with Mercury and Paris dressed in contemporary armor. Similarly, Minerva, Venus, and Juno wear jewelry of the period and sport the latest coiffures. Their awkward poses and the coy expression of one of the graces, who brazenly looks out at the spectator, serve to heighten the eroticism of the scene.

Cranach's interest in mythological subjects was no doubt reinforced by

Humanist scholars at the University of Wittenberg. Founded in 1502, the university had a distinguished faculty of Humanists teaching the classics and rhetoric, including Nikolaus Marschalk and Christoph Scheurl, among others. Such works as the *Reclining River Nymph at the Fountain* (1518) and *Venus with Cupid the Honey-Thief* (1530) were inspired by specific classical inscriptions. Cranach must have had help with these classical literary sources from his Humanist friends.

In 1508, Martin Luther was appointed professor of theology at the University of Wittenberg. Cranach knew him intimately. Cranach was a witness at Luther's wedding in 1525 and a godfather to his son Johannes. He also published some of Luther's writings and provided the designs for the title pages for two books by Luther published in 1518 and 1519. Cranach made several painted and printed portraits of Luther which serve to document Luther's life under the protection of Frederick III. Two of the most interesting of these are a painted panel and a woodcut, both of about 1521, which depict Luther in his disguise as Junker Georg after Luther's condemnation at the Diet of Worms.

The Lutheran message of direct redemption and the importance of faith alone in attaining salvation are themes that occur in several of Cranach's pictures and of those by Lucas the Younger. A late panel, often entitled the *Allegory of Redemption*, portrays the aging Cranach standing next to Luther beneath Christ on the Cross. Luther points to a passage in his translation of the Bible that promises direct salvation from Christ, while an arc of blood streams directly from the side of Christ onto Cranach's head. Begun by Cranach the Elder before his death, the work was completed by Cranach the Younger in 1555. A picture dating earlier in Cranach's career, the *Allegory of the Law and the Gospel* (1529), documents Luther's position that the Old Testament is incomplete without the New Testament. Such works by Cranach are clearly didactic, serving as a visual form to Luther's teachings.

Summary

Lucas Cranach, the Elder's lasting contribution to sixteenth century German art lies primarily in the quality of his works themselves. A prolific artist, no doubt aided by a well-supervised shop, Cranach produced a varied array of subjects in various media. They range in their scope from the naturalism of his portraits of real people to the impossible anatomy of his mythological nudes. Lacking the intellect of Albrecht Dürer's art or the sheer emotional power of Matthias Grünewald's paintings, Cranach's images seem more comfortable and less challenging. Yet Cranach was one of the first German artists to give visual form to early Reformation religious thought in his paintings, prints, and book illustrations. He developed conventions for illustrating classical mythology in an artistic tradition that had none. His art is a visual chronicle of the tastes and personalities of half a century of the

Wittenberg court, a society that had a profound impact on the intellectual, religious, and political formation of sixteenth century Germany.

Bibliography

Bax, D. *Hieronymus Bosch and Lucas Cranach: Two Last Judgment Triptychs*. Translated by M. A. Bax-Botha. New York: North-Holland, 1983. A detailed discussion of the subject matter of a painting attributed to Hieronymus Bosch in Vienna and a work related to it ascribed to Cranach in East Berlin. A focused study, the book concludes that Cranach copied the front of a now lost altarpiece by Bosch.

Christensen, Carl C. *Art and the Reformation in Germany*. Athens: Ohio University Press, 1979. Discusses more than a dozen paintings by Cranach and his shop that demonstrate subjects directly influenced by Protestant thought. There is also an excellent summary of Luther's theology and its relation to sixteenth century German art.

Cuttler, Charles D. *Northern Painting from Pucelle to Bruegel*. New York: Holt, Rinehart and Winston, 1968. A general survey of painting outside Italy during the Renaissance, the book devotes a separate chapter to Cranach's art. A short biography of Cranach is combined with a thorough stylistic survey of specific paintings and prints by the artist.

Falk, Tilman, ed. *Sixteenth Century German Artists, Hans Burgkmair the Elder, Hans Schäufelein, Lucas Cranach the Elder*. Vol. 11 in *The Illustrated Bartsch*, edited by Walter L. Strauss. New York: Abaris Books, 1980. Contains large illustrations of 155 engravings and woodcuts attributed to the artist. There is no commentary, but the illustrations provide an excellent resource of the prints by Cranach and his shop.

Friedländer, Max J., and Jakob Rosenberg. *The Paintings of Lucas Cranach*. Translated by Heinz Norden and Ronald Taylor. Ithaca, N.Y.: Cornell University Press, 1978. The new English translation, along with the original German publication, is largely a detailed catalog of nearly four hundred works ascribed to Cranach and to his sons. Many details of the 1932 catalog have been updated with a new introduction by Rosenberg.

Grossmann, Maria. *Humanism in Wittenberg, 1485-1517*. Nieuwkoop: B. de Fraaf, 1975. The author surveys the impact of German Humanism on the Reformation. Her chapter on the visual arts discusses Cranach's pictures in this context.

Hollstein, F. W. H. *Cranach-Drusse*. Vol. 6 in *German Engravings, Etchings, and Woodcuts, ca. 1400-1700*, edited by D. G. Boon and R. W. Scheller. Amsterdam: Menno Hertzberger. Provides lists of 140 prints and their locations by Cranach, the Elder, Cranach, the Younger, and impressions attributed to the Cranach workshop. Most entries are illustrated.

Schade, Werner. *Cranach: A Family of Master Painters*. Translated by Helen Sebba. New York: G. P. Putnam's Sons, 1980. The most comprehensive treatment of the subject to date. Schade's work discusses Cranach's life and art within the context of the contributions of his two sons. Profusely illustrated with many plates in color, the book also reprints in translation all documents relevant to the Cranach family with an extensive bibliography.

Snyder, James. *Northern Renaissance Art*. Englewood Cliffs, N.J.: Prentice-Hall, 1985. Intended as a general survey of Netherlandish, French, and German art, the book contains a separate chapter on Cranach. The author stresses Cranach's ties to Wittenberg Humanism and the Reformation aspects of his paintings.

Burton L. Dunbar III

SOR JUANA INÉS DE LA CRUZ
Juana Inés de Asbaje y Ramírez de Santillana

Born: November, 1648; San Miguel Nepantla, Mexico
Died: April 17, 1695; Mexico City
Area of Achievement: Literature
Contribution: Sor Juana is an outstanding poet of Mexico's colonial period. She is recognized as a key figure in Latin American literature and has the stature of an important Spanish poet of the seventeenth century.

Early Life

Juana Inés de Asbaje y Ramírez de Santillana was born in San Miguel Nepantla, Mexico, a small village in the foothills of the Popocatépetl volcano, probably in November, 1648. The traditional date of her birth, based on a biography by the Jesuit Diego Calleja, was November 12, 1651, but scholars have found a baptismal record for her parish for a female child dated December 2, 1648, which is believed to be hers. She is recorded as a "daughter of the Church," since her parents, Isabel Ramírez de Santillana and Pedro Manuel de Asbaje, were not officially married.

Juana Inés was one of six children, all illegitimate. Her father seems to have left when Juana Inés was very young, and she scarcely mentions him. After Captain Diego Ruiz Lozano entered the household, Juana Inés was sent to the house of her maternal grandfather, where she was reared and where she had access to a library. She learned to read at the age of three, and at the age of eight she composed a dramatic poem (*loa*) to the Eucharist. Eager to learn, she mastered Latin in about twenty lessons.

When she was sixteen, Juana Inés went to the viceroy's court as a lady of the viceroy's wife, the Marquesa de Mancera. She very soon became a favorite of the marquesa, and the two apparently shared a love of learning and of the intellectual life. At one point, the viceroy invited a group of about forty professors to question Juana Inés on her knowledge, and she astounded everyone with her answers. At this age, Juana was also a strikingly beautiful young woman.

A life at court did not provide a young woman in Juana Inés' circumstances with an opportunity for marriage, and she herself refers to a "total disinclination to marriage." Considering the options available to her, especially with her desire to continue studying, she chose, in 1667, to enter the Convent of the Discalced Carmelites. The order was too severe for her, however, and she became ill and left after three months. A year later, she entered the Order of Saint Jerome, where she remained for the rest of her life.

Life's Work

When Juana Inés took the veil in the Convent of Saint Jerome (San Jerónimo) on February 24, 1669, and officially became Sor Juana Inés de la Cruz, she was not yet twenty-one. She was from then on bound to the regulations and activities of the convent, which were not especially strict, but the communal life did provide interruptions which sometimes took her away from her studies. Nevertheless, she read broadly to fill in the many gaps in her education—she was essentially self-taught—and she also wrote extensively. From 1669 to 1690, she built up a considerable library collection for her use.

Sor Juana refers to her frail health on several occasions, and she was seriously ill with typhoid fever in 1671 or 1672. As a result, she wrote about the experience of death in a sonnet dedicated to "Laura" and a *romance* (a poem in octosyllabic verse with alternate lines of assonance) addressed to Fray Payo Enríquez de Rivera. Even her early writings show a sure skill in using the styles and forms of her times, and her own intelligence and sensitivity for nuances of meaning are evident.

Throughout her life, Sor Juana wrote many poems, but it is impossible to date them accurately since the originals have been lost and her style did not evolve. From the beginning, she showed a control of chiaroscuro and a sense of form and proportion. As is true of other works of the Baroque period, Sor Juana's poems are not personal revelations but rather a demonstration of talent in using correct form. Within a given form, individual talent emerges through ingenious use of well-known comparisons and images, or in the particular emphasis or tone.

In 1680, the Marqués de la Laguna was appointed viceroy, and the period of his reign, 1680-1688, was a very rich period in Sor Juana's intellectual life. She even heralded his arrival with a symbolic work entitled *El Neptuno alegórico* (1680; allegorical Neptune). Completely in tune with Baroque tradition, Sor Juana skillfully draws an allegorical portrait of the new viceroy using the device of an emblem or enigma. "Primero sueño" (first dream) begins with a poetic rendering of a slumbering world through mythology and imagery but develops into a philosophical argument on the relation of the intellect to the senses using the vocabulary and reasoning of Scholasticism. *El divino Narciso* (c. 1680; the divine Narcissus) is a sacramental play employing allegorical characters and representing the search of Human Nature (a woman) for Christ (in the form of Narcissus). Much of her other work consists of poems for special occasions.

In 1690, Sor Juana's *Carta atenagórica* (the Athenagoric letter) was published as a small pamphlet. The work, in the form of a letter, is a critique of a sermon given by the Portuguese Jesuit Antonio de Vieyra on Holy Thursday in 1650. She put her thoughts on paper at the request of someone with whom she had discussed the topic in casual conversation, and the letter came into the hands of Manuel Fernández de Santa Cruz, Bishop of Puebla, who wrote a brief prologue and had it published. This prologue, in the form of a letter signed Sor Filotea de la Cruz and dated November 25, 1690, did not forbid Sor Juana to study but did suggest that she study more in the area of sacred letters.

Three months later, on March 1, 1691, Sor Juana wrote her *Respuesta de la poetisa a la muy ilustre Sor Filotea de la Cruz* (1691; *Reply to Sor Filotea de la Cruz*, 1982). In this famous manuscript, she defends her thirst for knowledge. First, she recognizes her overpowering yearning to know and says that she learns not only from books but also from nature and everyday life. In essence, she defines herself as an intellectual. She then addresses the question of whether women should study. Since she is writing to the bishop, she readily agrees that she should study sacred works more, but the letter itself reveals a considerable amount of knowledge of the Bible and religious writers. In her argument, she reviews her own background and learning and even her decision to become a nun. Within the community, there was much opposition to her studies, and, although Sor Juana does not mention people by name, it is clear that she suffered because she could not quiet her intellect. The letter is a clearly considered and well-formulated argument, bringing to bear the use of reason as well as authority (a weaker argument). The letters caused some disagreement with the Church, and although the bishop favored Sor Juana, her own confessor, Jesuit Father Antonio Núñez de Miranda, broke ties with her. Then, Sor Juana decided to renounce the world by selling her library and giving the money to the poor. In addition, she signed an affirmation of faith in her own blood. When an epidemic struck the convent in 1695, Sor Juana helped the sick. She became ill and died from the disease on April 17, leaving unanswered the mystery of her renunciation.

Summary

Sor Juana Inés de la Cruz is a key figure in the history of Latin American literature, not only for her poetry but also for her important prose works *Reply to Sor Filotea de la Cruz* and *Carta atenagórica*, for which she is considered an early defender of women's emancipation. She believed that women, like men, should be allowed full intellectual development.

Sor Juana's poetic accomplishments, however, are what merit her a place in Latin American literary history. While Sor Juana's poetry was not original in the modern sense, wherein personal experience is important in poetry, she skillfully followed the tradition of the great Spanish writers Luis de Góngora y Argote and Pedro Calderón de la Barca. Her work is not distinctly American as opposed to peninsular Spanish, but she is honored as a Mexican poet nevertheless, because she was a part of the literature written in the New World and because she herself was a product of a criollo family. Her writings include an important body of lyric poetry, two comedies, and three religious allegories. The range of her abilities is reflected in her poetry, which could be intellectual or passionate, complicated or in popular style, witty or serious. Although she lived at the end of the Baroque period, the literature of which has been criticized as imitative and often extravagant, Sor Juana's poetry shows a skill and clearness in design which is exceptional and merits for her a distinguished place in the history of Spanish and Latin American literature.

Bibliography
Flynn, Gerard. *Sor Juana Inés de la Cruz*. Boston: Twayne, 1971. A very readable book. Introduces the reader to Sor Juana and her work. The first chapter gives biographical information, and the others review her poetry and drama. A discussion of the criticism of several authors is included, as are a number of quotations from Sor Juana's work with English translations provided by Flynn. Contains a selected bibliography of mainly Spanish-language sources.

Juana Inés de la Cruz, Sister. *A Woman of Genius: The Intellectual Autobiography of Sor Juana Inés de la Cruz*. Translated with an introduction by Margaret Sayers Peden. Salisbury, Conn.: Lime Rock Press, 1982. Contains a translation of Sor Juana's defense of her life, *Reply to Sor Filotea de la Cruz*. Also contains a list of basic sources at the end.

Montross, Constance M. *Virtue or Vice? Sor Juana's Use of Thomistic Thought*. Washington, D.C.: University Press of America, 1981. Examines Sor Juana's use of Scholastic doctrine and methodology, specifically the ideas of Saint Thomas Aquinas. The author analyzes the combination of belief and questioning in the *Carta atenagórica*, the *Reply to Sor Filotea de la Cruz*, and "Primero sueño." Extensive bibliography and the Spanish text of "Primero sueño" is included.

Paz, Octavio. *Sor Juana: Or, The Traps of Faith*. Translated by Margaret Sayers Peden. Cambridge, Mass.: Harvard University Press, 1988. A biography of Sor Juana by a leading Mexican poet, essayist, and cultural critic. Paz emphasizes Sor Juana's uniqueness as a poet and focuses on her struggle for her intellectual and creative life. Historical settings and traditions are detailed. Included are illustrations, among them portraits of Sor Juana, and a helpful listing of Spanish literary terms.

_____, ed. *Mexican Poetry: An Anthology*. Translated by Samuel Beckett. Reprint. New York: Grove Press, 1985. Contains a discussion of the place of Sor Juana in Mexican poetry as part of Paz's introduction to the history of Mexican poetry. Within the anthology itself are translations of twelve of Sor Juana's poems.

Royer, Fanchón. *The Tenth Muse: Sor Juana Inés de la Cruz*. Patterson, N.J.: St. Anthony Guild Press, 1952. A good introductory source. Each chapter is introduced with a translated quote from Sor Juana's work and traces the basic facts of her life along with interpretive commentary. An appendix includes some selected poems in Spanish as well as a short bibliography of Spanish-language sources.

Susan L. Piepke

GEORGES CUVIER

Born: August 23, 1769; Montbéliard, Württemberg
Died: May 13, 1832; Paris, France
Area of Achievement: Biology
Contribution: Cuvier was an anatomist who greatly extended the classification system of Linnaeus by dividing living organisms and the fossil record into phyla. He was also an antievolutionist, who adapted the theory that organic changes in the world were shaped by a series of catastrophes.

Early Life

Georges Léopold Chrétien Frédéric Dagobert Cuvier was the son of a retired French officer. His father had married late in life and had moved to Montbéliard. Montbéliard had been part of French Burgundy but came under the control of the Duke of Württemberg. The region kept the French language but adopted Lutheranism. His family had originally wanted young Cuvier to become a Lutheran minister, but he was denied a scholarship to theology school. In 1784, he found a patron in the wife of the governor of the city and was able to attend Caroline University, near Stuttgart. Although his initial studies were in legal and administrative areas, Cuvier befriended the zoology lecturer Karl Kielmayer, who taught him comparative anatomy and the intricacies of dissection. Cuvier was a short man with bright blue eyes and thick red hair. His weight increased throughout his life, with the result that he eventually was given the nickname "Mammoth."

Cuvier completed his studies in 1788, and for the next six years he served as a private tutor to a noble Protestant family in Normandy. During this time, the French Revolution was occurring, and, while many dramatic and far-reaching events were taking place in Paris, Cuvier lived his life quietly in the countryside. There he continued his dissection of various ocean organisms and recorded his work. An acquaintance suggested to Cuvier that he send his unpublished papers to Étienne Geoffroy Saint-Hilaire. Invited by Geoffroy to be his assistant at the Museum of Natural History, Cuvier went to Paris in 1795 and launched his career in science.

Life's Work

Once he settled in Paris, Cuvier's career progressed rapidly through the combination of his scientific accomplishments, his teaching abilities, and his administrative acumen. As a result of the dissections he performed in Normandy, he presented a paper in which he demonstrated that the classification of invertebrate animals into insects and worms could be reclassified into mollusks, crustaceans, insects, worms, echinoderms, and zoophytes. With his keen eye for detail and his ability to classify organisms accurately, he was appointed both professor of zoology and assistant professor of animal anatomy. For the rest of his life, promotions and honors came to him almost without pause. In 1800, he succeeded the eminent anatomist Louis Daubenton as a professor at the Collège de France and was given the responsibility of organizing the science departments of several lower schools. In 1808, Napoleon I made him university counselor, and he provided leadership in organizing the new Sorbonne in Paris. With the restoration of the monarchy in 1814, Cuvier continued to offer his services. Beginning in 1819, he chaired the Council of State in the Interior Department. He was made a baron in that same year, was elevated to the Legion of Honor in 1824, and became a Peer of France in 1831.

Cuvier's scientific accomplishments were the direct result of his position at the Museum of Natural History. The French government was committed to the creation of an internationally recognized research institution. Upon Cuvier's arrival, he immediately arranged to increase the anatomy collection. By 1804, he had increased this collection to three thousand items and by 1832 to more than thirteen thousand items. Without leaving Paris, Cuvier could dissect and prepare the anatomy of his organisms and create his classification systems for birds and fish. In fact little progress had been made before Cuvier in the classification of invertebrates. They were all thrown into a single catchall group called worms. In 1795, when Cuvier first arrived in Paris, he divided these into six new classes. By 1812, he was able to classify all animals into four phyla: vertebrates, mollusks, articulates, and radiates. Within these phyla, Cuvier discovered a number of new classes, orders, and families. Some of these had been grouped with others, and many were simply overlooked.

Cuvier's method of classification was a departure from the earlier Linnaean system, in which an organism had a number of independent and arbitrary characteristics. Taking a cue from Comte de Buffon, who treated organisms as a whole entity, Cuvier expanded this idea into the correlation of parts. Since all the functions of an organism are dependent on one another, the anatomical parts are also integrated in the organism. Through one well-preserved bone, it is possible to determine the class, order, genus, and in many cases the species of the animal. The application of this method not only produced rapid advances in the study of comparative anatomy but also was expanded to fossil remains. As early as 1804, Cuvier had tried to reconstruct the shape of the muscles of an extinct animal from the imprint left on the bones. The final step was to imagine a skin on this extinct animal, and it was resurrected.

Cuvier's contributions to anatomy and paleontology could have placed him among the earliest of the evolutionists. He found that several geological strata contained organisms peculiar to them. He also possessed ample evidence of extinction, since he examined the remains of an extinct elephant that differed significantly from any known living species. In addition, his knowledge of comparative anatomy was unequaled until the publication of Charles Darwin's theory of evolution. Cuvier, however, rejected all evolutionary explanations of his discoveries. One possible explanation for this position can be found in his belief that nature was an immense network that had remained fixed in place since the Creation. After 1812, he admitted that creation must have taken place over several stages, and he adapted Charles Bonnet's theory of catastrophism, which postulated that the world was totally flooded on several occasions. After each flood, life was created again, hence the various strata and different organic remains.

Although Cuvier was a devout Christian, his opposition to evolution could have originated from his intellectual makeup rather than from his religious beliefs. A review of his extensive writings shows that religious doctrines rarely entered his scientific work. Possibly, Cuvier rejected the notion of evolution because he did not see a chain of organisms that evolved from simple to more complex functions. His network was not a continuous one moving from a series of related species, but rather a discontinuous one in which each species was complete in itself, and the parts worked in total harmony. Also, the geological record of his time was limited and supported the conclusion that organic forms from one stratum could not be found in a later one. Later, when Cuvier found a similar organic form in several strata, he modified his catastrophe theory toward local events such as earthquakes, volcanic action, and mountain building.

Whatever Cuvier's reasons were for rejecting a theory of evolution, he became engaged in a famous academic conflict, beginning in 1802, that was to last until his death in 1832. The conflict involved his former friends Geoffroy and Jean-Baptiste de Lamarck. The conflict produced secret investigations on the religious beliefs of Lamarck and Geoffroy. Mummified animals were brought back from Egypt to demonstrate the transformation of species. In a further episode, Cuvier had erroneously classified an extinct crocodile, an event which brought Geoffroy to the attack. While this battle was vigorously fought among the combatants and their disciples, the press and political groups also entered the fray to champion their own views. Despite his power and prestige, Cuvier was unable to prevail in this dispute. As Cuvier lay dying, Sir Charles Lyell published his work on geology, which produced crucial evidence for Darwin's theory of evolution.

Summary

Georges Cuvier lived and worked in a world that was undergoing rapid change. The French Revolution dramatically altered European society and culture. Cuvier moved adroitly through a dangerously revolutionary Paris, rose to prominence under the empire of Napoleon, and maintained his administrative positions through the restoration of the monarchy and its fall in the July Revolution of 1830. He was a Protestant in a predominantly Catholic country, and he was a poor man who acquired wealth and titles. Even without his scientific contributions, his activities would rate a minor place in the history of France. He was a man who had extensive interests; indeed his personal library included more than nineteen thousand books covering history, law, and natural sciences. He absorbed this material and committed it to memory. With this knowledge, he completed a vast amount of work as secretary of the National Institute, and under Napoleon he shaped and changed the university system of France.

It was not a narrowness of vision which kept Cuvier from arriving at a theory of evolution or considering the merits of such an idea. He possessed a grand and ordered view of nature, along with an intricate knowledge of the anatomical parts of hundreds of species. For him, each organic form was already perfect, with not one evolving into greater complexity. Perhaps he understood too much to see the simple mechanism of change built into the individuals of a species. Without his discoveries in anatomy, paleontology, and the theory of correlation of parts, however, many others would have had to duplicate this work before the theory of evolution could have been developed.

Bibliography

Bourdier, Franck. "Geoffroy Saint-Hilaire Versus Cuvier: The Campaign for Paleontological Evolution (1825-39)." In *Towards a History of Geology*, edited by Cecil J. Schneer. Cambridge, Mass.: MIT Press, 1969. Covers the acrimonious conflict between Cuvier and Geoffroy through the differences in their temperaments and careers. The author's sympathies lie with Geoffroy, and he cites him as one of the great precursors to Darwin. Reviews some new sources of information to make his case.

Coleman, William R. *Georges Cuvier, Zoologist: A Study in the History of Evolutionary Theory*. Cambridge, Mass.: Harvard University Press, 1964. Covers Cuvier's zoological and anatomical work in detail. Several sections are too complex for the general reader, but the information on Cuvier's methodology and classification is valuable. Suggests that Cuvier's rejection of evolution is less influenced by his religious attitudes than by his intellectual makeup.

Eisley, Loren. *Darwin's Century: Evolution and the Men Who Discovered It*. Garden City, N.Y.: Doubleday, 1958. Presents Cuvier as a crucial predecessor to Darwin in the story of evolution. The sections on Cuvier are scattered in several parts of the text. Written in a simple style with ample information on Cuvier. An excellent overview of the history of evolutionary theory.

Mayr, Ernst. *The Growth of Biological Thought: Diversity, Evolution, and Inheritance*. Cambridge, Mass.: Harvard University Press, 1982. Mayr is the recognized authority on Darwin and the history of biological evolution. In each of the major sections of this work there are sections on Cuvier and his contributions to the world of biological ideas. The material can be difficult at times, but the treatment is definitive.

Nordenskiöld, Eric. *The History of Biology.* New York: Tudor, 1928. Chapter 2 of part 3 covers Cuvier's life and career. The topics include comparative anatomy, correlation of parts theory, paleontology, catastrophe theory, and the controversy with Geoffroy. Dated but competent.

Victor W. Chen

JACQUES DAGUERRE

Born: November 18, 1787; Cormeilles, near Paris, France
Died: July 10, 1851; Petit-Bry-sur-Marne, France
Areas of Achievement: Invention and technology
Contribution: Daguerre's greatest renown rests upon his contribution to the technology of photography. He achieved the earliest fixed-image photograph developed from a latent image. The process discovered by him produced a photograph on a polished iodized silver plate that was patented as the "daguerreotype."

Early Life

Jacques Daguerre's formal education in the schools of Orléans was brief and poor because of the distractions of the French Revolution. Fortunately, he revealed a gift for drawing early in his childhood, which, in some measure, offset the quality of his education. Daguerre was apprenticed by his father to a draftsman. Though the training in detailed exactitude was later to prove beneficial, it was Daguerre's wish to study painting. In 1804, his father allowed him to go to Paris for that purpose. He was apprenticed to the chief stage designer at the Paris Opera, with whom he lived and worked for three years.

At the end of this apprenticeship, Daguerre took employment with Pierre Prévost, a painter who had achieved a certain celebrity with his panoramas. These were representations akin to those currently called cycloramas. The viewer was situated at the center of a cylindrical painting of very large dimensions, comprising a single expansive view. Such paintings must be executed with scrupulous attention to accuracy of scale and fidelity to perspective. Once more, his experience in draftsmanship served him well. In 1810, one week before his twenty-third birthday, Daguerre married twenty-year-old Louise Georgina Smith, sister of a fellow employee at the Prévost studio. He continued his association with Prévost for six years after his marriage, starting an independent career only in 1816.

Daguerre quickly distinguished himself as a set designer, where an ability to achieve delightful illusions and exotic effects came fully into play. Until 1821, he was engaged in designing sets for some of the best-known theaters in Paris, and in 1819 the Académie Royale de Musique enlisted his widely acclaimed talents. For two years, he was one of the chief designers for the Académie.

Life's Work

During 1821 and 1822, Daguerre devoted much time and effort to the development of a new technique for creating scenes of very convincing realism that he called the "diorama." This new form of illusion was de-

veloped by Daguerre in conjunction with another former associate from Prévost's studio, Charles-Marie Bouton.

The diorama was clearly the product of a series of incremental advances
on previous techniques for creating visual illusion. The most recent, the
diaphanorama, was itself a departure from the panorama. Franz Niklaus
König, the creator of the diaphanorama, was Swiss by birth and was also an
experienced set designer.

König's effects were produced by painting with watercolors on transparent
papers, the backs of which he subsequently oiled to increase their translu-
cence. Displayed at a distance in darkened rooms, the paintings were illuminated by controlled, reflected light played on the back as well as the front,
the relative intensity of the light being adjustable in minute transitions. It is a
virtual certainty that Daguerre witnessed a display of König's ingenuity
when the latter traveled to Paris in 1821 and that his own diorama was
actually a refinement of the basic concept devised by König.

Daguerre and Bouton bought land and constructed a specially designed
structure. An enormous building was necessary because of the very large
paintings involved and the distance to be maintained between the paintings
and the viewers. The "picture rooms"—there were two—lay at the end of
corridors which were arranged like spokes radiating from the circular viewing salon, widening as they moved away from the audience. Viewers sat or
stood in a darkened, circular, revolvable salon that was positioned in such a
way that they could look down only one of the two corridors, at the end of
which was the scene.

After all the effects of the first scene had been rehearsed, the gallery faded
into darkness, and the salon was imperceptibly made to revolve to the position from which the second gallery could be brought into view by the gradual
introduction of light upon the second scene. Illumination was achieved by
light introduced through windows, controlled by shutterlike devices, sometimes colored by filters and conducted to the desired surfaces by reflection.
The structure itself and the ingenious system of illumination were so central
to the scheme that they were independently patented.

The paintings, which were periodically changed so that audiences could
return to see a new set of scenes, were executed upon both sides of a white
calico fabric, optimally translucent and prepared with sizing. The pigment
was suspended in a turpentine vehicle and applied to the fabric in as thin a
coat as would achieve the effect without causing complete opacity. The
painting was then shaded with translucent colors. By illuminating the painting first on one side and then the other and by using lights of various colors,
parts of the composition were made to disappear, while others seemed to
advance. It was possible in this manner to present a before-and-after history
of a scene, for example, a peaceful Swiss valley that fell victim to an
enormous landslide. By using several painted cloths in echelon with the

lighting such that the viewer could see through one, two, or more of them simultaneously, it was possible to achieve an astonishing degree of three-dimensional realism as well as to give the illusion of transitory atmospheric effects.

The diorama was received with enthusiasm, and Daguerre was made a Chevalier of the Legion of Honor in 1824; however, the enterprise appears never to have been much of a financial success. In March of 1839, a fire destroyed the Paris Diorama, which, because of the highly combustible materials it contained, was a constant danger.

By that time, Daguerre had brought to fruition his work on a means of fixing an image made upon a light-sensitive surface in a camera obscura. A man of his time, Daguerre was motivated not only by an interest in the accurate study of proportion and perspective but also by a desire for celebrity and wealth. Possibly this drive to distinguish himself explains why he periodically made claims to successes that proved to be false or that were only subsequently achieved.

Sometime during the year 1826, Daguerre learned of the work being done on heliography by Nicéphore Niépce. Niépce, in 1826, had produced the world's first photograph. Using a pewter plate coated with bitumen of Judea (asphaltum) and placed at the back of a camera obscura, he achieved an image of a scene from the second story of his country home. The process, however, required an exposure time of eight hours. Upon learning of this shortcoming in the exposure process, Daguerre at once approached Niépce by letter. By misrepresenting the extent of his own success, Daguerre drew a reluctant Niépce into a partnership. Having failed to secure any return on his own developments, Niépce on December 14, 1829, signed an agreement with Daguerre, who said that he had a strategy by which Niépce could profit from his discoveries. The partnership was entitled "Niépce-Daguerre," and by its terms Daguerre was obliged to "improve" a process of which Niépce was named "inventor." Daguerre was also to contribute a camera of an improved design, which he claimed to have developed and which would substantially reduce the exposure time. The camera, in the form described by Daguerre, did not exist. Daguerre, however, was twenty-two years younger than the senior partner, and Niépce hoped to enjoy the fruits of the great capacity for hard work and the unflagging optimism that characterized his new partner.

Daguerre learned from Niépce that it was not necessary to expose a plate until the image became visible on its surface; a faint or even completely invisible image could be brought out (developed) by chemical processes. Daguerre also seems to have learned from his partner that iodine could be used as the photosensitive coating to receive the image.

Niépce died in great poverty in 1833, before the partnership yielded any advantage to him. His son and legatee, Isidore, succeeded him as Daguerre's partner. At that time, the original problems remained unsolved: Images using iodine were negative, the exposure time remained seven to eight hours, and no means had been found to prevent the image from deterioration in light.

Daguerre, however, began to make critical discoveries after the death of Niépce. First, he made the discovery (evidently by the purest chance) that iodized silvered plates could be used as the surface upon which to secure light images in the camera. Then, sometime in 1837, he found (also quite by chance) that mercury vapors would precipitate out on the light-affected portions of an iodized silver surface. These two critical discoveries are credited entirely to Daguerre in spite of his haphazard methods. The great advantage in them was the production of a positive image at a substantial reduction in the exposure time, though he had not as yet discovered any means of making the image thus obtained permanent.

On May 9, 1835, Daguerre secured a modification of the partnership agreement. Isidore reluctantly signed, and Daguerre soon announced publicly that he had discovered a means of fixing permanently the images that he was securing. In fact, it was not until two years later, in May of 1837, that he made such a discovery.

Over the strong objections of Isidore, terms of the partnership were again revised. The names in the partnership were reversed, and it was made clear that Daguerre had pressed beyond mere improvement of someone else's discovery. Isidore was told that the new process (mercury development) reduced exposure time to four minutes. In truth, it still required twenty to thirty minutes of exposure to secure an image, which was still too long to make portraiture a practical possibility.

An effort to finance further development of the process through a public subscription failed in 1839. In March, the diorama was consumed in a spectacular fire. Daguerre was fifty-one, and his fortunes seemed to have hit a low point. He and Niépce decided to realize what they could by offering the process to the French government. They revealed the method to François Arago, a member of the Chamber of Deputies as well as president of the Academy of Sciences. Arago then secured the government's acceptance. Daguerre was made an Officer of the Legion of Honor, and both he and Niépce were given comfortable life pensions. The French government at once donated the process to the world at large.

Within months, a flood of developments vastly improved the quality and practicality of daguerreotypy. Among the more important of these were the use of thiosulfate as a fixative; a lens that corrected Daguerre's original mirror image; the introduction of the tripod and leather bellows, which made the camera more easily portable; and the discovery of bromoiodide and iodine bromochloride to increase significantly the sensitivity of plates, which, coupled with improved cameras, reduced exposure time to between 90 and 120 seconds for good-quality results.

Daguerre, much lionized for his discoveries, retired to a country estate at Petit-Bry-sur-Marne, where he died quite suddenly on July 10, 1851, at the age of sixty-three. The surviving daguerreotypes taken of their eponymous creator reveal a gentleman of ample but not excessive girth, a very round face still crowned by a full complement of curly, salt-and-pepper hair, a full mustache, and a look of fixed determination about the hooded eyes.

Summary

During an age when an individual's worth was considered to be the precise equivalent of his wealth and the self-made man was the social ideal, Jacques Daguerre, by hard work and seriousness of purpose, built upon native talents rather than education or social privilege to become both wealthy and famous. In the creation of the diorama, he produced not merely the most exciting optical illusion prior to motion pictures but also techniques that are still used in stage settings for the ballet and the opera to achieve mysterious or transitional effects.

Daguerre turned his attention to the emerging technology of photography when the diorama provided recognition but no appreciable wealth. Though the extent of his indebtedness to Niépce remains unresolved, it is certain that it was his own efforts that resulted in the first fixed-image photograph developed from a latent image. It is, therefore, equally certain that the foundation for the art in its present state was laid by Daguerre.

Bibliography

Bisbee, A. *The History and Practice of Daguerreotyping*. Dayton, Ohio: L. F. Clafting, 1853. Reprint. New York: Arno Press, 1973. An early and very clear description of the process used by Daguerre. This little book was written for the American public at the crest of the enthusiasm over the technology.

Eder, Josef Maria. *History of Photography*. Translated by Edward Epstean. New York: Columbia University Press, 1945. This book is annoyingly chauvinistic but sound in its scholarship. It is technically more informed than the Gernsheim work. Eder always thought that the critical discoveries were those of Niépce and evidently thought Daguerre not above taking credit for discoveries not, in fact, his own.

Gernsheim, Helmut, and Alison Gernsheim. *L. J. M. Daguerre (1787-1851): The World's First Photographer*. Cleveland: World Publishing, 1956. Rev. ed. *L. J. M. Daguerre: The History of the Diorama and the Daguerreotype*. New York: Dover, 1968. The only biography devoted to Daguerre's life and work. This study includes plates of the earliest efforts at photography and the two best daguerreotypes of Daguerre.

Rinhart, Floyd, and Marion Rinhart. *The American Daguerreotype*. Athens: University of Georgia Press, 1981. This book, which includes a number of

photographs of original daguerreotype equipment and some beautiful examples of the art, includes a brief account of its development.
Werge, John. *The Evolution of Photography*. London: Piper & Carter and
J. Werge, 1890. Werge emphasizes the haphazard nature of Daguerre's
research and recounts in detail stories that emphasize the utter happen-
stance by which the critical discoveries were made.

John Knox Stevens

GOTTLIEB DAIMLER

Born: March 17, 1834; Schorndorf (near Stuttgart), Württemberg
Died: March 6, 1900; Cannstatt, Germany
Areas of Achievement: Engineering, invention, and technology
Contribution: Daimler, as much as any one man, was the inventor of the first high-speed motor; because of his carburetion process and his development of light engine weight his motor became adaptable to driving both motor cars and aircraft.

Early Life

The second son of a master baker, Gottlieb Daimler was born in Schorndorf, Württemberg, on March 17, 1834. Daimler was relatively well educated. He attended public school, followed by two years of Latin school. One of young Daimler's closest friends was the son of a master gunsmith, under whose tutelage he apprenticed himself for three years until he produced a piece of work that qualified him as a journeyman. His work entailed precise drawings, which Daimler particularly loved and carried into later life with his depictions of plants and animals.

Journeyman status meant further training en route to mastery. Gottlieb went to work in Alsace, designing machine tools. Recognizing his educational deficiencies, particularly in mathematics, he soon applied his earned savings for two additional years of formal training, this time at the Stuttgart Polytechnic. While in Stuttgart, he came in contact with some of developing Germany's leading engineers such as Ferdinand von Steinbus. Steinbus, who had been instrumental in the industrial development of Württemberg, subsidized Daimler's further training in France and England, where he worked variously as a mechanic, foreman, and manager before returning to Württemberg as the manager of Bruderhaus of Rentlingen's—a highly esteemed firm of machine builders.

While at Bruderhaus, Daimler met Wilhelm Maybach, whose career he helped to shape and with whom he would later collaborate. Maybach, a remarkable young man twelve years Daimler's junior, had already demonstrated his manual skills and his grasp of mathematics, physics, and mechanical drawing. In 1868, when Daimler assumed the management of one of Karlsruhe's leading machine shops, he brought Maybach into his drawing office.

As the by-then-unified Germany rapidly industrialized under Otto von Bismarck and opportunities for skilled men blossomed, Daimler accepted a position with the firm of Otto and Langen in Deutz. Nikolaus August Otto and Eugen Langen furthered the practical design and production of an internal-combustion engine. Beginning in the 1860's, Étienne Lenoir made several hundred marketable gas (not gasoline) fired internal-combustion engines employed in machine shops and for pumping water. To Lenoir's impressive, if commercially unsuccessful work, Otto and Langen added the development, largely because of Daimler, of the first four-cycle engine, which in its operations is still the basis of most gasoline engines.

Life's Work

In his late forties, Daimler decided to leave his employers' Deutz plant and establish a plant for himself at Cannstatt in 1882. With him went Wilhelm Maybach, by then a masterful machine builder. Daimler's objective was to develop a practical, high-speed, gasoline-driven motor that would be adaptable to vehicle locomotion. By the beginning of the 1880's, Daimler's new four-stroke machines achieved between 150 and 180 revolutions per minute. At 250 revolutions per minute, however, there were problems with ignition and with the proper metering and timing of admixtures of gasoline and air. Daimler had resolved this problem in mechanical terms while working for Otto and Langen by introducing a flame carried in a special slide valve. This commercial result was Daimler's high-speed motor, capable of nine hundred revolutions per minute. Thirty thousand of these motors were sold internationally within the first decade of its development.

The problem that Daimler set out to resolve when he left Otto and Langen's remarkably inventive works had to do with the uses to which his inventions were put amid bitter international patent battles. Most of the Otto and Langen (or so-called Deutz) motors were sold to perform stationary functions. After years of losses and borrowing, Otto and Langen, to survive, addressed the available market for their product—customers who required stationary engines requisite to the needs of small workshops and mines. The production of moving vehicles, not only on the ground but also in the air, however, was what Daimler had in view.

At his Cannstatt workshop, he had by 1884 developed a high-speed gasoline engine in which the fuel for the combustion chambers was metered by a wick carburetor and ignited by an electric spark. It was a vertical engine which would soon be built in sizes from one-half to twenty-five horsepower with one, two, and four cylinders and eventually ran at six hundred revolutions per minute. Daimler claimed that he had created the basis for an entirely new industry.

He tested his new motor on a wooden cycle, which he drove in the garden of his Cannstatt home in November, 1885, and then on a boat, the first to be powered by a gasoline engine, both tests proving successful. By the following year, he had produced the four-wheeled Daimler carriage, which soon began making its appearance in Cannstatt and nearby Stuttgart. Its top speed was about six kilometers per hour. Daimler's motor, with improvements constantly insisted upon by Maybach, was swiftly patented. Maybach, meanwhile, urged Daimler to join his motor and chassis to form a single machine unit. Since Daimler was excited by prospects of mass-producing his vehicles as well as by turning a profit, he soon acquiesced and built a four-wheeled, gasoline-driven carriage that really was an automobile.

While late nineteenth century Germany furnished a marvelous environment for invention and technological innovation, and as a consequence had become one of the world's foremost industrial powers, Daimler's automobile did not become popular in that country. It remained for the French to lend the notoriety to Daimler's car that was essential to its popularity.

On July 1, 1894, the first international automobile race, along the one-hundred-kilometer Paris-Rouen road, was held. The winner was a Daimler machine that reached unprecedented speeds of up to 110 kilometers per hour. With world attention on the race, Daimler received eighty thousand francs in prize money. It was manifest at a practical level that the automobile was no longer a rich man's toy. The race had justified the previous formation of the Daimler Motoren-Gesellschaft in Cannstatt on January 28, 1890, a concern which became one of the world's great producers of automobiles.

Daimler and Maybach came to be driven less by pure technical considerations than by demands from prospective customers to increase the power of their automobiles from nine horsepower to thirty and forty horsepower. Under these immediate pressures, Daimler by 1900 developed and produced the first modern automobile, judged by power and appearance. Its name was "Mercédès."

Daimler did not live to enjoy the success of the first Mercedes after 1900. His health had been declining, and he was unable to bear the pressures under which he had worked for more than forty years. He died on March 6, 1900, in Cannstatt.

Summary

A brilliant technician and industrial entrepreneur, Gottlieb Daimler resolved the major problems that had plagued, and had thus retarded, the progress of men who had sought to design and produce automotive vehicles. His competence and technical skill exercised in the development of an efficient carburetor and a lightweight, gasoline-driven engine were responsible for the emergence of the world's first true automobile, the ultimate expression of which was the Mercedes. His vision was extraordinary as was demonstrated in 1897 by his recommendations to German authorities that they entertain plans for the creation of a motor-driven airship.

Daimler, like so many nineteenth century men of achievement, combined an extraordinary capacity for hard work with keen powers of observation and exceptional farsightedness. Daimler had spoken to his ultimate objectives while still a young man, and he never deviated from them.

Bibliography

Burstall, Aubrey F. *A History of Mechanical Engineering.* Cambridge, Mass.: MIT Press, 1965. Chapters 7 and 8, although they spend little time on Daimler, place him in context. Excellent schematic illustrations of the Otto engine and Daimler's 1897 gasoline engine. Directed to intelligent lay readers, it is richly illustrated. Contains reference footnotes, bibliographies, and an index.

Clark, Dugald. *The Gas, Oil, and Petrol Engine.* 2 vols. London: Basil Blackwell, 1916. Few other works so extensively trace the evolution of these varied engines and the problems that had to be resolved to render them effective. Volume 2 is particularly pertinent in regard to Daimler's achievements. While the work is old, it remains authoritative and is quite readable. Contains illustrations, bibliographical notations, and a useful index.

Field, D. C. "Internal Combustion Engines." In *The Late Nineteenth Century, c. 1850 to c. 1920.* Vol. 5 in *A History of Technology,* edited by Charles Singer, E. J. Holmyard, A. R. Hall, and Trevor Williams. Oxford, England: Clarendon Press, 1958. Clearly and authoritatively written for a general readership, this essay places Daimler's major contributions in context. There are many precise illustrations. Good select bibliographies follow this (and other) chapters, and there is a useful index for the entire volume.

Hill, Frank Ernest. *The Automobile: How It Came, Grew, and Changed Our Lives.* New York: Dodd, Mead, 1967. Intended primarily for high school readers rather than for college or university students. The early chapters, while somewhat simplistic compared to works cited above, nevertheless afford a sound general picture of Daimler's work. Includes photographs and an index.

Rae, John B. "The Internal Combustion Engine on Wheels." In *Technology in the Twentieth Century.* Vol. 2 in *Technology in Western Civilization,* edited by Melvin Kranzburg and Carroll Pursell. New York: Oxford University Press, 1967. Written by specialists for a general readership. Rae's chapter helps place the work of Daimler and other early automotive pioneers in an evolutionary context. Contains an extensive bibliography and an extensive index.

Rolt, Lionel Thomas C. *Great Engineers.* London: G. Bell, 1962. The only work in English that affords personal details on the life of Daimler and those with whom he worked and competed. Rolt, a British engineer, established himself as a fine, readable historian of engineers, precise and accurate without being pedantic. Contains a useful index.

Clifton K. Yearley

GEORGES DANTON

Born: October 26, 1759; Arcis-sur-Aube, France
Died: April 5, 1794; Paris, France
Areas of Achievement: Politics and government
Contribution: Danton was one of the principal leaders and shapers of the French Revolution. He became influential in molding modern conceptions of democracy, revolutionary politics, and the nation-state.

Early Life

Georges-Jacques Danton, like most of his future revolutionary associates, was born into a comfortably middle-class, provincial family. His father, Jacques Danton, who died when Georges was two years old, worked as a clerk for a local court. His mother, née Jeanne-Madelaine Camut, was remarried to an Arcis merchant, Jean Recordain, when Danton was ten. As the oldest male child, Danton received the best education his family could afford. After attending a local school for the primary grades, he was sent in 1773 to the Oratorian seminary at Troyes to complete his education. There, Georges studied a curriculum emphasizing science, history, and modern languages. Later, his critics would brand him "uneducated," probably because of his inability to read Latin and Greek and his unfamiliarity with classical texts. Nevertheless, by modern standards Danton's schooling was first rate. He mastered English and achieved a reading knowledge of Italian. As an adult, he showed an extraordinary command of the contemporary works of the Enlightenment, especially those of Voltaire, Comte de Buffon, and Jean-Jacques Rousseau.

Danton chose civil law as his career. After being graduated from Troyes, he attended the University of Reims and received his law degree in 1784. He then resided in Paris, where he competed with hundreds of other provincials for scarce legal business that barely provided a living. In 1787, however, Danton recouped his fortunes in an enterprising manner which would come to characterize him. On June 9, he was married to Antoinette-Gabrielle Charpentier, the daughter of a prosperous Parisian tax farmer and café proprietor. Using her dowry and loans from his father-in-law and a former mistress, Danton earlier had purchased an office as attorney to the King's Councils, a position which entitled him to present cases before the royal councils and commissions. When the French Revolution erupted in 1789, Danton owned a lucrative law practice and enjoyed the prestige proceeding from a close association with the Versailles court.

Life's Work

As befitted a beneficiary of the established regime, Danton was slow to involve himself in the revolutionary fervor rising around him. Once immersed in the enthusiasm which followed the storming of the Bastille (July 14, 1789), however, Danton rivaled all others in his fanaticism and devotion to political reform. Soon he became renowned for his unique oratory. Utilizing natural attributes—commanding height, intimidating size, and a stentorian voice— he demonstrated a capacity for incisive speech which motivated Parisian arti- sans, shopkeepers, and laborers to participate actively in the Revolution.

During this early period of revolutionary involvement, Danton's attentions were principally focused on Parisian politics. Although a supporter of the newly established constitutional monarchy, he rapidly developed a reputation for rabble-rousing and corruption. It was at this time that he pioneered the techniques of mob incitement and control which have since come to char- acterize successful revolutions. As an advocate of freedom of speech and of association—and to sustain his personal ambitions—he harangued the crowds and directed the resulting anger against more conservative constitu- tional monarchists, such as the Marquess de Lafayette and Jean Bailly.

The flight of the royal family to Varennes in June, 1791—King Louis XVI considered himself a prisoner of the revolutionaries—was a major turning point in Danton's career. Like many Frenchmen, he regarded the flight and other questionable royal deeds as evidence of Louis' treason. The king's actions radicalized Danton. He soon directed his demagogic activities toward deposing Louis and establishing a republic. The National Assembly's cha- rade that the royal family had been kidnapped further aroused Danton and many like-minded radicals. Against the constitutional monarchists' deter- mination to preserve Louis' powers, Danton helped organize a massive dem- onstration on July 17, at the Field of Mars, where thousands signed a petition demanding a new executive power. When the National Guard arrived to break up the crowd, shots were fired that killed fifty demonstrators. Hunted as one of those responsible for the incident, Danton fled to England, where he remained for only a short time.

By September, he had returned to Paris. During the next eleven months, the king and the constitutional monarchists played into the hands of the radicals, the former by vetoing the assembly's attempts to enforce clerical conformity to the nationalization of church property and activities, and the latter by declaring (April, 1792) and waging an unsuccessful war against Austria and Prussia. In July, the allied armies, assembled on the fron- tier preparing to invade France, issued the infamous Brunswick Manifesto, which threatened Paris with destruction if the people did not obey the will of the king. Danton and other republicans had little trouble transforming Pari- sian fear at the prospect of an allied invasion into a violent hysteria and hatred for Louis, whose communications with the Austrians and the French émigrés were well known. Danton was one of the principal organizers of the assault upon the Tuileries, the king's residence, on August 10. With the mob in control of Paris, direction of the Revolution fell largely into the hands of the radicals. The Legislative Assembly voted for the suspension of the king and for the calling of a national convention to draw up a new constitution. Danton was named Minister of Justice in the provisional executive council. A period of great personal achievement was to follow for him.

Danton served as Minister of Justice for only two months. During that time, he wielded greater power than Louis XVI had ever possessed. Relying on his abundant energy and determination, he dominated the provisional executive, requisitioning vast supplies of arms and recruiting thousands of volunteers for the French armies. On September 20, the allied invasion was turned back at the Battle of Valmy, a victory reflective of Danton's efforts. Shortly thereafter, he abandoned the ministry for a seat in the National Convention, where he and his followers aligned themselves with Robespierre and the Jacobins—the most famous of the Revolution's radicals.

As a deputy, Danton continued to strive tirelessly for the revolutionary cause. Denying charges of corruption—which were probably true—he involved himself deeply in foreign affairs. Between December, 1792, and March, 1793, he traveled to conquered Belgium four times to direct the installation of a revolutionary government there. In March and April—responding to French defeats in both Holland and Belgium—he mobilized 300,000 men for the armies and was instrumental in the creation of the Revolutionary Tribunal and the Committee of Public Safety, judicial and executive bodies designed to use authoritarian means to expedite and maximize the mobilization of people and resources for the war effort. During this period as a member of the Committee of Public Safety he supervised two departments, national defense and foreign affairs, making him for the second time the most powerful man in France.

These hours of triumph were marred by tragedy. In February, while in Belgium, Danton learned that his wife, Gabrielle, had died in childbirth. He was overcome with grief upon receiving the news but soon buried himself in politics and state business. A few months later, he married Louise Gely, who was fifteen years old and a friend of his family. His interest in his new wife probably lay mainly in the need to provide a mother for his two young sons.

On June 2, the Montagnards (radicals who included the Jacobins and Dantonists) purged the convention of the more moderate Girondins, leaving the direction of France completely under the control of Parisian extremists whose views were anathema to the majority of Frenchmen. Danton was a principal instigator of this coup. This was the high point of his power, however, as the Jacobins in subsequent months came increasingly to distrust his growing moderation.

By the summer of 1793, France had become once again a nation under siege. Great Britain and Spain had joined the powers already aligned against it, while counterrevolutionary movements controlled much of western and southern France. In response to the crisis, the Montagnards ruled the nation dictatorially through the Committee of Public Safety and the use of the Reign of Terror—the rounding up and executing of those suspected of opposing the Revolution or obstructing the war effort. Danton's solution to France's troubles was to negotiate with the enemies whose armies were pressing upon the frontier. The Jacobins considered his views to be a sign of weakness. They preferred to impose economic controls and mobilize the nation for an all-out struggle with internal and external foes. In July, Danton failed to win reelection to the committee, signaling his deteriorating political position. In October, Danton committed a fatal, inexplicable error by retiring to Arcis with his family for two months. In his absence, Robespierre and Louis de Saint-Just consolidated Jacobin control over the Revolution. When Danton returned in mid-November, they were powerful enough to move against him whenever they pleased.

By the early spring of 1794, the allied armies had been pushed back in several areas, while within France counterrevolutionary regions were undergoing slow pacification. As the crisis thus eased, Danton, seemingly unaware of the precariousness of his position, publicly called for relaxation of the Reign of Terror. His opponents moved swiftly against him. On March 30, he was arrested as an "enemy of the Republic." His trial before the Revolutionary Tribunal was farcical, and several times Danton jeered at absurd attempts to portray him as a "counterrevolutionary." Nevertheless, he was convicted and died, on April 5, 1794, on the guillotine.

Summary

Georges Danton's ambition found expression in pure demagoguery. A skillful orator and an adroit politician, he consistently demonstrated an uncanny ability to ascertain the desires of the Parisian lower classes and to identify himself quickly with them. Although Danton gained and retained power through unscrupulous manipulation of the electorate—and occasionally utilized the *sans culottes* as the bludgeon for his policies—his political career was distinguished by remarkable achievements in a very short time. Destruction of the monarchy, establishment of the republic, universal manhood suffrage, and abolition of imprisonment for debt—all of these landmarks of French history were given impetus through Danton's energy, both in his role as a popular mob leader and during his two brief tenures as unofficial chief minister of France. He was truly an architect of modern democracy and of the nation-state.

Bibliography

Christophe, Robert. *Danton: A Biography*. Translated by Peter Green. Garden City, N.Y.: Doubleday, 1967. A highly readable, dramatic account of Danton's life which captures the essence of his personality. Somewhat unreliable as to dates and facts.

Hampson, Norman. *Danton*. New York: Holmes & Meier, 1978. Scholarly and reliable, an excellent companion to the biography by Christophe. The bibliography cites nearly all the printed contemporary sources on Danton's life and the most important works by later historians.

Lefebvre, Georges. *The Coming of the French Revolution, 1789*. Translated by R. R. Palmer. New York: Random House, 1947. Introductory material for novices of the French Revolution. Although many historians disagree with Lefebvre's Marxist views, his interpretation continues to be popular in France. Covers only the early stages of the Revolution, 1787-1789.

Sydenham, M. J. *The French Revolution*. New York: G. P. Putnam's Sons, 1965. An introduction to its topic, which emphasizes the role of personalities and factions in shaping the Revolution. Includes a large bibliography and other valuable references for the beginner such as a detailed chronology, a map of Paris at the time of the Revolution, and an explanation of the revolutionary calendar.

Thompson, J. M. *The French Revolution*. Oxford, England: Basil Blackwell, 1943, rev. ed. 1985. An older narrative introduction with an updated (1985) bibliography. The latter cites the major printed primary sources on the Revolution while stressing more recent secondary works. Contains a host of valuable references.

Michael S. Fitzgerald

JACQUES-LOUIS DAVID

Born: August 30, 1748; Paris, France
Died: December 29, 1825; Brussels, Belgium
Area of Achievement: Art
Contribution: David was the founder of nineteenth century neoclassicism. His participation in the political events of his time directed not only the course of his own art but that of European painting as well.

Early Life

Jacques-Louis David's birth on August 30, 1748, coincided with the beginning of many profound political, social, and aesthetic changes in France. He was born in Paris into the merchant-and-artisan middle class, although his grandmother was the cousin of François Boucher, first painter to the king. During his early schooling, David was by all accounts an indifferent student who preferred drawing to any of his other studies. In 1764, at the age of sixteen, having declared his firm resolve to become a painter, David sought the help of Boucher. Although no longer accepting students himself, Boucher saw promise in the young David and advised that he study with Joseph Vien, a professor at the Royal Academy of Painting and Sculpture. Vien was, according to Boucher, a good painter and teacher, but somewhat cold. He advocated a return to classical antiquity as a source of moral as well as artistic inspiration; his own work, however, consisted mostly of superficial borrowings of classical motifs that lacked understanding of the true meaning of the classical spirit.

After two years in Vien's studio, David entered the academy as a student. In the light of his subsequent actions against the academy, it is important to note that at this time David did not question the academy's control over the arts in France. Accepting the academy's hierarchy of categories in painting, he aspired to the highest—that of history painting—and was determined to win the coveted Prix de Rome, which would allow him three years of study at the academy's branch in Rome and almost certainly guarantee his eventual membership in the academy. As an academician, eligible for the best royal commissions and allowed to exhibit his work at the Salon, he would be assured of a successful career.

After three unsuccessful attempts to win the Prix de Rome, David contemplated suicide. Even though he finally won the competition in 1774 with his *Antiochus and Stratonice*, he now harbored a bitter resentment of the academy's earlier rejections of his work, never forgiving the academicians for their failure to recognize the talent he was certain he possessed. In fact, his style at this time was fragmented, reflecting the many currents in French painting in the early 1770's—he painted classical themes with something of Vien's sense of theatricality and exaggerated dramatic effect, while his use of light and brushwork came from the rococo tradition.

While studying in Italy from 1778 to 1780, David was influenced by Greco-Roman classicism, the masters of the High Renaissance, and the early Baroque works of Caravaggio and the Carracci family. He went to Rome determined not to be seduced by classical antiquity, believing it to be lifeless and static. After studying classical sculpture and the Pompeian frescoes, however, he realized that he had based his work on a false principle. He sensed that he would have to repudiate everything he had once thought about art. The qualities of virtue, austerity, and moral strength which he saw in ancient classical art reinforced his own desires for simplicity and strength. His work soon began to evidence the characteristics that would mark his mature style: solidity of drawing, clarity of form and narrative structure, and a Caravaggesque realism of light and texture.

Life's Work

David's first public acclaim came with the exhibition of twelve paintings in the Salon of 1781, the most popular of which was *Belisarius*—the story of false accusation and unjust punishment in a past age, which viewers equated with a contemporary general falsely accused and executed for treason. In the next few years, David's reputation increased—he was praised by the encyclopedist Denis Diderot for his creation of a noble, didactic art, and he attained academy membership.

David's involvement with the political events of his day began with *The Oath of the Horatii* of 1785. This painting, with its theme of self-sacrifice for a noble cause, was perceived by viewers as a pictorial call to arms for the revolutionary sentiments rapidly gaining momentum in France. Just as he had done in *Belisarius*, David created a parallel between contemporary events and ancient history with this theme of the three Horatii who, united by a strict patriotic discipline of body and soul, swear an oath to fight to the death for their country, while the tragic personal loss which always accompanies heroic military feats is evidenced by the group of mourning wives and children who witness the oath. Then, with the exhibition of *The Death of Socrates* in 1787 and *Brutus Receiving the Bodies of His Sons* in 1789—both of which portray the same message of self-sacrifice for a greater good—David's reputation as a prophet of the Revolution was firmly established in the minds of the French public.

David, now a fervent Jacobin and friend of Robespierre, took a more active role in revolutionary events after the fall of the Bastille. He became the director of all revolutionary festivals. He was elected as a deputy to the National Convention, during which time he voted for the execution of the king in 1793, signed hundreds of arrest warrants during the Reign of Terror, and proposed the creation of national museums that he also helped to organize. In 1790, he had avenged himself upon the academicians by organizing other dissident artists into the Commune des Arts, and, in 1793, he persuaded the convention to abolish the academy, replacing it with a jury to supervise the awarding of Salon prizes. As the principal juror, David had become the virtual dictator of the arts in France. Always a reformer, he freed French art from some of the old academic constraints while he led the way toward a new academicism.

David's political activities continued to give direction to his painting. The prophet of the Revolution became the chronicler of the historic events of the present. His works of this period range from *The Oath of the Tennis Court* (1791)—commemorating the deputies of the Third Estate's writing of a new constitution—to his apotheosis of such slain republican heroes as Jean-Paul Marat, Vicomte Paul François Barras, and Paul Michel Lepeletier.

Political involvement, however, almost cost David his life. After the execution of Robespierre in 1794, David was arrested and, although his enemies demanded his death, he was imprisoned instead. An amnesty in 1795 set him free. While in prison, David—having vowed at his trial that he would henceforth attach himself to principles and not to men—began planning his next great classical painting, *The Battle of the Romans and Sabines* (1794-1799), a work which restored his artistic reputation.

His determination to avoid political involvements was quickly forgotten when, in 1797, he acquired a new patron and hero, Napoleon Bonaparte— then first consul and later Emperor of France. David became his court painter, documenting all the military splendor and pageantry of Napoleon's reign in portraits, in depictions of Napoleon leading his armies to victory, and finally in the coronation itself. David, who had earlier used history and mythology to refer to contemporary events, now turned contemporary events into new historical myths. His neoclassicism influenced everything from painting and sculpture to fashion and furniture design, and some of his most important works date from this period.

Unfortunately, David's political activities again proved to be his undoing. Napoleon's abdication and the First Bourbon Restoration of 1814 found David stubbornly maintaining his allegiance to the emperor, believing perhaps that his international reputation as an artist would protect him. During the Hundred Days, in fact, he met with Napoleon, who made him a Commander of the Legion of Honor, and he rashly signed the *Acte additionnel* (1815), again repudiating the rule of the Bourbon Kings of France. The Second Restoration, however, saw the enactment of a law banishing all who had signed the *Acte additionnel*, and David, at the age of sixty-seven, went into exile in Brussels.

Despite some attempts at reprisal by his enemies in France, David's last years in Brussels were happy and productive. Sale of his works brought him financial security, and he enjoyed a position of prominence within the artistic community. He painted continually, concentrating on portraits and mythological subjects such as *Cupid and Psyche* (1817) and *Telemachus and Eucharis* (1818)—themes which were less dangerous, perhaps, than the real or legendary histories of Greece and Rome which had served him so well during the politically active years of the Revolution, the Republic, and the Empire. He died peacefully at his home in Brussels on December 29, 1825, at the age of seventy-seven.

Summary

Jacques-Louis David's art, like his personality, was extremely complex. Friends described him as intense and dogmatic, sensitive and spartan—an assessment of character substantiated by the severe, doctrinaire classicism of his prerevolutionary works, all of which are remarkable for their stoicism and their sense of emotion held in check by icy control. David eventually realized that the success of these heroically ethical creations—which had proclaimed a new aesthetic and moral order—could not be repeated indefinitely, even by him. In 1808, he declared that the direction he had set for art was too severe to please for very long in France.

A different facet of David's personality was reflected in his attempt to separate artistic activity from the demands of morality by concentrating on purely aesthetic problems in *The Battle of the Romans and Sabines*—a work in which he modified the severity of his Roman classicism for a more Greek and abstract refinement. In his paintings of contemporary events during the Napoleonic era and in many of his portraits, David proved himself an acute observer of nature and a realist.

As the different goals and interests embodied in later nineteenth century movements such as Romanticism and Impressionism led artists to turn away from classicism, David's principles and his art were shunned, and his reputation went into an eclipse that lasted until 1913. At that time, an exhibition in Paris prompted an interest in his work which has continued to grow, and today he is acknowledged as the true founder of nineteenth century European neoclassicism.

Bibliography

Brookner, Anita. *Jacques-Louis David*. New York: Harper & Row, 1980. One of the most complete biographies, this book contains important documentation, never before published in English, of David's artistic sources and his political activities. Also contains an extensive catalog of paintings and drawings, although most plates are monochrome.

French Painting, 1774-1830: The Age of Revolution. Detroit: Wayne State University Press, 1975. Catalog of a French-American exhibition of paintings from the age of revolution. Excellent essays by foremost Davidian scholars discuss the artistic disunity of the era and analyze David's contribution to mainstream trends. Includes brief biographies of all exhibitors.

Friedlaender, Walter. *David to Delacroix*. Translated by Robert Goldwater. Cambridge, Mass.: Harvard University Press, 1952. Emphasizes the historical structure of French painting by studying the sources of various stylistic and intellectual currents of the period. Discusses classicism and other trends in David's art and the transformation of his principles by his followers.

Nanteuil, Luc de. *Jacques-Louis David*. New York: Harry N. Abrams, 1985. Detailed account of David's development from early styles through mature styles. Clear, concise discussion of political events which shaped his thinking. Excellent color plates of most significant works, with analysis of the formalistic elements of each.

Rosenblum, Robert, and H. W. Janson. *Nineteenth Century Art*. New York: Harry N. Abrams, 1984. Contains a perceptive analysis of David's style through the Napoleonic era, contrasting his use of classical sources to that of his contemporaries, and also relates his political allegiances to his painting. Continues with detailed accounts of David's followers and their efforts to maintain the neoclassical style in spite of the growth of Romanticism.

LouAnn Faris Culley

FERENC DEÁK

Born: October 17, 1803; Söjtör, Zala County, Hungary
Died: January 28, 1876; Pest, Hungary
Areas of Achievement: Government and politics
Contribution: Deák's persuasive and undaunting efforts brought about Hungary's most important compromise, the *Ausgleich*. He also led the liberals in the passage of much needed social reforms and was one of Hungary's greatest codifiers of progressive laws that brought Hungary out of feudalism.

Early Life

Ferenc Deák, Sr., a third-generation nobleman, followed the family tradition of increasing wealth and power through marriage. In the 1780's, he married Erzsébet Sibrik of Szarvaskend, the daughter of the deputy sheriff of Győr County. On October 17, 1803, their youngest of six children, Ferenc Deák, Jr., was born. Several days later, Erzsébet died of complications from childbirth. Consequently, her husband rejected his infant son and sent him to an uncle, József Deák. The family soon moved to Kehida, where Ferenc Deák, Sr., died on January 25, 1808. At that time, young Ferenc's elder brother, Antal, became his legal guardian.

Ferenc was tutored by a Franciscan until 1808. At that time, he started his formal education by attending elementary school at church schools in Kőszeg, Keszthely, and Pápa. In 1817, Ferenc was graduated from the *Gymnasium* in Nagykanizsa and then began his studies at the Royal Law Academy in Győr, where he excelled in German, Latin, and constitutional law and history.

Ferenc's future career and his thought processes were influenced by two major factors. First, he witnessed legislative resistance to royal decrees by local assemblies. Ferenc was maturing in an intense atmosphere of revolution and opposition to the Habsburg regime. In 1821, he attended, against royal mandate, the Assembly of Győr and witnessed its refusal to execute what it considered to be an unconstitutional royal decree. Then, he saw similar defiance in Zala County, when that assembly resisted the absolutism of the Metternich system. Zala County led the opposition against Austrian absolutism and Antal Deák led Zala County. The second major factor influencing Ferenc was the leadership of his brother. Antal advocated that loyalty to the dynasty should not prevent resistance to despotism and that local assemblies had a responsibility to resist any unconstitutional ordinances. He was well known throughout Hungary, and Ferenc was inspired by him.

In December, 1821, Ferenc was graduated from the Academy, and Zala County declared him legally of age. His first act was to emancipate his former wet nurse, symbolic of his future work in abolishing feudalism and in obtaining rights for all Hungarians. In November, 1822, Ferenc arrived in Pest and passed the bar examination with distinction on December 19, 1823. While in Pest, Hungary's cultural center, he came into contact with numerous cultural organizations. The most important of these was the *Auróra* circle, through which he developed lasting friendships with several liberal statesmen, politicians, and poets, many of whom greatly contributed to his intellectual development.

Ferenc began his public service at the county level by holding several unpaid positions. His first was given to him as a gesture of recognition for Antal's hard work. On December 13, 1824, Ferenc was elected notary to the County Commission for Orphans. He also held the position of county magistrate and was elected deputy high sheriff surrogate; however, he never took the latter post. When the national legislative body, the diet, convened in Pozsony in 1832, Antal represented Zala County as deputy. In January, 1833, he resigned and recommended Ferenc to replace him. On April 15, 1833, Ferenc was subsequently elected to a seat in the Lower House. With this position, his county service ended. His career as a national political figure began at this time and would influence Hungarian and Austrian history for the next forty-three years.

Life's Work

The 1830's and 1840's were critical years for Hungary. Plague, peasant revolts, and economic depression were widespread, and Hungary had a feudal constitution. Deák's experience at the county level enabled him to understand legal procedure and alerted him to Hungary's social, economic, and political problems. Thus, he joined the reform-minded liberals, led by Baron Miklós Wesselényi.

In 1836, Deák introduced his first legislative measure, calling for the emancipation of the serfs. When Ferdinand I vetoed the measure, Deák called an unofficial session of the diet. As a result of this episode, Deák was acknowledged as the leader of the liberals in the Lower House.

On May 2, 1836, Deák returned to Zala County to report on the proceedings of the diet. He also proposed a program of reforms, which was printed and published by the assembly and sent to other counties without royal approval. The Crown reprimanded the assembly and ordered all copies to be collected. The assembly rejected the reprimand, and Deák became the symbol of Hungarian progressive ideas. In appreciation for his legislative leadership, he was elected an honorary member of the Academy of Sciences on November 21, 1839.

Deák successfully concluded his first compromise during the Diet of 1839-1840. Many liberal leaders had been arrested in 1836, and Deák had offered his services as mediator; however, the Crown was unwilling to compromise. He then warned that if the Crown did not respect Hungarian laws and rights,

Hungary would employ passive resistance and defiance. Thus, on June 6, 1839, when Ferdinand summoned the diet, Deák recommended that they not discuss any royal proposals until all grievances were resolved. He met privately with an agent of the Crown in March, 1840, and achieved a compromise to the satisfaction of the liberals.

Deák entered the 1840's with hopes for a legal revolution that would transform Hungary from a feudal to a modern state through peaceful legislation. At the 1841 diet, he proposed drastic changes in the judiciary, but his legislative attempts all met with failure. Deák became apathetic and inactive; his aloofness began to compromise his influence. At this time, Lajos Kossuth assumed the leadership of the liberals. In 1846, Deák reluctantly helped write the Liberal Party platform, which called for universal reforms. This work promoted the unification of Hungary's first opposition party.

By August, 1847, Deák temporarily left Hungary, allegedly under doctor's orders. He was short and stocky, with great physical strength, but he was prone to sickness. In reality, however, he did not believe the liberals could achieve their goals at this time because of the stubbornness of the Crown. He realized the only course for Hungary was violence and revolution—actions which were against his values.

When the last feudal diet (1847-1848) was summoned, Kossuth sent a list of grievances (written by Deák) to Ferdinand I. By 1848, much of the empire was in revolt. Faced with chaos, Ferdinand consented to the list of demands and granted Hungary independence. The first elected parliament met in July, 1848, and passed a series of reforms known as the April Laws, ending feudalism and introducing a liberal form of government. Deák led the new Lower House and achieved the greatest social reforms of his legislative career. He was named Minister of Justice and succeeded in having his earlier judicial reform measures (of 1841) passed as the Press Act in 1848.

On September 11, 1848, Austria invaded Hungary. Deák abandoned his office, the ministry was in chaos, and counterrevolution began. On December 2, 1848, Ferdinand abdicated in favor of his nephew Francis Joseph I. Hungary considered the new ruler a usurper because he did not swear the required oath of loyalty to the Hungarian constitution. On April 14, 1849, the parliament deposed the Habsburg dynasty. Consequently, Francis Joseph ordered a massive assault on Hungary.

By August, 1849, the Hungarian revolution ended. Hungary was partitioned and placed under a repressive regime for many years. Most of the revolutionary leaders were either executed or exiled. Deák appeared before a military tribunal on December 14, 1849, and was interrogated for five months. Finally, he was released, as he had not supported the deposition of the royal dynasty.

From 1850 to 1859, Deák offered passive resistance to the Crown. In 1854, he sold the family estate and permanently moved to the Hotel Angol

Királyné in Pest. At this time, he became the director of the Hungarian Academy of Sciences. His passive resistance ended in December, 1860, when he was granted an audience with Francis Joseph. The two men immediately developed a mutual trust and respect for each other. Deák was honest, always spoke frankly, and was open-minded. He accepted Francis Joseph's offer to participate in the Lord Chief Justice's Conference (January 23 to March 3, 1861) aimed at reconciling Hungary's civil and criminal court procedures with Austria's system. On February 27, however, the Crown announced its intention to reduce Hungary to a province. Deák left the conference angrily, believing that revolution was Hungary's only hope of remaining autonomous.

He again became inflexible in his attitude toward the empire. In 1861, the Crown summoned the first diet in twelve years. This time, Deák represented Pest. Dissension among the liberals gave rise to two new political parties: the Party of Petition led by Deák and the Party of Resolution led by Count László Teleki. After Teleki committed suicide, Deák assumed the position of the leading statesman in Hungary.

With hostilities again developing, the Crown adopted more oppressive measures. Deák recommended a policy of passive defense to parliament, which was adjourned by the Crown on August 22, 1861. On November 5, 1861, Hungary became a province of the empire. From this position, Deák enjoyed his greatest level of prestige. He began to lay the foundations for a compromise. He anonymously wrote an article in *Pesti Naplo* entitled "Easter Article," followed by a series of similar articles. Through this vehicle he offered a solution to the volatile situation between Hungary and the dynasty. Deák knew that the time was right for compromise; Austria was nearly bankrupt and the empire's collapse was imminent.

Negotiations began and a new parliament was summoned in September, 1865. Deák's party won a majority of the seats. Deák began to shape Hungary's history and proved himself to be a practitioner of realpolitik. He did not create movements or ideas; he merely took advantage of situations, planned the right strategies, and knew how to manipulate the political forces that existed. For the first time in his long career, Deák exercised his very forceful and persuasive leadership ability. On December 20, 1865, the Deák Party Club was established to organize campaign strategies. Deák developed goals to be achieved and principles to be followed. He demanded discipline but never used force or humiliation to obtain his objectives.

On June 17, 1867, Austria went to war with Prussia. Deák now pushed for compromise. He met for a second time with Francis Joseph, and they agreed upon the *Ausgleich*, the Compromise of 1867. It provided for the following: the creation of the state of Austria-Hungary with a dual monarchy in the person of the emperor; the restoration of the Hungarian constitution of 1848; the separation of parliamentary bodies—the Hungarian Parliament would meet in Budapest and the Austrian parliament in Vienna; the joint administration of military and foreign affairs by delegates from the two parliaments and three joint ministers (foreign affairs, war, and finance); and the renewal of terms of the *Ausgleich* every ten years. There was some opposition to the *Ausgleich*, especially from Kossuth. Yet most Austrians and Hungarians rejoiced in the settlement, as it resolved a thirty-year-old conflict and provided stability for the empire (which lasted until World War I).

Deák also proposed a series of acts which created a new Hungary. The two most important were the Croatian-Hungarian Compromise and the Equality of the Nationalities Act. He finally saw fulfilled a lifetime of efforts to obtain and protect the rights of all people. Furthermore, Deák wanted Hungary to become a true democracy. After the *Ausgleich*, however, his party began to splinter, and his health deteriorated.

By 1871, Deák's era was coming to an end. His influence also began to wane, and he experienced legislative defeats. His last political act created the Parliamentary Liberal Party in 1873, with Kálmán Tisza as head, but liberalism was also beginning to decline. Deák's last speech was delivered to parliament on June 28, 1873. It was very reflective of his first presentation made forty years earlier in that his main emphasis was placed on the need for progressive legislation and liberalism.

In 1875, Deák was elected for the last time to parliament, but he was never seated. On January 28, 1876, he died in his hotel suite in Pest. The parliament, in his memory, commissioned a statue of him to be placed in front of the Academy of Sciences building in Budapest.

Summary

Ironically, while Ferenc Deák was the author of the greatest compromise in Hungarian history, he was very uncompromising on moral, constitutional, and social issues. He believed firmly in the Christian ideals of the brotherhood of all men and the stern morality of the ancient Hebrews. He emulated the Romans in their respect for the law and admired the Hellenistic culture for its love of beauty. These ideals were the basis for his moral standards and behavior.

His commitment to certain values became apparent when, on his second day as a freshman member of the diet, he broke with tradition and asked for the floor. It was here that he demonstrated for the first time his excellent oratorical skills and took the first step in his long journey toward making laws more humane and liberal.

Deák gained almost immediate recognition as a reformer. He spent the greater part of his life working toward creating a more liberal government in Hungary. He strove to remove the last remnants of feudalism and to achieve equality for all citizens through peaceful legislation. He strongly believed that law was the backbone of society. He therefore advocated changing unjust laws—not violating them. He worked earnestly at strengthening and modernizing the judiciary.

Deák was a man before his time. This was proved in his first legal case, which illustrated his basic philosophy. The case involved József Babics, a man charged with highway robbery, murder, and several lesser offenses. Deák admitted his client's guilt but not fault. The defense rested on the premise that society was responsible for Babics' actions because it had not provided him with an education and values. Deák lost the case, but he argued against capital punishment and for societal responsibility.

Deák's life's ambition was to achieve a true self-government for Hungary and to obtain the passage of liberal laws. He did not consider the *Ausgleich* the climax of his career. Instead, he viewed it as a necessary interruption to his real task, the completion of the work that the liberals had begun in Hungary during the Reform Era of the 1830's and 1840's. He attempted to create a truly democratic government and society; he sincerely cared about the deprived masses and sought reform in their name.

Bibliography
Jászi, Oscar. *The Dissolution of the Habsburg Monarchy*. Chicago: University of Chicago Press, 1929. This work contains an excellent bibliographical section for research on the Habsburgs, Austria, and Eastern Europe. Many of the works included, however, are in German. Describes Deák's political career from the 1830's through 1867 and his role in the Compromise of 1867.
Kann, Robert A. *The Multinational Empire: Nationalism and National Reform in the Habsburg Monarchy, 1848-1918*. 2 vols. New York: Columbia University Press, 1950. This work contains background information on the Austrian Empire. Addresses Deák's leadership ability and his drive for fair treatment of minorities. Volume 1 contains 444 pages with somewhat more emphasis on Deák's role in the government than the 423 pages of volume 2. Each volume contains an introduction and a notes section, and volume 2 has a selected bibliography and index.
Király, Béla K. *Ferenc Deák*. Boston: Twayne, 1975. An excellent although somewhat biased biography containing a chronology of the Deák family from 1665, when the family was ennobled, to Ferenc's death in 1876. Stresses Ferenc's devotion to his political career and also contains a thorough discussion of his private life. The 243 pages include notes, references, bibliographical sections, and an index.
May, Arthur J. *The Hapsburg Monarchy, 1867-1914*. Cambridge, Mass.: Harvard University Press, 1951. This work contains a notes section, a bibliography, and an index, and emphasizes Deák's work on the Compromise of 1867 and his role as the leader of the moderates. Also discusses his other political contributions, including his influence after the Compro-

mise of 1867. The 532 pages emphasize Deák's great negotiating skills, needed to placate the various minority groups in Hungary. Contains quotes taken from Deák's correspondences and speeches.

Murad, Anatol. *Franz Joseph I of Austria and His Empire*. Boston: Twayne, 1968. A standard biography of Franz Joseph, with an index, genealogical chart, and chronology from 1830 to 1916. Also contains a selected bibliography. Emphasizes details about the circumstances under which the Compromise of 1867 was agreed upon and Deák's role in obtaining Franz Joseph's approval as well as the relationship between Deák and such important revolutionaries as Count Gyula Andrássy.

Victoria Reynolds

RICHARD DEDEKIND

Born: October 6, 1831; Brunswick
Died: February 12, 1916; Brunswick, Germany
Area of Achievement: Mathematics
Contribution: Dedekind gave a new definition to the concept of irrational numbers, based exclusively on arithmetic principles. He helped clarify the notions of infinity and continuity and contributed to the establishment of rigorous theoretical foundations for mathematics.

Early Life

Julius Wilhelm Richard Dedekind was one of four children born to a well-established professional family in Brunswick. His father was a professor of jurisprudence at the local Collegium Carolinum, and his mother was a professor's daughter. In school, Dedekind was primarily interested in physics and chemistry, but when he enrolled in the Collegium Carolinum, it was as a student of mathematics. From a résumé, written somewhat later and in Latin, it is clear that this change was based on his dissatisfaction with the lack of rigor in the natural sciences.

In 1850, Dedekind was matriculated at the University of Göttingen, where he followed various courses in mathematics (studying under Carl Friedrich Gauss), astronomy, and experimental physics. In 1852, Dedekind presented his doctoral dissertation, which, in the opinion of Gauss, showed promise. At that time, the standard of mathematics at Göttingen was not very high, and Dedekind spent the following two years studying privately and preparing himself to become a first-class mathematician. No doubt his friendship with the brilliant Georg Friedrich Bernhard Riemann, at Göttingen at the same time, was also a positive influence. In fact, Dedekind attended Riemann's lectures even after he himself qualified as a university lecturer in 1854. When Gauss died in 1855, Peter Gustav Lejeune Dirichlet, previously professor in Berlin, succeeded him. Dedekind described Dirichlet's arrival in Göttingen as a life-changing event. Dedekind not only attended Dirichlet's lectures but also became a personal friend of the new professor.

Life's Work

In 1858, the Federal Institute of Technology in Zurich, Switzerland, appointed Dedekind as professor of mathematics on Dirichlet's recommendation. Riemann also applied for the post but his work was considered too abstract. Dedekind stayed in Zurich until 1862 and then accepted an invitation from his old college in Brunswick, which had become a polytechnic by then. While in Zurich, Dedekind taught differential and integral calculus and was disturbed by having to use concepts that had never been properly defined. In particular, he wrote: "Differential calculus deals with continuous magnitude, and yet an explanation of this continuity is nowhere given." He also deplored accepting without proof the belief that an increasing infinite sequence with an upper bound converges to a limit. He was dissatisfied that the notions of limit and continuity were based solely on geometrical intuition. On November 24, 1858, Dedekind succeeded in securing "a real definition of the essence of continuity." He waited until 1872 to publish this definition in book form, with the title *Stetigkeit und Irrationale Zahlen* ("Continuity and Irrational Numbers," translated in *Essays on the Theory of Numbers*, 1901).

Dedekind's problem was essentially that of irrational numbers, known already to the ancient Greeks. Rational numbers are dense in the sense that between any two rational numbers there is always another rational number, although there are infinitely many gaps between them. These gaps can be thought of as irrational numbers, and, before Dedekind began his work, they were characterized by infinite, nonrecurring decimal fractions. Dedekind devised a method, using "cuts," to define irrational numbers in terms of the rationals. If rational numbers are divided into two sets such that every number in the first set is smaller than every number in the second set, this partition defines one and only one real number. Should there be a largest or smallest number in one of the sets, the Dedekind cut corresponds to that rational number, while an irrational number is defined if neither set has a smallest or largest member. A Dedekind cut can be imagined as severing a straight line composed of only rational numbers into two parts. Rational and irrational numbers together form the set of real numbers, and this set can now be made to correspond to all the points of a straight line. With this method, Dedekind not only managed to define irrational numbers in terms of rationals without recourse to geometry but also showed that a line, and by implication three-dimensional space, is complete, containing no holes. Furthermore, Dedekind upheld his philosophical principles, according to which numbers do not exist in a Platonic sense but are free creations of the human mind.

Closely connected to this work was the introduction of the concept of "ideals." Dedekind edited and published Dirichlet's lectures on number theory after the death of the latter. Dedekind can, in fact, be considered the author of the book, since Dirichlet left only an outline plan for publication, and that was already based on Dedekind's notes. In the tenth supplement to the second edition of this influential book, Dedekind developed the theory of ideals, following to a certain extent a line Ernst Eduard Kummer had already taken. Dedekind, however, went far beyond Kummer, avoided his mistakes, and made the theory more exact.

Ideals are an extension and generalization of the common number concept. According to the fundamental theory of arithmetic, ordinary integers either are prime numbers or can be uniquely factorized into primes. Unique factorization is a useful feature but does not generally apply to all algebraic integers in a given algebraic number field, algebraic numbers being defined as the roots of polynomial equations with integer coefficients. With the introduction of ideals, unique factorization can be restored. Dedekind subsequently revised and further developed this theory. In an important paper coauthored by Heinrich Weber, the analogy between algebraic numbers and algebraic functions was demonstrated with the help of ideals.

In *Was sind und was sollen die Zahlen?* (1888; "The Nature and Meaning of Numbers," translated in *Essays on the Theory of Numbers*, 1901), Dedekind utilized the concept of what he called systems, which later became known as sets, and developed logical theories of original and cardinal numbers and of mathematical induction. In addition to contributing papers to mathematical journals, Dedekind coedited Riemann's collected works and supplied a biography of Riemann.

Dedekind stayed at Brunswick until his death and became a director of the polytechnic between 1872 and 1875. It seems that Dedekind was not offered the posts he would have accepted, while he refused the posts, most notably the one at Halle, that he was offered. Dedekind never married but lived with one of his sisters until her death in 1914. Although he lived in relative isolation, he was never a recluse. He was an excellent musician: He played the cello as a young man and the piano in later life. His portraits show a fine-featured man with thoughtful eyes; his character was described as modest, mild, and somewhat shy.

Summary

Although Richard Dedekind was a corresponding member of several academies and an honorary doctor of several universities, he never received the recognition he so fully deserved. It can be seen that his work was one of the most influential in shaping twentieth century mathematics. He is one of only thirty-one mathematicians meriting an individual entry in *Iwanami Sugaku Ziten* (1954; *Encyclopedic Dictionary of Mathematics*, 1977), in which he is described as a pioneer of abstract algebra. Transcending pure calculation, Dedekind made an attempt to find theoretical foundations to concepts used in algebraic number theory and in infinitesimal calculus. He defined and thereby created new mathematical structures that generalize the notions of number and serve as examples for further generalization.

Dedekind met Georg Cantor on a holiday in Switzerland and became his friend and also, at times, his frequent correspondent. Cantor submitted his theories to Dedekind for comment and criticism, and Dedekind was one of the first to support set theory in the face of hostility by other mathematicians. Independently of Cantor, he also utilized the concept of the actual, or concrete, infinite—a concept that was then regarded as taboo because there existed no theoretical foundation for its existence. Dedekind's work assisted in finding just such a foundation.

Bibliography
Bell, Eric T. "Arithmetic the Second." In *Men of Mathematics*. New York: Simon & Schuster, 1937. Reprint. New York: Penguin Books, 1965. This short chapter in a well-known collective biography of mathematicians discusses the life and work of Kummer and Dedekind. Bell makes a good attempt to explain the abstract and often difficult concepts that are necessary for the understanding and appreciation of Dedekind's work.
Dauben, J. W. *Georg Cantor: His Mathematics and Philosophy of the Infinite*. Cambridge, Mass.: Harvard University Press, 1979. Not a biography of Cantor, but a study of the emergence of a new mathematical theory. Dedekind's life, his work, and his influence on Cantor are featured extensively, but these references are dispersed throughout the book. Readers whose main interest is in Dedekind can rely on the well-constructed index and the twenty-four-page bibliography.
Edwards, Harold M. "Dedekind's Invention of Ideals." *The Bulletin of the London Mathematical Society* 15 (1983): 8-17. Traces the influences on Dedekind's set theoretic approach mainly to Dirichlet but also to Kummer and Riemann. Évariste Galois' influence was limited and resulted in steering Dedekind toward conceptual thinking as opposed to mere calculating. Dedekind went beyond Dirichlet, and against the accepted classical doctrine, by using completed infinites. The author stresses the innovative nature of Dedekind's theories and the analogy between cuts and ideals.
_____. "The Genesis of Ideal Theory." *Archive for History of Exact Sciences* 23 (1980): 321-378. Analyzes Kummer's, Leopold Kronecker's, and Dedekind's versions of the theory of ideal factorization of algebraic integers. The author advances the thesis that as Dedekind revised the theory several times to match his philosophical principles, it did not improve from the mathematical point of view, and the first formulation remained the best.
Gillies, D. A. *Frege, Dedekind, and Peano on the Foundations of Arithmetic*. Assen, the Netherlands: Van Gorcum, 1982. A short paperback with an adequate index and a list of references. Investigates the relationship between logic and arithmetic in the work of the three men. Gillies regards Dedekind as fundamentally a logician and compares him to Gottlob Frege, who denied that a set was a logical notion, and to Giuseppe Peano, who thought that arithmetic could not be reduced to logic.
Grattan-Guinness, I. "The Rediscovery of the Cantor-Dedekind Correspondence." *Jahresbericht der Deutschen Mathematiker Vereinigung* 76 (1974): 104-139. Recounts what happened to Dedekind's side of the correspondence, which seemed to have disappeared after the publication of the

mathematical extracts in 1937. Ninety-eight items are listed, including notes, drafts, and letters to Ferdinand Georg Frobenius and Weber in addition to the Cantor-Dedekind correspondence. Contains extracts from the letters in German, with connecting text in English. The reader gains some insight into why Dedekind refused the position offered to him at Halle.

Jourdain, Philip E. B. "Richard Dedekind (1833-1916)." *The Monist* 26 (1916): 415-427. Obituary article with long extracts from the English translation of Dedekind's works. Contains virtually no biographical details, but gives a clear explanation of the Dedekind cuts and mentions the connection between what Dedekind called systems and set theory introduced by Cantor. Ideals are not discussed. The importance of finding rigorous foundations to arithmetic is stressed.

Judit Brody

EDGAR DEGAS

Born: July 19, 1834; Paris, France
Died: September 27, 1917; Paris, France
Area of Achievement: Art
Contribution: Degas was one of the great figural painters and draftsmen of
the nineteenth century. His work combined a deep understanding of tradition with a commitment to innovative portrayals of modern life. His artistic independence was asserted in his role as one of the leading figures of
the Impressionist exhibitions of 1874-1886.

Early Life

Edgar Degas was born into a comfortable, upper-bourgeois Parisian family in 1834. His father managed the local branch of the family bank, head-
quartered in Naples, and his mother was the daughter of a cotton broker in
New Orleans. The family's social connections in France, Italy, and the
United States would play an important role in shaping Edgar's life and
character. Frequent visits to the Louvre, as well as to the homes of friends
who had substantial private collections, were regarded as an essential part of
the boy's upbringing. Edgar attended the prestigious Lycée Louis-le-Grand
in Paris, where he received his first instruction in drawing. Upon graduation
in 1853, he briefly studied law but soon turned his attention wholeheartedly
to a career in art.

Degas' early artistic training consisted of two stages: the period 1853-
1856, spent mostly in Paris, and the period 1856-1859, dominated by two
lengthy sojourns in Italy. In Paris, Degas studied under Louis Lamothe, a
follower of the disciplined classicism of Jean-Auguste-Dominique Ingres.
Working independently, Degas devoted much time to copying paintings in
the Louvre and prints in the Bibliothèque Nationale. In 1855, he enrolled in
the École des Beaux Arts. Instead of completing his formal studies and
competing for the coveted Prix de Rome, however, he decided to go to Italy
on his own. In Naples and Florence, where he visited relatives, and in
Rome, where he stayed at the French Academy, Degas' devotion to the art
of the past was expanded and deepened. At the same time, his contact
with other young French artists studying in Italy, such as Gustave Moreau,
helped turn his attention to the more recent achievements of artists such as
Eugène Delacroix.

Apart from many copies and sketches, the most important works produced
by Degas during these early years were portraits of family members. The
crowning achievement of these early portraits was *The Bellelli Family*, a
large painting of his Florentine relatives begun in Italy in 1858 and completed several years later in Paris. In its technical mastery and psychological
sensitivity, this painting announced the beginning of a major career.

Life's Work

The emergence of Degas' artistic personality during the 1860's was characteristically complex. Soon after his return from Italy, he established a studio in Paris and began to work on a series of large history paintings. Although inspired in part by the classical tradition, Degas' historical scenes tended to recast tradition through a disarming straightforwardness of treatment. The last of this group of pictures, *Scene of War in the Middle Ages*, was shown at the Salon of 1865 as Degas' first major publicly exhibited work. Ironically, that marked the beginning of Degas' public career and the end of his interest in history painting. The following year, he exhibited *The Steeplechase*, and in 1868 he showed *Mlle Fiocre in the Ballet "La Source."* The themes of the racetrack and the ballet proclaimed the artist's new commitment to the subject matter of contemporary life. This commitment would be a decisive factor in determining the subsequent course of his career.

Degas' interest in contemporary subjects was inspired and shared by a growing circle of progressive artists and writers with whom he began associating during these years. By around 1862, he had met Édouard Manet, leader of a new generation of artists devoted to painting modern life, and Edmund Duranty, a naturalist writer and critic who would become a champion of Degas' art during the 1870's. Through the frequent gatherings of artists at the Café Guerbois, Degas became familiar with Claude Monet,. Auguste Renoir, and other young artists who would eventually form the core of the Impressionist group. His keen, perceptive intellect and brusque humor soon established Degas' prominence within the group. Although his role would develop into one of dedicated leadership, he would always maintain a degree of the aloofness of an outsider. An intriguing glimpse of this complex personality is provided in the *Self-Portrait* of about 1863, in which confidence, irony, and self-consciousness seem to coexist behind a façade of bourgeois elegance.

The 1870's were both a climax and a turning point in Degas' career. His paintings of familiar urban entertainments such as the ballet achieved full maturity, and his circle of colleagues finally banded together and organized a series of independent exhibitions. At the same time, however, he experienced some unexpected setbacks. The Franco-Prussian War of 1870-1871 found him serving in the artillery, and at this time he began to have problems with his eyesight. His financial security was seriously compromised as a result of the failure of the family bank following his father's death in 1874. Degas' commitment to the risky venture of the independent exhibitions from the first show in 1874 until the last one in 1886 is all the more impressive in the face of these circumstances.

Degas' accomplishments as an artist during the 1870's were an extraordinary combination of fully realized maturity and restless experimentation. The ballet scenes were a dominant theme, beginning with such works as *The*

Orchestra of the Opera (c. 1870) and *The Dance Class* (1871), which established the performance hall and the rehearsal studio as the two realms of Degas' exploration of the dance. His portraits achieved new complexity and psychological depth, as exemplified by the group of paintings of his New Orleans relatives, done when the artist visited them in 1872-1873, and by various portrayals of friends and colleagues such as the portrait of Duranty of 1879. Several new themes were introduced or given greater prominence during the years of the Impressionist exhibitions, including the café and the café-concert, milliners, laundresses, and prostitutes. Along with these diverse themes, an increasing attention to varied techniques such as pastel, lithography, monotype, and sculpture contributed to the rich complexity of Degas' mature art.

The most decisive changes in Degas' later work were introduced in the years around 1880. The interest in sculpture was bold, experimental, and largely private. The subjects of the sculptures, especially dancers and bathers, paralleled the themes of his paintings at a time when pastel was increasingly replacing oil as his principal pictorial medium. The rich textures and glowing colors of the pastel bathers of the 1880's and 1890's represent the grand culmination of Degas' career. Seven such pictures were shown at the last Impressionist exhibit in 1886, including the famous *Woman Bathing in a Shallow Tub*. By presenting the nude in unconventionally natural poses seen from unexpected angles in realistic surroundings, these works revitalized tradition through an emphasis on the immediacy of experience and the ingenuity of artistic innovation.

Degas' late work was hampered by failing eyesight, although flashes of brilliance continued to appear until he finally had to stop painting entirely around 1908. He was able to turn his attention to collecting because of the rising prices he was receiving for his works, but for the most part the last years leading up to his death in 1917 were characterized by a frustrating inactivity and isolation.

Summary

Edgar Degas' artistic contribution can be summarized in terms of his complex relation to Impressionism. As a leading figure behind the Impressionist exhibitions, Degas made a historic commitment to artistic independence which would help set the stage for the development of modern art. His dedication to subjects drawn from modern life and to bold technical and stylistic innovation are aspects of his art which played an integral role within the group. On the other hand, he was persistently somewhat of an outsider whose attitudes and alliances increasingly factionalized the group. He particularly opposed the label Impressionist (he preferred "Independents") and its associations with a spontaneous, directly naturalistic art. Although his art was committed to contemporary subjects and steeped in observation and experience, Degas was never entirely a naturalist. In contrast to Monet, who rejected tradition and painted directly before his subjects in nature, Degas executed his works in the studio and relied heavily on calculation, imagination, and memory of earlier works of art. His artistic repertoire expanded from an early love of Ingres and the classics to include such nontraditional sources as Japanese prints and photography, but throughout his career Degas' art remained informed by other art as much as by nature. Even his favorite themes, such as the theater and the ballet, reveal an antinaturalistic orientation in which the artificiality of costume, pose, and stage set are celebrated. By studying the richness of life in a variety of such artificial contexts, Degas was creating an art dedicated to the modern city. By advancing the importance of direct experience and innovation in art without discarding the lessons of tradition, he was both contributing to the emergence of modernism and transcending it.

Bibliography
Adriani, Götz. *Degas: Pastels, Oil Sketches, Drawings*. Translated by Alexander Lieven. New York: Abbeville, 1985. The English translation of the catalog was produced in conjunction with the 1984 exhibition in Tübingen and Berlin. Includes a scholarly introductory essay, a well-documented catalog, and excellent illustrations.
Boggs, Jean Sutherland. *Portraits by Degas*. Berkeley: University of California Press, 1962. A classic study of an important, but often neglected aspect of Degas' art. The portraits are presented as being central to Degas' career. Careful analyses of sitters and their relations to the artist and his paintings are included.
Browse, Lillian. *Degas Dancers*. London: Faber & Faber, 1949. An early investigation of Degas' art from a thematic perspective, focusing on his most popular theme but presenting it in a more scholarly, interpretive context.
Degas, Hilaire Germain Edgar. *Degas: The Complete Etchings, Lithographs, and Monotypes*. Text by Jean Adhémar and Françoise Cachin. Translated by Jane Brenton. London: Thames & Hudson, 1974. A thoroughly illustrated and documented catalog of Degas' prints, with brief, informative introductory essays.
_____. *Letters*. Edited by Marcel Guérin. Translated by Marguerite Kay. Oxford, England: B. Cassirer, 1947. The English translation of the standard edition of the artist's letters. Provides important personal insights into his art, thought, and character.
_____. *The Notebooks of Edgar Degas*. Edited by Theodore Reff. 2 vols. Oxford, England: Clarendon Press, 1976. A carefully documented and annotated catalog of Degas' thirty-seven notebooks in the Bibliothèque Nationale in Paris. An indispensable publication on the artist's sources, development, and creative processes.

Halévy, Daniel. *My Friend Degas*. Translated by Mina Curtiss. Middletown, Conn.: Wesleyan University Press, 1964. A personal account of Degas during his later years, based on the journal Halévy began keeping in 1888 and continuing through the artist's death.

McMullen, Roy. *Degas: His Life, Times, and Work*. Boston: Houghton Mifflin, 1984. A comprehensive biography that is both scholarly and readable. Although considerable attention is given to major works, the emphasis throughout is on the artist's life and character. The best general biography in English.

Reff, Theodore, ed. *Degas: The Artist's Mind*. New York: Harper & Row, 1976. A collection of essays on various aspects of Degas' art. Most of the essays are revised versions of articles originally published in scholarly journals. A selection of important motifs, sources, and techniques are considered with a goal of better understanding Degas' artistic thought.

Dennis Costanzo

EUGÈNE DELACROIX

Born: April 26, 1798; Charenton-Saint-Maurice, France
Died: August 13, 1863; Paris, France
Area of Achievement: Art
Contribution: Delacroix, a powerful colorist, became the most important
figure in the development of the Romantic painting movement in France
in the nineteenth century. A prolific artist, he sought to stir viewers deeply
by appealing to their senses even though he chose to explore the dark side
of their human emotions.

Early Life

Eugène Delacroix was born in a Paris suburb called Charenton-Saint-
Maurice. His father, Charles, a schoolteacher, rose to become minister of
foreign affairs in 1795 under the revolutionary regime and French ambassador to the Netherlands some eighteen months later. His wife, Victoire
Oeben, descended from a distinguished family of royal cabinetmakers. Controversy surrounds Eugène's paternity. Some scholars maintain that his biological father was Talleyrand, one of Europe's most brilliant statesmen, to
whom the artist is said to have borne a striking resemblance.

While in Marseilles, as a result of an administrative appointment for his
father, Charles, the young Eugène exhibited a precocious talent for piano and
violin. His legal father died in late 1805, and Eugène's mother moved the
family back to Paris and enrolled Eugène at the Lycée Imperial, one of the
best schools in the capital. There Delacroix excelled in Latin, Greek, and
drawing. He also furthered his drawing skills by copying prints in the manner of the English caricaturist James Gillray, a practice which shaped a
career-long habit of seeking expressions of character and animated gestures.
When not yet eleven, Eugène had a fateful experience—a visit to the Louvre
on one of his free days. The sight of such pictorial variety, scale, and
technical mastery caused him to decide upon a painting career.

When Delacroix was seventeen, his career goal was aided by an introduction to Pierre-Narcisse Guerin, a successful painter and follower of Jacques-
Louis David, head of the neoclassical movement in art and practically an art
dictator under Napoleon I. In Guerin's atelier, Delacroix drew rigorously,
learning human anatomy from classical references. He enjoyed working on
large historical compositions involving faraway battles. While there he met
Théodore Géricault, once a Guerin pupil. The young Delacroix felt an immediate kinship with Géricault's ideas of infusing French art with sensuousness
plus an insistence upon spontaneity. Unfortunately, Delacroix was forced to
withdraw from Guerin's atelier after only six months, probably because he
could not afford the cost of tuition.

In 1816, Delacroix enrolled at the École des Beaux Arts. Orthodoxy ruled at this government-patronized school where all students progressed in basically the same manner. The primary methodology, like that for Guerin's classroom, was the study of classical form through seemingly endless copying of antique imagery from plaster casts, sculpture busts, coins, and, finally, male and female models. Delacroix was responsive to such instruction, but concurrently he searched for flexibility of expression and, on his own, explored the print-making mediums of etching and engraving as well as the new print form lithography.

Delacroix's growing need for emotional release was soon met by the emergence of a friendship with Géricault. The timing could not have been more propitious, as the slightly older Géricault was embarking on a sensational large work, *The Raft of the Medusa* (1819). Its subject, chosen to embarrass the restored monarchy of France with the hope of possibly becoming a success by scandal, depicts the moment of the initial sighting of the above-mentioned raft by a passing ship on the Atlantic horizon. The raft contained a dozen or so men who had survived twelve days adrift, their two ropes connected to lifeboats having been mysteriously cut within a day of abandoning the stranded and broken frigate *Medusa*. The ship had been on its way to Senegal with about four hundred passengers before running aground off the West African coast, thanks to an incompetent captain. Delacroix posed for the seminude figure lying face down near the edge of the raft in the central foreground. Though *The Raft of the Medusa* was overpoweringly raw, it proved to be the emotional elixir Delacroix was seeking. He may have been marked by its example, for his best paintings subsequently dealt with cruelty and death.

As with other artists falling under the perplexing umbrella of Romanticism, Delacroix's appearance and manner could be misleading. By age twenty, his aristocratic lineage was evident in his stiff posture and finely etched features. Fashion-conscious, he was one of the first to introduce the English-cut suit to Parisians, and to many people Delacroix was a pretentious dandy. Yet some historians suggest that the artist's elegant attire and fine manners were used to mock France's increasingly industrialized society, which he thought was crassly hopeful in its newfound material prosperity.

Delacroix also had a withdrawn and pessimistic nature, which he cultivated further by emulating the melancholic pathos in Dante's poetry and the works of George Gordon, Lord Byron. By contrast, the painter's work Delacroix most admired from the past was that of Peter Paul Rubens, whose high-keyed colors and dramatic action enthralled him. Yet it was Lord Byron who became a personal hero with a personality profile containing passion, bravery, elegance, melancholy, a love of freedom, and pessimism.

Life's Work

Desiring a successful career in painting, which in his day meant salon acceptance, Delacroix began a salon entry in 1821, one that would ideally attract critical reviews but not a storm of controversy. Touched by reading *The Inferno* from Dante's *The Divine Comedy*, he selected an episode from Canto VIII. Known by various titles, for example, *Dante and Virgil Crossing the Styx* and *The Bark of Dante*, the 1822 painting simulated the emotional potential and large scale of Géricault's *The Raft of the Medusa*, still fresh in Delacroix's memory. Unfortunately, polite taste, long accustomed to contained forms, polished technique, and clarity of color and values, was not ready for the ambiguous spaces and murky tones of Delacroix's painting.

Yet something more troublesome than salon taste marked Delacroix's subsequent career, namely the fact that many of his best paintings depicted injury, frenzy, and killing. He did not need to wait long for those types of thematic opportunities. In 1822, as many as twenty thousand Greeks on the island of Chios in the eastern Mediterranean were killed by invading Turks. Delacroix seized the chance to compose a potentially sensational work riding the crest of public interest in the war. Called *The Massacre at Chios* ("and the massacre of painting" by some of his contemporaries), it would seem to have been intended as a history set piece, except that the artist was basically apolitical.

A chance encounter with three landscape paintings by English Romantic painter John Constable at a Paris picture gallery may ultimately have been as important to Delacroix's subject and stylistic development as the gruesome massacre imagery. The artist noticed the application of color in bright flecks and dabs. Then he tested Constable's choppy, unblended color strokes and found, as did Constable, that a viewer's eyes mix the colors. The effects are not as crucial as Delacroix's intentions, which was not fidelity to atmospheric conditions but a contribution to a depressing mood combining murder and eroticism. From that point onward, color and a more vigorous painting method played a larger role in his art.

The Massacre at Chios shocked conservatives but enraptured youthful artists. It also stimulated Delacroix to explore more themes of death with erotic overtones. In fact, an immediate exploration of that sort was his entry for the 1827 Salon. Known as *The Death of Sardanapolus*, it was inspired by a Lord Byron play based upon the suicide of an Assyrian prince whom Byron named Sardanapolus. That world-weary aesthete choreographed his own conflagration as a final work of art. Through Byron, Delacroix illustrated the sickening preparations for the prince's funerary pyre, during which Sardanapolus watches without remorse as his favorite wives, horses, and dogs are killed in front of him by his officers.

The Death of Sardanapolus suffered disapproval by the press, and the French government refused to purchase it. Delacroix was warned by the head of the Academy of Fine Arts to refrain from painting any more like it for a long time lest he become ineligible for state commissions. Luckily for the artist, new officials, eager to overthrow the tastes of their predecessors, came to power in the aftermath of the July Revolution of 1830. Delacroix was soon in their good graces, and one of his few political paintings, *Liberty Leading the People*, was finished by late 1830. This painting became a much-copied icon of revolutionary propaganda, with versions appearing often as posters well into the twentieth century. It was born of a public uprising in Paris that Delacroix witnessed but in which he did not participate because, even here, he had little faith in the proletariat.

In *Liberty Leading the People*, a ragged army surges forward, stumbling over a barricade of paving stones, debris, and fallen comrades. They are led by a solidly built, resolute, young bare-breasted woman (Liberty), who holds a musket in her left hand and raises the flag of France with her right hand. The conflict stemmed from unresolved grievances of the Revolution in 1789 plus retrogressive decrees in July of 1830 by King Charles X, which dissolved the Chamber of Deputies, suspended freedom of the press, and overturned the voting rights of the merchant class and the new industrialists. Delacroix seemed to express perfectly the collective sentiment of the Parisians in revolt, perhaps even the universal will of ordinary citizens to revolt against intolerable conditions. Yet those were not his intentions. Nevertheless, the artist valued most the French flag defiantly raised by the spirit of Liberty, which was returned to the north tower of Notre Dame on July 28, 1832, and is visible at the extreme right of the composition.

The year 1832 was a turning point in Delacroix's development, for at that time he accepted an invitation to accompany Count Charles de Mornay on a goodwill trip to Morocco. The artist was asked to record picturesque events of a treaty-exploring journey which followed the recent French takeover of neighboring Algeria. In North Africa, Delacroix hoped to find brilliant colors, sensuality, and ferocity. Instead, he observed civility, dignity, simple life-styles, and a sense of unbroken traditions. From the first day ashore, he began to fill sketchbooks with drawings, watercolor vignettes, written notes on color, and descriptive details of his discoveries such as bright robes, exotic women, and non-European types of buildings. A short trip to Algiers was just as fruitful, for, once there, he realized a fantasy of long standing— entry into a harem. Two years after completing his North African trip, Delacroix produced an enchanting work drawn from that rare experience, *Algerian Women in Their Quarters*. In it, reverie and sensuality are fused and suspended.

The diaries and sketchbooks Delacroix filled sustained his art until his death in 1863. Equally remarkable is the fact that, despite the time lapse between the 1834 watercolor studies and the paintings derived from them, the latter did not lack freshness. The most popular works best typify Delacroix's taste for violence and cruelty: *The Lion Hunt* (1861) and *Arabs Skirmishing in the Mountains* (1862). For almost three decades, beginning in the 1830's, Delacroix was also involved with commissions sponsored by the government for major public buildings. There were church commissions, too. Altogether, they were exactly the type of employment to which most artists aspired at the time. Noteworthy contracts included wall and ceiling compositions at the National Assembly-Paris, the Luxembourg Palace (1845-1846), the Apollo Gallery at the Louvre (1850-1851), and the Church of Saint-Sulpice (1856-1861). Delacroix's last years were marked by failing health while he worked on these large projects. He died in 1863 in Paris after willing nearly six thousand works to public sale.

Summary
   Eugène Delacroix became the leading figure of the Romantic movement of painting in France and did so without trying. Actually, he may not have seen himself as a leader of anything. Like a number of major figures in art during his life, he was an enigma fraught with contradictions. For example, his thematic preferences ran quickly to scenes of high drama on the seas and depictions of fierce animal combat. Ironically, it was the gentle *Algerian Women in Their Quarters* which was later much admired, copied, and assimilated by artists of such stature as Pierre Renoir, Paul Cézanne, Henri Matisse, and Pablo Picasso.
   Delacroix's output was phenomenal, including 850 paintings, hundreds of watercolors, about sixty sketchbooks, many lithographs, thousands of drawings, a three-volume journal, and the beginnings of a dictionary of the fine arts. Furthermore, Delacroix, so full of energy, so prolific in his career, so strong-willed, seemingly had little faith in civilization. His pessimism, which was at first cultivated as a badge of distinction, eventually enveloped him like an unwelcomed, unshakable cloak. He is remembered as a rich colorist who painted dark themes. Delacroix died in 1863. By then Romanticism had been eclipsed by Édouard Manet's unvarnished naturalism in the 1863 Salon, which would lead to the emergence of the next major painting movement, Impressionism.

Bibliography
Delacroix, Eugène. *The Journal of Eugène Delacroix*. Translated by Walter
   Pach. New York: Crown, 1948. The first English translation of the artist's
   private thoughts recorded intermittently from 1822 to 1832 and from 1847
   to 1863. Perhaps the most relished are entries of his impressions of a six-
   month trip to North Africa in 1832. Delacroix's intentions toward his own
   art will be appreciated by those seeking to understand his state of mind
   when at work on key paintings.
Huyghe, René. *Delacroix*. New York: Harry N. Abrams, 1963. One of the
   best monographs on Delacroix to appear in English. Huyghe skillfully
   weaves quotations from the artist's journal and statements from Delacroix's

contemporaries with his own observations. Illustrations of key paintings are analyzed diagrammatically, stressing the compositional structure in Delacroix's aesthetics. Important themes or works in series are suitably illustrated in black and white as preparatory drawings, multiple painted versions, and lithographs.

Johnson, Lee. *The Paintings of Eugène Delacroix: A Critical Catalogue, 1816-1831.* 2 vols. Oxford, England: Clarendon Press, 1981. A publication of major importance. The first attempt at a complete compilation of Delacroix's paintings since the basic effort of Alfred Robaut in 1885. Johnson covers the artist's formative period and his early salon successes. He airs new data regarding problems of dating paintings, presents paintings absent in Robaut's books, offers new biographical information on several of Delacroix's portrait subjects, and relates pertinent drawings to their respective paintings.

Le Bris, Michel. *Romantics and Romanticism.* New York: Rizzoli, 1981. An intriguing and well-illustrated study of Romanticism as an international movement with roots in literature and folklore. By stressing themes and contextual tendencies, the book separates itself from watered-down profiles and superficial catalogs. Nineteenth century Romantic tendencies aptly explored include the appetite for death and pessimism, the desire to experience non-Western cultures, the yearning for lost worlds, and phantoms and the deadly sublime.

Prideaux, Tom. *The World of Delacroix.* Alexandria, Va.: Time-Life Books, 1966. A cultural-historical approach is used in this offering. Places Delacroix's art within the artistic and historical currents of his time. Prideaux weaves biography, politics and revolution, the painter's craft, and pedagogical issues into an engaging and lively text. A common thread of encounter in Delacroix's art is explored and found to be the result of a fertile imagination impelled toward invention and daring.

Trapp, Frank A. *The Attainment of Delacroix.* Baltimore: Johns Hopkins University Press, 1970. An ambitious monograph which addresses the artist's major works in dutiful fashion. The author's primary interests lie in Delacroix's paintings from literary sources and in themes from past history and current events. The last two chapters, which are entitled "Theory and Practice" and "Delacroix and His Critics," are perhaps the most welcome. The black-and-white illustrations are uneven in quality.

Tom Dewey II

LÉO DELIBES

Born: February 21, 1836; Saint-Germain-du-Val, France
Died: January 16, 1891; Paris, France
Area of Achievement: Music
Contribution: Delibes contributed significantly, as a composer, to the French
  ballet and opera of the nineteenth century.

Early Life

Clément-Philibert-Léo Delibes was born into a family which, on the maternal side, evinced musical talent. His grandmother was an opera singer, and his uncle, Antoine Édouard Batiste, was a noted organist and held important posts at the churches of Saint-Nicholas-des-Champs and at Saint Eustache. Clémence, Delibes' mother, was herself a musician, while his father, Philibert, worked as a civil servant in the postal service.

When Leo was eleven years old, his father died. His mother, who had provided her son with the fundamentals of music, moved the household to Paris. At this point, young Léo entered the Paris Conservatory and, in 1850, was awarded a *premier prix* in solfège. This skill in sight singing stood the future composer in good stead when he later turned his attention to opera. During his tenure at the conservatory, Delibes acquired skill as an organist through his study with François Benoist, a winner of the Prix de Rome in 1815 and a composer of ballets and operas, the two genres in which his pupil was eventually to make his mark. More important, Delibes studied composition with Adolphe-Charles Adam, a master of the opéra-comique (that is, *Le Postillon de Longjumeau*, 1836) and creator of such popular ballets as *Giselle* (1841) and *Le Corsaire* (1856). Adam, a pupil of François-Adrien Boïeldieu, became not only a mentor but also a partial father figure to his student.

Delibes' other musical enterprise as a youth included experience as a chorister at the Madeleine Cathedral and, on April 16, 1849, in the premiere of Giacomo Meyerbeer's *Le Prophète* at the Opéra. With the help of Adam, several professional positions were proffered him in 1853, and he thus found himself toiling as an accompanist at the Théâtre-Lyrique and as an organist at the Church of Saint Pierre de Chaillot. Despite his affinity for the organ (he worked as an organist steadily until 1871), Delibes developed an attraction for the theater. With the exception of a brief interlude as a critic (1858) for the *Gaulois hebdomadaire*, for which he wrote under the pen name Eloi Delbès, this attraction was cemented as early as 1856. In that year, his first stage work, *Deux sous de charbon*, was produced at Hervé's Folies-Nouvelles and received a favorable reception.

Life's Work

Delibes found the light opera, or operetta, to be a genre well suited to his talent and inclination. Over the next fourteen years, he provided some dozen such entertainments, a few of which were staged at Jacques Offenbach's theater, the Bouffes-Parisiens. Among them was the enormously popular *Deux Vieilles Gardes*. In his role as chorus master at the Théâtre-Lyrique, the young creator arranged the vocal score of Charles Gounod's *Faust* (1859) and worked also on two other major staples of the French operatic repertory, *Les Pêcheurs de perles* (1863) by Georges Bizet and *Les Troyens à Carthage* (1863) by Hector Berlioz. By 1864, in his role as chorus master at the Opéra, Delibes capitalized on the opportunities which presented themselves to him. His early successes were enlarged upon and solidified with the performance on November 12, 1866, at the Opéra, of the ballet *La Source: Ou, Naila*, on which he collaborated with the established Austrian-born composer, Ludwig Minkus. Delibes' contribution to the music for scenes 2 and 3 has been adjudged superior to Minkus' contribution to scenes 1 and 4. A year later, with a divertissement for a revivial of *Le Corsaire* by Adam, *Valse: Ou, Pas des Fleurs*, the composer had created for himself a considerable following. An opera bouffe entitled *La Cour du roi Pétaud*, produced on April 24, 1869, at Variétés, proved to be his final work in this genre.

The single most acclaimed composition by Delibes, the ballet *Coppélia: Ou, La Fille aux yeux d'émail*, was mounted on May 2, 1870, at the Opéra. The first ballet to use symphonic music throughout and to unify the dance and music into a homogeneity heretofore absent in this art form, *Coppélia* is based on Ernst Theodor Hoffman's story "Der Sandmann" (1816; "The Sandman," 1844). Set in two acts and three scenes, the work opens with a prelude; after the atmosphere has been created, there follow twenty musical numbers, the last of which comprises eight individual sections. The story line, which will be familiar to those who know Jacques Offenbach's *Les Contes d'Hoffmann* (1880), centers on the mechanical doll Coppélia, whose lifelike presence impels Franz, a young man who has become infatuated with her, to pursue her to the consternation of his fiancée, Swanhilda. Dr. Coppelius, the eccentric toymaker and magician who created the automaton, loves her as a daughter. When "the girl with the enamel eyes" is proved to be merely a toy, the lovers unite in marriage. It is at this juncture that number 20 of the score, "Festival of the Bell," with its eight sumptuous pieces featuring various uses of the bell, brings the ballet to a scintillating close. Assorted national dances such as the mazurka number 3, *Thème slave varié* number 6, the czardas number 7, and the bolero number 16 coupled with orchestral brilliance and coloration, contribute to the opulence of the composition.

In 1871, Delibes made the decisions to marry Léontine Estelle Denain and to devote himself entirely to composition; the latter determination caused him to refrain from time-consuming activity as an organist and chorus master. *Le Roi l'a dit*, Delibes' first major operatic opus, was produced on

May 24, 1873, at the Opéra-Comique. Its immediate success in Paris resulted in a performance in Antwerp (August 18, 1873) and, during the next year, performances in Vienna, Karlsruhe, and Prague. Returning to the ballet, the musician produced a second masterpiece in this genre with *Sylvia: Ou, La Nymphe de Diane*; it was premiered on June 14, 1876, at the Opéra. The story, based on Torquato Tasso's *Aminta* (1573), deals with Sylvia, a nymph of Diana, and her love affair with the shepherd Aminta. Interest and contrast are created by the involvement in the story of Diana, Eros, and Orion. Stylistically, this work differs from *Coppélia*; indeed, the political climate in France was also different. *Coppélia* was a creature of the Second Empire, a period in which Paris was the pleasure capital of the world. *Sylvia*, on the other hand, with its stylized mythology, came at a time when France, now a republic, retained strong memories of the Franco-Prussian War and the internal upheavals of the commune. The orchestral scoring in *Sylvia* reveals immediately a more serious emotionality of expression; there are, in addition, traces of Wagnerian influence. Distinguished musicians, among them Peter Ilich Tchaikovsky, who probably heard *Coppélia* during his several trips to Paris in the 1870's, was exposed to *Sylvia* in Vienna.

Now riding the crest of a triumphant wave, Delibes produced his three-act *drame lyrique*, *Jean de Nivelle*, on March 8, 1880, at the Opéra-Comique. It was very successful and received one hundred performances until January 6, 1881, at this theater. During the period 1880-1882, it was also performed in Stockholm, Budapest, Copenhagen, Vienna, Geneva, St. Petersburg, and Brussels. Oddly, after its revival at the Gaîté-Lyrique on October 5, 1908, it has fallen into oblivion.

Perhaps feeling a need to supplement his reputation as a composer with academic respectability, Delibes took a position as professor of composition at the Paris Conservatory in 1881, this despite admitted weaknesses in fugal and contrapuntal technique. Yet another side of this artist's talent emerges in the *Le Roi s'amuse*, *six airs de danse dans le style ancien*, written for a revival of Victor Hugo's *Le Roi s'amuse* (1832; *The King's Fool*, 1842), performed on November 22, 1882, at the Comédie-Française. Here, he reveals a distinct rapport for seventeenth century French classicism.

The three-act opera *Lakmé* premiered on April 14, 1883, at the Opéra-Comique. The exoticism of this work (the setting is India) in which the female lead, Lakmé, is the daughter of the Brahmin priest Nilakantha, has attracted audiences up to modern times. In this nineteenth century story, the British officer Gérald is in love with the heroine, much to her father's displeasure; indeed, the priest vows to kill the English suitor. When, however, Lakmé realizes that Gérald is torn between his duty and his love for her, she eases his burden by committing suicide. Of all its many excellences, the coloratura showstopper, the "Bell Song," remains a tour de force. From 1883 until his death, no other major work was completed by the composer, although an incomplete opera, *Kassya*, was produced on March 24, 1893, at the Opéra-Comique. Jules Massenet provided the orchestration but did not add the overture that Delibes did not live to compose.

Summary

Léo Delibes was described by French composer Henri-Charles Merechal as "restless, fidgety, slightly befuddled, correcting and excusing himself, lavishing praise, careful not to hurt anyone's feelings, shrewd, adroit, very lively, a sharp critic." This characterization aptly depicts those traits which most strongly affected the ballet master's creative path. The early works, notably the operettas, are always cited for their facile technique, their light and airy manner, and their elegance and wit. There is no plumbing of depths, no attempt at profundity. Delibes' operettas represent skillful treatment of a genre then in vogue and one which reached an apex of popularity in the hands of Offenbach, who, as a matter of interest, collaborated with Delibes on *Les Musiciens de l'orchèstre* (1861) and at whose theater Delibes produced nine of his light operas. Even at the height of his own fame, Delibes took time to complete Offenbach's *Belle Lurette* (1880) and *Mamzelle Moucheron* (1881).

As he matured, Delibes absorbed a variety of influences. Eclecticism as a *modus operandi* seems to have enabled the musician to create strikingly appealing dance numbers in *Coppélia* and *Sylvia*. In addition to the graceful turns of phrase, the orchestration reveals a genuine gift for originality. The use of alto saxophone in the barcarolle of *Sylvia* is a masterful stroke and one of the earliest efforts to make this instrument a viable member of the orchestra. The "Pizzicati" from the same ballet has been emulated by later composers. The oriental atmosphere in *Kassya* is skillfully wrought and is a portent of the direction in which Delibes was moving at his death.

Because his reputation had been solidified as a consequence of his stage works, there is a tendency to pay little heed to Delibes' many choruses, songs, piano pieces, and religious music such as the *Messe brève* for two equal voices with organ and string quartet, the *Ave maris stelle* for two voices, and the *Ave verum* for two voices. There is no uniformity of opinion with regard to Delibes' historical place. It is significant, however, that in his own lifetime he was elected a member of the Institut de France (1884). Delibes was viewed by the establishment as one worthy to carry on the French traditions deemed meritorious.

Because as a genre ballet has not attained the status of symphonic music, chamber music, or piano music, Delibes' position in the pantheon of musical celebrities has suffered, and because he was not a prolific composer, the total number of his works that survive in today's repertory is less than one dozen. Those who have seen or heard his best creations, however, have experienced an enchantment that lives long in the memory.

Bibliography
Curtiss, Mina. *Bizet and His World*. New York: Alfred A. Knopf, 1958. Contains useful and insightful information about the relationship between Delibes and Bizet.
Downes, Olin. *The Lure of Music: Depicting the Human Side of Great Composers, with Stories of Their Inspired Creations*. New York: Harper and Brothers, 1918. Contains an excellent essay on Delibes and his music, and takes the position that Delibes' ballets are far more than a potpourri of uninspired dance pieces.
Macdonald, Hugh. "(Clément Philibert) Léo Delibes." In *The New Grove Dictionary of Music and Musicians*, edited by Stanley Sadie, vol. 5. London: Macmillan, 1980. Probably the finest English-language reference article on Delibes. Includes a comprehensive list of works.
Studwell, William E. *Adolphe Adam and Léo Delibes: A Guide to Research*. New York: Garland, 1987. The heart of the section dealing with Delibes is a comprehensive annotated bibliography arranged topically and alphabetically. There is a valuable summary of Delibes' life and work, a discussion of the composer's relationship to his more illustrious contemporaries, and a commentary on the historical role of Delibes and his music's place in history. The bibliography includes four published writings of Delibes.
Van Vechten, Carl. "Back to Delibes." *Musical Quarterly* 8 (October, 1922). Perusing an old copy of *Coppélia*, Van Vechten credits the composer with revolutionizing the ballet by introducing a symphonic approach to the orchestration and by infusing his scores with melodic grace.

David Z. Kushner

RENÉ DESCARTES

Born: March 31, 1596; La Haye, Touraine, France
Died: February 11, 1650; Stockholm, Sweden
Areas of Achievement: Mathematics, philosophy, and physics
Contribution: Descartes' cardinal contribution is the extension of the mathematical method to all fields of knowledge. He is the father of analytic geometry and the author of the most universally appropriate version of mind-body dualism in the history of philosophy.

Early Life

René Descartes was born to one of the most respected families among the French-speaking nobility in Touraine. His father, Joachim, held the post of counselor to the Parlement de Bordeaux. Descartes' mother died of tuberculosis only a few days after giving birth to her son, leaving a frail child of chronically poor health to the sole care of his father. René's physical condition remained delicate until he was in his twenties.

Joachim Descartes was a devoted and admiring father, determined to obtain the best education for "his philosopher." When Descartes was ten, he was sent to the College of La Flèche, newly established by the Jesuits under the auspices of Henry IV.

Descartes was an exemplary student of the humanities and of mathematics. When, at the age of sixteen, he began his study of natural philosophy, he came to the insight which would later give rise to his revolutionary contributions to modern thought. Uncertainty and obscurity, he discovered, were hallmarks of physics and metaphysics. These disciplines seemed to attract a contradictory morass of opinions that yielded nothing uniform or definite. By contrast, Descartes' studies in mathematics showed him something firm, solid, and lasting. He was astonished to find that while mathematical solutions had been applied to scientific problems, the method of mathematics had never been extended to important practical matters. At La Flèche, Descartes concluded that he would have to break with the traditions of the schools if he were to find knowledge of any worth.

Descartes left his college without regret, and his father subsequently sent him to Paris. Social life there failed to amuse him, and he formed his most intimate friendships with some of France's leading scholars and teachers. When he was twenty-one, he joined the army but spent little time campaigning. In his spare time, he wrote a compendium of music and displayed his mathematical genius by instantaneously solving puzzles devised for him by soldiers in his company.

Descartes was housed with a German regiment in winter quarters at Ulm, waiting for active campaign, when the whole core of his subsequent thought suddenly took shape. On the night of November 10, 1619, after a day of intense and agitated reflection, Descartes went to bed and had three dreams. He interpreted these dreams as a divine sign that he was destined to found a unified science based on a new method for the correct management of human reason. Descartes' sudden illumination and resolve on that night to take himself as the judge of all values and the source of all certainty in knowledge was momentous for the world of ideas.

Life's Work

Descartes spent the next ten years formulating his method while continuing scientific researches, and occupied himself with travel in order to study what he called "the great book of the world." He had come to the view that systems of human thought, especially those of the sciences and philosophy, were better framed by one thinker than by many, so that systematizing a body of thought from the books of others was not the best method. Descartes wanted to be disabused of all the prejudices he had acquired from the books of others; thus, he sought to begin anew with his own clear and firm foundation. This view was codified in his first substantial work, *Regulae ad Directionem Ingenii* (1701; *Rules for the Direction of the Mind*, 1911). In this work, Descartes set forth the method of rational inquiry he thought requisite for scientific advance, but he advocated its use for the attainment of any sort of knowledge whatever.

Descartes completed a scientific work entitled *La Monde* in 1633, the same year that Galileo was condemned by the Inquisition. Upon hearing this news, Descartes immediately had his own book suppressed from publication, for it taught the same Copernican cosmology as did Galileo, and made the claim that indicted Galileo's orthodoxy: that human beings could have knowledge as perfect as that of God. A few years later, Descartes published a compendium of treatises on mathematics and physical sciences which were written for the educated but nonacademic French community; this work obliquely recommended his unorthodox views to the common men of "good sense" from whom Descartes hoped to receive a fair hearing. This work was prefaced by his *Discours de la méthode* (1637; *Discourse on Method*, 1649) and contained the *Geometry*, the *Dioptric*, and the *Meteors*.

Discourse on Method provided the finest articulation of what has come to be known as Descartes' method of doubt. This consisted of four logical rules: first, to admit as true only what was so perfectly clear and distinct that it was indubitable; second, to divide all difficulties into analyzable elements; third, to pass synthetically from what is easy to understand to what is difficult; and fourth, to make such accurate enumerations of the steps of reasoning so as to be certain of having omitted nothing. The method is fundamentally of mathematical inspiration, and it is deductive and analytical rather than experimental. It is a heuristic device for solving complex problems that yields explicit innovation and discovery. Descartes employed his method to this end in the tract on geometry when he discovered a way to resolve the geometric curves into Cartesian coordinates. Such an invention could hardly have come from the traditional Euclidean synthetic-deductive method, which starts from assumed axioms and common notions in order to generate and prove logically entailed propositions.

Descartes' new method was akin to those found in the writings of Francis Bacon and Galileo, and it was the architectonic of the new science. "Old" science, leftover from ancient and medieval researches, merely observed and classified, and explained its findings in terms of postulated natural purposes of things. The new science inaugurated in the seventeenth century sought, in Descartes' words, to make men the "masters and possessors of nature." This goal involved invention and discovery, the generation of new and nonspeculative knowledge, to be put in the service of practical ends. For Descartes and the other seventeenth century "new" scientists, human wonder and understanding were without intrinsic value; what was without practical use or application for mankind, Descartes remarked in *Discourse on Method*, was absolutely worthless. The new science aimed to create effects, not merely to understand causes.

Descartes intended his method not for mathematics and science only. He envisioned the unity of all knowledge. He employed his method in a purely metaphysical inquiry in *Meditationes de Prima Philosophia* (1641; *Meditations on First Philosophy*, 1680) to "establish something firm and lasting in the sciences." He fashioned in this a primary certainty by rejecting at the outset everything about which it was possible to have the least doubt.

He set aside as false everything learned from or through the senses, and the truths of arithmetic and geometry. Only the proposition, "I think, therefore I am," remained an indubitable truth. One cannot doubt one's existence, Descartes reasoned, without existing while one doubts. Thus, *cogito ergo sum* became his first and most certain principle. Further days of meditation on this principle revealed the certitudes that he was a substance whose whole essence it was to think, entirely independent of his body and of all other material things. His primary truth also enabled him to prove the existence of God.

In this one epochal week of meditations, Descartes made privacy the hallmark of mental activity, moved the locus of certitude to inner mental states, and rejected faith and revelation in favor of clarity and distinctness. Reason itself had previously governed the coherence of what had to be taken as truth; now inner representation, and its correspondence with the external, material world, governed the kingdom of relevant truth. Most philosophers after Descartes have followed his conception of inner representations as the foundation of knowledge of all outer realities. Only in the twentieth century has this position, and its attendant problems, been systematically examined and contested.

The years that followed the publication of *Meditations on First Philosophy* were marked by controversies resulting from attacks by theologians. Descartes' orthodoxy was impugned and his arguments were assailed. In 1647, formal objections to the Cartesian metaphysics, along with the author's replies, were published as a companion volume to a second edition of the *Meditations on First Philosophy* in French translation.

Descartes' next project was to be his last. *Les Passions de l'âme* (1649; *The Passions of the Soul*, 1650) was a treatise of psychology which explained all mental and physiological phenomena by mechanical processes. This work has striking moral overtones as well. Descartes' implicit prescription for the best human life is reminiscent of that of the ancient Stoics: Men should strive to conquer their passions in order to attain peace of mind. Descartes maintained in *The Passions of the Soul* that while people who feel deep passions are capable of the most pleasant life, these passions must be controlled with the intervention of rational guidance. In the end, he claimed that teaching one to be the master of one's passions was the chief use of wisdom.

In 1649, Descartes responded to the request of Queen Christina of Sweden to join a distinguished circle of scholars she was assembling in Stockholm to instruct her in philosophy. As a result of the Swedish climate and the rigorous schedule demanded by the queen, Descartes caught pneumonia and died the following year.

Summary

The thinking of René Descartes epitomizes the transition from the medieval epoch of the Western world to the modern period. Modern man came to deify personal freedom. This tendency originated with the privatization of consciousness and the drive to overcome the rigors of nature. For Descartes, only absolutely certain knowledge counted as wisdom. Descartes envisaged wisdom as having practical benefits for the many, as opposed to being a mere cerebral exaltation for the educated few. Descartes saw the improvement of the mental and physical health of mankind as being the best of these benefits of wisdom. This prospect was ratified by the enterprises of centuries to come.

Descartes was one of the pioneers of modern mathematics. He conceived the possibility of treating problems of geometry by reducing them to algebraic operations and devised the necessary means for making geometric operations correspond to those of arithmetic. He also introduced the notion of deducing solutions from the assumption of the problem's being solved. This has become such a fundamental technique in algebra and higher mathematics that one can scarcely imagine its having had a genesis. Descartes' radical distinction between mind and body and his revolutionary method of metaphysical inquiry have had a profound effect on the history of philosophy.

Bibliography

Balz, Albert G. A. *Descartes and the Modern Mind*. New Haven, Conn.: Yale University Press, 1952. Balz analyzes the pervasive influence of Cartesianism on the last three centuries. The analysis proceeds topically, with exposition of a particular facet of Descartes' thought and then analysis of its legacy.

Cottingham, John G. *Descartes*. New York: Basil Blackwell, 1986. Most commentators on Descartes' philosophy focus on his theory of knowledge; Cottingham takes a broader view of Cartesian philosophy and shows readers a profound Cartesian understanding of human nature. Excellent for beginning students, clear on and faithful to Descartes' texts.

Gaukroger, Stephen, ed. *Descartes: Philosophy, Mathematics, and Physics*. Totowa, N.J.: Barnes & Noble Books, 1980. Takes up Descartes' concern with providing a philosophical foundation for mathematical physics. Ten authors approach this theme from a variety of angles. Extremely well indexed.

Haldane, Elizabeth S. *Descartes: His Life and Times*. New York: American Scholar Publications, 1966. Artfully crafted, detailed (nearly 400 pages), but eminently readable biography of Descartes. Haldane is especially good at providing historical notes on circumstances which influenced Descartes' thought and development. Contains a good bibliography of studies of Descartes' philosophy.

Keeling, S. V. *Descartes*. New York: Oxford University Press, 1968. One of the best overviews of Descartes' thought and influence, this book connects Descartes' development to his thought, gives a systematic reading of his corpus, and critically analyzes the merits and defects of Cartesianism. Well indexed, with a substantial bibliography.

Kenny, Anthony. *Descartes: A Study of His Philosophy*. New York: Random House, 1968. A standard commentary for beginning students of Descartes' philosophy which gives particular emphasis to his epistemology. Treats philosophical issues topically in brief, clear chapters. Contains an abbreviated bibliography and a general index.

Patricia Cook

BARTOLOMEU DIAS

Born: c. 1450; probably near Lisbon, Portugal
Died: May 23?, 1500; at sea off the coast of Brazil
Area of Achievement: Exploration
Contribution: Dias was the first to command a sea expedition around Africa's Cape of Good Hope, a feat that had been attempted for more than fifty years before his success and one that led to the opening of sea trade between Portugal and the Orient.

Early Life

Bartolomeu Dias, like many Portuguese explorers of his time, remains an enigma. Nothing is known about his life except for an incomplete account of his voyage around the Cape of Good Hope in 1488 and two other references regarding one previous and one subsequent voyage. He may have been related to Dinis Dias, another Portuguese captain, who also explored the African coast in search of a sea route to the Orient in 1445. Dias had at least one brother, Pedro, who accompanied him on the historic voyage around the cape. Dias was undoubtedly from a poor social class, since most seamen and explorers shared a similar humble upbringing, some of them even having criminal records.

The major reason for the lack of any solid information about Dias is that virtually all the early Portuguese explorations were conducted under strict secrecy. Portugal and Spain were in fierce competition at the time, both attempting to discover the most profitable trade route to the Orient. Since land routes from Europe through the Middle East to Asia were nearly impossible to traverse because of the Muslim Empire's hostile monopoly of the area, a sea route around the uncharted seas of Africa seemed to be the only alternative.

More than fifty years before Dias' historic voyage, the idea of sailing past Cape Bojador (the bulging cape) located off the coast of the Sahara Desert in southern Morocco, was unheard of. There was a great fear that just south of this barren cape was the end of the world, where the sea boiled and monsters thrived. The man most responsible for stimulating interest in exploring the African coast in the hope of finding a trade route to the Orient was Prince Henry, third son of King John I and Queen Philippa of Portugal, later to be known as Prince Henry the Navigator. Henry's motivation for so fervently supporting sea exploration around Africa to Asia stemmed from his fierce hatred of the Muslims. He was a devout Christian and grand master of the militant Order of Christ, who believed that if he could locate the whereabouts of a legendary African empire ruled by a powerful Christian king called Prester John, Portugal could join forces with this influential king and overpower the Muslims, thus liberating the Holy Land and opening trade with Asia. By sending ships along the African coast, Henry planned to seek Prester John while simultaneously seeking a sea route to the Orient.

In 1433, Henry sent his first captain, Gil Eanes, with the explicit order to sail past the desolate and feared Cape Bojador. This was at a time when no reliable maps existed of the African coast, navigational equipment was primitive, and sailing ships were experimental, still evolving from a traditional small Mediterranean sailing vessel to a larger and more rugged European caravel specifically designed for long voyages. Eanes failed to conquer Cape Bojador on his initial voyage, but the following year he tried again and this time sailed one hundred miles past the intimidating cape. What followed over the next five decades was a painfully gradual exploration of the African coast by dozens of Portuguese captains. Key outposts and fortresses were established along the coast and a lucrative though cruel slave trade began.

The earliest reference to Dias is connected with the establishment of a major new fortress along the Guinea coast near Mina in 1481, twenty-one years after the death of Henry. Dias was one of the captains who sailed with the chief engineer of the project and who helped construct this key outpost. The principal explorer of this time, however, was Diego Cão, who, in two long voyages, sailed as far south as Cape Cross, fifty miles north of Walvis Bay in Namibia. Along the way, and under direction of King John II, Cão erected huge seven-foot limestone markers called *padrões*, which he mounted on prominent points where they could be seen by passing ships. When Cão died during his final voyage back to Portugal in 1485, preparations were made for the most ambitious voyage yet attempted by Portugal.

Life's Work

In August, 1487, John commissioned Dias to command another voyage, one of major importance. Secrecy surrounding the expedition was so intense that no official report exists of the voyage. The most up-to-date maps and navigational instruments of the time, as well as the best-equipped and most carefully prepared ships, were used. For the first time, a cargo ship, stocked with food and provisions, accompanied the two sailing ships.

Dias' principal crew members were all distinguished sailors; Pedro de Alenquer, one of the best-known mariners of the period, was chief pilot of Dias' ship, the *São Cristovão*. John Infante, a knight, captained the second ship, the *São Pantaleão*. Dias' brother, Pedro, captained the supply ship with the pilot John de Santiago, who had sailed previously with Cão. Also on board, as a junior pilot, was Bartolomeo Columbus, younger brother of Christopher Columbus. Along with the sixty crew members of the ships were six African captives, who carried precious metals and spices and were to be put ashore at various places along the coast to trade with the natives and to try everything possible to locate the elusive Prester John. Dias also carried three *padrões* to mark his progress along the coast.

Dias sailed without serious problems to Mina, the port he had helped establish six years earlier. He restocked his ships and then sailed as far as Port Alexander in Southern Angola, where he landed two of the African captives. Farther south near Cape Cross, Dias anchored the supply ship, and the two remaining ships sailed on, passing Cão's southernmost *padrōe* on December 1. One week later, the ships anchored in Walvis Bay, where they found protection from huge South Atlantic swells. Native villages could be seen nearby with the inhabitants herding cattle and sheep.

Two weeks later, they had sailed as far as Luderitz in southern Namibia, three hundred miles farther than any previous expedition. Because of continued foul weather, they anchored there for five days, while Dias put ashore another African emissary. When the winds became more favorable, they embarked again, only to encounter even more fierce weather. On January 6, 1488, Dias decided to sail into deeper waters, hoping to escape from the horrendous winds that had been battering them for a month. Dias and his crew had not been prepared for such harsh conditions, and they suffered horribly as the icy swells bashed their ships for thirteen days.

Finally, Dias gave the command to sail east in search of land. Yet no land was sighted on the eastern horizon. Dias swung from east to north in search of land, his crew becoming more and more frightened that they would never see land again. Finally, on February 3, land was sighted. Now, however, by their calculations, they were sailing east along the coast instead of south. Stunned and hardly believing the truth, Dias realized that during the thirteen days at sea fighting the storms, he and his crew had accomplished what so many before had attempted but failed to do. He had rounded the southernmost cape of Africa.

The weary mariners landed near Mossel Bay in South Africa and attempted to find provisions but were beaten back by hostile natives. They sailed to Algoa Bay and at last found refuge. Dias was elated with his achievement and erected his first *padrōe*. He was eager to continue on even farther and determined now to sail all the way to India. His crew, however, objected strongly. Many had died during the wicked storms and many more were sick. Provisions were nearly gone and the ships were tattered and badly leaking. Still, Dias wanted to continue, but the crew threatened to mutiny. Dias pleaded with his men, promising them great wealth if they would continue the great expedition. Second-in-command Infante, a knight with an aristocratic heritage and jealous of the low-born Dias, led the opposition, and in the end Dias was only able to persuade his men to proceed for three more days before turning back. To avoid dishonor, Dias made his officers and principal seamen sign a document which explained what had occurred. As the two ships turned back and passed the *padrōe* at Algoa Bay, Dias, according to a historian writing twenty years after the voyage, sadly bade farewell to the historic marker, "with as much pain and sentiment as if he were leaving a beloved son in eternal exile."

Six weeks later in April, they encountered the worst weather of the expedition and were forced to anchor for three weeks in South Africa's Cape Agulhas, where they overhauled their battered vessels. By the end of May, they were crawling once again along the coast. On June 6, they sighted the southernmost cape, the one they had passed in the terrible February storm. Because of the difficulties they had encountered in reaching this elusive location, Dias named it the Cape of Storms. Later, King John renamed it the Cape of Good Hope because of the promise it offered in the discovery of a sea route to India. Dias erected his second *padrõe* there and then retraced his course to Luderitz, where he placed the third and last *padrõe*.

After recovering and then burning his supply ship, Dias crawled up the African coast. He made several stops along the way and at one point rescued the shipwrecked crew of a previous Portuguese expedition. Finally, in December, 1488, after fifteen months and sixteen thousand miles, Dias and his crew sailed into Lisbon.

John was ecstatic. He was also determined to keep the success of the voyage a secret, however, and for the next eight years was able to suppress any information about the voyage as well as all other Portuguese voyages. One witness to Dias' historic return, the brother of one of the junior pilots, did make a notation in the margin of one of his books:

> Note: that in December of this year 1488, Bartolomeu Dias, commandant of three caravels which the King of Portugal had sent out to Guinea to seek out the land, landed in Lisbon. He reported that he had reached a promontory which he called Cape of Good Hope. . . . He had described his voyage and plotted it league by league on a marine chart in order to place it under the eyes of the said king. I was present in all of this.

The chronicler was Christopher Columbus, one of many who benefited from Dias' monumental achievement.

Summary

In addition to Columbus' note, only two other contemporary references to Bartolomeu Dias exist. First, he was influential in designing the ships that in July, 1487, carried Vasco da Gama around the Cape of Good Hope to India. Second, in March, 1500, less than a year after da Gama's historic return from India, Dias captained one of thirteen ships under the command of Pedro Álvars Cabral and sailed in search of an alternate route to the Orient. The result of this voyage was the exploration of the Brazilian coast of South America. Upon setting sail from Brazil to Africa, once again in search of the Cape of Good Hope and India, the expedition encountered a ghastly storm in late May, 1500. Four ships were lost with all crewmen. Dias was one of the casualties.

There is no underestimating the importance of Dias' greatest triumph. He had boldly attained the goal set by Prince Henry the Navigator in the early 1430's, to prove that there was a route around Africa to India that could be used to skirt the land routes monopolized by the Muslims. During his voyage, he accumulated valuable data which were used by John to plan the voyage that would ultimately result in Vasco da Gama's reaching India. He not only paved the way to the Orient but also inspired Christopher Columbus and later Ferdinand Magellan to seek their own routes to the Indies.

Dias, however, never reached the Orient himself. Another chronicler, writing sixty years after Dias' death, summarized Dias' achievement: "It may be said that he saw the land of India, but, like Moses and the Promised Land, he did not enter in." Ultimately, it was Dias, more than anyone before him, who made it possible for Portugal to dominate the Indian Ocean and secure the vast treasures of the Orient.

Bibliography
Buehr, Walter. *The Portuguese Explorers*. New York: G. P. Putnam's Sons, 1966. This juvenile book gives a detailed history of Prince Henry the Navigator, who was instrumental in igniting interest and financing the first voyages along the African coast. There is also a chapter on the development of the ships used by the Portuguese explorers and a chronicle of the most influential Portuguese captains with an account of Dias' voyage.
Hart, Henry H. *Sea Road to the Indies*. New York: Macmillan, 1950. Although the majority of the book chronicles the life and achievement of Vasco da Gama, the first part of the book is a detailed account of the Portuguese explorers who preceded him. Chapter 5 is dedicated to Dias and quotes from early Portuguese historians who later pieced together the long-suppressed details of Dias' voyage. Extensive bibliography of both English and foreign references.
Humble, Richard. *The Explorers*. Alexandria, Va.: Time-Life Books, 1978. Good overview of the most influential early explorers: Dias, Columbus, da Gama, and Magellan, the latter three all inspired by and benefiting from Dias' achievement. Excellent early maps, plus illustrations and text on the development of the ships and navigational equipment used for all the major voyages. Dias' voyage is described in chapter 1, "The First Giant Stride on the Route to India." Profusely illustrated; contains a selected bibliography.
Parr, Charles McKew. *So Noble a Captain*. New York: Thomas Y. Crowell, 1953. This biography on the life of Magellan contains a detailed description of Dias' voyage in chapter 1, plus information on Dias' influence on John and the building of the ships that da Gama used to sail to India. Extensive bibliography includes books on the history of Portuguese exploration, navigation, and sailing-ship construction.

Prestage, Edgar. *The Portuguese Pioneers.* New York: Macmillan, 1933. Covers in detail the history of Portuguese exploration from the late fourteenth century to the major expeditions of Dias, da Gama, and Cabral through the early sixteenth century. Dias' voyage is detailed in "Progress Under John II—the Voyage of Diego Cão—the Search for Prester John— the Voyage of Bartholomew Dias."

James Kline

DENIS DIDEROT

Born: October 5, 1713; Langres, France
Died: July 31, 1784; Paris, France
Areas of Achievement: Philosophy and literature
Contribution: As editor of and contributor to the *Encyclopedia*, Diderot codified and promulgated the views of the French Enlightenment. His posthumously published fiction has earned for him a prominent place in the pantheon of eighteenth century writers, and his philosophical works remain challenging and influential.

Early Life

The son of Didier and Angélique Vigneron Diderot, Denis Diderot was born on October 5, 1713, in Langres, France. Although the family was involved in trade—Didier Diderot was a master cutler and his wife the daughter of a tanner—a number of relatives had entered the Church, among them the canon of the cathedral at Langres. Diderot's brother, Didier-Pierre, and his sister, Angélique, would follow this ecclesiastical path, the former becoming a priest and the latter a nun. Diderot, despite his later atheism, also showed an early inclination in this direction. Tonsured at the age of twelve, he made the one-hundred-fifty-mile journey north to Paris three years later to study at the Jesuit Collège de Louis-le-Grand or the Jansenist Collège d'Harcourt; he may have taken courses at both. When he received his degree in 1732, though, it was from the University of Paris, and his interest had shifted to philosophy and rhetoric.

Since Diderot had abandoned a career in the Church, his father apprenticed him to the Parisian lawyer Clément de Ris. This field suited him no better than religion, and, after enduring two years of legal studies, Diderot turned to a life of letters. His father refused to approve of so uncertain a course, so for the next decade Diderot survived on the meager earnings he garnered as tutor and hack writer, supplemented by occasional small sums from his mother. On November 6, 1743, he married Anne-Toinette Champion, the daughter of a poor linen-shop owner; this step further alienated his father, who so opposed the match that he had Diderot locked up in a monastery to prevent the wedding. Diderot escaped; he realized, however, that he could not rely on his parents to support his family and recognized that he needed a secure source of income.

Life's Work

Diderot therefore turned to the booksellers, offering his fluency in English and his literary talent. In 1743 he translated Temple Stanyan's *Grecian History* (1707) for the publisher Briasson, who was sufficiently pleased with the result to ask Diderot for a French version of Robert James's *Medical*

Dictionary (1743-1745). At the same time that he was translating James's treatise, he was adapting the third Earl of Shaftesbury's *An Inquiry Concerning Virtue in Two Discourses* (1699). Much in Shaftesbury's work appealed to Diderot and deeply influenced his views. He admired the Englishman's tolerance and emphasis on reason, and he adopted the notion that religion and morality should be judged according to their social effects. Diderot also agreed with Shaftesbury that emotions play an important role in fostering socially proper conduct. He was less prepared to accept Shaftesbury's optimism, his notion of an innate aesthetic appreciation, and his criticism of organized religion.

Diderot's first original philosophical work, *Pensées philosophiques* (1746; English translation, 1819), written over Easter weekend, 1746, to earn fifty gold pieces for Madame de Puissieux, his mistress, built on this adaptation. Diderot was still not prepared to reject the Church—the fifty-first *pensée* reaffirms his belief in Catholicism—but he does urge that faith be tested by reason and that the passions, deemed by the orthodox to be dangerous, be seen as necessary to morality and creativity. Published anonymously, it was sufficiently impressive to be attributed to such well-known intellectuals as Voltaire or Étienne Bonnot de Condillac. It was also regarded as sufficiently radical to be condemned by the Parliament of Paris in July, 1746.

La Promenade du sceptique (1830) revealed Diderot's increasing doubts about religion; the manuscript was seized before publication, and the police began to watch Diderot closely. His bawdy satire on Louis XV and Madame de Pompadour, *Les Bijoux indiscrets* (1748; *The Indiscreet Toys*, 1749), further antagonized the authorities, and his *Lettre sur les aveugles à l'usage de ceux qui voient* (1749; *An Essay on Blindness*, 1750), which questioned the Deistic argument that cosmic order proves God's existence, led to his arrest and solitary confinement for three months in the fortress of Vincennes.

This experience shook him deeply. Previously he had published his controversial works anonymously; henceforth, he would rarely publish them at all. His reputation in the eighteenth century, therefore, was lower than it would become after his death. Much of his contemporary acclaim derived from the project that would occupy him for the next fifteen years, the *Encyclopédie: Ou, Dictionnaire raisonné des sciences, des arts, et des métiers* (1751-1772; *Encyclopedia*, 1965). His translations and other writings not only had exposed Diderot to new knowledge but also had made him a logical choice for coeditor, with Jean Le Rond d'Alembert, of the ambitious project to translate and supplement Ephraim Chambers' five-volume *Cyclopaedia: Or, Universal Dictionary of the Arts and Sciences* (1728).

As conservative opponents, who twice succeeded in having the *Encyclopedia* condemned, realized, the work was not an innocent compilation of existing knowledge. In its pages nature replaced providence, determinism superseded God's will as the guiding forces of the world. Instead of relying on authority and tradition, Diderot and his fellow philosophers urged readers to judge by experience and experimentation. In a world of monarchies, the article "Political Authority" proclaimed that "no man has received from nature the right to command other men. Freedom is a present from heaven, and every individual of the same species has the right to enjoy it as soon as he enjoys reason." By 1758, d'Alembert was sufficiently frightened by official reaction to resign as coeditor, leaving Diderot with the responsibility of writing and soliciting contributions to complete the seventeen volumes of text and twelve of plates.

In the midst of these labors, Diderot found time to produce a number of other works. The theater had long interested him. Late in life he would state that he had debated between studying at the Sorbonne and becoming an actor, and in his *Lettre sur les sourds et muets* (1751; *Letter on the Deaf and Dumb*, 1916) he claimed to know much of French drama by heart. In the latter half of the 1750's he indulged this interest by writing two plays, *Le Fils naturel* (1757; *Dorval: Or, The Test of Virtue*, 1767) and *Le Père de famille* (1758; *The Father of the Family*, 1770). As the subtitle of *Dorval* reveals, Diderot regarded these works, as he saw all of his writings, as having a moral purpose. In an article in *Encyclopedia*, he had spoken of actors' ability to engender in audiences the love of virtue, and an essay on Geneva, also in the *Encyclopedia*, by d'Alembert urged the city to permit dramatic productions because they promote morality.

In addition to reforming society, Diderot hoped that his plays would alter theatrical techniques and practices, which he regarded as unrealistic. To the published version of each play he added comments on stagecraft, urging actors to pretend that no audience faced them. He wanted the people onstage to interact naturally with one another, not perform for observers. Diderot also argues, in *Le Paradoxe sur le comédien* (1830; *The Paradox of Acting*, 1883), that the actor must be ruled by the intellect rather than by his emotions if he wishes to convey passion consistently. This view incidentally suggests that Diderot was beginning to question his earlier agreement with Shaftesbury on the primacy of sentiment in guiding action.

Questioning does not, however, mean rejecting. As he matured, Diderot would become increasingly skeptical—of his own views as well as others'—stating that "scepticism is the first step towards the truth." In *Le Neveu de Rameau* (1821; *Rameau's Nephew*, 1897), he seems to prefer Apollonian reason to Dionysian passion, but he also acknowledges the necessity of emotion for creativity. This same ambivalence shows itself in the aesthetic criticism that he wrote for Friedrich Melchior Grimm's *Correspondance littéraire* (1845-1857), a newsletter that circulated in manuscript, from 1759 to 1781. In an essay from 1766 on painting, he instructed the artist, "Move me, astonish me, rend me; make me shudder, weep, tremble; fill me with indignation." At the same time, he recognized that reason must balance enthusiasm.

Though uncertain about the means by which art should achieve its effects, Diderot had no doubt that its end must be the promotion of virtue. Hence, he preferred the sentimental paintings of Jean-Baptiste Greuze to the more sensuous works of François Boucher. Greuze appealed to the heart, Boucher only to the eye. Similarly, though he was an atheist, he admired religious art because it inspired virtuous feelings.

By the time his work on the *Encyclopedia* ended in 1765, Diderot had gained the reputation of being an important French intellectual. A flattering sign of Diderot's growing reputation came from Jean-Honoré Fragonard and Catherine the Great of Russia. In his series of paintings honoring the various arts, Fragonard chose Diderot to represent literature. His hair short, his forehead high, his mouth turned up in an enigmatic smile of reason, the philosopher holds a volume of the *Encyclopedia* and appears to be a Roman citizen wearing an eighteenth century dressing gown. Catherine the Great relieved Diderot of financial concerns in 1765 by buying his library for fifteen thousand livres and appointing him curator for life at a salary of another one thousand livres a year. She agreed not to take formal possession until after Diderot's death.

In 1773, Diderot went to Russia to thank the empress for her patronage. The trip inspired a number of works reflecting on politics and education, and during this time Diderot probably completed his best-known novel, *Jacques le fataliste et son maître* (1796; *Jacques the Fatalist and His Master*, 1797). A clever picaresque, it once more reveals Diderot's skepticism. Although he had, like Jacques, believed in determinism earlier in his life, he now questions this view. Despite Jacques's claim that no one has free will, he behaves as if he can choose whatever course of action he wishes to pursue, and the authorial intrusions indicate that chance rules the world. Readers may draw their own conclusions—or conclude nothing.

Similar doubts characterize other writings of this period. "Beware of those who impose order," he warned in the *Supplément au voyage de Bougainville* (1796; *Supplement to Bougainville's "Voyage,"* 1956). The dialogue form, which Diderot used repeatedly, allows for the presentation of various positions without requiring the author to endorse any. This method, drawn from Plato, appealed to Diderot because it was safe should authorities secure a copy of the manuscript, and it also permitted Diderot to explore various viewpoints. *Est-il bon? Est-il méchant?* (1781), his last and best play, questions, without deciding, whether one can be virtuous if one performs good deeds in a manner that embarrasses the beneficiaries. Skeptical to the end, Diderot's last words to his daughter were, "the first step towards philosophy is disbelief."

Summary

Since his death on July 31, 1784, Denis Diderot's reputation has grown.

With the benefit of the perspective brought by time, one can recognize the truth of Carl Becker's observation that Diderot epitomized his age, both in the profundity of his thought and in the occasional shallowness of his observations. One can appreciate more fully his courage in speaking out, guiding the *Encyclopedia* to completion despite an official ban, telling Catherine the Great that she should abandon autocracy for democracy, and the like. One of his essays was sufficiently bold in its criticism of the *ancien régime* to earn for him a severe reprimand from the police commissioner of Paris. With the publication of many of his best works, one can at last see his greatness as a writer as well as a thinker.

Even more important to the increasing appreciation of Diderot is the fact that his empiricism and skepticism match the modern mood. In his own day Voltaire referred to him as Socrates, a title that fits well. Like Socrates, Diderot questioned the accepted wisdom of his day, risked much for his beliefs, and contributed to the intellectual progress of his age. Writing of eccentrics, Diderot remarked, "If one of them appears in company, he is like a piece of yeast which ferments and restores to everyone a portion of his natural liberty. He shakes and stirs things up; he calls forth praise and blame; he brings out the truth." In these lines from *Rameau's Nephew* Diderot wrote his own epitaph.

Bibliography

Blum, Carol. *Diderot: The Virtue of a Philosopher.* New York: Viking Press, 1974. Focuses on Diderot's concern for a moral life and his intellectual quest to define what such an existence involves. A well-written study that draws on biography, letters, and published writings. Makes some useful comparisons between Diderot and Rousseau on the nature of virtue.

Darnton, Robert. *The Business of Enlightenment: A Publishing History of the "Encyclopédie," 1775-1800.* Cambridge, Mass.: Harvard University Press, 1979. This massive, prizewinning history of Diderot's great project is an important contribution to the growing number of studies devoted to publishing, bookselling, the reading public, and similar topics—placing ideas in the context in which they are disseminated. Illustrated, with a narrative bibliography and an index.

Fellows, Otis. *Diderot.* Boston: Twayne, 1977. A chronological overview touching briefly on almost all Diderot's works. Stresses Diderot's modernity and traces the evolution of his thought. A helpful, annotated bibliography concludes the work.

France, Peter. *Diderot.* New York: Oxford University Press, 1983. A good, short introduction concentrating on Diderot's ideas. Arranged topically rather than chronologically, covering Diderot's political, social, and aesthetic views. Includes a useful bibliography with brief annotations.

Undank, Jack, and Herbert Josephs, eds. *Diderot: Digression and Dispersion, a Bicentennial Tribute.* Lexington, Ky.: French Forum, 1984. Presents nineteen essays that cover Diderot's many activities and interests. In their diversity the contributions mirror the editors' view that Diderot did not seek unity but rather regarded diversity as the rule of nature.

Wilson, Arthur M. *Diderot.* New York: Oxford University Press, 1972. The definitive biography. Places Diderot within the context of the Enlightenment and emphasizes his courage in remaining as editor of the *Encyclopedia.* Considers the development of Diderot's ideas on such matters as religion, emotion and reason, order and diversity, determinism and chance.

Joseph Rosenblum

RUDOLF DIESEL

Born: March 18, 1858; Paris, France
Died: September 29, 1913; at sea, in the English Channel
Areas of Achievement: Invention and technology
Contribution: Diesel invented the diesel engine. His invention has found many applications—in automobiles, trucks, ships, and submarines, and for generating electricity.

Early Life

Born to Bavarian parents residing in Paris, Rudolf Diesel was exposed at an early age to the mechanical arts, both in his father's leather-goods shop and at the nearby Conservatoire des Arts et Métiers. The Diesel family fled to London in September, 1870, in the face of growing anti-German sentiment during the Franco-Prussian War. After eight weeks there, his father, realizing there were too many mouths to feed, sent twelve-year-old Rudolf to Augsburg, Bavaria, to live with an uncle.

Diesel's uncle enrolled him in a county trade school, where Diesel decided, at the age of fourteen, to become an engineer. At the trade school, he studied mathematics, physics, mechanical drawing, and modern languages. It was there also that Diesel realized that his life's ambitions would come true only through hard work and a mastery of science. In the summer of 1875, Diesel advanced to the next level of education in the German system by enrolling, on a scholarship, in the new Technische Hochschule in Munich.

At the Technische Hochschule, Diesel heard the lectures of Professor Carl von Linde on the subject of heat engines. He was particularly struck by the low efficiency of the steam engine and began to think about ways to improve that efficiency. The firm grounding in thermodynamics which he received from Linde's lectures later formed his approach to the problem of designing a better engine. In December, 1879, Diesel passed his final exams at the Technische Hochschule with honors and began his career as an engineer.

Life's Work

Linde, who had so impressed Diesel in school, became his first employer. Diesel took a job as the Paris representative of the refrigeration machinery business Linde had founded. By working with heat engines and heat pumps, Diesel gained experience with the subject which most interested him: thermodynamics.

For ten years, Diesel worked in his spare time on various heat engines, including a solar-powered air engine. A heat engine produces work by heating a working fluid; the fluid then expands and exerts pressure on a moving part, usually a piston. Like many of his contemporaries, Diesel investigated the use of ammonia, ether, and carbon dioxide as substitutes for steam as the working medium in a heat engine. He tried to build an ammonia engine but found ammonia too difficult to handle (even small leaks proved hazardous to the health of nearby workers). He then turned to air as a working medium for two reasons: It was abundant and the oxygen in air could support combustion, thus eliminating the need for a separate firebox.

Having thoroughly studied thermodynamics, Diesel understood the Carnot cycle and attempted to apply it to his new heat engine, in the belief that it would improve the engine's thermal efficiency. First published in 1824 by the French engineer Nicolas-Leonard-Sadi Carnot, the Carnot cycle describes the ideal heat engine of maximum thermal efficiency and consists of four phases: isothermal (constant temperature) combustion, adiabatic (no loss or gain of heat) expansion, isothermal compression, and adiabatic compression to the initial state. In order to realize the highest possible efficiency, Carnot noted, the heat to be converted into work must be added at the highest temperature of the cycle, and it must not raise the temperature of the cycle.

The difficulty of adding heat (through combustion) while maintaining a constant temperature did not daunt Diesel; he felt confident that he could design such an engine—an ideal Carnot engine. His solution was to heat the air by compressing it with a piston inside a cylinder. At the top of the stroke, the air temperature would be at a maximum. He would then add a small amount of fuel, which the high air temperature would ignite. The heat produced by combustion would then be offset by the tendency of the air temperature to drop as the piston moved down and the air expanded, thus producing isothermal combustion. While theoretically correct, this idea met with many practical difficulties, the most formidable being that the engine had to work at extremely high pressures in order to achieve maximum efficiency.

In Diesel's 1892 patent application for his engine, he listed isothermal combustion as the essence of his invention. A year later, Diesel published *Theorie und Konstruktion eines rationellen Wärmemotors zum Ersatz der Dampfmaschinen und der heute bekannten Verbrennungsmotoren* (1893; *Theory and Construction of a Rational Heat Motor*, 1894), in which he fully described his ideas and supported them with calculations and drawings. This book was important to Diesel as a way of promoting his ideas and thus gaining financial backing. With the endorsement of some of Europe's leading thinkers in thermodynamics, Diesel gained the support of two industrial giants: Krupp and Maschinenfabrik Augsburg. Under the agreement that he reached with these firms, Diesel received a good salary and the use of their facilities. Despite this boost, it would take him four years of hard work to begin to realize his dream of a more efficient engine.

In the process of writing his book, Diesel realized that the ideal engine he had envisioned would be almost impossible to build because of the high air pressures required by the theory, which were well beyond the practice of the day. Thus, he began, in 1893, to scale down his ideas and to settle for good, but less-than-ideal, efficiencies. Even with the changes in his theoretical goals, building a working engine proved to be a challenge. His first experimental engine, tested in late 1893, exploded upon ignition of the fuel. His second engine ran under its own power for a minute, but only at idling speed. Not until 1897 did a prototype run smoothly, but it had neither the reliability nor the economy to be a marketable engine. Furthermore, it operated at a thermal efficiency far below what Diesel had originally set out to achieve.

Despite the remaining problems, Diesel announced in June, 1897, at a meeting of the Society of German Engineers that his engine was ready to be sold. The resulting fiasco almost ruined Diesel financially, brought him to the brink of a nervous breakdown, and gave his engine a bad name. Continued refinement of the engine over the next five years, however, restored the diesel engine's reputation. It eventually gained a respectable share of the market, as the number of engines being sold every year increased steadily. By 1908, when Diesel's basic patent expired, the diesel engine was firmly established as an important type of power plant.

By 1912, doubts were being raised as to Diesel's role in the invention of the engine which bore his name. By some accounts, men other than Diesel—those who had taken his highly theoretical ideas and produced a working engine—deserved credit for the diesel engine. Those same critics saw Diesel as little more than a promoter. Diesel had always been highstrung (he was prone to migraines when under extreme stress) so it is not surprising that these criticisms stung him sharply. When he heard, in 1912, that a history of the diesel engine was being written, he countered with his own history, "Die Entstehung des Dieselmotors" (he published a book of the same title the following year). In November, 1912, he presented this paper at a professional meeting of engineers, at which two professors attacked him, pointing out that the diesel engine bore little resemblance to his original concept. At the same time Diesel was suffering these attacks upon his integrity, he was also suffering financial setbacks; bad investments had taken a heavy toll, despite good income from various sources. On the night of September 29, 1913, Rudolf Diesel disappeared from a steamer while crossing the English Channel. His son later identified the effects taken from a body at the mouth of the Schelde River as those of his father. The death was ruled a suicide.

Summary

The diesel engine of today bears little resemblance to Rudolf Diesel's original rational engine, but one is still quite justified in calling him the inventor. Few inventions spring from their creator's mind without the need to refine and improve them, and Diesel's brainchild was no exception. Significantly, Diesel kept a hand in his engine's development throughout the lengthy development period. Furthermore, today's engine retains three essential features of Diesel's original concept. First, all diesel engines are high-compression engines which use air as the working medium. Second, fuel is still injected into the cylinder at the end of the compression stroke. Third, it is still the heat of the compressed air which ignites the fuel.

Diesel engine production grew dramatically after Diesel's death. It is difficult to estimate the number of diesel engines in service, but the fact that millions are built each year throughout the world helps put their importance in perspective. The diesel engine's high thermal efficiency and the low cost of diesel fuel combine to make it an extremely economical engine. As a result, diesel engines have found a growing number of applications such as submarines, ships, locomotives, heavy road and off-road vehicles, passenger cars, and electric generating plants. These engines aptly carry the name of the man who worked so hard to make them a reality.

Bibliography
Bryant, Lynwood. "The Development of the Diesel Engine." *Technology and Culture* 17 (July, 1976): 432-446. A carefully documented case study of the nature of invention, development, and innovation. Contains a brief but useful discussion of the claims against Diesel in 1912. Highlights the many difficulties Diesel encountered in developing his engine and the many modifications to his original idea. Contains footnotes.

_____. "Rudolf Diesel and His Rational Engine." *Scientific American* 221 (August, 1969): 108-117. A careful examination of the intellectual evolution of the diesel engine. Well illustrated and written for the layman, the article explains each step in Diesel's progress toward the diesel engine of today. Contains an especially useful section, with graphs and illustrations, of the Carnot cycle—Diesel's starting point.

Diesel, Eugen. "Rudolf Diesel." In *From Engines to Autos: Five Pioneers in Engine Development and Their Contributions to the Automotive Industry*, by Eugen Diesel, Gustav Goldbeck, and Friedrich Schilderberger. Chicago: Henry Regnery, 1960. Written by Diesel's son, this is, nevertheless, a reasonably objective account of Diesel's life and work. Details of engine development follow a concise, ten-page summary of his early life. Suffers from a lack of documentation, but is notable for the insights it provides into Diesel's personality.

Grosser, Morton. *Diesel: The Man and the Engine*. New York: Atheneum, 1978. A very readable account of the development of the diesel engine from Diesel's original idea through the date of the book's publication. Generally dependable in technical details. Contains a glossary and a list of books for further reading, as well as photographs and illustrations.

Nitske, W. Robert, and Charles Morrow Wilson. *Rudolf Diesel: Pioneer of the Age of Power*. Norman: University of Oklahoma Press, 1965. Biography with two chapters at the end on the diesel engine in the modern world. Not totally reliable. Written mostly from secondary sources and without footnotes; as such, it offers little new information about Rudolf Diesel or his engine.

Brian J. Nichelson

DONATELLO
Donato di Niccolò di Betto Bardi

Born: c. 1386; Florence
Died: December 13, 1466; Florence
Area of Achievement: Art
Contribution: One of the first great European artists to articulate fully the principles of perspective, Donatello has had an incalculable influence on his successors, who have derived their inspiration from his highly naturalistic and intense dramatizations of the human form.

Early Life

Donatello's complete name was Donato di Niccolò di Betto Bardi. He was the son of a wool carder. Very little is known about his life, except what can be surmised from contemporary records (such as payments to him for commissioned work) and from a biographical sketch in *Le vite de' più eccellenti architetti, pittori, et scultori italiani* (1550) by Giorgio Vasari, an Italian architect, writer, and painter. Vasari, however, is not entirely reliable on the subject of his predecessors. It is known that Donatello lost his father while still a young boy, and that he lived with his mother until his middle forties, when she died. He never married. According to Vasari, the artist was a poor but generous man.

Donatello's native city of Florence had been an Etruscan city, founded before Rome. Florence had a long tradition as a center of commerce and pleasure, where a young man such as Donatello could learn art and the practical skills of business. He was trained in the Stonemasons' Guild and was the master of many crafts, including goldsmithing, the making of inlays, engraving, carving, and the application of stucco ornaments to furniture.

The first record of Donatello as an artist (May, 1403) puts him in the shop of Lorenzo Ghiberti, a pioneer in the use of perspective, a technique that gives depth and three-dimensional quality to paintings and relief sculpture. By 1406, Donatello was at work on small marble figures of prophets for the Porta della Mandorla of the Duomo of Florence. On February 20, 1408, he received his first major commission, for a marble figure of David.

Life's Work

Donatello's first major work, the *David* in the Palazzo Vecchio, is a marble figure measuring six feet, three and one-half inches. At his feet rests the massive head of Goliath. Standing above the head, with his legs parted, is a lithe, almost delicate David, draped in a close-fitting cloak that emphasizes the youthful muscularity of his figure. His long right arm accentuates the power of the slingshot throw that brought Goliath to earth. The fingers of the right hand are bent in a grasping pose and were probably meant to hold a sling which has been lost. There is great vitality and strength in the sculpture, even though David is not depicted in action, because of the economy and the expressive precision of the details Donatello dramatizes, such as the way the index and middle fingers of his left hand press against his torso. Although David is a religious figure and embodies a myth, he is presented as an individual, a remarkable personality worthy of close inspection.

With the marble figure of *Saint John the Evangelist*, now in the southern aisle of the Duomo of Florence, Donatello made a larger than life-size statue that surpasses the *David* in the dynamic rendering of personality. Working with a somewhat shallow block of marble, the artist shaped the upper half of the body in high relief, thus leaving enough marble for the seated figure's thighs. By giving the figure no back, he foregrounded those aspects of Saint John's person he wished to highlight. It is the saint's human qualities, his piercing eyes and grave demeanor, that rivet the viewer. With book in hand, held meditatively, he appears as the very embodiment of the prayerful man.

Saint George and the Dragon, a marble relief on the outside of the Or San Michele in Florence, is noteworthy for Donatello's use of mountain and forest landscape. As in his previous work, there is a beautiful rendering of naturalistic elements, a grounding in the reality of human emotions and settings. The representation of such scenes in the Middle Ages was more formulaic, more centered on a static composition of all the elements of the myth. In Donatello, rearing horse, rider, and dragon collide, so that the meaning of the myth arises primarily out of the sense of movement. Donatello's sculpture is not so much allegory (a pictorial evocation of myth) as it is an action in itself, a story evolving out of the artist's powerful dramatic technique.

The Feast of Herod (also known as the *Dance of Salome*), when compared to Pietro Lorenzetti's earlier painting of the same name, confirms Donatello's deft handling of realistic human figures in dramatic settings. In Lorenzetti's work, each of the seven figures is carefully spaced and distinctly visible in the foreground and background. The scene is frozen, made static, so that the picture is complete, the story intact. In Donatello's bronze relief for the Siena Cathedral font, five figures in the foreground of the right side of the relief draw back in horror at the presented head of John the Baptist. One man partially covers his face with his hand, as though the full sight of the head is more than he can bear. The other four figures are drawn back, but a woman in profile—perhaps the dancing Salome—stares fixedly at the head. These five figures are bunched together, obscuring a full view of their faces. Indeed, one face cannot be seen at all—only a headdress is visible. The realism, drama, and human complexity of the reactions to this atrocity demonstrate how intensely Donatello wished to convey the very life of events and personalities and not merely their symbolism. His use of composition to render the psychology of his subjects is evident in the left side of the bronze relief, where five distinctly positioned figures complete the fore-grounding of the work and relieve the congestion of the right side. There is an exquisite balance achieved in the framing of the scene, quite different from Lorenzetti's proportioning of space.

Between 1411 and 1427, Donatello received commissions to work on fig-ures of *Saint John the Evangelist* and *Saint George and the Dragon*, the *Sacrifice of Isaac*, the tomb of Baldassare Cossa (Pope John XXIII), the *Head of a Prophet*, the *Head of a Sibyl*, and others for the Or San Michele, the Opera del Duomo, and the cathedral of Orvieto—all in Florence. In 1430, he went to Rome for three years and carved several tombs. By 1433, he had returned to Florence to design several stained-glass windows, marble tombs, and bronze heads.

One of Donatello's most notable works from this period and said to have been his favorite is the so-called *Zuccone* (pumpkinhead, or baldhead). Again, it is the strong personality of the figure that is so commendable to modern taste. The long angular face, accentuated by the tilt of the head downward, the long loosely flexed right arm, with the right hand casually thrust inside a belt, are all aspects of a highly individualized figure. This is a person with his own peculiar outlook on the world, not simply a study of human form, and a figure with a posture that bends with life.

The bronze *David*, the *Equestrian Monument of General Gattamelata*, and *Mary Magdalen* are representative examples of the power and variety of Donatello's final period of creativity. It seemed to the artist's contemporaries that *David* was cast from life, so natural and playful does this slight figure appear. There is a joy and a lightness in this work that is entirely different from the earlier *David* in marble. The bronze statue of General Gattamelata, which stands in front of the Church Sant' Antonio in Padua, where the artist lived for nearly ten years, is a ruggedly determined depiction of the com-mander in chief of the Venetian military forces who died at Padua on Jan-uary 16, 1443. The tough, chiseled quality of the face, the tight, slight grim-ness in the lips bespeak a man girding himself for battle with the poised calm of a great leader. As Ludwig Goldscheider notes, the wood carving of Mary Magdalen is an especially vivid example of Donatello's final naturalistic phase. The roughly hewn wood exaggerates the worn, beaten-looking, bony face, with its broken-toothed, grotesque mouth, while the strong hands, with fingers not quite touching one another in the sign of prayer, suggest the spirituality that inheres in this crude body.

Summary

Donatello is regarded as one of the great innovators of Renaissance art. The bronze *David*, for example, is one of the first nude freestanding Renais-sance statues. His great contributions were recognized in his time, especially at Padua, where he was the head of an enormous workshop. In his last years, he created an extraordinary set of reliefs for the pulpits of San Lorenzo. Most of his work remains in Florence, although an unfinished *David* is exhibited at the National Gallery of Art in Washington, and a *Madonna* is in the Boston Museum.

The portrayal of human bodies is certainly one of Donatello's greatest achievements. The personality seems to express itself from within his dynamic figures, and there is never the sense that the faces he gives his figures are simply imposed upon them. In the perfect disposition of each physical feature, of every detail of clothing and setting, the artist perfects both the objective and psychological points of view. His figures are real people in a real world, observed with sharp accuracy.

Donatello can rightly be regarded as one of the precursors of modern art because his sculpture is autonomous, a thing in itself that is never simply illustrative of the subjects he carved and casted. Like his contemporary Fra Angelico, Donatello excels in the dramatization of whole scenes, relying not only on his deft manipulation of human figures but also on his profound understanding of architecture and of the spaces his figures and objects occupy. Where he differs from Fra Angelico is in the heroic quality of so many of his human figures. It is, in the last analysis, his ability to portray depth powerfully—in his human subjects and in his settings—that continues to make his work worthy of the most serious study.

Bibliography

Balcarres, Lord. *Donatello*. London: Duckworth, 1903. This study is still worth consulting for its detailed account of Donatello's career and its informative account of art history. Contains a large number of plates and an appendix of work lost or not executed. Out-of-date bibliography.

Goldscheider, Ludwig. *Donatello*. New York: Oxford University Press, 1941. Excellent reproductions of the artist's major sculptures with many plates focusing on interesting details. A well-written introduction to the significance of Donatello's work, a detailed catalog of major and minor sculpture, and an index of museums, collections, and places where Donatello's work appears make this an indispensable volume.

Janson, Horst Woldemar. *The Sculpture of Donatello*. 2 vols. Princeton, N.J.: Princeton University Press, 1957. Volume 1 is devoted to large black-and-white plates of the artist's work. Volume 2 contains a critical catalog that establishes accurate dating and documentation of Donatello's work. Extensive references to previous scholarship make this a dialogue between art historians as much as a discussion of Donatello's sculpture. Includes a very detailed and useful index.

Lightbrown, R. W. *Donatello and Michelozzo: An Artistic Partnership and Its Patrons in the Early Renaissance*. 2 vols. London: Harvey Miller, 1980. Although there is scant discussion of Donatello's individual works, this study provides excellent background for an understanding of the world in which Donatello worked. Should also be consulted for its glossary, a table showing popes in the fourteenth and fifteenth centuries, a chronology of Donatello, and beautiful plates with close-ups of the artist's greatest work.

Meyer, Alfred Gotthold. London: H. Grevel, 1904. Contains 140 black-and-white illustrations from pictures, etchings, and drawings, as well as detailed accounts of Donatello's art. The style is sometimes exaggerated. Scholarship superseded by more recent studies. Includes an index of artists.

Carl Rollyson
Lisa Paddock

GAETANO DONIZETTI

Born: November 29, 1797; Bergamo, Cisalpine Republic
Died: April 8, 1848; Bergamo, Austrian Empire
Area of Achievement: Music
Contribution: Donizetti was the most prolific composer of Italian operas in the first half of the nineteenth century. Though his works are uneven in quality, he was, at his best, the greatest and most vital exponent of Italian Romanticism before Giuseppe Verdi.

Early Life

Gaetano Donizetti was the fifth of six children born to Andrea and Domenica Nava Donizetti. He was born in a basement apartment, where, according to his later recollection, "no glimmer of light ever penetrated." His father, who discouraged him from pursuing a career as a composer, followed no particular trade; after 1808, he earned a miserable existence as the janitor of the local pawnshop.

In 1806, a free music school was established in Bergamo under the direction of Johann Simon Mayr. The eight-year-old Donizetti was one of the first students to enroll in the institution which would later bear his name (Istituto Musicale Gaetano Donizetti), and he continued his studies there until 1814. Donizetti's extraordinary fluency in composition in later years was a result at least in part of the rigorous training of Mayr, himself a successful composer of Italian operas.

At Mayr's urging, Donizetti went to Bologna to study counterpoint and fugue at the Liceo Filarmonico, then perhaps the most distinguished music school in Italy. His master in Bologna was the highly erudite Padre Mattei, who had formerly taught Gioacchino Rossini. Though Mattei did not inspire affection, Donizetti applied himself vigorously to the study of the contrapuntal forms; sixty-one exercises in his hand survive in manuscript.

Donizetti returned to Bergamo in 1817. Working with that facility and ease which was to mark his entire career, Donizetti composed four operas during a period of four years and a large body of nonoperatic works. In the latter category, Donizetti composed eighteen string quartets; though modest, these works have a certain vernal charm. Donizetti was also forced at this time to devote considerable energy to the avoidance of military service. With the help of a woman who admired his talent, Donizetti was able to purchase an exemption in 1818.

Donizetti had by this time matured into a well-favored young man. His passport of 1821 describes him as tall and slender, with blue eyes and chestnut hair; associates found him to be handsome, generous, and charming. As a young man, Donizetti was high-spirited; later, personal tragedies caused a melancholia to descend upon him.

Life's Work

Donizetti's career as a composer of opera was firmly launched in 1822, with the success of a serious opera in Rome. Donizetti was next offered a commission by the Teatro Nuovo in Naples. Then the most robust operatic center in Italy, Naples had been dominated musically by Rossini since 1815. Donizetti's first offering to the Neapolitan public, the semiserious opera *La zingara* (1822) was an immense success. For the next several years, Donizetti made Naples the base of his activities; like all successful opera composers of his day, however, he was forced to travel frequently.

Though none of the operas before *Anna Bolena* (1830) has maintained a place in the active repertory, Donizetti was stunningly productive during the fifteen-year span from 1822 to 1837. Donizetti completed forty-nine operas in this remarkably fertile period. All the subgenres of Italian opera are represented in the canon of Donizetti's works: opera buffa (comic opera), opera seria (serious opera), and opera semiseria.

Donizetti relied largely on the formal conventions of Italian opera as established by Rossini. Most of the scenes in Donizettian opera are reducible ultimately to an opening recitative (rapid declamation of text) and a section in a brisk tempo (*tempo d'attacco*), in which the dramatic situation is presented; a slow reflective aria; an interruption of mood in a faster tempo (*tempo di mezzo*); and a brisk concluding section replete with vocal fireworks (*cabaletta*). This formula could be applied to ensembles as well as to solo scenes; in the former case, the brilliant concluding passage was called the *stretto*. Yet Donizetti deployed the basic pattern in an infinite variety of ways; moreover, in his intuitive understanding of its dramatic potential, he surpassed Rossini. Donizetti was not an inventive harmonist, and his scoring sometimes consisted of the simplest accompaniment patterns repeated shamelessly; yet in dramatic pacing, in the creation of adrenaline-charged melodies, and in sheer élan, he had few peers.

Though earlier works had given ample indications of a strong talent, Donizetti did not reach artistic maturity until the composition of *Anna Bolena*. This work marks the ascendancy of the full-blooded Romantic melodrama in Italian opera. *Anna Bolena* is one of four Donizettian operas based on Tudor history. Donizetti created a score of great power and emotional sincerity. The work also marks the beginning of a preoccupation on the part of Italian composers with libretti which depict fallible women, in this case Anne Boleyn, in pitiable circumstances. In the moving final scene, in which Boleyn is alternately delirious and lucid before her execution, Donizetti offers a foretaste of the famous "mad scene" from his later opera *Lucia di Lammermoor* (1835).

Anna Bolena brought Donizetti international acclaim, and it probably marked the peak of his personal fortunes as well. Donizetti had been married, in 1828, to Virginia Vasselli. By all accounts, the union was a happy one. In the 1830's, however, three children born to them died in infancy, and in 1837, Virginia died of cholera. Donizetti never fully recovered from these losses, though he remained artistically productive for several years after Virginia's death.

The years between 1830 and 1837 constituted the zenith of Donizetti's career as a composer of Italian opera. In a series of striking works, including *Parisina* (1833), *Lucrezia Borgia* (1833), *Marino Faliero* (1835), *Lucia di Lammermoor*, and *Roberto Devereux* (1837), Donizetti solidified his achievement in the genre of the *melodramma* and also composed a comic opera of enduring charm in *L'elisir d'amore* (1832; the elixir of love). *Lucrezia Borgia*, an adaptation of Victor Hugo's play by Felice Romani, is a lurid drama steeped in violence and touching upon incest; in its sensationalism and explosiveness, Donizetti's setting adumbrates the *Verismo* opera school of the end of the century. Donizetti also happened upon a new musical texture for the setting of conversation in this work: The characters Rustighello and Astolfo chat in recitative in act 1, while a portentous motive sings in the orchestra (a device often credited to Verdi). *Marino Faliero*, with text supplied by Emanuele Bidera based indirectly on Lord Byron, prefigures Verdi's *I due Foscari* (1844), and *Simon Boccanegra* (1857) in its Venetian local color and its liberal political undercurrents. *Roberto Devereux* is the last of Donizetti's forays into Tudor history; his musical portrait of Elizabeth I in this work is one of his finest.

Lucia di Lammermoor has proved to be Donizetti's most durable work. It was his first collaboration with the distinguished librettist Salvatore Cammarano, and their joint effort is regarded by many as the touchstone of the entire bel canto repertory (as the works of Rossini, Vincenzo Bellini, Donizetti, and their contemporaries are collectively known).

In the final phase of his compositional career from 1838 to 1845, Donizetti was drawn into the orb of Parisian grand opera. He composed four operas to French texts for the stages of Paris; of these, the comic *La fille du régiment* (1840; the daughter of the regiment) and the serious *La favorite* (1840) became repertory staples. Donizetti's greatest achievement in the category of Italian opera buffa was also written for a foreign commission: His comic masterpiece *Don Pasquale* (1843) was written for the Théâtre Italien in Paris. Two serious operas with Italian texts, *Linda di Chamounix* (1842) and *Maria di Rohan* (1843), were commissioned by a Viennese theater.

Donizetti's life was rapidly approaching its own tragic denouement. In 1844, Donizetti began to show unmistakable symptoms of the last stages of syphilis. His condition deteriorated to the point where institutionalization was required in 1846. In 1848, Donizetti's died in Bergamo.

Summary

It was Gaetano Donizetti's misfortune to be the middle child in the family of nineteenth century Italian opera composers, preceded and followed by the more towering figures of Rossini and Verdi. Donizetti's primitive orchestrations and predictable melodic formulas were seen as tokens of his inferiority. A later generation of scholars has by contrast marveled at the professional standard Donizetti maintained given the conditions under which he worked. More detailed knowledge of his works has also bred increased respect; many effects associated with Verdi (or known through Sir Arthur Sullivan's parodies) have been found to be the products of Donizetti's imagination.

Appreciation of Donizetti's contribution has also been retarded by a lack of understanding of the subgenre in which he did his finest work, the *melodramma*. Modern critics have realized that the *melodramma* should not be judged according to the dramaturgical standards of a later generation. Texts which struck later generations as ludicrous were understood by Donizetti and his colleagues to be mere verbal semaphores reinforcing the profound emotional content of the music. Donizetti's role in the creation of the *melodramma* earns for him an honored place in the company of Victor Hugo, Hector Berlioz, and the other innovators who dismantled the edifice of artistic classicism.

Bibliography
Ashbrook, William. *Donizetti and His Operas*. Cambridge, England: Cambridge University Press, 1982. The definitive work in English on Donizetti. Part 1 offers biographical information; part 2 provides analytic comment on all the operas. Appendices supply synopses and information about Donizetti's librettists.
Ashbrook, William, and Julian Budden. "Gaetano Donizetti." In *The New Grove Masters of Italian Opera*. New York: W. W. Norton, 1983. Concise account of Donizetti's life and valuable analytic commentary by two first-rate scholars of Italian opera. Contains the most accurate catalog of Donizetti's works available.
Gossett, Philip. *"Anna Bolena" and the Artistic Maturity of Gaetano Donizetti*. New York: Oxford University Press, 1985. Detailed discussion of *Anna Bolena*, the watershed work in Donizetti's career. Gossett offers a revisionist view of Donizetti's achievement.
Tomlinson, Gary. "Italian Romanticism and Italian Opera: An Essay in Their Affinities." *19th Century Music* 10, no. 1 (1986). Useful essay suggesting that Donizetti was in the aesthetic vanguard of his day.
Weinstock, Herbert. *Donizetti and the World of Opera in Italy, Paris, and Vienna in the First Half of the Nineteenth Century*. New York: Pantheon Books, 1963. Full-length study of Donizetti's life aimed at a popular audience. Slightly out of date given the increase in scholarly interest in Donizetti, but highly readable.

Steven W. Shrader

DORGON

Born: November 17, 1612; Mukden, Manchuria
Died: December 31, 1650; Kharakhotun, China
Areas of Achievement: The military and politics
Contribution: Dorgon devised and implemented the political and military policies which led to the Manchu conquest of China. As regent over the first Ch'ing emperor, his measures contributed to the longevity of Manchu rule.

Early Life

Dorgon was the fourteenth son of Nurhachi, and one of three sons the Empress Hsiao-lieh bore to the Manchu ruler. Early in his life, there was a rumor that he was a favorite of Nurhachi and was slated to become his heir. More likely, Dorgon was one of the young men whom Nurhachi had chosen to participate in a leadership rotation. Not long after Nurhachi's death in 1626, however, one of the four senior administrators, Abahai, forced the suicide of Dorgon's mother in a successful effort to garner complete power for himself.

Abahai chose not to punish the sixteen-year-old Dorgon or his brothers but instead treated them well, with Dorgon and his brother, Dodo, each gaining control of a banner. In return, Dorgon served Abahai with dedication and courage and, during the period 1627-1636, participated in almost every military campaign. In 1636, when Abahai declared himself Emperor of the Ch'ing, Dorgon became a prince of the first degree with the designation Jui. Two years later, he assumed command of one of two giant armies which invaded China. Besides his military successes, Dorgon also possessed considerable diplomatic skills and was apparently admired by Chinese Mongols and Koreans.

Abahai also entrusted Dorgon with important administrative posts, and the latter was instrumental in the establishment of the Six Boards in 1631. Dorgon encouraged Abahai to treat the Chinese under Manchu control well in order to facilitate a future Manchu conquest of China. While Abahai accepted this advice, it apparently kindled the Manchu monarch's suspicions concerning Dorgon's ultimate agenda. Nevertheless, Dorgon served Abahai faithfully and continued to assume major responsibilities up until the death of the Ch'ing emperor in September, 1643.

Life's Work

Upon the death of Abahai, his eldest son, Haoge, and Dorgon competed for the Manchu throne. The successional dispute threatened to erupt into a civil war, with Haoge holding something of a military advantage. Dorgon, however, succeeded in obtaining a compromise. Abahai's five-year-old son,

Fu-lin, would become the heir and rule under the reign title Shun-chih. Until Shun-chih came of age, however, Dorgon and another Manchu prince, Jirgalang, were to act as regents.

Haoge and his supporters were mollified, expecting Jirgalang, who had enjoyed an outstanding military career, to be an effective deterrent to Dorgon's ambitions. They had not, however, counted on either Dorgon's political acumen or Jirgalang's distaste for civilian matters. Within months, Jirgalang was referring most important governmental affairs to Dorgon, and the latter was laying the foundations for Haoge's demise. By May of 1644, Dorgon had Haoge impeached for sedition and demoted to commoner. In 1647, Dorgon deposed Jirgalang, who had already been demoted to assistant regent, and had his own brother, Dodo, take his place. Finally, in 1648, Haoge himself was imprisoned and encouraged to commit suicide. Later, in 1650, upon the death of his own wife, Dorgon would marry Haoge's widow as a symbolic gesture of victory over his former rival.

During the course of this consolidation of power, Dorgon had himself repeatedly promoted in rank starting as uncle prince regent and culminating in 1648 with imperial father regent. In the same year, he was excused from prostrating himself before the emperor at audiences. Even as he was effecting a complete domination of the Manchu court, Dorgon was also leading the Manchus in their conquest of China and in the establishment of the Ch'ing Dynasty (1644-1911). Dorgon proved to be as clever at military diplomacy and administrative reform as he had been at conspiratorial court politics.

Within days of consolidating his power at Mukden, Dorgon had begun a massive invasion of Ming China, which had been weakened by a decadent court and constant internal upheavals. In April, 1644, Peking fell to a brutal bandit-rebel, Li Tzu-ch'eng, with the Ming emperor hanging himself near the palace. During this time, the Manchus were preparing an attack on Shanhai-kuan, which was being defended by General Wu San-kuei. News of the fall of Peking prompted Wu to invite Dorgon to participate in a joint venture to punish the bandit Li and to profit from captured booty. Dorgon, however, following the advice of several Chinese who served him, agreed to help punish Li but also made it clear that the Manchus intended to take over the Dragon throne. Dorgon called upon General Wu to surrender his troops and join the Manchus in recapturing Peking and eliminating Li. Using flowery sentences which promised to avenge the late Ming emperor's death, Dorgon's messages also pointed out the historical validity of the so-called Mandate of Heaven's being passed from the unworthy Ming to the worthy Ch'ing.

Unquestionably, these polished Chinese sentences were not the products of Dorgon himself but rather of advisers such as Fan Wen-ch'eng and Hung Ch'eng-ch'ou. Ultimately, however, it was Dorgon who realized the usefulness of ensuring that the Manchu invasion would not simply be another barbarian raid. Accordingly, Dorgon issued strict instructions to his officers and men to refrain from looting. After rushing to Shan-hai-kuan and accepting Wu San-keui's surrender and subordination, Dorgon marched to Peking.

Li Tzu-ch'eng had begun to attack Shan-hai-kuan but had retreated to Peking on news of the Manchu-Wu alliance. There, he crowned himself the Yung-Ch'ang emperor as his troops savagely pillaged the capital. On June 4, 1644, however, Li left after setting the palace and much of Peking ablaze. On the next day, to the amazement of those officials and residents who were anticipating a Chinese rescue army, Dorgon appeared and announced that the Manchus were there to receive the Mandate of Heaven. He promised Peking's residents and all Chinese that the Manchus would rule wisely and justly. Thus, with Dorgon as regent, Fu-lin began his rule over Ch'ing China.

During the rest of his regency, Dorgon consolidated Manchu control by mixing military action with the seduction of Ming military and civilian officials. Slowly but methodically, Ch'ing rule over China spread, and the waning hope of a Ming revival expired. In military action, Dorgon not only used his own trusted kin and supporters but also cautiously employed some of Haoge's former allies as well as Chinese. Dorgon was very successful at enlisting the allegiance of former Ming military officials, but he also knew how to employ civilian officials and draw good service from them.

Perhaps Dorgon's most impressive achievement was his ability to clean up the corruption that had characterized the Ming and yet do so with many of the same officials who had served in the corrupt administration. One action which improved morale among the Chinese officials and helped reduce corruption was the elimination of the power and influence of the palace eunuchs. Dorgon ordered that anyone who voluntarily castrated himself in order to become a palace eunuch would be decapitated.

The regent also reduced taxes and fought against venality, both at the court and in the countryside. He strove to maintain the examination system as a principal means of recruiting honest and conscientious Chinese officials to the Ch'ing administration. Areas which had suffered from the civil wars were often temporarily excused from taxes. Clearly, Dorgon was intent upon making Manchu rule as smooth and as acceptable to the Chinese population as possible. Yet, as his brother Abahai before him, Dorgon struggled with the question of the assimilation of the Manchus by the Chinese. Ultimately, his solution was a form of apartheid.

Initially, Dorgon vacillated over the previous policy of requesting Chinese under the Manchus to shave the front of their heads and wear their hair in queues. By 1645, however, Dorgon decided to demand this of all Chinese under the Ch'ing, as one means of separating the conquerors from the conquered. Dorgon rationalized that this policy would actually reduce tensions, but it was clear that he wished to avoid having his people assimilated by the Chinese. He gave much of the rich farmland surrounding Peking to Manchu troops and princes, and even had Chinese moved from the northern part of Peking to the south. While he recruited Chinese officials, he was also careful to leave the major positions in Manchu hands.

Having eliminated his major enemies and having achieved much success in ensconcing the Manchus in China, Dorgon began in the late 1640's to give up some of his previously rigorous regimen. He began to build a magnificent palace in Southern Jehol and was already at work stockpiling luxuries and concubines. It was not clear whether he intended to retire from active politics or to shift the focus of Manchu power from Peking to his future palace. In any case, while not quite recovered from an illness, he went on a difficult hunting trip, took ill at Kharakhotun, and died on the last day of 1650. He was buried with great honor, but his reputation would not last long after his death. By March of 1651, some of his former enemies assumed the regency and proceeded to withdraw most of Dorgon's honors and titles. His adopted son was forced to return to his previous family, and the records of Dorgon's achievements were rewritten in an unflattering manner. In 1773, however, the Ch'ien Lung emperor restored most of Dorgon's honors, and his name was celebrated in the Imperial Ancestral Temple.

Summary

A consummate factionalist player, Dorgon survived the deadly game of court politics resulting from the refusals by both Nurhachi and Abahai to designate heirs before they died. Had this been all, his career would have been historically insignificant. His legacy, however, was much more considerable. He surrounded himself with talented advisers and implemented their advice. He was thus instrumental in establishing the Ch'ing rule over China in a manner that would facilitate the longevity of Manchu rule. His insistence upon a form of dyarchy allowed the relatively unsophisticated Manchus an opportunity to mature into their role as overseers of a traditional Chinese government. Dorgon's policy with respect to eunuchs also prevented an endemic problem from ever developing to hinder Manchu rule.

Ultimately, however, Dorgon's hope that the Manchus would forever remain a separate people would fail. In measure, this was a consequence of his land policies. By distributing confiscated land among Manchus, he essentially laid the foundations for his people's eventual abandonment of hunting and pastoralism, the absence of which opened the door to rapid Sinicization. They would continue to rule China for more than two and a half centuries, but by becoming agriculturalists, they could not, as their Mongol neighbors had done, avoid assimilation and remain a separate people.

Bibliography

Hummel, Arthur W., ed. *Eminent Chinese of the Ch'ing Period (1644-1912)*. 2 vols. Washington, D.C.: Government Printing Office, 1943-

1944. Volume 1 contains an excellent biography of Dorgon.

Kessler, Lawrence D. *K'ang-hsi and the Consolidation of Ch'ing Rule, 1661-1684*. Chicago: University of Chicago Press, 1976. Although concentrating on the achievements of the K'ang Hsi emperor, the author provides some insight into the administrative beginnings of the Ch'ing Dynasty during the Dorgon regency.

Lee, Robert H. G. *The Manchurian Frontier in Ch'ing History*. Cambridge, Mass.: Harvard University Press, 1970. Essential reading for an understanding of frontier politics during Dorgon's life.

Michael, Franz. *The Origin of Manchu Rule in China: Frontier and Bureaucracy as Interacting Forces in the Chinese Empire*. Baltimore: Johns Hopkins University Press, 1942. A somewhat controversial, but still-incisive discussion of the frontier state and the processes undertaken by the early Manchu leaders to prepare for the conquest of China.

Oxnam, Robert B. *Ruling from Horseback: Manchu Politics in the Oboi Regency, 1661-1669*. Chicago: University of Chicago Press, 1975. In searching for the origins of the concept of regency and the nature of Oboi's policies, the author devotes considerable attention to the model provided by the Dorgon regency.

Wakeman, Frederic, Jr. *The Great Enterprise: The Manchu Reconstruction of Imperial Order in Seventeenth-Century China*. 2 vols. Berkeley: University of California Press, 1985. Destined to be a classic in the study of Chinese history. Wakeman presents a comprehensive study of the Manchu conquest and early rule over China. Volumes 1 and 2 devote much attention to Dorgon's career.

Hilel B. Salomon

FYODOR DOSTOEVSKI

Born: November 11, 1821; Moscow, Russia
Died: January 28, 1881; St. Petersburg, Russia
Area of Achievement: Literature
Contribution: One of the world's greatest novelists, Dostoevski summoned
   to imaginative life areas of psychological, political, and aesthetic experi-
   ence which have significantly shaped the modern sensibility.

Early Life

Fyodor Dostoevski is one of only two great nineteenth century Russian
writers—Anton Chekhov is the other—who failed, unlike Alexander Pushkin, Nikolai Gogol, Ivan Turgenev, Leo Tolstoy, and others, to be born into
the landed gentry. Whereas aristocrats such as Turgenev and Tolstoy depicted settled traditions of culture and fixed moral-social norms, Dostoevski
spent his early years in an atmosphere which prepared him to treat the moral
consequences of flux and change, and dramatize the breakup of the traditional forms of Russian society. His father, Mikhail Andreevich, derived
from the lowly class of the nonmonastic clergy, succeeded in rising to the
status of civil servant by becoming a military doctor and then became a
surgeon attached to a hospital for the poor on the outskirts of Moscow. His
mother, Marya Feodorovna, née Nechaev, was a merchant's daughter, meek,
kind, gentle, pious—obviously the inspiration for most of Dostoevski's fic-
tive heroines. The elder Dostoevski was not the repulsively dissolute prototype of Feodor Karamazov that many early biographies describe. He was,
however, while devoted to his family, extremely strict, mistrustful, irritable,
and easily depressed. The son was to acknowledge in later life his inheritance, from his father, of oversensitive nerves and uncontrollable explosions
of temper. In addition, Dostoevski suffered from epilepsy, a condition which
also ran in his family.

Fyodor was the second child and second son in the family. In 1838, the
elder Dostoevski sent his sons to St. Petersburg's Academy of Engineers,
determined to push them into secure careers despite their preference for
literary achievement. In February, 1839, the father suffered a partial stroke
when Fyodor failed to be promoted during his freshman year; in early June,
1839, Dostoevski's father died. All biographers assumed until modern times
that he had been murdered on his small country estate by peasants outraged
by his severity toward them. Joseph Frank, however, in *Dostoevsky: The
Seeds of Revolt, 1821-1849* (1976), the first volume of his monumental
biography of Dostoevski, shows that important new evidence points to the
probability of the elder Dostoevski's dying of an apoplectic stroke rather
than at the hands of killers. Nevertheless, Dostoevski all of his life believed
that his father had been murdered and therefore assumed a heavy burden of

parricidal guilt, for the peasants who—so he imagined—had killed his father were merely enacting an impulse which he had surely felt.

In August, 1843, Dostoevski was graduated from the academy and placed on duty in the drafting department of the St. Petersburg Engineering Command. He neglected his work, preferring to read widely among French and German Romantic authors. By far the deepest influence, however, was that of Gogol. In 1844, Dostoevski resigned from the army, published a translation of Honoré de Balzac's *Eugénie Grandet* (1833; English translation, 1859), and began to work on his first novel, which was published in January, 1846, as *Bednye lyudi* (*Poor Folk*, 1887).

This is a poignant story of frustrated love, told in the form of letters passed between a poor government clerk and an equally poor girl who lives near him. Dostoevski's insight into the tortures of humiliated sensibility constitutes his major departure from what is otherwise a Gogol-like protest against the upper class's condescension to the lower. The most influential literary critic of the 1840's, Vissarion Belinsky, hailed the book as Russia's first important social novel.

Belinsky was less enthusiastic about Dostoevski's second novel, *Dvoynik* (*The Double*, 1917), which also appeared in 1846. Gogol's fiction again served as the model, particularly "Nos" ("The Nose") and "Zapiski sumasshedshego" ("Diary of a Madman"). Dostoevski's protagonist, Golyadkin, a middle-ranking bureaucrat, is driven by inner demons. His unquenchable thirst for self-worth and dignity causes him to distort reality and create for himself a world that will mirror his self-conflicts. Golyadkin's split personality disintegrates into two independent entities: A double appears who confronts him with his worst faults, both reflecting the suppressed wishes of his subconscious and objectifying his accompanying guilt feelings. While Dostoevski erred in failing to establish a moral perspective from which the reader could evaluate Golyadkin either straightforwardly or ironically, he did succeed in hauntingly portraying, for the first time, the kind of obsessive, divided self that was to dominate his later, greater fiction.

Life's Work

Dostoevski's darkest decade began the night of April 22-23, 1849, when he was taken into police custody in St. Petersburg as a member of a circle headed by Mikhail Butashevich-Petrashevsky. A czarist court of inquiry concluded that fifteen of the accused, including Dostoevski, had been guilty of subversion and conspiracy. On December 22, 1849, the prisoners were taken to a public square and lined up before a firing squad. By prearrangement, literally in the last seconds before their expected execution, an aide-de-camp to the czar commuted their punishment to four years of hard prison labor and four additional years of military service as privates—both in Siberia. From this moment onward, the secular, progressive, idealistic influences from such writers as Friedrich Schiller, Victor Hugo, and George Sand, which had determined Dostoevski's previous philosophy, receded before the onrush of a spiritual vitality that overwhelmed him as a revelation. Always a believing Christian, he strove for the rest of his life to emphasize an ethic of expiation, forgiveness, and all-embracing love, based on a conviction of the imminence of the Day of Judgment and the Final Reckoning.

Some scholars interpret Dostoevski's consequent right-wing conservatism and mistrust of human nature as a psychic-emotive transformation caused by his disillusioning prison camp experiences. Joseph Frank takes a more acute view: Dostoevski came to regard each downtrodden convict as potentially capable of love and compassion but focused on the Russian peasant, regarding persons outside the Slavic culture and Orthodox faith as historically and religiously outcast. He became a fervent Slavophile, insisting that religious and cultural isolation from Western materialism had enabled the Russian people to avoid what he regarded as Europe's demoralization and decadence.

The Dostoevski who returned to St. Petersburg in mid-December, 1859, had matured enormously as a result of having confronted mortality, discovered the egotistic drives dominating his fellow convicts, and undergone a conversion crisis. In 1864, he published a novelette, *Zapiski is podpolya* (*Notes from the Underground*, 1918), written primarily as a satirical parody of the views expressed in Nikolay Chernyshevsky's didactic novel *Chto delat'?* (1863; *What Is to Be Done?*, c. 1863), which affirmed rational egotism as the panacea for all human problems. Not at all, says the Underground Man. He is a malicious, brilliantly paradoxical skeptic who challenges the validity of reason and of rational solutions. He insists that, above all, man is determined to follow his often foolish, perverse, and even absurd will. Against the Enlightenment premises of utilitarianism, order, and good sense, the Undergroundling opposes chaos, self-destruction, cruelty, and caprice. This work is now generally recognized as the central text in Dostoevski's canon, the prologue to his greatest novels. The problem he would now confront is how to preserve human freedom from nihilism, how to restrain its destructive implications.

Raskolnikov, the protagonist of *Prestupleniye i nakazaniye* (1866; *Crime and Punishment*, 1886), is another Underground Man, despising ordinary people and conventional morality. He commits murder to test his theory that an extraordinary person is beyond good and evil. He then suffers harrowing isolation and self-disgust. Only his growing love for the sacrificial Sonia will open him slowly to processes of compassion, remorse, and regeneration. Yet Raskolnikov's self-will continues to battle his surrender to selfless Christian atonement until his Creator finally nudges him into God's camp.

In *Idiot* (1868; *The Idiot*, 1887), Dostoevski presents a Christlike man, Prince Myshkin, yet shows all of his saintly virtues mocked by the world. Myshkin is innocent and gentle, a good-natured sufferer of insults who becomes involved in the whirlpool of others' egotistic drives; is broken by their pride, lust, avarice, and vanity; and ends back in the world of idiocy from which he had emerged. The love and sympathy he brings to the world only fans more intensely its flames of hate, resentment, and self-will.

Besy (1871-1872; *The Possessed*, 1913) is Dostoevski's bitterest and most reactionary novel. He bases his plot on a notorious historic episode: A Moscow student was murdered in 1869 by a group of Nihilists who followed Mikhail Bakunin's terrorist doctrines. Dostoevski fills this work with crimes, fires, debasements, and other forms of social and psychological chaos. The political drama centers on the Nihilistic leader Peter Verkhovensky, a cynical, slippery, vicious, and monstrously criminal man. Dostoevski also pursues a metaphysical drama at whose center stands his most enigmatic character, Nikolai Stavrogin, who is attracted equally to good and evil and is full of mystery, power, pride, and boredom. He dominates all events while remaining passive and aloof. He liberates himself from any fixed image by confounding everyone's expectations. He is a fallen angel, a Satan, who succeeds, unlike Raskolnikov, in destroying others without scruple or passion. His suicide is his only logical act.

Dostoevski's last novel, *Bratya Karamazovy* (1879-1880; *The Brothers Karamazov*, 1912), sums up his leading themes and ideas. Here Dostoevski tries for no less than a dramatization of the nature of humanity, caught in the conflicting claims of man's desire for sainthood, symbolized by the youngest brother, Alyosha; for sensuality, embodied by the lust-driven middle brother, Dmitry; and for intellectual achievement, exemplified by the eldest brother, Ivan. The last, a brilliant rationalist, organizes a revolt against a God-ordered universe in his powerful "Legend of the Grand Inquisitor," which denounces a world tormented with senseless, undeserved suffering. In the legend, Dostoevski, through Ivan, depicts man as weak, slavish, and self-deceptive, willing to renounce freedom and dreams of salvation in exchange for economic security and autocratic guidance. Like Raskolnikov and Stavrogin, Ivan believes that everything is permissible, including the murder of his depraved father. The counterarguments are mounted by the Elder Zossima and his disciple, Alyosha: "All are responsible for all." They preach and practice meekness, humility, compassion, and Christian commitment. Whether Dostoevski succeeds in refuting Ivan's skeptical secularism in this novel is questionable; most critics believe that he fails. He planned a sequel, with Alyosha as the dominant character, but died of a pulmonary hemorrhage in 1881, before he could write it.

Summary

Perhaps Fyodor Dostoevski's greatest literary achievement was to marry the novel of ideas to the novel of mystery and crime, thereby creating a philosophical novel-drama, or metaphysical thriller. To be sure, he has glaring faults: His construction and style are often congested; his tone tends to be feverish; his language has sometimes unnerving changes of pace and rhythm; his pathos can become bathos; he crowds his fiction with more characters, incidents, and ideas than most readers can reasonably absorb; and he can burden his plots with irrelevant excursions and pronouncements. Yet his vision, grasp, and skill in dramatizing the complexities and contradictions of man's nature exceed those of any other novelist. His psychology is amazingly modern in its emphasis on the irrational nature of man, on the human psyche as far subtler and more paradoxical than previous writers realized. He anticipates many of the findings of contemporary depth psychology in his awareness of the personality's duality, of the roles played by unconscious drives, and of the symbolic function of dreams. His is a creative process that grasps intuitively not only the outline but also the philosophical implications of events. His characters are wholly absorbed by their thoughts and emotions: They live as they think and feel, translating their ideas and passions into entirely appropriate actions. Dostoevski's hypnotic art, filled with a fury that sometimes verges on hysteria, prepares readers for the ideological and moral struggles that have characterized the twentieth century.

Bibliography
Dostoevsky, Fyodor. *The Brothers Karamazov.* Edited by Ralph Matlaw. Translated by Constance Garnett. New York: W. W. Norton, 1976. Includes relevant letters by Dostoevski and a dozen critical essays which suggest a diversity of approaches to the text: thematic, stylistic, mythological, structural, and religious.

_____. *Crime and Punishment.* Edited by George Gibian. Translated by Jessie Coulson. Rev. ed. New York: W. W. Norton, 1975. This valuable edition has extracts from Dostoevski's letters and notebooks and more than a score of outstanding critical essays representing distinguished Russian, Italian, and German as well as American scholarship; eight were not previously translated into English.

Frank, Joseph. *Dostoevsky: The Seeds of Revolt, 1821-1849.* Princeton, N.J.: Princeton University Press, 1976.

_____. *Dostoevsky: The Years of Ordeal, 1850-1859.* Princeton, N.J.: Princeton University Press, 1983.

_____. *Dostoevsky: The Stir of Liberation, 1860-1865.* Princeton, N.J.: Princeton University Press, 1986. Frank is engaged in one of the most ambitious and illuminating literary projects of the late twentieth century: a five-volume study of Dostoevski's life and career. Since Frank specializes in intellectual history, his study subordinates the melodramatic personal struggles that have dominated most biographies. Instead, he stresses the sociocultural context in which his subject lived and wrote, taking particular care to analyze the great contemporaneous issues in which Dostoevski participated. Indispensable.

Freud, Sigmund. "Dostoevsky and Parricide." In *Dostoevsky: A Collection of Critical Essays*, edited by René Wellek. Englewood Cliffs, N.J.: Prentice-Hall, 1962. Freud's famous essay traces Dostoevski's epilepsy and gambling mania to what the great psychoanalyst regards as his Oedipus complex and links the parricidal theme of *The Brothers Karamazov* and Dostoevski's trauma suffered after his father's death to his masochistic need for self-punishment to atone for his unconscious drive to kill his father. Though based on flawed historical sources, it remains a striking application of depth psychology to literature.

Mochulsky, K. V. *Dostoevsky: His Life and Work*. Translated with an introduction by Michael A. Minihan. Princeton, N.J.: Princeton University Press, 1967. Commonly regarded as the best one-volume interpretation of Dostoevksi. Mochulsky has a particularly brilliant analysis of *Crime and Punishment* as a five-act tragedy with a prologue and epilogue.

Gerhard Brand

ALEXANDRE DUMAS, *père*

Born: July 24, 1802; Villers-Cotterêts, France
Died: December 5, 1870; Puys, France
Areas of Achievement: Literature, theater, and drama
Contribution: Dumas was a major playwright who helped to revolutionize French drama and theater. He was one of the best historical novelists, publishing more than two hundred novels.

Early Life

Alexandre Dumas is usually designated *père* to distinguish him from his father and son of the same name. The son, known as *fils*, was also an important writer of drama and of fiction. Dumas' father was an impoverished, disillusioned general in Napoleon's Egyptian campaign. His prowess and exploits were models for the character Porthos and for many incidents in Dumas' works.

Dumas was born in the village of Villers-Cotterêts on July 24, 1802. His boyhood was spent there and in neighboring villages (Soissons and Crépy, for example). Early influences were his father, poachers with whom he lived and hunted in the nearby forest, and the sight of Napoleon I en route to and from Waterloo. An early visit to Paris brought him into contact with his father's friends, all field marshals under Napoleon. Dumas' early learning was limited to reading and penmanship, later enhanced only slightly by attendance at Abbé Grégoire's village day school. Literary influences were a production of William Shakespeare's *Hamlet* and reading the works of Friedrich Schiller, Johann Wolfgang von Goethe, Sir Walter Scott, and Lord Byron. At the age of fifteen, he was a clerk in a solicitor's office. At the age of eighteen, he met and collaborated on three vaudevilles with Adolphe de Leuven, a young Swedish aristocrat, who awakened him to drama. At this time he became a clerk to M. Lefèvre at Crépy.

In late 1822, following Leuven's return to Paris to attempt to stage the plays, Dumas and a fellow clerk went to Paris alternating walking and riding the clerk's horse, poaching game en route to barter for lodgings. At Paris, Dumas saw the Théâtre Française, met the famous actor François-Joseph Talma, attended a play, and received a touch on the forehead for luck; Leuven had been instrumental in arranging the meeting. Returning home, Dumas quit his job, pooled his assets, and re-embarked for Paris, this time in a coach.

Life's Work

After a series of successes and failures, Dumas became a major writer in several genres. His literary reputation rests primarily on his novels, his plays, his memoirs, and his many travel books, in which he recorded his experiences in as well as his impressions of Italy, Spain, Switzerland, Russia, Germany, the south of France, and Egypt.

From 1823 to 1844, although he published some fiction and other works, Dumas was primarily a playwright. His early success resulted partly from the acquaintances he made and partly from good luck. His first job at Paris was as a copyist for the Duke of Orléans, the future King Louis-Philippe, in whose palace was housed an important theater, the Comédie-Française. On attending the Théâtre Française, Dumas met the famous writer-theater critic Charles Nodier. Leading actresses often found Dumas attractive, and some were among his mistresses; Talma and other leading actors became his lifelong friends. Political figures, including the Marquess de Lafayette and Giuseppe Garibaldi, were his close associates and his commanders in two wars.

He found his dramatic calling with *Christine* (1830). Seeing a bas-relief depicting an assassination ordered by Queen Christina of Sweden, he studied the incident in a borrowed book. Collaborating with Leuven (the first of many collaborators for Dumas), he wrote the five-act verse drama in 1829. Through Nodier's influence, the play was accepted for staging, though such was delayed until the following year. Another historical drama, *Henri III et sa cour* (1829; *Catherine of Cleves*, 1831) was produced first. This work is historically significant because Dumas for the first time applied the methods of Sir Walter Scott to drama. A third important serious drama, *Antony*, was to appear in 1831 (English translation, 1904).

When the Revolution of 1830 began, Dumas began his career as a soldier, following duty and his current mistress to Villers-Cotterêts and Soissons and leading insurgents to victory at his birthplace. At Soissons, he and two students stormed and took an arsenal, recovering powder kegs in the face of a garrison. Disillusioned that his commander and friend Lafayette allowed Louis-Philippe to be chosen king and spurning minor posts offered him, he resigned from the new king's employ. The next year, his first child was born by Belle Krebsamer, another mistress.

Events of interest during 1832 and 1833 included a dispute over billing for *La Tour de Nesle*, which was a rewriting by Dumas of an inferior play by Frédéric Gaillardet, the latter being given first billing, and M. Three Stars (Dumas) second; after the latter was given top billing, Gaillardet went to court and also challenged Dumas to a duel. About the same time, Dumas inadvertently discovered the cure for cholera when he mistakenly took undiluted ether. During Mardi Gras, Dumas gave an extended dinner party to which important artists, writers, actors, and actresses were invited. Drawing on his boyhood acquaintances, the poachers, and bartering the excess of game for other provisions, Dumas did the cooking and fed more than one hundred guests.

Dumas returned to the theater to stage *Antony* and his most popular serious drama, *La Tour de Nesle* (1832; English translation, 1906). In 1841, he turned to comedy, staging two of his three best that year, *Mademoiselle de Belle-Isle* (1839; *Gabrielle de Belle Isle*, 1842) and *Un Mariage sous Louis XV* (1841; *A Marriage of Convenience*, 1899). The third was staged in 1843; later, in 1855, it was selected as a command performance by Queen Victoria upon hers and Prince Albert's visit to Paris.

Though Dumas had published fiction earlier and drama later, the real shift to fiction came in 1842, with the publication of his first great historical novel, *Le Chevalier d'Harmental* (1842; English translation, 1856). The following years saw the publication of his most popular, though not regarded as his best, novels, *Les Trois Mousquetaires* (1844; *The Three Musketeers*, 1846), *Le Comte de Monte-Cristo* (1844-1845; *The Count of Monte-Cristo*, 1846), and *La Tulipe Noire* (1850; *The Black Tulip*, 1851).

Dumas' recognized best novels are not always as well-known. *Le Vicomte de Bragelonne* (1848-1850; English translation, 1857), perhaps the most popular of these, is the sequel to *Vingt Ans après* (1845; *Twenty Years After*, 1846) and *The Three Musketeers*, forming with them a trilogy. As noted in the publishing dates, Dumas, like Charles Dickens, often issued his novels in serial form in journals. The following are also among his best works in this genre of historical fiction, *Les Quarante-cinq* (1848; *The Forty-five Guardsmen*, 1847), *Ange Pitou* (1853; *Taking the Bastille*, 1847), *Black* (1860; *Black: The Story of a Dog*, 1895), and *Conscience l'Innocent* (1852; *Conscience*, 1905).

In January of 1860, Dumas met Garibaldi and traveled with a letter from him. Dumas purchased a schooner, *The Emma*, sailing the Mediterranean with friends. Eventually, he joined Garibaldi's campaign with the same spectacular success he and his father had previously enjoyed in Egypt and France. In freeing Naples from the Bourbons, he avenged his father of the imprisonment and torture he had suffered at their hands. In Palermo, Dumas was popular as a writer and a hero until the political climate changed: Garibaldi, like Napoleon and Lafayette before him, swerved from complete dedication to republicanism. After supporting and later criticizing Garibaldi publicly, Dumas returned to Paris.

Having been regarded as the most important playwright and now the most famous novelist in France, the aging Dumas found his luck failing him. Having made a fortune and having wasted it through his lavish life-style and his unbridled generosity, he worked furiously trying to save his palatial estate and his tarnished reputation. As his method had always been to work with collaborators who supplied ideas and minor works, or who provided details and basic plots, to which Dumas gave his touch of literary genius, he was now faced with accusations and even suits charging him with plagiarism. Posterity has vindicated Dumas, since none of his collaborators has achieved anything of note unaided by him. His prolific productions came to be expanded by his need for money: He published novels in serials; he wrote accounts of his many travels (regarded as among the best travel literature); and he wrote and published *Mes Mémoires* (1852; *My Memoirs*, 1907-1909), sharing numerous details of his own experiences and observations as well as information about the people he had known, who numbered among them the most famous of his day. Eventually, after further travel, he lingered and died in bed at his son's estate in Puys.

Summary

In writing about Alexandre Dumas, *père*, one is overwhelmed not only by the amount that he wrote (estimates run from seven hundred to more than one thousand volumes) but also by the great volume of information, often of much interest, about the man, his family, and his famous acquaintances. He, like his characters, was lavish, demonstrative, flamboyant, wealthy, and generous, and quarreling and forgiving. A quadroon, he was descended from paternal grandparents of the lower aristocracy and of West Indian black ancestry. His physical appearance changed from slender and military to portly with a large overhanging belly. He had fuzzy hair, thick lips, and blue eyes. His tastes in clothing were extravagant. After being rebuked for presenting his mistress Ida Ferrier to the king, he was boxed into an unwanted marriage, which, as was his wont, he graciously accepted. He would have publicly acknowledged all three of his illegitimate children, but the mother of his younger daughter refused to permit this. His friend Victor Hugo lacked his fame but surpassed him in poetic ability. The two share credit for revolutionizing the theater of France.

Bibliography

Bell, A. Craig. *Alexandre Dumas: A Biography and a Study*. London: Cassell, 1950. Attempts to vindicate the genius of Dumas in the light of hostile critics, flippant biographers, and neglectful literary historians. Lists authentic and spurious works and provides an index.

Castelar, Emilio. "Alexandre Dumas." In *The Life of Lord Byron, and Other Sketches*. Translated by Mrs. Arthur Arnold. New York: Harper & Row, 1876. A chapter of rhythmic prose on Dumas in a collection composed of a lengthy life of Lord Byron and brief treatments of Dumas, Hugo, and three lesser-known writers.

Dumas, Alexandre. *An Autobiography-Anthology Including the Best of Dumas*. Edited by Guy Endore. Garden City, N.Y.: Doubleday, 1962. As the title suggests, included are excerpts from Dumas' own works, from *My Memoirs*, travel books, prose fiction, and others, interspersed with introductory comments by the editor, providing a running commentary on the life, writing career, and particular works.

_____. *The Road to Monte Cristo: A Condensation from the Memoirs of Alexandre Dumas*. Translated by Jules Eckert Goodman. New York: Charles Scribner's Sons, 1956. Goodman finds in the more than three thousand pages of the six volumes of the memoirs two types of material: much matter of lesser importance, since Dumas was paid by the line in his later years, and, interspersed among this matter, much that makes up an exciting and intriguing autobiography of Dumas for thirty years.

Maurois, André. *Alexandre Dumas: A Great Life in Brief.* Translated by Jack Palmer White. New York: Alfred A. Knopf, 1964. For the first reader of the life of Dumas, provides the basic facts in readable and limited fashion. Maurois is one of the recognized authorities on Dumas.

_____. *The Titans: A Three-Generation Biography of the Dumas.* Translated by Gerard Hopkins. New York: Harper & Row, 1957. Emphasis in the first of ten parts is devoted to Dumas and his young son. Parts 2 through 6 focus on Dumas, *père*, 7 and 8 on *père* and *fils*, 9 and 10 on *fils*. The same work was published in England under the title *Three Musketeers*.

George W. Van Devender

JEAN-HENRI DUNANT

Born: May 8, 1828; Geneva, Switzerland
Died: October 30, 1910; Heiden, Switzerland
Area of Achievement: Social reform
Contribution: Dunant is considered both the father of the International Red
   Cross and the cofounder of the World's Young Men's Christian Asso-
   ciation.

Early Life

The eldest of five children, Jean-Henri Dunant was born in Geneva,
Switzerland, at a time when there was great concern for a variety of humanitarian issues. His father, Jean-Jacques Dunant, was a prominent businessman who held a position in the Office of Guardianships and Trusteeships,
where he was charged with the welfare of prisoners and their families. His
mother, Antoinette Colladon, nurtured his religious convictions and liberal
humanitarian concerns. Dunant's interest in social issues was fostered early.
At the age of six, an encounter with chained convicts so moved him that he
vowed someday to help them. At thirteen, he was admitted to Geneva
College.

At eighteen, Dunant became active in the League of Alms, a Christian
organization whose members sought to aid Geneva's underprivileged, ill,
and imprisoned, and he soon assumed a leadership role. In 1855, Dunant
proposed international guidelines for a federation of young men's Christian
associations.

During that same period (1853-1859), Dunant was trying to earn his living
in the banking profession. In the course of his work, he was sent to Algeria
to manage the bank's interests, and there he succeeded in convincing many
wealthy and influential Genevans and French to invest in the mills at Mons-
Djémila. He sought additional land and water concessions from the French
government but was unable to gain his ends. Undaunted, in the spring of
1859 Dunant set out to bring his ideas for Algeria to the French emperor
Napoleon III, who was then on a campaign in Italy. Dunant followed the
advancing French troops through northern Italy. Although he never met the
emperor, his trip would set in motion a series of events that would forever
change the way conflicts would be waged.

Life's Work

On June 24, 1859, in pursuit of the emperor, Dunant arrived in the town of
Castiglione. All that day, only a few miles to the west, 150,000 French and
Allied forces and 170,000 Austrian troops were waging one of the bloodiest
conflicts of the nineteenth century, the Battle of Solferino.

Although it is not clear whether Dunant ever saw the fighting, he did see the casualties, estimated at forty thousand. He was so moved by the carnage and suffering that he spent the next eight days treating the wounded, seeking doctors, and procuring necessary medical supplies and food for the wounded of both sides. To the hundreds of wounded Dunant helped, the slender, handsome, dark-haired man in white became their symbol of hope. These eight days would serve as the focus for the remainder of Dunant's life.

Returning to Geneva, Dunant continued his business ventures but remained haunted by Solferino. In November, 1862, Dunant published *Un Souvenir de Solferino* (*A Memory of Solferino*, 1939), describing the plight of the wounded and proposing an organization of trained volunteers to aid them. Copies of the book were sent to influential people across Europe. Response to his book was profound. Gustave Moynier, a Geneva lawyer, recommended that a special committee be organized to promote Dunant's plans on an international scale. That permanent international committee consisted of Dunant, Moynier, Guillaume-Henri Dufour, Louis Appia, and Theodore Maunoir. The committee proposed an international conference to be convened in Geneva on October 26. During the summer of 1863, Dunant traveled throughout Europe, artfully convincing government after government to send representatives to the Geneva meeting. This conference was followed in August, 1864, by a second, officially sponsored by the Swiss government. The product of this second conference was an international treaty, the first of the Geneva Conventions, which served as the foundation for the International Red Cross and set guidelines for the treatment and status of the wounded during wars.

Dunant's role in the conference was insignificant. His strengths were in his ideas and in dealing with people on an individual basis. Some sources suggest that Dunant did not even attend the meetings of the second conference, but such accounts appear unfounded. As the conference came to a close, Dunant had to turn his attention to his own financial problems. Since his visit to Solferino, he had not paid enough attention to his Algerian investments.

Dunant's only hope for his ailing Mons-Djémila ventures was to get concessions from the French government. Yet even a meeting with the emperor in 1865 proved futile. In 1867, a rapid chain of events would lead Dunant to bankruptcy. In the early 1860's, Geneva had been hailing Dunant as one of its greatest sons, but after 1867, as the Calvinistic principles of the time dictated for the crime of bankruptcy, Genevans turned their backs on Dunant. Under these same rigid principles, he could never return to Geneva. In addition, under extreme pressure from Moynier, from whom he had become alienated, on August 25, 1867, Dunant was forced to resign from the international committee.

The period 1867-1887 was one of steady decline for Dunant, as he became an exile wandering about Europe. There were times when he was able to afford neither housing nor regular meals, and he slept on park benches or in train stations. Yet he continued to work for a variety of causes, including a Jewish homeland in Palestine, a world library, and a broadening of the Geneva Conventions to include guidelines for conducting warfare at sea and for treatment of prisoners of war.

As his means for survival slowly ebbed and a variety of health problems sapped his vitality, his brother Pierre brought him home to Switzerland. For the last twenty-four years of his life, the small village of Heiden would be Dunant's home. Extreme bitterness and an intense paranoia made even the closest relationships difficult for Dunant.

In 1895, Dunant allowed a young Swiss journalist to interview him. Largely because of these published interviews, the world became aware that the founder of the Red Cross was still alive. Although virtually forgotten for nearly thirty years, he now received honors. The culmination of these occurred in 1901, when Dunant, along with Frédéric Passy, was awarded the first Nobel Prize in Peace. Dunant died on October 30, 1910. In accordance with the conditions of his exile, Dunant's ashes were buried in an unmarked grave in Zurich.

Summary

The life of Jean-Henri Dunant is one of profound irony. On one hand, he was an idealistic humanitarian, who changed the conduct of warfare forever and who must be credited with the saving of millions of lives. The International Red Cross, the Geneva Conventions, and the Young Men's Christian Association stand as monuments to his great vision. On the other, he was a tragic victim of his own weaknesses. He experienced the tributes of royalty and the pain of extreme poverty.

Nevertheless, Dunant was consistent in the belief that he could make a difference in the world. In 1906 and 1926, the Geneva Conventions were expanded to cover the victims of naval warfare and prisoners of war, respectively, causes that Dunant had championed since the late 1860's. For his many accomplishments, it is only fitting that each year the world celebrates May 8, his birthday, as World Red Cross Day.

Bibliography

Deming, Richard. *Heroes of the International Red Cross*. New York: E. P. Dutton, 1969. Chapter 1 provides a condensed biography of Dunant that emphasizes his role as father of the Red Cross.

Dunant, Jean-Henri. *A Memory of Solferino*. Washington, D.C.: American National Red Cross, 1959. A short, moving description of the Battle of Solferino, Dunant's role in the aftermath, and the genesis of the principles that would ultimately inspire formation of the International Red Cross.

Gagnebin, Bernard, and Marc Gazay. *Encounter with Henry Dunant*. Translated by Bernard C. Swift. Geneva: Georg Geneva, 1963. A short, readable account of Dunant's life, supplemented by photographs, paintings, maps, and photocopies of published and unpublished manuscripts.

Kübler, Arnold. "Dunant." In *The International Red Cross Committee in Geneva, 1863-1943*. Zurich: Conzett & Huber, 1943. A short account of the unique circumstance that led Dunant to found the Red Cross, focusing on his efforts during and after Solferino.

Libby, Violet Kelway. *Henry Dunant: Prophet of Peace*. New York: Pageant Press, 1964. A longer biography that focuses on how the evolution of the religious and business climate within Dunant's Geneva both provided an ideal atmosphere to foster his humanitarian concerns and severely punished him for his business failings. Includes a short list of other sources.

Peachment, Brian. *The Red Cross Story: The Life of Henry Dunant*. Elmsford, N.Y.: Pergamon Press, 1977. A brief account of Dunant's life, intended for the younger reader.

Rich, Josephine. *Jean Henri Dunant: Founder of the International Red Cross*. New York: Julian Messner, 1956. A biography that focuses particularly on Dunant's relationships with his family. Also emphasizes Henri's lifelong concern with social causes.

Rothkopf, Carol Z. *Jean Henri Dunant: Father of the Red Cross*. New York: Franklin Watts, 1969. Follows Dunant's life but focuses on how the principles behind the Red Cross are deeply rooted in history. Provides a modest secondary bibliography.

Ronald D. Tyler

ALBRECHT DÜRER

Born: May 21, 1471; Nuremberg, Bavaria
Died: April 6, 1528; Nuremberg, Bavaria
Area of Achievement: Art
Contribution: Dürer has often been called the "Leonardo of the North" because of his diverse talents. Painter, graphic artist, and theorist, he moved in elite intellectual circles that included some of the most famous men of his time. As a graphic artist, Dürer has never been surpassed. He helped bring Italian Renaissance ideas to the art of northern Europe.

Early Life

Albrecht Dürer was born in Nuremberg at a time when that city was moving from its Gothic past to a more progressive style of Renaissance Humanism, exemplified by Vienna and Basel in northern Europe. His father, a goldsmith, had come from Hungary to Nuremberg, where he met and married Dürer's mother. The third of eighteen children, Dürer showed unusual artistic inclinations at an early age. After working with his father during his younger years, Dürer, at age fifteen, was apprenticed to Michel Wohlgemuth, head of a large local workshop that produced woodcuts for printers as well as painted altarpieces.

It was the custom for apprentices to complete their training period with a *Wanderjahre*, or wandering journey, in order to seek new ideas from outside sources before submitting their own *Meisterstück*, or masterpiece, to the guild so as to obtain a license as an artist within the city. Dürer, after completing three years with Wohlgemuth and becoming familiar with both painting and graphic technique, began his own journey. Little is known about the first year or so, but it is known that the young artist traveled to Colmar with the intention of working with the famed engraver and printer Martin Schongauer. Unfortunately, the older artist had already died before Dürer's arrival, so he journeyed to Basel to work with Schongauer's brother, Georg.

Dürer's intellectual curiosity and winning personality, affirmed by references in letters by his contemporaries, soon won for him valuable contacts in Basel. Designs in many of the illustrated books published there have been attributed to him, including those in the 1494 edition of Sebastian Brant's famous *Das Narrenschiff* (*This Present Boke Named Shyp of Folys of the Worlde*, 1509). Scholars agree that he did the frontispiece, *Saint Jerome Curing the Lion*, for *Epistolare beati Hieronymi* (letters of Saint Jerome), published in 1492 by Nikolaus Kessler.

In July of 1494, after a brief stay in Strasbourg, Dürer returned to Nuremberg to marry Agnes Frey, the daughter of a wealthy local burgher. Even considering that the marriage was an arranged one, as was the custom, the young couple seem to have been totally unsuited for each other. They had no children, and a few months after his wedding day Dürer went with friends to Italy, where he stayed for about a year.

Through his friendship with the Nuremberg Humanist Willibald Pirkheimer, a confirmed lover of classical objects, and through his own copying of prints by Italian masters, Dürer took full advantage of his stay in Italy. Drawings and watercolors of Venice, sketches of nudes and statuary, and especially his outdoor paintings of the Alps of the southern Tirol attest Dürer's fascination with the South and its artistic climate. A self-portrait done in 1498 shows the artist's conception of himself as a well-dressed, confident, and dignified young gentleman. Dürer early enjoyed an enviable reputation as a gifted artist and knowledgeable companion, and upon returning to Nuremberg he moved easily in the upper social and intellectual circles of that city. He was a good businessman and took advantage of the psychological impact of the projected year 1500, when the Last Judgment was supposed to occur, by completing German and Latin editions of the illustrated *Apocalypse* in 1498.

Life's Work

The awakening Renaissance and Humanistic tendencies in the previously Gothic North, along with the popularity of illustrated printed books, created a growing need for graphic artists. Dürer's graphic talents continued to deepen and become more refined. His mature works display a greater luminosity as well as a wider range of dark, light, and middle tonalities. By financing, illustrating, and printing *Apocalypse*, Dürer further enhanced his reputation as a master artist. An unusual *Self-Portrait* of 1500 reveals his mature self-esteem, as he shows himself remarkably like images of Christ. On the question of the role of artists—as craftsman or as creative genius— Dürer clearly assumed the latter designation.

Dürer took a second trip to Italy in the fall of 1505. By then, his reputation was widely established. *The Feast of the Rose Garlands*, made for the altar of the fraternity of German merchants in the Fondaco dei Tedeschi in 1506, is a large panel celebrating Christian brotherhood in the Feast of the Rosary. Perhaps this painting is an attempt to demonstrate the supremacy of Northern art. During his time in Italy, Dürer was especially fascinated by Italian theories of perspective and by studies of human proportions.

Two engravings by Dürer, *Adam and Eve* (1504) and *Melencolia I* (1514), illustrate the artist's complex personality and goals. Done very shortly before his second trip to Italy, *Adam and Eve* relied on Italian artists such as Andrea Mantegna and Antonio Pollaiuolo for a canon of the body's ideal beauty. Familiar with the writings of the classical writer Vitruvius on human proportions, Dürer chose two popular statues of antiquity, the Apollo Belvedere and the Medici Venus, as his models. Thus, the models of Italian classicism, only slightly altered in form, find themselves in Dürer's engraving, in a dark, Gothic northern forest. The Tree of Life with the parrot holds a plaque with the Latin inscription "Albertus Dürer Noricus faciebat 1504," demonstrating the artist's pride in his home city of Nuremberg. Dürer's usual signature is inconspicuously added. Eve receives the forbidden fruit from the center Tree of Knowledge. The Fall of Man results in the characters' loss of ideal form as well as loss of paradisiacal innocence; the animals at the first couple's feet symbolize the various human temperaments. The inevitable control these temperaments held on mankind after the Fall displays pessimism regarding the human condition as well as the northern taste for disguised symbolism. An uneasy tension exists between the Italianate classical figures and their northern environment.

Melencolia I was done seven years after Dürer's return from his second Italian trip. He was fully aware of the Italian Renaissance notion of the artist as a divinely inspired creature, but here Dürer shows in the large winged figure the personification of melancholic despair. The objects at her feet are tools for creating art, especially architecture, but they are useless in this context, as the seated figure suffers from the debilitating inactivity caused by the divine frenzy, or *furor melancholicus*. The idea is intensified by the bat, a symbol of the diabolical temperament, which carries the title banner across the sky. Thus, the message is clear that the artist, "born under Saturn" and endowed with potentially special gifts, is frustrated and unproductive in the search for an absolute beauty that only God knows. Both the *Adam and Eve* and *Melencolia I* engravings demonstrate Dürer's astonishing mastery of the medium in their complexity and luminosity.

Dürer's equal expertise with the woodcut medium is shown in *The Four Horsemen of the Apocalypse* (c. 1497-1498) from the *Apocalypse* series, which illustrates scenes from Revelation in the Bible. Dürer's rapid development of technique can be traced by comparing one of his earliest engravings, *Holy Family with the Butterfly* of about 1495, with a late work, the *Erasmus of Rotterdam* of 1526. In the former, some hesitancy can be seen in the cross-hatching of drapery folds and unconvincing variations of light and shade. In the mature work, one finds precise and sensitive modeling of forms, a broad range of light-and-shade tonalities, and a luminosity that bathes the figures in reflected light.

Among Dürer's many important patrons was Frederick the Wise, who commissioned a portrait and also asked Dürer to paint the altarpieces *Madonna and Child* (c. 1497) and *The Adoration of the Magi* (1504). In these paintings, Dürer demonstrates that he is primarily a graphic artist, as the paintings are more dependent on linear design than on color. Two paintings of Adam and Eve, done after Dürer's return to Nuremberg in 1507, indicate that he was influenced by premannerist tendencies found in Italian and German art of the early 1500's. The influence of Italian theory is also evident in his four-book study on human proportions, published shortly after his death. In 1511, Dürer published three picture books, *The Life of the Virgin*, *Great Passion*, and *Small Passion*. Some of the prints were issued as independent woodcuts.

During 1513 and 1514, Dürer issued three famous prints: *Knight, Death, and Devil*, *Saint Jerome in His Study*, and the *Melencolia I*. Had these been his only works, his fame would have been assured. In 1512, he was appointed court artist for Emperor Maximilian I, for whom he did a series of large woodcuts. In 1520, Dürer journeyed to western Germany and the Netherlands, and at this time did a portrait of King Christian II of Denmark, who was traveling through Antwerp.

Dürer's last major painting, *Four Apostles* (1526), is in many ways a memorial to the Reformation. He gave it to the city of Nuremberg, which had recently adopted Lutheranism as the official creed. The text below the figures issues a warning to the city to heed the words of the figures depicted—Peter, John, Paul, and Mark.

Summary

Albrecht Dürer was a man and an artist of exceptional talents who lived through a particularly crucial time in Germany, the age of the Reformation. Dürer was very much a man of his own time. A scholar and theorist as well as a gifted artist, he was cognizant of and contributed to the great accomplishments and ideas in art in the period between the late fifteenth and early sixteenth centuries in Europe. A careful scrutiny of his self-portraits alone suggests his growing self-awareness of the artist as no longer a mere anonymous craftsman but as an individual of extraordinary ability and special importance. Like one with whom he has often been compared, Leonardo da Vinci, Dürer approached art (that is, painting and the graphic arts) as one of the seven liberal arts rather than as a purely mechanical exercise. With his keen interest in Italian ideas of proportion of the human figure and of perspective, Dürer could be said to have almost single-handedly wedded Italian Renaissance to northern Gothic art.

Dürer was famous in his own time. On his late journeys to Antwerp and elsewhere, he was sought by the highest social and intellectual groups of the area. His diary and his theoretical writings show him to have been a person of broad knowledge and diverse interests. His treatise on proportions, together with that of Leonardo, constitutes a most important contribution to Renaissance art theory. Unlike Leonardo's works, Dürer's contributions became accessible to a large public through printed publication. Through his own use of Italianate classical models, Dürer increased public appreciation for classical art. In turn, Dürer influenced later Italian artists by his integrated style.

Dürer's late works, although fewer in number than his earlier output, do not diminish in power or originality. His great talents are particularly remarkable in the engravings and woodcuts, which he favored since they, unlike commissioned paintings, allowed him independence from patrons and served as a source of income through the popular prints. Dürer is one of the central figures of European art.

Bibliography

Anzelewsky, Fedja. *Dürer: His Art and Life*. London: Chartwell Books, 1980. A straightforward account of Dürer's life within the context of Renaissance and Reformation Europe. Special attention is paid to Dürer's writings, especially the treatises on art theory. Emphasizes Dürer's religious and humanistic beliefs. Good reproductions, many in full color. Useful bibliography.

Dürer, Albrecht. *The Intaglio Prints of Albrecht Dürer: Engravings, Etchings, and Drypaints*. Edited by Walter L. Strauss. New York: Kennedy Galleries, 1977. The most complete catalog of the intaglio prints in English. Illustrations after each catalog entry. Includes introduction, full catalog entries to all previous literature, and an annotated bibliography. Especially useful in that prints are reproduced in actual size. Important to an understanding of Dürer's graphics. Recommended for the general Dürer reader.

Panofsky, Erwin. *The Life and Art of Albrecht Dürer*. 4th ed. Princeton, N.J.: Princeton University Press, 1971. A paperback reprint of a classic, unmatched for sensitivity to and comprehensive analysis of Dürer's life and work. Omits now-outdated list of Dürer's works but retains excellent interpretive essays. Good illustrations. Very useful for student and general reader.

Rowlands, John. *The Age of Dürer and Holbein*. New York: Cambridge University Press, 1988. This book contains high-quality reproductions of Dürer prints and drawings as well as several watercolor studies. Surveys, through works in the British Museum and private and public British collections, art development from late Gothic style to Northern Renaissance naturalism. In addition to Dürer and Holbein, offers valuable coverage of their predecessors and contemporaries.

Russell, Francis. *The World of Dürer, 1471-1528*. New York: Time Books, 1967. An excellent text, introductory level, with many good reproductions, some full page and full color, as well as explanatory maps and graphics. Traces Dürer's development and life within the social, religious, and political context of his time. Chronology chart shows artists of Dürer's era. Limited but useful bibliography.

Scheller, Robert W., and Karel G. Boon, comps. *The Graphic Art of Albrecht Dürer, Hans Dürer, and the Dürer School*. Amsterdam: Van Gendt, 1971. This catalog is based on Joseph Meder's classic *Dürer—*

Katalog (Vienna, 1932) and is notable for making available in English the pioneering Dürer works by Meder and Hollstein. Excellent introductory section on Dürer as a graphic artist. Many prints, some of uneven quality. Valuable book for all levels.

Snyder, James. *Northern Renaissance Art: Painting, Sculpture, the Graphic Arts from 1350 to 1575*. New York: Harry N. Abrams, 1985. Full coverage of the Northern Renaissance, with an excellent chapter entitled "Albrecht Dürer and the Renaissance in Germany." Discusses in detail, with good reproductions, many examples of Dürer's graphic works and paintings. Text includes recent interpretations and theories. Includes a timetable of the arts, history, and science from 1300 to 1575. Valuable for the general reader.

Mary Sweeney Ellett

ANTONÍN DVOŘÁK

Born: September 8, 1841; Nelahozeves, Bohemia
Died: May 1, 1904; Prague, Bohemia
Area of Achievement: Music
Contribution: Dvořák was one of the most notable European composers of
the nineteenth century. He became one of the chief creators of the Czech
national style of music and also had a profound influence on the development of American music.

Early Life

Born into the family of a butcher-innkeeper in the small Bohemian village
of Nelahozeves, Antonín Leopold Dvořák did not seem destined to a musical
career. As was the case with other young men at that time, Antonín was
expected to carry on the family business, which his father had inherited from
his own father. In spite of these expectations, Antonín began to play the
violin with his father, who performed with the village orchestra at various
rustic festivals and ceremonies. The young Dvořák soon proved more capable than his father at the bow, and his musical promise attracted the notice of
the local schoolmaster, a musician named Josef Spitz.

From Spitz, Dvořák learned the elements of the violin. In 1853, Dvořák
was sent to his maternal uncle's house in Zlonice to continue his studies.
There, under the tutelage of Antonín Liehmann, Dvořák gained familiarity
with the viola, organ, and figured bass. Liehmann tutored the boy in modulation as well as extemporization, which he called "brambuliring." It was with
Liehmann that Dvořák first came into contact with the German language,
which, as Bohemia was then part of the Austrian Empire, was an important
prerequisite to further study. In order to perfect his German, he was sent to
live with a German family in the nearby village of České Kamenice.

In České Kamenice, Dvořák continued his musical progress under the
choirmaster at St. Jakub's Church, for whom he frequently substituted at the
organ. Liehmann's suggestion that the boy continue his musical studies at
Prague was received unfavorably by Dvořák's father, who asserted that there
was no money to finance such an undertaking. At Liehmann's insistence,
however, Dvořák's childless uncle agreed to pay for the boy's schooling at
the Organ Conservatory in Prague, which Dvořák entered in 1857. Dvořák's
musical talents rapidly developed at the conservatory under the guidance of
such men as Josef Leopold Zvonař (voice), Josef Bohuslav Foerster (organ),
and František Blažek (theory). Many of these men laid the initial foundations for the national style of Czech music.

During his days as a student, Dvořák found an extracurricular outlet for
his creativity in the orchestra of the musical society Cecilia, in which he
played viola. He participated in the weekly rehearsals of the society, which

was at that time under the direction of Antonín Apt, an ardent admirer of Robert Schumann and Richard Wagner.

Life's Work

Dvořák's musical career began at the end of the Romantic era in Bohemia. After the cultural renaissance of the Czech nation, the *národní obrození*, during which time poets such as Jan Kollár, František Čelakovský, and, above all, Karel Hynek Mácha carved out a wide area of cultural autonomy for the Czech nation, it became common for poets, musicians, and artists to find inspiration for their work in national hagiography and legend. In the 1860's, however, the vivid élan of Romanticism was slowing into the less revolutionary, nostalgic era of the Biedermeier. It is helpful to keep this literary distinction between Romantic and Biedermeier in mind when one speaks of the music of Dvořák. For, like the poet Karel Jaromir Erben, Dvořák, in this early period of his career, composed works suffused with languor and a certain *fin d'époque* melancholy. In addition to two symphonies which date from this period—the *Bells of Zlonice* in C minor and the Second Symphony in B flat major—the composer set Moravian poet Gustav Pfleger's "Cypress Trees" to music as a song cycle.

When the Czech National Opera opened in 1862, the members of the Cecilia society's orchestra formed its backbone. The contemporary atmosphere inspired Dvořák to compose his first venture for the musical stage: *Alfred* (1938), based on the lyric epic poem by Vítězslav Hálek. This work, however, was never produced onstage. Its overture was published in 1912—eight years after the composer's death—and is noted for its technical finesse.

Much of Dvořák's work predating 1870 was destroyed by the composer himself. In 1872, he took a curious journey back to the period of literary Romanticism in Bohemia. It was in this year that he set to music a few songs from the Ossian-like "Old Czech" forgeries of Václav Hanka—the *Rukopis královédvorský* and *Rukopis zelenohorský*. Like the literary works themselves, Dvořák's adaptations of the *Rukopisy* achieved some measure of fame beyond the borders of Bohemia. In 1879, they were published in German and English translation.

In 1873, Dvořák turned to a mode of composition which was to reward him with much musical success—the composition of quartets. One of the most beautiful of these works—written in this year of Dvořák's marriage to his former student Anna Čermáková—is the String Quartet in F minor, Op. 9. A growing sense of self-confidence, spawned perhaps by conjugal satisfaction, inspired Dvořák to resign from the National Opera and take a post in St. Vojtěch's Church. Then came the Symphony in D minor, Op. 13, which, however, was to lie dormant for a full twenty years.

The lure of the opera continued to be strong, and the year 1874 brought the composer's return to the operatic stage with the adapted puppet show *King and Collier*. The work was an immediate success, and Dvořák was hailed as a promising representative of a revivified Slavic music. Dvořák followed this event with another quartet, this time in A minor. The composer's career began to take off in earnest after these successes. In 1875, he was awarded a generous stipend from the Austrian government for his musical achievements; on the award's selection committee was Johannes Brahms, later to become Dvořák's lifelong friend. More chamber pieces and another collection of folk songs (the *Moravian Duets*) followed, as did the Symphony in F, Op. 24, which was to add greatly to the composer's renown abroad.

Personal tragedy struck the composer at the zenith of this fecund period. In 1876, while Dvořák was at work on another opera (*Wanda*, based on an ancient Polish legend), his daughter became sick and died. This painful occurrence inspired the composer to create one of his greatest musical works, the *Stabat mater*. This work made Dvořák's name famous in Great Britain, where he conducted the work himself to rave reviews in 1884.

Dvořák's steady, conquering march on the musical world was continued with his *Slavonic Dances*. Curiously enough, critics initally looked upon these works with coolness, as they were commissioned by the German music publishing firm of Simrock. Yet time has proven the great value of these sterling compositions, and the critics were soon silenced by voices such as Hans Richter's, who praised Dvořák's "God-given talent" after hearing the earlier *Symphonic Variations for Orchestra* (1877).

Dvořák consolidated his leading position among composers of the Czech national school during these years with the composition of various pieces of music deeply imbued with patriotic feeling. Such works are the *Hussite Overture* (1883), which contains as a theme the famous Hussite hymn "Ktož jste Boží bojovníci" ("You Who Art the Warriors of God"), and the tone poem suite *Ze Šumavy* (*From the Bohemian Forest*). Of special interest to the adept of comparative arts is Dvořák's chorale adaptation of Erben's Bürgeresque ballad *Svatební košile* (*The Spectre's Bride*).

About this time, Dvořák's fame began to burgeon in the Anglo-Saxon countries. In England, for example, his *Stabat mater* was hailed as "one of the finest works of our times" by a musical critic, when it was performed for the eight hundredth anniversary of Worcester Cathedral under the baton of the composer himself. For the next few years, Dvořák was to divide his time between the British Isles and his native Bohemia, where he had just acquired a peaceful, rustic cottage as a quiet retreat for composition. His Symphony in G, Op. 88, although dedicated to the Imperial Bohemian Academy for the Fine Arts, has become known as the "English Symphony," as it was published uncharacteristically in London. His popularity in England is attested by the Birmingham Festival's invitation to set John Henry Newman's *Dream of Gerontius* to music for the year 1891. The composer opted instead for something less literary: the *Requiem Mass*, Op. 89. This work was again received favorably when performed at the festival yet did not win for the composer the same high accolades as the seemingly unsurpassable *Stabat mater.*

Dvořák soon put the pen aside for conservatory instruction. In 1891, he accepted the chair of composition at the Prague Conservatory and embarked on a teaching career that was to last for five years and carry him across the ocean. Only one year after his appointment to the Prague professorship, he was granted a leave of absence by the institution to undertake similar duties at the New York Conservatory for what was at that time a generous salary.

The composer was to remain in America until 1896. From this stay in New York came what is perhaps his most recognizable work to the American ear, the Symphony in E minor, Op. 95, known popularly as *From the New World.* As George Gershwin was to do in the next century, Dvořák infused new blood into the musical scene by incorporating heretofore exotic musical elements—of Indian, African, and American flavor—into his strong European musical heritage. This last great work of his had enormous consequences for American symphonic music. Karel Hoffmeister goes so far as to suggest—with some justification—that Dvořák's impact on American music can be compared to that of George Frideric Handel on the music of England.

Dvořák returned from America to the hero's welcome which had greeted him constantly in these last few years of artistic grandeur. As his stay on American soil seemed to have affected his composition by introducing new motifs and styles in his European background, so his return to Bohemia reawakened his Slavic muse. Among his greatest successes from this last period of his life are the symphonic poems he composed, based on Erben's highly popular collection of folk-styled ballads entitled *Kytice* (*The Wreathe*) and his final great opera *Rusalka* (*The Water-Nymph*).

Dvořák's last effort in this field, the opera *Armida*, built around Jaroslav Vrchlický's libretto, ended in fiasco. It seems strange that the brilliant career of such an artist should end in failure, yet this is indeed what happened. Falling ill toward the end of March, 1904, the composer died on May 1. As a sign of the great esteem in which the Czech people held the composer, Dvořák was laid to rest on the grounds of the royal castle of Vyšehrad in Prague on May 5, 1904.

Summary

Antonín Dvořák is lauded as one of the greatest composers of the modern era. A technical genius whose absolute devotion to music gave birth to unforgettable symphonies, operas, and chamber works, Dvořák influenced and was highly regarded in his own day by colleagues such as Brahms and

Richter. As pedagogue, he left his unique mark upon musicians such as Oskar Nedbal, who came under his tutelage at conservatories in Prague and New York. Yet Dvořák is most widely known as the one composer who, more than anyone else in the late nineteenth century, popularized Slavic themes and musical styles to European and American audiences unaccustomed to the fertile region of East and Central Europe. In this, Dvořák can be compared to Frédéric Chopin, who preceded him in the early part of the century.

Dvořák is also remembered as a musical innovator who introduced American rhythms to the older traditions of Europe. He is unique in modern musical history as a composer who has had a profound effect on at least two, if not three (counting Germany), musical cultures—that of Bohemia and the United States—and deserves to be held in honor by the American, as well as the Czech, public as an illustrious founder of a musical culture which might have developed in a radically different fashion had he not participated in its nurturing.

Bibliography
Clapham, John. *Dvořák*. New York: W. W. Norton, 1979. Clapham's biography contains a wealth of information concerning the composer's life and compositions. Particularly valuable to the student who is interested in Dvořák's American years and his British successes. Some illustrative musical annotation, a "Catalogue of Compositions," a generous bibliography, and a helpful "Chronicle of Events" make this biography an excellent and easy-to-use reference tool. Black-and-white photographs.

Fischl, Viktor, ed. *Antonín Dvořák: His Achievement*. London: L. Drummond, 1943. Reprint. Westport, Conn.: Greenwood Press, 1970. This book is a helpful and enlightening collection of essays written by critics such as Edwin Evans, Thomas Dunhill, and Harriet Cohen. Topics discussed in the eleven papers cover every aspect of the composer's creative oeuvre, from his orchestral works and opera to his chamber music and sacral creations. An excellent text for both initiate and musically refined student because it presents Dvořák's life and compositional heritage in well-written, logically arranged sections.

Hoffmeister, Karel. *Antonín Dvořák*. Edited and translated by Rosa Newmarch. Westport, Conn.: Greenwood Press, 1970. This is a well-constructed biography, divided into two main sections. The first introduces the composer as a person and the second proceeds to a detailed discussion of his works, with generous snippets of musical notation which exemplify and reinforce the critical commentary. The reader, however, should be aware of a few minor miscues which detract from an otherwise excellent work. Hoffmeister at one point refers to a period in the composer's life as being quite "stormy and stressful," thus creating a misleading reference to the

German literary period *Sturm und Drang* (late eighteenth century). Also, the author suggests that the Czech national revival began in the mid-nineteenth century, when it actually began as early as 1785.

Moore, Douglas. *A Guide to Musical Styles: From Madrigal to Modern Music*. New York: W. W. Norton, 1942, rev. ed. 1962. Although not totally devoted to Dvořák, Moore's book is a concise, excellent introduction to the European musical heritage, with generous commentary on composers and musical styles which had a profound influence on Dvořák. Aids greatly in the understanding of the composer and his place in and significance for music. Generous musical annotation assists the adept in aurally experiencing the main points of the author's dialogue, while his easy style and helpful definitions make this book an indispensable tool for both beginning and advanced students of musical history.

Schonzeler, Hans-Hubert. *Dvořák*. New York: Marion Boyars, 1984. A contemporary, more in-depth biography of the composer than Hoffmeister's work. Many excerpts from the composer's own letters and writings make this work an especially interesting study. The book for those who wish to come to know Dvořák as a person rather than a composer. Contains sixty-seven well-chosen black-and-white photographs.

Charles Kraszewski

ELIJAH BEN SOLOMON

Born: April 23, 1720; Selec, Lithuania
Died: October 9, 1797; Vilna, Lithuania
Area of Achievement: Religion
Contribution: Elijah ben Solomon contributed to Talmudic and rabbinic literature by solving the most complicated questions of Jewish law and by writing commentaries and annotations to biblical, Talmudic, and Cabalistic books.

Early Life

Elijah ben Solomon was born on the first day of Passover in the year 1720 to Treina and Rabbi Solomon Zelman. Rabbi Solomon named his son Elijah in memory of his grandfather. Early in his childhood, Elijah manifested an intellect of gigantic potential. At the age of six, Elijah was able to study the Bible and the Talmud by himself. At six and a half, he delivered a lengthy discourse on Jewish law in the great synagogue in Vilna. When the boy was seven, Rabbi Abraham Katzenellenbogen of Brest Litovsk took him to study under Rabbi Moses Margalioth. Sometimes Elijah's comprehension was so swift that it was impossible for others to follow his thought. While boys of his age were laboring through the Pentateuch, Elijah could navigate through the vast sea of the Talmud and the Cabala.

Elijah also studied secular subjects—algebra, astronomy, geometry, geography, history, anatomy, and philosophy—in order to understand certain Talmudic laws and discussions. His main reason for studying astronomy was to comprehend the regulations of the Jewish calendar.

At age eighteen, Elijah married Hannah, the daughter of a rabbi. There is no doubt that much of Elijah's success was attributable to his happy marriage with Hannah. She was often the only person who had access to the secret retreats Elijah selected for his meditations. She brought him food and informed him about the happenings in the community. Elijah had full confidence in his wife, and she, an exceptionally pious and valorous woman, gave him full empathy.

At the age of twenty, Elijah decided to leave his wife and home in Vilna and wander throughout Europe. He had concluded that his store of knowledge was inadequate because of his seclusion. He wanted to gain a fuller understanding of Judaism by witnessing Jewish life in its various aspects, seeing the customs and traditions of diverse peoples. For eight years, he traveled, impoverished, through the kingdoms of Europe. For a while, he served as a tutor to Jewish children in an isolated village. There are interesting but unverified stories about Elijah's helping perplexed scholars to solve complicated problems. In one tale, a professor accosted him in Berlin and requested his help in solving an abstruse astronomical problem. Elijah solved the professor's problem with a sketch on a scrap of paper.

Elijah returned to Vilna as a recognized authority in Jewish law. Rabbis from all over Europe turned to him with their rabbinic legal difficulties. Again and again Jews in Vilna urged him to become the rabbi of Vilna, but Elijah refused. He would not even accept membership in the rabbinical board, but his opinion was sought on all important questions. Only on rare occasions would he publicly assert his great, though unofficial, authority. He preferred his status as a layperson.

Life's Work

Elijah settled in Vilna, where he would live for the remainder of his life. He received a weekly stipend from the community so that he could devote his entire time to study and writing. The money came from a legacy of his great-great-grandfather, Rabbi Moses Rivkes, to the community and was intended to help any descendant who devoted himself to the study of Judaism. Scholars soon acclaimed Elijah as the *Gaon* (Talmudic scholar par excellence), while the people called him *Hasid* (saint). These titles gradually took the place of his personal name.

Elijah lived in Vilna as a recluse, slept two hours a day, and took little nourishment. Despite his asceticism, Elijah was acclaimed throughout the Jewish world as the Talmudic scholar whose opinions on Jewish law were considered final. His views on contemporary communal problems were sought far and wide. In 1755, when Elijah was thirty-five years old, he was asked by the sixty-five-year-old Rabbi Jonathan Eybeschuetz to render an opinion concerning his controversy with Rabbi Jacob Emden.

Elijah was confronted with the problems of two eighteenth century movements, the *Haskalah* (enlightenment) and Hasidism. The Hasidic movement was founded by Ba'al Shem Tov. Ba'al Shem Tov taught that God should be served with joy and that asceticism might be the root of evil. Rabbis and scholars of the time were perplexed by the Hasidic movement, which gave a preeminent place in Judaism not to learning but to emotion and sentiment. It valued religious exultation over holy knowledge. As Hasidism extended its foothold in Eastern Europe, there emerged an antagonist movement, the *Haskalah*. The *Haskalah* called for rationalism and realism, and opposed the antirationalistic tendency of Hasidism. In their nascent forms, Hasidism and the *Haskalah* endangered the integrity of established Judaism; too much exultation in Hasidism and too much rationalism in *Haskalah*—either extreme undermined the Jewish tradition. Elijah, confronted with these extremes, tried to harmonize between the heart and the mind to prevent Judaism from being crushed between the *Haskalah* and Hasidism. He vehemently opposed Hasidism, which rejected the scholarly approach to the Torah that Elijah thought so important, and he supported the effort to excommunicate followers of Hasidism.

Elijah wrote more than seventy works and commentaries. More than fifty have been published, though others have been completely lost. He considered the *Shulhan Arukh* (book of codes) the gist of Talmudic law. Elijah wrote a commentary on the *Shulhan Arukh* known as the *Be'ur ha-Gra* (1803, 1806, 1819, 1856-1858; the commentary of the *Gaon*). In his commentary, he traced every statement, every decision, every custom and tradition to its mainspring, the Talmud.

Elijah wrote commentaries to nearly all the books of the Old Testament and to several books of the Mishnah. Elijah's writings cover the Cabala, algebra, trigonometry, astronomy, and grammar. He urged the translation of Euclid into Hebrew and examined the historical works of Josephus rendered into Hebrew. His favoring of secular study, however, does not place him in the camp of the *Haskalah*, which aimed at the substitution of reason for faith, though he was a critic of those scholars who relied too much on speculation. He was even critical of Maimonides for having interpreted certain passages of the Bible or Talmud in a philosophical manner, ignoring the simple meaning.

After Elijah reached the age of forty, he devoted most of his time to educating his disciples. He surrounded himself with a number of students who were gifted with brilliant minds and genuine piety. They became messengers in spreading the teachings of their beloved master. Elijah warned his students against wasting their precious time in *pilpul* (dialectic excess). He taught them to use clear thinking and to search for truth painstakingly. He provided his students with his corrected texts of the great books of halakic literature, the result of years of studying the Talmud. Elijah showed clearly that corrections made in the text of the Talmud could change the interpretation of the passage. He opened to his students a new frontier: critical examination of the text. Elijah advocated not only proper intellectual training but also the cultivation of morality. He held that, in order for Judaism to have its divine effect, the heart must be pure. He compared the Torah to rain. Just as rain nourishes the earth so the Torah purifies the soul.

Elijah also inspired Jews to emigrate to Israel. It was his lifelong dream to settle in the Holy land. He once undertook the dangerous and arduous trip but for unknown reasons decided to return to Vilna. The Vilna emigration, which he had encouraged, began in 1808, eleven years after his death; hundreds of Jews settled in Palestine. Six of his disciples headed the movement.

In a well-known legend, Elijah was passing through a crowd of playing children and noticed that they were shouting, *"Der Vilner Gaon, Der Vilner Gaon."* He stopped and said to the children, "If you only will it, you too, will become Geonim" (preeminent scholars). Elijah's humbleness belied his enormous intelligence and piety; few scholars have been as influential as he.

Summary

It is rare in Jewish history for one man to leave behind him a legacy of great works in rabbinic literature, significant individual contributions, noble deeds, and outstanding personal attributes. Elijah ben Solomon, revered by all, was such a man. His creations and involvement are those of a complicated individual and not simply reflections of the time and place in which he lived. An oustanding rabbi, codifier, scholar, thinker, author, and humanitarian, Elijah shared in the political, social, communal, and cultural trials and tribulations of his time, but he transcended these in continuing man's age-old examination of his purpose in life and his relationship to God and to his fellowman. His spirit and writings made important contributions to his generation, yet they continue to have meaning and will remain inspiring to future generations. His impact on the dissemination of the teachings of the Torah and on the establishment and maintenance of rabbinical seminaries is immeasurable. His contributions to rabbinic literature show him to be one of the most prolific and influential Talmudic scholars in Jewish history.

Bibliography

Dubnow, S. M. *History of the Jews in Russia and Poland.* Translated by I. Friedlander. Vol 1. Philadelphia: Jewish Publication Society of America, 1916. An excellent history of the period based on primary documents on the life and work of Elijah.

Graetz, Heinrich. *History of the Jews.* Vol. 5. Philadelphia: Jewish Publication Society of America, 1895. A scholarly source on the life of Elijah. Contains important information on the controversy between Elijah and the proponents of Hasidism.

Malamet, A., et al. *A History of the Jewish People.* Edited by H. H. Ben-Sasson. Cambridge, Mass.: Harvard University Press, 1976. Provides some background on Elijah's life and is an excellent source on the controversy over Hasidism.

Waxman, Meyer. *A History of Jewish Literature.* Vol. 3, *From the Middle of the Eighteenth Century to 1880.* New York: Thomas Yoseloff, 1960. An excellent work. Contains information on the life and writings of Elijah.

Zinberg, Israel. *A History of Jewish Literature.* Translated by Bernard Martin. Vol. 9, *Hasidism and Enlightenment (1780-1820).* Cleveland: Press of Case Western Reserve University, 1972-1978. A discussion of Elijah's thoughts on the controversy over Hasidism.

Lester Eckman

FRIEDRICH ENGELS

Born: November 28, 1820; Barmen, Prussia
Died: August 5, 1895; London, England
Areas of Achievement: Social reform, government, and politics
Contribution: In partnership with Karl Marx, Engels analyzed the origins
and nature of industrial capitalist society and worked to bring about the
overthrow of that society by a working-class revolution.

Early Life

Friedrich Engels was born into the social class whose domination he later
strove to overturn. His father, Friedrich, owned one of the principal cotton
mills in the Wupper Valley, in the Rhineland territory that Prussia had taken
over in 1815 after the Napoleonic Wars. It was assumed that young Friedrich, the first of nine children, would enter the family business, and university education was considered unnecessary for a business career; Friedrich
left grammar school in 1837 without taking the final examinations, having
shown strong academic skills, particularly in languages. His literary inclinations, he believed, could be pursued without academic credentials; indeed,
he became impressively self-educated.

By 1838, when he began a sort of businessman's apprenticeship in the
export business of a family friend in Bremen, Engels had already broken
away from the strong Pietist fundamentalist Protestantism of his family and
of Barmen. His letters also included sarcastic attacks on the Prussian king,
Friedrich Wilhelm IV, calling him oppressive and stupid. His taste in philosophy favored D. F. Strauss and the Young Hegelians, in literature, Heinrich Heine and the Young German movement. Engels had defined himself
as an alienated young man, but the newspaper articles that he wrote from
Bremen were generally amusing, mocking rather than vehement in tone,
though Engels did attack both capitalists and Pietists.

Engels returned to Barmen in 1841, and later that year went to Berlin to
do his military service as a one-year volunteer in the Prussian artillery. His
military duties, which he often avoided, were so undemanding that he was
able to attend lectures at the university, associate with enthusiastic young
radicals, and write copiously on political and philosophical issues. In October, 1842, his military service completed, he visited Cologne and the offices
of the *Rheinische Zeitung*, whose editor, Moses Hess, claimed credit for
converting Engels from generic revolutionary to communist.

From November, 1842, to August, 1844, Engels was in England, working
in the Manchester branch of his father's firm and preparing his vivid attack
on industrial capitalism, *Die Lage der arbeitende Klasse in England* (1845;
The Condition of the Working Class in England in 1844, 1887). In Paris, on
the way home from England, Engels met Karl Marx, beginning a partnership

that lasted till Marx's death. The two had met, coolly, in November, 1842. Now Engels' firsthand acquaintance with industrial society impressed Marx, who was beginning to interest himself in economic issues. The university-educated Marx, two years older than Engels, was profound, while Engels was quick; Marx mapped out huge projects that remained unfinished, and Engels responded to the needs of the moment. Together they attempted to change the world.

Life's Work

Marx and Engels defined their differences from other socialists of the day in their first collaborative writings and joined in organizing various revolutionary groups in Brussels, Paris, and London. One of these, the Communist League, aspired to be an international organization of the revolutionary working class, under the slogan "Workers of the World, unite!" Engels drafted this group's program and Marx revised it into *Manifest der Kommunistischen Partei* (1848; *The Communist Manifesto*, 1850). Although this program of a weak organization had little effect in 1848, it combined philosophy and economic history into a powerful prophecy that the course of history would soon make it possible to eliminate class rule and inaugurate true human freedom. The successes of the Industrial Revolution, carried out by the middle classes, were creating the conditions for a workers' revolution. Despite its dated denunciations of ephemeral leftist rivals, *The Communist Manifesto* remains the central expression of Marxism's ideas and style.

Revolution broke out in Paris in February, 1848, followed by upheavals elsewhere. Liberalism and nationalism were the issues of the day, not communism. Engels and Marx devoted their efforts to the *Neue Rheinische Zeitung*, published in Cologne, which advocated the unification of Germany as a democratic republic, ignoring for the moment the eventual goal of abolishing capitalism. Engels wrote caustically on the deliberations of the Frankfurt Assembly as that body failed to unite Germany, and he discussed revolution-related military campaigns in Hungary, Italy, and elsewhere. The authorities suspended the paper's publication in September and October, and Engels fled, taking an extended walking tour in France and returning to Cologne in January, 1849. He replaced Marx as editor-in-chief in April and May. In early May, uprisings occurred in several German areas, including Engels' hometown. He left Cologne to take part, but order was soon restored; he went back to Cologne, but the government, recovering its sense of initiative, shut down the *Neue Rheinische Zeitung* for good.

As revolutionary hopes faded everywhere in Europe, the Prussian king declined the invitation of the Frankfurt Assembly to serve as ruler of a new united Germany; only two small states supported the defiant, obviously doomed call to unite the country as a republic. Engels joined the volunteer corps, led by August Willich, as the revolutionary diehards held out for more than a month against overwhelming Prussian and other forces; he was among the last to cross into Switzerland. His sole experience of revolutionary combat showed the limitations of slogans and zeal against military organization.

Engels sailed from Genoa to London, already the refuge of Marx and many other revolutionary refugees. Debates on tactics and organization soon led to a split between the "party of the *Neue Rheinische Zeitung*," who argued that a real revolution would depend on years of preparation, education, and economic development, and those (including Engels' former commander Willich and other officers) who wished to revive the revolution by immediate conspiratorial and military action. As on several other occasions, Marx and Engels opposed more impatient revolutionaries. One consequence of this émigré discord (1850-1851) was that Engels took up the study of military science, to contest the opposing faction's monopoly on military expertise.

Bowing to economic necessity, Engels went to work at his father's company in Manchester. After his father's death in 1860, he became a partner in the firm, selling out his interest in 1869. His income from the textile mill, and later from successful investments, supported an official address where he met his business contacts, and a home where he lived with Mary Burns, a factory worker whom he had met during his visit to England in 1842-1844. It also furnished the chief, and often the only, source of support for the Marx family in London.

Until he was able to move to London in 1869, Engels corresponded daily with Marx. He wrote articles, often under Marx's name, for sale. When Eugen Dühring came forward with a rival socialist philosophy, Engels replied with *Herrn Eugen Dührings Umwälzung der Wissenschaft* (1877-1878; *Herr Eugen Dühring's Revolution in Science*, 1934), following Dühring into natural philosophy as well as politics. The work and an excerpt from it, *Die Entwicklung des Sozialismus von der Utopie zur Wissenschaft* (1882; *Socialism: Utopian and Scientific*, 1892), are Engels' best-known works, standing alongside *The Communist Manifesto* as summaries of Marxist thought, and sometimes accused of leading subsequent Marxists into simplistic materialist determinism. His foray into anthropology, *Der Ursprung der Familie, des Privateigentums und des Staats* (1884; *The Origin of the Family, Private Property, and the State*, 1902), has attracted some attention from feminist scholars. At great cost to his eyesight, Engels worked through vast quantities of overlapping, ill-organized drafts in Marx's wretched handwriting to produce volumes 2 and 3 of Marx's *Das Kapital* (1885, 1894; *Capital: A Critique of Political Economy*, 1907, 1908, best known as *Das Kapital*).

Described as military in bearing and nicknamed "General" by Marx's daughters after writing his brilliant articles on the Franco-Prussian War,

Engels made a specialty of military science. In addition to writing about wars and crises as bread-and-butter journalism, he studied war as a phenomenon which might improve or diminish the prospects of revolution. Some capitalist states were more regressive and obnoxious than others, and Engels and Marx were never indifferent to the wars of their lifetimes. The most important fruit of Engels' military studies was his conclusion, after the Austro-Prussian War of 1866, that all the great powers would have to adopt the Prussian-style universal-service army. That meant that there was hope for the revolution, despite the folly of insurrection against an intact army; a socialist electoral majority would be reflected by a majority in the ranks, and the army would vanish as a counterrevolutionary instrument.

After Marx's death in 1883, Engels found himself in the role of interpreter of Marx's theories and as leader of the movement. He dispensed encouragement and advice to the younger socialists and presided over splendid parties in celebration of holidays and socialist election victories. His companion Mary Burns had died in 1863, succeeded in Engels' household by her sister Lizzie, whom Engels married on her deathbed in 1878. Engels presided at the Zurich Conference of the Second International in 1893, the grand old man of a growing, confident, worldwide movement. When Engels died of throat cancer in 1895, his ashes were scattered in the sea off Beachy Head.

Summary
Friedrich Engels' name usually appears preceded by "Marx and." He was indeed important, not apart from Marx, but as a full partner in the creation of Marxism. In addition to providing Marx's material needs, protecting Marx's scholarly labors from interruption, and furnishing his friend vital psychological support for forty years, Engels brought to Marxism a quick intelligence and an acquaintance with the real world of capitalism. Involved in conceiving and elaborating all the varied aspects of Marxism and predominant in the crucial area of revolutionary tactics, Engels played an indispensable part in creating Marxism as an intellectual system and as a political and social movement.

Bibliography
Berger, Martin. *Engels, Armies and Revolution: The Revolutionary Tactics of Classical Marxism.* Hamden, Conn.: Archon Books, 1977. Emphasizes Engels' thought on war and military institutions as a key to Marxist views on international relations and the timing and tactics of revolution.
Henderson, W. O. *The Life of Friedrich Engels.* 2 vols. London: Frank Cass, 1976. A detailed study, strongest on Engels' business life in England.
Hunt, Richard N. *The Political Ideas of Marx and Engels.* 2 vols. Pittsburgh: University of Pittsburgh Press, 1974-1984. A standard account.

Differentiates Marx and Engels from both Leninist and Social Democratic varieties of Marxism.

Lichtheim, George. *Marxism: An Historical and Critical Study*. 2d rev. ed. New York: Praeger, 1965. An unusually coherent account of Marxism, placing Engels in context.

McLellan, David. *Friedrich Engels*. New York: Viking Press, 1978. A concise (120-page) introduction in the Modern Masters series, a by-product of the author's major Marx biography.

Marcus, Steven. *Engels, Manchester, and the Working Class*. New York: Random House, 1974. A perceptive study of Engels' *The Condition of the Working Class in England in 1844* as a literary work.

Mayer, Gustav. *Friedrich Engels: A Biography*. Translated by Gilbert Highet and Helen Highet. New York: Alfred A. Knopf, 1936. A condensation of the great two-volume German original (1934). Still a sound treatment.

Wilson, Edmund. *To the Finland Station: A Study in the Writing and Acting of History*. Garden City, N.Y.: Doubleday, 1940. A classic popular account of the development of Marxism. Contains a good sketch of the Marx-Engels relationship.

Martin Berger

DESIDERIUS ERASMUS

Born: October 27, 1466?; Rotterdam or Gouda, the Netherlands
Died: July 12, 1536; Basel, Switzerland
Areas of Achievement: Education, religion, and literature
Contribution: Of the intellectuals who transmitted and adapted the Renaissance spirit to northern Europe, Erasmus was the greatest. Taken together, his writings reflect a rare combination of practical Christian piety, biblical and patristic scholarship, and broad humanistic learning.

Early Life

Erasmus was born in Rotterdam, or possibly in the Dutch village of Gouda, on October 27 in the late 1460's (the exact year is disputed) to Margaret, a physician's daughter, and a priest probably named Gerard, for whom she served as housekeeper. As one of two illegitimate sons born to this couple, the sensitive Erasmus (he took the additional name Desiderius later in life) would endure shame and legal problems, but his parents lived together for many years and appear to have been devoted parents. Erasmus' childhood coincided with the ongoing war between the Duchy of Burgundy, which controlled Holland, and France. He grew to despise the Burgundian knights, whose cruelty belied the chivalric ideal expressed by Charles the Bold. He also developed an aversion to the provinciality and social rigidity of his homeland.

Around 1478, Erasmus' mother enrolled the two boys at a school in Deventer, about seventy-five miles inland, conducted by the Brethren of the Common Life, a lay society dedicated to the imitation of primitive Christianity. Although Erasmus later expressed contempt for the Brethren's teaching methods, both their piety and a humanistic strain which entered the school at this time helped shape the young student. His schooling at Deventer ended in 1483 or 1484, when the plague claimed the lives of both his parents. Three guardians appointed by his father sent Erasmus to another more conservative and even less congenial of the Brethren's schools for three additional years.

He entered the Augustinian priory at Steyn about 1487. There, the critical young man learned to dislike the ascetic routine and prevailing mysticism, but he enlarged his grasp of classical literature and wrote the first two of his many books, a conventional treatise on monastic life and a book of Latin verse. His years at Steyn climaxed with his ordination as priest on April 25, 1492.

Life's Work

About a year after his ordination, Erasmus accepted a post as Latin secretary to the ambitious Henri, Bishop of Cambray. While in his service,

Erasmus wrote, in the form of a Platonic dialogue, an attack on Scholasticism, the dominant philosophy of the Church, although the book remained unpublished for nearly thirty years. In 1495, Bishop Henri assisted Erasmus in gaining entrance to the University of Paris, a hotbed of Scholasticism, presumably to study for his doctorate in theology. At the College of Montaigu in Paris, he made Humanist friends, including an elderly man named Robert Gaguin, who had been a pupil of the noted Florentine Platonist Marsilio Ficino, and who now encouraged Erasmus to study the Neoplatonists. Constantly seeking the independence that would enable him to spend his life studying in reasonable comfort, he accepted in 1499 the patronage of the Englishman William Blount, Lord Mountjoy, and thus visited England for the first time. There he established friendships with leading scholars such as William Grocyn, Thomas Linacre, John Colet, and—preeminently—Sir Thomas More.

Already the wandering pattern of the man who later called himself a citizen of the world was being established. He returned to France the next year and began a routine of scholarly activity that included the study of Greek, the compilation of a book of proverbial wisdom, *Adagia* (1500; *Proverbs or Adages*, 1622), and a manual of Christianity written for the laity from the point of view of a monk who, at this point, was living in the manner of a principled Christian layman. *Enchiridion Militis Christiani* (1503; *The Manual of the Christian Knight*, 1533) became the best-known of his works in this genre. His study of Lorenzo Valla's exegesis of the New Testament, a work which he edited and published in 1506, quickened his determination to master the original Greek. After another sojourn in England with his Humanist friends there, he accepted a tutoring appointment which took him to Italy.

His work took him on a tour which included Turin, at whose university he received a doctorate in divinity in 1506, and Florence, Bologna, and Venice, where he met the distinguished printer Aldus Manutius, with whom he worked to produce a handsome revision of *Proverbs or Adages*. In Rome, he witnessed the growing corruption of the papal court, after which Mountjoy persuaded him to return to England. It has been argued that had the now influential Erasmus remained in Rome during the next crucial decade, he might have furthered the cause of reform, prevented the excommunication of Martin Luther, with whom he corresponded, and thus changed the course of religious history.

Upon his arrival in London, while awaiting the arrival of his books, he lived in Thomas More's house and wrote there a book, which he certainly did not consider among his most important but which, more than any other, has immortalized him: *Moriæ Encomium* (1511; *The Praise of Folly*, 1549). By a species of pun congenial to him and to his host, the title also signifies "the praise of More," though without any suggestion that More was foolish.

While the book is, like Sebastian Brant's *Narrenschiff* (1494; *Ship of Fools*, 1509), a satire on human folly, Erasmus' characterization of Folly is a rich and original conception depicting not only gradations of conventional foolishness but also ultimately figuring the Christian fool, whose folly is in reality wisdom.

Later, he became the first man to teach Greek at Cambridge. During his two and a half years on the faculty of the English university, he wrote *De Duplici Copia Verborum ac Rerum* (1512; *On the Twofold Abundance of Words and Things*, 1978, better known as *De Copia*), which would hold its place as a standard textbook on literary style for two centuries. Nevertheless, Erasmus was not happy at Cambridge, blaming the cold, damp climate for undermining his always frail health and finding Cambridge intellectually mediocre and provincial. His more enlightened Humanist English friends resided, for the most part, in London.

He was even less pleased with the prospect of returning to monastic life at Steyn, to which he was recalled in 1514, more than two decades after gaining permission to leave. Erasmus relayed his firm intention to return; it required, however, dispensation from Pope Leo X, which took him three years to acquire, to free himself from all possibility of further obligation to his order. While this appeal was pending, he completed his own Latin version of the New Testament, based on Greek manuscripts and more accurate in many (though not all) details than the standard Latin Vulgate. His translation reflected his conviction that Christ's teachings are easily understandable and not meant to be encrusted by the commentary of theologians. Strategically, he dedicated his work to Leo and also recommended that the Bible be translated into the vernacular tongues so that it might be accessible to the less educated.

Among his other works in this busy period were a nine-volume edition of the works of Saint Jerome and a manual, *Institutio Principis Christiani* (1516; *The Education of a Christian Prince*, 1936). Sharply contrasting with Niccolò Machiavelli's *Il principe* (wr. 1513; *The Prince*, 1640), Erasmus' advice to the prince included pleas for restraint in taxation and in the waging of war. Unlike Machiavelli, Erasmus regarded politics as a branch of ethics in the classical manner. Unenthusiastic about the tyranny of princes, Erasmus could see no other acceptable alternative to anarchy. In this work and in two other treatises of this period, Erasmus' thought tended toward pacifism, a shocking philosophy in an age that looked on the willingness to wage war as a certification of one's conviction.

During a stay at Antwerp in 1516-1517, Erasmus was painted by Quentin Massys, the first of three famous artists for whom he sat. In this portrait, Erasmus, then middle-aged, is at his writing desk, intently serious. Portraits by Albrecht Dürer and Hans Holbein the Younger a few years later interpret the Dutch scholar quite differently, but all three artists agree that Erasmus had a very long, somewhat aquiline nose, a wide mouth with thin lips, and a strong chin. Both Dürer and Holbein (in a late portrait of about 1532) endow the writer with a faint, enigmatic smile, which many viewers have seen as mocking human weakness as does his character Folly. All of these portraits show Erasmus wearing a flat cap.

From 1517 to 1521, Erasmus lived at Louvain. He published one of his most enduring works, *Colloquia Familiaria* (1518; *The Colloquies of Erasmus*, 1671), and also continued his task of editing the early fathers of the Church, spending all day and much of the night at his writing desk and turning out a stupendous volume of work for publication and hundreds— probably thousands—of gracefully written letters to correspondents all over Europe. Having made a number of severe criticisms of the Church, Erasmus received overtures from his fellow Augustinian Martin Luther, but while refusing for years to denounce Luther—many of whose famous ninety-five theses he anticipated—he did not support him either. In the interests of Christian unity, more important to Erasmus than most of the theological points on which Luther challenged the Church, he attempted to mediate the quarrel, but observing the intransigence of both Church and reformers, he refused an invitation to the Diet of Worms, where, in 1521, Luther's doctrines were condemned. Solicited by both sides but widely viewed as cowardly for his unwillingness to back either unequivocally, Erasmus made many enemies. Although he had little reason to fear the Protestant majority in Basel, where he lived during most of the 1520's, he refused to endorse even tacitly the city's denial of religious liberty to Catholic citizens and left for Freiburg in 1529.

He unsuccessfully urged the warring Christians to compromise and focus on the Turkish threat in the Balkans and continued to prepare editions of early Christian thinkers. In 1535, his own health failing, he learned of King Henry VIII's execution of his good friends More and Bishop John Fisher. In the final months of his life, he returned to Basel, dying there on July 12, 1536. In 1540, a wooden statue of Erasmus was erected in Rotterdam, the city he claimed as his birthplace, and Johann Froben published an edition of his collected works in Basel. The statue did not survive the Spanish occupation of the Netherlands and many of his books were burned, but the centuries that followed have proved Erasmus ineradicable.

Summary

Before the heyday of the Protestant Reformers, Desiderius Erasmus articulated his dismay at the excesses of an increasingly worldly and corrupt Church and urged a return to Christian essentials. His numerous editions of early Christian theologians and his Latin version of the New Testament signaled his contempt for the decadent but still-prevailing Scholasticism, while his manuals of practical piety reflected his conviction that what he called "the philosophy of Christ" was a simple and achievable attainment.

Erasmus' tolerance and pacifism, which owed something to his physical timidity but more to his capacity for rational analysis and insight into the futility of religious confrontation, turned both the Catholics and Protestants against him. In an ecumenically minded world, however, what appeared to his contemporaries as cowardice or indecisiveness looks more like wisdom.

As the greatest of the northern Humanists, he communicated not only the learning of the ancients but also their spirit of inquiry and independence to educated people of his time. He saw harmony in the best of classical and Christian thought. He also understood the potentialities of mass-produced books—a new development in his lifetime—and thus devoted his life to incessant writing. A bibliographical analysis by an Erasmian scholar in 1927 produced an estimate that two million copies of his books had been printed, one million of them textbooks. Erasmus never understood, however, why more people did not submit to the logic of his arguments. Paradoxically, his books enjoyed more popularity in the later sixteenth and seventeenth centuries, when his personal reputation was ebbing; today a torrent of scholarly works interpret his character much more favorably, but he is much less read. Only *The Praise of Folly* is still widely admired for its wit, subtlety, and the universality of its analysis of human folly. Readers who find their way to *The Colloquies of Erasmus*, however, discover that no writer since Plato has used dialogue so well to express his thought in a persuasive and readable form.

Taken as a whole, Erasmus' writings cast more light on the great European movements of his time—the Renaissance and the Reformation—than does the work of any other eyewitness. This wandering Augustinian monk was an intellectual seismograph who registered the brightest hopes and most profound disappointments of Western civilization in the stormy period of his life.

Bibliography

Bainton, Roland H. *Erasmus of Christendom*. New York: Charles Scribner's Sons, 1969. Probably the closest thing to a standard biography, Bainton's study has relatively little to say about Erasmus' more imaginative works but is particularly good on his less well-known ones. Scholarly, thoroughly documented, yet never ponderous, this book ably interprets Erasmus' complex relationships with Luther and other reformers.

Faludy, George. *Erasmus of Rotterdam*. London: Eyre & Spottiswoode, 1970. An excellent general reader's biography. Faludy explains the historical and intellectual contexts of Erasmus' work clearly and tactfully. He uses few footnotes but displays a thorough grasp of Erasmian scholarship.

Huizinga, Johan. *Erasmus and the Age of Reformation*. Translated by F. Hopman. New York: Harper & Row, 1957. Originally published as *Erasmus of Rotterdam* in 1924, Huizinga's biography has worn well. Not only was this Dutch scholar a recognized expert on Erasmus' era, but also he grasped the psychology of his subject as few other biographers have.

Mangan, John Joseph. *Life, Character, and Influence of Desiderius Erasmus of Rotterdam*. 2 vols. New York: Macmillan, 1927. Though dated in some of its interpretations, this lengthy biography prints translations of large chunks of Erasmus' writings, especially letters. Its last chapter contains extensive information on Erasmus' later influence as measured by editions and translations of his many works.

Phillips, Margaret Mann. *Erasmus and the Northern Renaissance*. London: English Universities Press, 1949. A somewhat elementary introduction to Erasmus and his age. Contains two chapters that can be especially recommended: "Portrait" and "The World Through Erasmus's Eye." Useful for beginning students of the Renaissance.

Smith, Preserved. *Erasmus: A Study of His Life, Ideals, and Place in History*. New York: Frederick Ungar, 1962. This reprint of a study published in 1923 views Erasmus as champion of "undogmatic Christianity" and thus emphasizes his subjects' relations with, and differences from, the Protestant Reformers. Less useful on the Humanist aspect. A patient, scholarly life with an extensive bibliography of nineteenth and earlier twentieth century studies, chiefly by European scholars.

Zweig, Stefan. *Erasmus of Rotterdam*. Translated by Eden Paul and Cedar Paul. New York: Viking Press, 1934. A lively popular life by a master of general readers' biographies. Although not always accurate in details or judicious interpretations, Zweig's life may well stimulate the beginning student of Erasmus to delve into more detailed and critical accounts of his life and achievements.

Robert P. Ellis

LEONHARD EULER

Born: April 15, 1707; Basel, Switzerland
Died: September 18, 1783; St. Petersburg, Russia
Areas of Achievement: Mathematics and physics
Contribution: Euler had a tremendous impact on almost all fields of mathematics, setting his contemporaries and those who followed on new and more fruitful courses. His founding of the field of analysis is particularly important, and his notations are in common use in mathematics today. He was one of the most prolific mathematical writers ever.

Early Life

Leonhard Euler was born to a Calvinist minister, Paul Euler, and his wife, Marguerite Brucker, the daughter of a minister, in Basel, Switzerland, on April 15, 1707. The family soon moved to Riehen. Little is known of Euler's childhood, but the information that is available indicates that his interest in mathematics was quite logical, for his father was an excellent mathematician in his own right.

Paul Euler had studied under Jakob I Bernoulli of the famous Bernoulli family of mathematicians while he was studying for his degree in theology. The elder Euler gave Leonhard his first instruction at home. During this period, the younger Euler studied some of the most difficult texts in mathematics available at the time. He later moved to live in Basel with his grandmother, where he went to the local school (*Gymnasium*). Euler was not satisfied with the mathematics instruction offered there and received private tutoring from Johann Burckhardt.

When Euler was almost fourteen, at his father's wish he entered the University of Basel to study theology. Although Leonhard was quite devout and worked dutifully, he had no desire to become a minister, and he filled his free time with mathematics. In fact, in time he received limited tutoring from Johann I Bernoulli. Bernoulli suggested texts for Euler and agreed to explain any difficulties during his free time on Saturdays. Since Euler did not want to disappoint Bernoulli, he worked very hard to ensure that he did not waste the professor's time.

Life's Work

In 1724, at age seventeen, Euler received his master's degree. His father was concerned about the progress Leonhard was making in theology, but the Bernoullis convinced Paul Euler that the young man was extremely gifted in mathematics and that the gift should not be wasted. Thus Euler was free at a very young age to pursue a career in mathematics. Euler began working independently and submitted a solution to a problem in navigation proposed by the Academy of Sciences in Paris in 1727. Although he only received an honorable mention, his name was placed before many of the people who could influence his career.

Unfortunately, there were many mathematicians who were not ready to accept one so young. When Euler applied for a post as professor of mathematics at the University of Basel, his name was not forwarded, probably because of his age. As such positions were rare in his home country, Euler was very discouraged, but the Bernoullis encouraged him with news of the newly formed Academy at St. Petersburg in Russia. This institution had a twofold purpose. Its members received a stipend to continue their own work, and, from time to time, the czar might pose practical problems to be solved by the members. Both Nikolaus and Daniel Bernoulli had positions there, and they wrote to him that there would soon be an opening in medicine. Therefore, Euler began to study anatomy so that he would be qualified. He received the appointment in 1727, and he traveled to Russia, intending to accept this medical position. The reigning monarch, Catherine I, died before he could take up his appointment, however, and he went into the mathematical group unnoticed in the change of regimes.

Although the political situation in Russia was not entirely satisfactory, the Russian academy offered Euler security and a good life-style, and except for a brief stint in Berlin, he made St. Petersburg his permanent home. His work for the first six years was fairly routine as a member of the physics staff, but in 1733 he became the leading member in mathematics when Daniel Bernoulli left to return home.

Euler, who had married Catharina Gsell and had begun a family, threw himself into his work with fervor. (Indeed, when Switzerland planned to published Euler's writings in the twentieth century, the editors were stunned by the amount of material found in St. Petersburg.) His works there were diverse, spanning navigation, cartography, ballistics, mechanics, measurement, and especially mathematics. During this first fourteen-year period in Russia, Euler wrote nearly one hundred articles and memoirs for publication. He also maintained correspondence with the most widely known European mathematicians, both for himself and in the name of the Academy of Sciences. Indeed, as the result of his strenuous pursuit of a Parisian prize in the field of astronomy, Euler developed an illness which resulted in the loss of sight in one eye.

In 1740, Euler was invited to Berlin by Frederick the Great of Prussia as part of the reorganization and refurbishing of the Berlin Academy of Sciences. Euler accepted this position, which he filled from 1740 until 1764. He also maintained his membership in the St. Petersburg Academy as well as in the Royal Society of London, to which he was elected in 1749. He continued to write for the Russian academy during this time as he was still in their employ. During his time abroad, Euler received a stipend from Russia as well as his recompense for his post in Berlin. While in Russia, he was supported well enough to have several servants. Euler and Frederick got along so poorly that at least once Frederick tried to remove him as the director of the Academy but was convinced by others that this would be a mistake. Nevertheless, Euler more than earned his pay. He worked on many applications for Frederick, including coinage, insurance, and pensions, and he held several administrative posts. In addition he produced almost three hundred mathematical papers and tutored some of Frederick's relatives.

By 1766, the situation with Frederick had become so bad that Euler, then fifty-nine, decided to accept the invitation of Catherine the Great to return to Russia. Since he had regularly sent memoirs back to that country and had enjoyed its financial support while in Berlin, the move seemed logical. He was to live there for the remainder of his life.

Soon after his return, Euler began to develop a cataract in his remaining eye. For a man of lesser gifts, blindness would have been a career-ending disability. Euler, however, began to train himself to solve problems mentally and dictate the results to others, principally his sons Johann Albrecht and Christoph, who were also mathematicians. He succeeded so completely that he was able to work in this fashion for another fifteen years, holding his post at the Academy and actually producing more papers than ever before. During this time, he produced some of his best work, including his discoveries about how the motion of the moon is affected by the forces of gravity from the earth and the sun. Although he did benefit from discussions with his peers, all the work had to be done without the aid of writing partial results or ideas. He also produced a monograph on integral calculus, work on fluid mechanics, and won a prize for work in astronomy.

Despite a lifetime of work, Euler was most comfortable with his family. A devoted family man, he even worked on mathematics while holding his children when they were small. Working with his sons in his later life was also quite fulfilling for him. Although he had chosen not to pursue theology as a youth, Euler never left his church, and he held daily services with his family. Euler's wife died in 1776, and he soon was married to his first wife's sister, with whom he lived until his death in St. Petersburg on September 18, 1783.

Summary

The extent of Leonhard Euler's work was vast. In mathematics, he developed much of the notation in current use, in addition to a considerable amount of theory. Euler was the first to treat trigonometry as a field in itself rather than a branch of geometry, and he developed spherical trigonometry. Thus, he led the way in its development as a discipline. He made great progress in calculus, writing two texts, *Institutiones calculi differentialis* (1755) and *Institutiones calculi integralis* (1768-1770), which are still used by mathematicians as reference works. Included in these books are several discoveries Euler made concerning differential equations and partial differential equations. Euler made significant refinements on the Fundamental Theorem of Algebra. He was also extremely interested in summation of infinite series and developed much of the basis upon which convergence theories would later be founded.

Although he produced a great quantity of work in physics, in part in response to requests by monarchs, Euler's major contribution in this field was his imposing analysis on mechanics. He was far more interested in the mathematical aspects of physical problems and thus was able to systematize his study. Euler published his results in *Mechanica sive motus scientia analytice exposita* (1736) and *Theoria motus corporum solidorum seu rigidorum* (1765). The former work was the first attempt to establish clear solutions to mechanical problems. Other sciences in which Euler worked are astronomy, navigation, and optics. Yet Euler's foremost field was mathematical analysis, a field which owes its foundation to Euler's book *Introductio in analysin infinitorum* (1748). Of particular interest to mathematicians is his development of function theory and notation.

The republication of Euler's work was begun in 1911 in Leipzig, Germany, and moved to Lausanne, Switzerland, in 1942. Three series have been produced, *Opera mathematica*, *Opera mechanica et astronomica*, and *Opera physica*, in which each work is reproduced in the original language of publication. Although only those papers which Euler personally prepared for publication are included, it is estimated that to include them all would take more than fifty volumes. Euler ranks as one of the most prolific mathematicians in history.

Bibliography
Bell, Eric T. "Analysis Incarnate." In *Men of Mathematics*. New York: Simon & Schuster, 1937. This book is a compilation of chapters which deal with major mathematicians from the early Greeks to the early twentieth century. The chapter on Euler includes both biographical information and a limited discussion on his work.
Boyer, Carl B. *A History of Mathematics*. New York: John Wiley & Sons, 1968. Boyer's book is a standard, though extensive, history, and his discussion of Euler and his work is both interesting and clear.
Eves, Howard. *An Introduction to the History of Mathematics*. New York: Holt, Rinehart and Winston, 1976. Although the treatment of Euler is extremely brief, Eves is excellent in the placement of Euler in the evolution of mathematics.
Struik, Dirk J. *A Concise History of Mathematics*. 3d rev. ed. New York: Dover, 1967. This is a standard history of mathematics, and the treatment of Euler and his work is concise yet informative.
Youschkevitch, A. P. "Leonhard Euler." In *Dictionary of Scientific Biog-*

raphy, vol 4. New York: Charles Scribner's Sons, 1971. This article is of particular note for at least two reasons. First, Youschkevitch is a Fellow of the Soviet Academy of Sciences, an outgrowth of the St. Petersburg Academy. As such, access to Euler's work has clearly been easy. Second, the article contains an extensive bibliography (seventy entries), which can lead an interested student into deeper study. The article itself is a clear exposition of Euler's life and work.

Celeste Williams Brockington

JAN VAN EYCK and HUBERT VAN EYCK

Jan van Eyck

Born: c. 1390; possibly Maastricht, Flanders
Died: July 9, 1441; Bruges, Flanders

Hubert van Eyck

Born: Before 1390; possibly Maastricht, Flanders
Died: Probably September 18, 1426; Ghent, Flanders
Area of Achievement: Art
Contribution: In paintings of unprecedented accuracy of observation and coherence of form, the van Eycks achieved a fusion of Christian religious content with a passionate devotion to visual fact.

Early Lives

The commonplace facts of the lives of Jan and Hubert van Eyck are almost entirely absent from the historical record. Jan's estimated year of birth, 1390, seems reasonable in view of the established details of his early career, as well as his date of death, 1441. Of Hubert, whose very existence has occasionally been called into question by scholars, evidence suggests that he was an elder brother; a taxation document from 1426 establishes that he died at about that time.

Both Hubert and Jan may have worked in The Hague from about 1415 to 1417, and it is certain that Jan was employed in that city from 1422 to 1424 by John of Bavaria, who as Count of Holland maintained his court there. A document indicates that Jan was accompanied in his work there by at least two assistants. In early 1425, civil war broke out in Holland, and Jan sought refuge in Flanders, where Hubert had already gone. On May 19, Jan van Eyck entered the service of Philip III, Duke of Burgundy. Philip the Good, as he was known, had a high regard both for Jan's artistic abilities and for his skills as a negotiator, since over the next several years Jan was engaged in various missions on Philip's behalf, including a journey in 1428 to negotiate Philip's marriage to Isabella, daughter of King John I of Portugal. Jan's role, at minimum, was to paint portraits of Isabella to help Philip come to a decision about the match. For the sake of security, two pictures were returned to Bruges, one by sea and the other by land.

Of the circumstances of Hubert's death, and of its effect upon the work in which he and Jan may have been jointly engaged, there is no documentation; their artistic and professional relationship can only be inferred from the paintings that have been attributed to them. A third brother, Lambert, who survived Jan, seems not to have been an artist.

Around 1432, Jan van Eyck bought a house in Bruges. By 1434 he had married, and in that year his son was born; a daughter was born several years later. Only the first name of Jan's wife, Margaretha, is known; of her social origins there is no record, but it may be assumed that a renowned artist of van Eyck's stature would seek a favorable marriage. Jan's portrait of her when she was thirty-three, painted in 1439, shows a woman of great intelligence, if not beauty. If Jan's painting of 1433, known as *The Man with the Red Turban*, is, as seems likely, a self-portrait, the modern viewer has a visual document of a prosperous fifteenth century husband and wife.

Life's Work

The dominant form of painting in northern Europe during the youth of Jan and Hubert van Eyck was manuscript illumination, a form that dominated the art of the Middle Ages and that was a particularly vital element of what came to be known as Gothic art. The small scale of manuscript illumination required extremely precise technique; that, and the need to include decorative elements and writing within the page, tended to favor qualities of abstract form and color rather than observation of nature. Around 1400, however, a trend toward naturalism in manuscript painting gained momentum in many northern European centers, including the region of Limbourg, near the van Eycks' birthplace. The origins of this new attention to natural appearances are varied, but the influence of Giotto di Bondone and his successors is certain. These fourteenth century Italian masters irreversibly influenced the depiction of the human figure, presenting it as a three-dimensional mass in an illusionistic space. The representation of natural light and the convincing portrayal of action and emotion were other progressive elements of Italian art which spread to major centers of artistic production in fifteenth century Europe.

In the earlier parts of their careers, the van Eycks were almost certainly occupied with manuscript painting. Probably the earliest works which could be attributed to Jan or Hubert are the *Heures de Turin* (the Turin hours), several paintings which were once part of a book of miniatures, *Très Belles Heures de Notre Dame*. This volume was the effort of many artists working over an extended period of time whose identities are elusive, but in the case of the *Heures de Turin*, the modernity of the use of space in landscape and the subtle modulation of tones suggest the involvement of artists of very progressive tendencies. No more likely candidates than the van Eycks have been proposed, but opinion has always been divided about which particular characteristics in the works can be attributed to Hubert and which to Jan, or in fact whether the works represent a collaborative effort at all. All that can be said with assurance is that the *Heures de Turin* represent the vital trends that reach fulfillment in later works of the van Eycks.

Generally accepted as a work of Hubert is *The Three Marys at the Sep-*

ulcher, a painting on a wooden panel that is substantially larger than a typical manuscript illumination. Although undated, it is considered a work of Hubert's mature years and exhibits many qualities thought to be uniquely his own, such as a sharply inclined ground plane, awkward perspective, and slender, small-headed figures. There is an intensity of narrative interest in the figures which is thought to be atypical of the work of Jan. Its great significance, however, is that, in it, the vigor and monumentality of the style of the *Heures de Turin* are rendered on a larger scale.

The scholarly problem of distinguishing between the work of Jan and Hubert van Eyck recurs in connection with the great polyptych, *The Ghent Altarpiece*, but here a consensus has emerged from decades of study. An inscription on the painting, placed there by order of the patron who commissioned it, states "Hubert van Eyck, the greatest painter who ever lived, began the work, which his brother Jan, the second in art, finished at the instigation of Jodocus Vijdt. With this verse, on 6 May [1432] he invites you to look at this work." Given such a documentary starting point, if the altarpiece were less complex, attribution of its design and execution would not be problematic. The altarpiece is, however, composed of twenty panels of differing shapes, dimensions, and representational scales. When closed, the work's eight exterior panels comprise an area 218 centimeters wide and 314 centimeters high; opened, its twelve panels together measure 455 centimeters in width. Within this impressive format, a multitude of figures is presented in an upper and lower register; centrally placed in the upper register is the seated figure of God, representing the Trinity. This figure, larger than life-size, is clothed in resplendent garments painted with an almost miraculous precision and vibrancy of color. To the left is the Virgin, and to the right is Saint John the Baptist. On either side of this central group are panels depicting angel musicians, and at the sides of this upper portion are the figures of Adam, on the left, and Eve, on the right.

The lower register consists of five panels which together form a continuous landscape. The large central panel, which is the width of the four flanking panels combined, is a scene of the Adoration of the Lamb representing Revelation 7:2-10: "After this I beheld, and, lo, a great multitude, which no man could number, of all nations, and kindreds, and people, and tongues, stood before the throne, and before the Lamb, clothed with white robes, and palms in their hands. . . ." The outer panels show the Just Judges, the Warriors of Christ, the Holy Hermits, and the Holy Pilgrims. In its entirety, the Adoration panels may be considered as the evocation of either an Earthly Paradise or the New Jerusalem. There is everywhere a profusion of grass, flowers, trees, and fruit, enveloped by a radiant, unifying light.

The consensus of scholars, which seems unlikely to be changed by further study, is that Hubert was largely responsible for the design of the altarpiece and for much of its execution, while Jan was the designer and painter of the figures of Adam and Eve and of parts of the rest, including the orange trees, palms, and cypresses of the Adoration of the Lamb. The question has been raised whether *The Ghent Altarpiece* was actually envisioned from the start in its present form by either Hubert or Jan, calling into question the unity of the overall structure. Yet few believe that the difference in scale, for example, of the figures in the upper and lower parts is anything but intentional; the contrast in scale seems visually and emotionally effective, and it is theologically sound.

With *The Ghent Altarpiece*, the technique of painting reached a degree of perfection that was the envy of painters in succeeding generations. The impression was given by the Italian artist Giorgio Vasari, writing in 1550, that Jan van Eyck had invented the technique of painting with oil. Oil had been used in the Low Countries as a medium before the van Eycks, but it is clear that the reputation for brilliance and subtlety gained by their works was in some measure the result of new methods in the preparation of paint, probably involving the use of a superior oil and more painstaking grinding of the pigment. The effects of their improvements were both aesthetic—a gain in the ease and flexibility with which paint could be applied—and physical, in that the paintings proved remarkably durable.

While working on *The Ghent Altarpiece*, Jan van Eyck accepted other commissions, but his next major works appeared after its completion in 1432. *The Arnolfini Wedding*, perhaps his best-known painting, was finished in 1434. It represents the wedding of Giovanni Arnolfini and Giovanna Cenami, natives of Lucca who resided in Bruges. It has been shown that each detail of the work has symbolic meaning and that the painting is in a sense almost a legal documentation of a wedding, with the two witnesses (the painter himself, and his wife—a priest was not strictly necessary) shown reflected in a convex mirror at the back of a small room in which the ceremony takes place.

The years which remained to Jan van Eyck were as productive as those preceding *The Arnolfini Wedding*. In addition to portraits of Arnolfini, Margaretha van Eyck, and others, he completed several panels in which the donor is represented appearing before the infant Christ and the Madonna in a contemporary setting. Of these, the finest is perhaps *Madonna with Chancellor Rolin*, which places the subjects in a beautifully rendered Romanesque palace, with a view of a city on a river receding to a distant mountain landscape.

Summary

Jan and Hubert van Eyck began their careers in a milieu where artistic endeavor tended to be anonymous and guilds controlled the standards and methods of production in the arts. Jan's career—there is no direct evidence of a "career" for Hubert, in this respect—demonstrated that an artist could achieve individual distinction and be recognized not merely by fellow artists but by citizens generally. Artists began to gain status beyond that of mere specialized craftsmen. Jan van Eyck's missions on behalf of his patron Philip the Good show that he was a trusted representative in political and personal matters, and one can infer that he was a man of substantial intellect.

Regardless of the credit due individually to Hubert or Jan in their works, each possessed a receptiveness to new ways of seeing the world, with the skill and sense of organization to complete projects of major physical and spiritual scope. On the slender evidence of Hubert's attributed works, one might say that he was the more passionate and Jan the more analytical personality. Both, however, presented the world as suffused with a unifying light and color which incarnate spiritual unity. The diversity of the natural world is seen with a fresh eye, but not as purely optical phenomena.

The paintings of the van Eycks belong to the first flowering of the Renaissance in the art of northern Europe. Their conquest of natural appearances, even though it was pursued in the realm of religious art, contributed to a process of secularization that affected all facets of life.

Bibliography
Baldass, Ludwig. *Jan van Eyck*. London: Phaidon Press, 1952. This major monograph on Jan van Eyck is exceptionally detailed both in text and illustrations. It gives a good account of the historical context of the van Eycks' work and has thorough appendices. The high-quality black-and-white reproductions are somehow more sympathetic to the works than those in most later publications.
Brockwell, Maurice W. *The van Eyck Problem*. Westport, Conn: Greenwood Press, 1971. Brockwell's long essay is a sort of case study of art historical inference, supposition, wishful thinking, and fashion, using *The Ghent Altarpiece* and the cloudy identity of Hubert van Eyck as the source material. The black-and-white illustrations are mediocre, and documentary material from several languages is not translated.
Faggin, Giorgio T. *The Complete Paintings of the van Eycks*. New York: Penguin Books, 1986. This volume, originally published in Italian in 1968 and subsequently updated, presents all the known paintings of the van Eycks. Major works are reproduced in color, many of them accompanied by enlarged details. The remainder of the reproductions are found in a separate section at the back of the book, which also contains extensive notes ranging from anecdotes to scholarly information. An introduction by Robert Hughes, though interesting, is not coordinated with the illustrations or the notes. A selection of comments on the van Eycks by writers through the centuries, a chronology, and appendices make this book useful and engrossing.
Panofsky, Erwin. "Jan van Eyck's Arnolfini Portrait." In *Renaissance Art*,

edited by Gilbert Creighton. New York: Harper & Row, 1970. This classic essay was first published in *The Burlington Magazine* in 1934, introducing the theory of "disguised symbolism," which became a standard tool of art history. Panofsky was one of the great scholars of art history, and he remains one of the most readable.

Van Puyvelde, Leo. *Flemish Painting from the Van Eycks to Metsys*. New York: McGraw-Hill, 1970. Readable but by no means authoritative, this book devotes about one-fifth of its pages to the van Eycks. Reproductions vary in quality from good to very good.

C. S. McConnell

LOUIS FAIDHERBE

Born: June 3, 1818; Lille, France
Died: September 29, 1889; Paris, France
Areas of Achievement: Colonial administration and the military
Contribution: Faidherbe, through war and diplomacy, laid the foundation of France's West African empire. He stemmed the Muslim military advance in West Africa but respected Islam. He improved Senegal economically, socially, and culturally. His generalship retrieved France's honor in the Franco-German War.

Early Life

Louis Léon César Faidherbe was born at Lille, France. His father, a moderately successful merchant, suffered imprisonment under Napoleon I. Louis studied at the Universities of Lille and Douai, the École Polytechnique, and the École d'Application. In 1842, he became a lieutenant in the Engineering Corps. In Algeria, where he was stationed from 1843 to 1846 and again from 1849 to 1852, Faidherbe embraced French imperialism and became adept in warfare. He showed ingenuity in designing and supervising a fort's construction in newly occupied Bou-Saada, where he commanded for two years. While in Algeria, Faidherbe experienced an intellectual awakening. He learned Arabic and read Ibn-Khaldūn's history of the Berbers. He developed respect for Arabo-Berber culture and for Islam. Nevertheless, he supported French conquest, whatever the tactics, because it benefited the so-called barbaric peoples.

In Guadeloupe, where he was stationed in 1848 and 1849, Faidherbe turned to republicanism and negrophilism, yet he did not allow these views to interfere with promoting French interests and his own career. The engineering detachment's reduction in Guadeloupe led to his recall and another stint in Algeria. In 1852, Faidherbe became subdirector of engineers in Senegal. He participated in seizing Podor and constructing its fort, attacking Diman's capital, and reinforcing Bakel's defenses in 1854. He wrote "Les Berbères" and began learning Wolof, Pular, and Sarakolé from his Sarakolé wife. He became interested in exploring the Niger River. Admiring Faidherbe's activities, major Bordeaux firms doing business with Senegal recommended him for Senegal's governorship.

Life's Work

Faidherbe served two terms as Governor of Senegal, 1854-1861 and 1863-1865. Determined to erect a stable *Pax Francia*, he instituted an aggressive policy of conquest and expansion of trade. He took decisive steps to advance eastward from St. Louis through the Senegal River valley and the vast Sudan region to Lake Chad. He even dreamed of a French African empire stretching from the Atlantic Ocean to the Red Sea. He sought to create a firm basis for its future development culturally as well as politically and economically.

Militarily, Faidherbe first sought to protect the gum trade along the Senegal River and to quell the Moorish Trarzas, who were raiding and opposing the Wolof peasants living along the river's south bank. In February, 1855, Faidherbe ordered his forces to expel Trarza clans from Walo. War ensued with Walo, whose leadership rebuffed Faidherbe's plan to "liberate" them; in April, Faidherbe had to fight the principal Trarza warrior clans. By the end of 1855, he had overcome Walo, which became the first sub-Saharan state dismembered and annexed by France. In 1858, having employed divide-and-conquer tactics, Faidherbe made treaties with the Trarzas of southern Mauretania. The Trarzas agreed to respect French traders and to commute the controversial "customs" charges into a fixed export duty of 3 percent.

Faidherbe's endeavor to end all African control over French navigation along the Senegal River, particularly the toll at Saldé-Tébékout in central Futa-Toro, brought greater hostilities. Conflict erupted with the traditional leaders of Futa-Toro and with the Tukolor Muslim reformer and state builder al-Hājj Umar Tal. In 1858-1859, Faidherbe forced the confederation of Futa-Toro to make peace with France on French terms. Faidherbe divided the confederation into four client states of France.

Faidherbe's greatest adversary, Umar, was the charismatic leader of the Tijaniyya fraternity in West Africa. Before Faidherbe's governorship, Umar had attacked the French because of their prohibiting the firearms trade in the Senegal valley. Faidherbe resisted Umar's thrust along the Senegal. In July, 1857, Faidherbe gallantly led a small force with fixed bayonets in relieving Médine from Umar's three-month siege. In 1860, Faidherbe negotiated a demarcation line along the Bafing River with Umar's emissary and provisionally agreed to send his own envoy to discuss future relations with Umar. Faidherbe hoped that, in return for political support and supplies of firearms, Umar would permit France to enact a line of fortified trading posts from Senegal to a base for navigation on the Niger. With Umar's cooperation, Faidherbe envisioned pushing French trade and influence downstream and averting the monopoly which Great Britain, through traders in the delta, threatened to establish over the Niger. Returning as governor in 1863, Faidherbe sent Lieutenant Eugène Mage to contact Umar. Eventually Mage negotiated a treaty with Umar's successor, Ahmadu Tal, wherein Ahmadu renounced holy war against France and permitted French trade and exploration in his territories, while France allowed him to buy goods in St. Louis. While fighting Umar, Faidherbe's forces gutted the principal villages of Buoye, Kaméra, and Guidimakha, after which Faidherbe made treaties with new client rulers in each state.

As early as 1859, Faidherbe had also turned his attention to the kingdom of Cayor. His aim was to prevent its warriors' interference in the collection of peanuts by peasants and to open a trail with three small forts placed along it and a telegraph line to link St. Louis to Dakar and Gorée via the coastal route. Faidherbe first tried peaceful means but, rebuffed by Damel Biraima, he used force. When Biraima died, Faidherbe claimed that Biraima had agreed on his deathbed to France's demands. Biraima's successor, Macodu, would not recognize the treaty. Faidherbe declared war and sought to replace Macodu with Madiodio. Thereupon Lat Dior progressed in seizing power. Faidherbe's replacement, Governor Jean Jauréguiberry, allowed Lat Dior to expel Madiodio and become ruler. In his second governorship, Faidherbe moved to restore Madiodio, who ceded more territory to France. As disorder still prevailed in Cayor, Faidherbe retired Madiodio and annexed the remainder of Cayor in 1865.

Faidherbe's military successes owed much to his personal touch. In 1857, he organized the Senegalese Riflemen. He created two battalions of volunteers recruited as much as possible from the free population of Senegambia. The first recruits were paid relatively well; they served short, two-year terms, wore special, colorful uniforms, were allowed a looser discipline than that of European troops, and received traditional food. Faidherbe labored in numerous ways in Senegal. He founded a school for the sons of chiefs, and lay schools for Muslims. He established scholarships for primary education in St. Louis and secondary education in France. He built small technical schools at Dakar. He opened a museum and a newspaper at St. Louis. Faidherbe founded the Bank of Senegal, laid out St. Louis afresh as befitted a capital city, promoted the export of groundnuts, made valuable and detailed studies of the indigenous people, and founded Dakar.

After the conclusoin of his second term as Governor of Senegal, Faidherbe returned to Algeria, where he spent the years from 1865 to 1870. In addition to his military duties, he gave considerable time to writing during this period. In December, 1870, Faidherbe became Commander in Chief of the Army of the North in the Franco-Prussian War. Despite fever and exhaustion, he commanded superbly in the Battles of Pont Noyelles, Bapaume, and St. Quentin. A confirmed republican, Faidherbe in 1871 declined election to the National Assembly because of its reactionary character. In 1879, he accepted election to the Senate. In 1880, he became Grand Chancellor of the Legion of Honor. He continued his writing until his death, in 1889. After a public funeral in Paris, he was buried in Lille.

Summary

Louis Faidherbe stood center stage in modern French imperialism. He initated firm French control of the Senegal valley, which became the springboard for further expansion in West Africa. By opening the trade of Senegal, he provided the means for reaching the Niger Basin. His plan for railroad construction eventually materialized. His proposal, rejected by his superiors, for France and Great Britain, and France and Portugal mutually to arrange exchange of territories in West Africa would have created the French Gambia valley. Faidherbe grappled firmly but humanely with Islam in West Africa. He used war and diplomacy to stop the westward push of the great Al-Hājj Umar Tal. Faidherbe's policy of opposing Christian proselytism of Muslims caused a lasting prestigious francophile Muslim community and tradition in Senegal.

Faidherbe further affected West Africa. In Senegal, his governorship distinguished priorities and allocated limited resources. Faidherbe started new public works and aided the peasants. His policies of non-French settlement and restricted assimilation into French citizenship became models for French West Africa. Faidherbe accomplished still more. He reorganized the Legion of Honor and reformed its educational work. He wrote extensively on ancient Egypt, Carthage, Numidia, the Franco-Prussian War, West Africa, and army reorganization. His scholarship gained for him election to the Academy of Inscriptions and Belles-Lettres.

Bibliography
Abun-Nasr, Jamil M. *The Tijaniyya: A Sufi Order in the Modern World.* London: Oxford University Press, 1965. An excellent, impartial treatment of the movement led by Faidherbe's major foe, Umar. Clear analysis of the reasons for the clash between Faidherbe and Umar, the warfare between the French and Umarians, and the negotiations bringing peace. A fine map, footnotes, a bibliography, and an index.
Barrows, Leland C. "Faidherbe and Senegal: A Critical Discussion." *African Studies Review* 19 (April, 1976). A scholarly and detailed study of Faidherbe's governorship of Senegal. Presents the background for his work. Critical of Faidherbe's so-called radicalism, especially his stand on slavery and his ambiguity in defining the positions of blacks and mulattoes. Stresses Faidherbe's militarism as his chief contribution to the creation of French West Africa.
Cohen, William B. *Rulers of Empire: The French Colonial Service in Africa.* Stanford, Calif.: Hoover Institution Press, 1971. Cohen emphasizes Faidherbe's founding of a workable administrative organization in West Africa, which remained unchanged and, indeed, lasted with few modifications until the very end of the French occupation. Extensive endnotes and a bibliography. Contains a map, illustrations, and tables.
Hargreaves, John D. *Prelude to the Partition of West Africa.* New York: St. Martin's Press, 1963. Pinpoints Faidherbe's faith in the possibilities of penetrating the Sudan by the upper Senegal route and his freedom from strong anti-Muslim prejudice achieved during service in Algeria. Good on Anglo-French relations in West Africa. Contains a useful annotated bibliography, an index, and maps.

Howard, Michael. *The Franco-Prussian War: The German Invasion of France, 1870-1871*. New York: Macmillan, 1961. Shows that Faidherbe's object was not to defeat the enemy but to pin down the greatest possible number of Germans and, by attacks, to facilitate Paris' relief. Seventeen maps, a select bibliography, and an adequate index.

Kanya-Forstner, A. S. *The Conquest of the Western Sudan: A Study in French Military Imperialism*. Cambridge, England: Cambridge University Press, 1969. Underlines Faidherbe's vigor and his envisioning the future French African empire most clearly. Notes the declining fortunes of Senegal following his departure in 1865 but the revival of his Niger plan after 1876. Contains valuable footnotes, a bibliography, an index, and two maps.

Klein, Martin A. *Islam and Imperialism in Senegal: Sine-Saloum, 1847-1914*. Stanford, Calif.: Stanford University Press, 1968. Stresses Faidherbe's laying the foundation of France's West African empire in spite of the skepticism of France's government and its reluctance to sanction an aggressive policy. Recognizes Faidherbe's imagination. A first-rate consideration of Faidherbe's relations with the Senegambian rulers. Notes Faidherbe's compromise with slavery but his enlightened outlook toward Islam. Very good maps, charts, and lists of African rulers and French officials. Splendid glossary, notes, and bibliography.

Robinson, David. *The Holy War of Umar Tal: The Western Sudan in the Mid-Nineteenth Century*. Oxford, England: Clarendon Press, 1985. A reliable account of Faidherbe's encounter with Umar. Shows Faidherbe's ingenuity: use of intelligence reports and manufacturing his own propaganda to counter the appeal of Umar's holy war. Contains an excellent map, with tables, notes, and a bibliography.

Erving E. Beauregard

ALESSANDRO FARNESE

Born: August 27, 1545; Rome
Died: December 2-3, 1592; Arras, France
Area of Achievement: The military
Contribution: Combining prodigious military ability and political talent, Farnese came close to retaking all of the Netherlands for Spain before imperial distractions and drains on Philip's finances elsewhere combined to undermine his achievements.

Early Life

Alessandro Farnese had illustrious ancestry. His great-grandfather on his father's side, for whom he was named, was Pope Paul III. His mother, Margaret of Austria, was the natural daughter of the Emperor Charles V. Two years after his birth, his father, Ottavio Farnese, inherited the Duchy of Parma. Alessandro and his twin, Carlo (named for his maternal grandfather), were the only children of his parents' marriage. Carlo died within a few months of birth, making Alessandro the only legitimate heir to Ottavio and a treasured only child to Margaret.

In 1556, to cement the alliance between his father and Philip, the regent of Spain, Alessandro was sent to Brussels to reside at the Spanish court. For the next nine years, until his marriage and subsequent return to Parma, Alessandro would serve as a hostage to his family's good faith and would complete his education in the Low Countries and Spain. He studied for a time in the great university town of Alcalá de Henares, where his course of study, shared with his contemporaries the Crown Prince Don Carlos and his uncle Don Juan of Austria, was designed by his uncle Philip II. Although Alessandro and Don Carlos found a common interest in military science, it was his young uncle Don Juan who became his closest friend. The young Italian nobleman was well received at the Spanish court in Madrid and admired for his manners, linguistic ability, and skill in the military arts.

After the number of plans to ally the house of Farnese with other prominent families fell through, at length a suitable match was approved by his father and Philip II. In November, 1565, Alessandro married Princess Maria of Portugal. The bride was considerably older than the groom, and she was considerably more enamored of him than he was of her, but it proved a fruitful marriage, producing two sons and a daughter before Maria died. After the marriage, the young couple settled in Parma, where Alessandro found that the combination of matrimony and the quiet life made him restless. After much pleading and many frustrations, he received the opportunity to join in the Crusade against the Turks in 1571, serving under Don Juan.

Life's Work

The campaign against the Turks gave Farnese a chance to demonstrate his military prowess and personal courage. He joined the expedition with three hundred soldiers and eighty-two knights from the Duchies of Parma and Piacenza. Don Juan gave him charge of several Genoese galleys in the international fleet. Farnese acquitted himself well at the Battle of Lepanto, personally leading the boarding party which captured the treasure ship of the Turkish fleet. After this great victory, which made Don Juan a national hero, life quieted down again for Farnese until 1577, when he was given command of the relief forces sent to assist Don Juan, now governor of the rebellious Low Countries. In the Netherlands campaigns of the next fifteen years, Farnese would establish a reputation for military genius and political astuteness which would outstrip that of his illustrious uncle. Farnese's army reached the scene of the fighting in time to tip the balance in the Battle of Gembloux in December, 1577. Using a brilliantly conceived strategy, Farnese surprised the rebel army and triggered a rout which completely destroyed it. Farnese quickly became Don Juan's best and most trusted commander, and when this revered leader lay dying in October, 1578, he appointed Farnese as his interim successor. Philip II made the appointment as governor of the Low Countries permanent.

Now in his early thirties, Farnese was described as having

> black, closely-shorn hair . . . erect and bristling. The forehead was lofty and narrow. The features were handsome, the nose regularly aquiline, the eyes well opened, dark, piercing . . . he was of middle stature, well formed, and graceful in person, princely in demeanor, sumptuous and stately in apparel.

He was revered by his men and respected by his enemies for his intelligence, personal bravery, and skill.

As governor of the Low Countries, Farnese combined military genius with an effective diplomacy. Through organizational skill and the sheer force of his personality, he molded an army of disparate elements into an efficient fighting machine which struck fear into the hearts of the enemy. In particular, he was effective in his utilization of mercenary troops. As a negotiator, he utilized the knowledge of the tensions and jealousies within the Netherlands nobility, gained both from his youthful experiences there and from intelligence from an extensive network of spies. He won defections to the Spanish side using a combination of persuasion and bribery, offered with the utmost delicacy and graciousness. That not only conserved men and money but also allowed Farnese to concentrate his forces on those towns still resisting. By these methods, Farnese became the most successful of Philip's governors of the Spanish Netherlands.

Between 1579 and 1585, Farnese systematically reconquered most of the southern provinces, earning a place in history as the creator of modern Belgium. He reached the high point of his military success in the summer of 1585, with the successful culmination of the Seige of Antwerp. He seemed poised to complete his task of subjugating all the rebellious provinces until international politics, in the form of English aid, intervened in 1586. This aid stiffened Dutch resistance and turned Philip's attention toward invading England, which he believed would secure England for Catholicism, perhaps gain for him the throne, and solve the thorny problem of the Netherlands once and for all. Farnese played a major role in the preparation of the Invincible Armada. Philip requested plans for an invasion of England from his greatest sailor, the Marquis of Santa Cruz, and his greatest soldier, Alessandro Farnese. Farnese's original plan was for a secret operation ferrying some thirty thousand crack troops across the Channel in barges to link with an uprising of English Catholics. The Marquis of Santa Cruz recommended a large fleet of five hundred vessels carrying sixty thousand soldiers, capable of defeating the English fleet. Philip's plan combined parts of both. Spain would assemble a large fleet with Spanish infantry on board to escort an invasion force from the Netherlands to England.

Farnese recommended October, 1586, for the invasion, but delays in the assembly of the fleet in Lisbon made this impossible. By the time the Armada sailed in the summer of 1588, Farnese's reinforcements were greatly depleted by illness and desertion after months of inactivity. Logistical problems and communication breakdowns between Farnese and the Duke of Medina Sedonia, the Armada commander, doomed the invasion even before the defeat of the Armada at Gravelines and its destruction by storms as it attempted the circuituous voyage home.

After the Armada disaster in 1588, Farnese's position in the Netherlands became progressively weaker. Spanish finances, stretched to pay for the Armada, were chronically inadequate to meet Farnese's needs. His unpaid troops began to be hard to control. Worse, perhaps, Dutch resistance was bolstered by this clear sign that the Spanish were not invincible. Events in France, also triggered partly by the Armada, distracted Philip, with consequences harmful to the Spanish Netherlands.

The civil war in France had worsened, and with the assassinations of the Duke of Guise and the Cardinal of Lorraine at the hands of Henry III, and Henry's subsequent assassination in August, 1589, Philip saw not only a chance to defeat the Protestant forces of Henry of Navarre but also an opportunity to put himself or his heirs on the throne of France. To these ends, he put the Netherlands on the back burner and ordered Farnese to take an army into France in 1590 to relieve the Siege of Paris by Henry and the Protestants.

Farnese relieved Paris, but at the cost of a serious deterioration in his position in the Netherlands. While still struggling to regain control of the situation in the Low Countries, Farnese was again ordered into France in 1591, over his strenuous objections, to help the forces of the Catholic League. He succeeded in that, but the campaign cost him dearly, both personally and as a commander. He returned to Flanders in 1592 a sick man. He was ordered back to France in 1592 and died at Arras in December. At his death, he was unaware that Philip had sent an envoy with orders to replace Farnese and send him back to Madrid to face charges of defrauding Philip of the money sent to finance military operations in the Low Countries.

Summary

In spite of Philip's ultimate distrust and rejection of him, Alessandro Farnese served his monarch well, often at personal sacrifice. The demands of his governorship separated him from his home and family. He was unable to return to Italy when his wife died in 1577 or when his only daughter married. He became Duke of Parma and Piacenza at his father's death in 1586, but, unable to leave his post in the Netherlands, had to appoint his seventeen-year-old heir, Ranuccio, to serve in his place. An extensive correspondence between father and son indicates a high degree of interest in the affairs of Parma despite Farnese's major responsibilities in the Low Countries. Despite a growing weariness with the incessant war in the Netherlands, Farnese would not live to retire in peace to rule his inheritance. He died while obediently making one more march into France at the order of his monarch.

Bibliography

Lynch, John. *Spain Under the Hapsburgs*. 2nd ed. 2 vols. New York: New York University Press, 1981. Volume 1 addresses Farnese's career in the service of Spain. Lynch takes a very positive view of Farnese's character and abilities and is sympathetic to the constraints and frustrations under which he had to operate in dealing with Philip II. Extensive notes provide citations of mostly foreign-language sources.

Mattingly, Garrett. *The Armada*. Boston: Houghton Mifflin, 1959. The most readable account of the invincible Armada. Mattingly highlights Farnese's important role in the planning and implementation of the attempted invasion of England. Defends Farnese's actions in preparing his army to invade England, seeing his lack of preparedness to embark his men in August, 1588, as a sign of his military acumen.

Merriman, Roger Bigelow. *The Rise of the Spanish Empire in the Old World and in the New*. Vol. 4, *Philip the Prudent*. New York: Cooper Square, 1962. Addresses the reign of Philip. Contains a significant amount of material about Farnese in all aspects of his service to the Crown. Merriman's coverage of Farnese is less extensive and his writing is less colorful than that of John Motley, but his treatment of Spain and Farnese is far more objective.

Motley, John Lathrop. *The Rise of the Dutch Republic: A History*. 3 vols. New York: Harper & Brothers, 1852. Volume 3 contains extensive references to Farnese during his involvement in the Netherlands campaigns from 1577 to 1584. Motley has a strong anti-Spanish bias, but the work is useful because it is based on published narratives and documents from the period. Motley admires Farnese's military and political genius, even though it worked against what Motley considers to be the forces of modernism and progress.

_____. *The United Netherlands: A History from the Death of William the Silent to the Twelve Years' Truce, 1609*. 4 vols. London: John Murray, 1904. A continuation of the history of the Netherlands, picking up in 1584 where *The Rise of the Dutch Republic* ends. Volumes 1, 2, and 3 contain extensive discussions of Farnese's service as governor of the Low Countries from 1584 to his death in 1592. This work has the same drawbacks and strengths as Motley's other volumes.

Parker, Geoffrey. *The Dutch Revolt*. Ithaca, N.Y.: Cornell University Press, 1977. A good summary of Farnese's successes and failures in the Netherlands campaigns, based heavily on archival sources. Parker admires Farnese and ascribes much of the blame for his failures to lack of consistent financial support and leadership from Philip.

Victoria Hennessey Cummins

GUSTAV THEODOR FECHNER

Born: April 19, 1801; Gross-Särchen, Prussia
Died: November 18, 1887; Leipzig, Germany
Areas of Achievement: Philosophy and physics
Contribution: Fechner is widely regarded as the founder of psychophysics, or the science of the mind-body relation, and as a pioneer in experimental psychology. His most important contributions are a number of quantitative methods for measuring absolute and differential thresholds that are still employed by psychologists to study sensitivity to stimulation.

Early Life

Gustav Theodor Fechner was born in the village of Gross-Särchen, near Halle in southeastern Germany, the second of five children of Samuel Traugott Fechner and Johanna Dorothea Fischer Fechner. His father was a progressive Lutheran preacher, who is said to have astounded the local villagers by mounting a lightning rod on the church tower and by adopting the unorthodox practice of preaching without a wig. Although he died when Gustav was only five years old, already the young Fechner was infused with his father's fierce intellectual independence and his passion for the human spirit.

Fechner attended the *Gymnasium* at Soran, near Dresden, and was matriculated in medicine at the University of Leipzig in 1817. He was not a model student, opting to read on his own rather than attend lectures. During this period, Fechner became disenchanted with establishment views: He professed atheism and was never able to complete the doctorate which would have entitled him to practice medicine. His studies were not a waste of time, however, since he began composing satires on medicine and the materialism which flourished in Germany during this period. Some fourteen satirical works were published by Fechner under the pseudonym "Dr. Mises" between 1821 and 1876.

In 1824, Fechner began to lecture on physics and mathematics at the University of Leipzig without any remuneration. Translating scientific treatises from French into German (about a dozen volumes in six years), although onerous work, helped him to make a living. He managed to publish numerous scientific papers during this period, and a particularly important paper on quantitative measurements of direct currents finally secured for him an appointment with a substantial salary as professor of physics in 1834.

This period marked the happiest time in Fechner's life. The year before his appointment, he had married Clara Volkmann, the sister of a colleague at the university. The security of a permanent position and marital bliss did nothing to dampen his enthusiasm for hard work; an enviable social life was simply incorporated into his already cramped schedule. Evenings at the local symphony conducted by Felix Mendelssohn were regular events to which, on occasion, the Fechners were accompanied by Robert and Clara Schumann, his niece by marriage.

Fechner's idyllic life was shattered in 1839 by an illness that forced him to resign his position at the university. At first, he experienced partial blindness caused by gazing at the sun through colored glasses as part of a series of experiments on colors and afterimages; depression, severe headaches, and loss of appetite soon followed. For three years, Fechner sheltered himself in a darkened room, and his promising career seemed to be over. One day, however, he wandered into his garden and removed the bandages that had adorned his eyes since the onset of his illness. He reported that his vision not only was restored but also was more powerful than before because he could now experience the souls of flowers. After the initial trauma of restored eyesight faded, Fechner recovered with a revitalized religious consciousness. It was this newfound awareness of the importance of the human spirit that marked the beginning of Fechner's mature period.

Life's Work

The focal point of Fechner's work was a deep-seated antipathy toward materialism, or the view that nothing exists except for matter and its modifications. His first volley against materialism was the enigmatic *Nanna: Oder, Über das Seelenleben der Pflanzen* (1848; Nanna, or the soul life of plants), which advanced the notion that even plants have a mental life. Three years later, his *Zend-Avesta: Oder, Über die Dinge des Himmels und des Jenseits* (1851; *Zend-Avesta: On the Things of Heaven and the Hereafter,* 1882) proclaimed a new gospel based on the notion that the entire material universe is consciously animated and alive in every particular. The phenomenal world explored by physics, Fechner asserted, is merely the form in which inner experiences appear to one another. Since consciousness and the physical world are coeternal aspects of the same reality, materialism (or what Fechner referred to as the "night view") must be repudiated because it examines the universe in only one of its aspects.

More pertinent, Fechner submitted that his alternative "day view" dissolves the traditional problem of the mind-body relation. There is no need to worry about how the physical is converted into the mental, because mind and body are not distinct kinds of things. All that one needs is to display the functional relationship between consciousness and its physical manifestations. Since it was uncontested that physical qualities could be measured, Fechner discerned that he would have to specify a means for measuring mental properties if the scientific establishment was to be convinced that his alternative program represented a legitimate contender to materialism.

The German physiologist Ernst Heinrich Weber had submitted in 1846 that a difference between two stimuli (or an addition to or subtraction from one or the other stimulus) is always perceived as equal if its ratio to the stimulus remains the same, regardless of how the absolute size changes. If a change of one unit from five can be detected, Weber's result specifies that so can a change of ten from fifty, of one hundred from five hundred, and the like. On the morning of October 22, 1850, Fechner discovered what he regarded as the fundamental relation between the mental and the physical world. Where Weber's result was restricted to external stimulation, Fechner posited a general mathematical relationship between stimulus and sensation, such that for every increase in stimulation there is a corresponding increase in sensation. This functional relationship is now known as the Weber-Fechner law. It asserts that the psychological sensation produced by a stimulus is proportional to the logarithm of the external stimulation.

Although Fechner's law represents a development of Weber's work, he did not rely on Weber's substantive result. Indeed, it was Fechner who realized that his psychophysical principle corresponded to Weber's result and gave it the name Weber's law. Perhaps he was overly generous. Weber's result conflicts with low stimulus intensities. By incorporating the activity of the subject's sensory system into the equation, Fechner was able to overcome this difficulty.

Fechner's law is a genuine psychophysical law in the sense that it relates mental phenomena to external stimulation. Comparing it with Sir Isaac Newton's law of gravitation, Fechner laid out his ambitious program for a science of the functional relations of mind and body in his classic work, *Elemente der Psychophysik* (1860; *Elements of Psychophysics*, 1966). Along with his method for measuring the relationship between psychological and physical phenomena, Fechner refined three methods—the method of barely noticeable differences, the method of right and wrong cases, and the method of average error—for measuring thresholds, or the point at which a stimulus (or a stimulus difference) becomes noticeable or disappears. These techniques for measuring sense discrimination are still prominent in psychological research. Fechner also established the mathematical expressions of these methods and contributed to the literature a series of classical experiments on human sensitivity to external stimulation.

Fechner's program for a psychophysics attracted few converts. Vocal opponents, such as William James, the eminent American philosopher and psychologist, objected that mental properties are not quantifiable. Fechner sought to measure sensations by measuring their stimuli, but he furnished no independent evidence for the presupposition that it is sensations that are measured. This objection was significant granted that there was good reason to suppose that sensations cannot be measured. Sensations are not additive; a larger sensation is not simply a sum of smaller sensations. Anything that is not additive, Fechner's opponents declared, cannot be measured. What he had measured, rather, was observer response to stimulation; Fechner had produced an account of sensitivity and so had confused the sensation with the excitation of the subject.

These and related objections led to the downfall of psychophysics. Although Fechner's ideas were examined by Hermann von Helmholtz, Ernst Mach, and other scientists who were interested in related subjects, Fechner's attempt to place the mental on a par with the physical was dismissed as pure whimsy. The failure of Fechner's program, however, does not diminish his importance as a philosopher. Fechner's methods for measuring sensitivity were assimilated into the basis of empirical psychology. Since Fechner's methods presume that chance is a characteristic of physical systems, Fechner achieved a measure of victory over materialism. If he was right, mental phenomena could not be straightforwardly reduced to matter and its modifications.

Although Fechner continued to contribute to the literature on psychophysics, he turned to other matters late in his life. An interest in aesthetics proved to be a rather natural development of his interest in stimulation and his longstanding affection for the arts. The culmination of his work on the study of beauty was *Vorschule der Aesthetik* (1876; introduction to aesthetics), which argued that aesthetics is the study of the objects that produce aesthetic experiences. This work proved to be seminal in the history of experimental aesthetics.

Summary

Gustav Theodor Fechner was a man of great erudition—not only was he a physicist and a philosopher but also he was the author of a detailed theological theory, a poet, and a satirist. What united his diverse pursuits was a struggle to reconcile the empirical rigor of the exact sciences with a spiritual conception of the universe. Although Fechner's attempt to place consciousness on a par with the physical was rejected by the scientific community, his vision helped to lay the foundations for the emerging science of empirical psychology.

Fechner's greatest contributions, the functional proportion between sensation and stimulus and his numerous techniques for measuring psychological response to stimulation, do not compare favorably with the concept of universal gravitation. Fechner's philosophy of nature as consciously animated and alive in every particular was rejected by the scientific community, and so his contributions did not revolutionize science. Yet without his techniques for measuring psychological variables, the science of empirical psychology would not have reached maturity.

Bibliography
Boring, Edwin G. *A History of Experimental Psychology*. 2d ed. New York: Appleton-Century-Crofts, 1950. A comprehensive account of the emergence of experimental psychology. Although Boring credits Fechner with

laying the foundations for empirical psychology, he contends that it was merely an unexpected by-product of Fechner's philosophical interests.

Fechner, Gustav Theodor. *Elements of Psychophysics*. Translated with a foreword by Helmut E. Adler. New York: Holt, Rinehart and Winston, 1966. The author's introduction provides an overview of the problem concerning the mind-body relation and an outline of his program for a science of psychophysics. The translator's foreword places Fechner's contributions in their nineteenth century historical context.

James, William. *The Principles of Psychology*. New York: Henry Holt, 1890. Reprint. New York: Dover, 1950. Contains a faithful presentation of Fechner's contributions and a searching critique of his philosophical outlook. Perhaps the best indicator of why psychophysics fell into disfavor.

Savage, C. Wade. *The Measurement of Sensation: A Critique of Perceptual Psychophysics*. Berkeley: University of California Press, 1970. A thorough discussion of the central philosophical issues in the measurement of sensation. The excellent bibliography is a useful guide to the wealth of literature on this topic.

Snodgrass, Joan Gay. "Psychophysics." In *Experimental Sensory Psychology*, edited by Bertram Scharf. Glenview, Ill.: Scott, Foresman, 1975. A concise introduction to the history of psychophysical theory and its methods. For the technically minded reader, the analysis of the relationship between Weber's result and Fechner's psychophysical law helps to illustrate Fechner's contributions to the measurement of sensation.

Brian S. Baigrie

FERDINAND II

Born: July 9, 1578; Graz, Austria
Died: February 15, 1637; Vienna, Austria
Area of Achievement: Monarchy
Contribution: While Emperor of the Holy Roman Empire from 1619 to 1637, Ferdinand II sought to restore Roman Catholicism to the Protestant areas of the Empire and to assert Habsburg political hegemony throughout the Empire. His efforts directly resulted in the Thirty Years' War in Germany, one of history's most devastating wars.

Early Life

Ferdinand II was born in Graz, Austria, on July 9, 1578, the eldest son of Archduke Charles of Inner Austria (Styria) and Maria of Bavaria. The Europe into which he was born was filled not only with political struggles between dynastic, territorial states but also with religious strife between various Protestant denominations and Roman Catholics. The Holy Roman Empire itself was a microcosm of these conflicts. German princes, especially Protestant ones, and the Roman Catholic Habsburg emperor were continually at odds over the definition of the Empire. Further complicating this situation was the dream of a catholicized, consolidated Europe and Empire held by both the Austrian and the Spanish branches of the Habsburg family.

Ferdinand's father, a devout Roman Catholic and brother of the Emperor Maximilian II, was archduke of a principality which was predominantly Protestant. Of necessity, in 1578 he had granted religious guarantees in the form of a "religious pacification" to the Lutheran dominated Estates, the representative assembly of nobles of Inner Austria. Yet he was determined that his son would not be influenced by Lutheranism, which he viewed as dangerous not only spiritually but also politically. He sent Ferdinand to the Jesuit University of Ingolstadt, where the young man studied between 1590 and 1595. Also attending the university was his cousin and future brother-in-law, Maximilian I of Bavaria. It was there that Ferdinand learned the fundamental tenets which were to guide him throughout his life: unswerving loyalty to the Roman Catholic church, the responsibilities of a Christian prince, and a belief in the divine right doctrine of "one ruler, one religion." It was also there that he learned to depend upon the Jesuits for their advice and counsel, something he was to do for the remainder of his life.

With his father's death in 1590, Ferdinand, as a minor, ruled through a regency until 1596. Upon gaining power, he immediately demonstrated that he had learned his Ingolstadt lessons well. His first action was to refuse to confirm the "religious pacification" that his father had issued. He then set about restoring Roman Catholicism in his lands by expelling the Protestant preachers and teachers, closing or destroying the Protestant churches, confiscating the property of Protestant nobles, and offering nonnoble Protestants a choice of exile or conversion. This confessional absolutism resulted in Ferdinand's establishing religious uniformity within his domain within a relatively short period of time. By removing the base of support for his Protestant nobles, he was able simultaneously to destroy potential opposition to his absolutism by forcing the Estates to accede to his demands. In this undertaking, Ferdinand was confident that his was a mission in the service of the Church. His success led him to intrigue to gain the succession to the imperial throne, where he could continue his mission on a broader scale.

Life's Work

The Holy Roman Empire of the early seventeenth century was an empire in name only. Since the mid-fourteenth century, the crown of emperor had been elective, and the princes' jealously guarded their prerogatives, won at great cost. The Reformation, which had begun with Martin Luther's declarations in Saxony, had accelerated the forces of fragmentation. Religious coalitions of princes resulted in frequent wars; by 1555, the Empire was on the verge of political and religious anarchy. In that year, the Peace of Augsburg fixed the limits of Lutheranism but ignored Calvinism altogether. Afterward, weak or otherwise occupied emperors were neither able to enforce the treaty nor to enhance the power of either the Habsburgs or Roman Catholicism.

When Emperor Rudolf II died heirless in 1612, and his brother and successor Matthias appeared destined to do the same, it was deemed imperative by the Spanish-Bavarian factions at the imperial court that the best candidate be elected emperor. With Ferdinand's record of devotion to Roman Catholicism and his strong-willed leadership with his own domain to recommend him, the Archduke of Inner Austria was the obvious choice. To the German princes of all religions, the move was greeted with trepidation. Still, as the result of no small degree of behind-the-scenes manipulating, Ferdinand was crowned King of Bohemia in 1617 and of Hungary in 1618. He was elected Emperor of the Holy Roman Empire in 1619. When he moved to Vienna, he took with him his closest associates, especially his Jesuit confessor, William Lamormaini, and those who had served him well in catholicizing Inner Austria.

That such a person would be crowned particularly concerned Bohemian Protestant nobles, who had had little influence on the choice of their king. Fearing the loss of their religious privileges, held since the time of John Hus, in May, 1618, they revolted and declared the Calvinist Frederick V of the Palatinate as their choice as King of Bohemia. That was the opening event of the Thiry Years' War. Although the Bohemians briefly besieged Vienna, they were soon placed on the defensive. Ferdinand was supported by Spanish Habsburg troops and by the Catholic League of German princes under the leadership of Maximilian I of Bavaria. Opposing the Catholic forces was the Protestant Union, an amalgam of Lutheran and Calvinist princes who were divided in their support of the Bohemian rebels. Accordingly, Ferdinand was able to crush the rebels as well as to occupy the Palatinate.

During the Bohemian phase of the Thirty Years' War, many Lutheran princes had remained neutral. Ferdinand's actions after his victory was to send a corporate chill of horror through their ranks. As he had once done in Inner Austria, he now restored Bohemia to Roman Catholicism and instituted political absolutism through the Jesuits, the Inquisition, and confiscation. He executed the leaders of the revolt, destroyed the Bohemian Estates, confiscated vast tracts of land, ruined the town-centered economy, and expelled Protestants by the thousands. What had been a vibrant, Protestant, town-oriented society was transformed into a rural, agricultural latifundia under Jesuit domination. The thoroughness of the undertaking resulted in the Protestant princes of the Empire allying themselves with the Lutheran King of Denmark and declaring war on the emperor.

The Danish phase of the Thirty Years' War resulted in the virtual ascendancy of the Habsburgs over the Holy Roman Empire, something that had not existed for centuries. The long-standing weaknesses of the Austrian Habsburgs had been a shortage of income and a reliance upon the military strength of allies. The confiscations of land and the concomitant destruction of the burgher class in Bohemia had greatly added to the imperial treasury. The large-scale economic depredations resulted in a disastrous inflation which Ferdinand's advisers used to his financial advantage. Just as significant was the emergence of Albrecht Wenzel von Wallenstein as general of the imperial army. That lessened Ferdinand's reliance upon the military forces provided by his Spanish Habsburg cousins and the Catholic League. Wallenstein was a great general who completely defeated the Protestant forces by 1629 and dominated the entire German area of the Empire. He was also able to implement a system of support for his army that cost the emperor virtually nothing, thereby freeing him from dependence upon the generosity of the Catholic League.

Ferdinand, as undisputed master of the Empire, now sought to apply his fundamental tenets to the Empire itself. In March, 1629, he issued the Edict of Restitution, which ordered the return to the Roman Catholic church of all property confiscated by Protestants since the Peace of Augsburg. Had this been successful, Ferdinand would have established imperial ascendancy throughout the Empire. His action, however, succeeded only in uniting Protestant and Catholic princes against him. Their combined efforts resulted in Wallenstein's dismissal in 1630, thereby depriving the emperor of a major factor in his successes. The Edict of Restitution also resulted in further consequences. The French, who wanted to block the Habsburgs wherever possible, agreed to support financially the efforts of Gustavus II Adolphus of Sweden, who was alarmed by the strong Habsburg forces on the Baltic shoreline. In 1630, the Swedish king invaded the Empire, driving imperial and Catholic League forces back to Austria. Ferdinand recalled Wallenstein, who checked the Swedish advance. The death of Gustavus II Adolphus at Lützen in 1632 ended the brilliant skein of victories for the Protestants, and the Swedish phase of the Thirty Years' War became a virtual stalemate.

The strains of war and rule left Ferdinand prematurely aged. He acquiesced to the dismissal and assassination of Wallenstein in 1634. He then turned much of the work of government over to his very capable son, Ferdinand III. As the war had degenerated into a desultory conflict during which the civilian population suffered greatly, his son was largely responsible for the Peace of Prague (1635), which reconciled most of the German princes with the emperor. This peace effectively terminated Ferdinand's dream of a Catholic, Habsburg Holy Roman Empire. Sadly for Germany, the war, which began as a religious/political struggle within the Empire, had become a part of a European-wide war between the Bourbons and the Habsburgs. The Thirty Years' War would not end until France, Sweden, and Spain were in agreement; that would not occur until 1648. Ferdinand himself died in Vienna on February 15, 1637.

While the Thirty Years' War dominated most of Ferdinand's actions during his life as monarch, there were other aspects of his life that are worth mentioning. He was a stout, blond, blue-eyed man who was kind and benevolent to those he loved. He was devoted to his family. He was twice married, in 1600 to Maria Anna of Bavaria, sister of Maximilian I, and, following her death in 1616, in 1622 to Eleonora Gonzaga, sister of Vincenzo II of Mantua. He was the father of six children. In his personal life, he was frugal; in his public life, he was as ceremonious as the occasion demanded. He was also a patron of the arts, especially music and the theater. He did not look the part of a zealot, but he most assuredly was as far as his religion was concerned.

Summary

The significance of Ferdinand II in history is based upon his unyielding belief in the Roman Catholic faith. Although he could be kind and benevolent on some matters, his Catholic convictions were an all-consuming passion. He lived the Catholic life; he was pious and virtuous. He attended masses at all hours of the day and night; he favored priests and relics; he went on pilgrimages; and he relied on his Jesuit confessors and advisers. Just as devoutly as he believed in his faith, so too did he devoutly believe that Protestantism meant heresy and disloyalty. Therefore, Protestantism had to be ruthlessly extirpated. Had he been in a position of insignificance, his zealotry would have perhaps been inconvenient, but not dangerous. As an archduke and an emperor, his actions led to great changes in Central Europe.

While the Thirty Years' War was for many a political conflict, there is no disputing that for Ferdinand it was for Catholicism first and political gain second. Other powers may have used the war for political gains; Ferdinand used it for the Counter-Reformation. No other explanation of his activities in Inner Austria, his crusade in Bohemia, or his issuance of the Edict of Restitution can suffice. Perhaps naïve, and certainly bigoted, Ferdinand missed a golden opportunity to unite or at least to control the Holy Roman Empire for the Habsburgs. In sum, Ferdinand II was an exceptionally diligent monarch who worked long hours with his ministers in an effort to carry through his fundamental tenets.

Bibliography

Evans, R. J. W. *The Making of the Habsburg Monarchy, 1550-1700*. New York: Oxford University Press, 1979. Evans focuses upon the Central European Counter-Reformation and its socioeconomic consequences, as well as upon the interaction between regions of the Empire and the imperial government. His prime focus is upon intellectual and social history.

Königsberger, H. G. *The Habsburgs and Europe, 1516-1660*. Ithaca, N.Y.: Cornell University Press, 1971. Studies the history and the aims of the Habsburgs during the century and a half of their dominance of the European state system. Focuses primarily upon the Spanish Habsburgs, but the Thirty Years' War is covered in some detail.

Lockyer, Roger. *Habsburg and Bourbon Europe, 1470-1720*. New York: Longman Group, 1974. An excellent introduction to the themes, events, and personages that dominated Europe during the period discussed.

Parker, Geoffrey, ed. *The Thirty Years' War*. New York: Routledge & Kegan Paul, 1984. Ten historians collaborated to provide this account of the war. It is the best single work for providing the reader with an overview of the conflict and with pertinent bibliographical information.

Steinberg, S. H. *The Thirty Years War and the Conflict for European Hegemony, 1600-1660*. New York: W. W. Norton, 1967. This eclectic and very readable account of the period views the Thirty Years' War as part of the European-wide struggle for a balance of power. According to Steinberg, religion, while important, was secondary to the political motives of the combatants.

Wedgwood, C. V. *The Thirty Years War*. London: Jonathan Cape, 1938. Wedgwood follows the traditional German interpretation of a largely German war which devastated the German economy and German life. According to this thesis, the war was the last of the religious wars which began in the 1520's and which was exploited by outside powers for their own political ends.

William S. Brockington, Jr.

FERDINAND II and ISABELLA I

Ferdinand II

Born: March 10, 1452; Sos, Spain
Died: January 23, 1516; Madrigalejo, Spain

Isabella I

Born: April 22, 1451; Madrigal, Spain
Died: November 26, 1504; Medina del Campo, Spain
Areas of Achievement: Monarchy, the military, politics, and government
Contribution: The Catholic monarchs directed Spain's transition from medieval diversity to national unity. They achieved governmental and ecclesiastical reform, and established a continuing Spanish presence in Italy, America, and northern Africa.

Early Lives

Ferdinand and Isabella were each born to the second, much younger wives of kings. A much older half brother stood between each of them and the throne; their siblings died with considerable suspicion of poisoning. Thus the young prince and princess grew up the focus of intrigue. Their marriage represented an alliance between Ferdinand's father, John II of Navarre (from 1458 of Aragon), and a faction of Castilian nobles, including his mother's kinsmen, the Enríquez family, and Isabella's protector, Archbishop of Toledo, Alfonso Carrillo.

John II of Castile, Isabella's father, died when she was three and her brother Alfonso less than a year old. Their mother, Isabella of Portugal, withdrew to her cities of Arevalo and Madrigal to maintain her independence. This dowager queen, a woman of exemplary piety, became increasingly unstable, and King Henry IV, Isabella's half brother, brought the children to his court in 1461. In 1462, young Isabella stood sponsor at the baptism of the king's daughter Juana. Henry had married Juana of Portugal, mother of Princess Juana, within a year after his divorce from his first, childless wife, Blanche of Navarre, on the grounds of his own impotence. Princess Isabella and her brother Alfonso, who died in 1465, became involved in several plots that included challenging the legitimacy of Princess Juana, deposition of Henry, and various plans for Isabella's marriage, which led to her union with Ferdinand of Aragon in 1469.

Her isolated childhood and her preferred semi-isolation at Henry's gay court caused Isabella to grow up pious and rather bookish. Gonzalo Chacón, chosen by their mother to supervise Isabella and Alfonso, proved a guiding influence in her early life and later. This man had been a confidant of Álvaro de Luna, John II's great Constable of Castile. A description of the princess at the time of her marriage tells of golden red hair, gray eyes with long lashes and arched brows, and a red-and-white complexion. A long neck and slim, erect posture set off her face and gave an effect of dignity and majesty.

Ferdinand early became the focus of a quarrel between his father and his own half brother, Prince Charles of Viana, who was supported by the City of Barcelona. Almost from birth, the boy participated in Barcelona's elaborate ceremonies, and at the age of ten he and his mother, Queen Juana Enríquez, were besieged in Gerona by the Barcelona army and rescued by his father. Though Ferdinand had tutors and attendants to teach him to read and ride, his father was his great teacher. John II of Aragon involved his son in war and government as much as the boy's years allowed. Aragonese politics involved the same kind of intrigue as Castile's but were complicated by the complex nature of the Crown, which included Aragon, Catalonia, Valencia, Mallorca, Sardinia, and Sicily. In 1468, John II entitled Ferdinand King of Sicily, a position that gave him superior rank to his bride and that gave them both status in their struggle against Princess Juana and her uncle-fiancé, King Afonso V of Portugal, to win Castile.

Ferdinand's portraits show a red-and-white complexion with dark eyes and a full mouth. He wore his dark brown hair rather long, in the style of the day; his hairline began early to recede noticeably. In riding, warfare, athletics, and dancing, he performed with perfect skill and ease.

Life's Work

During the first decade of their marriage, Ferdinand and Isabella struggled to establish themselves in Castile, first to gain the good graces of Henry IV and, after his death, to dominate the barons. Men like Carrillo changed sides as it suited their interests; having supported Isabella, Carrillo turned to Princess Juana when it became clear that the newlyweds would not take direction from him. An incident in the early stages of the war against Portugal limns the characters of the young couple. When cautious, shrewd, self-confident Ferdinand withdrew, avoiding a confrontation at Toro in July, 1475, rather than risk defeat, his insecure, impetuous, chivalric wife gave him a very chilly homecoming. His victory on March 1, 1476, near Toro (at Peleagonzalo) was more a victory of maneuver than a battle, and historians dispute the question of who actually won. In this period, Isabella played a role of great importance. For example, when the Master of the Crusading Order of Santiago died in 1475, she pressured its members into accepting her husband as their leader. That same year, the monarchs put under royal control the militia and treasury of the Holy Brotherhood, the medieval alliance of Castilian cities. With these forces and loyal barons, they subdued the others. Nobles who would not accept royal authority had their castles destroyed. By 1481, Ferdinand and Isabella stood masters of Castile. The longevity of

Ferdinand's father, who died in 1479, preserved control in Aragon, while Ferdinand and Isabella won Castile.

The next decade brought the glorious conquest of the Kingdom of Granada. In the medieval tradition, King Abu-l-Hassán had adopted an aggressive attitude during the Castilian disorders; now his son Muhammad XI (or Boabdil to the Spanish) faced a united Aragon and Castile. In the period 1482-1492, the "Catholic Monarchs," as Pope Alexander VI called Ferdinand and Isabella, waged continuing warfare against the Muslims. Ferdinand headed Castilian forces in this great adventure and so consolidated his personal leadership. Isabella's role in providing funds, men, and supplies confirmed the essential importance of their partnership. Muhammad's surrender ended the 780-year Christian reconquest of Iberia and brought Spain's middle ages to an end; that same year, sponsorship of the first Christopher Columbus voyage and a decree expelling Jews from Castile signaled the beginning of Spain's modern age.

The years from the victory in Granada to Isabella's death brought signal triumph and personal disappointment. In 1495, Ferdinand and Isabella launched a war commanded by a Castilian nobleman, Gonzalo Fernández de Córdoba, against Aragon's traditional enemy, France, for control of the Kingdom of Naples. Continued by their successors, this struggle brought Spain's domination of Italy. A series of marriage alliances further strengthened them against France. The Portuguese alliance always remained paramount. Their eldest daughter, Isabella, married, first Prince John, son of John II of Portugal, and, after his death, King Manuel I. When this Isabella died, Manuel married her sister María. Typical of the new era of peaceful relations with Portugal, the 1494 Treaty of Tordesillas amicably adjusted the 1493 Papal Line of Demarcation which, consequent to the Columbus voyage, had divided the non-European world into Spanish and Portuguese hemispheres. Ferdinand and Isabella's only son, John (who died in 1497), married a Habsburg and their second daughter, Joan, married Philip of Burgundy, who was also a Habsburg. Ferdinand and Isabella's daughter Catherine (of Aragon) embarked on a tragic career in Tudor England as wife of Prince Arthur and later of King Henry VIII.

After Isabella's death, her husband continued their life's work, his course shaped by a series of accidents. Castile passed to the control of Joan and her Habsburg husband, and Ferdinand married a second wife, Germaine de Foix. Ferdinand and Germaine's son died soon after his birth. Joan's mental instability and her husband's death in 1506 restored Ferdinand's position as regent, now for Joan's son Charles (later King Charles I of Spain and Emperor Charles V). Yet only Ferdinand's military defeat of the Andalusian nobles made the regency effective. A series of ventures in North Africa culminated in the 1509 conquest of Oran, financed by Archbishop of Toledo Francisco Jiménez de Cisneros. A final triumph came in the conquest of

Spanish Navarre in 1512, realizing the claim of Queen Germaine to that region. This conquest rounded out Spain's national boundaries; for the rest of his life, Ferdinand devoted himself to aligning Spanish policy with that of the Habsburgs.

Summary

In many ways, Ferdinand II and Isabella I superintended a transition to the national and cultural unity that provided the base for Spain's modern world influence. Though they left local affairs largely in the hands of barons and city oligarchies, the Royal Council provided a protobureaucratic center. This council took charge of the Holy Brotherhood, and one of its members became president of the *Mesta*, Castile's great sheepherders' guild. Through meetings of the Cortes and the junta of the Holy Brotherhood, the monarchs maintained contact with representatives of the cities, and *corregidores* acted as their agents in the cities. If Spain's laws remained as diverse as the multiplicity of its political units, Ferdinand and Isabella ordered compilations of Castile's medieval laws and their own proclamations as a guiding framework. They themselves traveled constantly through their kingdoms, providing personal justice.

Their strengthening of the Catholic culture and fostering of a Spanish national type made Spain a leader in the Catholic Reformation in Europe and the world. A papal decree in 1478 established the Spanish Inquisition under royal control to ferret out crypto-Jews. Combined with edicts in 1492 and 1502 obliging Jews and Muslims respectively either to convert or to leave Castile, the Inquisition largely established a Christian norm in place of medieval cultural diversity. Later it repressed Protestantism in Spain. In Aragon, Ferdinand reactivated the older Papal Inquisition, but the appointment of Tomás de Torquemada as High Inquisitor for both kingdoms and the establishment of a Council of the Inquisition made it a national institution. Appointment in 1495 of Isabella's confessor, the ascetic, selfless Jiménez de Cisneros as Archbishop of Toledo, in contrast to the lusty and ambitious Carrillo, acted to reform and control the Church. (Jiménez became High Inquisitor in 1507.) Jiménez de Cisneros' reform of the Spanish Franciscans and his founding of the University of Alcalá de Henares show a more positive dimension. The university adopted the Erasmian approach of using Renaissance scholarship for religious purposes.

Certainly no act of the reign had greater long-range impact than sponsorship of Columbus. Though Castile had engaged in conquest of the Canary Islands since 1479, the American voyages looked beyond Africa to world empire. Hampered by very limited revenues, Ferdinand and Isabella continued their sponsorship of this enterprise when significant monetary returns seemed problematical. The new American empire posed unprecedented problems of distance and dimension involving treatment of the Indians and control of Columbus' enormous claims as discoverer. Their development of viceregal authority went beyond anything in the tradition of Aragon, the conquest of the Canaries, or the feudalism of the Reconquest.

Bibliography
Hillgarth, J. N. *The Spanish Kingdoms, 1250-1516.* Vol. 2, *1410-1516, Castilian Hegemony.* Oxford, England: Clarendon Press, 1978. A work of solid scholarship, following recent Spanish interpretations with special emphasis on the reign of Ferdinand and Isabella. The great advantage of the book lies in its consideration of events in Aragon and the other Spanish kingdoms.
Kamen, Henry. *Spain, 1469-1714: A Society in Conflict.* London: Longman, 1983. This book reviews material covered in J. H. Elliott's 1963 book, *Imperial Spain.* Provides an up-to-date view of Spain's Golden Age. Both utilize recent Spanish scholarship and considerably revise older interpretations. Kamen, also author of a book on the Spanish Inquisition, here pays attention to the needs of students, providing both an introduction and a reference tool.
Lunenfeld, Marvin. *Keepers of the City: The Corregidores of Isabella I of Castile.* Cambridge, England: Cambridge University Press, 1987. Based on archival research, this book is the sort of institutional history that has made possible the new interpretations of the subject. Lunenfeld has also written a similar book on the Council of the Holy Brotherhood.
Merriman, R. B. *The Rise of the Spanish Empire in the Old World and the New.* Vol. 2, *The Catholic Kings.* New York: Macmillan, 1918. A monumental work with narrative detail not found elsewhere in English, but for this reign the book is otherwise superseded by the books of Hillgarth and the others cited above. Its interpretations are outmoded, and its facts not always reliable. Its long reign as the standard English work on Ferdinand and Isabella partly explains the even longer reign of William Prescott's biography.
Miller, Townsend. *The Castles and the Crown: Spain, 1451-1555.* New York: Coward & McCann, 1963. Although written with a lively style and based on chronicles, this book does not take account of recent scholarship. Its interpretations are of the Prescott school.
Nader, Helen. *The Mendoza Family in the Spanish Renaissance, 1350-1550.* New Brunswick, N.J.: Rutgers University Press, 1979. A work of solid scholarship with a very important focus on a great baronial family. The Mendozas and their ilk were as important in this reign as the Kingdoms of Castile and Aragon.
Prescott, William H. *History of the Reign of Ferdinand and Isabella, the Catholic.* 3d rev. ed. 3 vols. New York: Hooper, Clark, 1841. The pioneering work in English that is also the longest. Many of Prescott's

interpretations and his scholarship are inevitably and completely outdated. The book, for example, overemphasizes Isabella's importance by denigrating Ferdinand. Like Miller's books, it can still be read for pleasure.

Walsh, William Thomas. *Isabella of Spain, the Last Crusader.* New York: Robert M. McBride, 1930. Deserves attention as a long, detailed work that is a biography of the queen, not a history of the reign or a study of Spain in her times.

Paul Stewart

PIERRE DE FERMAT

Born: August 17, 1601; Beaumont-de-Lomagne, France
Died: January 12, 1665; Castres, France
Area of Achievement: Mathematics
Contribution: Fermat, though a lawyer and jurist, made several pivotal discoveries in the foundations of analytical geometry, differential calculus, and probability theory. His main achievements, however, were in number theory, in which he established the basis of the modern theory and formulated two fundamental theorems that still bear his name.

Early Life

Pierre de Fermat was born in a provincial village northwest of Toulouse in the Gascony region of southern France. His father, Dominique, was a well-to-do leather merchant and petty official; his mother, Claire, née de Long, belonged to a prominent family of jurists. Pierre, his brother Clement, and his two sisters acquired primary and secondary education at the local monastery of Grandselve. Pierre then attended the University of Toulouse, from which, having decided on a legal career, he entered the University of Law at Orléans, where he earned a bachelor of civil laws degree in 1631. Shortly before graduation, he purchased an office in the Parlement of Toulouse; shortly after, he married a distant cousin, Louise de Long, and settled down to a long and apparently uneventful career as a civil official and legislator. For the next thirty-four years, he fathered five children, served capably in office, and overtly did little to distinguish himself. Few records remain of his life, beyond the normal transactions of the bourgeois.

The single remaining portrait of Fermat, apparently done when he was around forty-five, shows a round, somewhat fleshy face, with arched brows, a large straight nose, and a small, rather delicate mouth. The large eyes, the most prominent feature of his face, seem unfocused, as though staring at something deep within. On the whole, he looks remote, withdrawn, aloof, and a bit patrician—a proper image for a provincial jurist.

He looked undistinguished largely because he wanted to. His life spanned a turbulent period in French history, when distinction often led to disgrace or at least to difficulty. Fermat avoided this adroitly, and he therefore gained stability and a measure of leisure, allowing him to pursue his real interest: mathematics. Mathematics had not yet become a profession, hence, it could be pursued as a hobby. Fermat became one of the greatest mathematical hobbyists of his or of any other time. His correspondence is filled with the most daring mathematical speculations ever recorded, all the more striking because he strenuously resisted publication or any kind of public recognition. Publication might have jeopardized his stability, his security, and his serenity.

Life's Work

Fermat's major achievements lie in the field of his great love, number theory; but he anticipated these with striking discoveries in other analytical areas, which, characteristically, he neglected to publish, thereby allowing others—notably René Descartes and Blaise Pascal—to gain credit that was properly his. Thus, for example, he anticipated the fundamental discovery underlying the differential calculus thirteen years before the birth of Sir Isaac Newton and seventeen years before that of Gottfried Leibniz; yet they are commonly given independent credit for that finding. He did this in a characteristic way. The basic problem of differentiation is to determine the rate of change of a system at a particular instant in time. This is commonly represented by the attempt to draw the straight-line tangent to the graph of a continuous function—that is, to discover how to construct a line tangent to any point of a given curve. After Descartes had invented a coordinate system, constructing the graph itself was relatively easy. The difficulty lay in determining the tangent, for it changed at every point in the curve. The inventors of the calculus solved this simply by visualizing what would happen to a given tangent as it approached a given point—that is, by seeing how the tangent changed as the distance between it and the point dwindled to nothing. Once they had seen this in their imagination, they could proceed to create algebraic or graphical means of specifying it; this was done by determining the limiting values of the y-component divided by the x-component as both approached zero simultaneously. This sounds complicated, and is extremely difficult to visualize without graphic demonstration and some knowledge of trigonometry, but these problems had real physical applications which had to be determined before modern physics and the technology based on it could be carried out.

Fermat made a second discovery in this new differential calculus closely related to the first. Basic algebra presents equations in which one quantity is expressed in terms of another: $y = 4t$ for example. This means that the value of y can be determined by calculating the value of $4t$. From another point of view, the value of y depends on t, or y depends on t, or y is a function of t: $y = f(t)$, in algebraic notation. In this particular instance, the function can be graphed as a straight line, and the calculations for applications are quite simple. When the graph is a complex curve, however, in many practical applications it is necessary to find the maximum and minimum values of the function. Fermat derived a way to do this simply, both graphically and algebraically. Beginning with his earlier observations about tangents, Fermat reasoned that the highest and lowest values of any function would be found at the highest and lowest points of the curve. Observation would show this easily on a graph. Furthermore, these tops and bottoms would occur only where the tangents became parallel to the horizontal axis—that is, where the equation of the tangent became zero. To find them, he had only to set the tangent equation equal to zero and calculate the point. This discovery, relatively simple, had vital and far-reaching effects.

Fermat himself occasionally dabbled in particular applications of his general theorems. In one case, he turned his attention to optics and the problems of determining how a ray of light will behave when it reflects from or is refracted through a surface. In the process of studying this, he discovered what has come to be called the principle of least time, which is the fundamental principle of quantum theory, particularly in its mathematical aspect of wave mechanics. A ray of light passes from point A to point B, undergoing several reflections and passing through several surfaces. Fermat proved that regardless of deviations, the path the ray must take can be calculated by a single factor: The time spent in passage must be a minimum. On the strength of this theorem, Fermat deduced that, in reflection, the angle of incidence equals the angle of reflection and, in refraction, the sine of the angle of incidence equals a constant multiple of the angle of refraction in moving from one medium to another.

Fermat was also an innovator in analytic geometry, anticipating Descartes in the process but characteristically refusing to declare his precedence by publishing his findings. In fact, he went beyond Descartes and made the crucial applications on which all further progress in the discipline depended. Fermat was the first to postulate a space of three dimensions, thereby laying the basis for modern multidimensional analytic geometry. Like most of his other discoveries, this marked a true turning point, for the great difficulty in this method of analysis is going from two to three dimensions. Moreover, in making this transition, Fermat also corrected Descartes in the classification of curves by degrees of equation. Descartes, assuming proprietary rights as the assumed inventor of the system, at first balked at accepting the corrections of an amateur but had to concede in the end. Yet true credit for this invention was denied Fermat for centuries. Similarly, not until 1934 did anyone discover that Newton had borrowed the fundamental theorem of the differential calculus from Fermat.

Any of these discoveries alone would have sufficed for the life's work of any mathematical genius. For Fermat, however, these were mere incidents; his principal mathematical occupation was the theory of numbers, a field in which he made his major achievements. This field concerns itself with the most basic of all topics in mathematics: the simple whole numbers and their common relationships and properties. Although basic to mathematics and simple in the beginning, the problems presented here have led to the most abstract theories, all of which have not yet been explicated.

Fermat began by concentrating on prime numbers—those numbers greater than one which have no divisors other than 1 and the number itself: 2, 3, 5, 7, 11, and the like. In working with these numbers, Fermat routinely presented his theorems without proofs, or without proving them completely, or simply with hints about the methods he used to discover them. Furthermore, he sometimes happened to be completely—or partly—wrong. Something like that took place in his formulation of what came to be known as Fermat's numbers: the series 3, 5, 17, 257, 65537. All of these numbers are found by the same process of raising 2 to a further power of 2 itself raised to a sequential power of 2. Fermat asserted that every number so found is a prime. He was right for the first five numbers, but the next two that follow are not primes. Thereafter in the sequence, there seems to be no general rule, though that could not be determined until the development of modern computers. The amazing point is this: Fermat was wrong, but these numbers still turned out to have significant applications in physics.

Fermat's greatest accomplishments in number theory are found in two theorems that still bear his name: Fermat's theorem and his last theorem. The first can be stated simply: If n is any whole number and p is any prime, then $n^p - n$ is divisible by p. Typically, he gave this without proof, and one was not presented until fifty years after his death. Yet the proof depends on only two facts: that a given whole number can be made only by multiplying primes, and that if a prime divides a product of two numbers then it divides at least one of them. Yet it also depends on the use of the principle of mathematical induction, which was first formulated during Fermat's lifetime. That Fermat had formulated this principle independently is clear from this theorem and from his description of a method he called "infinite descent," already suggested in the account given of his method of tangents.

Fermat's so-called last theorem grew out of his fascination with the kind of equations called Diophantine—equations with two or more unknowns requiring whole number solutions. Fermat accomplished much with these equations. For example, he asserted that the equation $y^3 = x^2 + 2$ has only one solution: $y = 3$, $x = 5$. As usual, he gave no proof; yet he must have had one, since one eventually emerged. This has been true of all the theorems he posited, with the single exception of the last theorem, which states that there are no solutions to equations of the type $x^n + y^n = z^n$. Yet, though no proofs have been found, neither have any solutions, even by computers.

Summary

The significance of someone such as Pierre de Fermat is difficult to state directly or simply, since he worked solely in the area of abstract mathematics and produced few tangible or readily measurable results. It is even more difficult with him than with other mathematicians because he refused publicity; at his death, few could have been aware that one of the world's truly seminal minds was passing away. Furthermore, many of his discoveries were paralleled by other workers; it would be easy to dismiss him as interesting but not particularly significant, but such a judgment would not do him justice.

So many of his discoveries were pivotal: They provided a necessary impetus to the opening of several new and rich fields of inquiry. While it is true that others paralleled some of his work, in most cases he provided the catalyst. In analytic geometry, for example, Descartes preceded him in print, but Fermat made the absolutely necessary transition to the third dimension; he also corrected Descartes' formulation of the degrees of the equations. Without these contributions, Cartesian analysis could not have become a formidable instrument in the development of mechanics and the incipient engineering of the Industrial Revolution. Similarly, Newton and Leibniz could not have begun differential calculus without Fermat's work on tangents and slopes. Finally, whole areas of analysis in physics remain indebted to Fermat.

Bibliography
Beiler, Albert H. *Recreations in the Theory of Numbers: The Queen of Mathematics Entertains*. 2d ed. New York: Dover, 1966. Less technical in approach than many books in number theory. Beiler provides a solid introduction to the problems that Fermat attacked and his methods of solution. Fairly readable but requires some advanced mathematics.
Bell, Eric T. *Men of Mathematics*. New York: Simon & Schuster, 1937. The best general introduction to the major figures in classical mathematics. Demands little more than a general aptitude for mathematical thought. His discussion of Fermat covers all major topics with style and wit.
Burton, David M. *The History of Mathematics: An Introduction*. Boston: Allyn & Bacon, 1984. This is a standard text in the history of mathematics, written for readers with some knowledge of advanced mathematics. The approach is oriented toward problem solving, so that it re-creates the process of mathematical discovery, which is particularly good for understanding Fermat.
Kline, Morris. *Mathematical Thought from Ancient to Modern Times*. New York: Oxford University Press, 1972. An excellent general history of mathematics, this work pays more attention to the general relation of mathematics to cultural background than most. It contains a clear, succinct account of Fermat's contributions, but it does not treat his work as an entity.
Mahoney, Michael Sean. *The Mathematical Career of Pierre de Fermat (1601-1665)*. Princeton, N.J.: Princeton University Press, 1973. A good work for the professional historian of mathematics or science. Can be used profitably by the general reader because of the quality of the writing and the clarity of the exposition. The mathematical explanations are fully detailed and in general not overly technical.

James Livingston

JOHANN GOTTLIEB FICHTE

Born: May 19, 1762; Rammenau, Saxony
Died: January 27, 1814; Berlin, Prussia
Area of Achievement: Philosophy
Contribution: Fichte's philosophy of ethical idealism served as the pivotal theory in the development of Idealism within the German philosophical community. His emendations of Immanuel Kant's conception of the human mind paved the way for the development of Absolute Idealism by Georg Wilhelm Friedrich Hegel.

Early Life

Johann Gottlieb Fichte was born into poverty. His father, Christian Fichte, managed only a meager living by making and selling ribbons. At an early age, Johann displayed severe conscientiousness, stubbornness, and tremendous intellectual talents. As legend has it, a local nobleman, Baron von Miltitz, missed the Sunday sermon and was informed that Johann could recite it verbatim. The baron was so impressed with this feat that he undertook to have the poor boy formally educated. Fichte was sent to the school at Pforta (1774-1780). This was followed by studies in theology at the Universities of Jena, Wittenberg, and Leipzig. No longer supported by Miltitz, Fichte was forced to terminate his education in 1784 and support himself by tutoring. Yet his proud temperament and radical ideas forced him to change locations frequently. In 1788, he traveled to Zurich as a tutor for a wealthy hotel owner. There he befriended Johann Kasper Lavater, the most important pastor of Zurich, with whom he came to share theological interests. Lavater in turn introduced him to Inspector Hartman Rahn (a brother-in-law of the poet Friedrich Klopstock). Fichte fell in love with the inspector's daughter Johanna. Because of his financial situation, however, they remained unmarried for several years.

Life's Work

During his engagement, Fichte studied the work of Immanuel Kant, the dominant philosopher in Germany during this period and the figure responsible for Fichte's intellectual development. Initially, Fichte endorsed the doctrine of determinism. He became convinced, however, that a philosophical reconciliation between determinism and human freedom was possible within a Kantian framework. In fact, Fichte was so enthusiastic about Kant's philosophy that he traveled to Königsberg to meet the aging savant but received a rather cold reception.

In spite of this rebuff, Fichte immediately went to work on his first major philosophical treatise, *Versuch einer Kritik aller Offenbarung* (1792; *Attempt at a Critique of All Revelation*, 1978), in which he interpreted revealed religion in terms of Kant's moral theory. He argued that the experience of duty (the analysis of which he deduced from Kant) is the real supernatural element in human life; in short, one's experience of the moral law is one's experience of the divine. Thus, revealed religion amounts to an acknowledgment of being bound by a principle (of morality) which cannot be deduced from the world of sensation.

When the work was published, the author's name was omitted and the reading public assumed that Kant was the author. Eventually, Kant denied authorship, praised the work, and cited the rightful author. This error on the part of the publisher made Fichte's career. The year after publication he married Johanna.

After their marriage, Fichte and his wife continued to live in Switzerland. During this time, Fichte published two pamphlets anonymously, *Zurückforderung der Denkfreiheit von der Fürsten Europens* (1793; reclamation of the freedom of thought from the princes of Europe) and *Beitrag zur Berichtigung der Urteile des Publikums über die französische Revolution* (1793; contributions designed to correct the judgment of the public on the French Revolution). In these works, he was influenced by Gotthold Ephraim Lessing's concerns with freedom of thought and toleration and defended the ideal of free speech as an inalienable right. Unfortunately, these political views earned for him the label of a radical.

In 1794, at the age of thirty-two, he was appointed to a professorship at the University of Jena on the recommendation of Johann Wolfgang von Goethe. Fichte had been working on foundational problems in epistemology and metaphysics for some time and now combined these domains of philosophical investigation into a science of knowledge, the *Wissenschaftslehre*. His first major texts on the subject, *Über den Begriff der Wissenschaftslehre* and *Grundlage der gesamten Wissenschaftslehre* (combined translation as *The Science of Knowledge*, 1868), were published the same year of his appointment.

Kant lies at the basis of all Fichte's writings, but even though Fichte embraced Kant's moral philosophy, he completely rejected Kant's metaphysical notion of the thing-in-itself (*Ding-an-sich*). This concept refers to that which lies "behind" and causes experience. Yet there can be no answer to the question of whether the world is identical to the way it is experienced (since an answer would entail taking a viewpoint which stands above experience and measuring its correspondence). Since one cannot know in principle if there is perfect correspondence between one's experience and the thing which causes that experience, one is forced to conclude that the thing-in-itself is absolutely unknowable. Since Fichte rejected the notion of such a cause of experience, only the phenomenal realm was left. This is the starting point of all idealistic philosophies, the world as it appears in one's experience.

The great problem for Fichte was to account for the fact that experiences are of two sorts, namely subjective and objective, or what appears as coming from one's own mind and what does not. The philosopher conceptually isolates the two fundamental facts of experience, the subject and the object, and attempts to explain all experience in terms of one or the other. The attempt which begins with the object (of experience) must ultimately make recourse to the thing-in-itself and is labeled dogmatism by Fichte. The other approach, idealism, begins with the subject (of experience) and explains experience ultimately through recourse to the thought which lies behind the conscious subject. Only this approach allows for freedom of action. Most important, Fichte argued that the choice between these two is ultimately based on the character of the philosopher. Since freedom belongs to the realm of the subject, a philosopher aware of and concerned with the fact of freedom will choose idealism.

Within this general idealistic approach, Fichte argued that there are three fundamental principles which characterize the metaphysical structure of the universe. All the particular sciences are derived from these principles, which do not admit of further justification or grounding. The first, and logically ultimate principle, is "the ego posits itself," or, in effect, reality is conceived of as activity. Fichte has already ruled out the thing-in-itself, so reality is not ultimately material, it is ideal, or thought or spirit. Yet even as ideal, the fundamental nature of reality is not substance, it is thought activity. This activity is the absolute ego, by which Fichte does not mean the individual self, soul, "I," or whatever might be meant by the term "ego" in contemporary psychology. He means the primordial, total, infinite activity of existence. The second principle is that this prime activity creates for itself a "field." The transcendental ego posits the non-ego and in so doing limits and defines itself by creating the domain within which it realizes itself. The third principle is that the absolute spirit posits a limited ego in opposition to a limited non-ego. One now has the particular subjects and objects of empirical knowledge, that is, knowers and what is known.

In Kant's philosophy, the concept of the transcendental ego had served the function of making the experience and moral action of the individual possible. Fichte argued that a transexperiential, unindividuated ego was the ground or source of all being, including finite, experiencing selves.

In the following years, Fichte developed the ethical aspect of his philosophy. In 1796, he published *Grundlage des Naturrechts nach Principien der Wissenschaftslehre* (*The Science of Rights*, 1886, 1889) and in 1798 he published *Das System der Sittenlehre nach den Principien der Wissenschaftslehre* (*The Science of Ethics as Based on the Science of Knowledge*, 1897).

In Fichte's moral philosophy, the choices of the individual are expressions of the striving of the absolute ego, if the individual acts in accord with the moral law. The free activity of the absolute spirit has as its end increased self-determination or definition (as free, self-defining activity). Since the absolute ego expresses its free, determining activity through individual selves, each individual self strives to determine itself to strive after complete freedom. Thus, freedom itself becomes the end of moral activity. With these developments of his moral philosophy, Fichte had become the preeminent philosopher in Germany.

While at Jena, Fichte coedited a monthly philosophical journal, the *Philosophisches Journal einer Gesellschaft teutscher Gelehrten*. In 1798, he published an article in this journal entitled "Concerning the Foundation of Our Belief in Divine Government of the World," in which he argued that if the world is considered from a standpoint outside itself, then it is seen to be only a "reflection of our own activity." Accordingly, God is not needed to explain the existence of the sensed world. Fichte iterated an identification of God with the moral order of the universe (equating God with the absolute ego). On the basis of these claims, he was charged, in a series of anonymous pamphlets, with atheism and unfitness for teaching. The Saxon government ordered the Universities of Leipzig and Wittenberg to impound all copies of the journal in which the articles appeared and requested the governments of the neighboring German states to follow suit. Fichte responded by publishing two essays insisting that his views were not atheistic though they differed from the Judeo-Christian conception of a personal God. The Grand Duke of Weimar was finally approached concerning the issue and, because he was dedicated to free research, would have been content with a censure of Fichte. Anticipating this, Fichte declared in writing to the authorities that he would not submit to censure which, when acknowledged by the government, was tantamount to dismissal. Fichte left the university in 1799 and settled in Berlin. Surprisingly, though Goethe had supported Fichte's acceptance at Jena, he now became an ardent supporter of his dismissal. In addition, Kant published a statement in which he emphatically separated his own philosophy from that of Fichte's.

In the year after his dismissal, Fichte published a popularization of his moral views, *Die Bestimmung des Menschen* (1800; *The Vocation of Man*, 1848). In 1805, Fichte accepted a professorship at Erlangen. Yet within two years he returned to Berlin and shortly thereafter published *Reden an die deutsche Nation* (1808; *Addresses to the German Nation*, 1922). In this work, he advocated national educational policies which emphasized the development of the individual's conscience and capacity for moral action. When these traits were fully realized in adulthood, according to Fichte, the German people would be worthy of being spiritual leaders of the world. Fichte believed that the German people were best fitted for such leadership because Napoleon I had betrayed the ideals as expressed in the French Revolution.

Fichte's metaphysics took on deeply religious overtones toward the end of his life. He came to equate the absolute ego with the god of traditional religion. In 1806, he published *Die Anweisung zum seligen Leben: Oder, Auch die Religionslehre* (*The Way Towards the Blessed Life*, 1844). In this work, Fichte claimed that the whole purpose of life is to attain knowledge of and love of God.

The final university appointment came for Fichte in 1811, when he was made rector of the newly formed University of Berlin. Because his temperament made it difficult to work with him, he did not remain at this post for long. He did continue to lecture throughout 1812-1813. During these years, Johanna worked at a hospital nursing the sick and those wounded in the Napoleonic Wars. In the course of her work, she contracted a fever and while Fichte was nursing her back to health he also became ill. The malady proved fatal in his case, and he died on January 27, 1814.

Summary

Johann Gottlieb Fichte exercised a tremendous influence on philosophy in Germany. He personally knew the leading figures of the Romantic movement. While he was Fichte's student in 1796, Friedrich von Schlegel closely followed the intellectual footsteps of his master. Schlegel later turned to Baruch Spinoza and Gottfried Leibniz and eventually became the most prominent leader of the German Romantic movement. Friedrich Wilhelm Joseph von Schelling, a professor at Jena, argued that the absolute ego could be apprehended in a direct intuition (and not merely posited by pure practical reason as in Fichte's system). One of Schelling's early journal articles was a comparison of the philosophies of Fichte and Spinoza. Fichte met Friedrich Schleiermacher during his Berlin years. He was, however, very critical of the free morals and glorification of sentimentality of the Romanticists and quickly dissociated himself from the movement.

Most important, Fichte influenced Hegel, who had succeeded Fichte in 1800 as professor of philosophy at Jena. Hegel's first book was a comparison of the philosophies of Fichte and Schelling. Fichte's change of the Kantian transcendental ego into an unindividuated absolute activity paved the way for Hegel's development of Absolute Idealism. Fichte's philosophy also influenced Thomas Carlyle.

In his own day, Fichte was respected as much for his moral character as for his philosophy. He was regarded as extremely conscientious, self-demanding, and disciplined. The epigraph on his tomb reads "Thy teachers shall shine as the brightness of the firmament, and they that turn many to righteousness as the stars that shine for ever and ever."

Bibliography

Adamson, Robert. *Fichte*. Edinburgh: William Blackwood and Sons, 1881.

Contains a long biography. Devoted to tracing the evolution of *The Science of Knowledge* from early phase to later phase. Argues that this philosophy never rids itself of subjective idealism and that only in its earlier formulations was the doctrine influential.

Everett, Charles Carroll. *Fichte's "Science of Knowledge": A Critical Exposition*. Chicago: S. C. Griggs and Co., 1884. Compares Hegel's and Arthur Schopenhauer's philosophies to Fichte's. Argues that Fichte fails to reconcile the concept of finitude with the doctrine of the absolute. More than half of the work is devoted to exposition of Fichte's three fundamental principles.

Fichte, Johann Gottlieb. *Fichte: Early Philosophical Writings*. Translated and edited by Daniel Breazeale. Ithaca, N.Y.: Cornell University Press, 1988. Contains a long biographical introductory essay by the translator and a substantive preface to each of the ten selections.

Gopalakrishnaiah, V. *A Comparative Study of the Educational Philosophies of J. G. Fichte and J. H. Newman*. Waltair: Andhra University Press, 1973. Stresses the importance of the university to the community, the social function of education, and the provision of scientific research by the university in Fichte's educational theories and contrasts these themes with their contraries in Newman.

Hohler, T. P. *Imagination and Reflection: Intersubjectivity Fichte's "Grundlage" of 1794*. The Hague: Martinus Nijhoff, 1982. Devoted to the problem of finitude and the philosophy of the "I" in Fichte's early writings only. Argues that the transcendental "I" is essentially and inherently intersubjective; that is, intersubjectivity is argued to be a transcendental constituent of "I-ness."

Talbot, E. B. *The Fundamental Principle of Fichte's Philosophy*. New York: Macmillan, 1906. Concentrates on the changes that Fichte made in his fundamental principle between the early and later periods of his development. Argues that differences noted by critics are overstated and that the fundamental characterization as activity remains constant throughout.

Mark Pestana

JOHANN BERNHARD FISCHER VON ERLACH

Born: July 20, 1656 (baptized); Graz, Austria
Died: April 5, 1723; Vienna, Austria
Area of Achievement: Architecture
Contribution: The founder of the Austrian Baroque, Fischer von Erlach was
the pivotal figure in the artistic life of late seventeenth century and early
eighteenth century Austria, creating an architectural style which embodied
the imperial pride of the revived Habsburg Empire.

Early Life

Johann Bernhard Fischer von Erlach was born in Graz in 1656. His father,
Johann Baptist Fischer, was a local sculptor with sufficient means to send his
son, whom he had trained as a sculptor and stucco worker, to Italy to complete his artistic education. It was natural that he should go south for his
apprenticeship. The lands of the Austrian Crown had long been little more
than an artistic extension of the Italian Baroque, with itinerant architects,
painters, and stucco workers from northern Italy, especially from the Como
region, disseminating there the aesthetic canons of the Jesuit-dominated
Counter-Reformation. Fischer would be the first native Austrian to challenge
this virtual monopoly of the Italians, and in so doing would become the
father of the Austrian and German Baroque. Nevertheless, his sojourn in
Italy proved immensely rewarding. Although the exact length of his stay is
unknown, he seems to have spent at least twelve years there between the
early 1670's and around 1686, working and studying first in Rome and then
in Naples. In Rome, Gian Lorenzo Bernini was still alive, and Francesco
Borromini was not long dead. The work of both greatly influenced the young
Fischer, but he seems to have been especially fascinated by Borromini. Italy had much to teach him, but he was no mere architect's apprentice or a
hanger-on in artists' ateliers. Already he possessed a voracious appetite for
reading and learning, and a boundless intellectual curiosity which, in time,
would make him something of a Renaissance man.

By 1687, Fischer had returned to Graz and, by 1690, he was established
in Vienna. Between 1688 and 1689, he worked (with the Italian Lorenzo
Burnacini) on the Dreifaltigkeitssaule, or Pestsaule, the sculptured column
erected by Leopold I in the Graben to commemorate a recent visitation of
the plague. In 1688, he also began his first major architectural commission,
for Count Michael Althan, at Schloss Frain (Vranov, Czechoslovakia), on a
magnificent cliff-top site, where he designed a freestanding domed Ahsen-
saal, a hall in which the count's ancestors were commemorated, with ten
niches in which stood life-size statues of ancestors, and with a frescoed
ceiling representing the familial virtues of the Althans. The painter was
Johann Michael Rottmayr, a native Austrian from the Salzkammergut, who

later worked with Fischer in Salzburg and in the Karlskirche.

By now, Fischer had attracted the attention of the Habsburg court, and on the occasion of the crowning of Leopold's heir (the future emperor Joseph I) as King of the Romans in 1690 he was commissioned to construct an elaborate triumphal arch, for which the exuberant design still exists. Thereafter, he was appointed architectural tutor to Joseph, presumably on the strength of his growing reputation as the first Austrian architect to rival the ubiquitous Italians (Leopold was committed to reducing French and Italian influences at his court). He was also ennobled (hence, the von Erlach). On his accession in 1705, Joseph appointed Fischer von Erlach chief imperial inspector of buildings and festivities. The emperor stood as godfather to the architect's eldest son, Joseph Emanuel, who was to pursue a distinguished career as an architect in his own right. It was Joseph who requested Fischer von Erlach to design for him a palace at Schönbrunn to outshine Versailles. Although the palace was never built, the design survives and has been described as "one of the great visions of architectural history."

Life's Work

During the first fifteen years of the eighteenth century, Fischer von Erlach achieved his full stature as an architect. It was during these years that he set his distinctive mark upon Vienna with his many commissions for town palaces for the nobles of the empire, who were eager to employ the emperor's favorite in building residences which would advertise both their wealth and their taste. The first of such commissions was the palace which he built for Prince Eugene between 1695 and 1700 on the narrow Himmelpfortgasse, later to be enlarged by his rival, and the prince's favorite architect, Johann Lucas von Hildebrandt. He gave it a Roman façade of the kind which would become his hallmark and designed a *Treppenhaus* (an entrance hall with a double staircase) which ranks as one of the finest examples of a form for which the Austrian and German Baroque is rightly famous. Here, the upper level of the staircase is supported by magnificent muscular atlantes such as he would employ again with such effect in the Batthyány and Trautson palaces and in the Bohemian Chancellery.

Eugene's town palace was followed by the construction of the Batthyány palace (1699-1706), the Klesheim palace at Salzburg (1700-1709), the Bohemian Chancellery (1708-1714), the Trautson palace (1710-1716), the Schwarzenberg palace (1713-), and the Clam-Gallas palace in Prague (begun in 1713). Yet notwithstanding these secular commissions, mainly in Vienna, Fischer von Erlach had also established a reputation as an ecclesiastical architect, primarily through his work at Salzburg. Largely because of an idiosyncratic dislike of Italian craftsmen on the part of the reigning prince-archbishop of the city, Johann Ernst von Thun-Hohenstein, Fischer von Erlach replaced Johann Caspar Zuccalli as court architect and was commissioned to build there the Dreifaltigkeitskirche (the Church of the Holy Trinity, 1694-1707), the Kollegienkirche (the Collegiate Church of the Benedictine University, 1696-1707), and the Ursulinkirche (the Church of the Ursuline Convent, 1699-1705). In 1709, the archbishop died, and since his successor preferred to employ Hildebrandt, Fischer von Erlach's connection with the archiepiscopal city came to an end. There was also a hiatus in his church-building until 1715, when he began work upon his ecclesiastical masterpiece, the Karlskirche.

By then, however, he had become by far the most celebrated architect in the emperor's dominions. With his acute intelligence and his wide-ranging interests, there was much of the scholar about him, as well as the artist, and it should come as no surprise to find him a correspondent of the philosopher Gottfried Leibniz. Indeed, it has been suggested that Fischer von Erlach aspired to create in stone a transcendent vision of the harmony and order inherent in the mind of the Leibnizian "Divine Mover." In 1712, he dedicated to Charles VI in manuscript a lavishly illustrated history of architecture. Published in an expanded version in 1721 and translated into English in 1730, it was to be one of the most influential architectural treatises of the eighteenth century. It was characteristic of Fischer von Erlach's intellectual curiosity that his researches led him far beyond the world of classical antiquity, to Egypt, the Middle East, and the Orient. He seems, for example, to have had an appreciation for Islamic architecture rare among Europeans at that time and indeed for another two centuries.

In 1713, the plague again struck Vienna, and in fulfillment of a vow made at that time to Saint Carlo Borromeo for the city's deliverance, the emperor determined to construct a great basilica for the saint facing across what was then open ground toward the Hofburg, the imperial palace. Leading architects of the day such as Hildebrandt were invited to submit designs, but it was Fischer von Erlach's which was accepted, and in 1715 he began work upon his masterpiece. The foundation stone was laid in 1716, but it was not until 1738 that the Karlskirche was finally dedicated. At the time of Fischer von Erlach's death in 1723, however, the frame of the church was already standing (the dome and the dome drum being completed during 1723-1724), and under the direction of Joseph Emanuel Fischer von Erlach, the dead architect's son, whom Charles VI held in great esteem, the project went forward in accordance with the original design.

The internal arrangements of the Karlskirche center on a longitudinal oval at right angles to the façade, crowned by a mighty dome, but it is the façade of the Karlskirche which gives it a unique place among Baroque churches. As was his custom, Fischer von Erlach designed the front exterior with great care. The central section was to consist of a Roman portico, behind which would be seen the great high-drummed dome above the nave. The portico was then linked to two rather squat campanili by concave walls, in front of which were to stand two immense columns derived from Trajan's column in Rome and similar to a pair which had been originally incorporated into his grandiose design for Schönbrunn. Both columns were to be encircled, like their Roman original, by commemorative bas reliefs, in this case, illustrating the life of Saint Carlo Borromeo.

Just as Fischer von Erlach did not live to see the completion of the Karlskirche, so he did not see the completion of his other masterpiece, the Hofbibliothek, or imperial library. The Hofburg, for generations the Vienna residence of the Habsburgs, had deteriorated greatly, and Charles VI turned to Fischer von Erlach for a master plan for its renovation. Between 1716 and 1720, therefore, the latter drew up designs for an imperial library as the first stage of the rebuilding. It was to represent, symbolically, a temple of knowledge and science, perhaps reflecting the ideas of Leibniz, who certainly took a great interest in its design. Delays resulting from lack of funds and the declining health of the architect meant that the finished building, erected between 1722 and 1738, was as much the work of Joseph Emanuel Fischer von Erlach as it was of his father. Nevertheless, the son was meticulous in following his father's original plan, although he himself deserves full credit for the quality of the finished interior, with its ceiling frescoes by Daniel Gran, who had worked with both father and son on the Schwarzenberg palace.

Summary

One of the most original architects of the late Baroque, Johann Bernhard Fischer von Erlach was the founder of the *Kaiserstil*, or imperial style, which spread from Austria, in one form or another, throughout the Holy Roman Empire. Possessing an equal aptitude for ecclesiastical and secular building, he left an indelible mark upon the landscape of Vienna. Yet unlike many of his contemporaries, Fischer von Erlach was no mere technician: Rather, he was the embodiment of the notion (perhaps derived from Leibniz) that the architect could be both the formulator and the interpreter of the ideals of the age, an assumption as implicit in his great treatise on world architecture as it was in the elaborate symbolism of the Karlskirche and the Hofbibliothek.

Bibliography

Aurenhammer, Hans. *J. B. Fischer von Erlach*. Cambridge, Mass.: Harvard University Press, 1973. This is the only book available in English devoted solely to Fischer von Erlach. As such, it must be regarded as an invaluable study.
Fergusson, Frances D. "St. Charles' Church, Vienna: The Iconography of Its Architecture." *Journal of the Society of Architectural Historians* 29 (1970): 318-326. A detailed account of the imperial symbolism attached to

the building and decoration of the Karlskirche. Essential reading.

Fischer von Erlach, Johann Bernhard. *Entwurff einer historischen Architektur, in Abbildung unterschiedener berühmten Gebäude, des Alterthums und fremder Völcker.* Ridgewood, N.J.: Gregg Press, 1964. Fischer von Erlach's treatise on the history of architecture has been reprinted in the second edition of 1725, together with the English translation of 1730, entitled *A Plan of Civil and Historical Architecture, in the Representation of the Most Noted Buildings of Foreign Nations, Both Ancient and Modern.*

Norberg-Schulz, Christian. *Late Baroque and Rococo Architecture.* New York: Harry N. Abrams, 1974. An outstanding survey of its subject, excellently illustrated with photographs and ground plans.

Sedlmayr, Hans. *Johann Bernhard Fischer von Erlach.* Vienna: Herold, 1956. The definitive monograph on the architect. (In German.)

Tapié, V. L. *The Age of Grandeur: Baroque and Classicism in Europe.* Translated by A. Ross Williamson. London: Weidenfeld & Nicolson, 1960. Virtually an instant classic upon publication, this book provides the best general background to the art and aesthetics of Baroque Europe.

Wangermann, Ernst. *The Austrian Achievement, 1700-1800.* London: Thames & Hudson, 1973. An excellent introduction to Austria's golden age, setting Fischer von Erlach's activities in historical perspective.

Gavin R. G. Hambly

GUSTAVE FLAUBERT

Born: December 12, 1821; Rouen, France
Died: May 8, 1880; Croisset, France
Area of Achievement: Literature
Contribution: The most influential European novelist of the nineteenth century, Flaubert, who is most famous for his masterpiece *Madame Bovary*, is regarded as the leader of the realist school of French literature.

Early Life

Born in Rouen, Gustave Flaubert was the son of Achille Cléophas Flaubert, a noted surgeon and professor of medicine, and Caroline (Fleuriot) Flaubert, a woman from a distinguished provincial family. As a child Flaubert was high-strung, delicate, and precocious. He developed a love of literature early.

In his adolescence, Flaubert became attracted to the Romantic movement. Consequently he declared a hatred for bourgeois values and a passionate devotion to art; he maintained these attitudes throughout his life. They were strengthened through his youthful friendship with Alfred Le Poittevin, a young philosopher, whose pessimistic outlook affected Flaubert deeply. Another formative influence was his father's practice and teaching of medicine, which led him to value the discipline, intelligence, and clinical eye of the surgeon and helped shape his own approach to his literary materials.

In 1836, at the age of fifteen, Flaubert met Élisa Schlésinger, a married woman eleven years his senior, and succumbed to a devastating romantic passion for her which was destined to remain unrequited and to serve in his mind as an ideal which was never to be reached in his subsequent relationships with women.

Flaubert was sent to Paris in the autumn of 1842 to study law, a profession which did not attract him. He was committed to literature but reluctant to publish his work and susceptible to episodes of serious depression. In January, 1844, he gave up the study of the law upon suffering a nervous breakdown that was then diagnosed, probably erroneously, as epilepsy. Following a yearlong recuperation, he began to devote his time and energy to literary creation and to turn away from his earlier romantic subjectivism.

Flaubert's father died in January, 1846, leaving him an inheritance which enabled him to pursue his literary career full-time. His sister Caroline died the following March, leaving an infant daughter. Flaubert and his mother adopted the child and began living at their estate at Croisset, near Rouen, where he spent most of the remainder of his life. In July, 1846, Flaubert met the poet Louise Colet in Paris, and began a tempestuous, intermittent affair with her that ended ten years later, in 1856.

In 1847, Flaubert went on a walking tour through Brittany with his writer friend Maxime Du Camp and wrote about the tour in *Par les champs et par les grèves* (with Du Camp; *Over Strand and Field*, 1904), which was published posthumously (1885). At this time, he was also engaged in writing the first version of *La Tentation de Saint Antoine* (1874; *The Temptation of Saint Anthony*, 1895), begun in 1846. Although he expended much energy and care on the manuscript, his friends found it florid and rhetorical and advised him to burn it. Disheartened, he set it aside and set out with Du Camp in November, 1849, on travels through Egypt, Palestine, Syria, Turkey, Greece, and Italy. Upon his return to Croisset in the summer of 1851, he was preparing to begin a very different kind of novel.

Life's Work

Flaubert spent the next five years of his life hard at work on *Madame Bovary* (1857; English translation, 1886). In the first two months of 1857, the French government brought Flaubert to trial, charging him with writing an immoral work, but he was acquitted and *Madame Bovary* won widespread success.

In the writing of *Madame Bovary*, Flaubert found himself, both as a man and as an artist. The novel relates dispassionately the story of a young provincial girl whose incurably romantic notions about life and passion lead her to adultery, financial ruin, and suicide. Her yearnings are of a kind with which Flaubert himself had been all too familiar, as is evidenced in his famous remark, "Madame Bovary, c'est moi" (Madame Bovary is myself). In projecting his own temperament upon this fictional character and subjecting it to relentlessly objective scrutiny, Flaubert was working to exorcise inner weaknesses that had bedeviled him all of his life.

Flaubert's painstaking care with the observation of concrete facts and psychological details in *Madame Bovary* and his constant concern to present his materials impersonally constituted a revolution in the art of the novel and earned for him recognition as the leader of a new realist school of literature. This designation is misleading, however, and, in fact, somewhat ironic. Flaubert himself detested it, commenting, "People think I am in love with reality, though I hate it; for it is out of hatred of realism that I undertook the writing of this novel."

It is important to note the prevailing idealism in Flaubert's temperament and art. He saw art as an escape from life's ugliness; the paradox of *Madame Bovary* is that it takes a story that is essentially sordid and commonplace and transforms it into a vessel of beauty. The medium of this transformation is Flaubert's language: Through his ideas about and use of this medium, he has come to epitomize the dedicated literary artist. He refused to rush his art, and would spend hours in anguish searching for the right word or phrase to express his vision.

From *Madame Bovary* Flaubert turned to the subject of ancient Carthage;

in 1862, he published *Salammbô* (English translation, 1886), a minutely researched novel whose fictitious narrative is set against the actual historical background of the 240-237 B.C. uprising of the mercenaries against Carthage. *Salammbô* was a popular success, but, to Flaubert's disappointment, it failed to win approval from the critics.

After writing three unsuccessful plays, Flaubert took up for extensive revision the manuscript of *L'Éducation sentimentale* (1869; *A Sentimental Education*, 1898). The novel, which Flaubert called a "moral history of the men of my generation," is set in Paris in the 1840's, and fictionalizes Flaubert's personal experiences within the panoramic and solidly realized historical context of France under the July Monarchy. Flaubert considered this novel his masterpiece, but the reviews were very unfavorable and the reading public unsympathetic.

Other troubles also plagued Flaubert in his last years. He was beset by financial problems after sacrificing his own fortune in 1875 to save his niece's husband from bankruptcy. He was, nevertheless, highly respected by other writers and generous in his advice to young authors, including Guy de Maupassant—who became his disciple—as well as Émile Zola and Alphonse Daudet. He formed friendships with the novelists Ivan Turgenev and George Sand.

Flaubert's last novel, which he left unfinished, was *Bouvard et Pécuchet* (1881; English translation, 1896). He interrupted his work on this long novel in 1875-1877 to write *Trois Contes* (1877; *Three Tales*, 1903), three stories that display the range and diversity of Flaubert's art and received immediate recognition. *Bouvard et Pécuchet* is a portrayal of human folly and frailty, specifically in its modern manifestation as an uncritical confusion of science and truth.

Flaubert died at home in Croisset after suffering a stroke on May 8, 1880. He was buried in Rouen.

Summary

Gustave Flaubert greatly influenced the development of the modern novel. In the historical context of French literature, his work forms a bridge between romanticism and realism, and his art arises out of the conflict within his mind and temperament between these two tendencies. *Madame Bovary* has been called the first modern novel and is widely hailed as one of the greatest works of fiction ever written.

Although he was a kindhearted man and a loyal friend, Flaubert's vision of life in his fiction was tragic and pessimistic. It epitomizes for many a quintessentially modern outlook. His ironic stance; his understanding of solitude, ennui, suffering, and loss; his dissatisfaction with materialistic and empty bourgeois values and the pursuit of ideal beauty; and his fascination with the destructive force of time and the preserving power of memory are attitudes that are found in the works of many writers of the late nineteenth and twentieth centuries. His understanding of human psychology was precise and deep. Flaubert's painstaking devotion to style and form raised the status of the novel to a form of high art and made him a model of the literary artist for subsequent generations of writers and readers.

Bibliography
Bart, Benjamin F. *Flaubert*. Syracuse, N.Y.: Syracuse University Press, 1967. This lengthy and comprehensive critical biography makes copious use of Flaubert's letters, private papers, and drafts for his novels to present a detailed account of his life, of his aesthetic, and his ideas about prose fiction.
Brombert, Victor. *The Novels of Flaubert: A Study of Themes and Techniques*. Princeton, N.J.: Princeton University Press, 1966. A thorough study of the texture, structure, patterns, and themes in Flaubert's fiction, stressing the nonrealistic and autobiographical aspects of his art. Brombert argues that Flaubert is essentially a tragic novelist.
Buck, Stratton. *Gustave Flaubert*. Boston: Twayne, 1966. A comprehensive and authoritative introduction, for students and general readers, to Flaubert's novels and correspondence. Buck traces the evolution and composition of each of Flaubert's novels, describes their nature and contents, and assesses their artistic importance.
Culler, Jonathan. *Flaubert: The Uses of Uncertainty*. Ithaca, N.Y.: Cornell University Press, 1974. A sophisticated study, with a critical approach influenced by structuralism. Culler addresses Flaubert's early writings in sequence, demonstrating in them predominant themes, especially human stupidity and irony, in the later novels, which he then treats at length together. Culler concludes by discussing Flaubert's writings in terms of their value and sources of interest for modern readers.
Flaubert, Gustave. *The Letters of Gustave Flaubert*. Selected, edited, and translated by Francis Steegmuller. 2 vols. Cambridge, Mass.: Harvard University Press, 1980-1982. Flaubert's letters are crucial to an understanding of his personality, life, and works. This edition, which includes authoritative notes, appendices, indexes, and illustrations, presents Flaubert's letters from 1830 through 1880.
Nadeau, Maurice. *The Greatness of Flaubert*. Translated by Barbara Bray. New York: Library Press, 1972. A general introduction to Flaubert's life and career by the editor of the author's complete works. Nadeau stresses Flaubert's lifelong and never fully realized quest, as he became an artist, for a coherent sense of his own identity. Nadeau characterizes Flaubert's work as a body of "social, philosophical, and moral criticism."
Spencer, Philip H. *Flaubert: A Biography*. New York: Grove Press, 1952. A sensible and highly readable narrative that provides a vivid introduction to

Flaubert's life. Spencer views Flaubert in terms of an interrelated set of conflicts between self and society, idealism and disillusionment, beauty and ugliness, and escapism and commitment, and explores these conflicts as they manifest themselves in his life and motivate him as an artist.

Starkie, Enid. *Flaubert: The Making of the Master.* New York: Atheneum, 1967. Starkie draws previously unused materials from manuscripts, notes, and letters in this comprehensive and well-documented critical biography of Flaubert through 1857, concluding with a study of *Madame Bovary*, its antecedents, its publication and censorship trial, and Flaubert's aesthetic doctrine. Includes illustrations, bibliography, notes, and index.

_____. *Flaubert, the Master: A Critical and Biographical Study, 1856-1880.* New York: Atheneum, 1971. In this, the sequel volume to her *Flaubert: The Making of the Master* (1967), Starkie presents a sympathetic and thorough analysis of Flaubert's life and art after the publication of *Madame Bovary.* She argues that Flaubert's later works represent the fundamental aspects of his genius. Includes illustrations, bibliography, notes, and index.

Vargas Llosa, Mario. *The Perpetual Orgy: Flaubert and Madame Bovary.* Translated by Helen Lane. New York: Farrar, Straus & Giroux, 1986. A thoroughgoing study of Flaubert's art in *Madame Bovary* by the celebrated Peruvian novelist. Vargas Llosa begins by charting vividly his particular experiences with this novel. He then addresses in depth the biographical, historical, and geographical origins of *Madame Bovary*, and analyzes important recurring themes and innovative techniques.

Eileen Tess Tyler

CHARLES FOURIER

Born: April 7, 1772; Besançon, France
Died: October 10, 1837; Paris, France
Areas of Achievement: Social reform and social science
Contribution: Fourier was one of the founding fathers of nineteenth century
Utopian socialism. Although the few experiments in building a model
community based upon his theories proved short-lived, Fourier's writings
have continued to attract interest.

Early Life
François-Marie-Charles Fourrier (he stopped using the second *r* apparently
when he was eighteen) was born on April 7, 1772, at Besançon, France, a
town near the Swiss border, the fifth child and only son of a prosperous cloth
merchant. In 1781, his father died, leaving him a substantial inheritance. He
attended the local Collège de Besançon, where he received a solid if uninspiring classical education. His ambition appears to have been to study military engineering at the École de Génie Militaire, but he lacked the noble
status requisite for admission. He was apprenticed to a cloth merchant around
1790, first at Rouen, then at Lyons. He was ill-suited for, and unhappy in,
the world of business.

Fourier was involved in the savagely suppressed 1793 counterrevolutionary uprising in Lyons against the Convention (central government). As a
result, he was imprisoned and narrowly escaped execution. In 1794, he was
called for military service; he was discharged two years later. Although the
details remain unclear, he lost the bulk of his inheritance. He thereafter
worked as a traveling salesman and then as an unlicensed broker. He also
began writing short articles and poems, which appeared in the Lyons news-
papers starting in 1801. He set forth an outline of his developing ideas in
two papers written in late 1803, "Harmonie universelle" and "Lettre au
Grand-Juge." In 1808, he published—anonymously and with a false place
of publication to protect himself against prosecution by the authorities—his
first major work, *Théorie des quatre mouvements and des destinées géné-
rales* (*The Social Destiny of Man: Or, Theory of the Four Movements*,
1857). In 1812, Fourier's mother died, leaving him a modest lifetime annu-
ity. The money allowed him to devote himself full-time to elaborating his
ideas in a projected *Grand Traité* (great treatise). Although he never finished
this great treatise he did publish in 1822 his two-volume *Traité de l'association domestique-agricole* (later retitled *Théorie de l'unité universelle*; *Social Science: The Theory of Universal Unity*, 185?). A briefer and more
accessible statement of his position would appear in his *Le Nouveau Monde
industriel et sociétaire: Ou, Invention du procédé d'industrie attrayante et
naturelle distribuée en series passionées* (1829).

Fourier never married, appears to have had no lasting romantic attachment, and lived most of his life in cheap lodging houses and hotels. He was a deeply neurotic personality—what the French call a *maniaque* (crank). There is even evidence that he seriously thought himself to be the son of God. As he grew older, he became increasingly paranoid about his supposed persecution by his enemies. His jealousy of rival would-be saviors of humanity resulted in an 1831 pamphlet, *Pièges et charlatanisme des deux sectes Saint-Simon et Owen, qui promettent l'association et le progrès* (traps and charlatanism of the Saint-Simonian and Owen sects, who promise association and progress). The last of his major writings to be published during his lifetime was the two-volume *La Fausse Industrie morcelée, répugnante, mensongère, et l'antidote, l'industrie naturelle, combinée, attrayante, veridique, donnant quadruple produit et perfection extrème en tous qualités* (1835-1836). A manuscript entitled *Le Nouveau Monde amoureux*—written around 1817-1818 and demonstrating the central place in his thinking of his vision of a sexual revolution—was not published until 1967.

Life's Work

Fourier's starting point was his repudiation of the eighteenth century philosophes, who had enthroned reason as mankind's guide. He dismissed reason as a weak force compared to the passions, or instinctual drives. He postulated the existence of twelve fundamental human passions. These in turn fell into three major categories. There were the so-called luxurious passions (the desires of the five senses of sight, hearing, taste, smell, and touch); the four group, or affective, passions (ambition, friendship, love, and family feeling or parenthood); and the serial, or distributive, passions (the "cabalist" desire for intrigue, the "butterfly" yearning for variety, and the "composite," or desire for the simultaneous satisfaction of more than a single passion). Fourier held that since all the passions were created by God, they were naturally good and harmonious. Thus, they should be allowed the freest and fullest expression. He preached that mankind had achieved sufficient mastery over the forces of the natural world to make possible the satisfaction of all human wants.

The trouble was that in capitalist society—which Fourier in his sixteen-stage scheme of human history termed civilization—most people found their passions repressed or, even worse, so distorted as to become vices. What was required was a new social order that would channel the passions in salutary directions. His ideal world—which he called Harmony—was a paradise of sensuous enjoyments: a continuous round of eating, drinking, and lovemaking. The prerequisite for its attainment was a properly designed community, or phalanx, which would constitute the basic social unit. Each phalanx would consist of sixteen hundred to two thousand persons. This number would allow inclusion within the phalanx of the full range of different individual personality types and thus of potential combinations of passions. There were, he calculated, no more than 810 fundamentally different varieties of men and the same number for women. The perfect society required that each type interact with all other types.

All the members of the phalanx would live in one large building, known as the phalanstery. He even specified the architectural design: a building about six stories high, consisting of a long main body and two wings with inner courtyards and a parade ground immediately in front. Almost always, individuals would not engage in their occupations or pastimes alone or as part of a haphazard gathering, but rather as members of scientifically arranged groupings. Individuals with the same interests would voluntarily form a small group, and groups with like occupations would similarly combine naturally into what he termed a series. This organizational scheme would give full scope simultaneously to the cooperative and competitive impulses, because each group would consist of volunteers passionately devoted to the purpose of the group and the different groups would vie with one another to win the praise of the other members of the phalanx.

Boredom would be eliminated because of frequent changes in jobs and sex partners. Phalanx members would work at any given task typically only one hour per day, with two hours as the maximum. Leadership would be similarly rotated depending upon the activity. Most important, phalanx members would join only those groups and series that attracted them. Within each group, they would perform only that part of the work that appealed to them. Thus, for example, the would-be Nero would find an outlet for his bloodthirsty tastes by working as a butcher. This matching of job with personality was the fundamental difference between Civilization and Harmony. "In the former," Fourier explained, "a man or a woman performs twenty different functions belonging to a single kind of work. In the latter a man performs a single function in twenty kinds of work, and he chooses the function which he likes while rejecting the other nineteen."

Fourier did not propose to abolish private property. He allowed differential rewards for those with superior creative abilities and, accordingly, differences in the degree of pleasures according to resources. Even the poorest in the phalanx would lead much richer and more pleasurable lives than was attainable by even the richest in the existing society. As for who would do society's so-called dirty jobs, he had a simple answer: children. "God," he explained, "gave children these strange tastes to provide for the execution of various repulsive tasks. If manure has to be spread over a field, youths will find it a repugnant job but groups of children will devote themselves to it with greater zeal than to clean work."

A revolutionary educational policy was at the heart of Fourier's system. Whereas civilized education repressed the faculties of the child, the new education that he envisaged would be aimed at developing all the child's physical and intellectual faculties, especially the capacities for pleasure and enjoyment. He most antagonized contemporary opinion—and dismayed even many of his disciples—by his advocacy of free love. He was convinced that the amorous desires of most people were polygamous. He thus attacked the family as the number-one example of an unnatural institution, stifling both men and women. Marriage in contemporary society, he charged, was "pure brutality, a casual pairing off provoked by the domestic bond without any illusion of mind or heart."

From 1822 on—except for a brief return to Lyons in 1825—Fourier lived in Paris. He was constantly appealing to would-be patrons to finance the establishment of an experimental phalanx to provide scientific proof of the correctness of his theories. Every day on the stroke of twelve noon, he would return to his lodgings to await the arrival of the hoped-for benefactor. He was the target of frequent newspaper ridicule, but he attracted a small but loyal band of disciples. In 1832, the first Fourierist journal, *Le Phalanstère*, was launched; the same year witnessed the first attempt to establish a model phalanx at Condé-sur-Vesgre. From 1833 on, Fourier suffered from worsening intestinal problems that sapped his health. For the last year of his life, he was an invalid confined to his apartment. On the morning of October 10, 1837, the building concierge found him dead, kneeling by his bed dressed in his frock coat.

Summary

Charles Fourier himself constitutes a fascinating psychological problem, given the contrast between his free-ranging, sensual imagination and the crabbed drabness of his personal life. Much of his writing is simply incoherent—rambling, repetitive, and filled with invented pseudoscientific jargon. He goes into flights of fantasy—such as his portrayal of the planets copulating, his prophecy of the oceans turning into lemonade, his vision of the pests of man, such as fleas, rats, crocodiles, and lions, becoming transformed into more pleasant species, anti-fleas, anti-rats, anti-crocodiles, and anti-lions—that raise questions about his sanity. Yet his vision of a freer, happier, and more harmonious social order to replace the poverty, misery, and conflict of early industrial society exerted a strong attraction upon his sensitive-minded contemporaries, ranging from the young Fyodor Dostoevski to the New England Transcendentalists assembled at Brook Farm.

Although all the attempts to establish a model phalanx proved failures, Fourier has received renewed attention as the prophet of what have become the animating values for much of Western society—liberation of the senses from the repressions of middle-class life, exaltation of the instincts, and an all-pervading impulse toward self-gratification. He has attracted perhaps most interest as the precursor of the sexual revolution because of his calls for freedom from sexual taboos, his attacks on the barrenness of the marriage relationship, and his implicit assumption that there was no such thing as a sexual norm. He anticipated Sigmund Freud in key respects, particularly in his recognition of the importance of the sexual drive and the mechanisms for its repression and sublimation. Fourier's direct contribution to these later developments was minor, if not nil. Yet he was a more astute reader of human nature—and thus of the future—than the eighteenth century philosophes whom he so strongly attacked.

Bibliography

Altman, Elizabeth C. "The Philosophical Bases of Feminism: The Feminist Doctrines of the Saint-Simonians and Charles Fourier." *Philosophical Forum* 7 (Spring/Summer, 1974): 277-293. A laudatory examination of Fourier's advanced (at least from a present-day feminist perspective) ideas concerning the stifling effects of middle-class marriage upon women and his egalitarian views about the role of women in the phalanx.

Beecher, Jonathan. *Charles Fourier: The Visionary and His World.* Berkeley: University of California Press, 1986. An impressive piece of research into the extant published and manuscript materials on Fourier, this work should remain for the foreseeable future the definitive biography. The book is divided into three major parts: Part 1 details Fourier's life up to 1822; part 2 is an in-depth explication of his ideas; and part 3 traces his efforts to publicize and implement his program.

Fourier, Charles. *The Utopian Vision of Charles Fourier: Selected Texts on Work, Love, and Passionate Attraction.* Edited and translated by Jonathan Beecher and Richard Bienvenu. Boston: Beacon Press, 1971. As the subtitle indicates, the book contains English translations of selections from Fourier's writings. The editor-translators have avoided the temptation of pruning the nonsense and even gibberish with which Fourier filled so many of his pages; students without a knowledge of French thus can get at least a taste of Fourier's style. The seventy-five-page introduction provides an excellent, relatively brief introduction to Fourier's thinking.

Manuel, Frank E. *The Prophets of Paris.* Cambridge, Mass.: Harvard University Press, 1962. The author has written a perceptive account of five late eighteenth/early nineteenth century French prophets of a transformed social order—Anne-Robert-Jacques Turgot, Marquis de Condorcet, Comte de Saint-Simon, and Auguste Comte, along with Fourier. Manuel explains the similarities and differences in their ideas. He gives a sympathetic appraisal of Fourier as Freud's precursor in his psychological insights.

Poster, Mark, ed. *Harmonian Man: Selected Writings of Charles Fourier.* Garden City, N.Y.: Doubleday, 1971. Although Poster's introduction is short, the volume offers a handy selection of translated excerpts from Fourier's writings. Approximately half of the selections are nineteenth century translations, mostly by Arthur Brisbane. The rest—including excerpts from *Le Nouveau Monde amoureux*—were translated for this volume by Susan Ann Hanson.

Riasanovsky, Nicholas V. *The Teaching of Charles Fourier*. Berkeley: University of California Press, 1969. A lucidly written, comprehensive, and systematic analysis of the major themes in Fourier's thinking that should be the starting point for any serious examination of his ideas. An admirer of Fourier, Riasanovsky makes him appear too sensible and perhaps too modern by downplaying the fantastic and bizarre elements in his writings.

Spencer, M. C. *Charles Fourier*. Boston: Twayne, 1981. The volume includes a brief biographical sketch along with a summary of the major points in Fourier's thinking. Yet Spencer's own interest lies on the aesthetic side, and he has suggestive comments about Fourier's influence on French literature from Charles Baudelaire to the Surrealists.

John Braeman

JOSEPH FOURIER

Born: March 21, 1768; Auxerre, France
Died: May 16, 1830; Paris, France
Areas of Achievement: Mathematics and physics
Contribution: In deriving and solving equations representing the flow of heat in bodies, Fourier developed analytical methods which proved to be useful in the fields of pure mathematics, applied mathematics, and theoretical physics.

Early Life

Jean-Baptiste-Joseph Fourier, twelfth child of master tailor Joseph and ninth child of Édmie, became an orphan at the age of nine. He was placed in the local Royal Military School run by the Benedictine Order and soon demonstrated his passion for mathematics. Fourier and many biographers after him attribute the onset of his lifelong poor health to his habit of staying up late, reading mathematical texts in the empty classrooms of the school. He completed his studies in Paris. He was denied entry into the military and decided to enter the Church and teach mathematics.

Fourier remained at the Benedictine Abbey of St. Benoit-sur-Loire from 1787 to 1789, occupied with teaching and frustrated that he had little time for mathematical research. Whether he left Paris because of the impending revolution or because he did not want to take his vows is uncertain. He returned to Auxerre and from 1789 to 1794 served as professor and taught a variety of subjects at the Royal Military School. The school was run by the Congregation of St. Maur, the only religious order excluded from the post-revolutionary decree confiscating the property of religious orders.

Fourier became involved in local politics in 1793 and was drawn deep into the whirlpool as internal unrest and external military threats turned the committees on which he served into agents of the Terror. Fourier made the mistake of defending a group of men who turned out to be enemies of Robespierre. He was arrested and very nearly guillotined, spared only by the death of Robespierre. He became a student at the short-lived École Normale, mainly to have the opportunity to go to Paris and meet Pierre-Simon Laplace, Joseph-Louis Lagrange, and Gaspard Monge, the foremost mathematicians in France. In 1795, the École Polytechnique was opened, and Fourier was invited to join the faculty, but he was arrested once again, this time by the extreme reactionaries who hated him for his role in the Terror, even though he did much to moderate the excesses of the Terror in Auxerre. As with many other aspects of Fourier's life during the Revolution, the exact reason for his release is unknown. In any case, he was released and occupied himself with teaching and administrative duties at the École Polytechnique.

In 1798, Fourier was chosen to be part of Napoleon I's expedition to

Egypt. Fourier was elected permanent secretary of the newly formed Institute of Egypt, held a succession of administrative and diplomatic posts in the French expedition, and conducted some mathematical research. Upon his return to France in 1801, Fourier was named by Napoleon to be the prefect of Isère, one of the eighty-four newly formed divisions of France. It is during his prefecture that Fourier began his life's work.

Life's Work

Fourier's work in the development of an analytical theory of heat diffusion dates from the early 1800's, when he was in his early thirties, and after he had distinguished himself in administration of scientific and political institutions in Egypt. He had demonstrated a talent and passion for mathematics early, but he had not yet made significant contributions to the field. It was during whatever time he could spare from his administrative duties as prefect that he made his lasting contribution to physics and mathematics.

Fourier remained at Grenoble until Napoleon's downfall in 1814. He turned a poorly managed department into a well-managed one in a short time. It is not clear why Fourier began to study the diffusion of heat, but in 1804 he began with a rather mathematically abstract derivation of heat flow in a metal plate. He conducted numerous experiments in an attempt to establish the laws regulating the flow of heat. He expanded the scope of problems addressed, polished the mathematical formalism, and infused physical concepts into the derivation of the equations which expressed heat flow. He presented in 1807 a long paper to the French Academy of Sciences, but opposition from Laplace and others prevented its publication. At issue was a fundamental disagreement over mathematical rigor and the underlying physical concepts.

Laplace's first objection was that Fourier's methods were not mathematically rigorous. Fourier claimed that any function could be represented by an infinite trigonometric series—a sum of an infinite number of sine and cosine functions each with a determinable coefficient. Such series were instrumental in Fourier's formulation and solution of the problems of the diffusion of heat. Only later were Fourier's methods shown to be strictly rigorous mathematically. The second objection concerned the method of derivation. Laplace preferred to explain phenomena by the action of central forces acting between particles of matter. Fourier, while not denying the correctness or the usefulness of that approach, took a different approach. Heat, for Fourier, was the flow of a substance and not some relation between atoms and their motions. He attempted, successfully, to account for the phenomenon of heat diffusion through mathematical analysis. His paper of 1807 languished in the archives of the Academy of Sciences, unpublished.

As a result of his work in Egypt and his position as permanent secretary of the Institute of Egypt, Fourier edited and wrote the historical introduction to the *Description de l'Égypte* (1809-1828; description of Egypt). He worked on this project from around 1802 until 1810.

A prize was offered in 1810 by the Academy of Sciences on the subject of heat diffusion, and Fourier slightly revised and expanded his 1807 paper to include discussion of diffusion in infinite bodies and terrestrial and radiant heat. Fourier won the prize, but he had faced no serious competition. The jury criticized the paper in much the same way as the 1807 paper had been criticized, and again Fourier's work was not published. Eventually, after years of prodding, the work was published in 1815.

Fourier was probably not very happy being virtually exiled from Paris, the scientific capital of France. He seemed destined to live out his days in Grenoble. With Napoleon's abdication in April, 1814, Fourier provisionally retained his job as prefect during the transfer of power to Louis XVIII. He also managed to alter the route Napoleon took from Paris to exile in Elba, bypassing Grenoble, in order to avoid a confrontation between himself and Napoleon. Upon Napoleon's return in March, 1815, Fourier prepared the defenses of the town and made a diplomatic retreat to Lyons. Fourier returned before completing the journey upon learning that Napoleon had made him prefect of the Rhône department. He was dismissed before Napoleon fell once again.

Fourier's scientific work began again after 1815. One of his former pupils was now a prefect and appointed Fourier director of the Bureau of Statistics for the Seine department, which included Paris. He now had a modest income and few demands on his time. Fourier was named to the Academy of Sciences in 1817. During the next five years, he actively participated in the affairs of the Academy, sitting on commissions, writing reports, and conducting his own research. His administrative duties increased in 1822, when he was elected to the powerful position of permanent secretary of the mathematical section of the Academy. His *Théorie analytique de la chaleur* (1822; *The Analytical Theory of Heat*, 1878) differs only slightly from his 1810 essay. The papers he wrote in his later years contained little that was new. He led a satisfying academic life in his last years, but his health began to deteriorate. His rheumatism had returned, he had trouble breathing, and he was very sensitive to cold. Fourier died from a heart attack in May, 1830.

Summary

The core of Joseph Fourier's scientific work is *The Analytical Theory of Heat*. This work is basically a textbook describing the application of theorems from pure mathematics applied to the problem of the diffusion of heat in bodies. Fourier was able to express the distribution of heat inside of and on the surface of a variety of bodies, both at equilibrium and when the distribution was changing because of heat loss or gain.

He significantly influenced three different fields: pure mathematics, applied mathematics, and theoretical physics. In pure mathematics, Fourier's most lasting influence has been the definition of a mathematical function. He realized that any mathematical function can be represented by a trigono-metric series, no matter how difficult to manipulate the function may appear. Some scholars single out this as the stepping stone to the work of pure mathematicians later in the century, which resulted in the modern defini-tion of a function. Additional influences are that of a clarification of a nota-tional issue involving integral calculus and properties of infinite trigonomet-ric series.

Applied mathematics has been influenced to a great extent by Fourier's use of trigonometric series and techniques of integration. The class of prob-lems that Fourier series and Fourier integrals can solve extends far beyond diffusion of heat. His methods form the foundation of applied mathematics techniques taught to undergraduates. Some mathematicians before him had used trigonometric series in the solutions of problems, but the clarity, scope, and rigor that he brought to the field was significant.

His influence in theoretical physics is more subdued, perhaps because of the completeness of his results. There was little room for others to extend the physical aspects of Fourier's work—his results did not need extending. Other branches of physics appear to have been influenced by his approach, and a direct influence on the issue of determining the age of the earth by calculating its heat loss has been documented.

Bibliography
Bell, Eric T. *The Development of Mathematics*. 2d ed. New York: McGraw-Hill, 1945. Presents a narrative history of the decisive epochs in the de-velopment of mathematics without becoming overly technical. Chapter 13 is where the most references to Fourier may be found.
Fourier, Joseph. *The Analytical Theory of Heat*. Translated by Alexander Freeman. New York: G. E. Stechert, 1878, reprint 1945, 1955. Fou-rier's preliminary discourse to his most famous work explains in very clear terms what he is attempting in the work. Devoid of technical mat-ters, this book offers the reader a glimpse of why Fourier has achieved the status he has.
Fox, Robert. "The Rise and Fall of Laplacian Physics." *Historical Studies in the Physical Sciences* 4 (1974): 89-136. This paper presents a descrip-tion of the research program of Laplace, which dominated French science at one of its most successful periods, from 1805 to 1815. Fourier led the revolt against this program.
Friedman, Robert Marc. "The Creation of a New Science: Joseph Fourier's Analytical Theory of Heat." *Historical Studies in the Physical Sciences* 8 (1977): 73-100. This paper concentrates on conceptual and physical issues rather than the mathematical aspects stressed in most older works. Also

discusses how Fourier's philosophy of science compared to that of his contemporaries.

Grattan-Guinness, Ivor, with J. R. Ravetz. *Joseph Fourier, 1768-1830: A Survey of His Life and Work, Based on a Critical Edition of his Monograph on the Propagation of Heat, Presented to the Institute de France in 1807.* Cambridge, Mass.: MIT Press, 1972. Intertwines a close study of Fourier's life and work with a critical edition of his 1807 monograph. The 1807 monograph is in French, but everything else is in English. Contains a bibliography of Fourier's writings, a list of translations of his works, and a secondary bibliography.

Herivel, John. *Joseph Fourier: The Man and the Physicist.* Oxford, England: Clarendon Press, 1975. While this work does not claim to be the definitive biography of Fourier, it goes much further than any other work written in English. Although the book is almost devoid of technical detail, the prospective reader would benefit from a knowledge of the history of France from 1789 to 1830.

Roger Sensenbaugh

GIROLAMO FRACASTORO

Born: c. 1478; Verona, Venetian Republic
Died: August 6, 1553; Incaffi, Venetian Republic
Areas of Achievement: Medicine, philosophy, astronomy, and literature
Contribution: Fracastoro clearly described contagious diseases, and his pro-
phetic hypotheses on their causes foreshadowed by centuries the modern
understanding of microbial infections.

Early Life

Girolamo Fracastoro was born into an old and distinguished Veronese
family. His grandfather had been a physician to the reigning Scala family of
Verona. After training at home, he was sent to the University of Padua,
where he was entrusted to an old family friend, Girolamo della Torre, who
taught and practiced medicine there. Before his medical studies began, Fracastoro, following a well-established practice, pursued the liberal arts, which
also included mathematics and astronomy, under Nicolo Leonico Tomeo and
philosophy under Pietro Pomponazzi. Among his teachers of medicine was
Alessandro Benedetti, through whom he could come in contact with the
Ferrarese humanistic medics, as well as with Girolamo della Torre and his
son Marcus Antonio della Torre. Among his fellow students were the future
cardinals Ercole Gonzaga, Gasparo Contarini, and Pietro Bembo, through
whom he might have met members of the Aldine circle at Venice. He also
befriended Giovanni Battista Ramusio, who gained fame in later life as a
geographer.

Barely finished with his studies at Padua, Fracastoro was there appointed
lecturer in logic in 1501 and the next year became an anatomical councillor,
thus starting a traditional academic career in medicine. By 1508, wars interrupted his academic career and the remainder of his life was spent at Verona,
practicing medicine or managing his private landed estate at Incaffi. From
1505, when he had been elected to the College of Physicians at Verona, he
remained its faithful member. His hour of glory arrived in 1545, when the
pope made him physician of the Council of Trent.

Life's Work

Venice had always maintained close ties with Constantinople, and when
Padua came into its hands in 1404, Greek influence became dominant there
as well. While in other parts of Italy Humanists strove to revive Roman glo-
ries, Venice was more interested in resurrecting the achievements of the
Greeks. At the University of Padua the prevailing form of Aristotelianism,
originally developed by the Parisian Averroists, was one in which Aristotle
was not perceived as the ultimate "master of those who know," and his
theories and methodologies were constructively criticized. Philosophical con-

siderations were subordinated to his scientific work. Theology and meta-physics in general were gradually replaced by a closer study of nature. It was at the University of Padua that Fracastoro's scientific outlook was formed.

The work that brought most fame to Fracastoro was a lengthy narrative poem *Syphilis sive morbus Gallicus* (1530; *Syphilis: Or, A Poetical History of the French Disease*, 1686), written in verses similar to Vergil's *Georgics* (c. 37-29 B.C.). Fracastoro started working on this poem as early as 1510, but it was not until 1525 that it was presented in two books to Pietro Bembo, who at the time was considered to be the premier stylist. When it finally appeared in print in 1530 at Verona, it consisted of three books of some thirteen hundred hexameters.

In the first book, Fracastoro describes the horrors of the disease that had recently appeared in Europe and in a few years after 1495 spread across the whole continent. The disease was supposedly controlled by the sublime in-fluence of the planets, which could be interpreted as the council of gods. The epidemic of syphilis was reminiscent of previous plagues and gave Fra-castoro an opportunity to make allusions to pagan science, where the cosmic change is transmitted by the Lucretian seeds (*semina*) through the air.

The second book is devoted to cures. Fracastoro opens by describing his times, an age when disasters have been compensated for by the voyages of discovery. By judicious selection, he lists various cures and preventatives for the disease, setting the whole in a bucolic mood. He concludes the book with the myth of Ilceo, a shepherd in Syria, who, like Adonis, kills a stag sacred to Diana. As a punishment, he is stricken with a dreadful malady of the skin for which there is no remedy. Ilceo, through a dream, is directed to the underworld, where he is met by the nymph Lipare, who instructs him to wash himself in the river of flowing silver (mercury), which allows him to shed his skin like a snake and in this way rid himself of the disease. The whole is permeated with the influence of Vergil.

Book 3 contains another extended myth forming a short epos, on Christo-pher Columbus' voyage to the West Indies and the discovery of the Holy Tree, the guaiacum, which is a specific remedy against syphilis, which was endemic among the natives. The origin of this disease is explained by two stories. In the first, the natives are represented as survivors of Atlantis, which was destroyed by earthquakes and floods for its wickedness and af-flicted by this dreaded disease. In the second story, Syphilis, another shep-herd, blasphemed against Apollo the sun god and encouraged his king, Al-cithous, to assume the prerogatives of a god. As a punishment, he was stricken by Apollo with this pestilence. After proper expiatory sacrifices were performed, Juno and later Apollo relented, the healing tree was pro-vided by the gods, and Syphilis was cured.

It has been suggested that the subjects treated in this poem are but a pretext for positing the much deeper problem of the mutations that take place in nature. Nature constantly creates and destroys, distributing misery and happiness, without being influenced in any way by man's prayers and supplications. It is only through science that man can hope to tame nature and make it work for his benefit.

In 1538, Fracastoro published a work on astronomy, *Homocentricorum sive de stellis* (homocentricity on the stars), which he dedicated to Pope Paul III. He tried to represent the motions of the planets without having recourse to the epicycles or eccentrics and relying solely on circular motions about a single center (homocentric spheres). In this work, he was following the notions of two students of Plato, Eudoxus and Callippus, rather than ideas presented by Aristotle and developed by Ptolemy. Fracastoro's theory represents one of the last attempts to solve the planetary riddle before Nicolaus Copernicus.

This same book also contained his tract, this time of medical interest, *De causis criticorum dierum libellus* (1538), in which Fracastoro rejected the astrological explanation of the critical days as being dependent on the quarters of the moon, a notion which had been accepted by Galen. Fracastoro postulated his theory on two grounds: that ascription of critical days to the virtue of number was false, because neither number nor quantity can be the principle of action, and that the days of a disease seldom coincided with the phases of the moon. Fracastoro did not reject critical days as such, but he believed the causes underlying them have to be sought in the nature of the disease itself, that is, qualitative and quantitative alterations of the humors.

Many scholars have praised Fracastoro as a forerunner of the germ theory of infectious diseases, ascribing to him prophetic intuition. Most of his thinking on this subject is found in his *De contagionibus et contagiosis morbis et eorum curatione libri tres* (1546; *De contagione et contagiosis morbis et eorum curatione*, 1930), but one should remember that this tract is preceded in the same volume by his *De sympathia et antipathia rerum* (1546; on the attraction and repulsion of things), in which he stated that without understanding sympathy and antipathy one cannot deal with contagion. It is based on ancient theories of the continuity of nature and avoidance of a vacuum as well as the tendency of the elements toward their own natural places and the attraction of like for like. All of it is expounded in terms of Aristotelian philosophy, without any trace of experimental method. As far as contagion is concerned, Fracastoro postulated three means by which disease can be spread: by simple contact, as in the case of scabies or leprosy, by *fomites*, such as clothing or bedsheets, or at a distance, through the propagation of *seminaria morbi* (seeds of contagion), which propagate either by joining humors that have the greatest affinity or by attraction, penetrating through vessels. These *seminaria* proliferate rapidly in the human body and cause the humor to which they have closest affinity to putrify. He believed, however, that these seeds of contagion perish in a dead body. As far as his explanations are concerned, Fracastoro remains a product of his time, but, when he concerned himself with observed clinical phenomena, he demonstrated an acute ability in differential diagnosis.

Among his philosophical works, one must count three dialogues dealing with poetics, the intellect, and the soul: *Naugerius sive de poetica dialogus* (1549; English translation, 1924), and "Turrius sive de intellectione dialogus" and "Fracastorius sive de anima dialogus," which were published posthumously. The first of these is a panegyric of poetry as the most complete of the arts and the most useful. The second discusses such psychological problems as cognition, mind-object relationships, and the location of memory. It is interesting to note that Fracastoro perceived man as a microcosm. The last dialogue was claimed to have been written to denounce the teachings of his professor at Padua, Pomponazzi, who promoted the idea that the human soul is perishable; yet not one harsh word can be found against him in this work. Basically, it is an attempt to reconcile Aristotle with Christianity, relying not on dogmatic assertions but on experimental procedure and critical reasoning, which he was forced to abandon when he realized to which conclusions it was leading. In the end, Fracastoro himself was forced to assume a theological position.

Fracastoro produced various other shorter works of literary as well as scientific interest, some of which were printed centuries after his death, on August 6, 1553. He remains an exemplar of Italian Humanism, who, contrary to accepted wisdom, began to show interest in natural sciences.

Summary

Girolamo Fracastoro better than anyone else demonstrated the aspirations as well as the limitations of premodern science. To him poetry was the preferred vehicle to transmit information, and he was more concerned with demonstrating to his readers his classical erudition than his medical acumen. He can easily stand for the typical post-Renaissance man, who is clearly exhibiting his intellectual roots. He is almost an exact replica of Dante, though more than two centuries separate them and no one reading Vesalius would realize that he and Fracastoro were contemporaries. Yet most people tend to accept the great anatomist as a typical representative of the medical mentality of his age and try to make Fracastoro fit that mold. The fundamental difference between Fracastoro and Dante was their attitudes toward authority. Dante lived in a world of tamed Aristotelianism, where natural philosophy was still the preserve of the theologians, whereas Fracastoro was educated by physicians who believed in the separation of the two realms of theology and science; it was this new attitude that made the scientific revolution possible.

Bibliography

Fracastoro, Girolamo. *Fracastoro's Syphilis*. Translated with introduction, text, and notes by Geoffrey Eatough. Liverpool, England: Francis Cairns, 1984. Written mainly from the point of view of a literary scholar who stresses Fracastoro's poetic achievements. Contains a detailed analysis of the poem *Syphilis*. Includes a computer-generated word index.

Greswell, W. Parr, trans. *Memoirs of Angelus Politianus, Joannes Picus of Mirandula, Actius Sincerus Sannazarius, Petrus Bembus, Hieronymus Fracastorius, Marcus Antonius Flaminius, and the Amalthei*. Manchester, England: Cadell and Davies, 1805. An early biography of Fracastoro, based primarily on an even earlier life by F. O. Mencken. It is concerned primarily with Fracastoro as a literary figure. Especially good on reporting on his contemporaries' opinions about him. Contains notes and observations by Greswell.

Rosebury, Theodor. *Microbes and Morals: The Strange Story of Venereal Disease*. New York: Viking Press, 1971. Two chapters are devoted to Fracastoro, dealing specifically with syphilis as a medical problem. This book presents the best semipopular treatment of the origins of syphilis and whether it was brought from the Americas by the sailors of Columbus.

Thorndike, Lynn. "Fracastoro (1478-1553)." In *A History of Magic and Experimental Science*, vol. 5. New York: Columbia University Press, 1941. A short critical treatment of Fracastoro's scientific contributions. Thorndike was one of the first to realize that the Middle Ages were not quite as dark or the Renaissance quite as brilliant as was commonly accepted. In making this point, Thorndike uses evidence skillfully.

Truffi, Mario. "Fracastor's Life." In *Syphilis*, by Hieronymus Fracastor. St. Louis: Urologic & Cutaneus Press, 1931. A rather laudatory treatment of Fracastoro, written by a physician and therefore slanted more toward medical aspects of his life. A good counterbalance for the previous entry.

Leonardas V. Gerulaitis

JEAN-HONORÉ FRAGONARD

Born: April 5, 1732; Grasse, France
Died: August 22, 1806; Paris, France
Area of Achievement: Art
Contribution: One of the foremost painters of the eighteenth century and praised for the gaiety of his style and composition, Fragonard is renowned for his depictions of French high society in the years immediately preceding the Revolution.

Early Life

The son of a Grasse merchant, Jean-Honoré Fragonard was brought to Paris at the age of fifteen. His father had been ruined by bad investments, and Fragonard was apprenticed to a notary. Showing no talent for the law but already exhibiting signs of his artistic gift, he was taught by several important French masters, including the great landscape painter Jean Siméon Chardin and François Boucher. Boucher's influence proved the strongest, and Fragonard's work has often been compared to his teacher's, especially in its delightful depiction of frivolous French court life and the pleasures of the flesh.

A precocious talent, Fragonard won the Prix de Rome (one of the most coveted prizes in France) when he was only twenty. Beginning in 1756, he spent six years in Italy drawing monuments, ruins, Italian gardens, and copying works by Giovanni Battista Tiepolo and learning to emulate his sunny palette and sense of drama. For the most part, Fragonard was not drawn to Renaissance art but rather to landscapes and bacchanalian scenes.

Shortly after his return from Italy in the early 1760's, Fragonard painted a series of landscapes in rather dark, realistic tones to presage a shift in public taste away from the elaborate and fanciful decorativeness of rococo art. It may have been in response to this new seriousness in the public mood that the artist searched for a safe subject that would guarantee his full membership in the French Academy.

Life's Work

To become a member in the French Academy, Fragonard painted *Corésus Sacrificing Himself to Save Callirhoé* (c. 1761-1765), which was soundly praised by the critics and satisfied the Royal Academicians, who were looking for first-rate history painters to serve the needs of the state. Marion L. Grayson has called the painting "a scene of strange and violent pagan passions," and R. H. Wilenski has referred to it as "rather simple and severe with few of the impetuous curves that characterise his later drawing." Yet it is recognizably in Fragonard's manner, rendered with his characteristic flair for presenting voluptuous women. The painting pleased Fragonard's conservative contemporaries, but this stylish artist never returned to this kind of conventional work. Instead, he changed almost immediately to portraying risqué scenes from private life that made him something less than a respectable figure.

The Swing (c. 1766), perhaps Fragonard's most famous painting, epitomizes the artist's willingness to delineate titillating scenes which his contemporaries avoided. Gabriel-François Doyen had been approached by the Baron de Saint-Julien to paint his mistress on a swing being pushed by a bishop, and the baron wanted himself put somewhere in the composition, where he could have a good view of the charming lady's legs. Doyen was taken aback by the proposition and did not accept the commission, although he suggested the witty innovation of having the lady's slipper fly into the air to be caught by cupids. Fragonard not only accepted the baron's salacious conceit but also exaggerated it by showing the lady at the height of her swing kicking one leg high up against a cloudy background, sending her slipper upward toward a statue of a cupid while the baron (reclining on the ground) obtains a tantalizing glimpse of his lover. On the lady's other side, her husband (who seems to be amused) thrusts his arms forward, having pushed her high into the air. The picture forms a neat triangle, with the lady at its apex, her companions below taking different sorts of pleasure from her own gay recreation.

This has been called a naughty picture. It is also a brilliant evocation of sophisticated French court society before the Revolution, in which ladies and gentlemen indulged their fantasies, took lovers with considerable panache, and in general adopted a worldly attitude toward sin. If this painting was shocking, it was so only in the sense that an artist of Fragonard's stature would indulge his patron's whims so directly and flamboyantly. Technically, the artist's contemporaries recognized that his painting was a tour de force. The setting is beautifully realized: The lady swings into the light out of the cozy shadiness of the bushes and trelliswork. In the flowing folds of her dress, she appears as an airy creature, suspended between the yearning arms of two men. Indeed, the entire effect of the painting is of lightness and of fancy—the playfulness of desire.

With *The Swing*, Fragonard gained a reputation for pandering "to the tastes of a morally and esthetically decadent few," as Grayson puts it. His work provided elegant decoration for the residences of the rich and the highborn. Between 1770 and 1775, he painted the *Progress of Love* series of Madame du Barry, the mistress of Louis XV. His portraits rival those of Peter Paul Rubens in their supple rendering of human flesh, yet Fragonard's expressionistic brushwork gives his female figures an ethereal, almost spiritual quality—especially in portraits where a young woman is posed, quill in hand, about to write a letter, or is pictured with a letter in one hand while she places her other hand to her cheek as she reads with a serene, contented expression. In such works, the paint looks as though it has been swirled onto the canvas in one extremely graceful movement. Fragonard is said to have accomplished some of these portraits in an hour's time, a stunning feat of artistic inspiration and control.

Fragonard married in 1769, an important step for a painter who could have continued to frequent the salons of his patrons and remain outside the realm of respectable domesticity. Instead, he chose to pursue a more conventional existence, which had remarkable consequences for his work. Beginning in the 1770's, the painter turned to scenes of home life and family life. In *The Good Mother* (c. 1770-1772), for example, he took up Jean-Jacques Rousseau's conceit that the best education was to be got at home and that society should return to its origins in nature. Rousseau was reacting against the elaborate artifice of a society that had paid Fragonard handsomely for celebrating its sexual games and intrigues. Now Fragonard, with a home life of his own, and in a society moving toward the utter seriousness of a revolution that would overthrow the decadent court, was showing that he, too, had values that transcended what was merely fashionable. In a country that was gearing up for massive social change, *The Good Mother* emphasized continuity, security, and protectiveness. The subject is pictured in a luxuriant garden—more a fantasy or wish fulfillment than a real place—with a babe on her lap, another asleep beside her, and a third wide-awake, somewhat older child behind her pouring water into a bowl while the mother dips a cloth, evidently about to wash her infant's face. The harmony and peacefulness of this scene is echoed in many other paintings—in settings where a motherly figure is portrayed with children gathered about her teaching them the alphabet, where daily life and domestic pursuits are given a uniquely sincere value.

Horace Shipp has pointed out that these two phases of Fragonard's work—his erotic portrayals of courtly society and his charmingly serious evocations of family life—constitute different veins of influence stemming from his apprenticeship to Chardin (the man of the people who found in their homely lives and scenes his inspiration) and Boucher (the fantastic colorist and decorator who gave a rococo flourish to the sexually titillating lives of the richly privileged). For a time, in other words, Fragonard was able to mirror and to capitalize upon the contradictions of his society which was, at turns, attracted to domestic stability, dignified and historical themes, moralizing stories based on pagan subject matter, romantic landscapes, and classical subjects (Roman ruins and sculpture). It was only in his last years, in the period of the Revolution, that the artist's complex attitude toward his paradoxical culture was incapable of coping with enormous, abrupt change.

Summary

In his last years, Jean-Honoré Fragonard came under the protection of

Jacques-Louis David, who became, in Wilenski's words, the "art-dictator" of the Revolution. David believed that Fragonard had painted many masterpieces, and he was able to secure for his older contemporary a secure position as a museum curator. Yet the temper of the times had clearly turned against an artist who could easily, if unfairly, be accused of frivolousness and of idealizing the lives of the idle rich. The very gorgeousness of Fragonard's technique, his extraordinary facility with paint, was condemned for its seductiveness. By 1806, when Napoleon decreed that all artists and their studios must be removed from the Louvre, Fragonard, then seventy-four, was forced to find a new home and place to work. On August 22, 1806, Fragonard, hot from a long walk, sat down at a café to eat an ice and died of a stroke.

In the years since his death, Fragonard has come to be valued for his style, for the way he is able to endow the slightest subject matter with elegance and wit. In discussing one of his great landscapes, *The Fête at Saint-Cloud* (c. 1778-1780), Raymond Mortimer marvels at the witty, seductive, and kind look at nymphs, at a "Nature in gauze and feathers, a millinery of trees, under which to be private" and imagines a modern rake exclaiming, "Oh, to have lived when frivolity could be thus poetical." Mortimer notes that Fragonard's scenes never really existed, that they are highly idealized— expressions of fantasy, not reality. Fragonard's work still has the power to disturb viewers who demand a politically engaged and socially responsible art and to indulge viewers who find satisfaction in admiring the artist's technique and his ability to suggest a world where the art of living and where the artist's talent predominate.

Bibliography

Fragonard, Jean-Honoré. *Fragonard Drawings for Ariosto*. Essays by Elizabeth Mangan, Philip Hofer, and Jean Seznec. New York: Pantheon Books, 1945. The essays discuss Fragonard as draftsman, illustrated editions of Ariosto's *Orlando Furioso*, and Fragonard as an interpreter of Ariosto's long narrative poem that features the adventures of Roland and Charlemagne's other knights in wars against the Saracens. Notes, a bibliography, and 137 black-and-white plates make this a comprehensive study of the artist as illustrator.

Grappe, Georges. *Fragonard: La Vie et L'Œuvre*. Monaco: Les Documents D'Art, 1946. The text is useful only for readers of French, but the volume also contains thirty-two large black-and-white plates of the artist's most important works.

Grayson, Marion L. *Fragonard and His Friends*. St. Petersburg, Fla.: Museum of Fine Arts, 1982. A catalog of an exhibition, held November 20, 1982, through February 6, 1983. Sixty black-and-white plates document the place of Fragonard's art in his time, with examples of his painting and of engravings made by others of his work. Included in the exhibition is work by Boucher, Chardin, and many of Fragonard's other contemporaries and teachers. Notes on individual plates explain the background of the work. Grayson's biographical and critical introductions to Fragonard and his contemporaries are succinct and insightful and make this catalog an extremely valuable study.

Muehsam, Gerd, ed. *French Painters and Paintings from the Fourteenth Century to Post-Impressionism*. New York: Frederick Ungar, 1970. Contains two illustrations of Fragonard's work and excellent excerpts from studies of his painting. A detailed bibliography and indexes help organize and structure this anthology of criticism.

Shipp, Horace. *The French Masters: A Survey and Guide*. London: S. Low, Marston, 1931. One of the older histories of French art, but still a competent and succinct treatment of Fragonard's place in the context of his teachers and successors. Several black-and-white plates, a chronology of important dates in French history, and an index make this a convenient, accessible source of study.

Wilenski, R. H. *French Painting*. Rev. ed. Boston: Charles T. Branford, 1949. Contains an excellent section on Fragonard's life, his oeuvre, and his accomplishments as an artist. Several black-and-white plates give a representative survey of his work. A judicious and well-indexed study.

Carl Rollyson

FRANCIS I

Born: September 12, 1494; Cognac, France
Died: March 31, 1547; Rambouillet, France
Areas of Achievement: Monarchy and patronage of the arts
Contribution: Francis I, France's Renaissance monarch, increased the power of the Crown within France, led his country in a series of wars against the Habsburgs, created a glittering court, and helped to introduce the Italian Renaissance into France.

Early Life

When Francis was born to Charles d'Angoulême and his young wife, Louise of Savoy, he was not expected to become King of France. Only after Charles VIII died childless three years later, making Francis' cousin King Louis XII, did he become next in line to the throne. Indeed, not until Louis died in 1515 without having fathered a son was it absolutely certain that the twenty-year-old Francis would take the throne. After the somber last years of his aged, weary predecessor, Francis on his accession represented youth, vigor, and enthusiasm to his subjects. He had developed into a tall, athletic man with a lively and expressive, rather than handsome, face. His education in academics and statecraft had been haphazard at best, and his great passions were for the chase and for seduction, rather than for the sedentary arts of statesmanship. Throughout his reign, Francis maintained a court notorious for its elegance, gaiety, and erotic exuberance. Notwithstanding his sensual self-indulgence, this cheerful, gracious, and dashing young man would become one of France's most respected sovereigns.

Life's Work

The land to which Francis fell heir in 1515 was growing steadily in prosperity, population, and power. The ravages of the Hundred Years' War were a rapidly fading memory, and the feudal dynasties which had checked the power of France's kings for so long had mostly disappeared. The nobles were clamoring for the adventure, glory, and profits of conquest, and their young king was eager to oblige them. In July, 1515, Francis led an army into northern Italy, continuing Louis XII's policy of seeking to control the wealthy Duchy of Milan. In September, he won the greatest victory of his reign at the Battle of Marignano. Charging joyously at the head of his cavalry, Francis shattered the dreaded Swiss pikemen. This left him the master of Milan and the dominant power in northern Italy, a happy situation which would not last long. The deaths of Ferdinand of Aragon in 1516 and of the Emperor Maximilian in 1519 made their grandson, Charles V of the house of Habsburg, ruler of Spain and its possessions in the New World, of Austria, of the Burgundian lands, and of much of Italy as well. When Charles was elected Holy Roman Emperor in 1519, France was virtually encircled by his power.

Francis spent much of the rest of his reign fighting with Charles, trying to maintain his own power in Italy and to prevent Charles from dominating all of Europe. In 1525, Charles's armies routed the French at the Battle of Pavia, and Francis learned the folly of a king trying to lead his troops in the field: He was captured, and Charles replaced him as the dominant power in Italy. Francis was forced to spend the next year as Charles's prisoner in Spain, gaining his release only by agreeing to a humiliating treaty. Once free, Francis swiftly repudiated the treaty and resumed hostilities. In a series of punishing wars over the following two decades, joined at various times by Venice, England, the Papacy, Protestant German princes, and even—to the horror of all Christendom—the Turks, Francis struggled unsuccessfully to regain Milan and to break the Habsburg hold on Italy. This great contest, the rivalry between the house of Habsburg and the French Crown, would continue to dominate European power politics until the eighteenth century.

Francis was able to mobilize his kingdom's human and material resources in the service of his Italian ambitions to an extent which would have dazzled his predecessors. Many scholars, impressed by the obedience and support which he commanded, have regarded him as a key figure in the development of France's absolute monarchy. There are strong arguments in favor of this view. Public opinion and the most important French political theorists of the time, reacting against the civil wars and vulnerability to invasion which had bedeviled France in earlier centuries when the Crown was weak, were inclined to stress the absolute nature of the royal prerogative. Tracts such as Guillaume Budé's *De l'institution du prince* (1547, wr. 1518) argued that the king's power was limitless and that he was not bound to respect any rights of his subjects.

Without question, Francis himself subscribed wholly to Budé's views. Throughout his reign he showed little inclination to let any considerations of customs or rights, no matter how venerable, interfere with the accomplishment of his desires. As he was energetic, charming, intelligent, and determined enough to win the respect and support of most of the politically active population of his kingdom, Francis was generally successful. He was able to absorb into the royal domain the vast holdings of Charles, Duke of Bourbon, after Bourbon betrayed him in 1523. Francis also reformed and centralized the fiscal administration of the Crown, and he significantly increased the control of the central government over its provincial officials. He was able repeatedly to bulldoze his way past objections to his policies and edicts voiced by the Parlement de Paris, ignoring its traditional function as a check on the legal absolutism of French kings.

Francis' most important struggles with the Parlement concerned religion. In 1516, fresh from his great victory at Marignano, he negotiated the Concordat of Bologna with the pope. This agreement restored the Papacy's right to tax the French church, in exchange for confirming and extending Francis' power over appointments to high church offices in France. The Parlement's genuine outrage over this double blow to the independence of the French church was contemptuously rejected by Francis, who forced the body to register the Concordat in 1518. The Parlement was equally distressed by Francis' reluctance to persecute religious dissidents, particularly the adherents of the new Protestant ideas which began seeping into France as early as 1519. Again, however, their remonstrances went unheeded by the king. Not until the mid-1530's, when Francis himself became concerned about the increasing radicalism of the reformers, did he inaugurate systematic persecution. By this time, though, the new ideas had become too strong to be dislodged without a protracted, agonizing struggle.

Francis was obviously a far stronger king, more securely in control of his government and his kingdom, than any of his predecessors. That does not, however, mean that his power was absolute. Francis' subjects, particularly the nobles and the wealthy bourgeoisie, continued to possess independent military and political strength which Francis was forced to respect. That can be seen most clearly in the field of finance. Even though Francis' extravagance and his endless wars left him chronically in need of funds, he did not dare to raise taxes enough to meet his needs. He knew too well that his subjects could still rebel against him if he pushed his prerogative too far, infringing on what they considered to be their own traditional rights. That was shown in 1542, when an attempt to impose new taxes in the southwest of France provoked a serious armed rebellion.

For the most part, therefore, Francis had no choice but to raise the money he needed by a series of expedients which inevitably undermined royal power in the long run. He sold public offices and titles of nobility, he sold royal lands, and he borrowed. Thus, he bequeathed to his son and heir, Henry II, a number of officials who could neither be fired nor relied upon, shrunken revenues from the royal domain, and a discouraging mound of debts. Clearly Francis' absolutism did not include unlimited power to tap the wealth of his subjects. In addition, though the Parlement and other institutions had been cowed into obedience by Francis, once his strong hand was removed from the scene they lost little time in reasserting themselves under his successors. Francis as an individual was popular and respected enough to get most of what he wanted done, but his reign does not appear to have left the monarchy as an ongoing institution significantly stronger than it had been before.

Francis is more admired today for his role as a generous and discriminating patron of culture than for his political or military policies. Throughout his life, Francis maintained a lively interest in intellectual and artistic pursuits, particularly after his early campaigns in Italy exposed him to the

Humanism of the Renaissance there. Back in France he established lecture-ships in classical Latin and Greek, in Hebrew, and in mathematics, which would ultimately evolve into the Collège de France. He was an avid amasser of both books and manuscripts, and his collections would form the nucleus of the Bibliothèque Nationale, the French national library.

Francis' generosity toward artists attracted Leonardo da Vinci, Benvenuto Cellini, Andrea del Sarto, and other Italian masters to France, helping to establish the Renaissance style there. Many of their works, including Leo-nardo's *Mona Lisa*, have remained among the treasures of France ever since Francis' reign; indeed, Francis' extensive collection of paintings and other artworks have become the nucleus of the collection of the Louvre. Francis' interest in the arts can also be seen today in the numerous châteaus which he built or modified, again spreading Renaissance styles into France. Among the most notable are those of Chambord, Blois, and Fontainebleau. At these and similar palaces, Francis did much to introduce a still-coarse and tur-bulent French nobility to a more elegant, sophisticated, and graceful way of life. His reign significantly improved the manners, if not the morals, of the French elite.

Summary

As a man Francis I is best remembered for his charm, the refinement and elegance which he brought to the French court, and for his numerous love affairs and gallant dalliances. As a king he was popular and successful, though not a reformer or innovator of great significance. While it is an exag-geration to regard him as an absolute monarch or even as a major architect of the absolute monarchy of the late seventeenth century, he made the power of the Crown felt in France to an unprecedented extent during his reign. As a statesman his wars against Charles V, even though unsuccessful, did keep France independent and established it even more firmly as one of the great powers of Europe. As a patron of culture he is largely responsible for spreading the styles and standards of the Italian Renaissance into France, raising the level of civilization there and endowing his kingdom with many lasting treasures.

Bibliography

Hackett, Francis. *Francis the First*. Garden City, N.Y.: Doubleday, 1935, reprint 1968. A highly readable, romantic popular biography, but dated and not always judicious in its conclusions. Hackett's enthusiasm for psy-choanalyzing Francis and other figures unfortunately entailed the con-struction of great edifices of interpretation on flimsy foundations of fact. No notes or bibliography.

Knecht, R. J. *Francis I*. Cambridge, England: Cambridge University Press, 1982. This study will remain the standard English-language biography of Francis for some time to come. Thoroughly researched, elegantly written, and soundly argued, it is a splendid example of modern scholarship. Its 431 pages of text intelligently cover all aspects of Francis' reign and are supplemented by an extensive bibliography. A detailed index increases the usefulness of the work.

_____. *Francis I and Absolute Monarchy*. London: Historical Association, 1969. This brief pamphlet argues cogently in favor of regarding Francis as an absolute monarch. It is basically a response to the work of Major, cited below.

McNeil, David O. *Guillaume Budé and Humanism in the Reign of Francis I*. Geneva: Librairie Droz, 1975. Concentrates on religious and intellectual developments during Francis' reign, centering on the life and works of Budé. McNeil also discusses Budé's significant role in the politics of the times. Contains a comprehensive bibliography on the subject.

Major, J. Russell. *Representative Institutions in Renaissance France, 1421-1559*. Madison: University of Wisconsin Press, 1960. This controversial, seminal volume by a great scholar argues that the absolutism of Francis and other sixteenth century French kings has been much exaggerated. Should be read in conjunction with the works by Knecht cited above.

Salmon, J. H. M. *Society in Crisis: France in the Sixteenth Century*. New York: St. Martin's Press, 1975. Though the bulk of this book deals with the religious conflicts of the second half of the century, the opening chapters contain a serious analysis of all aspects of the France of Francis I. Economic and social structures, the institutions of government, and cultural developments, rather than narrative political history, are emphasized. A detailed index, an extensive bibliography, genealogical charts, and a glossary of French terms help make this work an excellent reference.

Seward, Desmond. *Prince of the Renaissance: The Golden Life of François I*. New York: Macmillan, 1973. A beautifully illustrated and lively, though brief and rather superficial, popular biography. Very thorough on Francis' patronage of the arts but tends to exaggerate his role in shaping French culture. The work must also be used with caution on diplomacy and government, as Seward tends to let his flair for the colorful and the dramatic get the best of his judgment. Skimpy bibliography and few notes.

Garrett L. McAinsh

FRANCIS JOSEPH I

Born: August 18, 1830; Schönbrunn Palace, near Vienna, Austria
Died: November 21, 1916; Schönbrunn Palace, near Vienna, Austria
Area of Achievement: Government
Contribution: The reign of Francis Joseph I was one of the longest in European history. Ascending the throne at the age of eighteen, he eventually became the living symbol of an imperial ideal of government doomed to vanish at his death, which occurred near the end of World War I.

Early Life
The person who had the most profound effect upon the character of Francis Joseph was his mother, Princess Sophie of Bavaria. This younger daughter of Maximilian I married Charles Francis, the second son of Emperor Francis I, in 1824, and, until the birth of her first son, she devoted her time to mastering the bewildering etiquette of the Austrian court as well as the maze of imperial politics.

The heir to the throne, Archduke Ferdinand, was mentally handicapped and suffered from epilepsy. It was expected that the crown would pass to Sophie's retiring and irresolute husband. Since she was already regarded as the best political mind in the family, few had any doubts about who would govern the empire. Metternich, the man who had redrawn the map of Europe in 1815, dashed Sophie's hopes by arranging a marriage for the hapless Ferdinand and persuading the emperor that his heir was capable of ruling Austria. In 1835, Francis died and Ferdinand ascended the throne.

Archduke Charles Francis was a loving and devoted father to his children, but their mother was in charge. Although young Francis had been given a household of his own at birth, his mother totally controlled his upbringing. Slowly, the charming prince began to evolve into a devout and gallant young gentleman. Although he was not a scholar, Francis was a conscientious student, but his real love was military science. At the age of thirteen, he was appointed a colonel of dragoons and began to train seriously for a career as a soldier. The handsome, graceful youth proved an instant favorite who fit easily into the carefree world of Vienna in the last years before the Revolution of 1848.

The events that shook the foundations of the empire between March and December of 1848 provided the opportunity for which the Archduchess Sophie had long waited. With Metternich a fugitive in England, she easily persuaded her husband to renounce his claim to the throne in favor of their eldest son. On December 2, 1848, Emperor Ferdinand gladly abdicated in favor of his nephew, who assumed the name Francis Joseph in memory of Joseph II, the great reforming emperor of the late eighteenth century. As the imperial family journeyed from Vienna, however, it was the new empress-mother who was busily charting the course of the new reign, not the young emperor.

Life's Work

During the first three years of his reign Francis Joseph demonstrated his hostility to liberalism and constitutional government by methodically revoking most of the changes which had been made by the revolutionaries. Even freedom of the press was denied lest criticism of the regime become too widespread. With the confidence of youth, the emperor sought to fashion a centralized absolutism in which all power and responsibility would reside in him. While a number of worthy administrative reforms were made to implement this policy, he totally ignored the potent force of nationalism. When the Hungarians under Lajos Kossuth resisted, their fledgling republic was crushed by troops sent from Russia by Czar Nicholas I, who was delighted to further the cause of reaction.

When a Hungarian patriot tried unsuccessfully to assassinate Francis Joseph in February, 1853, the young sovereign's sense of mission only deepened. He believed that he had been sent to revive the defunct Holy Roman Empire in partnership with a revitalized Roman Catholic church. Apart from this rather grand scheme, his foreign policy was rather erratic and unimpressive.

Against his mother's wishes Francis Joseph married his sixteen-year-old cousin, Elizabeth of Bavaria, on April 24, 1854. Unfortunately for the young couple, Sophie decided to mold her niece into her image of an empress. Elizabeth was equally determined to resist, and the struggle of these two strong-willed women eventually led to an estrangement between Francis Joseph and his wife. Sophie then assumed the responsibility for rearing her three grandchildren while their mother frequented fashionable spas, seeking to restore her health.

At the moment his personal happiness began to vanish, the emperor was forced to face the loss of all of his Italian possessions except Venetia. The combined armies of France and Piedmont-Savoy defeated the Austrians at Solferino on June 24, 1859. This bloody battle and the peace terms arranged at Villafranca the next month forced Francis Joseph to make some drastic changes in the way in which the empire was governed.

The liberals, whom the emperor had rejected at the beginning of his reign, were now wooed with the creation of an imperial parliament, whose membership was effectively restricted to the moneyed classes. The Hungarians, Poles, and Czechs refused to cooperate, but Francis Joseph proceeded with his plan for a largely German legislature. Having lost most of his Italian possessions, the emperor turned his attention to regional affairs. His dream of an Austrian-led central Europe brought Francis Joseph unwittingly into conflict with Otto von Bismarck.

In 1864, Bismarck lured the Austrians into a war against Denmark to prevent the incorporation of the largely German duchies of Schleswig and Holstein into that kingdom. The war lasted barely six months, and with its end the control of Schleswig passed to Prussia and the control of Holstein to Austria. While he diplomatically isolated Austria, Bismarck began a war of nerves over the administration of Holstein. Goaded beyond endurance, Austria went to war against Prussia in June, 1866. On July 2, 1866, the Prussians and their allies won a decisive victory at Königgrätz. Francis Joseph was forced to acquiesce to the absorption of most of northern and central Germany into the Prussian dominated North German Confederation. There were repeated calls for the emperor's abdication in favor of his younger brother Maximilian. The final humiliation was the seizure by Italy of Venetia with the blessing of Prussia.

To prevent the complete disintegration of the empire, Francis Joseph agreed to the Compromise of 1867, which created an independent Hungary within a dual monarchy. As Emperor of Austria and King of Hungary, he presided over a government which shared control of foreign affairs, armed forces, and finances between Vienna and Budapest. Shortly after his coronation in Hungary in June, 1867, Francis Joseph learned of the death of Maximilian before a firing squad in Mexico. For three years Maximilian had been emperor of that turbulent country with the support of the French, but the desertion of his allies left him at the mercy of his rebellious subjects.

The death of his brother was the first of a series of personal tragedies which haunted the remaining years of Francis Joseph's life. When Sophie died in 1873, the possible reconciliation between her son and daughter-in-law did not take place; instead, the gulf that separated them grew wider. Although intelligent and liberal in his political outlook, Crown Prince Rudolf did not display the same dedication to duty which his father prized, nor was his personal life exemplary. When Rudolf and his mistress committed suicide in January, 1889, the very foundations of the empire were shaken. The empress never recovered from her son's death, and her wanderings became more aimless until she died at the hands of an assassin in Geneva in September, 1898.

Francis Joseph's last years were marred by the murder of his nephew and heir, Franz Ferdinand, at Sarajevo in June, 1914, and by World War I. A man of peace, he would have preferred to spend his last days with his grandchildren. Instead, he died like a good soldier immersed in war-related work on November 21, 1916.

Summary

The rapid disintegration of the Austro-Hungarian Empire in the last months of the war surprised a number of experts. It had survived so many crises since the end of the Napoleonic era, including revolution and the constantly disruptive force of nationalism, that it seemed eternal. Francis Joseph I was the force that held together the diverse elements that composed his empire. The ideas which he brought to the throne were those of his mother, Metternich, and Felix Schwarzenberg, his first prime minister. As he matured, these youthful ideas were modified or discarded. Personal tragedy tempered his nature and endeared him to his people.

It may well be that he perceived the incurable weaknesses in his empire long before they became apparent to others, but with a tenacity born of adversity he devoted his life to preserving the rather antiquated structure. With age and infirmity, he was forced to curtail his public duties and leave the cares of state to lesser men. By then he was already a legend, almost a national icon. He was the one element that held the Austro-Hungarian Empire together, and when he died, it died with him.

Bibliography
Bagger, Eugene S. *Francis Joseph, Emperor of Austria-King of Hungary.* New York: G. P. Putnam's Sons, 1927. This standard biography, while almost contemporary with its subject, remains a work of solid and reliable scholarship. The author tends to avoid an in-depth analysis of private and personal matters in favor of a strict historical narrative. It should be read as background to other later works.
Crankshaw, Edward. *The Fall of the House of Habsburg.* New York: Viking Press, 1963. The bulk of this work is devoted to the reign of Francis Joseph and the collapse of the Austro-Hungarian Empire after his death. Well-written and well-documented. Contains a useful bibliography.
McGuigan, Dorothy Gies. *The Habsburgs.* Garden City, N.Y.: Doubleday, 1966. Although a general history of the Habsburg Dynasty, one quarter of this work is devoted to Francis Joseph. The notes and bibliography are extremely valuable. Useful for its sensitivity to the forces that destroyed the empire and to the destiny that trapped the last Habsburgs.
Marek, George R. *The Eagles Die: Franz Joseph, Elisabeth, and Their Austria.* New York: Harper & Row, 1974. The rather complicated, yet tragic relationship between Francis Joseph and his wife is the theme of this work. The men and women who influenced their lives are carefully profiled. The portrait of the emperor is particularly sensitive and complete.
May, Arthur J. *The Habsburg Monarchy, 1867-1914.* Cambridge, Mass.: Harvard University Press, 1951. The primary focus of this work is the period from the Compromise of 1867 to the outbreak of World War I. A work of depth and scholarship. The chapter notes are particularly valuable.
Wandruszka, Adam. *The House of Habsburg: Six Hundred Years of a European Dynasty.* Translated by Cathleen Epstein and Hans Epstein. Garden City, N.Y.: Doubleday, 1964. Gives a valuable overview of the entire

dynasty with a brief but incisive treatment of Francis Joseph. The genealogical charts are particularly useful.

Clifton W. Potter, Jr.

CÉSAR FRANCK

Born: December 10, 1822; Liège, Belgium
Died: November 8, 1890; Paris, France
Area of Achievement: Music
Contribution: Franck's mastery of the principles of orchestration and the harmonic theories of the nineteenth century made him the acknowledged leader of French music of the era and one of the world's great composers.

Early Life

César Auguste Franck was the firstborn son of a minor bank official who had come from Aix to settle in Liège in 1817 and had married a German woman in 1820. Nicholas-Joseph, the father, was an ambitious, frustrated man. Himself a lover of music and amateur musician, he curried the favor of the writers and artists of Liège and transferred his thwarted ambition for fame and fortune onto César, who early displayed musical ability. Nicholas-Joseph arranged a strict schedule for the boy, forcing him to rigorous study of the piano and composition. By the time César was eight years old, the elder Franck enrolled him at the local conservatory, where his musical aptitude gained for him the notice of his teachers.

In 1835, when Franck was thirteen, his father sent him to Paris to study counterpoint and harmony under the most notable music masters of the day. Eager to succeed through the merits of his son, Nicholas-Joseph arranged a number of public concerts at which his young son performed as a prodigy, along with such established musicians as Franz Liszt. At these concerts, Franck played some of his own compositions. Though competent, they were undistinguished.

Realizing that a foreigner had very little chance to make his way into the musical establishment of Paris, Nicholas-Joseph became a naturalized French citizen and won for Franck the right to enroll in the prestigious Paris Conservatory in 1837. Franck's talents were so extraordinary that by the end of the first year he had taken a special first prize for playing a difficult piano piece, astonishing his examiners by transposing the work into another key while sight reading.

For four years the young Franck pursued his studies, especially of the organ, an instrument which was to be a crucial factor in his career. Then—probably at his father's perverse insistence—Franck resigned from the conservatory in 1842. His father had arranged a series of weekly concerts to be held in his own home and Franck obligingly performed, playing some of his own pieces—fantasias, adaptations of tunes from popular light operas, and other theatrical music. He also composed a set of four piano trios (1843), works which brought him some serious attention, but by and large the music of this concert period was more attuned to public taste and personal profit than to serious artistic concerns.

Gradually, Franck grew restive under the despotism of his father. Though he had made a number of artistic friendships through his father's contrivances—people such as Franz Liszt and Hector Berlioz—Franck bridled under his father's overbearing control, which forced him to produce the kind of music which the old man thought would advance his son's, and his own, career.

One such composition was *Ruth* (1846), an oratorio composed from earlier musical jottings. Based on the Old Testament story of Ruth and Boaz, the work comprised fifteen numbers, and when first performed drew a number of serious reviews. Critics noted its simplicity, its almost childlike directness, and though the work was a failure it remains the first major achievement of the composer, one that he would come back to and revise some thirty years later.

Meanwhile, Franck had met and fallen in love with one of his piano pupils, Félicité Saillot-Desmousseaux, whose parents were actors in the Comédie Française. Franck married Saillot in February, 1848. The marriage signaled a formal break with his father; Franck was now on his own.

Retiring from public music, Franck began making his living primarily as a teacher, as accompanist at a conservatory in Orléans and, significantly, as organist at the Church of Saint-Jean-Saint-François-au-Marais and, more important, at the Church of Sainte-Clotilde. These were key events in his artistic career. The modern organ of Franck's time, especially the wonderful instrument at Sainte-Clotilde, was capable of producing a wide range of tones and orchestral coloring and presented Franck with the opportunity of developing a musical technique based on this symphonic capability. For the rest of his life Franck was to dedicate himself to the mastery of the organ, though his duties as church organist kept him, for almost two decades, from creating any music more significant than improvisational pieces and routine liturgical works. Thus, from the late 1840's to the beginning of the Franco-Prussian War in 1870, Franck lived and worked in virtual obscurity.

Life's Work

In retrospect, this obscurity was a period of creative gestation during which Franck worked out his musical ideas. *Six Pièces* (1862) were short, improvisational experiments filled with a majestic tonality and a melodiousness which were to characterize his later masterpieces. Liszt, who was one of Franck's earliest and most important friends, regarded these pieces as worthy of comparison to those of Johann Sebastian Bach.

Meanwhile, the contacts he had made during a thirty-year career as musician, teacher, and minor composer began to bear fruit. Liszt had been playing Franck's 1843 trios in Germany and had gained for the composer some small measure of fame. Additionally, Franck's mastery of the organ now brought him into contact with French musicians who specialized in that instrument. The Franco-Prussian War raised French nationalistic sentiment, so that by late 1871 a group of French composers and musicians organized the National Society of Music. Its purpose was to promote, through concerts, the music of French composers. At fifty, Franck was the oldest in the group, but he was to become one of its most important artists.

The years immediately after Franck's fiftieth birthday were central in his career as a composer. He was appointed professor of the organ at the conservatory in 1872, and though the position did little for him financially it did establish his preeminence and brought his music more serious attention. Parts of his oratorio *Ruth*, which had lain in comparative neglect since the late 1840's, were given fresh performances. Amid such renewed interest in his music, Franck determined to compose an ambitious work.

The work was *Rédemption* (1873), which Franck conceived as a symphonic poem for orchestra and voice. The text is in three parts. Part 1 tells of man's paganism and his expectations of the coming of Christ. Part 2 records man's Christian joy through the centuries, and part 3 laments the Fall of Man and contemplates a second redemption through prayer.

Though the obvious religiosity of the subject deeply appealed to the composer, the work was a resounding failure, not only because of poor copies of the orchestration and bad conducting but also because the piece lacked dramatic tension. Nevertheless, *Rédemption* is important in the Franck canon as a transitional work, particularly the section of symphonic interlude, bearing characteristics of harmony and tonality that distinguish the best of Franck's music.

Despite this setback, however, Franck continued his duties as teacher, establishing a profound influence on the younger generation of French composers and musicians who embraced his ideas of harmony and the relationship of chords and keys. One of his pupils, Vincent d'Indy, a composer in his own right and one of Franck's first biographers, records his famous impression of Franck at the organ, his flowing white hair and whiskers setting off his dark, piercing eyes.

In 1874, Franck first heard the prelude to Richard Wagner's *Tristan und Isolde* and was reassured about his own harmonic techniques. The following year, Franck composed *Les Éolides*, first performed in Paris in 1876. A major orchestral work, this symphonic poem is the first composition which fully integrates structure and tonality, combining lyrical delicacy with structural grace. *Les Éolides* introduced the last phase of Franck's achievement. The work ushered in a period of creative efflorescence that continued unabated until the composer's death some fifteen years later. At the age of fifty-three, when most composers had already completed most of their best work, Franck was just beginning to produce his masterpieces.

Les Béatitudes was completed in 1879 and published the following year. A large-scale oratorio based on Christ's Sermon on the Mount, the work is impressive in its structural integrity and its use of certain keys to denote psychological states. Also in 1879, Franck astonished the musical world with one of his greatest works, *Quintet in F Minor for Piano and Strings*. Filled with dramatic energy and passion, it still retains a formal structure that provides a balance and cohesiveness, making the quintet among the composer's most popular works. Still another oratorio, *Rebecca*, appeared the following year, but it was the two symphonic poems, *Le Chasseur maudit* (1882) and *Les Djinns* (1884), and the *Variations symphoniques* (1885) that finally established Franck as one of France's greatest composers. These works are characterized by a lush harmony within a tightly structured cyclical form, a technique of restating themes and chords as a principle of musical organization.

The awarding of the Legion of Honor to Franck in 1885 was a tribute no less to his achievement as a composer as to his standing as a professor and his character as a man. Such official recognition was thus the culmination of the public's belated acknowledgment. With the *Sonata in A Major for Violin and Piano* (1886), he produced a masterpiece of chamber music—concise, eloquent, and finely structured. It is one of his most popular compositions.

At the height of his creative powers, Franck climaxed his career as a composer in the production of his only symphony, the magnificent *Symphony in D Minor*. For sheer expressiveness, controlled by classical form, and as an example of chromatic richness and harmonic beauty, the symphony ranks as the composer's crowning work. Though it earned for him a mixed reception at its first performance—some of the criticism leveled particularly at the use of the English horn in the first movement—the symphony has never lost its appeal. It is regarded by many as one of the great symphonies of the world.

The *String Quartet in D Major* (1889), his last major composition, is also one of his best. Typical of his greatest work, the quartet is masterfully structured, melodically rich, a superb example of the cyclical form at its most subtle and concise.

In October, 1890, still involved in several projects, Franck caught cold. By November, his condition worsened. Pleurisy developed and he died on November 8.

Summary

Among great composers, César Franck was the least prolific. He contributed only one symphony to the orchestral repertory and only three major works in chamber music. Yet the quality of these compositions assures for Franck a place as the foremost composer of absolute—that is, nonprogrammatic—music in France during the nineteenth century.

Though he wrote numerous choral works throughout his career, his genius was not as a composer for the voice. His oratorios, while creditable, lack the texture of harmonic fullness, even the drama, of his orchestral scores. His opera *Hulda*, written hastily between 1884 and 1886, was never produced during Franck's lifetime; another, "Ghiselle" was never completed. Neither is of any consequence.

Yet in his symphonic poems, his chamber music, and his symphony, Franck led the way among all French composers of the nineteenth century. In a period when French music was dominated by theatrical forms, especially the opera and operetta, Franck looked back to the classical forms of Bach and Ludwig van Beethoven and created works of forceful and melodic character. As a teacher, Franck influenced a generation of French composers who carried their master's dedication to well-designed harmonic structure into the twentieth century.

Bibliography
Davies, Laurence. *César Franck and His Circle*. Boston: Houghton Mifflin, 1970. A classic study not only of Franck but also of his influence on the lives and works of his pupils and musical descendants. Such composers as Ernest Chausson, Henri Duparc, and Vincent d'Indy brought to their music the principles of their master, who must thus be considered a precursor of modern music.
Demuth, Norman. *César Franck*. London: Dennis Dobson, 1949. A musical study of the composer with copious examples of notation and scoring. Suggests that Franck was a pioneer in the creation of the symphonic poem. A good biography, though rather technical for the lay reader.
Indy, Vincent d'. *César Franck*. Translated by Rosa Newmarch. London: John Lane, 1910. An important early biography, representing the biased view of one of Franck's pupils. Himself a composer, d'Indy writes reverently of Franck and his music, glorifying the composer in tones amounting almost to deification. Assessments aside, historical details are accurate.
Ulrich, Homer. *Chamber Music*. 2d ed. New York: Columbia University Press, 1966. A good, brief examination of Franck's chamber works, noting particularly their cyclical form. A basic knowledge of musical composition would help the lay reader to appreciate fully Franck's structural methods.
_____. *Symphonic Music, Its Evolution Since the Renaissance*. New York: Columbia University Press, 1952. Views Franck as a late Romanticist and notes his mastery of the cyclical form, with several examples of notation. Interesting reference to Franck's skill as master organist and the effect of such on his orchestral writing.
Vallas, Léon. *César Franck*. Translated by Hubert Foss. Reprint. Westport, Conn.: Greenwood Press, 1973. The avowed purpose of this study is to demythologize the life and work of Franck as established by d'Indy and others. Though accurate, it devotes as much space to Franck's choral

music as to his more important orchestral works and is thus somewhat too detailed.

Edward Fiorelli

FREDERICK I

Born: July 11, 1657; Königsberg, East Prussia
Died: February 25, 1713; Berlin, Prussia
Areas of Achievement: Monarchy and statecraft
Contribution: Frederick I is noted principally for having crowned himself
    King in Prussia in 1701, thus transforming his noncontiguous territories
    into the Prussian monarchy.

Early Life

In 1688, Frederick William, the Great Elector, the father of the modern
Prussian state, was succeeded by his son, Frederick. The physically robust
and energetic father stood in stark contrast to his languid son. Frederick,
who was born in 1657, was burdened physically and psychologically by a
humped back. He had suffered to no avail at the hands of doctors and
charlatans, who vainly offered to correct his handicap. His later quest for a
crown can be interpreted, at least partly, as an attempt to compensate for this
disability, which led the Berliners to refer to him as "crooked Fritz."

In 1674, Frederick's path to the electorship was cleared when his elder
brother died. It was rumored, however, that the crown prince had been poisoned by his stepmother, Dorothea of Holstein-Glücksburg. Dorothea was
attempting to persuade Frederick William to bypass his sons by his deceased
first wife, Louise Henriette of Orange, and bequeath his territories to the
sons she had borne him. In 1687, when Frederick's younger brother also
died, Frederick fled Berlin in fear of his life. Eberhard von Danckelmann,
the tutor, confidant, and friend of the young prince, assumed the role of
protector to Frederick after the death of the prince's elder brother. When
Frederick William died, it was Danckelmann who engineered the invalida-
tion of the great elector's will, which called for a division of his territories
between Frederick and his half brothers.

Danckelmann's service was not sufficient protection from the wrath of
Frederick. Danckelmann's power and accomplishments had roused envy and
opposition. The enmity of Frederick's wife, Sophie Charlotte, who despised
Danckelmann's rigidity and parsimoniousness, was especially damaging to
Danckelmann's position. It was, however, Danckelmann's opposition to
Frederick's desired crown, because of the expenses connected with maintaining a royal court, that finally alienated Frederick. At the end of 1697, Dank-
kelmann was arrested and charged with an array of offenses. While none of
the major charges could be proved, Frederick's determination to be rid of
this encumbrance to his ambition caused him to condemn Danckelmann to
ten years of imprisonment in the fortress of Peitz.

The diligent, thrifty, and impeccably honest Danckelmann was succeeded
by a trio of dishonest sycophants, who ingratiated themselves to Frederick

through flattery and support for his financially costly building programs and court, the expenses of which doubled to a half million taler between 1687 and 1711. Johann Wartenberg, Alexander Wartensleben, and August Wittgenstein, the "three woes," grew rich as they mismanaged the state and amassed a significant debt. Prussia's foreign policy was rudderless during this period. Frederick's pursuit of a crown was his only consistent objective. Frederick was at war for twenty-two of his twenty-five-year reign, not because he was warlike but because he drifted along without objectives and put his troops at the paid service of others. The incompetency of Frederick's advisers and Prussia's financial exhaustion account for Prussia's failure to take advantage of the Great Northern War to wrest territory from Sweden. A plague and famine in 1709, coupled with military expenses, finally rendered the corrupt incompetents intolerable. An investigation by Crown Prince Frederick William led to the ouster of the advisers in 1711 and the establishment of administrative reforms when he became king in 1713.

Life's Work

Frederick's desire for a crown was fueled by the augmentation of the rank and prestige of his neighbors. His cousin, William of Orange, had become King of England in 1689. Ernest Augustus, the Duke of Brunswick, was elevated to the rank of Elector of Hanover, and the English crown would in all probability pass to that family in the future. A crown had already been placed on the head of Frederick Augustus, the Elector of Saxony, who had mounted a throne as King of Poland in 1697. Frederick's regal obsession, however, was not rooted solely in his love of rank and show. He was offended by the relegation of the Brandenburg delegation to an inferior place in the negotiations at Rijswijk in 1697, following the War of the League of Augsburg. Not only was Brandenburg treated in a demeaning fashion but also its interests, despite its contribution to the war effort, were ignored by its allies.

Frederick's opportunity came with the death of Charles II of Spain in November, 1700, and the approach of the War of Spanish Succession. Holy Roman Emperor Leopold I agreed to purchase the support of eight thousand Brandenburger troops in his struggle against the French. The agreed price was Leopold's recognition of Frederick as King in Prussia. On November 16, 1700, a contract was signed in which Leopold agreed to recognize Frederick's royal status "with regard to the duchy of Prussia." Prussia lay outside the Holy Roman Empire, and in that respect the qualifying limitation suited Leopold. It was also important to Frederick, because his father had gained the right of complete sovereignty over East Prussia in 1660. As a result, kingship in Prussia would not be limited by any theoretical feudal encumbrances. On January 18, 1701, at the castle in Königsberg, Frederick, in the presence of the Prussian Estates, placed a crown upon his own head and then crowned his wife. Frederick postponed an anointing by Lutheran churchmen to emphasize his complete independence and autonomy from any other power, religious or secular.

Frederick's quest for a crown was not solely an act of vanity. Titles and formalities still had considerable substance, and the gaining of a crown bestowed upon Brandenburg-Prussia an increase in prestige and power. Frederick gained for his state an increase in rank commensurate with the increase in strength gained for it by Frederick William. Although the emperor had limited his recognition to "King in Prussia," Frederick ignored that limitation. Elector Frederick III was rapidly transformed into King Frederick I of Prussia. The army was referred to as the "Royal Prussian Army," and the bureaucracy in each of the separate provinces as the "Royal Prussian Administration." The crown, thus, provided a further symbolic unity to the administrative centralization that had been promoted by the great elector. It also served as a potent symbol which bound the Junker class more closely to the Prussian rulers.

Frederick also aspired to build upon the work of his father and to transform Berlin into a suitable capital for the new Prussian kingdom. He enlarged the Hohenzollern Palace and built a massive arsenal. In the cultural arena, the accomplishments of Frederick far exceeded those of his father. Aided by his charming and intellectually lively wife, Frederick attempted to make his court a cultural center. Gottfried Wilhelm Leibniz was the most renowned of the intellects attracted to Berlin, and he was appointed the first president of the Prussian Academy of Sciences, which was established in 1701. Frederick also patronized the pacesetting University of Halle, which was established in 1694 and subsequently trained competent and progressive jurists and civil servants for the Prussian state.

Summary

Frederick I was neither a powerful nor an especially successful monarch. He did, however, contribute to the development of the Prussian state by acquiring a royal title, preserving the army, which had been crafted by his father, and patronizing intellectual institutions, which would promote the development of a capable cadre of civil servants. Although Frederick showed little direct interest in his army, he maintained its size and added to its spirit by transforming it into a royal army. In imitation of Louis XIV, he outfitted its different regiments in distinctive uniforms. He also increased royal control over the military by appropriating to himself the right to appoint and promote all officers. Though Frederick did not lead the Prussian army in battle or even use it to add significantly to his territory, he did not let it atrophy and handed on to his son a force which Frederick William I would be able to build into the renowned fighting force of Frederick the Great.

Bibliography

Ergang, Robert. *The Potsdam Führer: Frederick William I, Father of Prussian Militarism.* New York: Columbia University Press, 1941. Ergang provides a brief but colorful summary of the character and achievements of Frederick I in this excellent study of his son, Frederick William I.

Fay, Sidney B. *The Rise of Brandenburg-Prussia to 1786.* New York: Holt, Rinehart and Winston, 1937. Fay's book is an excellent introduction to and summary of Prussian history through the reign of Frederick the Great. The treatment of Frederick I is very brief, but his place in Prussian history and his accomplishments are precisely delineated.

Fischer-Fabian, S. *Prussia's Glory: The Rise of a Military State.* Translated by Lore Segal and Paul Stern. New York: Macmillan, 1981. Fischer-Fabian, a German, wrote this book for a broad audience. He tells an interesting and gossipy story but offers little historical analysis to shed light on Prussian development.

Frey, Linda, and Marsha Frey. *Frederick I: The Man and His Times.* Boulder, Colo.: East European Monographs, 1984. The only biography of Frederick in English. Provides an overview of Frederick. The authors are not very successful in their attempt to revise the general assessment that Frederick was a rather weak and ineffectual monarch. The Freys are most successful in their treatment of Frederick's foreign policy, wherein they admit that many of his policies were ill-conceived.

Holborn, Hajo. *A History of Modern Germany.* Vol. 2, *1648-1840.* New York: Alfred A. Knopf, 1968. In the second of this three-volume history of Germany, Holborn briefly discusses Frederick. His treatment of Frederick's foreign policy is more positive than the usual assessment. He argues that Frederick's participation in the War of the Spanish Succession was beneficial insofar as it freed Germany from the dominating pressure of France.

Ranke, Leopold von. *Memoirs of the House of Brandenburg, and History of Prussia During the Seventeenth and Eighteenth Centuries.* Translated by Sir Alex Duff-Gordon and Lady Duff-Gordon. Reprint. Westport, Conn.: Greenwood Press, 1968. Ranke attempts to judge Frederick I in the context of his age. In Ranke's opinion, though Frederick shared his period's taste for ostentatious display, he did not neglect the task of increasing the power of the state.

Bernard A. Cook

FREDERICK HENRY

Born: January 29, 1584; Delft, Holland
Died: March 14, 1647; The Hague, Holland
Areas of Achievement: The military and politics
Contribution: Frederick Henry succeeded through his military and diplomatic abilities in completing successfully the Eighty Years' War for the Independence of the Dutch United Provinces from Spain and in establishing the House of Orange as the hereditary sovereign of the new nation.

Early Life

The seventh child of William the Silent by William's fourth wife, Louise de Coligny, daughter of the French Huguenot leader Gaspard de Coligny, Frederick Henry, Count of Nassau and Prince of Orange, was born on January 29, 1584, less than six months prior to the assassination of his father on July 10, 1584, at Delft by Balthasar Gerard. Although his mother probably intended him for a career in France, his half brother Maurice of Nassau, who was also William the Silent's successor in the struggle against Spain, directed him toward a life of service to the Dutch. Educated at the University of Leiden, elected a member of the Council of State while still a very young man, a participant in foreign negotiations, and a close companion of his brother on the latter's military campaigns, Frederick Henry acquired at an early age a firm foundation in the twin arts of diplomacy and military matters. Handsome, with a mustache and a small beard beneath thick black hair, a high forehead, and dark piercing eyes, possessed of noble bearing, renowned early for his gallantry in arms, and the first of his house with the ability to speak the Dutch language without a foreign accent, he endeared himself quickly both to the army and to the Dutch people. Unfortunately, during most of his life he suffered grievously from gout, ultimately dying of its complications. In 1624, at the age of forty, largely on the urging of his brother Maurice, who had no children of his own, Frederick Henry married the intelligent and ambitious Amalia von Solms, who proved to be not only a devoted wife but also perhaps Frederick Henry's shrewdest adviser throughout the remainder of his career.

Life's Work

The Netherlands, originally under the dominance of the Catholic Habsburgs of Spain, was divided at the time of the death of Maurice on April 23, 1625, into two parts: the southern part, primarily Roman Catholic (and now the modern countries of Belgium and Luxembourg), under the control of Spain, and the northern part, primarily Dutch Protestant but containing many Roman Catholics and consisting of eight provinces, struggling for its independence. Seven of the eight northern provinces were loosely bound together in a confederation congress called the States-General, which tried, sometimes successfully, sometimes not so successfully, to unite all eight provinces into uniform action against the Habsburg Spanish overlord.

On the death of his brother, Frederick Henry was quickly elected by five of the eight northern provinces of Holland, Zeeland, Utrecht, Overyssel, and Gelders as stadholder (chief executive officer) to replace Maurice and was appointed by the States-General captain-general and admiral-general of the confederation or union, as well as head of the Council of State. Friesland, Groningen, and Drente retained their own stadholders, while Drente, although a northern province, was not then a member of the States-General.

Where William the Silent had been the spirit of the revolution of the Dutch northern provinces, he lacked the military ability to go with it; where his son Maurice had the military ability, he lacked the gift of diplomacy that would have made the military struggle easier. In Frederick Henry, both military ability and diplomacy were present, so that on occasion he was able to make the conflicting interests of Calvinists and Roman Catholics work together in the northern provinces, persuade the proud province of Holland to work together with the States-General, and convince the French Cardinal Richelieu to give aid to the Protestant Dutch struggle against the Catholic Spanish Habsburgs.

His first consideration lay in securing the southern and eastern borders of the union against Spanish attack, and here he demonstrated his enormous ability in besieging fortresses with success. The 1627 campaign was marked by the brilliant capture of Grol, a town on the eastern frontier, and in 1629 the even more brilliant conquest of 's Hertogenbosch. In this campaign, Frederick Henry exhibited an ability not only to obtain the highest efficiency from his soldiers but also to win their hearts, something made all the more difficult by the fact that where the Dutch war of independence had become a training ground for military men from a variety of countries, of the eighteen regiments under him at 's Hertogenbosch, three were Netherlanders, one Frisian, one Walloon, two German, four French, three Scottish, and four English. Although he was unable to take Dunkirk in 1631, a Spanish fleet of thirty-five large vessels and a number of smaller ships carrying stores and munitions were destroyed on September 12 in the Battle of the River Slaak, while in 1632 the eastern frontier was strengthened by the capture of the city of Maastricht. These setbacks brought the Archduchess Isabel, Habsburg regent of the Netherlands, to an effort at negotiations. Matters of religion and trade, however, interfered: The Spaniards insisted upon the elimination of heresy in the Netherlands; the Calvinists in the United Provinces pressed for the restriction of Roman Catholicism; and the merchants of Amsterdam wished an elimination of trading restrictions against them that Spain was not willing to grant.

The failure of these negotiations and the need for money led Frederick

Henry to achieve an almost miraculous alliance with Cardinal Richelieu's France. Spain and France were both Catholic, but as they were political enemies France was loath to see the Netherlands in Spanish hands. Although the Dutch were primarily Protestants and heretics in the eyes of Cardinal Richelieu, he needed the Dutch fleet to help blockade the French Huguenot port of La Rochelle, which he was besieging. Despite the objections of French Catholics on one side and Dutch Calvinists on the other, a defensive and offensive alliance was concluded between the Dutch and the French in the early part of 1635. By the terms of the agreement, any conquests in the southern Netherlands were to be divided between them; neither nation was to conclude peace without the consent of the other; and each was to provide for field action an army consisting of twenty-five thousand foot soldiers and five thousand cavalry.

In 1637, the important city of Breda in the province of Brabant fell to the Dutch, giving the Dutch Republic the security of three great frontier fortresses: 's Hertogenbosch, Maastricht, and Breda. The following year, at the great Battle of the Downs, Lieutenant-Admiral Maarten Harpertszoon Tromp debilitated a powerful Spanish fleet under the command of Antonio de Oquendo. For the Dutch, this battle was comparable to the defeat of the Spanish Armada of 1588, and it ended any attempt of the Spaniards toward dominance on the sea. The following year, however, Frederick Henry's campaign against the frontier town of Hulst ended in failure, made even more disappointing by the death in that campaign of Count Henry Casimir of Nassau-Dietz, who was stadholder of the three provinces of Groningen, Friesland, and Drente. Groningen and Drente chose Frederick Henry to be their stadholder in place of Henry Casimir, which strengthened the union, but Friesland chose to elect William Frederick, the younger brother of Henry Casimir, as its stadholder. On May 12, 1640, Frederick Henry had gained sufficient prestige to enable him to marry his son William to Mary, the eldest daughter of Charles I of England, by which he hoped to add England's aid to that of France. The rift between the two branches of the house of Nassau eventually was healed when, three or four years after the death of Frederick Henry, William Frederick in 1651 married Frederick Henry's daughter Albertine Agnes.

During the Civil War in England, in which the Puritan Parliament under the leadership of Oliver Cromwell rebelled against Charles I, Frederick Henry's sympathies were with Charles. Henrietta Maria, Charles's wife, who resided at The Hague during the early stages of that revolt, pressured Frederick Henry to come to the aid of her husband, but that statesman was much too prudent not to know that the Calvinists in the northern provinces would never do again as they did in France—come to the aid of a non-Calvinist king against their fellow Calvinists. They were already dissatisfied with an alliance that in its ultimate effects permitted France to enlarge itself in the southern Netherlands at the expense of Spain, and Frederick Henry himself came to realize that it was far too dangerous to his country to permit a powerful France to take the place of a much weaker Spain in the southern Netherlands.

When religion was involved, Frederick Henry always had to be prudent. The insistence by Spain that the Inquisition be introduced into the Netherlands to crush the Protestants was the original spark which inflamed the Protestants of the northern provinces to their war for independence under William the Silent in 1568. That portion of the Reformed church in the northern provinces, the Calvinists, demanded the complete suppression of Roman Catholicism. Those Protestants of the Dutch provinces who were more worldly and more tolerant of Catholicism so long as they themselves could practice their own religion were called Remonstrants, or Arminians, after the Amsterdam preacher Jacobus Arminius, while the Calvinists were called Counter-Remonstrants. The Synod of Dort, under the dominance of the Counter-Remonstrants and Maurice's armed forces, condemned the Remonstrants and had their major leader, Jan van Oldenbarneveldt, put to death. Yet the realities of the situation outweighed the theories of the Calvinists, and in the course of time the Dutch of the northern provinces, and Frederick Henry, came to see that Catholics and Protestants could live together as Dutchmen, tolerant of one another's religious beliefs, in a country independent of Spain. Therefore, like the merchant-burghers of Amsterdam, Frederick Henry concluded that so long as the northern Dutch provinces had secured their borders it would be better to make peace with Spain.

In the meantime, the Dutch were expanding both in the West and East Indies. On May 9, 1624, under Piet Hein, a Dutch fleet captured Bahia in Brazil from the Portuguese, who were then under Spanish domination, and when Bahia was recaptured by the Spaniards on April 28, 1625, Piet Hein recaptured it on March 23, 1627. The following year, Piet Hein started attacking the treasure ships bringing gold and silver from the New World back to Spain, while other attacks on Spanish shipping led the way toward a gradual extension of Dutch control in Brazil. In the East Indies, Dutch naval supremacy over all European rivals became especially evident, so that soon rich cargoes were flowing back to Amsterdam from Amboina, Banda, the Moluccas, Java, Formosa, and even Japan. Where the Dutch West India Company had been successful in planting colonies, the Dutch East India Company had been successful in planting colonies and developing a rich trade as well in the spices and jewels that Europe prized most, both companies acting with the encouragement of Frederick Henry.

After the campaign against Hulst, Frederick Henry, age sixty-three, was broken in health, suffering badly from gout, with rapidly failing faculties of mind, spirit, and body. On March 14, 1647, he died and was buried with great pomp beside his father William and his brother Maurice in Delft. By the *Acte de Survivance* of April 19, 1631, almost sixteen years before, the States-General had declared the son of Frederick Henry, William, to be heir to his father's offices of Captain-General and Admiral-General of the United Provinces, giving Frederick Henry something of the position of a sovereign prince. Therefore, on Frederick Henry's death, his son succeeded him in his various offices and honors as William II.

Spain, its treasury empty, its gold galleons attacked by Dutch, French, and English buccaneers, and facing French armies at the Pyrenees, Portugal, and Catalonia in revolt, was ready for the peace that came about at Münster, on January 30, 1648, in which Spain recognized the independence of the Dutch Republic and brought an end to the so-called Eighty Years' War.

Summary

The stadholdership of Frederick Henry has been called the Golden Age of the Dutch Republic, in that Netherlanders were enormously productive in many fields of learning: law, philosophy, painting, letters, science, and seafaring. As a human being, Frederick Henry with his natural characteristics of military ability, tolerance, and humanity, was able not only to win for his country her independence but also to stand as a model of the religious tolerance, kindliness, and practical wisdom for which the Dutch people became so well known.

Bibliography

Edmundson, George. "Frederick Henry, Prince of Orange." In *The Cambridge Modern History*, edited by A. W. Ward, G. W. Prothero, and Stanley Leathes, vol. 4. Cambridge, England: Cambridge University Press, 1906. The best survey in English of the career of Frederick Henry from 1625 through his death and the Treaty of Münster. Although there is virtually nothing regarding Frederick Henry's life prior to 1625, the author gives a fine chronological presentation of the subject's work after that time. The concluding portion, dealing with the Dutch overseas activities in the Western Hemisphere and in the East Indies, is concise and easy to understand. There is, however, relatively little explanation of the religious conflict between Catholic and Protestant and little real explanation of the conflict between the Remonstrants and the Counter-Remonstrants or the conflict between the province of Holland and the States-General.

Geyl, Pieter. *The Netherlands in the Seventeenth Century*. Vol. 1, *1609-1648*. Rev. ed. London: Ernest Benn, 1961. For the seasoned student of history. Deals with the period starting with the twelve-year armistice of 1609 through the Peace of Westphalia, ending the Thirty Years' War, of which the Treaty of Münster, which ended the Eighty Years' War, was a portion. Very little is given about the life of Frederick Henry prior to his becoming stadholder in 1625, and relatively little about himself as a person.

_____. *Orange and Stuart, 1641-1672*. Translated by Arnold Pomerans. New York: Charles Scribner's Sons, 1970. Chapter 1, "Frederick Henry of Orange and King Charles I, 1641-47," deals more with the politics of the marriage of Frederick Henry's son William to the eldest daughter of England's Charles I, than with the life and personality of Frederick Henry. Yet it does much to explain the difficult position in which Frederick Henry found himself, between the Calvinists on one side and the non-Calvinist Stuarts on the other, both of whom he sought to please.

Schama, Simon. *The Embarrassment of Riches: An Interpretation of Dutch Culture in the Golden Age*. New York: Alfred A. Knopf, 1987. Although this book does not discuss Frederick Henry and the military situation in the Dutch Republic, it presents an extensive kaleidoscope of Dutch life during that period: homelife, eating habits, the business world, trade, the making of money, the care of children, painting, and the Dutch mentality in general.

Robert M. Spector

FREDERICK THE GREAT

Born: January 24, 1712; Berlin, Prussia
Died: August 17, 1786; Potsdam, Prussia
Areas of Achievement: Government and politics
Contribution: As King of Prussia, Frederick II raised the power and prestige of his state from a status of relative obscurity to that of one of Europe's most powerful nations. Through despotic but progressive policies at home and spectacular victories in war, he earned recognition as Frederick the Great.

Early Life

One of Prussia's greatest kings, Frederick II was the son of Frederick William I and Princess Sophia Dorothea of Hannover. As prince and heir to the throne, Frederick had to study government and military matters, as his father prescribed, but the prince found them boring. Frederick William was anti-intellectual and cared only for his army, but Prince Frederick, under the influence of his tutor Duhan de Jandun, developed a passionate love for French language and culture. Relations between father and son became extremely hostile, and the king often beat his son and berated him in public. The queen, on the contrary, encouraged her son's cultural inclinations.

As tensions with his father became unbearable, the prince tried to flee to England with two companions, but all were caught and arrested. Frederick William threatened to remove Prince Frederick from the royal succession if he ever rebelled again, and he imposed upon his son a regimen of training in state and military affairs, which his instructors pursued mercilessly.

At his father's insistence, Frederick married Princess Elizabeth Christina of Brunswick-Bevern in 1733, a loveless union without progeny. By that time, Frederick had capitulated to paternal demands, and, through services he performed in the province of Neumark, he gained a measure of respect from his father.

From 1735 to 1740, Frederick lived at Rheinsberg, an estate north of Berlin. There he enjoyed fellowship with learned friends, played his flute, read, and wrote under the influence of the French philosophes. He corresponded with the brilliant French scholar Voltaire, and he composed *Anti-Machiavel* (1740), a critique of amoral politics. While at Rheinsberg, Frederick improved his relationship with the king by completing all assigned duties competently.

Life's Work

On May 31, 1740, the quasi-reformed prince became King Frederick II, monarch of Europe's thirteenth largest state. He brought to the throne the conviction that the ruler was the first servant of the state. An atheist, he rejected the theory of divine right monarchy and began to cement his rule. He worked relentlessly for the kingdom, and he expected his subjects to do the same. Frederick made heavy demands upon the nobles, especially for military service. He managed to increase the army from 80,000 eventually to 200,000 men.

Although while at Rheinsberg Frederick had written against amoral politics, as king he made pragmatism the basis of his policy. A striking evidence of this may be seen in his seizure of Silesia from Empress Maria Theresa, which initiated the War of the Austrian Succession. His late father had allowed Austria to decide his foreign policy and had signed a pragmatic sanction, by which he recognized Maria Theresa's right to succeed to the Habsburg throne. Frederick, however, revived a dubious Prussian claim to parts of Austrian Silesia, which he invaded in December, 1740. In this struggle, Prussia allied with France and Bavaria, both of which Frederick deserted once he had realized his objective. Victory enabled him to increase his kingdom by about a third and thereby acquire territory rich in agricultural lands and mineral resources. His skillful military leadership and the performance of his army impressed all the great powers. In his memoirs, the king admitted that he had taken Silesia simply to strengthen Prussia, and he did not think it necessary to justify that move morally.

Frederick's impressive triumph over Austria produced a general alarm about his intentions toward Europe as a whole. The Habsburgs remained unreconciled to their losses, and Maria Theresa branded Frederick "the robber of Silesia." She concluded alliances with Russia, Saxony, and France. Frederick had unwittingly effected a diplomatic revolution, which confronted Prussia with a coalition of Europe's three largest states. Although Frederick was able to gain the support of Great Britain, the future looked bleak for Prussia. Rather than wait to be attacked, Frederick launched a preemptive strike against Saxony, thereby beginning the Seven Years' War.

Frederick had no illusions about the dangers that confronted Prussia. He instructed his mistress to pay no ransom should he be captured and his army to wage war as though he were there. He carried poison, apparently to end his life rather than fall into enemy hands. He led combat operations personally and often exposed himself to danger. The king's heroism had an inspiring effect upon his troops and contributed to some amazing victories over much larger enemy forces.

At first, the Prussian armies won resounding victories and inflicted heavy casualties upon their foes. Finally, however, the sheer weight of numbers took its toll, and Prussia could not replace its losses. Defeat appeared certain, but Empress Elizabeth of Russia died in 1762 and left the throne to Peter III, a peculiar personality with an obsessive admiration for Frederick the Great. Russia withdrew from the war. This reenergized the Prussian effort, and by 1763 all combatants were nearing exhaustion. The Treaty of

Hubertsburg ratified Prussian possession of Silesia and left Frederick's kingdom the chief power in central Europe.

By 1763, the prestige of Prussia and her heroic king were at their height. No other power could afford to ignore Prussia, whose interests would have to be considered in all significant international matters. Frederick knew this and took full advantage of this hard-won status.

After his great victory of 1763, Frederick made the security of his domain his chief concern. His kingdom was powerful and prosperous as a result of success in postwar reconstruction, and he intended to keep it that way. National security required rapprochement with recent enemies; Frederick therefore turned to Russia, where Catherine the Great had replaced Peter III, her murdered husband, in 1762. Catherine required, as the price of an agreement, Frederick's cooperation in the partition of Poland, over much of which Russia exercised control, and where a succession crisis had erupted. In 1772, Russia, Austria, and Prussia collaborated in dividing about a third of Poland among them.

In domestic affairs, Frederick's achievements are almost as impressive as his triumphs in war and diplomacy. Frederick aspired to be an enlightened ruler. He sought the good of his subjects, but he never relinquished despotic authority over them. He maintained the traditional class structure by relying upon the nobles to fill the army officer corps and the most important posts in the state. He nevertheless enacted many reforms that improved life for all classes of society.

To combat waste and corruption, Frederick eliminated the sale of government offices and conducted regular audits of state funds. He protected peasants against abusive landlords, and he made the dispensation of justice more equitable than ever before. He banned the use of torture for crimes other than treason.

Frederick had no faith, but he believed that religion has social utility by teaching public morality. He respected the rights of Catholics in occupied Silesia, but he pressured priests to support his policies. He employed Jesuits to teach in some schools even after the pope had dissolved that order. The king granted both toleration and citizenship to Jews in his dominions, although Protestantism remained the dominant faith in Prussia. Frederick actually ridiculed Christianity as a superstition. Some of his French critics complained that the only real liberty in autocratic Prussia was the freedom to scorn religion. Frederick could afford to tolerate diverse religions because he was indifferent toward all of them.

Frederick's economic policies reflect his subscription to mercantilism, a government-regulated economy. Salt, coffee, and tobacco were state monopolies, and families were required to buy a stipulated amount of salt annually. When he opened crown lands to settlement, the king required colonists to pay him dues. They could not leave the land without finding replacements, and they were subject to forced labor. Many features of feudalism remained in Prussia long after they had disappeared in France.

The king owned a third of Prussia's agricultural lands, and he regulated timber, iron, and lead production. Frederick required farm workers to learn the art of wool spinning, and he gave free looms to immigrant weavers. He was a paternalist, who sought to direct the profits from state enterprises toward the public welfare. He assumed that no one knew better than he what was good for his subjects. Yet his economic policies protected the old class structure and thereby retarded the growth of a vigorous middle class. The king placed taxation in the hands of French revenue agents, who were more efficient than any officers who might have been recruited in Prussia. Although government income increased considerably, the presence of foreign officials caused much resentment, which the monarch chose to ignore.

The Seven Years' War exhausted Frederick, and he retired to the seclusion of Potsdam and thereafter seldom appeared in public. In old age, he became irritable and sometimes irrational. When, for example, some Berlin magistrates rendered a verdict that angered him, the king sentenced them to forced labor for a year, despite his subscription to the rule of law.

Summary

Voltaire, who had been a sort of philosopher-in-residence at the palace from 1750 to 1753, bestowed upon Frederick the title "the Great." The king's remarkable achievements surely justify that appellation, but Frederick was, nevertheless, an authoritarian ruler, a militarist at times, and an advocate of enlightenment only insofar as it would strengthen the state and his control over its affairs. In military matters, he was one of the greatest commanders in history.

Subsequent events seem to indicate that Frederick's Prussia depended too much upon him personally, and when he was gone, his far less able successors were unable to maintain the strength it needed. The Napoleonic Wars brought humiliating defeats, but, on the foundation that Frederick the Great laid, Otto von Bismarck built the mighty German empire, Europe's most powerful state, by the opening of the twentieth century.

Bibliography

Asprey, Robert B. *Frederick the Great*. New York: Ticknor & Fields, 1986. A work of fine scholarship that reveals extensive research. The lucid style makes it interesting reading for practically all readers. Places the subject into the context of the times and skillfully evaluates his role in history.

Daniels, Emil. "Frederick the Great and His Successors." In *The Cambridge Modern History*, edited by A. W. Ward et al., vol. 6. Cambridge, England: Cambridge University Press, 1909. Although this treatment appeared years ago, it remains a highly useful analysis that contains extensive coverage of Frederick's economic policies and their far-reaching effects. Frederick is portrayed as a progressive ruler with a keen understanding of his nation's needs and policies that improved the quality of life for his subjects and greatly enhanced Prussia's international standing.

Horn, D. B. *Frederick the Great and the Rise of Prussia*. New York: Harper & Row, 1964. This delightfully written work is a combination biography and political history of Prussia in the eighteenth century. Although intended for general readers rather than scholars, it displays the author's erudite research beneath his skillful style.

Johnson, Hubert C. *Frederick the Great and His Officials*. New Haven, Conn.: Yale University Press, 1975. In addition to his great military accomplishments, Frederick demonstrated unusual managerial abilities in supervising the administration of his state politically and economically. This scholarly examination tells the story of Prussia's development under her king's scrupulous and relentless direction. This is a book for readers who have some previous knowledge of the subject and his period of history.

Paret, Peter, ed. *Frederick the Great: A Profile*. New York: Hill & Wang, 1972. Despite his overwhelming importance in European history, Frederick has always been a controversial figure. Paret has united diverse interpretations of Frederick's policies and his role in history. This is a very convenient means by which readers may ascertain quickly how the career of Frederick has impressed a variety of scholars.

Ritter, Gerhard. *Frederick the Great: A Historical Profile*. Translated by Peter Paret. Berkeley: University of California Press, 1968. This is a widely acclaimed critical biography by a renowned scholar of German history. It may be one of the finest works of its kind to appear. Full appreciation of Ritter's treatment requires some previous acquaintance with Prussian history and Frederick's role in it.

Simon, Edith. *The Making of Frederick the Great*. Boston: Little, Brown, 1963. This vivid biography in popular style in the work of a skilled professional writer is likely to remain a favorite among general readers. It is not, however, an adequately critical treatment and thus will not satisfy the requirements of historians.

James Edward McGoldrick

FREDERICK WILLIAM, THE GREAT ELECTOR

Born: February 16, 1620; Berlin, Brandenburg-Prussia
Died: May 9, 1688; Potsdam, outside Berlin, Brandenburg-Prussia
Areas of Achievement: Government and the military
Contribution: Frederick William was the first gifted ruler of the Hohenzollern family. He was the founder of the Prussian army and bureaucracy, and laid the basis for the future strength of the Brandenburg-Prussian state.

Early Life

Frederick William was born in Berlin on February 16, 1620, the son of the Elector of Brandenburg George William of the house of Hohenzollern and his wife, Elizabeth Charlotte, the granddaughter of William I of the house of Orange. Frederick William's early years were clouded by Brandenburg's financial exhaustion and military vulnerability during the Thirty Years' War. When the electorate of Brandenburg was threatened by Albrecht Wenzel von Wallenstein's imperial soldiers, Frederick William, then seven years old, was moved for safety into the fortress of Küstrin. For five years, he remained at the fortress, growing both physically and intellectually under the direction of his Rhenish tutor. When Frederick William was fourteen, he was sent to continue his education in the security of the Netherlands, where his relative Frederick Henry of Orange was stadtholder.

Frederick William became Elector of Brandenburg upon his father's death on December 1, 1640. The prospects of the twenty-year-old elector were dim. His territories had been devastated by the Thirty Years' War, the population of Brandenburg had been cut nearly in half, agriculture and commerce had collapsed, and much of his land was occupied by foreign armies. The local estates in all the elector's territories continued their resistance to any increase in taxation or strengthening of the central government. This sad state was compounded by the fact that the army that was passed on to the young elector consisted of only five thousand largely worthless men.

Life's Work

Even before his father's hated Catholic adviser Adam von Schwarzenberg died in March, 1641, Frederick William reappointed Schwarzenberg's Lutheran and Calvinist opponents to the Privy Council. To these the new elector added his young and energetic friends, Conrad von Burgsdorf, Joachim Friedrich von Blumenthal, Count Georg Friedrich von Waldeck, and Otto von Schwerin. In the face of overwhelming Swedish power, Frederick William placed his army on the defensive. At the same time that he sought an armistice with the Swedes, he purged the chaff from his army and, with a remaining core of about twenty-five hundred men, began rebuilding his army numerically and morally. By the end of the Thirty Years' War, the force had grown to almost eight thousand disciplined, loyal, and well-paid men. This credible army won respect for Brandenburg in the deliberations leading to the Treaty of Westphalia.

Frederick William, at the beginning of his reign, had gone to Warsaw and given homage to Władysław IV to ensure his status in the Duchy of Prussia, which was held as a fief of Poland. He then went to Königsberg and, after confirming the traditional rights of the Prussian Estates, received their support. After winning a truce with Sweden in July, 1641, he attempted to gain Swedish-occupied Pomerania and the Baltic coast by marrying the Swedish Queen Christina. Rebuffed by her, Frederick William in 1646 turned to the Netherlands, from which he gained an alliance and a wife, Louise Henriette, the daughter of Frederick Henry of Orange.

At Westphalia in 1648, Frederick William was able to win legal recognition for his fellow Calvinists and the termination of the princes' right to compel religious conformity. He failed, however, to secure his claim to all of Pomerania. The Swedes retained western Pomerania and the port of Stettin, while Frederick William received only the eastern half and the lesser port of Colberg. He did receive some compensating parcels of territory, including Minden and a future claim to Magdeburg, which contributed to the expansion and strengthening of Brandenburg.

During the Northern War between Sweden and Poland, Frederick William pursued a vacillating and self-serving course, switching from neutrality to the side of Sweden and finally to that of Poland. As a result of these maneuvers, he was able to win from Poland the recognition of his sovereignty in Prussia, which was confirmed in the Treaty of Oliva in 1660. With his expanded army, which had grown to twenty-seven thousand men during the war, and the recognition of sovereignty in Prussia, which lay outside the Holy Roman Empire, Frederick William increased his stature to that of a European sovereign.

Realizing the importance of his army for both his external and internal policies, Frederick William maintained a strong standing force in peace time, which could be doubled in size at time of war. The elector's army in 1686 numbered thirty thousand, second only to the Austrian army among the German states. During peace, the soldiers were utilized for public-works projects, such as the construction of the canal linking the Oder and Elbe rivers, which made Berlin the center of transportation in north Central Europe. Frederick William established for the army a central command, which developed into a permanent general staff. The officials and bureaus, which he initiated to provide financial support for the army, developed into a centralized and professional bureaucracy.

State interest and shifting alliances continued to characterize Frederick William's subsequent military policy but with much less success than in the

Northern War. During the Dutch War, Frederick William ran Louis XIV's Swedish allies out of western Pomerania, winning for himself the appellation "Great" for his victory at Fehrbellin on June 28, 1675. He, however, was betrayed at the peace conference by his Dutch and imperial allies. Forced to return his conquests, the Great Elector turned to the French, until he was repelled by Louis's revocation of the Edict of Nantes in 1685 and Louis's increasingly aggressive anti-German policy.

If the Northern War raised Frederick William's external status, it also enabled him to augment his power within his territories and advance the cause of centralization. When he assumed the electorship, Frederick William had conciliated the local estates. Taking advantage of the unsettled foreign scene in 1653, he was able to extract a six-year tax grant from a united Diet of the Brandenburg Estates. In 1655, at the outbreak of the Northern War, when the Brandenburg Estates refused an additional tax, Frederick William used his army to collect his desired tax and to extort additional funds from the chastened estates. When the six-year tax of 1653 expired in the middle of the war, Frederick William merely continued to collect the tax, and never again called together the Brandenburg Diet.

Frederick William coopted the district directors, who had acted as elected representatives of the estates, by simultaneously appointing them war commissioners. These local administrative officers were thus gradually transformed into loyal agents of the central government. He also appointed war-tax commissioners to collect taxes in the towns. These officials gradually took total control over the town administration and thus destroyed the self-government which the towns had exercised. The western territories of Kleve and Mark were able to resist this centralizing destruction of local traditional rights and representation somewhat more successfully than Brandenburg, but Frederick William asserted his right to station troops permanently in those territories, and their Estates, though they continued to meet, did grant the taxes requested by the elector.

It was in eastern Prussia that the struggle between Frederick William and the estates was most bitter. The estates there had won broad rights by appealing to the kings of Poland against their Hohenzollern dukes. The Prussian Estates claimed that these privileges recognized by Frederick William in 1640 had not been erased by the Treaty of Oliva. Frederick William's close associate Otto von Schwerin summoned a Great Diet and offered to recognize most of the privileges of the estates in return for their recognition of the elector's sovereignty. The estates, led by Hieronymus Roth, a leading magistrate of Königsberg, rejected the offer. Eventually Frederick William himself went to Königsberg and had Roth arrested and tried before a special commission. Despite pleas for clemency, Frederick William condemned Roth to life imprisonment. Persuaded by Frederick William's forcefulness, the estates in 1663 recognized his sovereignty and in return had their privileges confirmed.

The next diet, which met in 1669, haggled over the elector's tax request. This diet, however, was cowed when another leading dissident, Christian Ludwig von Kalckstein, was executed for treason. After 1680, Frederick William collected a regular military tax from Prussia through a rural land tax and an excise tax in Königsberg. With city and countryside divided, the estates atrophied and in 1705 ceased to function.

Summary

Frederick William, the Great Elector, was the first truly gifted Hohenzollern ruler. He laid the foundations for the greatness of Brandenburg-Prussia. When he became elector in 1640, he faced a formidable challenge. He had to establish internal order and to secure his territories against predatory foreign powers. He also had to build a credible military from practically nothing. With the army, he secured Brandenburg against outsiders and asserted the authority of the central government over the defenders of local interests and rights. Having forcibly asserted his power to tax at will, he was able to expand his army and enlarge the state's developing bureaucracy. He ran roughshod over traditional rights but did establish the order and security craved by many of his subjects after the calamity of the Thirty Years' War, and he laid the foundations of later Prussian absolutism.

Bibliography

Carsten, F. L. *The Origins of Prussia*. Oxford, England: Clarendon Press, 1954. Carsten's book is a first-rate scholarly study, more than one-third of which is devoted to Frederick William and his accomplishments. Carsten details the elector's use of his army to replace the power of the provincial *Landtag* with his own absolute authority.

Fay, Sidney Bradshaw. *The Rise of Brandenburg-Prussia to 1786*. New York: Holt, Rinehart and Winston, 1937. This is an excellent introduction to and summary of Prussian history, including the reign of Frederick William. Fay clearly summarizes both internal and external developments under Frederick William and describes well the bureaucracy that the elector developed.

Holborn, Hajo. *A History of Modern Germany*. Vol. 2, *1648-1840*. New York: Alfred A. Knopf, 1968. In this second of his three-volume history of Germany, Holborn gives a brief but perceptive overview of Frederick William's career and achievement.

Koch, H. W. *A History of Prussia*. New York: Longman, 1978. Koch presents an uncritical and rather old-fashioned treatment of Prussian history. One chapter is on Frederick William and emphasizes that Frederick William, rather than actually making Prussia a great power, laid the basis for future Prussian greatness.

Nelson, Walter Henry. *The Soldier Kings: The House of Hohenzollern*. New

York: G. P. Putnam's Sons, 1970. Nelson's study of the Hohenzollerns is intended for a popular audience. Nelson stresses the improbable accomplishment of the elector, laying the basis for a great state in his poor, sparsely populated, disjointed, and exposed territories.

Schevill, Ferdinand. *The Great Elector.* Chicago: University of Chicago Press, 1947. Schevill's book is the standard English-language study of Frederick William. Schevill is largely noncritical and laudatory. He excuses Frederick William's deviousness and violation of traditional privileges, or protoconstitutional rights, by appealing to expediency. According to Schevill, Frederick William's willfulness and brutal pursuit for additional power were justified by the end result: the construction of the basis for the modern state of Prussia.

Bernard A. Cook

GOTTLOB FREGE

Born: November 8, 1848; Wismar
Died: July 26, 1925; Bad Kleinen, Germany
Area of Achievement: Mathematics
Contribution: Frege is the founder of modern symbolic logic and the creator of the first system of notations and quantifiers of modern logic.

Early Life

Friedrich Ludwig Gottlob Frege was the son of the principal of a private, girls' high school. While Frege was in high school in Wismar, his father died. Frege was devoted to his mother, who was a teacher and later principal of the girls' school. He may have had a brother, Arnold Frege, who was born in Wismar in 1852. Nothing further is known about Frege until he entered the university at the age of twenty-one. From 1869 to 1871, he attended the University of Jena and proceeded to the University of Göttingen, where he took courses in mathematics, physics, chemistry, and philosophy. By 1873, Frege had completed his thesis and had received his doctorate from the university. Frege returned to the University of Jena and applied for an unsalaried position. His mother wrote to the university that she would support him until he acquired regular employment. In 1874, as a result of publication of his dissertation on mathematical functions, he was placed on the staff of the university. He spent the rest of his life at Jena, where he investigated the foundations of mathematics and produced seminal works in logic.

Frege's early years at Jena were probably the happiest period in his life. He was highly regarded by the faculty and attracted some of the best students in mathematics. During these years, he taught an extra load as he assumed the courses of a professor who had become ill. He also worked on a volume on logic and mathematics. Frege's lectures were thoughtful and clearly organized, and were greatly appreciated by his students. Much of Frege's personal life, however, was beset by tragedies. Not only did his father die while he was a young man but also his children died young, as did his wife. He dedicated twenty-five years to developing a formal system, in which all of mathematics could be derived from logic, only to learn that a fatal paradox destroyed the system. During his life, he received little formal recognition of his monumental work and, with his death in 1925, passed virtually unnoticed by the academic world.

Life's Work

Frege's first major work in logic was published in 1879. Although this was a short book of only eighty-eight pages, it has remained one of the most important single works ever written in the field. *Begriffsschrift: Eine der Arithmetischen Nachgebildete Formelsprache des reinen Denkens* (conceptual treatise: a formula language, modeled upon that of arithmetic, for pure thought) presented for the first time a formal system of modern logic. He created a system of formal symbols that could be used more regularly than ordinary language for the purposes of deductive logic. Frege was by no means the first person to use symbols as representations of words, since Aristotle had used this device and was followed by others throughout the history of deductive logic.

Earlier logicians, however, had thought that in order to make a judgment on the validity of sentences, a distinction was necessary between subject and predicate. For the purposes of rhetoric, there is a difference between the statements "The North defeated the South in the Civil War" and "The South was defeated by the North in the Civil War." For Frege, however, the content of both sentences conveyed the same concept and hence must be given the same judgment. In this work, Frege achieved the ideal of nineteenth century mathematics: that if proofs were completely formal and no intuition was required to judge the correctness of the proofs, then there could be complete certainty that these proofs were the result of explicitly stated assumptions. During this period, Frege began to use universal quantifiers in his logic, which cover statements that contain "some" or "every." Consequently, it was now possible to cover a range of objects rather than a single object in a statement.

In 1884, Frege published *Die Grundlagen der Arithmetik* (*The Foundations of Arithmetic*, 1950), which followed his attempt to apply similar principles to arithmetic as his earlier application to logic. In this work, he first reviewed the works of his predecessors and then raised a number of fundamental questions on the nature of numbers and arithmetic truth. This work was more philosophical than mathematical. Throughout the work, Frege enunciated three basic positions concerning the world of philosophical logic: Mental images of a word as perceived by the speaker are irrelevant to the meaning of a word in a sentence in terms of its truth or falsity. The word "grass" in the sentence "the grass is green" does not depend on the mental image of "grass" but on the way in which the word is used in the sentence. Thus the meaning of a word was found in its usage. A second idea was that words only have meaning in the context of a sentence. Rather than depending on the precise definition of a word, the sentence determined the truth-value of the word. If "all grubs are green," then it is possible to understand this sentence without necessarily knowing anything about "grubs." Also, it is possible to make a judgment about a sentence that contains "blue grubs" as false, since "all grubs are green." His third idea deals with the distinction between concepts and objects. This distinction raises serious questions concerning the nature of proper names, identity, universals, and predicates, all of which were historically troublesome philosophical and linguistic problems.

After the publication of *The Foundations of Arithmetic* Frege became known not only as a logician and a mathematician but also as a linguistic philosopher. While the notion of proper name is important for his system of logic, it also extends far beyond those concerns. There had existed an extended debate as to whether numbers such as "1,2,3, . . . " or directions such as "north" were proper names. Frege argued that it was not appropriate to determine what can be known about these words and then see if they can be classified as objects. Rather, like his theory of meaning, in which the meaning of a word is determined by its use in a sentence, if numbers are used as objects they are proper names.

His insistence on the usage of words extended to the problem of universals. According to tradition, something which can be named is a particular, while a universal is predicated of a particular. For example, "red rose" is composed of a universal "red" and a particular "rose." Question arose as to whether universals existed in the sense that the "red" of the "red rose" existed independently of the "rose." Frege had suggested that universals are used as proper names in such sentences as "The rose is red."

Between 1893 and 1903, Frege published two volumes of his unfinished work *Grundgesetze der Arithmetik* (the basic laws of arithmetic). These volumes contained both his greatest contribution to philosophy and logic and the greatest weaknesses of his logical system. Frege made a distinction between sense and reference, in that words frequently had the same reference, but may imply a different sense. Words such as "lad," "boy," and "youth" all have the same reference or meaning, but not in the same sense. As a result, two statements may be logically identical, yet have a different sense. Hence, $2 + 2 = 4$ involves two proper names of a number, namely "$2 + 2$" and "4," but are used in different senses. Extending this idea to a logical system, the meaning or reference of the proper names and the truthvalue of the sentence depend only on the reference of the object and not its sense. Thus, a sentence such as "The boy wore a hat" is identical to the sentence "The lad wore a hat." Since the logical truthvalue of a sentence depends on the meaning of the sentence, the inclusion of a sentence without any meaning within a complex statement means that the entire statement lacks any truthvalue. This proved to be a problem that Frege could not resolve and became a roadblock to his later work.

A further problem which existed in *Grundgesetze der Arithmetik*, which was written as a formal system of logic including the use of terms, symbols, and derived proofs, was the theory of classes. Frege wanted to use logic to derive the entire structure of mathematics to include all real numbers. To achieve this, Frege included, as part of his axioms, a primitive theory of sets or classes. While the second volume of *Grundgesetze der Arithmetik* was being prepared for publication, he received a letter from Bertrand Russell describing a contradiction that became known as the Russell Paradox. This paradox, sometimes known as the Stranger Loop, asks, Is "the class of all classes that are not members of itself" a member of itself or not? For example, the "class of all dogs" is not a dog; the "class of all animals" is not an animal. If the class of all classes is a member of itself, then it is one of those classes that are not members of themselves. Yet if it is not a member of itself, then it must be a member of all classes that are members of themselves, and the loop goes on forever. Frege replaced the class axiom with a modified and weaker axiom, but his formal system was weakened, and he never completed the third volume of the work.

Between 1904 and 1917, Frege added few contributions to his earlier works. During these years, he attempted to work through those contradictions which arose in his attempt to derive all of mathematics from logic. By 1918, he had begun to write a new book on logic, but he completed only three chapters. In 1923, he seemed to have broken through his intellectual dilemma and no longer believed that it was possible to create a foundation of mathematics based on logic. He began work in a new direction, beginning with geometry, but completed little of this work before his death.

Summary

In *Begriffsschrift*, Gottlob Frege created the first comprehensive system of formal logic since the ancient Greeks. He provided some of the foundations of modern logic with the formulation of the principles of noncontradiction and excluded middle. Equally important, Frege introduced the use of quantifiers to bind variables, which distinguished modern symbolic logic from earlier systems.

Frege's works were never widely read or appreciated. His system of symbols and functions were forbidding even to the best minds in mathematics. Russell, however, made a careful study of Frege and was clearly influenced by his system of logic. Also, Ludwig Wittgenstein incorporated a number of Frege's linguistic ideas, such as the use of ordinary language, into his works. Frege's distinction between sense and reference later generated a renewed interest in his work, and a number of important philosophical and linguistic studies are based on his original research.

Bibliography

Bynum, Terrell W. Introduction to *Conceptual Notations*, by Gottlob Frege. Oxford, England: Clarendon Press, 1972. An eighty-page introduction to the logic of Frege. While sections of the text on the logic are not suited for the general reader, the introductory text is clear, concise, and highly accessible. The significant works by Frege are outlined in simple terms, and the commentary is useful.
Currie, Gregory. *Frege: An Introduction to His Philosophy.* Brighton, England: Harvester Press, 1982. Discusses all the major developments in

Frege's thought from a background chapter to the *Begriffsschrift*, theory of numbers, philosophical logic and methods, basic law, and the fatal paradox. Some parts of this text are accessible to the general reader; other parts require a deeper understanding of philosophical issues.

Dummett, Michael A. E. *Frege: Philosophy of Language.* London: Duckworth, 1973. One of the leading authorities on the philosophy of Frege. The advantage of this text over others, is that Dummett is in part responsible for the idea that Frege is a linguistic philosopher. Somewhat difficult but good introduction to Frege.

Grossmann, Reinhardt. *Reflections on Frege's Philosophy.* Evanston, Ill.: Northwestern University Press, 1969. Delineates three major areas of Frege's thoughts as found in *Begriffsschrift* and *The Foundations of Arithmetic*, and describes the distinction between meaning, sense, and reference. Within these areas the author writes an exposition on a few selected problems which are of current interest.

Kneale, William, and Martha Kneale. *The Development of Logic.* Oxford, England: Clarendon Press, 1962. Three chapters in this work are very useful. Chapter 7 covers Frege and his contemporaries, Frege's criticism of his predecessors, and Frege's definition of natural numbers. Chapter 8 covers Frege's three major works and outlines his contributions to the world of logic. Chapter 9 covers formal developments in logic after Frege and reveals his pivotal position in the development of modern symbolic logic.

Victor W. Chen

FRIEDRICH FROEBEL

Born: April 21, 1782; Oberweissbach, Thuringia
Died: June 21, 1852; Marienthal, Thuringia
Area of Achievement: Education
Contribution: Froebel founded the first kindergarten. He believed in the underlying unity in nature, for him God, and emphasized that schools should provide pleasant surroundings, encourage self-activity, and offer physical training for children.

Early Life

The unhappiness of Friedrich Wilhelm August Froebel's childhood affected his entire life. Born on April 21, 1782, to Johann Jakob and Eleonore Friderica Froebel, Friedrich was left motherless when he was nine months old. His father, a Lutheran pastor, was aloof and pompous. Upon his second marriage, he lost interest in Friedrich, who was still too young for school. After Johann's wife bore their child, Friedrich was treated like an interloper. His stepmother addressed him in the formal third person rather than in the familiar second person normally used with children.

The father considered his son stupid and rebellious. He conveyed these feelings to Friedrich, who developed a sense of personal unworthiness. When Friedrich began school, his father insisted that he attend the girls' school, making Friedrich feel more unusual than he already considered himself.

When he was ten, Friedrich was sent to live with a kindly uncle in Stadt Ilm, remaining there for five years. On his return home, however, the antagonisms that plagued his earlier days resurfaced, so his father apprenticed him to a woodcutter at Neuhof, the former home of educational reformer Johann Heinrich Pestalozzi, where he stayed for two years.

At seventeen, Friedrich visited his brother, a medical student at the University of Jena. Although he was ill-prepared for the university, Froebel attended elementary lectures in philosophy, the sciences, and mathematics until he was jailed by the university for indebtedness. After his father reluctantly posted his bail, Froebel drifted for five years. After a flirtation with architecture, he turned to tutoring, and found that he loved teaching.

In 1805, Froebel made his first short visit to Yverdon, where Pestalozzi had just established his experimental school. After a brief stay in Frankfurt, he returned to Yverdon to spend four years as an assistant to Pestalozzi. He perceived that Pestalozzi's approach failed both to interconnect the subjects being taught and to give much attention to the students' spiritual connection with the universe. These reservations spurred Froebel into formulating his own philosophy of education.

Life's Work

When Froebel completed his four-year stay at Yverdon in 1810, he returned to Frankfurt as a tutor. He soon decided, however, that he had a dual destiny. On the one hand, he saw himself as a potential educational reformer. On the other, he was trying to find a unity in nature, an explanation of the mysteries of existence. Accordingly, he was enrolled in the University of Göttingen in 1811, first studying ancient languages in his search for the underlying unity in existence. He then turned his attention to mathematics, the sciences, and philosophy, subjects to which he had been exposed at Jena.

In 1812, Froebel moved to the University of Berlin to study crystallography; his interest in this subject was awakened by an essay he had written on the symbolism of spheres the preceding year at Göttingen. By 1813, he was assistant curator at the university's museum of mineralogy. He continued his research in crystals, viewing them always as symbols of an underlying unity.

Although Froebel was offered a teaching position at the University of Berlin in 1816, he believed that his greatest contribution could be made by opening a school. In that year, in a humble cottage not far from Pestalozzi's Neuhof, he founded the Allegemeine Deutsche Erziehungsanstalt (universal German institute of education). The student body consisted of five of Froebel's nephews. His declared purpose was to teach people how to be free, something that he himself was still in the process of learning.

By 1817, the school had grown. Froebel moved it to more imposing quarters in nearby Keilhau. He was soon joined by Wilhelm Middendorff and Heinrich Langethal, friends he had made in 1813 during his brief service in the military. The school almost foundered in 1818 after Froebel's marriage to Wilhelmine Hoffmeister aroused contention in the closely knit school community. The origins of the discord are perhaps attributable to homosexual overtones, overt or covert, in Froebel's relationship with Middendorff and Langethal. One of Froebel's brothers rescued the school with both funds and a new approach to running its business. The school's enrollment rose to sixty.

As the enterprise succeeded, Froebel became increasingly absolutist, autocratic, and tyrannical. Students began to rebel against him, and word reached public officials that all was not well at the institution. An official investigation cleared the school of the charges against it, but the damage had been done. By 1820, Froebel's influence was minimal, although he was associated with the school until 1831. From the Keilhau experience Froebel wrote *Die Menschenerziehung* (1826; *The Education of Man,* 1885), which details his philosophy of teaching children to age ten.

Essentially, the book is guided more by intuition than reason. It is based on nothing resembling scientific method. Froebel's stated aim is to help his students unlock what is inside them and to find a harmony between their inner selves and the external world, which to Froebel is the entire universe. The approach is mystical and shows Froebel as a deeply religious man who, presuming a divine origin for the universe, proceeds to suggest ways to bring human beings into a balance with that divine, creating force. As Froebel searched for absolutes, his search made him increasingly absolutist.

Froebel believed that everything, no matter how small, has a purpose. His scheme of education was to lead people to discover that purpose. He agreed with Pestalozzi's belief that, because the universe is constantly changing, nothing in life is static. This reasoning led him quite naturally to a dynamic *Weltanschauung*. For Froebel, people are themselves an inherent part of all activity. They can be guided by skillful teachers, but real teaching proceeds only from self-activity. Froebel's conception of human development is not one in which infancy, childhood, youth, and maturity are separate entities, but one in which these stages are entities evolving into subsequent stages of which they are forever parts. Such speculation suggests the taxonomies of such educational theorists as Benjamin S. Bloom and Lawrence Kohlberg and also presages Sigmund Freud.

Froebel, like Jean-Jacques Rousseau, presumed that children are inherently good. He thought that evil resulted from bad education. He considered the ideal educational institution to be the earliest one—the family—at whose heart, he believed, is the mother as chief teacher of the young. Froebel's own education lacked the fundamental ingredient of effective learning—a mother who both loved and taught. Froebel virtually deified mothers, and in so doing, moved in the direction of what was to be his greatest educational contribution, the kindergarten—literally a garden whose blossoms are children. Froebel was rationalizing guilt feelings about what he perceived as his own evil when he wrote that wickedness proceeds from a mother's neglect of her young child.

Froebel left Keilhau in 1831 and went to Switzerland, where he opened a school; he opened a second at Lucerne. Soon, however, he was forced to disband these schools, partly because Lucerne's Catholic populace was suspicious of him and partly because his nephews, his former students at Keilhau, bore him great animosity and did everything they could to discredit him. By 1833, Froebel had developed a plan for the education of Bern's poor, but he had yet to find his real vocation.

In 1835, Froebel was appointed director of the orphanage at Burgdorf, the site of some of Pestalozzi's pre-Yverdon teaching, and he operated the orphanage according to Pestalozzi's methods, training teachers at the orphanage and teaching the children. At Burgdorf, Froebel began to concentrate on the education of young children and especially of those normally considered too young for school. He left Burgdorf in 1836 to go to Berlin, where he studied nursery schools.

In 1837, at the age of fifty-five, Froebel established a school in Blankenburg, not far from Keilhau, for the training of very young children. He called it a *Kleinkinderbeschäftigungsanstalt* (an institution for the occupation of small children), but in 1840 he changed the name to the less cumbersome, more familiar kindergarten. In this school, he instituted his method of teaching through gifts and occupations. Children received, over a period of time, ten boxes of gifts, objects from which they could learn, and they also were assigned ten occupations, activities that would result in their creating gifts.

Part of Froebel's technique was to devise games to interest and actively involve children both physically and mentally. He recorded these techniques in *Die Pädagogik des Kindergartens* (1862; *Friedrich Froebel's Pedagogics of the Kindergarten: Or, His Ideas Concerning the Play and Playthings of the Child*, 1895), published posthumously. His most successful book of that period was *Mutter- und Kose-lieder* (1844; *Mother-Play and Nursery Songs*, 1878), a book containing fifty original songs and finger plays that would help mothers interact with their infants. This book attracted an enthusiastic following.

Successful though Froebel's first kindergarten was in many respects, it fell into debt by 1844, and he had to disband it. People expressed great fears about kindergartens, worrying about the political and religious philosophies to which very young, impressionable children were exposed in Froebel's institution, which enrolled students from ages one through seven. By 1851, the Prussian government had banned kindergartens as threats to society. Meanwhile, Froebel's influential nephews worked hard to discredit him.

On June 21, 1852, a year after he married Luisa Leven, his second wife, who was thirty years his junior, Froebel died at Marienthal, his kindergartens banned in Prussia until 1860.

Summary

Friedrich Froebel's experimental school, the kindergarten, has affected education and society significantly. Froebel had vigorous supporters, among them his widow and the Baroness Berthe von Marenholtz-Bülow, both of whom traveled widely to disseminate his ideas. Indeed, Charles Dickens wrote a favorable account of a kindergarten he had seen.

Mrs. Carl Schurz and her sister, both trained by Froebel, imported the kindergarten to the United States in 1855, establishing a German-language kindergarten in Watertown, Wisconsin. Elizabeth Peabody established the first English-language kindergarten in the United States in Boston in 1860.

The term *kindergarten* has survived in the United States, although it now frequently designates that single year before a child enters the primary grades. The kindergarten as Froebel perceieved it now exists in the United States as the preschool, attended by infants of several weeks to children of four or five.

Bibliography

Downs, Robert B. *Friedrich Froebel*. Boston: Twayne, 1978. An accurate, brief overview of Froebel. Solid presentation of facts, although generally short on analysis. The book serves the basic purpose for which it is intended, that of informing the reading public and college undergraduates.

Froebel, Friedrich. *Autobiography of Friedrich Froebel*. Translated and annotated by Emilie Michaelis and H. Keatley Moore. Syracuse, N.Y.: Bardeen, 1889. Froebel's only autobiographical record exists in two long letters, one written to the Duke of Meiningen in 1827, the other to Karl Krause in 1828. These letters, well translated and accurate, along with Johann Barop's notes on the Froebel community, comprise this useful volume. Helpful for biographical details.

Kilpatrick, William H. *Froebel's Kindergarten Principles Critically Examined*. New York: Macmillan, 1916. Despite its age, an indispensable book for Froebel scholarship because it describes how the intractability of the International Kindergartners Association, founded in 1892, eventually clashed with Granville Stanley Hall's more scientifically devised psychological approach to early childhood education. An accurate, objective assessment of an important topic.

Lawrence, Evelyn, ed. *Friedrich Froebel and English Education*. New York: Philosophical Library, 1953. Six British educators discuss Froebel's influence on the schools of Great Britain and on education in general. A balanced view of Froebel's contributions outside Germany.

Marenholtz-Bülow, Berthe von. *Reminiscences of Friedrich Froebel*. Translated by Mary Mann. Boston: Lee and Shepard, 1895. This book by one of Froebel's former students and staunchest supporters provides important details about his later years, during which he was implementing his concept of the kindergarten.

R. Baird Shuman

ANDREA GABRIELI

Born: c.1520; in or near Venice
Died: 1586; Venice
Area of Achievement: Music
Contribution: Gabrieli was one of the most versatile musicians of his genera-
tion. His compositional output includes sacred vocal music, secular vocal
music, instrumental ensemble music, and organ music.

Early Life

Very little is known about Andrea Gabrieli's early life. He was probably
born in the northern (or Canareggio) section of Venice. Although most biographers have stated that he was born around 1510, the lack of available
information on Gabrieli until the 1550's suggests a birth date of around
1520. It is possible that he may have received some early training from the
organist at San Geremia in Canareggio (Baldassare da Imola), and that he
may have been a singer at St. Mark's Cathedral in Venice in 1536, although
there is no documentation to prove either of these assumptions. Nor is there
evidence to suggest that he was a pupil of Adrian Willaert, the chapel master
of St. Mark's at that time.

Since Gabrieli's first published composition appears in a 1554 collection
of madrigals by Vincenzo Ruffo, it is possible that he may have been a
musician at the Verona cathedral, where Ruffo worked during the 1550's.
The first indication of Gabrieli's activities as a church organist dates from
1557-1558, when he was organist at San Geremia. Although he competed
unsuccessfully for the position of second organist at St. Mark's Cathedral in
1557, he must have already been an accomplished organist, for he was a
member of the Accademia della Fama in Venice by 1558.

Perhaps the most significant event in Gabrieli's musical training is his
connection with the court of Munich during the early 1560's. As court organist to Duke Albrecht V of Bavaria in 1562, he accompanied the duke on
several journeys and became friends with the duke's music director, Orlan-
dus Lassus. Before his period at the court of Munich, Gabrieli had published
only four compositions, all madrigals that suggest the influence of Cipriano
de Rore. This contact with Lassus heavily influenced Gabrieli's many subsequent publications of both sacred and secular compositions and assured his
future position as one of the most important musicians in Venice.

Life's Work

Gabrieli became second organist at St. Mark's in 1564. His growing popularity in Venetian musical life is attested to by the fact that he composed
ceremonial music for various state occasions—the visit of Archduke Karl of
Graz (1569), the festivities after the Venetian republic's victory against the

Turks (1571), and the visit of King Henry III of France (1574). During these mature years, he also attracted a number of talented students, including Hans Leo Hassler, Ludovico Zacconi, and his nephew Giovanni Gabrieli. He became first organist at St. Mark's in 1584, a position which he retained until his death late in 1586.

Unfortunately, much of Gabrieli's music was published late or posthumously, making it difficult to trace the development of his musical style. For this reason, his life's work is best discussed by types of compositions, divided into the following categories: madrigals, villanelle, sacred vocal music, ceremonial music, instrumental ensemble music, and keyboard music. Gabrieli's seven books of mature madrigals were published between 1566 and 1589. With these collections, he established himself as a master of the lighter type of madrigal that became a fashionable reaction to the serious, avant-garde madrigals of many late sixteenth century composers. Petrarch's texts are set in a less serious style, and many madrigals use the lighter pastoral verses of such poets as Battista Guarini and Torquato Tasso. Gabrieli achieves a less contrapuntal, more appealing style in these madrigals through the use of closely spaced imitative entries and through a greater tendency toward homophonic writing with various combinations of voices. Some phrases have two melodic voices and a harmonic bass, a tendency that anticipates the texture of Baroque music. The harmonic style shows a preference for major triads and a feeling for tonal clarity resulting from the use of few altered notes. In these madrigals, Gabrieli is still attentive to the words but avoids the manneristic tendency to disturb the musical flow of a composition by his lighter treatment of the texts.

Gabrieli also contributed to the development of the villanella, a light type of secular vocal composition that was a reaction to the more serious sixteenth century madrigal. He composed two types of local Venetian villanelle, greghesche and giustiniane, both influenced by the villanelle of Lassus. Greghesche have verses that characterize *commedia dell'arte* figures and are written in a mixture of Venetian and Greek. Giustiniane have texts that repeat certain syllables to portray the stuttering of a Venetian patrician. In most cases, both types of pieces have three voice parts that move in a simple, homophonic style.

Gabrieli's sacred music also shows the influence of Lassus and suggests that he may have been attentive to the requirements of the Council of Trent. The words are easily understood because of the tendency toward homophonic writing, the syllabic text setting, and the clear-cut phrases. These masses and motets are generally diatonic with a harmonically oriented bass. Like Lassus, Gabrieli was interested in setting the penitential psalms to music. His *Psalmi Davidici* (1583; psalms of David) reflect the Council of Trent's goals by taking a greater interest in sonority, simplifying the texture, and avoiding obvious word painting.

Gabrieli's ceremonial music includes compositions set to both sacred and secular texts. His eight-voiced madrigal "Felici d'Adria" was composed in 1567 for the visit of Archduke Charles of Carinthia to Venice. In the *Concerti*, published posthumously by his nephew Giovanni in 1587, motets for eight or more voices are found that have texts dealing with major festivals of the Venetian year. Some ceremonial works by Gabrieli have separate choirs that alternate unpredictably in phrases of different lengths. At other times, he creates variety by constantly changing the grouping of the voices and by mixing homophonic with contrapuntal writing. His last occasional music may have been written for the opening of the Teatro Olimpico in Vicenza, for which he composed sixty-four choruses to a translated version of Sophocles' *Oidipous Tyrannos* (c. 429 B.C.; *Oedipus Tyrannus*).

Gabrieli's contributions to the development of instrumental music have never been fully appreciated. For four-part instrumental ensembles, Gabrieli composed a number of ricercars that are suitable for many combinations of early string or wind instruments. His interest in thematic unity is clearly seen in these ricercars, which are usually based on one or two melodic ideas that are repeated extensively in all four instrumental parts. He achieves variety by writing duet passages, by alternating overlapping imitative entries with entrances of the thematic material that do not overlap, and by developing one thematic idea sometimes and juxtaposing two thematic ideas at other times.

Gabrieli composed several types of pieces for keyboard instruments: intonazioni, toccate, canzone, and ricercar. His intonazioni and toccate reflect the spirit of sixteenth century improvisation and could have served as preludes to other compositions. Gabrieli composed two types of keyboard canzone, those that are not based on vocal compositions and those that are based on secular chansons of well-known composers. The canzone that are not derived from vocal works are characterized by the imitation of a number of successive thematic ideas and have sections in contrasting meters and tempos. Those that are based on chansons follow their vocal models but add extensive ornamentation.

Some of Gabrieli's keyboard ricercars are freely composed, while others are based on vocal compositions. Those belonging to the latter category do not follow the vocal model as closely as Gabrieli does in his canzone. In these ricercars, each melodic motive is treated at greater length than in the vocal model itself. Thus, instead of imitating each motive once in each of the four polyphonic parts, they show their clearly instrumental character by normally having five to ten imitative entries for a melodic motive. The freely composed ricercars can be divided into three categories: those that have one thematic idea prevailing throughout, those that employ two complimentary thematic ideas, and those that have a number of thematic ideas that are derived from the opening idea. Some of the imitative entries over these thematic ideas overlap in typical Renaissance fashion. At other times, the imitative entries anticipate Baroque fugal procedure by not overlapping. Some ricercars demonstrate Gabrieli's contrapuntal skill by lengthening the thematic idea to two or four times the length of the original note values (augmentation), or by inverting the melodic intervals of the thematic idea. Whatever the special devices, the opening thematic idea or one of the other main thematic ideas is present most of the time.

Summary

During his lifetime, Andrea Gabrieli made significant contributions to many of the genres current in his day—secular vocal music, sacred vocal music, ceremonial music, and keyboard music. His villanelle and madrigals are important to the development of secular vocal music, for they represent a lighter alternative to the more serious, highly expressive avant-garde madrigals that many other composers were writing. Because of their humorous texts, his villanelle are important predecessors of the early seventeenth century madrigal comedies by Adriano Banchieri and Orazio Vecchi. His sacred vocal music reflects the needs of the Council of Trent; the simpler textures and diatonic style of writing served as a model for other composers wishing to compose in a style acceptable to the Catholic church. His ceremonial music influenced other composers, particularly because of the changing textures or the alternation of separate choirs. Although the origins of Baroque style lie primarily in the works by those composers who believed in more serious text expression, Gabrieli's vocal works do anticipate certain Baroque traits in their tendency toward homophonic writing, clear-cut phrases, a simpler harmonic style, and an increased vertical orientation.

Gabrieli's greatest impact, however, was in the realm of keyboard music. His intonazioni and toccate reveal much about sixteenth century improvisation. His sectional canzone anticipate the early Baroque canzona and sonata, while his chanson-based canzone are excellent examples of Renaissance ornamentation practices. Gabrieli's ricercars, because of their tendency toward thematic unity, the persistent use of imitation, and the use of special contrapuntal devices, foreshadow the fugal procedures of the seventeenth century. Although the works of Gabrieli are not as well known as those of his nephew Giovanni, Andrea is far more significant, for he contributed to a wider variety of vocal and instrumental genres than did his nephew and had a greater influence on more composers. He helped to make Venice one of the most important centers of musical activity in Europe.

Bibliography

Apel, Willi. *The History of Keyboard Music Before 1700.* Translated by Hans Tischler. Bloomington: Indiana University Press, 1972. The most thorough description of Gabrieli's keyboard music. Stresses the importance of Gabrieli's ricercars as predecessors of the Baroque fugue and describes his canzone, intonazione, toccate, and organ masses.

Arnold, Denis. "Ceremonial Music in Venice at the Time of the Gabrielis." *Proceedings of the Musical Association* 82 (1955/1956): 47-59. States that music for separated choirs fulfilled the need for ceremonial music on important festive occasions in Venice. Discusses Gabrieli's role in the history of Venetian ceremonial music and describes the major influences on his music for separated choirs.

——————. *Giovanni Gabrieli and the Music of the Venetian High Renaissance*. New York: Oxford University Press, 1979. Although primarily about Andrea Gabrieli's nephew, this book contains some useful biographical information and general discussions of Gabrieli's motets, masses, instrumental ensemble music, and keyboard music. Emphasizes the influence of Gabrieli upon his nephew but clearly distinguishes their musical styles.

Einstein, Alfred. *The Italian Madrigal*. Translated by Alexander H. Krappe, Roger H. Sessions, and Oliver Stunk. Princeton, N.J.: Princeton University Press, 1949, 2d ed. 1971. A dated but useful discussion of Gabrieli's villanelle and madrigals. Emphasizes Gabrieli's role in the development of the madrigal and suggests that his light madrigals reflect sixteenth century Venetian life. The musical style of several madrigals is described in detail.

Gabrieli, Andrea. *Andrea Gabrieli: Complete Madrigals*. Vols. 41-52. Edited by A. Tillman Merritt. Madison, Wis.: A-R Editions, 1981-1984. The introduction contains information about Gabrieli's life and musical style. It also lists the major sources of his vocal and instrumental works. All the volumes have detailed discussions of the texts and music edited in each volume.

John O. Robison

GIOVANNI GABRIELI

Born: c. 1556; Venice
Died: August 12, 1612; Venice
Area of Achievement: Music
Contribution: Gabrieli was one of the most gifted of the Venetian school of composers of the Renaissance and Baroque eras. Through his teaching of northern European students, particularly Heinrich Schütz, and the wide circulation of his published music north of the Alps, Gabrieli is considered an important influence on the development of German music during the Baroque period.

Early Life

Very little is known of Giovanni Gabrieli's early life, as is typical for composers of the Italian Renaissance. Unlike the greatest artists, musicians were usually regarded as servants, not celebrities. Even the year of his birth is unknown, since the notice of his death in the records of his parish church lists his age at death as fifty-six, while the Venetian public-health records give it as fifty-eight. His parents were Pietro de Fais, a weaver, and Paola, the sister of Andrea Gabrieli (c. 1520-1586), a noted composer. Sadly, many documents relating to his life may have been destroyed by Napoleon I's armies in 1797, and others at the end of World War II in 1945.

Giovanni's first teacher was his uncle, with whom he went to Munich, probably in 1575, as a musician at the court of the Duke of Bavaria, Albrecht V. In Munich, Giovanni was associated with a number of other noted composers besides his uncle, notably Orlando de Lassus. Two other gifted composers he came to know in his formative years became lifelong friends, Giuseppe Guami, another musician at the Bavarian court, and Hans Leo Hassler, a student of Andrea. Giovanni's adoption of his uncle's surname and his painstaking editing of his uncle's works after Andrea's death indicate his closeness to his relative and teacher. Giovanni's own pupil Schütz was to be another close friend.

It is clear that Gabrieli made friends easily and that many of his friends throughout his life were other musicians, including several Germans. It is quite possible that at least some of Gabrieli's recognized influence on the development of German early Baroque music came about through his friendships as well as his gifts. That would not be unique in musical history. Some of the influence of the Netherlands school may have been as a result of the attractive personalities of its members, particularly Johannes Ockeghem and Lassus. During the classical period, Franz Joseph Haydn's good nature may have contributed to his success. Unfortunately, much more is known about the lives and personalities of Ockeghem, Lassus, and Haydn than is known about the life and personality of Gabrieli.

Life's Work

Gabrieli was already a respected composer when he returned to Venice, sometime between 1579 and 1584. In 1584, he was hired as a temporary organist at St. Mark's Basilica and won the permanent post of second organist the following year. He was to hold it for life. St. Mark's had two organs in lofts at the north and south ends of the building, so there were always two organists. During Gabrieli's tenure, a third (chamber) organ was added. Normally the organists used only one and played on alternate Sundays, but on great feast days all three organs would be used. There was no difference in salary and responsibilities between the first and second organists. When Giovanni was hired, his uncle was the first organist. From 1588 to 1591, the first organist was Giovanni's friend Guami, while for the remainder of Giovanni's life, the other organist was Paolo Giusto. In 1585, Giovanni became organist for a lay religious society, the Scuola Grande di San Rocco. Both posts required the organist to compose as well as to play, which was a general requirement for salaried organists and music directors (*Kappelmeisters*) until about the beginning of the nineteenth century.

At St. Mark's, Gabrieli had the use of one of the largest and best-trained musical establishments in Europe, partly built by his uncle during the twenty years (1566-1586) Andrea was an organist at the basilica. The paid permanent ensemble included thirty or more singers and four instrumentalists (two cornets and two trombones). Moreover, Gabrieli could draw on far larger resources on special occasions, such as great feasts of the Church and public festivals. Since many of his instrumental pieces called for strings, woodwinds, and additional brasses, it is clear that Gabrieli regularly hired additional musicians. These could have come from many sources and may have included women as well as men.

Venetian *ospedales* (foundling homes and orphanages) included such excellent music instruction that, a century later, Antonio Vivaldi's girls at the Pietà are thought to have been the best ensemble in Europe, providing the orchestra for all of his works and the soloists for all of his concertos, except those for violin. Other resources that could be drawn on included church choirs, the professional trumpeters who accompanied the Doge, and the musicians of the several religious confraternities, among them Gabrieli's own Scuola Grande di San Rocco. Very few other cities had such numerous, varied, and talented bodies of musicians available, and Venetian composers from Adrian Willaert to Vivaldi made full use of them. It was this unmatched abundance of players and singers that helped attract talented composers to Venice and that helped to make the Venetian school distinct from the musicians of other Italian regions. Venetian music, like Venetian painting, imparts a feeling of opulence. Some of Gabrieli's best works drew on all of these resources, stretched them further than had earlier Venetian composers, and achieved a kind of massive grandeur which was opulent even by

Venetian standards and entirely appropriate to the richness of St. Mark's.

Associated as he was with St. Mark's and other religious bodies, a great part of Gabrieli's output was of sacred music. He wrote madrigals while in Bavaria, but, apparently, very few after he returned to Venice. There is no evidence of his ever having written dance music. Instead, he devoted himself to the composition of religious works, primarily for St. Mark's, and ceremonial music for both St. Mark's and the religious processions of the Scuola Grande di San Rocco.

Venetian composers, starting with Willaert, who introduced Venice to the advanced ideas of the Netherlands school to which he belonged, had made use of the large size, multiple organs and choir lofts, and long echoes of St. Mark's by separating their choirs and placing choirs or sections in different parts of the cathedral, often with instrumentalists, chiefly trombones, trumpets, and bassoons. They might play and sing together or antiphonally—choirs answering one another. Called *cori spezzati*, they made the listener seem to hear the music as coming from different directions, and, if all musicians were playing and singing, from all directions. Ideally suited to St. Mark's, this practice lasted longer in Venice than anywhere else in Italy. Gabrieli was the last major Italian composer to use *cori spezzati* in his church pieces, and he also introduced the practice into his many canzonas, short works for instruments, usually brasses and organ. The effects were rich and majestic, even by Venetian standards.

Cori spezzati composition and performance endured much longer in Germany than in Italy, for a variety of reasons. The Germans, on the whole, were more religious than the Italians. Gabrieli's successors at St. Mark's, Claudio Monteverdi and Giacomo Carissimi, were the last significant Italian religious composers before Vivaldi. Even Monteverdi's operas and madrigals are at least as well known as his sacred music. Secular music, not sacred, was what the Italian public wanted. In Germany, on the other hand, the chapel, not the opera house, was where the audience went to hear music. German and Austrian composers continued to write large quantities of church music, Catholic and Protestant, throughout the seventeenth and eighteenth centuries. Many German cathedrals were as suited to separated choirs as St. Mark's. Indeed, many composers who worked in Germany, including Andrea Gabrieli and Lassus, composed for *cori spezzati*. Another reason for its survival in Germany was that Venetian works were common and appreciated north of the Alps. Many German musicians had studied in Venice because of the excellence of its resources and teaching. Moreover, Venice was then the most important center for music publication. The publication of Gabrieli's own works, begun during his lifetime with madrigals composed while he was in Bavaria, continued with *Sacrae symphoniae* (1597) and the posthumous *Canzoni e sonate* (1615). Many works still remained in manuscript at that time. In 1956, Denis Arnold began publishing Gabrieli's complete works, but some lost ones have been discovered during the 1980's.

As little is known of Gabrieli's later years as is known of his early life. It is probable that he married and had a large family, and it is certain that he spent a good part of his spare time in the German community, where he had many friends. Aside from this, it is known only that he died from kidney stones after a long illness in 1612.

Summary

Giovanni Gabrieli's place in history seems secure. Unlike the works of most early Baroque and Renaissance composers, his choral works, in particular, sometimes were performed during the nineteenth and early twentieth centuries. His popularity resulted from one of the earliest important musicological studies, Carl von Winterfeld's *Johannes Gabrieli und sein Zeitalter* (1834), which reintroduced his work at a time when practically no Renaissance and early Baroque music was played or sung, except for that of Giovanni Pierluigi da Palestrina. While Winterfeld's work contained a number of exaggerated claims for Gabrieli that later scholars have rejected, the work did influence continuing research on and performance of the Venetian master. Winterfeld was particularly interested in Gabrieli's choral works, while later studies have concentrated more upon his instrumental pieces.

Gabrieli and his younger Roman contemporary, Girolamo Frescobaldi, are usually considered the most important Italian organ composers. In Gabrieli's case, his fame rests on a number of pieces ranging from ricercars, toccatas, and fugues, all exercises in theme and variation, to intonations, short pieces of a few bars which introduce longer works, usually for choir, organ, and instruments. Gabrieli's compositions for instrumental ensembles have especially interested modern musicologists and performers, particularly brass players. Musicologists see them as leading directly to the sonata and concerto. While some are for strings and organ and others for strings, organ, and winds, many are for brass or brass and organ. Since the brass repertory is rather limited, Gabrieli is a favorite of most brass ensembles. In composing some of his instrumental music, Gabrieli was one of the first composers to specify whether music should be played loudly or softly.

The vocal music of Gabrieli and his German admirers, such as Schütz and Michael Praetorius, has frequently been recorded. Massive works requiring multiple choirs, vocal soloists, organs, and brasses placed in different positions in echoing cathedrals are a perfect subject for stereophonic and quadrophonic recording. A few contemporary musical groups and composers have composed and performed works for *cori spezzati*.

Bibliography

Arnold, Denis. *Giovanni Gabrieli and the Music of the Venetian High Renaissance*. New York: Oxford University Press, 1979. This is the fullest and most readable biography of Gabrieli in English. Arnold sees Gabrieli as a brilliant conservative, a late sixteenth century Bach.

Grout, Donald Jay. *A History of Western Music*. Rev. ed. New York: W. W. Norton, 1973. This fine general work is useful in placing Gabrieli and other composers in perspective.

Kenton, Egon. *Life and Works of Giovanni Gabrieli*. Rome: American Institute of Musicology, 1967. A highly technical work for the professional musician, musicologist, or music historian. Kenton's work is of value to the amateur student chiefly as a second opinion to balance that of Arnold.

Robertson, Alec, and Denis Stevens, eds. *A History of Music*. Vol. 2, *Renaissance and Baroque*. New York: Barnes & Noble Books, 1965. Like that of Grout, this is a general work. Its particular value for the student is in putting Gabrieli and other Renaissance and Baroque composers in perspective in the European musical scenes of their times.

Selfridge-Field, Eleanor. *Venetian Instrumental Music from Gabrieli to Vivaldi*. New York: Praeger, 1975. In chapter 4, which is devoted to Gabrieli, Selfridge-Field portrays him as playing a crucial role in the creation of the Baroque era and in anticipating the concerto and the sonata.

John Gardner

GALILEO

Born: February 15, 1564; Pisa, Republic of Florence
Died: January 8, 1642; Arcetri, Republic of Florence
Area of Achievement: Astronomy
Contribution: Galileo helped establish the modern scientific method through his use of observation and experimentation. His work in mathematics, physics, and astronomy made him a leading figure of the early scientific revolution.

Early Life

Galileo Galilei was the first of seven children born to Vincenzo Galilei and Giulia Ammanati. His father was a cloth merchant as well as a noted musician who wrote several treatises on musical theory. The Galileis were a noble Florentine family that over the years had lost much of its wealth. It was for financial reasons that Vincenzo left Florence and moved to Pisa to establish his textile trade.

At the age of ten, Galileo and his family returned to Florence. His early education was directed by his father with the help of a private tutor. He also spent some time at the monastery of Santa Maria di Vallombrosa. The content of Galileo's elementary education is unknown, but it was probably humanistic in character. His father urged him to pursue university studies which would lead to a lucrative profession.

Following his father's wish, Galileo enrolled as a student of medicine at the University of Pisa in 1581. He showed little interest in his medical studies; it was mathematics that captured his attention. A year after enrolling at the university, Galileo made his legendary discovery of the isochronal movement of pendulums by observing a chandelier in the Pisa cathedral. He confirmed his theory regarding the equal movement of pendulums by conducting a series of experiments. He continued an independent study of science and mathematics, finally convincing his father to allow him to abandon his medical studies. Galileo withdrew from the University of Pisa in 1586 without receiving a degree, and he returned to his family.

Upon his return to Florence, Galileo studied a wide range of literary and scientific texts. In addition, he delivered a series of popular lectures on the *Inferno* of Dante's *La divina commedia* (c. 1320; *The Divine Comedy*, 1802) at the Florentine Academy. In 1589, he used the influence of friends to obtain an appointment as a lecturer of mathematics at the University of Pisa. His return to Pisa marked a productive and enjoyable time for the young scholar. He conducted a series of experiments relating to falling bodies and wrote a short manuscript which challenged many traditional and generally accepted teachings about physics. In addition to his scholarly activities, Galileo was known for his quick wit, biting sense of humor, and excellent debating ability. Once again his friends intervened on his behalf to arrange an appointment, in 1592, to a more prestigious chair of mathematics at the University of Padua.

Life's Work

It was at Padua that Galileo began his life's work which would bring him both fame and controversy. He quickly established himself as an excellent and popular teacher, both in terms of public lectures and private tutoring. He also wrote a series of short manuscripts on a variety of technical and practical issues. In 1597, he constructed a "military compass" to assist artillery bombardments and army formations.

Although Galileo's invention of the military compass brought him acclaim and a good source of additional income, it was his work in the study of motion and astronomy that firmly established his reputation as a leading scientist. In 1604, a new star could be seen, and its sudden appearance prompted a fierce debate. According to the dominant theory of the time, Earth was the immovable center of the universe. Based on the work of Aristotle and Ptolemy, most scholars believed that the planets, sun, and stars rotated around a stationary Earth. The universe was thought to reflect a perfect and unchangeable order that had been created by God. The new star raised a problem of how to account for its presence in an already complete and perfectly ordered universe.

The intensity of this debate reflected a larger controversy regarding the work of Nicolaus Copernicus. Copernicus claimed that Earth and the other planets orbited the sun, and the stars were fixed or stationary. The appearance of a new star provided a tangible point of reference to settle a much larger scientific and theological debate on the structure and nature of the universe. It was a debate Galileo wanted to enter. As his correspondence with the astronomer Johannes Kepler indicated, Galileo found Copernicus' thesis convincing, but he lacked the necessary instrument to test the theory. This problem was remedied in 1609 when on a visit to Venice, Galileo learned about a new "eye-glass by means of which visible objects, though very distant from the eye, were distinctly seen as if nearby." Based on this limited information, Galileo returned to Padua to design and build his own telescope.

With this new instrument, Galileo turned his gaze toward the sky. He saw that the moon was not a smooth sphere, as previously assumed, but had many craters and mountains. These geological characteristics implied that Earth was not a unique or central planet in the universe. While observing Jupiter, he discovered four moons, disproving the assumption that Earth was the only planet to be orbited by a natural satellite. His observations of Venus forced Galileo to conclude that its phases could not be accounted for within the traditional geocentric model of the universe but could only be explained in terms of the Copernican heliocentric system. His study of the sun revealed its spots implying that it was spherical and rotated on its axis as did Earth.

In 1610, Galileo published his findings in his *Sidereus Nuncius* (*The Sidereal Messenger*, 1880). The book was quite popular and was translated and reprinted in a wide variety of languages. The book implied a strong support of the Copernican solar system. The vast number of stars and movement of planets which Galileo observed could only be explained in the context of a heliocentric model wherein Earth and the other planets orbit the sun, and the stars are fixed points of light which only appear to move because of Earth's orbital path.

The Sidereal Messenger brought Galileo international fame and set the stage for future controversy. The University of Padua granted him a professorship for life. Instead of accepting the offer, however, he resigned in order to return to Florence and become the grand duke's chief philosopher and mathematician. The move marked a fateful change for the scientist.

A year after his return to Florence, Galileo made a triumphant visit to Rome. He lectured widely, demonstrated his telescope, and debated a variety of scientific issues. Although he was well received by both the pope and papal court, there were signs of growing opposition to his work. Some theologians claimed that Copernicus, and therefore Galileo, was in conflict with the Bible and the doctrines of the Church regarding the central role and location of Earth in God's created order. Galileo was warned that he should teach and discuss the Copernican system only as a speculative theory and not as a truthful representation of the universe. In 1615, Copernicus' book, *De revolutionibus orbium coelestium* (1543; *On the Revolutions of the Celestial Spheres*, 1939), was placed on the Catholic church's index of banned publications. In response to this censorship, Galileo refrained from any public comment on astronomy for a number of years, turning his attention to navigational problems. In 1618, however, three comets appeared, and a Jesuit astronomer maintained that their appearance disproved Copernicus. Galileo broke his silence with the publication of *Saggiatore* (1623; the assayer). The brief tract not only refuted the attack against Copernicus but also presented an elegant argument in behalf of free scientific inquiry.

As the controversy surrounding this episode subsided, Galileo began writing his most important and controversial book, *Dialogo sopra i due massimi sistemi del mondo, tolemaico e copernicano* (*Dialogue Concerning the Two Chief World Systems, Ptolemaic and Copernican*, 1661), published in 1632. Its purpose was to present an "inconclusive" comparison between the Ptolemaic and Copernican models of the universe. Although Galileo carefully presented the various claims in terms of competing theories, it was apparent that he believed that the Ptolemaic geocentric theory was false and that the Copernican heliocentric theory was true. Although the book had received the Catholic church's imprimatur, it was placed on the index of banned books shortly after its publication. A few months later, the Office of the Inquisition summoned Galileo to Rome to stand trial for heresy. What was at stake was whether he had defied a papal ban "to hold, defend, and teach the Copernican doctrine." More important, the Church's authority and ability to enforce compliance with its teachings were also at issue.

After a five month trial, Galileo was convicted because he "held and believed false doctrine, contrary to the Holy and Divine Scriptures." The punishment would be a public prohibition of *Dialogue Concerning the Two Chief World Systems* and a prison sentence. Galileo, however, was given an opportunity to recant, which he accepted, swearing, "I will never again say or assert . . . anything that might furnish occasion for a similar suspicion." Theological authority, for the time being, had silenced the claims of scientific observation.

Summary

For the rest of his life Galileo remained under house arrest, first in the village of Siena and later in Arcetri. He was not allowed to take any extensive trips or to entertain many guests. Following the death of his favorite daughter in 1634, he lived a lonely life and became blind in 1637. Despite the attempt to isolate him from the world, his fame grew—such noted figures as Thomas Hobbes and John Milton went out of their way to visit him shortly before his death.

His legacy was to establish science, based on observation and experimentation, as an important intellectual and social force in the world. Unlike Copernicus or Kepler, he was not a systematic or speculative thinker, preferring to base his work on a careful inquiry into the causes of natural phenomena. As indicated by his various inventions, he was also interested in applying his knowledge to practical problems.

Galileo marked an important break between theology and science that was not easily or quickly bridged—Copernicus and he were not removed from the Church's index of banned books until 1835. Yet despite his conviction for heresy, history has judged his right to seek after truth quite differently. According to legend, as Galileo signed his recantation following his trial, he mumbled, *"Eppur si muove"* ("And yet it [Earth] moves"). Although Galileo never spoke these words, the legend's existence and endurance is a fitting indication of the eventual support he received not only for his work but also for the right of the scientist to engage in free and open inquiry.

Bibliography

Boas, Marie. *The Scientific Renaissance, 1450-1630*. New York: Harper & Row, 1962. A detailed historical account of the major scientific discoveries and conflicts during the Renaissance. Provides good background material regarding the work and accomplishments of Galileo.

Fermi, Laura, and Gilberto Bernardini. *Galileo and the Scientific Revolution*. New York: Basic Books, 1961. A concise and highly sympathetic biography. The book includes a limited number of illustrations and an appendix which presents a translation of Galileo's first tract, "The Little Balance."

Geymonat, Ludovico. *Galileo Galilei*. New York: McGraw-Hill, 1965. A highly detailed biography which concentrates on examining the development of Galileo's thinking. Particular attention is placed on reconstructing his emerging philosophy of science.

Koyré, Alexandre. *Galileo Studies*. Translated by J. Mepham. Atlantic Highlands, N.J.: Humanities Press, 1978. A highly technical and critical examination of the scientific and mathematical principles used by Galileo in his various observations and experimentations.

Kuhn, Thomas S. *The Copernican Revolution: Planetary Astronomy in the Development of Western Thought*. Cambridge, Mass.: Harvard University Press, 1957. A detailed historical review of the debate inspired by Copernicus. The dramatic intellectual and social implications of the change from a geocentric to a heliocentric worldview are also examined.

Redondi, Pietro. *Galileo: Heretic*. Translated by Raymond Rosenthal. Princeton, N.J.: Princeton University Press, 1987. A comprehensive and critical examination of Galileo's trial before the Inquisition. Particular attention is directed toward examining the motivations and issues at stake for the Catholic church in the trial.

Ronan, Colin A. *Galileo*. New York: G. P. Putnam's Sons, 1974. A standard biography which not only provides numerous details about Galileo's life but also places them within the larger context of the intellectual changes taking place. The book also contains numerous illustrations and photographs.

Brent Waters

ÉVARISTE GALOIS

Born: October 25, 1811; Bourg-la-Reine, near Paris, France
Died: May 31, 1832; Paris, France
Area of Achievement: Mathematics
Contribution: Galois produced, with the aid of group theory, a definitive answer to the problem of the solvability of algebraic equations, a problem that had preoccupied mathematicians since the eighteenth century. Consequently, he laid one of the foundations of modern algebra.

Early Life

Évariste Galois' father, Nicolas-Gabriel Galois, was a friendly and witty liberal thinker who headed a school that accommodated about sixty boarders. Elected mayor of Bourg-la-Reine during the Hundred Days after Napoleon's escape from Elba, he retained office under the second Restoration. Galois' mother, Adelaïde-Marie Demante, was from a long line of jurists and had received a more traditional education. She had a headstrong and eccentric personality. Having taken control of her son's early education, she attempted to implant in him, along with the elements of classical culture, strict religious principles as well as respect for a stoic morality. Influenced by his father's imagination and liberalism, the eccentricity of his mother, and the affection of his elder sister Nathalie-Théodore, Galois seems to have had a childhood that was both happy and studious.

Galois continued his studies at the Collège Louis-le-Grand in Paris, entering in October, 1823. He found it difficult to adjust to the harsh discipline imposed by the school during the Restoration at the orders of the political authorities and the Church, and, although a brilliant student, he was rebellious. In the early months of 1827, he attended the first-year preparatory mathematics courses taught by H. J. Vernier; this first exposure to mathematics was a revelation for him. He rapidly became bored with the elementary nature of this instruction and with the inadequacies of some of his textbooks and began reading the original works themselves.

After appreciating the difficulty of Adrien-Marie Legendre's geometry, Galois acquired a solid background from the major works of Joseph-Louis Lagrange. During the next two years, he attended Vernier's second-year preparatory mathematics courses, then the more advanced ones of L. P. E. Richard, who was the first to recognize Galois' superiority in mathematics. With this perceptive teacher, Galois excelled in his studies, even though he was already devoting much more of his time to his personal work than to his classwork. In 1828, he began to study some then-recent works on the theory of equations, on number theory, and on the theory of elliptic functions.

This was the time period in which Galois' first memoir appeared. Published in March, 1829, in the *Annales de mathématiques pures et appliquées* (annals of pure and applied mathematics), it demonstrated and clarified a result of Lagrange concerning continuous fractions. While it revealed a certain astuteness, it did not demonstrate exceptional talent.

Life's Work

In 1828, by his own admission Galois falsely believed—as Henrik Abel had eight years earlier—that he had solved the general fifth-degree equation. Quickly enlightened, he resumed with a new approach the study of the theory of equations, a subject which he pursued until he elucidated the general problem with the aid of group theory. The results he obtained in May, 1829, were sent to the Academy of Sciences by a particularly competent judge, Augustin-Louis Cauchy. Fate was to frustrate these brilliant beginnings, however, and to leave a lasting impression on the personality of the young mathematician.

First, at the beginning of July, his father, a man who had been persecuted for his liberal beliefs, committed suicide. A month later, Galois failed the entrance examination for the École Polytechnique, because he refused to use the expository method suggested by the examiner. Barred from entering the school which attracted him because of its scientific prestige and liberal tradition, he took the entrance examination for the École Normale Supérieure (then called the École Préparatoire), which trained future secondary school teachers. He entered the institution in November, 1829.

At this time he learned of Abel's death and, at the same time, that Abel's last published memoir contained several original results that Galois himself had presented as original in his memoir to the Academy. Cauchy, assigned to supervise Galois' work, advised his student to revise his memoir, taking into account Abel's research and new results. Galois wrote a new text that he submitted to the Academy in February, 1830, that he hoped would win for him the grand prix in mathematics. Unfortunately, this memoir was lost upon the death of Joseph Fourier, who had been appointed to study it. Eliminated from the competition, Galois believed himself to be the object of a new persecution by both the representatives of institutional science and society in general. His manuscripts preserve a partial record of the revision of this memoir of February, 1830.

In June, 1830, Galois published in *Bulletin des sciences mathématiques* (bulletin of mathematical sciences) a short note on the resolution of numerical equations, as well as a much more significant article, "Sur la théorie des nombres" (on number theory). That this same issue contained original works by Cauchy and Siméon-Denis Poisson sufficiently confirms the reputation that Galois had already acquired. The July Revolution of 1830, however, was to initiate a drastic change in his career.

Galois became politicized. Before returning for a second year to the École Normale Supérieure in November, 1830, he had already developed friendships with several republican leaders. Even less able to tolerate his school's strict discipline than before, he published a violent article against its director in an opposition journal. For this action he was expelled on December 8, 1830.

Left alone, Galois devoted most of his time to political propaganda. He participated in the riots and demonstrations then agitating Paris and was even arrested (but was eventually acquitted). Meanwhile, to a limited degree, he continued his mathematical research. His last two publications were a short note on analysis in the *Bulletin des sciences mathématiques* of December, 1830, and "Lettre sur l'enseignement des sciences" (letter on the teaching of the sciences), which appeared on January 2, 1831, in the *Gazette des écoles*. On January 13, he began to teach a public course on advanced algebra in which he planned to present his own discoveries; this project appears not to have been successful. On January 17, 1831, Galois presented the Academy a new version of his memoir, hastily written at Poisson's request. Unfortunately, in Poisson's report of July 4, 1831, on this, Galois' most important piece of work, Poisson suggested that a portion of the results could be found in several posthumous writings of Abel and that the rest was incomprehensible. Such a judgment, the profound injustice of which would become apparent in the future, only encouraged Galois' rebellion.

Arrested again during a republican demonstration on July 14, 1831, and imprisoned, Galois nevertheless continued his mathematical research, revised his memoir on equations, and worked on the applications of his theory and on elliptic functions. After the announcement of a cholera epidemic on March 16, 1832, he was transferred to a nursing home, where he resumed his investigations, wrote several essays on the philosophy of science, and became immersed in a love affair which ended unhappily. Galois sank into a deep depression.

Provoked into a duel under unclear circumstances following this breakup, Galois sensed that he was near death. On May 29, he wrote desperate letters to his republican friends, hastily sorted his papers, and addressed to his friend Auguste Chevalier—but intended for Carl Friedrich Gauss and Carl Gustav Jacob Jacobi—a testamentary letter, a tragic document in which he attempted to outline the principal results that he had attained. On May 30, fatally wounded by an unknown opponent, he was hospitalized; he died the following day, not even twenty-one years of age.

Summary

Évariste Galois' work seems not to have been fully appreciated by anyone during his lifetime. Cauchy, who would have been able to understand its significance, left France in September, 1830, having seen only its initial outlines. In addition, the few fragments published during his lifetime did not give an overall view of his achievement and, in particular, did not provide a means of judging the exceptional interest of the results regarding the theory of equations rejected by Poisson. Also, the publication of the famous testamentary letter does not appear to have attracted the attention it deserved.

It was not until September, 1843, that Joseph Liouville, who prepared Galois' manuscripts for publication, announced officially that the young mathematician had effectively solved the problem, already investigated by Abel, of deciding whether an irreducible first-degree equation is solvable with the use of radicals. Although announced and prepared for the end of 1843, the memoir of 1831 did not appear until the October/November, 1846, issue of the *Journal de mathématiques pures et appliquées*, when it was published with a fragment on the primitive equations solvable by radicals.

Beginning with Liouville's edition, which appeared in book form in 1897, Galois' work became progressively known to mathematicians and subsequently exerted a profound influence on the development of modern mathematics. Also important, although they came too late to contribute to the advancement of mathematics, are the previously unpublished texts that appeared later.

While he formulated more precisely essential ideas that were already being investigated, Galois also introduced others that, once stated, played an important role in the genesis of modern algebra. Furthermore, he boldly generalized certain classic methods in other fields and succeeded in providing a complete solution and a generalization of problems by systematically drawing upon group theory—one of the most important structural concepts which unified the multiplicity of algebras in the nineteenth century.

Bibliography

Bell, Eric T. *Men of Mathematics*. New York: Simon & Schuster, 1937. Historical account of the major figures in mathematics from the Greeks to Giorg Cantor, written in an interesting if at times exaggerated style. In a relatively brief chapter, "Genius and Stupidity," Bell describes the life and work of Galois in a tone that both worships and scorns the young mathematician and mixes fact with legend in his discussion.

Boyer, Carl B. *A History of Mathematics*. New York: John Wiley & Sons, 1968. In this standard and very reputable history of mathematics, Boyer devotes a brief section to Galois. Galois is described as the individual who most contributed to the vital discovery of the group concept. The author also assesses Galois' impact on future generations of mathematicians. Includes charts, an extensive bibliography, and exercises for the student.

Infeld, Leopold. *Whom the Gods Love: The Story of Évariste Galois*. New York: Whittlesey House, 1948. This biography takes great license with the facts (many of which are unknown) of Galois' life and creates an interesting, if fictional, account. The author, maintaining that biography always mixes truth and fiction, puts Galois' life in the historical context of nineteenth century France by creating scenes and dialogues that might have occurred. Contains a bibliography.

Kline, Morris. *Mathematical Thought from Ancient Times to Modern Times.* New York: Oxford University Press, 1972. In this voluminous work, the author surveys the major mathematical creators and developments from its beginnings through the first few decades of the twentieth century. The emphasis is on the leading mathematical themes rather than on the men. The brief section on Galois gives some biographical information and discusses the mathematician's work in finite fields, group theory, and the theory of equations.

Struik, Dirk J. *A Concise History of Mathematics.* Vol. 2, *The Seventeenth Century-Nineteenth Century.* New York: Dover, 1948. In this book devoted to a concise overview of the major figures and trends in mathematics during the time period covered, a brief section is devoted to Galois. The author spends approximately equal time discussing Galois' life and major achievements, and views the mathematician both as a product of his times and as a unique genius.

Genevieve Slomski

LUIGI GALVANI

Born: September 9, 1737; Bologna, Papal States
Died: December 4, 1798; Bologna, Papal States
Areas of Achievement: Physiology and physics
Contribution: Galvani contributed to physiological studies on the electrical stimulation of nerves and muscles. His most important discovery was the production of electric current from the contact of two different metals attached to a frog, which led to the invention by Alessandro Volta of the electric battery.

Early Life

Luigi Galvani was born on the Via de' Maggi in Bologna. He was the third of four children born to Domenico and Barbara Foschi Galvani and was baptized Alyosio Domenico. His family was well known in Bologna, going back in local records to 1267. Deciding early to pursue a medical career, he entered the University of Bologna, where he studied philosophy and medicine under some of the leading teachers of his time. Under Domenico Galeazzi, he developed a special interest in anatomy. After receiving his degree in medicine and philosophy in July, 1759, he wrote his doctoral thesis on the human skeleton. This was a study of the structure, function, and pathology of bones, describing their anatomical and chemical composition, their growth patterns, and their diseases.

In 1762, Galvani married Lucia Galeazzi, the only daughter of his teacher, Galeazzi, who had served four terms as president of the Bologna Academy of Science. For several years, Galvani served as an honorary lecturer in anatomy at the University of Bologna and as an instructor at the affiliated Institute of Science, while conducting some medical and surgical practice and anatomical research. He was installed by the Senate of Bologna in 1766 as curator and demonstrator of the anatomical museum at the university. In 1768, he became a paid lecturer, and in 1773 he was promoted to the rank of professor of anatomy and surgery. His demonstrations made his lectures popular, though he was not regarded as an eloquent lecturer.

Galvani's early research efforts were devoted mostly to anatomical topics relating to birds. He published an article on the kidneys of birds in 1767 that described the three-layered ureteral wall and its peristaltic and antiperistaltic movement (contractions) when irritated. He also devoted several papers to the anatomy of the ear in birds. When Galeazzi died in 1775, Galvani succeeded him as lecturer in anatomy, having already succeeded him as president of the academy in 1772. Finally, in 1782, the Senate of Bologna elected him professor of obstetric arts at the Institute of Science.

Life's Work

Galvani's most important work began in the 1770's with a shift in emphasis from anatomical concerns to physiological studies on nerves and muscles in the frog, leading to a particular interest in animal electricity. In 1772, he presented a paper to the Institute of Science on the Hallerian theory of irritability, based on the work of the Swiss physician Albrecht von Haller, who had demonstrated muscle contractions by stimulating muscle and nerve tissues. Two more papers were presented to the institute in 1773 and 1774 on muscle movements in frogs and on the effect of opiates on frog nerves. These studies led to a series of experiments in the late 1770's on electrophysiology, in which he stimulated muscles by electrical means.

Earlier work on animal electricity had been done by several researchers in Italy. Electricity had been used to stimulate muscles in 1756 at Bologna, and it had been suggested that nerves conduct a so-called electric fluid and perhaps even excite it. Giambatista Beccaria, professor of physics at the University of Turin, used electricity to stimulate the muscles of a living rooster and published correspondence on his electrical research which supported and extended the ideas of Benjamin Franklin on atmospheric electricity.

By 1780, Galvani had acquired an electrostatic machine and a Leyden jar for producing and storing electric fluid, and after 1783 his major field of research became animal electricity. He prepared frogs for electrical stimulation by dissecting the lower limbs as a unit with the spinal column attached by the crural nerves (the nerves that act on the leg muscles). By touching the conductor of his electrostatic machine to the spinal cord resting on a pane of glass, he could observe the contractions of the muscles in the legs when the machine was discharged. Galvani also experimented with the effects of atmospheric electricity on warm-blooded animals, assisted by his nephew Camillo Galvani. In September, 1786, he recorded a frog-muscle contraction when the nerve was touched by scissors during an electrical storm.

In the autumn of 1786, Galvani began to observe some surprising phenomena that led to his discovery of current electricity in contrast to the static electricity used in his experiments. These observations started when an assistant touched a scalpel to the medial crural nerve of a frog preparation and observed violent contractions even though the electrostatic machine was disconnected and at some distance away on the table. Another assistant, his wife, Lucia, according to some accounts, noticed that this happened at the same moment that a spark was discharged from the electrical machine. Galvani confirmed this effect by several experiments in which contractions were induced whenever the nerve was touched by a grounded conductor at the same time that a spark was drawn from a disconnected electrical machine. To see if this induction effect would result from natural electricity, he fastened some prepared frogs by brass hooks in their spinal cord to an iron railing surrounding a balcony of his house and observed contractions when lightning flashed. The most suprising result was that contractions continued to occur even after the sky cleared, and these were intensified when the brass hook in the spinal cord was pressed against the iron railing. At first, Galvani viewed the frog preparation as a sensitive electroscope, but then he suggested that perhaps electric fluid was produced within the assembly of frog and metals, independent of any external electrical source.

Galvani confirmed this result indoors by placing the frog preparation on an iron plate and pressing the brass hook against it. He showed that the strength of the contractions depends on the kind of metals used, and that nonmetals such as glass and resin produce no effect. He also did a series of experiments with metallic arcs connected between the leg muscles and the hook in the spinal cord, and again showed that the kind of metals in the arc and hook determined the strength of the contractions. Thus, he clearly demonstrated the main features in his discovery of "galvanism" by producing an electric current from the contact of two dissimilar metals in a moist environment. He thought, however, that this environment must include animal tissues and that they were the source of the electricity. Thus, he believed that he had confirmed the existence of animal electricity, which was viewed by some in the eighteenth century as a vital force distinct from natural electricity such as lightning, and the artificial electricity produced by friction, as in electrostatic machines.

After five years of careful research, Galvani published the results of his work, *De viribus electricitatis in motu musculari commentarius* (1791; *Commentary on the Effect of Electricity on Muscular Motion*, 1953). This four-part essay reviewed the effects of artificial electricity on muscular motion, similar effects produced by atmospheric electricity, his observations and ideas in support of animal electricity, and his final conclusions and conjectures. In the last section, he compared the muscle to a Leyden jar in which the nerve becomes positively charged while the muscle becomes negatively charged, and a metal contacting both would cause a discharge of electric fluid and the associated contractions.

Galvani's *Commentary on the Effect of Electricity on Muscular Motion* aroused considerable interest among scientists, and his experiments were repeated by many. Volta, professor of physics at the University of Pavia and already famous for his work in electricity, pursued the theory of animal electricity but became skeptical after it occurred to him that the metals might be the source of the electric fluid, with the frog legs serving only as a kind of electroscope. By the end of 1793, he had rejected animal electricity in favor of his "contact" theory, in which electric fluids are produced by the mere contact of two dissimilar metals.

A long debate followed from these two interpretations, leading to many ingenious experiments by both Galvani and Volta. Galvani showed that contractions resulted from two pieces of the same metal, which Volta explained by differences in metal composition. Much of Galvani's defense was continued by his nephew Giovanni Aldini, son of his sister Caterina and later professor of physics at Bologna. The controversy spread to other scholars at Bologna versus those at Pavia, physiologists versus physicists, animalists versus metalists; despite their differences, Galvani and Volta remained on friendly terms.

In the last years of his life, Galvani suffered many difficulties, but he managed to continue his work. His wife died childless in 1790 at the age of forty-seven. In 1794 and 1797, he announced two experiments in which contractions were produced merely by touching frog nerves to muscles without any metals. During this time, he made a sea voyage along the Italian coast to collect marine torpedoes and showed that their strong electrical discharge is generated by structures similar to nerves and muscles. Although these results supported his theory of animal electricity, they also led Volta to his invention in 1799 of the bimetallic pile (electric battery), requiring no animal tissues. Galvani died in the house of his birth the year before Volta's invention. Earlier that year, he was dismissed from the university and lost his salary when he refused to take an atheistic oath of allegiance to the Cisalpine Republic created by Napoleon I. He left his microscope to Aldini, his electrical machine to his nephew Ludovico Galvani, and his manuscripts to another nephew, Camillo Galvani.

Summary

Luigi Galvani was a modest and deeply religious man, whose achievements were the result of hard work and careful experimentation. His many contributions are often obscured by Volta's discovery of a source of constant electric current, which ushered in the electrical revolution of the nineteenth century; yet Galvani provided the generative spark. His early contributions to the pathology of bones and the comparative anatomy of birds would have been sufficient to secure his reputation. His investigations of the ear in birds included many original and valuable observations.

All of Galvani's writings show exhaustive thoroughness, but this is especially true of his electrical experiments. His observations of electrostatic induction, including the inductive effects of lightning discharges on his frog preparations, anticipated the discovery of the propagation of radio waves. His most important contribution, however, was his observations and description of the production of electric fluid from the contact of two metals with his frog preparations. This led directly to the investigations by Volta of what he called "galvanism" and the invention of the electric battery. Thus, Galvani's name has been immortalized in words such as "galvanometer" and "galvanized."

The publication of Galvani's *Commentary of the Effect of Electricity on Muscular Motion* and the subsequent Galvani-Volta debate stimulated much research in both physics and physiology. Although Galvani failed to see the full significance of his discovery of galvanism, he proceeded to demonstrate the electrical nature of the nervous fluid. His defense of animal electricity led to experiments that in effect marked the beginning of electrophysiology. His demonstrations that frog-leg contractions result from contact between nerve and muscle even without metals led to the discovery in the 1840's of the electrical nature of nerve impulses by Emil Du Bois-Reymond and others. The life and work of Luigi Galvani are too important to be dismissed as merely a confused preface to the discovery of methods to produce electric current and the electrical revolution that followed.

Bibliography

Dibner Bern. *Galvani-Volta: A Controversy That Led to the Discovery of Useful Electricity.* Norwalk, Conn.: Burndy Library, 1952. Contains a brief description of the historical background and scientific work of Galvani, the defense of his ideas by Aldini, and the controversy with Volta. There is also an original translation of the first experiment, establishing the existence of electricity in living tissues, published anonymously in 1794.

Galvani, Luigi. *Commentary on the Effect of Electricity on Muscular Motion.* Translated by Robert Montraville Green. Baltimore: Waverly Press, 1953. The twelve-page introduction is an interesting discussion and evaluation of Galvani's life and work. Includes an original work by Aldini. Also translated by Margaret Foley for Burndy Library in 1953.

Hoff, Hebbel E. "Galvani and the Pre-Galvanian Electrophysiologists." *Annals of Science* 1 (1936): 157-172. This article contains a description of Galvani's three early experiments and his theory of animal electricity. Hoff then discusses the background of his work by tracing the history of electrical stimulation over the previous fifty years following the invention of the Leyden jar.

Lenard, Philipp. *Great Men of Science: A History of Scientific Progress.* New York: Macmillan, 1933. A twelve-page chapter entitled "Luigi Galvani and Alessandro Volta" gives a brief and readable account of the life and work of Galvani, and the development of his work by Volta.

Potamian, Michael, and James Walsh. *Makers of Electricity.* New York: Fordham University Press, 1909. A twenty-nine-page chapter entitled "Galvani, Discoverer of Animal Electricity" gives an interesting and readable account of Galvani's life and work, though it contains some historical inaccuracies.

Joseph L. Spradley

VASCO DA GAMA

Born: c. 1460; Sines, Portugal
Died: December 24, 1524; Cochin, India
Areas of Achievement: Exploration and the military
Contribution: Da Gama was the first European during the Age of Discovery
to reach India by sailing around Africa. His voyage culminated decades of
Portuguese efforts at exploration and began Portugal's era as a spice em-
pire.

Early Life

Vasco da Gama was born about 1460 (although possibly as late as 1469)
at the small coastal town of Sines in southern Portugal. His parents, Estevano da Gama and Isabel de Sodre, were members of ancient but poor
families of the lesser nobility. Their marriage produced four children, of
whom Vasco was the third son. His two elder brothers were Paulo and Estevano (or Ayres), and there was a sister named Theresa. When he reached the
proper age, Vasco was sent to school at the inland town of Evora. What he
studied, however, is not known, and little other information survives concerning his early life.

All da Gama men had a reputation for bravery. That reputation was supplemented by a certain notoriety for being quarrelsome and unruly people.
According to tradition, Vasco da Gama repelled by sheer force of personality
the alcalde and night watch of Setubal during a nocturnal confrontation. His
first documentable historical appearance occurred in 1492, during a diplomatic crisis between King John II of Portugal and Charles VIII, the King of
France. As part of the effort to prepare Portugal for the possibility of a war,
the king sent da Gama to Setubal to take care of affairs in the Algarve. The
Portuguese king's choice for this important assignment reflected his great
confidence in da Gama, which was based on the young man's successful but
unspecified service in the fleet, probably against pirates. Some historians
also speculate that various undocumented and secret Portuguese voyages of
exploration in the southern Atlantic and along the East African coast took
place during the last years of the 1480's and the first years of the 1490's. It
is also thought that, if so, da Gama may have commanded one or more of
these expeditions.

Life's Work

King John II had long planned a follow-up expedition to Bartolomeu Dias'
discovery of the Cape of Good Hope in 1488, but various circumstances had
delayed it. Originally the king wanted to appoint Estevano da Gama as
commander of the expedition, and when he died the post devolved on his son
Vasco by at least December, 1495. It may even have been first offered to da

Gama's elder brother Paulo, who declined because of ill health.

Da Gama's expedition consisted of four ships, which departed from Portugal on July 8, 1497. His objectives were to find a sea route to India, to engage in the Eastern spice trade, and to make contact and treaties with local Christian rulers. The expedition was primarily one of exploration and not trade. Arriving at Santiago in the Cape Verde Islands on July 27, the expedition rested and then took to the high seas on August 3, steering a southwesterly course and ignoring the coastal route used by Diogo Cão and Dias.

The Portuguese were attempting to take advantage of favorable wind patterns which, on this occasion, turned out to be abnormally weak. Turning eastward after a long passage, they did not sight land until November 4, at about the region of Santa Helena Bay. It was an impressive navigational accomplishment for that age. Next, da Gama's fleet rounded the Cape of Good Hope on November 22, after which they broke up their supply ship and distributed its contents. As they sailed up the eastern coast of Africa, scurvy began to appear in the crew, but they soon contacted Arab traders and obtained supplies of fresh fruit. On March 29, 1498, they arrived at the hospitable city of Malindi, where they took on a skillful pilot, probably the famous Ahmed ibn Madgid. With his aid, they proceeded northward and caught the monsoon, which quickly transported the expedition to the Malabar coast of India on May 18. They arrived at the town of Capocate on May 20 and on May 21 went ashore, where they met two Spanish-speaking Tunisian merchants, who exclaimed, "May the Devil take you! What brought you here?" The Portuguese replied, "Christians and spices." That exchange foreshadowed the type of reception that they would continue to receive in India during their visit.

It was not until May 30, 1498, that da Gama managed to get an audience with the Samorin of Calicut, the most powerful local ruler and controller of the spice trade. By that time, the Portuguese had discovered that their trade goods were better suited for the primitive Hottentots of southern Africa, while the sophisticated Hindus held the scruffy Portuguese and their goods in contempt. At the same time, da Gama remained hopeful because of his mistaken belief that the Hindus were Christians of some sort. Mutual suspicions grew, however, and the Portuguese only managed with the greatest of difficulty to trade their shoddy cargo for some spices and precious stones. About August 12, they approached the samorin for permission to depart; he refused and instead took some hostages. The Portuguese retaliated by taking some Indian hostages on August 19. An exchange was negotiated and then made on August 29. Da Gama sailed the next day, although he had to fight a short battle with some of the samorin's navy. Steering north, the expedition stopped at Angediva Island for a rest.

Da Gama and his fleet left Angediva Island on October 5. Unfortunately on this passage they encountered very unfavorable winds as the monsoons had not yet shifted, and so little progress was made. Scurvy broke out with great intensity, and eventually thirty men died. After the monsoons arrived, the Portuguese finally sighted Africa on January 2, 1499. Losses among the crew forced them to abandon one vessel at Malindi before they went on to Portugal. Da Gama split the expedition at the Cape Verde Islands and rushed his ailing brother Paulo to the Azores in the vain hope of saving his life. Meanwhile, another captain, Nicolau Coelho, sailed for Portugal and arrived on July 10. It was not until late August or early September, 1499, that da Gama reached Lisbon, where he received an enthusiastic reception.

King Manuel rewarded da Gama with the title of Admiral of the Sea of the Indies and made him proprietary owner of his birthplace, Sines. Sometime between 1499 and 1502, da Gama married Catarina d'Atayde. He also prepared detailed sailing instructions for the expedition of his successor, Pedro Cabral, in 1500. That expedition resulted in even greater hostilities between the Portuguese and the Muslim merchants of Calicut. Apparently dissatisfied with Cabral's performance, Manuel named da Gama commander of the next expedition to India. This expedition's purpose was conquest, not trade, and was the most powerful fleet yet sent to the Indian Ocean. It consisted of fifteen ships under the command of da Gama and another five ships under his brother Estevano. They sailed for India in February and March, respectively. Arriving off the Malabar coast, da Gama intercepted a Muslim ship full of pilgrims returning from Mecca; he massacred the passengers and burned the ship. He proceeded to Calicut on October 30, where he demanded the expulsion of the hostile Muslim merchant community. When the samorin refused, the Portuguese shelled the city. Next, they visited the friendly cities of Cochin and Cananore and picked up a cargo of spices. They then returned to Portugal and arrived home on September 1, 1503. Da Gama left five ships behind under the command of Vincente Sodre to protect Cochin and the Portuguese factory there. These expeditions of Cabral and da Gama forced the Portuguese into a policy of conquest, as the Muslim merchants persuaded the Mamlūks of Egypt and the Gujaratis to form an alliance to drive the intruding Portuguese from the Indian Ocean.

After the expedition of 1502-1503, da Gama returned to private life. His resentment over what he considered inadequate rewards for his great achievements simmered. In 1518, Manuel managed to placate him somewhat by appointing him Count of Vidigueira. Meanwhile, the Portuguese empire in the East, which had been established by his great successors Francisco de Almeida and Afonso de Albuquerque, began to flounder under a series of incompetent and corrupt governors. In 1524, King John III appointed da Gama Viceroy of India. Da Gama left for India on April 9, 1524, and, immediately upon his arrival at Goa, began restoring discipline and harassing Portugal's enemies. Traveling to Cochin, he arrested the departing Governor Duarte de Menezes, but overexertion and the tropical climate worked their ill effects on the now elderly da Gama. He died on December 24, having barely begun the much-needed reformation of the Portuguese spice empire.

Summary

The years 1498-1945 have been dubbed the "Vasco da Gama Epoch" in Asian history. That era basically consisted of Europe's navies' dominating Asian coastlines, which further resulted in European control of the Asian economy and politics; da Gama had begun this domination. The goods he brought to Calicut may have been inferior; he and his men may have been almost intolerably dirty and rude by Hindu standards. Yet they possessed decisive superiority in one crucial area: Their ships were more seaworthy and far more heavily armed with cannons than any Asian ships. As a result, da Gama and his successors were able to create a vast spice empire in spite of vigorous Muslim and Hindu resistance. Only a similarly and even more heavily armed European rival, the Dutch, was able to dislodge the Portuguese from their monopoly of the spice trade.

Da Gama served the Portuguese crown as well as any man, exhibiting bravery, cunning, and authority. Yet he was not an indispensable man; Portugal possessed many men like da Gama. It was da Gama's good fortune to be at the right place to obtain the assignment that would make his name live forever. In fact, if he held the same opinions as his descendants, the immediate material rewards of his voyages mattered far more to him than a permanent and respected place in history based on his achievements in Asia.

Bibliography

Cortesão, Armando. *The Mystery of Vasco da Gama.* Coimbra, Portugal: Junta de Investigacoes do Ultramar, 1973. The "mystery" is whether any Portuguese voyages of exploration took place between Dias' discovery of the Cape of Good Hope in 1487 and da Gama's voyage to India in 1497. Cortesão contends that such voyages did take place and that da Gama actually commanded at least one of them.

Diffie, Bailey W., and George D. Winius. *Foundations of the Portuguese Empire, 1415-1580.* Minneapolis: University of Minnesota Press, 1977. This detailed and authoritative survey of the early phase of Portuguese trading and colonial enterprise is excellent for obtaining a reasonably detailed introduction to da Gama's career, along with placing it firmly in its historical context. Particularly useful for debunking various misconceptions and myths associated with the Age of Discovery.

Hart, Henry H. *Sea Road to the Indies: An Account of the Voyages and Exploits of the Portuguese Navigators, Together with the Life and Times of Dom Vasco da Gama, Capitão-Mor, Viceroy of India, and Count of Vidigueira.* New York: Macmillan, 1950. Covers both the background to and the substance of da Gama's explorations and the conquests in the Indian Ocean. Detailed and contains many interesting anecdotes. Unfortunately, the author takes an uncritical approach to the sources and should be read with caution.

Jayne, Kingsley Garland. *Vasco da Gama and His Successors, 1460-1580.* Reprint. New York: Barnes & Noble Books, 1970. Originally published in 1910, this well-written study is still worth consulting. The account of da Gama's first voyage is quite detailed. Furthermore, unlike most books dealing with the founding of the Portuguese spice empire, Jayne's narrative supplies information about da Gama's years of retirement between his second voyage to India in 1502-1503 and his viceroyalty in 1524.

Nowell, Charles E. "Vasco da Gama—First Count of Vidigueira." *Hispanic American Historical Review* 20 (August, 1940): 342-358. This useful article discusses the reasons for da Gama's being neglected by biographers and blames the situation on the lack of information about his youth and personality. Existing printed primary sources are then described and evaluated. Da Gama is assessed as a product of his times.

Pearson, M. N. *The Portuguese in India.* Cambridge, England: Cambridge University Press, 1988. Largely dealing with the late fifteenth through the mid-seventeenth centuries, this authoritative volume is the most recent study of Portuguese activity in India. Supplies the Asian context for da Gama's voyages along with an up-to-date bibliography for further reading on the topic.

Sanceau, Elaine. *Good Hope: The Voyage of Vasco da Gama.* Lisbon: Academia Internacional da Cultura Portuguesa, 1967. This well-written book basically is a detailed narrative of da Gama's first heroic voyage to India. Its author has written extensively on the history of Portuguese exploration. Unfortunately, the scholarly level of her historical methods is sometimes not high enough to satisfy many academic historians.

Ronald Fritze

LÉON GAMBETTA

Born: April 2, 1838; Cahors, near Toulouse, France
Died: December 31, 1882; near Paris, France
Areas of Achievement: Government and politics
Contribution: Gambetta, one of the most vocal critics of the Second Empire
of Napoleon III in the 1860's, became the virtual dictator of France in
1870 during the resistance to the Prussian invasion. He was one of the
most prominent and the most popular republican politicians of the period.

Early Life

Léon Gambetta was born in 1838 in Cahors, in southern France. His
Italian grandfather had moved his family to the region in 1818, and the
Gambettas became shopkeepers. In 1837, Gambetta's father, Joseph, married
Marie Magdeleine Massabie, the daughter of a local chemist; Gambetta's
family, on both sides, might best be described as lower-middle-class. Gam-
betta's father wished him to follow in the family business, but in 1857
Gambetta went to Paris to study law. He had long been an opponent of the
Second Empire of Napoleon III, and in the 1860's he began to write and
speak against the regime. He made his mark during that decade in his defense of various individuals accused of political crimes against the Empire.
In 1869, he was elected to the French Legislative Assembly, representing
the southern city of Marseilles though he had also been victorious in the
working-class Parisian district of Belleville. Though young, he was already a
recognized leader of the opposition.

Throughout his life, Gambetta suffered from various medical problems,
including the loss of an eye as a child. He was of less than average height
and put on substantial weight as a young man, but his long hair and his pronounced nose gave him a dramatic appearance, especially in profile. This imposing physical presence was complemented by a charismatic rhetorical style.

Life's Work

In 1870, France and Prussia went to war as a result of Otto von Bismarck's
Machiavellian diplomatic machinations. The French public demanded war,
and although Napoleon III's own inclinations were toward peace, he led
France against its enemy from across the Rhine. This action proved disastrous. Napoleon was captured and soon abdicated, French armies were defeated, and in Paris on September 4, 1870, the former regime was replaced
by a republic and a government of national defense was established. The
new government was composed primarily of those elected to represent the
various Parisian districts in the previous year's election. Gambetta, who had
been elected from Belleville, became minister of the interior. As Prussian
troops approached Paris, it was decided to establish another governmental

presence in Tours, and soon the decision was made to reinforce the Tours government with Gambetta, the youngest member of the cabinet. In Tours, he became minister of war as well as minister of the interior and became the most powerful individual in France.

Earlier, Gambetta had joined with a number of his fellow republicans to warn against the war with Prussia, but, unlike some of his republican allies, Gambetta was no pacifist. He fervently believed in France and was willing to resort to arms to save France and the republic. In Tours, Gambetta faced what he considered internal treason as well as foreign invasion; the result was that by the end of the year Gambetta had become in effect dictator of France. Some of his critics had their doubts.

Although impressively assembled, the French troops were no match for the Prussians. Gambetta wished to continue the war, but as the winter elapsed the opinion of the French public turned toward peace. Eventually, Gambetta was forced to give way, and he resigned on February 6, 1871. He had both saved France's honor and left a residue of considerable controversy.

In the elections to the National Assembly which followed, Gambetta was victorious in ten different constituencies but chose to represent a department in Alsace, fated to be lost, along with Lorraine, to Germany as a result of the peace. When the treaty was accepted, Gambetta resigned in protest, the cause of the lost provinces remaining of paramount concern to Gambetta and to France. In the following months, Gambetta attempted to recover his damaged health, and in July he was again elected to the assembly, choosing to represent working-class Belleville.

In the years which followed, Gambetta's prestige and influence remained widespread. Fully committed to the ideals of the republic, he initially demanded that the assembly be quickly dissolved and a new one elected with the clear objective of producing a republican constitution. He feared, along with many other republicans, that the existing assembly was too monarchist in sentiment, intent on restoring either the house of Bourbon or that of Orléans. He particularly feared a Napoleonic revival. Gambetta was also concerned about the power of the Church. Sympathetic to the positivism of Auguste Comte, he had few orthodox religious feelings. His animosity toward the Church was based less on its claims to spiritual truth than on its institutional influences on French society, particularly in education.

In time, Gambetta began to believe that the assembly could in itself become safely republican and that there might be no need to call a new constituent assembly. That required compromise on his part, particularly in his acceptance of a senate, which many conservatives demanded as a curb on the democratically elected Chamber of Deputies. Accepting a senate not chosen directly by the voters, he argued that democratic reforms could be made in the future, but his willingness to compromise gained for him a reputation as an opportunist.

The future of the republic remained problematical during the early 1870's. In 1875, the assembly adopted, by a narrow vote, a method to choose the eventual successor to the President of France, the conservative Marshal Mac-Mahon, thus transforming the provisional republic into a more permanent one. There was no formal constitution, merely the acceptance of a series of laws which established the powers of the president, a Senate, and a Chamber of Deputies.

Gambetta, as he had earlier, pushed for Republican Union, the name of his bloc in the Chamber of Deputies, but there were more radical republicans to the Left and more conservative republicans to the Right. While no socialist, Gambetta did believe in the right of labor to organize and the necessity for some government regulation of business. Unlike many of his fellow republicans on both the Right and the Left, Gambetta, the nationalist, believed in the need for a strong government, both internally and externally. In 1876, he was chosen head of the important Budget Committee of the Chamber of Deputies. In early 1879, he became president of the chamber, a position of considerable prestige but which compromised Gambetta's political leadership. Many argued that the president of the chamber should remain above the party fray, but it was difficult for Gambetta to distance himself. Soon some claimed that Gambetta was wielding hidden power. Many predicted that Gambetta would soon become premier and form his own government, but MacMahon's successor, the conservative republican Jules Grevy, refused to summon Gambetta, a longtime rival, until November, 1881.

Only then did Gambetta form his long-awaited Grand Ministry. There were great expectations, but, for both personal and political reasons, Gambetta was unable to fulfill his ideal of republican unity. Many of the most prominent of his republican colleagues refused to join his government, and he was forced to rely upon his own often young and untried supporters. He himself often acted too imperiously when several years earlier he might have been more accommodating. In attempting to strengthen the central government, he alienated various local interests; in advocating railroad regulation, he caused consternation among some conservative republican businessmen. He took the Foreign Affairs ministry himself and was particularly concerned to ally France with England in Egypt.

The issue which caused his downfall was an issue with which he was long associated. Gambetta, in order to create a stronger unity among republicans, had long urged that deputies should be selected not from individual districts but collectively representing larger areas. For once, Gambetta's opportunism failed him, and the legislature, elected by individual districts, was unwilling to adopt a different system, especially so early in its term of office. Also, many were suspicious of Gambetta's possible dictatorial bent, and when he lost a key vote in the chamber, his government resigned after only seventy-four days.

Summary

Léon Gambetta was only forty-three years old when he resigned. His health had long been poor, and after resigning he took time away from politics to recover his strength. When he returned, he took up the cause of military reform. Gambetta's reputation ever since 1870 had been connected to the fortunes of the military, and many accused him of being too adventurous, particularly in his desire to regain Alsace and Lorraine. Gambetta was conscious of those accusations, and while he never forgot the lost provinces he remained hopeful that someday Germany might be willing to exchange them for overseas territory. Unlike many of his countrymen, Gambetta was interested in colonial development, both in Africa and in Southeast Asia. A colonial empire would add to France's strength; in addition, colonies might someday be traded for Alsace and Lorraine.

On November 27, 1882, while handling a revolver, Gambetta accidentally shot himself in the hand. The wound, itself minor, became infected. Gambetta gradually weakened, dying on the last day of the year. He was given a state funeral, and his body, at his father's demand, was buried in Nice. In 1920, with the return of Alsace and Lorraine after World War I, Gambetta's heart was placed in the Pantheon in Paris, coinciding with the golden jubilee of the Third French Republic, the republic to which he had been so committed.

An oft-expressed criticism of Gambetta was that he was too closely tied to the working classes of Belleville and that they would ensure that his words and actions would remain too radical for the moderate inclinations of most French voters. Yet he did not see himself as representing only the working classes. He did speak of the "new social strata" which would come to power under the republic, but for Gambetta that controversial phase referred not to the working classes exclusively but rather to the majority of the French population, including the middle classes, which, he argued, had been excluded from power under the kings and emperors of France's past. Gambetta was always more a political than an economic radical, committed to majority political rule instead of advancing the claims of particular economic classes. In that he was a nineteenth century liberal, not a Marxist. Still, his opponents accused him of revolutionary radicalism.

Léon Gambetta's career had been full of paradoxes: a half-Italian who personified French patriotism; a moderate republican who in the eyes of many epitomized revolutionary radicalism; a pragmatic politician accused of being both an ideologue and an opportunist; a representative of the proletariat, or the middle classes, who wished to become dictator. When he died, some argued that he was still posed between Left and Right, and it is impossible to say in which direction he might have turned. What can be said is that he dominated French politics from 1870 until his death in 1882 as did no one else of that time.

Bibliography

Brogan, D. W. *France Under the Republic: The Development of Modern France (1870-1939)*. New York: Harper & Brothers, 1940. Brogan's elegantly written study of the Third Republic is considered one of the classic historical accounts of the subject. Gambetta plays a significant role in the first part of the work, sometimes published separately under the title *From the Fall of the Empire to the Dreyfus Affair*.

Bury, J. P. T. *Gambetta and the Making of the Third Republic*. London: Longman, 1973. The author is the major English biographer of Gambetta. In *Gambetta and the National Defense* (1970), he analyzed Gambetta's role during the Prussian invasion of France in 1870-1871. Here he carries the story of Gambetta and the Third Republic through 1877.

_____. *Gambetta's Final Years: "The Era of Difficulties," 1877-1882*. New York: Longman, 1982. Bury concludes his exhaustive study of Gambetta. The author is sympathetic toward his subject, finding Gambetta to be perhaps the crucial figure in the founding of the Third Republic. Bury is not uncritical, however, suggesting that in his later years Gambetta's judgment was corrupted by his power and popularity.

Deschanel, Paul. *Gambetta*. New York: Dodd, Mead, 1920. Written by a later President of the Third Republic. Well-written and sympathetic to the subject. Less a scholarly work than an interpretation of Gambetta's contributions to later French history.

Horne, Alistair. *The Fall of Paris: The Siege of the Commune, 1870-71*. New York: St. Martin's Press, 1965. The author is a specialist in modern French history. Horne presents a very readable story of the aftermath of the Franco-Prussian War, in which Gambetta plays a central role.

Mayeur, Jean-Marie, and Madeleine Reberioux. *The Third Republic from Its Origins to the Great War, 1871-1914*. Cambridge, England: Cambridge University Press, 1984. This valuable work is more analytical and more structured than Brogan's work, which was published a generation earlier. Gambetta plays a major role in the early chapters.

Stannard, Harold. *Gambetta and the Foundation of the Third Republic*. London: Methuen, 1921. Like Deschanel's, this study of Gambetta was also written soon after Germany's defeat in World War I. In contrast to Deschanel, however, Stannard is not French, and although he admires Gambetta Stannard is more critical. Suggests that regardless of Gambetta's own motives, some of his statements and actions did seem to imply, to others, the turn toward dictatorship.

Eugene S. Larson

GIUSEPPE GARIBALDI

Born: July 4, 1807; Nice, France
Died: June 2, 1882; Caprera, Italy
Area of Achievement: The military
Contribution: Hero of the Risorgimento, Garibaldi inspired Italy to unite
under the leadership of Victor Emanuel of Piedmont and Sardinia. His
victory over Naples was the key achievement in bringing about a unified
Italy and capped a life devoted to wars of liberation.

Early Life

Giuseppe Garibaldi was born in Nice on July 4, 1807, the son and grandson of sailors. Nice was, in 1807, a French town, but it was ceded to the
Kingdom of Sardinia and Piedmont in 1815. Garibaldi is said to have learned
to speak and read Italian from a priest, who also taught him the history
of Italy and filled him with an enthusiasm for his country. His youth was
marked by numerous events, some difficult to distinguish from the legends
that naturally arise around a charismatic figure. One such story describes an
escape with friends from school at age fourteen, including the seizure of a
sailboat and embarkation in it for Constantinople. Garibaldi's disinclination toward disciplined intellectual activity induced him to leave school at an
early age and to embark upon a career as a seaman, and he first pursued a
sailor's life working on cargo ships in trade with the eastern Mediterranean
and Black Sea.

On one of his voyages, a shipmate informed him of an organization inspired by the Italian nationalist leader Giuseppe Mazzini, Young Italy,
pledged to the cause of liberating Italy from foreigners. By 1834 an ardent
member of the society, Garibaldi participated in a plot to seize a ship in the
port of Genoa; the plot was discovered and Garibaldi fled to Marseilles,
where he learned from an Italian newspaper that he had been condemned to
death.

From Marseilles, Garibaldi sailed for South America, reaching Rio de
Janeiro. Brazil and the republic Rio Grande do Sul were at war. Talking to
some prisoners, Garibaldi quickly resolved to help the small state in its war,
and the rest of his twelve years on the continent were spent fighting for Rio
Grande in its war with Brazil and for Uruguay in its war with Argentina. He
fought primarily at sea as a pirate, attacking Brazilian shipping until 1843,
when he formed an Italian legion, whose "uniform" consisted of red shirts
(from a happy opportunity to buy at a good price shirts otherwise destined
for workers in slaughterhouses). During this time, he carried off (1839) and
later married Anna Maria Ribeiro da Silva, who shared his exploits and
glory until her death in 1849.

In South America, Garibaldi practiced and mastered the techniques of guerrilla fighting that were to serve him in Italy. He also learned how to command and inspire men. In later life, he was criticized for being a rather lax disciplinarian, but it may be said in his defense that comradeship is perhaps better than strict discipline at inspiring a volunteer guerrilla army. Surely he gained more experience in military matters than any other Italian of his generation.

His greatest battles were perhaps fought toward the end of his South American exile, in behalf of Uruguay. His victory at Sant'Antonio in 1846 won for him fame in Italy, where a sword of honor was inscribed for him. In 1847, commanding the defense of the capital, Montevideo, he met Alexandre Dumas, *père*, whose life of Garibaldi added adventures to an already adventuresome life.

Life's Work

Early in 1848, news reached Garibaldi of the revolutions taking place in Europe, and, together with his wife and children and many members of his Italian legion, he set sail for Italy, intending to participate in the war for independence against Austria. In Italy, his offers to fight were rebuffed first by Pope Pius IX, then by King Charles of Piedmont-Sardinia. Garibaldi and his men fought for Charles anyway and engaged in several bloody fights at Como, Varese, and Laveno. His troops were finally scattered, and Garibaldi retired into Switzerland. Soon afterward, he made his way to his childhood home of Nice, where he and his wife enjoyed a few months of domestic life.

The intense fervor to unify Italy, still seen as a visionary and quixotic dream by all but the most ardent followers of Mazzini, stirred Garibaldi to go to Rome when, with the pope in flight, an opportunity presented itself in late 1848. There he tried to organize Rome's independence, but, when the French planned to reinstate the pope as head of the government, Garibaldi fought against the French siege of the city. Although victory was highly unlikely, Garibaldi, his men, and indeed the people of Rome fought gallantly for nearly three months, ringing the bells of the city at the approach of the French and erecting barricades in the streets to prevent or delay their entrance. Eager not to fall into the hands of French and papal supporters, Garibaldi and about four thousand of his men began a retreat across Campagna to the Adriatic. The enemy pursued him hotly, and Garibaldi was compelled to hasten his retreat. He managed to escape, but at the cost of his dear wife, who died from the exertions.

A fugitive again, unwelcomed by the King of Piedmont-Sardinia, hunted by the Austrians, Garibaldi left his children with his parents in Nice and went to live and work on Staten Island, New York. He soon returned to sea and became the commander of a Peruvian sailing vessel. Learning in 1853 of the death of his mother and the repeal of the order banishing him from Italy, he returned to Nice. In 1856, he bought a parcel of land on the island of

Caprera, between Sardinia and Corsica, and planned to retire. In 1859, when the war of France and Sardinia against Austria broke out, King Victor Emmanuel of Piedmont-Sardinia and his minister Count Cavour invited Garibaldi to form an army and fight with them. He formed the Cacciatori delle Alpi and achieved notable success by guerrilla maneuvers in the Tirol region of the Alps.

In May, 1860, Garibaldi set sail for Sicily with about one thousand volunteers, later to be celebrated in Italian history as the mythical *Mille*, who made the Italian peninsula into a modern nation. His aim was ostensibly to aid an insurgent revolt against Sicily's master, Naples. Garibaldi landed at Marsala amid artillery fire from several Neapolitan frigates and at once met with success. With additional volunteers constantly joining his ranks, he defeated the Neapolitan army at Calatafimi and marched toward Palermo, the largest and most important city in Sicily. The city was well fortified with Neapolitan soldiers, but, after several feints, Garibaldi entered the city in the dawn of May 26 and had the city in his control by mid-morning. Additional volunteers kept coming from all Sicily to join him, and the Neapolitan troops withdrew. He declared himself dictator and established provisional governments throughout the island. Taking advantage of his victories, he hastened across the Strait of Messina and charged through Calabria to Naples, which he entered on September 7, 1860. As "Dictator of the Two Sicilies" he fought a battle against a Neapolitan army in October. By then, his army had increased to thirty thousand, the largest number of men Garibaldi had ever commanded, and it held the line victoriously at the Volturno River.

Plebiscites conducted throughout the southern peninsula and in Sicily gave Garibaldi the authority to present these lands to Victor Emanuel. When the king arrived in November, Garibaldi met him ceremoniously, but when the king and his court—perhaps anxious about some of Garibaldi's radical and revolutionary ideas, perhaps envious of Garibaldi's enormous popularity— would not grant him powers over these newly added lands, Garibaldi retired to his home in Caprera. His retirement was short-lived. In April, 1861, he was elected to the Chamber of Deputies, where he opposed Cavour and the king. He also caused embarrassment when in July, 1862, he appealed to Hungary to revolt against Austria. When some of his officers were arrested, Garibaldi threatened to attack Rome. Slipping through a blockade of Napoleon III, he landed in Italy and, with more than two thousand of his followers, fought a battle near Aspromonte. Garibaldi was badly wounded and imprisoned but was soon released and returned to Caprera. Though he had seemed to be independent, it became clear that he was working with the king to effect Rome's accession to the kingdom. Between 1867 and 1871, Garibaldi participated in two more campaigns, another unsuccessful expedition to the Papal States and an attempt to help France in its war with Prussia. He then retired to his home in Caprera, wrote his memoirs, and tried to overcome the infirmities of age and of a body scarred with thirty battle wounds. He died in 1882.

Summary

Few in their own lifetimes enjoyed as much repute as did Giuseppe Garibaldi. Abraham Lincoln invited him to take a command at the beginning of the Civil War; unhappy with Lincoln's refusal to take a stronger stand against slavery, however, Garibaldi refused. When in 1864 Garibaldi went to England, he was received by thousands of well-wishers. The peoples of the world recognized in Garibaldi a man sincere in his love of freedom, a man selfless in his devotion to his cause, a man absolutely incorruptible. Because he was uncompromisingly idealistic, he was an inspiration to his people; indeed, more than Mazzini, Cavour, or even Victor Emanuel himself, Garibaldi represented the spirit of Italian unification.

Garibaldi's military successes were perhaps also a manifestation of his character and most particularly of his courage. What academy-trained military man would have ventured the risks he did and against such overwhelming odds? Indeed, the very riskiness of his adventures often secured their success, for surprise was easier to achieve when the hazards seemed overwhelming. Garibaldi stands as one of the great patriots of all time, a "hero of two worlds" and for all times. If he was at times overcredulous and naïve, such may be attributed to his good heart, the same good heart which was the source of his heroic splendor.

Bibliography

Garibaldi, Giuseppe. *Autobiography of Giuseppe Garibaldi*. Translated by A. Werner, with a supplement by Jessie White Mario. London: W. Smith and Innes, 1889. A two-volume translation of Garibaldi's memoirs, certainly the starting place for serious study of Garibaldi. The supplement provides insights by one of the subject's friends.

Hibbert, Christopher. *Garibaldi and His Enemies: The Clash of Arms and Personalities in the Making of Italy*. Boston: Little, Brown, 1966. Deliberately not a social history. The subtitle suggests its focus: the personalities and events out of which came the Risorgimento. A less flattering biography than older accounts.

Mack Smith, Denis. *Garibaldi: A Great Life in Brief*. New York: Alfred A. Knopf, 1956. A readable biography, providing a portrait of Garibaldi as more a passionate than an intellectual figure.

_____, ed. *Garibaldi*. Englewood Cliffs, N.J.: Prentice-Hall, 1969. A biography put together from original documents, here all conveniently translated into English.

Ridley, Jasper. *Garibaldi*. New York: Viking Press, 1976. A highly detailed and massive biography, perhaps relying too much on secondary sources for Italian history, but vivid in its portrayal of Garibaldi as a personality.

Trevelyan, G. M. *Garibaldi's Defence of the Roman Republic (1848-9)*. Reprint. London: Longmans, Green, 1949.

_____. *Garibaldi and the Thousand (May, 1860)*. Reprint. London: Longmans, Green, 1948.

_____. *Garibaldi and the Making of Italy (June-November, 1860)*. Reprint. London: Longmans, Green, 1948. For many years the most widely read books about Garibaldi in the English-speaking world. Notable for their romantic portrait of Garibaldi as hero.

James A. Arieti

PAUL GAUGUIN

Born: June 7, 1848; Paris, France
Died: May 8, 1903; Atuana, Marquesas Islands
Area of Achievement: Art
Contribution: Gauguin epitomized a rejection of nineteenth century realism and its final phase, Impressionism, in favor of a new approach to painting based on primitive art; a simplification of lines, colors, and forms; and a suppression of detail, all intended to enhance the intellectual-emotional impact of a work of art. His program amounted in fact to a deliberate overthrow of the primacy of the optical sensation that had dictated all art since the Renaissance and is therefore the single most revolutionary thought introduced by a nineteenth century artist.

Early Life

An extraordinary childhood and youth preceded Paul Gauguin's entry into the bourgeois world of business and finance. His parents, Clovis and Aline, active in liberal circles, felt forced to flee Paris (after the *coup d'état* of Napoleon III in 1851) and to seek refuge in Peru, where Aline's uncle, Don Piot Tristán y Moscoso, who would soon adopt her as his daughter, lived a life of leisure and luxury. Clovis died during the ocean voyage, but Aline, with children Marie and Paul, arrived in Lima to remain there for four years. Although only a small child during his stay in Lima, Gauguin was never to forget that country. Indeed, his persistent longing for the faraway and exotic no doubt had its roots in his rich, unencumbered childhood years in Peru.

Mother and children returned to France in 1855, and Paul spent the next seven years as a solitary, morose, and withdrawn schoolboy who learned "to hate hypocrisy, false virtues, tale-bearing, and to beware of everything that was contrary to my instincts, my heart, and my reason." In his seventeenth year, he hired on as a seaman on a ship sailing to South America, beginning a career that would keep him at sea for six years, part of that time as an enlisted man in the French navy.

Aline, who died at age forty-two in 1865, had appointed a business friend as guardian to her children, and it was through him that Gauguin in 1871 became a stockbroker, sufficiently successful to offer marriage to a Danish woman, Mette Sophie Gad, in 1873. In his financial career, he met Émile Schuffenecker, a Sunday painter who convinced Gauguin to take up the same hobby; his interest in art, together with a reasonable affluence that enabled him to become an art patron, brought him into contact with Camille Pissarro, the paterfamilias of the Impressionist group, whose influence is readily detected in Gauguin's early, still-hesitant paintings. In 1883, by now the father of five children, he resigned as a stockbroker to devote all of his energy to the arts.

Life's Work

Gauguin's first official entry into the art world took place in 1876, when he exhibited a canvas in the Impressionist style at the annual Parisian Salon. From 1879 until 1886, he showed in the last five exhibits of the Impressionists. Shortly thereafter, with his family settled in Copenhagen, he set out for Central America, working for a time on the construction site of the Panama Canal, then stopping in Martinique, where he produced his first canvas depicting a tropical paradise, a view of the Bay of Saint-Pierre, still in the Impressionist spirit, yet with a color vibrancy that reflects his emotional reaction to the subject.

Back in France in 1888, he took up residence in Pont-Aven, Brittany. "I love Brittany," he said in a letter to Schuffenecker. "I find here the wild and the primitive. When my clogs ring out on its granite soil, I hear the low, flat, powerful note I seek in painting." Joining him in Pont-Aven were Émile Bernard and Louis Anquetin, young experimental painters whose ideas were close to Gauguin's. All three felt moved by the rich colors of medieval enamelwork and cloisonné, and favored reducing visual phenomena to abstract lines and flat colors, a pictorial method clearly employed by Japanese printmakers, whose works were then much in vogue. Gauguin's Brittany paintings, such as *The Vision After the Sermon* (1888), must be seen as an affirmation of these ideas, with its use of receding planes of flat primary colors enclosed by angular, dark lines and dramatized by a drastic perspective. The result is an overall effect far removed from any visual reality. This intense concentration on the visual and emotional totality of the subject rather than on its separate components, the synthetic view, would characterize the majority of Gauguin's paintings. The landscape and people of French Polynesia, where he spent most of his creative life, tended to mellow his temperament and turn his pictures into vibrantly colorful, sinewy linear, often mysteriously muted paeans to primitive nature. On his return to Paris from Pont-Aven in the summer of 1888, he met Vincent van Gogh, and that fall joined van Gogh in Arles in the Midi of France. In spite of turbulent conflicts during the three months they spent together, the Arles experience left its positive impact on both artists, as seen in canvases of closely related subjects produced during their joint outings in the fertile Provençal countryside.

In 1889, during the World's Fair in Paris, Gauguin and his friends from the artist colony in Pont-Aven arranged a private exhibit of one hundred of their works in an Italian bistro within the fairground, Café Volpini. Hardly taken seriously by the public at that time, the Volpini Exhibit is today considered one of the milestones in nineteenth century art. While the exhibitors called themselves "Impressionists" and "Synthetists" they had clearly abandoned the gracefully textured, retinally oriented approach of Claude Monet, Pierre-Auguste Renoir, and Pissarro. Instead, they presented pictures with large patches of contrasting colors separated by dark lines, minimal emphasis on depth and perspective, and, in Gauguin's case, a steady procession of peasants at their melancholy tasks or in worshipful contemplation.

During his stay in Brittany, and more so after his return to Paris in 1890, Gauguin continually toyed with the idea of settling in a more exotic part of the world, preferably with fellow painters in a new "Barbizon" of primitive nature, but if necessary he would go alone. Prior to his departure for Tahiti in the spring of 1891, his Paris friends—and by now there were many of them, artists, writers, government officials—eased his transition, helping him with an auction of his works, which brought a substantial amount of money, and arranging a farewell banquet presided over by Stéphane Mallarmé, the avant-garde poet.

During the two years of his first stay in Tahiti, Gauguin produced some of his most stunning canvases depicting the landscape, the people, and a civilization of beauty and innocence in the process of vanishing. A Tahitian landscape with a village surrounded by wildly exotic, swirling trees, backed up by mountains in sharp, receding planes and surmounted by white clouds against a cerulean sky, is reminiscent of his landscapes in Brittany, except that the dark, angular lines separating the color surfaces in the Brittany scenes have yielded to softer, more undulant patterns in this new, exotic setting. Similarly, his depiction of people of Tahiti, though in form and color resembling his efforts in Brittany, has something new and mysterious in it, close-up views mostly of women, singly or in clusters, with guarded, secretive mien and in hushed poses of ritual solemnity. "Always this haunting silence," Gauguin wrote in a letter to his wife. "I understand why these individuals can rest seated for hours and days without saying a word and look at the sky with melancholy."

Despite his enchantment with the Polynesian ambience, however, he felt confined and out of touch with the art world. Besides, he was financially destitute, incapable of providing for his daily bread. He decided to return to France and succeeded in finding a lender to advance his travel expenses. In the early fall of 1893, he was back in Paris with his Tahitian paintings, preparing for an exhibit and hoping for wide acceptance. His display of more than forty canvases generated few sales, and even his presentation to the French state of the magnificent *Ia Orana Maria* (1891; we hail thee, Mary) was rejected. A few close supporters, Edgar Degas and Mallarmé among them, helped Gauguin—Degas by making a purchase and Mallarmé by praising the Tahitian works.

Such signs of approval, however, were scarce, and Gauguin soon regretted his return to the insensitive, overcivilized world he had once abandoned. An unfortunate altercation during a visit to Brittany left him hospitalized and maimed, and an encounter with a Parisian prostitute resulted in syphilis. All of this resulted in a life of creative stagnation and physical agony, and as soon as he was able to move about he began to prepare for his second and final journey to Tahiti. A major sale of his paintings and belongings was arranged to finance the venture, and, planning to issue a catalog of the items on view, he asked a new acquaintance, the dramatist August Strindberg, to write a preface. In a long and detailed letter, Strindberg enumerated the reasons for his refusal to do so. Yet it appears that he understood Gauguin's creative impulse, sensed its depth. Gauguin, detecting a positive note in Strindberg's rejection, printed the letter as the preface. The sale, however, was a failure. In fact, in a letter to his wife, he records a detailed account showing a net loss of 464 francs. Nevertheless, with the assistance of several picture dealers and a guarantee that they would market his subsequent works, he was able to raise a sum sufficient for the voyage and his immediate subsequent needs; he left France in June of 1895, never to return.

In his second Tahitian period, Gauguin produced one hundred paintings, more than four hundred prints, and numerous pieces of sculpted wood. In addition, he wrote hundreds of letters, an intriguing journal, and reworked text and illustrations in his *Noa Noa* (English translation, 1919), published in France in 1900.

During his first stay, his works, like his visual reactions to life in Brittany, had reflected the primal quality of the Tahitian landscape, the natural innocence of a people still close to the beginnings of time, and the legendary quality of Tahitian spirituality. Thus, desiring to share his experiences with the art audience at home, he had attempted to serve as a messenger from a remote world and a civilization still unspoiled yet inevitably doomed. In his second stay, he found these subtle links with the past already severely eroded through Western colonization. His works from this final period are therefore more introspective and deliberately ponderous. Typical of this approach is his monumental masterpiece *Where Do We Come From? What Are We? Where Are We Going?* (1897-1898), "designed to embody a total philosophy of life, civilization, and sexuality." As in early Renaissance altar panels, it is a work whose imagery transcends time and place, a composite of ritual episodes moving from the outer perimeter toward a central, all-embracing Godhead. A significant and influential aspect of his last Tahitian stay is found in a series of tropical woodblocks carved and hand printed in 1898-1899. Viewed in sequence as in a frieze, they seem to constitute a summary of his visual and spiritual experiences in the land and society he had adopted.

Gauguin never denied his admiration for certain other artists of the nineteenth century, and among his last works are paintings reminiscent of Eugène Delacroix's epochal depictions of women of Morocco, nudes and horses clearly indebted to Degas, and still-lifes of fruits and flowers echoing those of van Gogh painted in Arles.

Still on his easel at the time of his death was his final work, *Breton Village Covered by Snow*. Painted in feverish, death-conscious agony, it is a profoundly melancholy dream evoking the beginnings of a career devoted to a futile search for an earthly paradise.

Summary

Paul Gauguin was the first nineteenth century artist to move away from naturalism to a world of visual dreams inspired by the primitive magic of the medieval past and intensified by a direct exposure to societies less marred by Western civilization. From childhood experiences in Latin America and a turbulent youth at sea and in the Caribbean, he was irresistibly drawn to the untamed and the exotic, finding part of it in a Brittany still steeped in its past and more in the faraway islands of the South Seas. With their purity of line and surface, vibrancy of color, and subtle evocation of the human condition in a tenuous state of innocence, his paintings opened up entirely new vistas in the world of the arts, through the depiction of rare and exotic subject matter. They also paved the way for equally bold strivings among artists of future generations. "I wanted to establish the right to dare everything. My capacity was not capable of great results, but the machine is none the less launched. The public owes me nothing . . . but the painters who today profit from this liberty owe me something."

Bibliography

Andersen, Wayne. *Gauguin's Paradise Lost*. New York: Viking Press, 1979. An American scholar's attempt at reaching an understanding of the artist's psychological development through a parallel probing of his works and writings.

Brettell, Richard, et al. *The Art of Paul Gauguin*. An exhibit catalog prepared by Richard Brettell, François Cachin, Claire Freches-Thory, and Charles F. Stuckey, with assistance from Peter Zegers. Boston: New York Graphic Society Books, 1988. Numerous catalogs have been issued in conjunction with the many exhibits of Gauguin's works mounted worldwide. The exhibit jointly sponsored by the National Gallery and the Art Institute of Chicago was accompanied by a catalog so comprehensive, so authoritative, and so richly illustrated that it supersedes all previous efforts in that direction. Drawn from collections in North and South America, Europe, and Asia, the exhibit included 280 separate items, nearly all described in terse but excellent articles.

Danielsson, Bengt. *Gauguin in the South Seas*. Translated by Reginald Spink. Garden City, N.Y.: Doubleday, 1966. A Swedish anthropologist and explorer, the author is the only Gauguin biographer intimately familiar with the artist's Tahitian people, their mores, and their land, and he succeeds in conveying to the reader the artist's enchantment and frustrations as he pursues his dream. In a series of photographs inspired by Gauguin's paintings, Danielsson shows both the continuity and the disruption of the civilization the artist depicts.

Gauguin, Paul. *The Intimate Journals of Paul Gauguin.* Translated by Van Wyck Brooks, with a preface by Émile Gauguin. London: W. Heinemann, 1923. The original manuscript, finished in 1903, has the title *Avant et après* and was published in facsimile editions in 1913 and 1953. The English edition was endorsed by Gauguin's son, who in his preface says, "These journals are the spontaneous expression of the same free, fearless, sensitive spirit that speaks in the canvases of Paul Gauguin."

_____. *Paul Gauguin: Letters to His Wife and Friends.* Edited by Maurice Mallinge. Translated by Henry F. Stenning. Cleveland: World Publishing, 1949. This collection sheds much light on the strained relationship between the artist and his estranged wife, Mette Gad, who at the time of Gauguin's first stay in Brittany returned with their five children to her childhood home in Copenhagen. Characterized by Gauguin's continual quest for understanding and her pervasive bitterness, the letters also contain much information on his creative activities.

Gauguin, Pola. *My Father, Paul Gauguin.* Translated by Arthur G. Chater. New York: Alfred A. Knopf, 1937. Written by Gauguin's youngest son, an artist and art historian who lived in Norway, this biography draws much of its information from family letters and documents whose content up to that time had been unavailable to the public. Remarkably dispassionate in its narration, it tends to counterbalance the relentless bitterness of Gauguin's wife.

Gray, Christopher. *Sculpture and Ceramics of Paul Gauguin.* Baltimore: Johns Hopkins University Press, 1963. Gray's volume spans Gauguin's entire career and shows how his early efforts in ceramics foreshadowed the three-dimensional works produced in Tahiti. An appendix twice the size of the principal text contains a detailed catalog of the artist's known works in these media.

Rewald, John. *Post-Impressionism: From Van Gogh to Gauguin.* 3d rev. ed. New York: Museum of Modern Art, 1979. This magnificently illustrated work by a principal authority in late nineteenth century European painting presents the total fabric of the Post-Impressionist movement in which van Gogh and Gauguin occupied centerstage, with many others playing supporting roles.

Reidar Dittmann

CARL FRIEDRICH GAUSS

Born: April 30, 1777; Brunswick, Germany
Died: February 23, 1855; Göttingen, Lower Saxony
Areas of Achievement: Mathematics, astronomy, and physics
Contribution: Gauss, one of the greatest scientific thinkers of all time, often ranked with Archimedes and Isaac Newton, made significant contributions in many branches of science. Perhaps his greatest achievement was that he arrived at the two most revolutionary mathematical ideas of the nineteenth century, non-Euclidean geometry and noncommutative algebra.

Early Life

Carl Friedrich Gauss was born into a family of town workers who were struggling to achieve lower-middle-class status. Without assistance, Gauss learned to calculate before he could talk; he also taught himself to read. At the age of three, he corrected an error in his father's wage calculations. In his first arithmetic class, at the age of eight, he astonished his teacher by instantly solving a word problem which involved finding the sum of the first hundred integers. Fortunately, his teacher had the insight to furnish the child with books and encourage his intellectual development.

When he was eleven, Gauss studied with Martin Bartels, then an assistant in the school and later a teacher of Nikolay Ivanovich Lobachevsky at Kazan. Gauss's father was persuaded to allow his son to enter the *Gymnasium* in 1788. At the *Gymnasium*, Gauss made rapid progress in all subjects, especially in classics and mathematics, largely on his own. E. A. W. Zimmermann, then professor at the local Collegium Carolinum and later privy councillor to the Duke of Brunswick, encouraged Gauss; in 1792, Duke Carl Wilhelm Ferdinand began the stipend that would assure Gauss's independence.

When Gauss entered the Brunswick Collegium Carolinum in 1792, he possessed a scientific and classical education far beyond his years. He was acquainted with elementary geometry, algebra, and analysis (often having discovered important theorems before reaching them in his books), but he also possessed much arithmetical information and number-theoretic insights. His lifelong pattern of research had become established: Extensive empirical investigation led to conjectures, and new insights guided further experiment and observation. By such methods, he had already discovered Johann Elert Bode's law of planetary distances, the binomial theorem for rational exponents, and the arithmetic-geometric mean.

During his three years at the Collegium, among other things, Gauss formulated the principle of least squares. Before entering the University of Göttingen in 1795, he had rediscovered the law of quadratic reciprocity, related the arithmetic-geometric mean to infinite series expansions, and conjectured the prime number theorem (first proved by Jacques-Salomon Hadamard in 1896).

While he was in Brunswick, most mathematical classics had been unavailable to him. At Göttingen, however, he devoured masterworks and back issues of journals and often found that his discoveries were not new. Attracted more by the brilliant classicist Christian Gottlob Heyne than by the mediocre mathematician A. G. Kästner, Gauss planned to be a philologist, but in 1796 he made a dramatic discovery that marked him as a mathematician. As a result of a systematic investigation of the cyclotomic equation (whose solution has the geometric counterpart of dividing a circle into equal arcs), Gauss declared that the regular seventeen-sided polygon was constructible by ruler and compasses, the first advance on this subject in two thousand years.

The logical aspect of Gauss's method matured at Göttingen. While he adopted the spirit of Greek rigor, it was without the classical geometric form; Gauss, rather, thought numerically and algebraically, in the manner of Leonhard Euler. By the age of twenty, Gauss was conducting large-scale empirical investigations and rigorous theoretical constructions, and during the years from 1796 to 1800 mathematical ideas came so quickly that Gauss could hardly write them down.

Life's Work

In 1798, Gauss returned to Brunswick, and the next year, with the first of his four proofs of the fundamental theorem of algebra, earned a doctorate from the University of Helmstedt. In 1801, the creativity of the previous years was reflected in two extraordinary achievements, the *Disquisitiones arithmeticae* (1801; *Arithmetical Inquisitions*, 1966) and the calculation of the orbit of the newly discovered planet Ceres.

Although number theory was developed from the earliest times, in the late eighteenth century it consisted of a large collection of isolated results. In *Arithmetical Inquisitions*, Gauss systematically summarized previous work, solved some of the most difficult outstanding questions, and formulated concepts and questions that established the pattern of research for a century. The work almost instantly won for Gauss recognition by mathematicians, although readership was small.

In January, 1801, Giuseppi Piazzi had briefly discovered but lost track of a new planet he had observed, and during the rest of that year astronomers unsuccessfully attempted to relocate it. Gauss decided to pursue the matter. Applying both a more accurate orbit theory and improved numerical methods, he accomplished the task by December. Ceres was soon found in the predicted position. This feat of locating a distant, tiny planet from apparently insufficient information was astonishing, especially since Gauss did not reveal his methods. Along with *Arithmetical Inquisitions*, it established his reputation as a first-rate mathematical and scientific genius.

The decade of these achievements (1801-1810) was decisive for Gauss. Scientifically it was a period of exploiting ideas accumulated from the previous decade, and it ended with a work in which Gauss systematically developed his methods of orbit calculation, including a theory of and use of least squares. Professionally this decade was one of transition from mathematician to astronomer and physical scientist. Gauss accepted the post of director of the Göttingen Observatory in 1807.

This decade also provided Gauss with his one period of personal happiness. In 1805, he married Johanna Osthoff, with whom he had a son and a daughter. She created a happy family life around him. When she died in 1809, Gauss was plunged into a loneliness from which he never fully recovered. Less than a year later, he married Minna Waldeck, his deceased wife's best friend. Although she bore him two sons and a daughter, she was unhealthy and very often unhappy. Gauss did not achieve a peaceful home life until his youngest daughter, Therese, assumed management of the household after her mother's death in 1831 and became his companion for the last twenty-four years of his life.

In his first years as director of the Göttingen Observatory, Gauss experienced a second burst of ideas and publications in various fields of mathematics and matured his conception of non-Euclidean geometry. Yet astronomical tasks soon dominated Gauss's life.

By 1817, Gauss moved toward geodesy, which was to be his preoccupation for the next eight years. The invention of the heliotrope, an instrument for reflecting the sun's rays in a measured direction, was an early by-product of fieldwork. The invention was motivated by dissatisfaction with the existing methods of observing distant points by using lamps or powder flares at night. In spite of failures and dissatisfactions, the period of geodesic investigation was one of the most scientifically creative of Gauss's long career. The difficulties of mapping the terrestrial ellipsoid on a sphere and plane led him, in 1816, to formulate and solve in outline the general problem of mapping one surface on another so that the two were "similar in their smallest parts." In 1822, the chance of winning a prize offered by the Copenhagen Academy motivated him to write these ideas in a paper that won for him first place and was published in 1825.

Surveying problems also inspired Gauss to develop his ideas on least squares and more general problems of what is now called mathematical statistics. His most significant contribution during this period, and his last breakthrough in a major new direction of mathematical research, was *Disquisitiones generales circa superficies curvas* (1828; *General Investigations of Curved Surfaces*, 1902), which was the result of three decades of geodesic investigations and which drew upon more than a century of work on differential geometry.

After the mid-1820's, Gauss, feeling harassed and overworked and suffering from asthma and heart disease, turned to investigations in physics. Gauss accepted an offer from Alexander von Humboldt to come to Berlin to work. An incentive was his meeting in Berlin with Wilhelm Eduard Weber, a young and brilliant experimental physicist with whom Gauss would eventually collaborate on many significant discoveries. They were also to organize a worldwide network of magnetic observatories and to publish extensively on magnetic force. From the early 1840's, the intensity of Gauss's activity gradually decreased. Increasingly bedridden as a result of heart disease, he died in his sleep in late February, 1855.

Summary

Carl Friedrich Gauss's impact as a scientist falls far short of his reputation. His inventions were usually minor improvements of temporary importance. In theoretical astronomy, he perfected classical methods in orbit calculation but otherwise made only fairly routine observations. His personal involvement in calculating orbits saved others work but was of little long-lasting scientific importance. His work in geodesy was influential only in its mathematical by-products. Furthermore, his collaboration with Weber led to only two achievements of significant impact: The use of absolute units set a pattern that became standard, and the worldwide network of magnetic observatories established a precedent for international scientific cooperation. Also, his work in physics may have been of the highest quality, but it seems to have had little influence.

In the area of mathematics, however, his influence was powerful. Carl Gustav Jacobi and Henrik Abel testified that their work on elliptic functions was triggered by a hint in the *Arithmetical Inquisitions*. Évariste Galois, on the eve of his death, asked that his rough notes be sent to Gauss. Thus, in mathematics, in spite of delays, Gauss reached and inspired countless mathematicians. Although he was more of a systematizer and solver of old problems than a creator of new paths, the very completeness of his results laid the basis for new departures—especially in number theory, differential geometry, and statistics.

Bibliography

Bell, Eric T. *Men of Mathematics*. Reprint. New York: Simon & Schuster, 1961. Historical account of the major figures in mathematics from the Greeks to Giorg Cantor, written in an interesting, if at times exaggerated, style. In a lengthy chapter devoted to Gauss titled "The Prince of Mathematicians," Bell describes the life and work of Gauss, focusing almost exclusively on the mathematical contributions. No bibliography.

Boyer, Carl B. *A History of Mathematics*. New York: John Wiley & Sons, 1968. In "The Time of Gauss and Cauchy," chapter 23 of this standard history of mathematics, Boyer very briefly discusses biographical details of Gauss's life before summarizing the proofs of Gauss's major theorems. Boyer also discusses Gauss's work in the context of the leading contemporary figures in mathematics of the day. Includes charts, an extensive bibliography, and student exercises.

Buhler, W. K. *Gauss: A Biographical Study*. New York: Springer-Verlag, 1981. The author's purpose is not to write a definitive life history but to select from Gauss's life and work those aspects which are interesting and comprehensible to a lay reader. Contains quotations from Gauss's writings, illustrations, a bibliography, lengthy footnotes, appendices on his collected works, a useful survey of the secondary literature, and an index to Gauss's works.

Dunnington, Guy Waldo. *Carl Friedrich Gauss, Titan of Science: A Study of His Life and Work*. New York: Exposition Press, 1955. Gauss and the times in which he lived are depicted to reveal the man as well as the scientist. Contains the largest bibliography yet published and includes appendices on honors and diplomas, children, genealogy, a chronology, books borrowed at college, courses taught, and views and opinions.

Turnbull, H. W. *The Great Mathematicians*. New York: New York University Press, 1962. Useful as a quick reference guide to the lives and works of the major figures in mathematics from the Greeks to the twentieth century.

Genevieve Slomski

JOSEPH-LOUIS GAY-LUSSAC

Born: December 6, 1778; Saint-Léonard-de-Noblat, France
Died: May 9, 1850; Paris, France
Areas of Achievement: Chemistry and physics
Contribution: A preeminent scientist of his generation, Gay-Lussac helped
   prepare the way, through his discoveries in chemistry and physics, for the
   modern atomic-molecular theory of matter. His investigations of gases led
   to the law describing how they react with each other in simple proportions
   by volume, and his chemical investigations led to the discovery of a new
   element, boron, and to the development of new techniques in qualitative
   and quantitative analysis.

Early Life

Joseph-Louis Gay was born on December 6, 1778, at Saint-Léonard-de-
Noblat, a small market town in west central France. He was the eldest son of
five children of Antoine Gay, a lawyer and public prosecutor, who, to distinguish himself from others called Gay, later changed his surname to Gay-
Lussac, after the family property in the nearby hamlet of Lussac. Joseph-
Louis used this expanded name throughout his life. His early education from
a priest and his comfortable social and economic position were ended by the
Revolution of 1789, and in the turbulent years that followed, his teacher fled
the country, and his father was arrested.

With the fall of Robespierre in 1794, the Revolution took a more moderate
direction, and Gay-Lussac's father was freed. Antoine Gay-Lussac was then
able to send Joseph-Louis to Paris to continue his education at religious
boarding schools. His father expected him to study law, but Gay-Lussac
became increasingly interested in mathematics and science. His excellent
record in mathematics gave him the opportunity to enter the École Polytechnique, then a young but already prestigious revolutionary institution for
the training of civil and military engineers. Gay-Lussac completed his studies there with distinction, and he was graduated in November, 1800. He then
entered the École des Ponts et Chaussées. He saw engineering not as a career
but as a position to fall back on if he did not succeed in pure science.

During these years of study, Gay-Lussac came under the wing of Claude
Louis Berthollet, a distinguished chemist and former companion to Napoleon I in Egypt. In his triple role as teacher, father-substitute, and patron,
Berthollet became the most important influence on Gay-Lussac's life. Some
of Gay-Lussac's greatest early work was done at Berthollet's country house
at Arcueil, where important scientists would gather and where the Society of
Arcueil was later formed. Gay-Lussac continued his studies at the École des
Ponts et Chaussées, but his relationship with the school grew more nominal
as he spent more and more time on scientific research at Arcueil.

Life's Work

Gay-Lussac's initial research was of considerable importance both because of its permanent scientific value and because it marked his successful initiation into a career of pure science. In 1802, after painstaking measurements, he showed that many different gases expand equally over the temperature range from 0 to +100 degrees Celsius. Despite the thoroughness of his studies and the significance of his results, Gay-Lussac is not generally credited with the discovery of the quantitative law of the thermal expansion of gases. Some chemists recalled that Jacques Charles, a French physicist, had found in 1787 that certain gases expanded equally, but Charles had also found that other gases, those that dissolved in water, had different rates of expansion. Since Charles never published his work and since he did not completely understand the phenomenon of thermal expansion, many scholars believe that justice demands that this discovery should be known as Gay-Lussac's law.

Gases were central to another of Gay-Lussac's early research projects. In the early nineteenth century, scientists debated whether the percentage of nitrogen, oxygen, and other gases was different in the upper and lower atmosphere. A similar diversity of opinion existed about the behavior of a magnet at low and high altitudes. To resolve these differences, Gay-Lussac and Jean-Baptiste Biot, a young colleague, made a daring ascent from Paris in a hydrogen-filled balloon on August 24, 1804. By observing oscillations of a magnetic needle, they concluded that the intensity of the earth's magnetism was constant up to four thousand meters, but they did not have time to collect samples of air. Therefore, to answer the question about the atmosphere's composition, Gay-Lussac made a solo balloon ascent over Paris on September 16, 1804. He reached a height of more than seven thousand meters, an altitude record that would remain unmatched for a half century. He discovered that the temperature of the atmosphere decreased by one degree Celsius for every 174-meter increase in elevation. When he analyzed the air samples that he had collected, he found that the composition of air was the same at seven thousand meters as it was at sea level (his technique was not sensitive enough to detect the differences that were later found).

Shortly after the balloon flights, Gay-Lussac began to collaborate with Alexander von Humboldt, a Prussian nobleman, world traveler, and scientist. Gay-Lussac had just received an appointment to a junior post at the École Polytechnique when he met Humboldt, who was interested in his analysis of the atmosphere. Humboldt and Gay-Lussac agreed to collaborate in a series of experiments on atmospheric gases. Their research led to a precise determination of the relative proportions with which hydrogen and oxygen combine to form water: almost exactly two hundred parts to one hundred parts by volume. Though they were not the first to discover this 2:1 ratio (Henry Cavendish had noted it in 1784), the experiment convinced

Gay-Lussac that scientists should study the reactions of gases by volume instead of by weight.

Because of the fruitfulness of their collaboration, Gay-Lussac wanted to accompany Humboldt on a European tour he was planning, to make a systematic survey of magnetic intensities. Gay-Lussac was granted a leave of absence from the École Polytechnique, and in March, 1805, he and Humboldt embarked on a year of travel through Italy, Switzerland, and Germany. Through their tour, Gay-Lussac made many contacts with important physicists and chemists such as Alessandro Volta, the inventor of the electric battery. A tangible result of his European travels was a paper on terrestrial magnetism. Because of this and other studies, he was elected in 1806 to the National Institute (the revolutionary replacement for the Royal Academy of Sciences). Although this was a major step in Gay-Lussac's career, his base of operations remained the École Polytechnique and Arcueil.

In 1807, Gay-Lussac completed a series of experiments to see if there was a general relationship between the specific heat of a gas and its density. Specific heat is a measure of a substance's capacity to attract its own particular quantity of heat. For example, mercury has less capacity for heat than water; that is, mercury requires a smaller quantity of heat than does water to raise its temperature by the same number of degrees. Gay-Lussac knew that the compression of gases was accompanied by the evolution of heat and their expansion by the absorption of heat, but he wanted to find the relationship between the absorbed and evolved heat. Through an ingenious series of experiments, he discovered that the heat lost by expansion was equal to the heat gained by compression, a result significant in the history of physics, particularly for the law of the conservation of energy.

Although Gay-Lussac had studied the 2:1 chemical combination of hydrogen and oxgen in 1805, he did not generalize his results until 1808, when he again became interested in gas reactions. At that time, he began his long collaboration with Louis Jacques Thenard, a peasant's son who had risen from laboratory boy to Polytechnique professor. In one of their early experiments, they heated a mixture of calcium fluoride and boric acid in an iron tube. Instead of getting the expected fluorine, they obtained fluoric acid (now called boron trifluoride), a gas which, on coming into contact with air, produced dense white fumes that reminded them of those produced by muriatic acid (now called hydrogen chloride) and ammonia. In fact, they found that boron trifluoride and ammonia reacted in a 1:1 ratio by volume, just as hydrogen chloride and ammonia did. With these and other examples from his own experiments, along with results reported by others in various papers, Gay-Lussac felt secure enough to state that all gases combine in simple volumetric proportions. He announced this law, now known as Gay-Lussac's law of combining volumes, at a meeting of the Société Philomatique in Paris on December 31, 1808. This law would later be used to teach students about the evidence for the atomic theory, but at the time of its proposal Gay-Lussac rejected John Dalton's atomic theory.

Despite Gay-Lussac's important research at the École Polytechnique and Arcueil, his career was stalled. During the years 1808 and 1809, his friends tried to lobby on his behalf for a position commensurate with his accomplishments. The death of Antoine Fourcroy in 1809 provided the opportunity for which Gay-Lussac's friends had been waiting, and on February 17, 1810, Gay-Lussac became Fourcroy's successor to the chemistry chair at the École Polytechnique. Another reason for this activity on Gay-Lussac's behalf was his impending marriage to Geneviève-Marie-Joseph Riot, to whom he was married in May, 1809. The marriage was a happy one, eventually producing five children.

During the time that Gay-Lussac's friends were trying to find him a position, Gay-Lussac and Thenard were doing important work on the alkali metals. These soft metals with great chemical reactivity had recently been isolated by Humphry Davy, the great English chemist who would become Gay-Lussac's competitor in many discoveries. Davy had used the giant voltaic batteries at the Royal Institution to discover sodium and potassium. Because of the rivalry between Great Britain and France, Napoleon ordered the construction of an even larger collection of batteries at the École Polytechnique, and he urged Gay-Lussac and Thenard to do experiments with this voltaic pile. Ironically, they actually found that they could ignore electrolysis and use chemical means to produce large quantities of sodium and potassium. Davy's electrical method had liberated only tiny amounts of the new metals, whereas Gay-Lussac and Thenard's method of fusing potassium and sodium salts with iron filings at high temperatures produced great amounts of sodium and potassium more cheaply.

Gay-Lussac and Davy were both interested in isolating the element contained in boric acid. On June 21, 1808, Gay-Lussac and Thenard heated boric acid with potassium in a copper tube, producing a mixture of products, one of which was the new element. Their first published claim to the discovery of boron was in November, a month before Davy submitted a similar claim to the Royal Society. They delayed publishing their discovery because they wanted not only to decompose boric acid but also to recompose it.

After their work on boron, Gay-Lussac and Thenard examined oxymuriatic acid. At the beginning of the nineteenth century, chlorine was called oxymuriatic acid because chemists thought that it was a compound of oxygen and muriatic acid. This belief was based on its preparation by heating muriatic (now called hydrochloric) acid with a substance such as manganese dioxide with its abundance of oxygen. Gay-Lussac and Thenard were therefore astonished when they passed oxymuriatic acid gas over red-hot charcoal and the oxygen which was supposedly in the acid refused to combine with the charcoal. This led them to doubt that the gas contained oxygen and to suggest that it might be an element. Historians of chemistry usually report that Davy first recognized the elementary nature of chlorine, because in Gay-Lussac and Thenard's report in the 1809 volume of the Arcueil Memoires, which was known to Davy, they conservatively stated that their experiments caused them to doubt the existence of oxygen in oxymuriatic acid, whereas Davy in 1810 unambiguously stated that it was an element, for which he proposed the name chlorine.

In addition to the misconception about chlorine, chemists of the time were also grappling with a faulty theory of acids since Antoine Lavoisier had earlier proposed that all acids contained oxygen. Until Gay-Lussac's research on iodine in 1814 and on prussic acid in 1815, he had accepted Lavoisier's theory of acidity. Gay-Lussac's discovery and investigation of hydriodic acid reopened the question for him, and he concluded that hydrogen, not oxygen, was necessary to convert iodine to an acid. He clearly stated that hydrogen played the same role for one class of substances that oxygen did for another. He introduced the concept and name "hydracid" for the first class, and his studies of hydrogen chloride, hydrogen iodide, and hydrogen fluoride prepared the way for a new theory of acids.

Gay-Lussac's early work was based on the recognition, common among chemists since the eighteenth century, that each substance possessed a unique chemical composition that could be represented by a unique formula. During the 1820's, Gay-Lussac and other chemists discovered pairs of compounds, each member of which had the same number of the same atoms but with quite distinct properties. Gay-Lussac straightforwardly interpreted this phenomenon, called isomerism, as a result of the different atomic arrangements in the two substances. This idea, that different structures result in different chemical properties, would become an extremely important theme in the history of modern chemistry.

During the final decades of Gay-Lussac's career, he turned his attention more and more to applied science. The economic needs created by his growing family caused him to do more industrial research, where the financial rewards were greater than in theoretical work. Particularly noteworthy was his development of a superior method of assaying silver using a standard solution of common salt. This precise method, which he developed after he became Chief Assayer to the Mint in 1829, is still used.

In 1832, Gay-Lussac accepted a distinguished position at the Museum of Natural History. In his last years, he worked so hard to provide for his family that he produced little theoretical work, but he continued to reap honors for his brilliant early discoveries. In 1839, he became a Peer of France, even though his election was accepted reluctantly by those who thought that he worked too much with his hands to be a gentleman. He had a brief political career in the 1830's, after which he held a number of advisory positions, where he used his technical knowledge to suggest improvements in such industrial chemical processes as the production of gunpowder and oxalic acid. He died in Paris on May 9, 1850, lamenting his departure from the world just when science was becoming interesting.

Summary

The quest for laws dominated Joseph-Louis Gay-Lussac's scientific life. He believed that if a scientist lacked this desire, then the laws of nature would escape his attention. His most important discovery was the law of combining volumes, which helped pave the way for the modern atomic-molecular theory of matter.

Gay-Lussac managed to pass relatively unscathed through three political revolutions. Nevertheless, his life reflected the social and political changes taking place around him. His education occurred largely in schools founded or modified by the Revolution. Berthollet and the Society of Arcueil, the shapers of Gay-Lussac as a scientist, owed much to the patronage of Napoleon. During the 1830's and 1840's, under Louis-Philippe, Gay-Lussac became a conservative member of the professional class or upper bourgeoisie. Through all these changes he continued to be a French patriot. This chauvinism surfaced in his scientific controversies with the British chemists Humphry Davy and John Dalton.

Just as his political life was a curious blend of liberalism and conservatism, so too was his scientific life. In his early career, devoted to pure science, he made so many important discoveries in so many areas that no one in post-Napoleonic France could teach chemistry without frequent references to his work. During the Restoration, however, he made few contributions to pure science, and he seemed to many young scientists to represent an enervating conservatism. For example, he adhered to the caloric theory of heat (heat as a substance) rather than embracing what most scientists saw as the superior kinetic theory (heat as motion). Despite these weaknesses in his later career, Gay-Lussac's place in the history of science is secure. His achievements in chemistry, physics, meteorology, and geology led him to become a central figure in the French scientific establishment, and he was influential in shaping such institutions as the École Polytechnique and the Museum of Natural History. His facility in applying chemistry to practical problems set an example that had wide repercussions later in the century. He also had great influence internationally—he emerges as a key figure of European science in the first third of the nineteenth century.

Bibliography

Crosland, Maurice. *Gay-Lussac, Scientist and Bourgeois*. New York: Cambridge University Press, 1978. Crosland takes a thematic rather than a strictly chronological approach to the life and work of Gay-Lussac. He relates Gay-Lussac both to the history of science and to contemporary social and political history. His account, which is refreshingly frank in dealing with issues of scientific rivalry and academic politics, is intended for historians of science as well as for social and economic historians, but because Crosland explains the science of the times so well, his work should be accessible to a wider audience.

_____. *The Society of Arcueil: A View of French Science at the Time of Napoleon I.* Cambridge, Mass.: Harvard University Press, 1967. This book contains an important account of the social context of Gay-Lussac's early work. Crosland also uses Arcueil to make some good general points about the nature of patronage and about French science.

Ihde, Aaron J. *The Development of Modern Chemistry.* New York: Harper & Row, 1964. Ihde, who taught the history of chemistry for many years at the University of Wisconsin, emphasizes the period from the eighteenth to the twentieth century. His approach is more encyclopedic than analytic, but descriptive enough so that it is readable by high school and college chemistry students. Contains an extensive annotated bibliography.

Scott, Wilson L. *The Conflict Between Atomism and Conservation Theory, 1644-1860.* New York: Elsevier, 1970. Scott focuses on the conflict between groups of scientists over the issue of whether force (later called energy) is conserved when one hard body strikes another. This debate had important implications for the atomic theory, and Gay-Lussac's ideas and experiments were integral to it. The book is based on extensive research, but because the author can tell a story and explain scientific concepts clearly, his account is accessible to readers without any special scientific knowledge.

Szabadvary, Ferenc. *History of Analytical Chemistry.* Elmsford, N.Y.: Pergamon Press, 1966. This book, first published in Hungarian in 1960, is a detailed account of the historical development of analytical chemistry. Gay-Lussac's contributions to qualitative and quantitative, gravimetric and volumetric analysis are extensively discussed. The book is based largely on original sources and is intended for the reader with some knowledge of chemistry.

Robert J. Paradowski

ALBERICO GENTILI

Born: January 14, 1552; Castello di San Ginesio, Ancona, Papal States
Died: June 19, 1608; London, England
Area of Achievement: Law
Contribution: Gentili, a precursor of Hugo Grotius, brought the study of
international law into modern times by recognizing that all the states of
Europe belonged to one community of law, by applying the principles of
morality to international law and particularly to war, and by separating
international law from its religious basis (though not from morality) and
placing it instead upon a basis of practicality.

Early Life

Known also by the Latin name of Albericus Gentilis, Alberico Gentili was
born in the ancient town of Castello di San Ginesio in the march of Ancona
in the Apennines facing the Adriatic Sea. One of seven children born to
Matteo, a physician, and Lucretia, Alberico was educated in law at the
University of Perugia, where one of the most celebrated teachers was Ri-
naldo Rodolfini. Shortly after being graduated on September 22, 1572, with
a doctor's degree in civil law, Alberico was elected a judge at Ascoli and
then in 1575 elected to the office of advocate in San Ginesio.

In 1579, the family was broken up by Matteo's and Alberico's religious
tendencies toward Protestantism and their flight in order to escape the Inquisition, with the youngest son, Scipio, to Laibach in Carniola, Austria,
where Protestantism was still tolerated. Unwilling to leave, Lucretia stayed
behind with the remainder of her children. Thereafter, an additional split in
the family occurred when Matteo, remaining for a time in Laibach, sent
Alberico to England and Scipio to universities in Germany and the Low
Countries. Not long afterward, finding that Austrian policy toward Protestantism was changing, Matteo followed his son to England and died there in
1602. Scipio eventually found fame as a scholar, poet, jurist, and professor
of law at Altdorf, where he died in 1616.

Life's Work

Reaching England in August of 1580, after brief stays in Tübingen and
Heidelberg, Gentili met, through the small congregation of Italian Protestants in London, a number of distinguished people, including Robert Dudley,
Earl of Leicester, who had been chancellor of the University of Oxford since
1564. From Dudley, Gentili obtained a letter of recommendation to the authorities of the university describing Gentili as one who, "being forced to
leave his country for religion, is desirous to be incorporated into your University, and to bestow some time in reading and other exercise of his profession there." Granted small amounts of money for his support, he took up

residence in Oxford, receiving his degree on March 6, 1581, and thereupon devoted himself to teaching and writing. His activities in writing were so extensive as to produce until the end of his life at least one book each year, beginning with *De iuris interpretibus dialogi sex* (1582; six dialogs), which was dedicated to the Earl of Leicester.

When the Spanish ambassador to England was found plotting against Queen Elizabeth I in 1584, Gentili and John Hotoman were consulted by the Crown as to the course of action to be followed by the English government. Largely on their advice, the ambassador was treated with civility and permitted to leave the country unharmed. Gentili's research into the field of foreign ministries led to the publication of his *De legationibus libri tres* (1585; *Three Books on Embassies*, 1924).

In the autumn of 1586, through the influence of the queen's close adviser Sir Francis Walsingham, Gentili accompanied Horatio Pallavicino as ambassador to the elector of Saxony in Wittenberg, but returned to England in 1587 to be appointed regius professor at Oxford, on June 8, 1587. The experience in Germany elevated further his interest in international law and led to the publication of his major work: *De iure belli libri tres* (1588-1589; *The Three Books on the Law of War*, 1931), a work in three volumes that appeared again in a thorough revision in 1599. In 1589, he married Hester de Peigni, and the couple eventually had five children.

In the meantime, Gentili's knowledge was being called more and more into service for actual trial work before the courts in London, where he came to reside. He was admitted in 1600 to Gray's Inn (one of England's Inns of Court), leaving his duties at the University of Oxford more frequently to a deputy. In 1605, Gentili was nominated by the Spanish ambassador to England, Don Petrus de Zunica, with permission of King James I, to be advocate to the Spanish embassy of Philip III of Spain and his successors. England was neutral in the struggle then occurring in the Spanish effort to quell the Dutch Protestant revolt, with the result that many cases involving the British merchant marine came before the English Court of Admiralty. Gentili's notes on these cases were collected and published by his brother Scipio in 1613, five years after Gentili's death, under the title *Hispanicae advocationis libri duo* (*The Two Books of the Pleas of a Spanish Advocate*, 1921).

Gentili suffered obscurity in the light of Hugo Grotius' work until Gentili's achievement was largely uncovered by Thomas E. Holland of the University of Oxford in 1874; much of what is known of Gentili is the result of Holland's original research. Holland encountered two forces in opposition to the resurrection of Gentili's reputation: the first originating in the Roman Catholic church, which had centuries before placed Gentili's name in the Index of heretics whose writings were not to be read, and the second, among the Dutch, who carefully guarded any diminution in the reputation of their compatriot Hugo Grotius. Not until 1877 was a monument to Gentili placed in St. Helen's Church, Bishopsgate, where he was buried, and a new edition of *The Three Books on the Law of War* was published. In 1908, a statue of Gentili was unveiled in his native town.

Of the many books that Gentili wrote, he is best known for *Three Books on Embassies*, *The Three Books on the Law of War*, and *The Two Books of the Pleas of a Spanish Advocate*. Although he dealt with the practicalities of modern life, divorcing his ideas from the mere dogmas of any specific religion, as the basis for his thought, he infused morality into the foundation of international behavior. In this respect, he departed from the concepts of Niccolò Machiavelli's *Il principe* (wr. 1513, pb. 1532; *The Prince*, 1640) in that he viewed good faith, proper behavior among nations, honesty, and respect as the truly effective qualities, whether in war or peace, among the community of nations. Drawing upon his scholarship and experience, Gentili, in the first book of *Three Books on Embassies*, gives his definition of legations and their history. The second book discusses the rights and immunities of ambassadors in foreign lands, and the third book discusses the behavior and conduct of ambassadors and ministers to foreign countries.

In Gentili's opinion, war is *publicorum armorum justa contentio* (the community clothed in arms for a just cause). As to the definition of the term "just," Gentili said that justice expresses not only law but also what is from all perspectives righteous, as exemplified by self-defense, the defense of others, necessity, and the vindication of natural and legal rights. He believed in honest diplomacy, even among warring enemies, and eschewed verbal trickery. He approved strategy but not perfidy, for example. He also analyzed the treatment of prisoners of war, the taking of hostages, the burial of the dead after battle, behavior toward noncombatants, and the rights of noncombatants. In *The Two Books of the Pleas of a Spanish Advocate*, Gentili displays his concern for the neutral rights of nonbelligerents. Acting as counsel for Catholic Spain against the Protestant Netherlands, in determining the claimed right of the Netherlands to capture Spanish prizes in English waters, Gentili presented a strong statement of territorial sovereignty, jurisdiction of sovereignties over adjacent seas, and the rights of both belligerents and neutrals.

In his last will, made in London, Gentili expressed the desire that he be buried as closely as possible to his father and that all of his unpublished manuscripts, except those referring to the Spanish advocacy, be destroyed, as he considered the remainder of his manuscripts too unfinished to be preserved. The first request was carried out, and he was buried beside his father in the churchyard of St. Helen's, Bishopsgate. The destruction of the manuscripts apparently did not take place, because twenty-eight volumes came into the possession of a book collector in Amsterdam and were thereafter purchased from his successors in 1804 for the Bodleian Library in Oxford, where they remain.

Summary

Alberico Gentili has been heralded as the first knowledgeable author of modern international law and the first clearly to define its subject matter. Francis Bacon insisted on an empirical or inductive method of achieving a true science, as distinct from the deductive, a method that Gentili maintained is the true method of determining international law: that is, to examine the behavior and situation of states, and the changes of society, and, by a process of induction, to modify, cancel, and adjust international law to suit the specific circumstances as newly discovered facts and situations become available. He conceived of nations as a community of states; he believed in freedom of the seas and in the freedom of intercourse among nations; he insisted that the monarch or leader of a nation exists for the state, not the state for the monarch; and he opposed war generally but recognized that, if war must take place, it must be conducted with honor insofar as war and honor can coexist. In addition to international law, Gentili gave attention in his writings to other controversies of his time, including the limits of sovereign power, the problem of remarriage, the union of England and Scotland, the respective jurisdictions of canon and civil law, and the use of stage plays for the airing of legal and moral questions.

Bibliography

Gentili, Alberico. *De iure belli libri tres*. 2 vols. Oxford, England: Clarendon Press, 1933. In the Classics of International Law series. The first volume is a photocopy of the original edition in Latin; the second volume contains the English translation by John C. Rolfe and a superb introduction by Coleman Phillipson. This introduction deals with the precursors of Gentili, the place, life, and works of Gentili, his position in law, and his method and conception of law.

———————. *De legationibus libri tres*. 2 vols. New York: Oxford University Press, 1924. This is also in the Classics of International Law series. The first volume is a photocopy of the Latin edition of 1594; the second volume contains the translation by Gordon J. Laing, with an introduction by Ernest Nys dealing with a good concise presentation of the life of Gentili.

Holland, Thomas Erskine. *Studies in International Law*. Oxford, England: Clarendon Press, 1898. The article on Gentili was delivered at All Souls College, November 7, 1874, and, after some additions by Holland, was translated into Italian by Count Aurelio Saffi, thereby reviving both an interest in and a knowledge of Gentili. The first part of the article gives a substantial chronology of Gentili's life; the second part gives an assessment of his work in international law. Includes an appendix with information on the background of the Gentili family, the controversy over the dates of Gentili's birth and death, his will, his published and unpublished writings, and the revived interest in the subject as a result of the lecture.

Phillipson, Coleman. "Albericus Gentilis." In *Great Jurists of the World*, edited by Sir John MacDonnell, vol. 2. Boston: Little, Brown, 1914. Part of the Continental Legal History series. A brief summary of the facts of Gentili's life, with extensive analysis of his three main works.

Simmonds, K. R. "Some English Precursors of Hugo Grotius." *Transactions of the Grotius Society* 43 (1962): 143-157. This is a paper originally read before the Grotius Society on May 1, 1957, dealing with the English precursors of Hugo Grotius in international law, including Gentili. Contains only a brief presentation of Gentili's life and place in the field of international law.

Walker, Thomas Alfred. *A History of the Law of Nations: From the Earliest Times to the Peace of Westphalia, 1648*. Vol. 1. Cambridge, England: Cambridge University Press, 1899. Presents a few facts of Gentili's life but is largely concerned with the content of *The Three Books on the Law of War*.

Robert M. Spector

THÉODORE GÉRICAULT

Born: September 26, 1791; Rouen, France
Died: January 26, 1824; Paris, France
Area of Achievement: Art
Contribution: Géricault helped to move French art away from neoclassicism, which was dominant between the revolutionary and Napoleonic eras, into new, more modern directions. Nineteenth century Romantic and realistic painters alike claimed to have been inspired by his work.

Early Life

Jean-Louis-André-Théodore Géricault was a descendant of a respectable Norman line. His father, Georges-Nicolas Géricault, a prosperous lawyer and later businessman, was forty-eight at the birth of his only child. His mother, Louise-Jeanne-Marie (née Caruel), had turned thirty-nine.

The Géricaults moved to Paris around 1796. Théodore soon entered boarding school and in 1806 commenced study at the Lycée Impérial, an academy known for its fine, classical education. Only an average student, he nevertheless showed artistic talent. Théodore also was fortunate to have been taught by Pierre Bouillon, winner of the 1797 Grand Prix de Rome. Géricault later competed for this government-sponsored award, which carried with it art study in Italy.

The death of his mother in 1808 caused Théodore to reconsider his circumstances. It also brought him closer to home: Théodore decided that he had had enough of academic training and decided to live with Georges-Nicolas. Furthermore, his mother's large estate and his father's business interests allowed the young man to devote himself wholly to art, without concern for finances. One obstacle remained: Georges-Nicolas objected to Théodore's career pursuit. With moral support from his maternal uncle, Jean-Baptiste Caruel, the younger Géricault allegedly went to work but actually entered the studio of Carle Vernet. Thus, Géricault eased his way into art.

Life's Work

According to the professional codes of the day, enrollment in a master's studio was the first of many steps toward status as a painter. Géricault's affinity for Vernet, primarily an equestrian artist, appears logical: One of Géricault's first actions after the death of his mother had been to buy a horse.

As a teacher, Vernet ran a very loose studio, providing his own atmosphere and personal warmth but little artistic direction. Géricault nevertheless maintained a lifelong enthusiasm for both riding and equestrian art. The early twentieth century Parisian critic Louis Dimier ventured, "Only when it came to horses did he paint to perfection." This verdict is open to much scrutiny. It may be more accurate to say that Géricault took equestrian painting from a rather stodgy, still form and gave it life, placing the animals in motion and illustrating their diverse work and sporting roles. To do that, he frequently employed gouache or watercolor washes with brown ink or pencil on beige paper. Yet the artist used oils for his larger, more ambitious works.

After spending roughly two years in Vernet's studio, Géricault may have felt the need for a more rigorous, professional approach. He then became affiliated with Pierre Guérin, a painter who had attained considerable renown in his day and owed inspiration to the revered Jacques-Louis David. A method instructor, Guérin required his students—Eugène Delacroix also was one of them—to paint antiquarian and heavenly subjects. Géricault, however, asserted his individuality. During a particular session, he first began to copy, then radically alter, the composition of his master's work. When queried by a perturbed Guérin, the younger artist allegedly responded, "I had taken it into my head to inject some energy into it, and you can imagine how that turned out." Géricault stayed with the classical painter for only eleven months, into 1811. He then studied independently, frequenting the Louvre. Most authorities admit that the young artist was influenced by the warm colors, brush techniques, and lifelike images of Peter-Paul Rubens, Titian, and the Italian masters.

If scholars disagree on Géricault's style, perhaps this stems from the fact that contemporary French society underwent many changes very quickly— from the turbulent Revolution to the Napoleonic conquests to the restoration of the Bourbon monarchy. Some of the democratic ideals advocated during the Revolution, for example, harked back to classical Greece and Rome; hence, the philosophical commitment and tremendous popularity of the neo-classicist David. Napoleon I, on the other hand, sought to ennoble his own image and contributions. In 1810, the emperor identified two thematic classifications—historic and current—by which the government-sponsored Salon was to judge its art competition. Napoleon also brought to Paris cultural riches from his far-flung conquered lands, rendering the Louvre a truly eclectic treasure chest. Thus, Géricault benefited from a much broader exposure than did, for example, David.

If influences were widening, the attainment of status followed an established track. Géricault therefore enrolled in the École des Beaux Arts and, because of his affiliation, began to enter competitions. Certainly the largest and best known of these, the Salon, accepted his *Charging Chasseur* for its 1812 exhibition. Géricault's work depicted a mounted officer of the Imperial Guard, poised for action. Although executed quickly, it won critical acclaim, more so, in fact, than any of Géricault's subsequent Salon showings. The *Charging Chasseur*—with its warm colors and effective sense of light and motion—also emphasized the artist's interest in military subjects.

Two years later, the Salon displayed both the *Charging Chasseur* and a new creation, the *Wounded Cuirassier* (1814). Reception this time proved to be rather poor. The less buoyant tone of the *Wounded Cuirassier* followed Napoleon's military losses, but the critical ambivalence also may be attributed to stylistic factors and disappointment over the painting's failure to fulfill expectations.

In 1816, Géricault vied for the top award: the Prix de Rome. When he did not capture the honors, he decided to finance his own studies in Italy. Personal as well as art-related reasons motivated him: Géricault had become involved with Alexandrine-Modeste de Saint-Martin Caruel, his uncle's young wife. Perhaps the painter was depressed over this relationship, or maybe he sought foreign refuge before the family became embroiled in a full-fledged scandal. His affair with Alexandrine, continuing after his return from Italy, never proved to be happy, although it produced one son, Georges-Hippolyte, in 1818.

Géricault's Italian odyssey lasted for a year, during which time he became entranced with the work of Michelangelo and other masters. The youthful painter also witnessed a uniquely Roman event, the riderless horse race of Barberi, which meshed his artistic and equestrian interests. Although Géricault rendered many sketches of this intended life-size project, it remained unfinished. Most authorities agree that the tall, slender, handsome painter—with his curly reddish-blond hair and deep-set eyes—was suffering from a lack of confidence. The artistic grandeur of Rome possibly aggravated his perceived inadequacies.

Returning to France in September, 1817, Géricault resumed his friendship with Horace Vernet, the son of his former teacher and an artist in his own right. It was under Vernet's influence that Géricault first produced lithographs, again using military subjects as a theme. Unfortunately, the works hardly sold. Knowing of Géricault's financial independence, his art publisher even advised him to seek another career.

Disappointed over the lithographs and with his child on the way, Géricault spent eighteen intensive months preparing the most important work of his life, *The Raft of the Medusa* (1818-1819), which was based on a controversial contemporary event. A government frigate, the *Medusa*, sank off the coast of Africa, largely because of the incompetence of its captain, who owed his commission to political patronage. The errant officer also retained the most serviceable lifeboats for himself and his friends, forcing the rest of the passengers to construct a raft from the sinking ship's parts. Of the 149 people stranded aboard the improvised vessel, only fifteen survived. Cannibalism, among other horrors, had occurred.

Géricault tackled his project in the manner of a chronicler: He interviewed the survivors and went to local hospitals and morgues to observe the dead and dying. Intensely committed to a realistic portrayal, he prepared numerous sketches. A model, possibly commenting on this frenetic process, said, "Monsieur Géricault had to have complete silence, nobody dared speak or move near him; the least thing disturbed him."

The dramatic, monumental masterpiece—measuring sixteen by twenty-four feet—appeared in the Salon of 1819 but bore the brunt of debate. Disparate factions blamed one another for the circumstances that ultimately determined the *Medusa*'s fate, and many argued about Géricault's political interpretations. Writing in typically partisan journals, art critics also viewed the painting harshly. Its dark tones and frank depiction of human torment also worked against it. Still, the Salon awarded Géricault a medal for his labor of love. One judge even commissioned him to do another painting. Fatigued from the intensive preparation and controversial aftermath of *The Raft of the Medusa*, however, Géricault transferred the proposed assignment to his friend Delacroix. French art circles may have been divided in their assessment of *The Raft of the Medusa*, but in 1820 an English gallery owner invited Géricault to show his work in London, where it was praised. The painting subsequently traveled to Dublin.

Géricault returned to Paris in December, 1821. The following year, a friend who specialized in mental disorders commissioned the artist to paint portraits of ten psychiatric patients; five of these portraits survive. Notwithstanding the radical changes in psychiatry, the series deserves respect for its realistic approach: a study of men and women with problems rather than the subhumans popularly perceived during the early nineteenth century.

A normal existence, and therefore painting, would become increasingly difficult for Géricault toward the end of his life. In 1822, he suffered two falls while horseback riding. Undaunted, he continued to pursue his favorite sport and also to sketch more advanced versions of *African Slave Trade* (1823) and *Liberation of the Prisoners of the Spanish Inquisition* (1823). Both of these paintings took an enlightened view; the second was critical of the restored Bourbon monarchy.

Géricault never allowed his wounds to heal properly. By 1823, the riding injuries caused his spine to deteriorate. Doctors operated several times but ultimately failed to save him. Géricault died on January 26, 1824, at the age of thirty-two.

Summary

The three paintings that Théodore Géricault exhibited during his lifetime currently hang in the Louvre, testimony to his endurance as an artist. When his studio was cleared for sale ten months after his death, many works surfaced, far more than had been known to exist.

Géricault likely doubted his compositional and drawing skills and, therefore, sketched numerous life studies before proceeding with a master painting. Once confident of his ability to portray people and events realistically, he added the motion, lighting effects, and drama which often characterize him as a Romantic. If experts disagree on Géricault's style, they also ponder his social consciousness. The artist, in his later years, expanded his repertoire from military and equestrian themes to controversial political subjects and studies of the downtrodden. During his British tenure, for example, he sketched a public hanging, a paralytic woman, and an impoverished man. Géricault nevertheless became increasingly enamored of the relatively highbrow, distinctly English, equestrian crowd.

The artist's premature death left his life open to speculation and, occasionally, legend. Yet, from 1824 through much of the twentieth century, various patrons of the arts—collectors, gallery owners, scholars, and museum directors—have shown consistent interest in what now appear to be his prodigious efforts.

Bibliography

Canaday, John. *The Lives of the Painters*. Vol. 3, *Neoclassic to Post-Impressionist*. New York: W. W. Norton, 1969. A chapter describing the classic-Romantic schism in France contains a short synopsis of Géricault's life and creative output. The painter appears as a prominent force, whose work embodied a number of nineteenth century trends.

Eitner, Lorenz. *Géricault*. Los Angeles: Los Angeles County Museum of Art, 1971. Text accompanies this catalog of 125 paintings (plates) displayed during a 1971 exhibition. The introductory chapter mostly discusses the posthumous fame and changing perceptions of Géricault's art. Also includes a ten-page timeline and a table of exhibitions and literature.

_____. *Géricault: His Life and Work*. Ithaca, N.Y.: Cornell University Press, 1982. Fusing biography and art history, nearly four hundred pages yield a comprehensive study of Géricault. Extremely useful for assessing the creative process: how his original ideas and subject matter changed during the course of a painting. Contains many color and black-and-white plates.

Grunchec, Philippe. *Géricault's Horses: Drawings and Watercolors*. New York: Vendome Press, 1985. Although more than an equestrian artist, Géricault elevated the genre to new heights and broadened its dimensions. This book examines horse painting as the primary nexus between the master's career and outside life. Contains a bibliography, a chronology of exhibitions, and numerous plates, most of which are in color.

_____. *Master Drawings by Géricault*. Washington, D.C.: International Exhibitions Foundation, 1985. Heavily illustrated with reproductions of Géricault's sketches, this work seeks to demonstrate his stylistic and thematic tendencies. Text also discusses friends and other artists who influenced him, as well as the posthumous dispersal of his art. Contains a timeline and a well-annotated list of paintings.

Lethève, Jacques. *Daily Life of French Artists in the Nineteenth Century.*
Translated by Hilary E. Paddon. New York: Praeger, 1972. The book
offers insights into how artists lived, executed and marketed their work,
and gained recognition. Students of Géricault will find several interesting details and quotations, but the most important contribution is an
understanding of the institutions (such as the Salon) which made an
impact upon his professional career. Contains notes, a bibliography, and
illustrations.

Lynn C. Kronzek

CONRAD GESNER

Born: March 26, 1516; Zurich, Swiss Confederation
Died: December 13, 1565; Zurich, Swiss Confederation
Areas of Achievement: Philology, medicine, and natural history
Contribution: Gesner was a Renaissance man, who collected, studied, and
   published the works of earlier literary, medical, and natural history authorities; he also compiled encyclopedic surveys of earlier scholarship
   in these fields. Equally as important, however, was Gesner's extension of
   knowledge, particularly in the fields of philology and natural history.

Early Life
Conrad Gesner was one of many children of Ursus Gesner, a Zurich fur-
rier, and Agathe Frick. His family formed an undistinguished branch of a
Swiss family that would become famous for having produced several acclaimed scholars, physicians, and scientists in the sixteenth through eighteenth centuries. Conrad was the godson and protegé of the Swiss Protestant
reformer Huldrych Zwingli, and during his early school years he lived with
an uncle, a minister, who engendered in him an interest in theology and
botany. First Gesner attended the Carolinum, then he entered the Fraümun-
ster seminary, in Zurich. There, in the Humanist tradition, he studied the
Latin classics. After the death of both Zwingli and Gesner's father on the
battlefield at Kappel in defense of Zwingli's reformed religion in 1531,
Gesner left Zurich for Strasbourg. There he expanded his study of the ancient languages by studying Hebrew with Wolfgang Capito at the Strasbourg
Academy.
   After his interest in theological studies waned, Gesner began to study
medicine alongside his studies of ancient languages. Gesner traveled to
Bourges and then to Paris for medical studies. In 1535, he returned to
Strasbourg, then to Zurich. In Zurich, Gesner married a young girl from a
poor family, whose later ill health placed great strain on his meager financial
resources. They lived for some time in Basel, before moving to Lausanne.

Life's Work
From 1537 until 1540, Gesner held the first chair of Greek at the Lausanne
Academy, after which he resigned his position in Lausanne and moved to
Montpellier to continue medical and botanical studies. He received a doctorate in medicine at Basel in 1541. Later that year, Gesner settled in Zurich,
where he became the city's chief physician. In Zurich, Gesner also held the
chair of philosophy. In 1552, a serious illness sapped his strength. Gesner
lived on the edge of poverty, but about this time he was awarded the position
of *canonicus* in an attempt to improve his financial situation. Although Gesner's health suffered during the last ten years of his life, in 1555 the Zurich

city magistrates appointed Gesner professor of natural history. He held this professorship until his death during an epidemic of the plague in Zurich in 1565. Gesner's scholarship centered on philology, medicine, and natural history. His work in natural history, which interested him most, was in the fields of botany, zoology, paleontology, and crystallography.

Proficient in many languages, Gesner undertook numerous philological and linguistic studies. His most significant contribution in philology is his four-volume *Bibliotheca universalis* (1545-1555), a biobibliography of all Greek, Latin, and Hebrew writers, ancient to contemporary, known in Gesner's day. Considered the first great annotated bibliography of printed books, it established Gesner's reputation as a philologist and put him in contact with many contemporary scholars. Gesner also published translations and editions of many classical texts. In linguistics, he produced a Greek-Latin dictionary, one of the first studies ever attempted in comparative grammar, in which he cataloged around 130 ancient to contemporary languages and dialects. Gesner also prepared editions and compilations of classical medical texts, as well as publishing original treatises on medical and pharmaceutical topics.

Gesner's observation of plants, a result of his philological work, led to his interest in their medical uses. He collected and read widely in classical botanical works, from which he extracted information for encyclopedic publications such as his *Historia plantarum et vires ex Dioscoride, Paulo Aegineta, Theophrasto, Plinio, et recētioribus Graecis* (1541; the history of plants and their powers from Dioscorides, Paulo Aegineta, Theophrastus, Pliny, and the more recent Greek authors).

Gesner also developed an interest in plants and animals, and, like most sixteenth century botanists, he focused upon collecting, describing, and classifying both known and newly discovered plants. Along with other northern botanists, Gesner increased the number and accuracy of available empirical descriptions of plants in several ways. He recorded many original empirical observations, and he provided numerous descriptions of new and little-known plants. For example, his treatise *De tulipa Turcarum* (1561; on the Turkish tulip) was the first descriptive monograph on that plant. One of the leaders of the trend toward realistic illustrations, this botanist himself drew more than fifteen hundred plates for his *Opera botanica* (1751-1771; botanical works), which contained the bulk of his botanical writings. Gesner also encouraged observation of plants by founding a botanical garden and a natural history collection in Zurich.

Gesner is especially noteworthy in this period for the system of botanical classification he developed. Gesner grouped plants according to whether they were flowering or nonflowering and vascular or nonvascular, among other things. Upon the suggestion of Valerius Cordus, Gesner also chose a plant's organs of generation, the flower and fruit, as the key characteristics by which to classify it. In addition, Gesner first advanced the idea of natural families, and in so doing he moved biological classification toward natural systems. He distinguished different species of a genus and was the first botanist to utilize seeds to establish kinship between otherwise dissimilar plants.

Among Gesner's contributions to zoology can be listed editions of earlier zoological treatises, but his most important accomplishment in this field was the publication of his monumental, five-volume *Historiae animalium* (1551-1587; history of animals). In *Historiae animalium*, Gesner included all animals described by earlier authorities, generally without questioning the real existence of the animal or the validity of the description. He classified members of the animal kingdom according to the Aristotelian scheme, and within each group he arranged individual animals alphabetically by name. For each animal included, Gesner listed all known names, as well as the animal's range and habitat, habits, diet, morphology and anatomy, diseases, usefulness (including medical uses), and role in literature and history. The work is heavily illustrated, containing a woodcut for every animal. Many of the illustrations, drawn by the author himself, are quite novel and show evidence of careful empirical observation.

In Gesner's only publication in the field of paleontology, *De rerum fossilium, lapidum, et gemmarum maximè, figuris et similitudinibus liber* (1565; on the shapes and resemblances of fossils, stones, and gems), Gesner used the term "fossil" to refer to any object dug from the earth. He included extinct vegetable and animal forms, now rightly called fossils, in this group, but he also included minerals, ores, shells, stone axes, pencils, and other debris in the same category. Although Gesner did regard some exceptional fossils as petrified animals, for the most part he accepted the traditional theory that they were figures formed in stone by astral influences, by subterranean vapors, or by internal vegetative forces during the growth of the surrounding stone. In his classification of these objects, Gesner abandoned the medieval alphabetical system. Instead, Gesner divided his fossils into fifteen categories, using the criteria of their geometric shapes or resemblance to a variety of inanimate and living things. Gesner placed crystals in his first category (fossils whose forms are based upon geometric concepts) and described them according to the angles they exhibited. His *De rerum fossilium* was the first work on fossils to contain a significant number of illustrations, as well as one of the earliest works to include illustrations of crystals.

Summary

As a Renaissance Humanist, Conrad Gesner placed great value on studying previous scholarly works; in so doing, he accumulated an encyclopedic knowledge of the arts, the sciences, and medicine. Gesner also collected, edited, and published the works of selected literary, medical, and natural history writers, from the Greek and Latin classics to his own day. He is credited with collecting and surveying a vast amount of previous knowledge in encyclopedic publications in philology and natural history. He was one of the earliest and best postmedieval encyclopedists. In philology, his work initiated modern bibliographical studies and earned for him the title "father of bibliography." Writing just before European biologists were swamped by the deluge of new plant and animal forms from the New World and the microscopic realm, Gesner sought to collect previous knowledge about the living world, and his massive histories of plants and animals are testaments to his industry. Of the few zoological encyclopedias produced in the sixteenth century, Gesner's *Historiae animalium* ranks as the best, and it immediately earned for him an international reputation. Moreover, Gesner made original contributions to the fields of philology, medicine, botany, zoology, and geology. In philology, his research in comparative linguistics was unprecedented.

In extending knowledge, however, Gesner's most important contribution was to natural history. He was among the first early modern authors to question earlier biological accounts and to present firsthand descriptions and illustrations based on his own observation of nature. In botany, Gesner offered improved illustrations and innovative classification schemes. In presenting a scheme of classification according to structure, particularly according to the reproductive organs, Gesner advanced an idea that would later transform the study of botany. Although Gesner exerted little influence upon contemporary natural historians, in the eighteenth century the biologist Linnaeus acknowledged his debt to Gesner's focus on floral structures and the nature of seeds in botanical classification. Today the plant family *Gesneriaceae*, composed of about fifteen hundred species of plants, is named in Gesner's honor.

Gesner also contributed to the sweeping changes under way in the fields of zoology and geology in the sixteenth and seventeenth centuries. His *Historiae animalium*, a landmark in the history of zoology, occasionally displays a critical attitude when presenting collected knowledge. The studies of animal physiology and pathology presented there have led some historians to consider Gesner the founder of veterinary science. The *Historiae animalium* is also significant in the history of zoology because it introduced new and accurate descriptions and illustrations of the animal world. So innovative was that zoological work that Georges Cuvier considered it to be the founding work of modern zoology. Finally, even in his last treatise on fossils, Gesner broke ancient and medieval bonds. His classification and illustrations of fossils set the stage for the development of modern paleontology and crystallography.

Bibliography

Adams, Frank Dawson. *The Birth and Development of the Geological Sciences*. Reprint. New York: Dover, 1954. Adams' excellent history of geology includes the best account in English of Gesner's system of fossil classification, two pages of reprinted illustrations of fossils from *De rerum fossilium*, as well as a brief biography.

Bay, J. Christian. "Conrad Gesner (1516-1565): The Father of Bibliography." *Papers of the Bibliographical Society of America* 10, no. 2 (1916): 53-86. The best existing biography of Gesner in English. Focuses on Gesner's contribution to bibliographic studies and places it within the context of the humanistic studies of the Reformation. Contains a helpful bibliography of the early editions of Gesner's *Bibliotheca universalis*, *Historiae animalium*, and supplements to them where applicable.

Crombie, A. C. *Medieval and Early Modern Science*. Vol. 2, *Science in the Later Middle Ages and Early Modern Times, XIII-XVII Centuries*. Garden City, N.Y.: Doubleday, 1959. Offers a general description of Gesner's work in botany, zoology, and paleontology. Gesner is placed within the broader history of these sciences.

Debus, Allen G. *Man and Nature in the Renaissance*. New York: Cambridge University Press, 1978. Debus presents a very good, brief, and somewhat detailed account of Gesner's *Historiae animalium*. Chapter 3, "The Study of Nature in a Changing World," is especially recommended for placing Gesner's scholarship in natural history within the context of Renaissance science.

Reed, Karen M. "Renaissance Humanism and Botany." *Annals of Science* 33 (1976): 519-542. This excellent article describes the translating, collecting, and other work of the Renaissance Humanists in botany in the late fifteenth and sixteenth centuries. Reed gives an account of the milieu in which Gesner's work took place.

Topsell, Edward. *The Historie of Foure-Footed Beastes*. New York: Da Capo Press, 1973.

──────────. *The Historie of Serpents*. New York: Da Capo Press, 1973. Both of these works are based heavily upon Gesner's work. They are recommended reading as primary documents illustrating Gesner's zoological work.

Martha Ellen Webb

LORENZO GHIBERTI

Born: c. 1378; Pelago, near Florence
Died: December 1, 1455; Florence
Area of Achievement: Art
Contribution: Ghiberti's sculpture for the baptistery in Florence is often con-
sidered the first example of Renaissance art in Italy.

Early Life

Lorenzo Ghiberti was born in Pelago, near Florence, into a family connected to the arts. His father was a goldsmith, and Ghiberti was educated in
that craft, which went beyond the obvious training in mechanical skill to an
understanding of the problems of design and a general theoretical knowledge
of art. Ghiberti began his career as a fresco painter, and he painted a very
good fresco in the palace of Sigismondo Malatesta, the ruler of Rimini. He
had probably gone there first to avoid the plague which had infested Florence, but in 1401 he was urged to return to Florence in order to enter a
competition for a commission to produce a set of doors for the baptistery
there, a building of considerable age and reputation to which the Pisan
sculptor Andrea Pisano had added a much-admired set of decorated bronze
doors in the 1330's.

The competition for this major project was formidable and included Fi-
lippo Brunelleschi, who had a considerable reputation. Ghiberti was still
relatively unknown, and his credentials rested on his skills not as a sculptor
but as a goldsmith and fresco painter. According to one report of the contest,
the list of candidates was eventually reduced to Brunelleschi and Ghiberti,
and the suggestion was made that the two men collaborate. Brunelleschi may
have withdrawn because of a reluctance to work in tandem or because of
friendship with Ghiberti. Whatever the case, Ghiberti was awarded the commission, and the rest of his artistic life was spent, in the main, on his work
on the doors, since the first set (begun in 1403) led his sponsors to order a
second set in 1425.

Life's Work

The baptistery of the cathedral at Florence is separated from the main
building, standing a street's width to the west of the entrance to the church.
It is a very old building, built on the site of a Roman ruin, and may have
been begun as early as the fifth century. Dressed in green-and-white marble,
it is a work of art in its own right. In the early 1300's, however, the Guild of
Cloth Importers, which had assumed the responsibility for decorating the
building, had Pisano, a Pisan sculptor, add a double-leaf door to the south
side of the building. It was the first major use of bronze in Florence and
proved a great artistic success, clearly indicating in its fundamentally Gothic

elements the influence of classical design. This development was a precursor to the change in artistic sensibility which led to the beginnings of Renaissance sculpture.

If Pisano's door suggested that the Gothic world was passing, it has been said that Ghiberti's execution of the second set of doors marks the beginning of the Renaissance in Florence—and the beginning of the grandest period in the use of bronze sculpture in the city. It would be unfair to patronize Pisano and his work on the baptistery; Ghiberti, while generally thought to be the finer artist, had the advantage of Pisano's example, both technically and artistically. Bronze sculpture was a lost art in the Middle Ages, and Pisano had been obliged to bring a bell maker in from Venice to cast his doors. Ghiberti spent years training his crew in the art of bronze casting, and in the process he added to the sophistication and subtlety of the very difficult technique of that art. More important, perhaps, was the way in which Ghiberti took the design of the doors forward into the wider, freer, more dramatic world of Renaissance art.

The simplest, crudest definition of the birth of the Renaissance is that the sensibility (social, religious, aesthetic—indeed, psychological) of Italy turned from Heaven to the world, from God to man, to an appreciation of the fact that life need not simply be a preparation for the afterlife but was an exciting, potentially wide-ranging celebration of existence, however fragile that existence might be. In Greek and Roman sculptures, the artists found their models for such expressions of exultation and confidence in man at his best. The body became the outward, aesthetic sign not only of the beautiful soul (in Neoplatonic terms) but also of the beautiful life, the boundless possibilities for the individual and for the state. That beautiful body shows up stunningly in Ghiberti's work on the doors. Indeed, Ghiberti's competition piece, which was set for all the competitors, probably shows this shift most clearly—how the Gothic inclination toward flatness and rejection of realism and drama had (with Pisano's help) been overcome. Isaac, on his knees, his glowingly muscled torso turned in *contrapposto*, his head skewed to expose his neck to Abraham's knife, is a gorgeous young man, sculpted tenderly, with an appreciation for the human body.

The Ghiberti doors did not, however, stop at graceful celebrations of human comeliness. Ghiberti's subjects were quite properly religious, and in his accommodation of the human figure to the stories from the Bible, he also added a realistic sense of place and a sense of psychological moment. The north door was his first commission; it took twenty-one years (from 1403 to 1424) to complete it. (Donatello, who was to become a far greater sculptor than his master, was a member of Ghiberti's young crew.) The subjects of the twenty-eight panels included figures from the New Testament, Evangelists, and the Fathers of the Church.

Yet such seemingly austere subjects did not deter Ghiberti from putting into play a much more dramatically exciting conception of how the panels could be used. There is something flatly stagy about the Pisano work; it is splendidly worked technically, but it is somewhat stiff. Ghiberti, however, takes to the contours of the Gothic borders of the panels (a holdover from the Pisano design) with ease and makes use of the space much more gracefully. Pisano's work is clearly rectangular, set tightly inside the flow of the margins; Ghiberti worked his design into the concave spaces, achieving a sense of space, of depth into the panels. He also possessed a deeper understanding of how to make the figures tell a story that would appeal to the emotions.

Ghiberti's determination to make his art real, to give it depth, was his greatest gift. His second set of doors, which took up the last half of his career, were begun in the mid-1420's and not completed until 1452. They are considered his masterpiece, and they allowed him to extend himself in ways which were severely limited in the earlier work. He was able to break away from the small panels into ten larger, rectangular spaces, which gave him not only more room but also a shape he really understood. As John Pope-Hennessy, one of his best critics, said, it is important to remember that he was a painter and that he knew how to put more than one thing into a seemingly flat, extended area.

With the second set, Ghiberti continued his biblical tales, often working a series of incidents into the bronze in ways which led to the culminating moment with considerable dramatic skill. He knew how to tell a story, and he knew how to divide his space horizontally, vertically, or diagonally in order to make the divisions support the narrative sequence of the various scenes. Also, he was much better at creating a sense of internal space within the panels.

Although Ghiberti's international reputation rested heavily on his work on the doors, he was not confined to working on them exclusively. He was equally adept at two-dimensional design, and his windows for the cathedral, if less well known, are also masterpieces. His window depicting the Assumption of the Virgin is strongly realistic not only in its portrayal of the Virgin's clothing but also in its depiction of her as a poignant young human being. Enthroned in a triumphant circle of swirling angels, she is proportionally sized to give a sense of depth.

There are also a handful of freestanding statues by Ghiberti in Florence. The first of these, a figure of Saint John the Baptist (1412-1416), is important for being bronze (Florentine sculptors normally worked in marble), but it is also significant because it strongly reveals an aspect of his work which can sometimes be missed in the enthusiasm for the revolutionary aspects of his bronze sculpture. This piece is clearly of an earlier time, an example of what is called the International Gothic style, and underlines the point that Ghiberti never entirely broke free from late Gothic tendencies, which can be seen closely entwined with the classical elements in all of his work, particularly in the graceful, sweeping postures which his figures often affect.

As is often the case at the beginning of a change in the artistic sensibility, Ghiberti was soon overshadowed by younger men, such as Donatello and Nanni di Banco, who were less encumbered by the last vestiges of the Gothic and whose work is less stylized, less elegantly mannered, and just slightly further down the line toward the new Humanism in their more realistic vivacity. Still, Ghiberti's work on the baptistery, particularly in the later door, called the "Porta del Paradiso," shows that he broke with tradition more as he grew older. At the National Gallery in Washington, D.C., there is a terra-cotta sculpture of the Madonna and Child—intimate, natural, and lyrically serious—which is attributed to Ghiberti; if it was indeed executed by him, it is clear that there were moments when Ghiberti was as much a Renaissance artist as Donatello.

In his later years, he kept a journal of his ideas as a practicing artist, *I commentarii* (c. 1447; commentaries), in which he discussed not only the technical aspects of his craft but also the relation of art to society, morals, and religion. That modest pride can be seen again on the Paradise door; in one of the ornamental roundels that decorate the frame, Ghiberti's bald, round head, his arched eyebrows, and his slightly pawky look suggest that he was a man well satisfied with what he had wrought.

Summary

If Pisano was the man responsible for bringing bronze to Florence, then Lorenzo Ghiberti was the artist who established its use as a medium for expressing the glorious aspirations of the Renaissance. Taking the example left by Pisano almost seventy years previous, he brought it into the mainstream of intellectual and aesthetic expression. Clearly a lesser artist than Donatello, Ghiberti was no less a major contributor to the aesthetic perfection of Florence, and his doors on the baptistery in Florence well deserve the attention they have always received. Indeed, a walk around the outside of the baptistery is a journey not only through time but also through the process whereby a civilization moves forward, in this case from modest intimations of things to come in the Pisano door through the surprising leap forward in Ghiberti's first door to the aesthetic triumph of the second door.

Bibliography

Avery, Charles. *Florentine Renaissance Sculpture*. London: John Murray, 1982. This handsome, modest paperback is well illustrated. Its first three chapters lead the reader into the late Gothic and on to the Renaissance, putting Ghiberti firmly between his predecessor, Pisano, and his successor, Donatello.

Borsook, Eve. *The Companion Guide to Florence*. London: Collins, 1966.

A guidebook to the city, this volume will help place Florence's artists in context.

Godfrey, F. M. *Italian Sculpture: 1250-1700*. New York: Taplinger Publishing, 1967. A well-illustrated, step-by-step historical survey beginning with the Romanesque period and ending with the Baroque. With very clear, helpful comments on Ghiberti.

Krautheimer, Richard. *Lorenzo Ghiberti*. Princeton, N.J.: Princeton University Press, 1956. This work may be somewhat daunting to the lay reader, but it is worth the effort.

Pope-Hennessy, John. *The Study and Criticism of Italian Sculpture*. Princeton, N.J.: Princeton University Press, 1980. Includes a detailed essay on Ghiberti by an expert on the subject. Excellent illustrations.

Seymour, Charles. *Sculpture in Italy: 1400 to 1500*. Harmondsworth, England: Penguin Books, 1966. Particularly good on the detail of the bronze doors. Contains a chapter on the competition which resulted in Ghiberti's winning the commission.

Charles Pullen

VINCENZO GIOBERTI

Born: April 5, 1801; Turin, Kingdom of Sardinia
Died: October 26, 1852; Paris, France
Areas of Achievement: Philosophy, religion, government, and politics
Contribution: Gioberti contributed the first comprehensive political program
for the Risorgimento—the Italian national unification movement. He rep-
resented the progressive Catholic political tradition in nineteenth century
Italy and sought to redefine the Church's political role in the process of
creating the new Italian nation.

Early Life

Vincenzo Gioberti was born in Turin on April 5, 1801. He lost his father,
Giuseppe, at an early age, and his mother, Marianna Capra—a learned and
deeply religious woman—died on December 24, 1819. Gioberti received his
education from a school run by a Catholic religious order—the Fathers of
the Oratory, in Turin. Despite his ill health as a child, he studied diligently
and demonstrated a particular interest in the writings of the Italian poet
Vittorio Alfieri and the French philosopher Jean-Jacques Rousseau. Gioberti
entered the religious order but apparently without much enthusiasm. In his
studies for the priesthood, he became convinced of the need for religious
reform and for the reconciliation between the Christian faith and modern
science. After earning a theology degree in 1823, Gioberti joined the faculty
of the theological college at the University of Turin. He was ordained a
priest in 1825. The following year, he received an appointment as chaplain
to the royal court of King Charles Felix of Piedmont-Sardinia.

Gioberti's service to the Savoy monarch in Turin did not alter his personal
aversion to political authoritarianism. As a young man, he harbored the
democratic and nationalist sentiments of many educated Italians in the early
nineteenth century. The Italy of Gioberti's youth existed only as a "geographical expression"—an odd assortment of kingdoms, duchies, and prin-
cipalities running the length of the Italian peninsula. Italians, inspired by the
political ideas and events of the French Revolution, nurtured their aspirations for an independent, united Italy. The obstacles to unification were
immense. Much of northern Italy was part of the Austrian Empire; Spanish
royalty ruled southern Italy and Sicily; and the pope exercised sovereignty
over a large part of the central region. Moreover, the European powers had
agreed to maintain the status quo in Italy, even by military intervention if
necessary. Many Italian nationalists, in their hopes for unification, looked to
the strongest independent Italian state—Piedmont-Sardinia—for leadership.
The conservative Savoy monarchs, however, had no desire to encourage
political upheaval, nor did they wish to offend the Papacy or the European
powers. Without the leadership of the Savoy monarchy or any other political

authority, the task of Italian unification fell to a loosely connected network of secret patriotic societies. Gioberti's political activity began with his involvement with these conspiratorial organizations.

Life's Work

Gioberti first established contact with a secret society in 1828, when he traveled through northern Italy. During these travels (under the constant surveillance of the Austrian police), he also met with Giacomo Leopardi and Alessandro Manzoni, two leading nationalist writers. Later, he became acquainted with Young Italy, the republican society founded by Giuseppe Mazzini in 1831. He openly sympathized with Young Italy until Mazzini sponsored an unsuccessful insurrection in Piedmont in 1834.

Because of his preaching on civic and political matters, and his radical religious opinions, Gioberti was dismissed from the royal court in May, 1833. Shortly thereafter, he was arrested and imprisoned on the charge of advocating a republican form of government and distributing copies of Mazzini's newspaper *Young Italy* among Piedmontese soldiers. Given the choice between a lengthy prison sentence or exile, he left for France in September, 1833.

After a year in Paris without finding means for study or suitable employment, he accepted a teaching position at the Gaggia College in Brussels. There he began an intense period of writing. He published studies of aesthetics and the supernatural, a critique of Jesuit doctrines, and an introduction to philosophy. His most important work, *Del primato morale e civile degli italiani* (on the moral and civil primacy of the Italians), was published in two volumes in 1843.

In *Del primato morale e civile degli italiani*, Gioberti presented a far-ranging theological and historical justification for Italian independence and unity. He recounted Italy's past greatness as the center of the Roman Empire and Christian civilization. He reminded Italians of the moral and political legacy that they had bequeathed to the modern world, and he called on his country to resume its historic role as a leader among nations. In his program for a new Italy, he envisioned a federation of independent states, free from foreign rule, united under the aegis of a papal president, and protected by the strong military arm of the House of Savoy. Gioberti dismissed the idea of unification through a popular insurrection as dangerous and impractical. Instead, he looked to the rulers of each Italian state to demonstrate their patriotism and their political wisdom by enacting progressive reforms and joining the national federation on a voluntary basis. Gioberti's outline for Italian independence and unification included several practical suggestions: abolishing tariffs and duties; standardizing weights, measures, and currency; and other forms of economic cooperation.

With *Del primato morale e civile degli italiani*, Gioberti established his reputation as the leading theorist of Italian unification. The tedious, seven-hundred-page work was widely read and discussed, despite the ban on its circulation outside Piedmont. *Del primato morale e civile degli italiani* lifted the morale of Italian nationalists. Both King Charles Albert of Piedmont-Sardinia and Pope Pius IX came under its spell. Gioberti's program for unification inspired political moderates to action. Many nationalists in the upper classes feared the economic and social upheaval that might accompany unification. They were wary of any participation of the masses in the unification movement, and they found much assurance in Gioberti's idea of creating an Italian nation "from above."

Some Italian nationalists, even among the moderate element, were skeptical of Gioberti's proposals. He gave no indication of how to deal with Austria and its powerful army in northern Italy. His hopes for political cooperation among the rulers of the Italian states seemed hopelessly naïve. The most controversial point was the idea of a pope as president of a federation of Italian states. Gioberti's critics scoffed at the notion that the pope could have any positive role in Italian unification. Their criticism was well justified. The Papal States had a reputation unsurpassed in Europe for political oppression, corruption, and misrule. The Papacy stood as a defender of the old order and an obstacle to political progress. Many nationalists believed that unification would be completed only when the pope surrendered civil authority over his territory and allowed Rome to become the capital of the new Italian nation. Yet when Pius became the new pontiff in 1846, the political climate in the Papal States changed markedly. The youthful, energetic ruler immediately instituted a series of democratic reforms within the Papal States, disbanded his mercenary army, and granted amnesty to political prisoners. His popularity grew throughout Italy, and he won support even among anticlerics. The explosion of revolutionary sentiment in 1848 eventually overtook the pontiff's program of reform, and Pius retreated behind a wall of intransigent conservatism. For a time, however, Gioberti's idea of a liberal pope seemed to be vindicated.

Gioberti's writing won for him national renown. He was recognized as the leader of the *Veri italiani* (true Italians), a circle of distinguished political moderates living in exile, and began corresponding with Charles Albert. The king, in turn, recognized his achievement by granting him an annual pension, which Gioberti donated to the church charity in Turin. While residing in Paris in 1846, he was elected to the Subalpine (Piedmontese) Parliament. He returned to Turin after almost fifteen years in exile, a celebrated figure in Italian political life. When he traveled through northern Italy, crowds greeted him as a national hero. In July, 1848, he was elected president of the Chamber of Deputies. In December, the king invited him to form a government.

Gioberti's tenure as prime minister was short and undistinguished. He lacked the requisite political skills and the ability to compromise. Somewhat vain and aloof, he refused to consult with his cabinet and advisers. His ineptness became apparent during a crisis in foreign affairs. An insurrection in Rome had driven the pope from the city. Gioberti sought ways to restore him to power before the European governments intervened. His attempts failed. The French army occupied the Papal States and ended the short-lived Roman Republic. The popular uprisings of 1848—particularly the one in Rome—left Pius frightened, embittered, and vindictive. He disavowed all progressive ideas and reforms, placed Gioberti's *Del primato morale e civile degli italiani* on the Index (list of works banned by the Church), and restored authoritarian rule to the Papal States.

Gioberti resigned in February, 1849, over the crisis in Tuscany. A popular uprising there had opened the way for unification with Piedmont. He refused to send troops to secure the region, and Austrian forces eventually restored order. In the spring of 1849, he accepted the post of ambassador to France and remained in Paris until his death. His frustrating experience in Italian politics led him to write *Il rinnovamento civile d'Italia* (the civil renewal of Italy) in 1851. By this time, he had accepted the position of other political moderates that national unification was possible only under the auspices of the King of Piedmont-Sardinia. Gioberti died suddenly on October 26, 1852, leaving many of his writings unfinished.

Summary

In calling for papal leadership in Italy, Vincenzo Gioberti revived Guelphist politics—a tradition that dated from the Middle Ages, when the popes vied with the Holy Roman Emperors for political power in Europe. As a neo-Guelphist, he sought to restore papal authority as the moral and political arbiter of Christian nations. His critics dismissed this as a medieval solution to a modern problem, but some of Gioberti's ideas were validated by subsequent events. His belief that Italy needed to build a strong navy and acquire a colonial empire reflected foreign-policy goals followed by Italian governments until the end of World War II. The idea of making Italy "from above" was ultimately affirmed in the statesmanship of Count Cavour. For all of his assurances of the "moral and civil primacy of the Italians," Gioberti actually had little faith in the political maturity of his countrymen. He believed in paternalistic, Christian government—"everything for the people, nothing by the people." As he had envisioned, Italy was unified without the involvement of most Italians, but this lack of popular participation in the unification process ultimately proved a source of political weakness for the new Italian state.

Bibliography

Berkeley, C. F. H. *Italy in the Making*. Vol. 1. Cambridge: Cambridge University Press, 1932. This survey of Italian unification is a helpful source.

The author, sympathetic to the Catholic church and the moderate political elements in the unification movement, deals at length with Gioberti's intellectual and political contributions.

Coppa, Frank J., ed. *Dictionary of Modern Italian History*. Westport, Conn.: Greenwood Press, 1985. Contains a brief biography of Gioberti taken from Italian sources.

Gioberti, Vincenzo. *Essay on the Beautiful*. Translated by Edward Thomas. London: Simpkin and Marshall, 1860. An English translation of one of Gioberti's several published works.

Grew, Raymond. *A Sterner Plan for Italian Unity: The Italian National Society in the Risorgimento*. Princeton, N.J.: Princeton University Press, 1963. Places Gioberti in the broader context of the moderate political tradition in the unification movement.

Mack Smith, Denis. *The Making of Italy, 1796-1870*. New York: Harper & Row, 1968. A survey of the Italian unification movement, more balanced than Berkeley's history in its assessment of Gioberti and the political moderates.

Michael F. Hembree

GIORGIONE

Born: c. 1477; Castelfranco, Republic of Venice
Died: c. 1510; Venice
Area of Achievement: Art
Contribution: The Renaissance celebration of the ordinary human being enjoying the pleasures of the natural life not in the great public paintings, but in the intimacy of the small canvas, suitable for displaying in the simple living room, found its painter in Giorgione, the master of the private moment.

Early Life

Giorgione is one of the great mysteries of art history. Little is known of his life, early or middle, and there is no late since he died so young. Of that death, there is some certainty, since comment is made upon it in a letter. He was probably born in the Veneto in the small town of Castelfranco, probably of humble parents. He was probably known originally in Venice as Giorgio da Castelfranco, although Giorgio seems to have given way to the Venetian version of the same name, Zorzo.

Given the extent of his career in Venice, it is likely that Giorgione came into the city sometime around 1500, and joined the workshop of Giovanni Bellini. He seems to have established a reputation for himself quickly, and in the decade left to him he established himself not only as a painter but also as a fresco artist, and several fresco façades on buildings throughout the city are supposed to have been painted by him, none of which is extant. The source for any knowledge of him lies mainly with the painter-historian Giorgio Vasari, who presents a romantic picture of a handsome, diminutive, gregarious man, socially popular and eagerly sought after for his art. Yet Vasari wrote some thirty years or more after Giorgione's death, and there was a tendency in biography at that time to romanticize subjects. Still in existence, however, is a 1507 document in which Giorgione is commissioned to do a painting for the Doge's palace; evidence of a quarrel over a fee for a fresco, which was settled by a panel of adjudicators, including Giovanni Bellini, in Giorgione's favor; and a letter announcing his death.

It is likely that Bellini was Giorgione's teacher as well as employer, since much of what would be seen as Giorgione's style can be traced to certain aspects of Bellini's own work. Whatever the facts, Giorgione was busily at work in the middle of the first decade of the sixteenth century. His was a short career, but he was to be mentioned as one of the great painters by Baldassare Castiglione in *Il libro del Cortegiano* (1528), and Marcantonio Michiel, in *Notizia d'opere di disegno* (wr. 1525-1543, pb. 1800), lists sixteen paintings by Giorgione in Venetian collections and numerous fresco commissions. Hardly a handful of these paintings is extant.

Life's Work

Vasari speaks confidently of Giorgione as one of the best painters in the "modern style," linking him with Leonardo da Vinci, Raphael, Michelangelo, and Correggio. His modernity, however, is somewhat peculiar to himself, and he is best understood as being at once one of the innovators of the early Renaissance style in painting and an individual stylist of peculiar felicities, which made him so popular with Venetian collectors of paintings. His best work is not public; rather, it is private.

Painting during the Middle Ages was, in general, at the service of the church and state, recording high moments in the histories of those two mainstays of medieval society. In the fifteenth century, particularly in the later years, there was an inclination in the social and religious sensibility to put some emphasis upon the life of the individual, to see life as not simply a vale of tears leading to eternal salvation or damnation but as a place of some pleasure in and of itself. This vague tendency to think about life as worth living began tentatively to reveal itself in the arts thematically, tonally, and technically. Bellini, for example, continued to paint Madonnas, but in his later work the modeling of the figures became less dry and stiff, and tended to dwell on the physical beauty of the human subjects with considerable tenderness. Occasionally, Bellini would go even further in his exploration of the beauty of the human form. His *Toilet of Venus* (1515) is a quite magnificent painting per se; it is a painting clearly in the full flow of Renaissance enthusiasm for the human body and the richness of life at its best. Two other aspects of Bellini's work had influence on Giorgione. Tonally, Bellini brought to his Madonnas and to his altarpieces a kind of dreamy hush, a low-keyed softness that is perhaps best exemplified in what are called his *sacra conversazione* paintings, in which the Madonna and Child are adored quietly by a combination of contemplative saints and angels playing musical instruments. This "tonality" was taken out of the sacred realm with great success by Giorgione. Giorgione was also indebted to Bellini in part for his landscapes. Bellini used landscapes in the common tradition of the time as backgrounds for his enthroned Madonnas. These works tend to be somewhat stiffly idealized versions of the local landscapes, but they also tend to become softer and more natural as Bellini's career progressed. Giorgione noticed Bellini's idea of the softened natural scene and created his own version of it.

What is immediately apparent in Giorgione's work is how felicitously he adopted the then new ideas of allowing human feeling and pleasures onto the face of the work of art and how the use of oils and canvas, both relatively new elements in painting at the time, allowed Giorgione much greater ease in expressing himself. Bellini worked mainly in tempera on wood, and he stayed with the wood in his early oils. Yet younger artists such as Giorgione made the double jump to oils and to canvas, which allowed them to escape the dryness of tempera and the stiffness of modeling, and to achieve great subtlety in the use of color.

Giorgione proved to be the master of the new mode of wedding canvas and oil, and he developed the reputation for modeling through color rather than through line, a technique which was to become the touchstone of Venetian art. In a sense, modern art began with Giorgione. The idea that art could be used for the simple purpose of enriching life by its very presence without necessarily illustrating some historical or religious act of importance and that the artist might make a living providing canvases of modest size, illustrating modest moments of common life, is an obvious aspect of Giorgione's career. He seems only occasionally to have done public commissions, and his patrons, so far as is known, were not the most important members of Venetian society. His patrons tended to be people of property but not of particularly imposing reputation or power, as had usually been the case of patrons prior to this time and would continue to be the case in the career of painters such as Titian.

What might have happened had Giorgione lived is another matter. Titian might have begun as Giorgione's pupil, or both painters might have been with Bellini. What is known is that in the early years of his career, Titian, who was slightly younger than Giorgione, was closely associated with him. They often worked together, and, after Giorgione's death, Titian finished some of Giorgione's work. Indeed, they were so similar stylistically that some paintings, including the famous *Concert Champêtre*, are sometimes credited to Giorgione and sometimes to Titian. Whatever the case, Titian went on to an international career, and it is presumable that, given his early reputation, Giorgione might have taken a similar road to wider reputation had he lived.

Giorgione left, however, a group of quite enchanting paintings, almost all of which have a worldwide reputation and at least two of which, the *Concert Champêtre* (if it is his, or partly his) and *The Tempest* (c. 1505), are among the best-known paintings in the world. These paintings seem to say something about life, which, like poetry, is virtually untranslatable into rational concepts. The tender, soft sweetness of the painting, the colors, the posture of the participants, the opulent dreaminess, the hints of symbolism not quite fully formed, and the elegiac pastoral melancholy come together in surprisingly uncluttered masterpieces of very modest size. These qualities are the signature of Giorgione and can be seen to a slightly lesser extent in his altarpiece at Castelfranco and in *The Three Philosophers* (c. 1510) in Vienna. The paintings seem to say something beyond their content, while drawing the viewer to a kind of hypnotic conclusion that whatever the meaning may be matters little in the face of such glorious modeling, rich coloring, and consummate rendering, particularly of the human body. Giorgione did not live long enough to paint anything of a lesser order.

Summary

What Giorgione did was to free painting from the institutions that had fostered and dominated it through the Middle Ages. That dominance did not diminish immediately, but painters, and to a lesser extent sculptors, were to discover a new market for their work, a market which was to allow them the opportunity to experiment with new themes. Giorgione also helped to educate the public that art was not only a reminder of social, political, and religious responsibilities but also a medium of pure pleasure.

The fact of Giorgione's popularity is an indication of the developing Renaissance sensibility. It was one thing for Giorgione to make paintings of simple, intimate moments of innocent encounter; it is the mark of the great artist to meet instinctively that inchoate appetite of society, vaguely struggling to understand its desire to celebrate and enjoy life rather than simply bear it with religious stoicism. A Giorgione painting, small enough to be hung in a living room, had nothing to do with religion, or history, or politics, or worldly success; it had to do with the beauty of nature and of human beings, and with the sympathetic connections of humanity with landscape. His paintings provided the example of a metaphysical tenderness, which was later pursued by painters such as Antoine Watteau, Jean-Baptiste-Siméon Chardin, and Paul Cézanne. After Giorgione, paintings no longer had to stand for something but could be something, a center for contemplative pleasure by the individual. It was more than the discovery of the innocent subject that made Giorgione important. He was one of the first and also one of the finest practitioners of oil on canvas, immediately capable of understanding how that combination made painting more lushly bright and how paint, used tonally, could be used as a medium for supple draftsmanship, which would be one of the distinguishing marks of Venetian painting. Art became part of ordinary life, not simply a record of its more glorious moments. With the intimate Giorgione, art entered the home and made way for the modern idea of the artist as the glory of humanity. The artist was to become as important as the art.

Bibliography

Beck, James. *Italian Renaissance Painting*. New York: Harper & Row, 1981. Giorgione's contribution can be best understood in the light of the whole movement of art as it works its way out of the medieval period into the early stages of the Renaissance. This sensible survey is easily understood.

Berenson, Bernhard. *The Italian Painters of the Renaissance*. New York: Meridian Books, 1957. Berenson, one of the great critics of Italian art, puts Giorgione in the context of Venetian painting and Venetian social history.

Phillips, Duncan. *The Leadership of Giorgione*. Washington, D.C.: American

Federation of Arts, 1937. A charming book, somewhat heavy on speculation, but wide-ranging in the associations it brings to the contemplation of the mystery of Giorgione's career.

Pignati, Terisio. *Giorgione*. Translated by Clovis Whitfield. New York: Phaidon Press, 1971. A scholars' text, dealing briskly, but with confident economy, with the problem of the life and the canon.

Vasari, Giorgio. *Lives of the Artists*. Translated by George Bull. Baltimore: Penguin Books, 1965. An inexpensive paperback in which the facts (if they are that) of Giorgione's life and art are presented by a near contemporary. Other artists of the time are also represented and form a valuable frame for considering Giorgione.

Charles Pullen

CHRISTOPH GLUCK

Born: July 2, 1714; Erasbach, Upper Palatinate
Died: November 15, 1787; Vienna, Austria
Area of Achievement: Music
Contribution: Gluck established a new style of opera that marked the end of the Baroque and the beginning of the classical era in music. Many of his stage works represent a turning point in the balance between counterpoint and homophony, between vocal display and musical drama.

Early Life

Christoph Gluck was born the son of a forester and huntsman, a profession followed by several of his ancestors. The young Gluck's early training remains a matter of conjecture, but he traveled to Prague in late adolescence and probably enrolled at the University of Prague, although he did not complete his studies there. His musical experiences during this period involved private study, a position as church organist, and surely much exposure to Prague's vigorous musical life, dominated by Italian composers, operas, and oratorios. Travels took him to Milan, where he was engaged in the private orchestra of Prince Antonio Melzi and where he came under the influence of the Italian symphonist Giovanni Battista Sammartini, through association, if not through direct study. Gluck's first appearance as an opera composer took place in Milan with *Artaserse* (1741), a success followed by seven more Italian operas in the next four years. In 1745, he visited London for the production of two more operas, works derived largely from his Milan scores. The composer's views on melody may have been born at this time; Gluck is said to have noted that simplicity exerted the greatest effect on English audiences and that he subsequently tried to write for the voice in a simpler, more natural manner.

Many of Gluck's works during the following years were constructed with borrowings from his own earlier compositions, but *Semiramide riconosciuta* (1748) was performed with great success in Vienna and was recognized as a totally new work both in its musical materials and in the sense of musical drama which it projected. Gluck traveled to Hamburg and Copenhagen later that same year, establishing a widening reputation as an opera composer and conductor. In Copenhagen, he met the critic Johann Adolph Scheibe, who probably influenced Gluck to some degree in the question of the connection between the opera overture and music of the opera which followed it, an idea later promoted by Gluck himself.

Gluck's marriage in 1750 to the daughter of a wealthy Viennese merchant brought him a dowry and connections at the Viennese court which assured his financial independence, a consideration important for any composer contemplating new ventures.

Life's Work

In 1752, Gluck was appointed *Konzertmeister* in the household of the imperial field marshal in Vienna, a position giving him a secure base of operations in the very heart of the Austrian Empire. In the ensuing years, he produced a number of operas which won the favor of the royal family, and his growing reputation led to a commission for an opera to be presented during the 1756 carnival season in Rome. Through the influence of one of his Roman patrons, Gluck was awarded the papal title Cavalier of the Golden Spur. Upon his return to Vienna, an appointment to adapt several French *opéras comiques* for the stage brought him into contact with a good troop of French actors, and the first *opéra comique* of his own, *La Fausse Esclave* (1758), was a success noted for its coordination of music and drama. Around 1760, Gluck was introduced to the Italian author and dramatist Raniero Calzabigi; their first collaboration, the ballet-pantomime *Don Juan: Ou, Le Festin de Pierre* (1761), was unusually well received. This was followed by *Orfeo ed Euridice* (1762), a major success which marked a turning point in the history of opera and the cornerstone of Gluck's lasting fame as an opera composer. It is probable that some of the traditions of vocal display to which singers and audiences were accustomed endured in early performances of this work. Yet the score avoids the entrenched pattern of alternating recitative and aria; the comparatively uncluttered vocal lines allow for a sense of dramatic projection of text; the orchestra supports the dramatic events onstage; and chorus and ballet are incorporated into the score in a masterful way.

Gluck continued to work at adapting French *opéras comiques* for the Viennese stage, traveling frequently between Paris and Vienna. He collaborated once again with Calzabigi for *Alceste* (1767), a second reform opera in the spirit of *Orfeo ed Euridice*. In the preface to the published score of *Alceste*, he set forth his musical goals in matters of opera: Music should follow the poem, not be overburdened with ornaments; the tripartite aria should not interfere with the sense of the plot; the overture should be in keeping with the action that follows; and all should be executed with the goal of achieving a beautiful simplicity. Gluck later acknowledged that Calzabigi was responsible for many of these ideas. It is also clear that similar thoughts were widespread among the literati of the time. Yet, to the composer's lasting credit, it was the unusually expressive quality of the music in both works which established them as milestones in the history of opera.

Gluck continued his operatic activity in Vienna; the third reform opera, *Paride ed Elena* (1770), was less successful than its predecessors and, for that or for other reasons, represented Gluck's last joint venture with Calzabigi. In spite of the personal fortune achieved with the aid of his wife's dowry, Gluck, always noted for a degree of parsimony, felt driven to extra effort to recover losses on some theatrical investments in Vienna. The operatic scene in Paris seemed to offer the most ready profits, and most of the next decade was spent in travels between Vienna and the French capital. *Iphigénie en Aulide* and a French version of *Orfeo ed Euridice*, both produced in Paris in 1774, show a continued development of his sense for music and drama. In 1777, Gluck was in Paris once again, where he was drawn into a controversy between his own supporters and those favoring the older Italian opera as it was represented in the works of Niccolò Piccinni. It was proposed that both composers should set the story of *Roland*, by Philippe Quinault, but Gluck, upon learning that Piccinni was already at work on that libretto, withdrew and put forth instead his setting of Quinault's *Armide* (1777). This work was performed four months before Piccinni's *Roland*; while it did little to affirm the superiority of one style over another in the opinion of the factious Parisian public, *Armide* did establish a distinction between the style of Gluck's operas and the traditional *opéra seria*. On his next return to Paris, another setting of a classic tragedy, *Iphigénie en Tauride* (1779), proved to be Gluck's greatest success. His musical depiction of characters and the suggestion, by the orchestra, of character traits and ideas not directly present onstage were qualities later expanded by nineteenth century opera composers, particularly Richard Wagner.

Gluck's last years in Vienna were marked by continuing composition and several efforts to revive some of his works for the Paris stage, despite a series of debilitating strokes. He was in contact with the young Wolfgang Amadeus Mozart, an aspiring composer for the stage whose natural gifts far surpassed Gluck's, but who still must have assimilated much from the many rehearsals of the German version of *Iphigénie en Tauride* he attended. A few days before his death, Gluck gave to Antonio Salieri, his supposed successor, a *De profundis* which Salieri conducted at the composer's funeral on November 17, 1787. Gluck's tombstone reflected something of the esteem he enjoyed in the eyes of his contemporaries; he was described as "An upright German man, a devout Christian, a faithful husband . . . great master of the noble art of music."

Summary

Christoph Gluck, with the possible exception of Claudio Monteverdi, may be described as the earliest composer of opera to maintain a place in the functioning repertory. He effectively wrought significant and lasting changes in what was a widespread yet decadent art form. For all of his influence, his work represents a synthesis at least as much as an innovation; many of his ideas had been expressed before he gave them musical shape and substance. He realized the ideals of the eighteenth century Enlightenment in matters of naturalness, balance, and clarity in his reform operas of the 1760's, and continued this development in varying degrees in the works which followed.

In specifically musical matters, Gluck achieved in the opera a new balance between music and drama; he avoided the vocal display and stereotyped librettos which had made opera into a notorious spectacle; the orchestra contributed to the dramatic presentation through careful use of instrumental timbre and thematic interplay with the vocal parts, and the overture became an integral part of the score rather than a dispensable introduction. These changes in style mark Gluck as one of the major creative figures who established the principles which underlay musical classicism of the late eighteenth century.

Bibliography

Cooper, Martin. *Gluck*. New York: Oxford University Press, 1935. An extended monograph by a recognized authority on Gluck and his music. Contemporary events are chronologically presented to illustrate the composer's activities as a response to the milieu of the musical theater in which he worked. Most valuable is the closing chapter examining Gluck's position in the history of music.

Einstein, Alfred. *Gluck*. Translated by Eric Blom. London: J. M. Dent, 1936. Reprint. New York: McGraw-Hill, 1972. Although somewhat dated in its style, this remains a standard and comprehensive English-language monograph on Gluck. The survey of life and works is sometimes colored more by the author's erudite opinion than by scholarly objectivity. Supplemented by useful appendices, including a catalog of works, a list of persons with whom Gluck worked, a bibliography, and an excerpt from Gluck's correspondence.

Grout, Donald Jay. *A Short History of Opera*. 3d ed. New York: Columbia University Press, 1988. A concise, direct approach to the complete scope of opera, with a significant portion devoted to Gluck, his works, and his influence. One of the most accessible and current sources available.

Howard, Patricia. *Gluck and the Birth of Modern Opera*. London: Barrie & Rockliff, 1963. A stylistic study cast in a historical perspective which treats Gluck and his works, particularly his reform operas, as part of the second (modern) stage of opera following its beginning in the early seventeenth century.

_____, ed. *C. W. von Gluck: "Orfeo."* Cambridge: Cambridge University Press, 1981. A series of substantial essays by various authors addressing the first and most famous of Gluck's reform operas. The essays can be grouped into the historical, the analytical, and those examining the impact of critical writing about this particular work. Select bibliography and discography, the latter often overlooked in most critical studies of major musical works.

Ratner, Leonard G. *Classic Music: Expression, Form, and Style*. New York: Schirmer Books, 1980. Within a comprehensive examination of musical style in the eighteenth century, Gluck and his operatic achievements are presented as the principal manifestation of a "high style" in musical theater specifically and in the later years of the classical era in general. Comparisons between settings by Gluck and others of the same plot, *Iphigénie en Tauride*, serve to illustrate the specific stylistic differences between Gluck and his contemporaries.

Wellesz, Egon, and Frederick Sternfeld, eds. *The New Oxford History of Music*. Vol. 7, *The Age of Enlightenment*. London: Oxford University Press, 1973. Gluck's Italian and French operas are addressed separately; the discussion of Gluck's work in Paris is particularly valuable in that he is presented clearly as a musical iconoclast facing an aristocratic, autocratic society rather than a prophet of later operatic venues for a middle-class public. Perhaps the best discussion available of his French operas.

Douglas A. Lee

AUGUST VON GNEISENAU

Born: October 27, 1760; Schildau, Saxony
Died: August 23, 1831; Posen, Pomerania
Area of Achievement: The military
Contribution: As a Prussian field marshal and member of King Frederick William III's Military Reorganization Commission, Gneisenau fashioned the Prussian strategy that finally defeated Napoleon I in the campaigns of 1813 and 1814 and played a key role in reforming the Prussian army into the most professional military force in nineteenth century Europe. Gneisenau's organizational and operational reforms survive today as accepted elements in most of the world's armies.

Early Life

The scion of a noble but poor German military family, August von Gneisenau was born near Torgau, Saxony, during the Seven Years' War. His father, an artillery lieutenant in the Austrian army, abandoned him to friends who reared him in near poverty. A moneyed maternal grandfather subsequently assumed responsibility for the young orphan and entrusted his education to Jesuits. With the death of his benefactor, young Gneisenau inherited enough money to attend Erfurt University from 1777 to 1779. With his inheritance depleted, Gneisenau prematurely left the university, joined a local Austrian regiment as a cavalry subaltern, and fought against Prussia in the 1778 War of Bavarian Succession.

He subsequently joined the army of Bayreuth-Ansbach, a tiny principality that hired out its soldiers to the highest bidder. It was within this context that Gneisenau, now a lieutenant of chasseurs, traveled to North America in 1782 to fight as a British mercenary against the American colonists. He arrived too late to fight, but he came upon and embraced new concepts that would later define his role as a leading Prussian military reformer: the belief in a politically active citizenry and the use of open order tactics by civilian militias in warfare.

Gneisenau returned to Europe after one year and personally petitioned Frederick the Great to allow him to join the Prussian army. In 1786, he received a commission as a first lieutenant in the infantry. Although he did participate in the Polish campaign of 1793-1794, Gneisenau served for the next twenty years in different Silesian garrisons, where he immersed himself in military studies and further developed the unique blend of combat and staff skills for which he is rightfully famous.

Gneisenau was an undistinguished forty-six-year-old captain when war broke out between France and Prussia in 1806. On October 14, 1806, he commanded a company of infantry at the Battle of Jena and experienced at first hand Napoleon's annihilation of the once-invincible Frederican army.

The defeat was a profound blow to Gneisenau, but even more devastating was the complete indifference shown by the Prussian middle class to the loss of the army. In fact, their perception of the army as a royal instrument promoting reactionary interests was in direct contrast to the nascent "people in arms" concept Gneisenau had seen in the Colonies.

Gneisenau adopted the citizen-soldier concept in his 1807 defense of Kolberg, a Pomeranian coastal town situated on the Baltic Sea and besieged by the French. Gneisenau's defense of Kolberg was the only successful Prussian military operation at the time and was directly attributable to his deliberate attempt to transform the local civilians from detached bystanders into active defenders who fought with the same spirit as his regular troops. Gneisenau's success earned for him the highly prized Pour le Mérite award, a promotion to lieutenant colonel, and the notoriety that laid the foundation for his major accomplishments.

Life's Work

Subsequent to the Prussian debacle at Jena-Auerstadt, King Frederick William III established the Military Reorganization Commission on July 25, 1807. Its charter was to review the army's performance and propose necessary reforms. Major General Gerhard von Scharnhorst, after rejecting a position as the director of an English artillery school, became chairman of the commission. Gneisenau, who saw himself as Scharnhorst's "Saint Peter," also became a member, as did two other protégés, Majors Karl Grolman and Herman von Boyen. Carl von Clausewitz, although never a full member of the commission, worked indirectly with it as Scharnhorst's aide. With royal sanction, these five military reformers would resurrect a new Prussian army from the ashes of the one previously destroyed by Napoleon. Gneisenau's influence was second only to Scharnhorst's; with the latter's premature death in 1813, he became the most prominent military reformer.

Gneisenau and his peers quickly ascribed the Prussian defeat to an outdated military and a reactionary society. The Frederican army that faced Napoleon relied on rigid tactics, brutal and unenlightened discipline, and overcentralized control. Common people, in turn, felt no sense of responsibility toward the state and greeted Prussian military failures with apathy. Gneisenau and the other reformers decided to reverse the situation, but they realized that to be competitive the Prussian army would have to revise its tactics, organization, and working relationship with civilians completely. A mere reorganization of the old-style army would not suffice.

Gneisenau also realized that the reformers needed to inspire a new loyalty to the state; they had to transform Prussian subjects into self-motivated citizens, inspired by patriotism and a belief in national honor. Yet Gneisenau believed that a people's army was impossible if Prussia did not change from a feudal society, dominated by landed Junkers, into a liberal, constitutional monarchy. In Gneisenau's estimation, neither a serf in hereditary bondage nor a member of the middle class restricted from local government or the officer corps would develop a devotion to the state in the absence of basic social and political rights. The regeneration of the Prussian military would occur only through the reformation of the state.

Gneisenau and the other commission members quickly introduced a number of enduring military reforms. In contrast to the murderous discipline of the past, an edict issued on August 3, 1805, introduced a humane system of rewards and punishments that deliberately limited corporal punishment. Humane treatment, the reformers hoped, would inspire soldiers to become self-motivated and thus develop a more enduring commitment to both the army and the state. Grolman, with the active support of Gneisenau, sponsored an August 6, 1808, decree that transformed the officer corps into a meritocracy, where members of the middle class could enter and succeed based on their demonstrated performance rather than on their family background.

A third innovation was the introduction of professional military education. By 1810, the Prussian army had reorganized all of its schools and introduced the prototype for the *Kriegsakademie*, the first modern war college. Those who attended the college received a liberal education that included, for the first time, a systematic study of war. Thanks to Gneisenau and his fellow reformers, war was no longer for a brave dilettante but for cool professionals who subjected it to lifelong study.

Gneisenau also supported Baron Heinrich von Stein, the king's chief minister and a fellow reformer on the Military Reorganization Commission, who laid the foundation for a War Ministry responsible for directing, coordinating, and controlling the Prussian army. The nascent General Staff, organized within the General War Department of the War Ministry, would begin to flourish as the intellectual center of the German military under Helmuth von Moltke, the Elder.

Gneisenau's most cherished reforms, however, were the most imperfectly realized. He and the Military Reorganization Commission called for universal conscription as early as 1808, but Frederick William, who feared the destruction of the monarchy in a civil war between economic classes, balked at the idea of a nation in arms. It was only in 1814, when the defeat of Napoleon seemed possible, that Frederick William accepted national conscription. The principle survived, but Gneisenau did not see a lasting union of regular soldiers and militia into a military force crusading for freedom in Europe. The militia (*Landwehr*) enjoyed a brief, independent life but ultimately was subsumed under regular army control beginning in 1819.

Gneisenau worked hard for the above reforms and functioned as chief of the fortifications and engineering corps until Napoleon forced a powerless Frederick William to dismiss Stein and other reformers. In disgust, Gneisenau resigned and quietly undertook missions to Great Britain, Russia, and

Sweden in order to muster support against France. His passionate humanism now focused on liberating Europe from Napoleon. When Prussia discarded its role as an unwilling satellite to France, Gneisenau returned to active service as Scharnhorst's *Ia*, or first general staff officer. When Scharnhorst died in June, 1813, Gneisenau became chief of the General Staff and served Marshal Gebhard von Blücher. In this capacity, Gneisenau planned the Prussian strategy for the major campaigns of 1813-1814, including the Battle of Leipzig.

During this phase of his career, Gneisenau introduced battlefield innovations that had a lasting influence. He was the first to make the chief of staff of a major command equal in responsibility with the commander. He believed that this arrangement would strengthen the General Staff system and establish spiritual unity between staff officers and combatants. He also developed the practice of issuing clear and comprehensive objectives while leaving room for the combat commander to exercise individual initiative and freedom of action. Gneisenau directly influenced Clausewitz's subsequent theory of war by insisting that the goal of an army was not to engage in maneuver warfare but to destroy enemy forces directly. Finally, he was an early practitioner of the battle of encirclement, later used with great success by Helmuth Karl Bernhard von Moltke and Alfred von Schlieffen. For these innovations and other successes, Frederick William ennobled Gneisenau in 1814.

Upon Napoleon's return from Elba in March, 1815, Gneisenau once again became Blücher's chief of staff. Each was good for the other: Gneisenau's powerful intellect and organizing skills tempered Blücher's mercurial personality and bulldog tenacity. It was Gneisenau, with prodding from Grolman, who at the Battle of Ligny decided not to retreat toward Prussia but north to Wavre, Belgium. Thus, when the Battle of Waterloo hung in the balance, the Prussians tipped it in the Duke of Wellington's favor by attacking the French flank. The murderous pursuit of the French troops that followed was yet another example of Gneisenau's vigorous style of war.

With the final defeat of Napoleon, Gneisenau fell into disfavor. The absence of a common foe enabled the reactionary Junkers to reverse the more extreme changes he and the other reformers had introduced. Gneisenau subsequently resigned in 1816. He became governor of Berlin in 1818 and a field marshal in 1825. In 1831, during the Polish Revolution, he commanded the army of occupation on Prussia's eastern border. While on border duty, both he and Clausewitz, now his chief of staff, died of cholera.

Summary

As a reformer and combatant, August von Gneisenau had a lasting and widespread influence. He and the other Prussian reformers on the Military Reorganization Commission forever changed the character of modern armies. Following the Prussian example, rival powers introduced universal conscription and opened the officer corps to those with talent, regardless of their social background. They increasingly relied on nationalism rather than harsh discipline to motivate troops. They also formalized their military establishments by introducing war ministries, professional military education, and the General Staff system. Gneisenau was instrumental in developing and popularizing these innovations.

Yet he was bitterly disappointed in two respects. Prussia, rather than becoming a liberal constitutional monarchy, remained thoroughly autocratic. As a result, the army remained an isolated enclave of military technicians rather than a democratic institution manned by enlightened citizen soldiers who had a personal investment in supporting their government. Gneisenau overestimated the state's willingness to turn over a new leaf. Instead, the pattern for future Prussian jingoism was set.

As a combatant, Gneisenau believed that the army was the enemy's "center of gravity" and thus had to be destroyed. A vigorous pursuit was part of the process. Both concepts found expression in Clausewitz's *Vom Kriege* (1832-1834; *On War*, 1873), which later had an impact on German strategy and tactics (beginning in the Wars of German Unification). Given the influence of these combat techniques and his earlier organizational reforms, Gneisenau's sustained influence on modern military establishments is undeniable.

Bibliography
Britt, Albert Sidney. "Field Marshal August Neidhart von Gneisenau." In *The Consortium on Revolutionary Europe, 1750-1850: Proceedings, 1983*, edited by Clarence Davis. Gainesville: University of Florida Press, 1985. A basic treatment of Gneisenau's accomplishments that tries to prove that he was an outstanding example of ability improved by study.
Craig, Gordon. *The Politics of the Prussian Army, 1640-1945*. New York: Oxford University Press, 1956. Craig's seminal work traces the role of the army in modern German history. Gneisenau and the reformers receive a sympathetic look for their attempts not only to resurrect an army but also to change a society.
Dupuy, Trevor Nevitt. *A Genius for War: The German Army and General Staff, 1807-1945*. Englewood Cliffs, N.J.: Prentice-Hall, 1977. Dupuy performed statistical analyses of World War II battles and discovered that German combat effectiveness per man was better than for the Allies. He concludes that the Germans developed the ability to institutionalize military excellence. Analyzes how the Germans did this, beginning with Gneisenau and the reformers in 1807. The specific details on Gneisenau are valuable but limited.
Goerlitz, Walter. *History of the German General Staff, 1657-1945*. Trans-

lated by Brian Battershaw. New York: Praeger, 1953. This German historian traces the growing incompatibility between the German army and a society evolving toward a democratic-capitalistic system. Goerlitz identifies Gneisenau's zealotry as one reason that the reformers fell so quickly into disfavor. He also treats Gneisenau's impact as a combatant.

Ritter, Gerhard. *The Sword and the Scepter: The Problem of Militarism in Germany.* Translated by Heinz Norden. Coral Gables, Fla.: University of Miami Press, 1969. As the title implies, this three-volume study analyzes the growth of German militarism from 1740 to the present. Gneisenau receives a factual review for reform efforts that unwittingly created the possibility for subsequent military adventurism.

Peter R. Faber

BORIS FYODOROVICH GODUNOV

Born: c. 1551; place unknown
Died: April 23, 1605; Moscow, Russia
Areas of Achievement: Government and politics
Contribution: Godunov provided a brief period of stability between the harsh
   rule of Ivan the Terrible and the unsettled period of the Time of Troubles.

Early Life

Boris Fyodorovich Godunov was born about 1551. His father, Fedor Ivanovich, was a moderate landowner in Kostroma on the Volga River. Most
sources claim that the Godunovs were Tartar in origin and could trace their
Muscovite service to approximately 1330. At best, Godunov's education was
limited. He was superstitious, which was not unusual for his time. Following
his father's death, Godunov became connected with his uncle, Dmitri
Ivanovich Godunov. Through the association, the younger Godunov became
a member of the *Oprichnina*, which was organized by Ivan the Terrible to
restructure Muscovy (modern Moscow) and provide a secret police.

Godunov's career began to advance rapidly in 1570, when he married
Maria, the daughter of Grigori Malyuta, a trusted and loyal supporter of
Ivan. Thus entrenched at court, Godunov became a constant companion to
the czar's sons and a member of Ivan's personal entourage. Ivan selected
Godunov's sister, Irina, to be the wife of Fyodor, his second son. This relationship proved beneficial for Godunov when Ivan's death in 1584 brought
the feebleminded Fyodor to the throne. Ivan had previously killed the eldest
son in a fit of rage.

There was a drastic difference between the court of Ivan the Terrible and
the one ruled by Fyodor and Godunov. Ivan's years had been full of violence
and death. The court of Fyodor and Godunov was peaceful and quiet. Ever
careful to govern jointly in their names, Godunov was the actual ruler. While
many of the princely boyars resented the rise of Godunov to power, the
English actually called him "Lord Protector" of Muscovy.

Life's Work

To many, Godunov was a handsome and striking figure. He was average
in height. He was outwardly kind and possessed a captivating charm. To
those who were of princely origin, he displayed an appropriate degree of
subservience. Many contemporaries commented on his concern for the poor
and observed that Godunov did not like to see human suffering.

One of Godunov's major achievements was the establishment of the Moscow Patriarchate. Muscovites considered themselves the "Third Rome." To
enhance this claim, they demanded that their church be raised to the position
of a patriarchate. This dream became possible when Jeremiah II, the Pa-

triarch of Constantinople, came to Muscovy in 1589 to collect alms for the church. Godunov prevailed upon him to approve the establishment of a patriarchate for Muscovy. After much consideration, Jeremiah agreed, even allowing the Russian metropolitan Iov to fill the position. The Council of Eastern Churches officially recognized the decision in the spring of 1590.

Perhaps the most significant event in Godunov's career, however, was the death in May, 1591, of the young Dmitry, the son of Ivan by his seventh wife, Maria Nagoi. While the boy's possible claim to the throne was weak since his mother's marriage was uncanonical, he would have been a serious claimant to the throne when Fyodor died without heirs. Godunov immediately appointed a special commission of inquiry to determine what had happened to Dmitry. The official story that emerged was that, while playing a game with friends, the nine-year-old boy suffered an epileptic fit and killed himself with a knife. Some doubted that story.

Another major crisis began to emerge in the late 1590's because of a decline in population in certain areas of Muscovy. In an attempt to keep people on the lands, Godunov issued in 1597 a decree that ordered all peasants who had deserted the lands since 1592 to be returned to their landlords. This limiting of peasant movement greatly aided the establishment of serfdom.

On January 7, 1598, Fyodor died without heirs, which caused much fear in Muscovy. To Muscovites, the end of a dynasty was similar to the end of the world. The czar was considered a Godhead, closer to God than even the patriarch. With the end of the dynasty, many believed that God's favor had been withdrawn.

According to church sources, Fyodor appointed his wife, Irina, to be the ruler. She refused the position, desiring to enter the church instead. Some supporters urged her to reign but to allow Godunov to rule as he had done under Fyodor. She refused. Meanwhile, Godunov had retired to a monk's cell to await the outcome. Undoubtedly, Godunov planned his election. He realized that he had to be careful as there were several other possible claimants to the throne. His most serious opponent was Fyodor Nikitich Romanov from the powerful Romanov family.

The Patriarch Iov and his party came to Godunov and pleaded with him to take the throne. Godunov knew the boyars would accept him only if they could limit the czar's authority. Since he refused any conditions, he told Iov that he would accept the throne if a *zemsky sobor* (assembly of the land) asked him to do so. Iov immediately called an assembly that, according to custom, contained clergy, boyars, gentry, and merchants to meet in February, 1598. The assembly offered the crown to Godunov, who accepted. The boyar dominated duma, however, did not like the election.

Godunov had many plans for his reign. To solidify his dynasty, he tried to arrange a European marriage for his daughter, Kseniya. His first attempt was with the exiled Gustavus of Sweden, but this failed. He then attempted to arrange a marriage with Duke Johann, the brother of Christian IV of Denmark. Johann died, however, before a marriage could take place. Realizing that Muscovy needed Western technology, Godunov hired many European doctors, engineers, and military men. Though not formally educated himself, he wanted to establish a university in Moscow. When this idea failed, he sent eighteen students to study in Europe, but none ever returned.

Heavy rains began to fall during the spring of 1601 and continued for ten weeks; the grain could not ripen. In mid-August, severe frosts killed what few crops that grew in the fields. Grain stocks were soon exhausted, and by the winter the people were starving. Muscovy had entered the period known as the Time of Troubles. Nothing Godunov did seemed to help. He opened many granaries in Muscovy and distributed their contents to the people, and he launched a massive building program to increase employment. Yet people still died. To Muscovites, a famine signified a visitation of God's displeasure, and they worried.

Godunov became paranoid. He was convinced that plots were being hatched against him. He counteracted with an elaborate system of spies, who performed effectively. Indeed, they discovered a serious plot concerning the young Dmitry, who had supposedly died in 1591. The false Dmitry, as he is portrayed, appeared in Poland claiming to be the real Czar of Moscow. While King Sigismund III of Poland refused to grant the pretender any official support, the monarch allowed the false Dmitry to raise money and men. With this and strong support from the Catholic church, the false Dmitry invaded Muscovy to claim the throne. Godunov asserted that the false Dmitry was really the monk Grigorii Otrepev, who had at one time been in the employ of the powerful Romanov family, Godunov's major continuing opposition.

Godunov continued to fight the invasion, but on April 23, 1605, he died unexpectedly. His sixteen-year-old son, Fyodor, succeeded him, but the false Dmitry seized control of the throne within six weeks. A popular theory concerning Godunov's death is that he had been poisoned at the dinner table. The more likely story is that he died of heart disease, as he had experienced severe troubles with his heart since suffering a stroke in 1604.

Summary

Boris Fyodorovich Godunov stands as a significant figure in the history of Muscovy. Following the rule of the powerful Ivan, who literally reshaped the state in a brutal fashion, Godunov provided a brief period of peace and governmental reorganization. Fyodor was not able to rule effectively; therefore, Godunov was forced to do so. He reestablished respectable relationships with the West, advocating trade and closer contacts. He wanted European technology and European educational standards for his people. One of his most notable accomplishments was the establishment of the patriarchate. Godunov loved power and proved effective at using it.

Despite his accomplishments, Godunov remains a puzzle to contemporary historians. When the Orthodox church accepted the false Dmitry as the legitimate czar, Godunov became the recinarnation of evil, an attempted murderer. Seventeenth and eighteenth century Russian historians apparently accepted the premise that Godunov attempted to have the young boy killed and thus greatly condemned him. The official Russian version was established by a noted Russian historian, N. M. Karamzin, who painted Boris as nothing more than a power-hungry despot who deserved what happened to him. In the West, Godunov is primarily known through a drama written by Alexander Pushkin, who took his position from Karamzin. Another vehicle of knowledge about Godunov comes from the opera composed by Modest Mussorgsky, who was influenced by Pushkin. In all probability, a historical consensus on Godunov is unlikely.

Bibliography
Emerson, Caryl. *Boris Godunov: Transpositions of a Russian Theme*. Bloomington: Indiana University Press, 1986. The author attempts to examine Godunov as he has appeared in the different periods of literature. He explains how Godunov has evolved in literature and how various writers treat him. The notes are valuable in gathering bibliographical information.
Graham, Stephen. *Boris Godunof.* New Haven, Conn.: Yale University Press, 1933. Reprint. Hamden, Conn.: Archon Books, 1970. Graham does not like Godunov. He attempts to present the good points of Godunov, but it is very obvious that this is a major effort. Contains a short bibliography.
Grey, Ian. *Boris Godunov: The Tragic Tsar*. New York: Charles Scribner's Sons, 1973. This book tends to be one of the most apologetic books in English on the subject. Grey depicts Godunov as an able, honest, and even humane ruler. Furthermore, Grey sees him as a person whom historians have slandered. In his attempt to explain Godunov in a good light, Grey often loses sight of his subject. Makes good use of most published biographies. Easy to read and has an adequate bibliography.
Platonov, S. F. *Boris Godunov: Tsar of Russia*. Translated by L. Rex Pyles. Gulf Breeze, Fla.: Academic International Press, 1973. Platonov presents a rather colorful account of his subject's life with the aim of restoring Godunov to his proper place in historical scholarship. Provides a satisfactory overview of the subject. Contains a short bibliography from the translation and one from the author which is in Russian.
_____. *The Time of Troubles: A Historical Study of the Internal Crisis and Social Struggle in Sixteenth and Seventeenth Century Moscow*. Translated by John Alexander. Lawrence: University Press of Kansas, 1970. Platonov offers a picture of the entire period of Russian history

known as the Time of Troubles. The work has approximately thirty-seven pages on Godunov and is a good, brief account.

Skrynnikov, Ruslan G. *Boris Godunov.* Edited and translated by Hugh F. Graham. Gulf Breeze, Fla.: Academic International Press, 1982. Skrynnikov published several articles on Godunov during the 1970's. He is generally favorable toward Godunov. He disputes the prevailing view that Godunov's family was descended from Tartar nobility and claims that the story was created to make Godunov appear more in the line of royalty. A straightforward account. The bibliography is short and entirely in Russian, as are most of the notes.

Vernadsky, George. *A History of Russia.* Vol. 5, *The Tsardom of Moscow, 1547-1682.* New Haven, Conn.: Yale University Press, 1969. Vernadsky is a Russian émigré who has written many books on Russian history, including the multivolume *A History of Russia.* Generally, he presents a balanced but brief view of Godunov. He has a large bibliography for the entire period.

Eric L. Wake

JOHANN WOLFGANG VON GOETHE

Born: August 28, 1749; Frankfurt am Main
Died: March 22, 1832; Weimar, Saxe-Weimar-Eisenach
Areas of Achievement: Theater, drama, literature, and science
Contribution: Goethe, whose lyric, dramatic, and narrative talents produced literary works of lasting influence on the Western tradition, is considered to be one of the greatest German writers. An amateur scientist and able administrator, Goethe was a truly gifted man of his time.

Early Life

Johann Wolfgang von Goethe was born into a financially well-established family in the cosmopolitan city of Frankfurt am Main. His father, Johann, was a serious man, who retired from his law practice early and devoted himself to the education of his children. His mother, Katharine Elisabeth, was of a more lighthearted nature and stimulated the imaginative and artistic faculties of her children. From 1765 to 1768, Goethe studied law (at his father's request) at the University of Leipzig. In August, 1768, he became gravely ill with a lung ailment and returned to Frankfurt to recuperate. He remained there with his family until March, 1770, and then moved to Strassburg to complete his studies.

Life's Work

From April, 1770, to August, 1771, Goethe studied law in Strassburg; the period was a pivotal one for his development. He was of a literary nature and had never been interested in pursuing a law career. In Strassburg, he met Johann Gottfried Herder, an intense and brilliant man of letters, who encouraged Goethe's writing efforts. In Sesenheim, a small village outside the city, Goethe wooed a young woman, Frederike Brion, who inspired some of his best early poetry. His poems brought a vitality and freshness of image and theme to the discourse of the lyric. During the first half of the eighteenth century, German letters had reached a stasis in that the various genres had become rather mannered and stylized, often under the influence of prior Latin and French models. Goethe's older contemporaries, such as the poet Friedrich Klopstock and the dramatist Gotthold Lessing, had begun to create a new vision of the literary arts, and Goethe brought this impetus to fruition. He is considered a major representative of the dynamic *Sturm und Drang* (storm and stress) period of German literature.

Filled with youthful bravado and creative energy, the young Goethe was a genial spirit—discussion of the creative genius was current at the time—and his early poems and plays are populated with titanic individuals involved in great deeds. His play *Götz von Berlichingen mit der eisernen Hand* (1773; *Götz von Berlichingen with the Iron Hand*, 1799) is fueled by the dramatic energy of the Shakespearean stage and portrays the monumental life of a renegade knight in the late Middle Ages as he struggles to maintain his independence against the imperial intrigues of the Bamberg court. After receiving his law degree, Goethe began a practice in the city of Wetzlar and became involved with another woman, Charlotte Buff, who was engaged at the time. In great emotional distress, he left the city in 1772. His epistolary novel *Die Leiden des jungen Werthers* (1774; *The Sorrows of Young Werther*, 1779) is partly autobiographical and relates the tragic fate of a young man who is caught in a love triangle and whose intense emotions drive him to suicide. The book was a European best-seller and the favorite reading matter of Napoleon I.

In 1775, Goethe was appointed adviser to Karl August, the young Duke of Weimar, and moved to that city. He became involved with various administrative projects (such as road construction and mining) in the small duchy. In Weimar he also made the acquaintance of an older woman, Charlotte von Stein, who sought to cultivate the rather impetuous young writer. At the Weimar court, Goethe matured under her maternal guidance, and his literary production exchanged its *Sturm und Drang* intensity for the more measured tone and form of the neoclassical movement of the late eighteenth century. His play *Iphigenie auf Tauris* (1779; *Iphigenia in Taurus*, 1793) was written in iambic meter and presents an adaptation of the play by Euripides that deals with a part of the legendary Trojan War. Iphigenia was the daughter of King Agamemnon, who sacrificed her to the gods so that the Greek fleet might find favorable winds for their journey to besiege Troy. Goethe's version stresses in the title figure a vision of the ethically exemplary individual whose behavior exerts a morally didactic influence of moderation and mutual respect upon those around her.

From 1786 to 1788, Goethe traveled extensively in Italy and then returned to the Weimar court. In July, 1788, he met a young woman, Christiane Vulpius, with whom he lived in a common-law marriage for many years and with whom he had several children. Goethe continued to serve in various official capacities (including theater director) in Weimar, while working on his literary projects. After Goethe returned from his trip to Italy, he composed the *Römische Elegien* (1793; *Roman Elegies*, 1876), love poems that were modeled after the classical elegy form. His *Bildungsroman*, or novel of education, *Wilhelm Meisters Lehrjahre* (1795-1796; *Wilhelm Meister's Apprenticeship*, 1824) established the model for this narrative subgenre. It deals with the developmental years of a businessman's son as he seeks his place in life and becomes involved with a group of actors on their travels through Germany. Through a series of trials and errors, he encounters a number of different individuals and attains in the end what Goethe held to be a well-rounded personality, that is, one whose contemplative-artistic and practical-committed sides have achieved a degree of harmony. A life dedicated to the service of humanity is presented as the ultimate goal of Wilhelm's development. At this time, Goethe befriended the contemporary German poet and dramatist Friedrich Schiller, and the two maintained an active correspondence and collaborated on a well-known literary journal. During these years, Goethe was also actively engaged in various kinds of scientific research, especially comparative morphology and the theory of light refraction. He is credited with the discovery of a particular small bone in the human jaw. In *Zur Farbenlehre* (1810; *Theory of Colors*, 1840), he sought, in a fanciful way, to counter the prevailing light refraction theory of Sir Isaac Newton.

In 1809, Goethe started writing his autobiography, *Aus meinem Leben: Dichtung und Wahrheit* (1811-1814, 1833; *The Autobiography of Goethe*, 1824). During this same year, he also wrote another novel, *Die Wahlverwandtschaften* (1809; *Elective Affinities*, 1849), a complex text which uses the symbolic image of chemical attraction and repulsion to examine the conflicting interactions of fated passion and moral self-restraint in four individuals. In the following years, Goethe published another volume of poetry, *West-östlicher Divan* (1819; *West-Eastern Divan*, 1877), a collection of love lyrics influenced by the fourteenth century Persian poet Hāfez.

In 1808, Goethe published the first part of his dramatic poem *Faust: Eine Tragödie* (1808; *The Tragedy of Faust*, 1823), his best-known and most widely read work. The final editions are written in a variety of metrical patterns and rhyme schemes. He had begun working on an early version of the story—a late medieval legend that had become a popular chapbook in 1587—during his student stays in Strassburg. It is the story of a learned man, a scholar and professor named Heinrich Faust, who makes a pact with a devil, Mephistopheles, in order to gain a godlike understanding of the universe. In the first part, the devil rejuvenates the aging Faust, and the latter falls in love with an innocent young girl named Gretchen. Through the diabolical aid of Mephistopheles that leads to the deaths of Gretchen's mother and brother, Faust manages to seduce Gretchen, and she becomes pregnant. Faust abandons her; she murders her baby and goes insane with guilt. The first part concludes with Gretchen's execution and Faust's despair over what he has done. The second part of the Faust tragedy was published in 1833 and is a highly symbolic text in which Faust falls in love with the beautiful Helen of Troy. As an old man, he devotes himself to working on the behalf of humanity. When Mephistopheles comes to claim his soul at the moment of death, God intervenes and Faust receives the pardon of divine grace.

Earlier versions of the Faust story, such as the chapbook or Christopher Marlowe's *Doctor Faustus* (c. 1588), are didactic tales that illustrate the essentially corrupt nature of man. These Faust figures seek wealth and secular power. In these versions, Faust's soul is condemned to Hell. The character of Goethe's Faust, however, remains unique and is intended to represent the true spiritual nature of all human beings, that is, a striving for godlike perfection. His Faust seeks divine knowledge and not merely wealth and worldly prestige. The beginning of the poem contains a prologue in Heaven, in which Mephistopheles wagers with God that he can corrupt Faust, and the latter becomes thereby a kind of Everyman figure. The terms of the pact Mephistopheles makes with the scholar is that the former can satisfy Faust and cause him to say yes to the moment and cease striving for ever-greater knowledge. Although Faust makes serious mistakes in his quest for absolute knowledge, he never stops his efforts and is thus true to his divine nature. He is therefore saved from eternal damnation.

During Goethe's later years, he was honored as an internationally respected man of letters. Goethe died in Weimar on March 22, 1832. His last words were reputedly "More light!"

Summary

Johann Wolfgang von Goethe is a good example of the eighteenth century ideal of the Renaissance man. Like his American contemporary Thomas Jefferson, Goethe sought to encompass many fields of endeavor, from science and political affairs to the various genres of literature. It is in this latter area that he is most famous, and his role in the history of German literature is unparalleled. His literary production in poetry, drama, and fiction set standards that following generations of authors found hard to surpass.

Goethe revitalized the German lyric tradition. His *Erlebnislyrik*, or poetry of the individual's emotional or subjective experience, established a tradition that influenced nineteenth century German poets such as Annette von Droste-Hülshoff, Nikolaus Lenau, and Eduard Mörike. His dramatic works, along with those of Schiller, comprise today's repertoire of classical German theater. His version of the Faust story has been seen as an exemplary tale of the true nature of modern man. His narrative texts, especially the novel of education *Wilhelm Meister's Apprenticeship*, influenced nineteenth century examples of this genre such as the works of the Austrian Adalbert Stifter and the Swiss Gottfried Keller. His highly symbolic yet realistic narrative *Elective Affinities* also helped to further the tradition of the modern novel.

Goethe's personal philosophy—as expressed in his literary works—went through a development that echoes the general trends of European culture. His early works, with their emphasis on feeling over intellect as a mode of knowing, are essentially Romantic and follow the rebellious and emotional spirit of other writers and thinkers such as Jean-Jacques Rousseau. As he grew older, and in the bloody aftermath of the French Revolution, Goethe tended toward a more conservative point of view and believed that a stoic attitude of self-control, as well as hard work in the service of mankind, was the best that an individual could contribute to the progress of history. Goethe seemed to prefigure the spirit of resignation that informed much of German and European culture and philosophy during the latter half of the nineteenth century. As a leading figure in the literary arts of his age and beyond, Goethe helped to direct the course of German literature and thought.

Bibliography
Dieckmann, Liselotte. *Johann Wolfgang von Goethe*. Boston: Twayne, 1974. A good general introduction to Goethe's life and major texts that adopts a traditional critical perspective. Includes an annotated bibliography.
Fairley, Barker. *A Study of Goethe*. New York: Oxford University Press, 1947. An older but classic introduction to Goethe and his writings that is organized by both topics and periods of the author's life. Contains an index.
Gray, Ronald. *Goethe: A Critical Introduction*. Cambridge: Cambridge University Press, 1967. An excellent, thorough study of Goethe's life and major writings by a respected scholar. Contains a selected bibliography and notes.
Hatfield, Henry. *Goethe: A Critical Introduction*. New York: New Directions, 1963. A well-respected introductory survey of the author's life and works that is organized chronologically and gives some background information on the period. Contains a brief bibliography and illustrations.
Reed, T. J. *Goethe*. New York: Oxford University Press, 1984. A brief but informative and well-written introduction to Goethe's life and works that covers all the major texts and is organized by topics. Contains annotated suggestions for further reading and an index.
Van Abbé, Derek. *Goethe: New Perspectives on a Writer and His Time*. London: Allen & Unwin, 1972. A brief yet interesting overview of Goethe's life and works organized in terms of thematic topics. Contains background information on the period.

Thomas F. Barry

VINCENT VAN GOGH

Born: March 30, 1853; Zundert, the Netherlands
Died: July 29, 1890; Auvers-sur-Oise, France
Area of Achievement: Art
Contribution: During his brief artistic career, van Gogh gave expression to a
passionate vision of nature and humanity. Following his death, his paintings came to be acknowledged by critics and the public as constituting one
of the highest achievements of nineteenth century art.

Early Life

Vincent Willem van Gogh was born in Zundert, the Netherlands, on
March 30, 1853. His father, the Reverend Theodorus van Gogh, was thirty-
one years old at the time of Vincent's birth; his mother, Anna Cornelius
Carbentus, was three years older than her husband. Among van Gogh's three
sisters and two brothers, Vincent was to be close only to his brother Theodorus (called Theo), who was an important influence in his life. Vincent's
family had been established for generations in the Dutch province of North
Brabant, near the southern border with Belgium. Among his ancestors could
be found preachers, craftsmen, and government officials, and his living relatives included several uncles prominent in business and government. Vincent's father, a Protestant minister, was a handsome man but not a gifted
preacher. Working quietly in several rural parishes until his death at age
sixty-two, he was able to provide for his family in a respectable but modest
fashion.

Vincent enjoyed a happy childhood and was especially attached to the
natural world; drawings he made as early as age eleven show a keen observation of plant life. His skill at drawing, which seems to have been fostered by
his mother, does not foreshadow his later artistic genius, but it testifies to his
capacity for solitary concentration. The recollection of Vincent's sister Elizabeth was that Vincent could be unapproachable and that he enjoyed solitude. Yet if he seems to have had a somewhat changeable personality as a
boy, his education proceeded normally when he was sent at age twelve to a
boarding school in the nearby village of Zevenbergen, from which he progressed to a state secondary school in the town of Tilburg. By age fifteen, he
was well on the way to being a literate, if not yet sophisticated, young man.

After more than a year at home in Zundert, Vincent left in the summer of
1869 to work as a junior clerk in the branch of the French firm of Goupil and
Sons in The Hague, a post for which his uncle Vincent, a partner in the firm,
had recommended him. He enjoyed his work, found favor with his employers, and was transferred after four years to the London branch of the
firm. Beginning with this period, there is a substantially continuous documentation both of Vincent's activities and of his emotional and intellectual

experiences, for in August, 1872, he and Theo began a correspondence that was to last to the end of the artist's life.

In the summer of 1874, the first of several romantic disappointments struck van Gogh, when he declared his love for his landlady's daughter, Eugénie. Finding that she was engaged and had been playing upon his innocent devotion, he was cast into a despair, which he was unable to dispel during a three-month assignment to Goupil's Paris gallery. Returning to his London job in January, 1875, he once again failed to win Eugénie's love, and his distress, now colored by religious concerns, was intensified. In May he was permanently transferred to Paris, where his spiritual preoccupations distracted him from his work and led to his dismissal from Goupil's in March, 1876.

Van Gogh returned to England the following month and took an unpaid position in Ramsgate as a teacher of French, German, and arithmetic. In July, he changed jobs again, teaching at a boys' school in Isleworth and preaching occasionally. The prospect of a religious vocation began to dominate his thoughts, but with his health failing he returned to his parents' home, which was now in Etten. Soon after, his uncle found him another job in a bookstore in the city of Dordrecht, but by May, 1877, van Gogh had determined to study for admission to the faculty of theology at the University in Amsterdam. For a little more than a year, he studied Greek and Latin with a congenial young Jewish scholar, Mendes da Costa, but in July, 1878, declaring his inability to learn these languages, he enrolled in a preparatory course for evangelists in Brussels. Failing to qualify for a regular parish, van Gogh was given a trial appointment as a missionary in the Borinage, a coal-mining district of Belgium, but the church authorities soon dismissed him for his unconventionally zealous behavior. Continuing his work alone, van Gogh seems to have gone through a period of extreme spiritual crisis, during which he began to draw the very people to whom he had been preaching. In the autumn of 1880, believing that his destiny was to be an artist, van Gogh left the Borinage for Brussels, seeking advice there from painters and attempting to improve his drawings.

During the following spring and summer, van Gogh was again in Etten, where a second disappointment in love occurred. At his parents' home he met a recently widowed first cousin, Kee Vos Stricker, and fell in love with her, but she fled to her parents when van Gogh declared his affection. In this affair, van Gogh's capacity for creating strained relationships with those closest to him had reached a new peak, and as a result he left again for The Hague, where he established a small studio in January, 1882, and lived with a prostitute, Clasina Hoornik, known as "Sien."

Life's Work

Through his employment at the Goupil establishments, van Gogh had been exposed to much art that was merely fashionable, but he had also seen the paintings of notable French and English painters such as Jean-François Millet, Thomas Gainsborough, and John Constable. In his own early work, however, he was guided less by artistic precedents than by a profound urge to render the life of laboring peasants and miners and to evoke compassion for the suffering of his fellowman. Van Gogh was, from the start, temperamentally incapable of following a commonplace path in his art, but he valued the advice of his fellow painters, including popular ones such as his cousin by marriage, Anton Mauve, from whom he received instruction in The Hague during the winter of 1881-1882. Perhaps for family considerations, van Gogh's uncle, Cornelius, also lent the struggling artist encouragement in 1882 by commissioning from him a series of drawings of city views, but it was Theo's regular allowance that kept van Gogh from abject poverty throughout his artistic career. Just as important, Theo gave moral support to his erratic and socially inept elder brother, becoming a spiritual as well as financial guardian. He was also the recipient of much of van Gogh's best work, as van Gogh did not sell a painting until the last year of his life.

Van Gogh's passionate devotion to his artistic self-education yielded solid results during his stay in The Hague; to the emotional conviction of his drawings he was able to add increasing fluency of form. His subjects, principally peasants and workers, are often shown in a wintry landscape that seems both accurately rendered and true to the artist's social vision. There is experimentation with materials, but it is always aimed at rendering a particular subject rather than at producing an attractive appearance.

In the summer of 1883, van Gogh began to work in earnest with oil paints and during the next two years, living again at home with his parents in the village of Nuenen, he produced dozens of canvases of the countryside and its people. The culmination of this work is a masterpiece, *The Potato Eaters*, completed in October of 1885. It is a canvas approximately three feet high and four feet wide, depicting a family of five peasants seated around a rough table, about to eat a meal of boiled potatoes. Each figure, including that of a girl whose face cannot be seen, is a distinct portrait of human dignity in the face of adversity. Darkly monochromatic and roughly textured, *The Potato Eaters* is an uncompromising study of the human condition and has none of the sentimentality that van Gogh sometimes found appealing in other artists and writers.

The year 1885 brought important new influences to van Gogh. In October, he saw old master paintings in the Rijksmuseum in Amsterdam and found special inspiration in the work of Rembrandt and Frans Hals. In late November, while studying briefly in Antwerp, he first saw Japanese prints, which were just beginning to be widely appreciated in Europe. The clarity and brilliance of the Japanese woodblock print, together with the freshness of van Gogh's seventeenth century Dutch predecessors, helped change his conception of light and color, which had been dominated by earth colors and dark tones. Early in 1886, this change was accelerated by his move to Paris, where the Impressionist painters were gaining recognition for their innovative style of rendering effects of light and color by applying brilliant, unblended pigments to their canvases. Van Gogh was soon associating with the Impressionists and befriending such artists as Camille Pissarro and Henri de Toulouse-Lautrec. Theo, as a representative of the new owners of Goupil's, was an agent for Impressionist paintings and fueled van Gogh's appreciation and understanding of them.

In the summer of 1886, Theo and Vincent took an apartment together in the Paris suburb of Montmartre. Despite the deep affection of the brothers for each other, their relationship was often strained almost to the breaking point; perhaps the remarkable progress of van Gogh's painting was Theo's reward for tolerating his volatile and inconsiderate brother. For van Gogh, however, the Paris years of 1886 and 1887 were a time of relative stability. He became acquainted with many personalities with valuable experiences and opinions to share. Among these were artists such as Émile Bernard, who later wrote perceptively about van Gogh, and the celebrated Julien Tanguy, an art-supply dealer who offered a haven—and quiet financial help—to many painters who were subsequently recognized as leading artists of their day. Van Gogh's 1887 portrait of "Père" Tanguy shows the quiet gentleman seated against a wall on which Japanese prints—which he also sold—are hung. In this celebrated work, van Gogh unites his affection for Tanguy and his reverence for Japanese art with a Postimpressionist technique likely borrowed from Paul Signac.

After a remarkable two years in Paris, van Gogh may have believed that he had exhausted the city's possibilities; in any case, the stress underlying his relationship with Theo could not continue indefinitely, and in February, 1888, he left Paris abruptly for the town of Arles, near the Mediterranean coast, arriving on February 20. The south of France had then, as it has continued to have, rich associations for artists. In addition to the many reminders of classical Latin culture, the climate, light, and atmosphere could be powerful stimuli to creative work. In van Gogh's case, Arles and its environs was in some sense the cause of the astonishing outpouring of drawings and paintings that occurred between February, 1888, and May, 1890.

Ironically for an argumentative person such as van Gogh, he had been preoccupied by the idea of creating a brotherhood of artists, and his move to Arles was partly intended as a step in that direction. In the early months in Arles, he associated with several artist acquaintances, but more typically he formed friendships with local people such as the postman Joseph Roulin, whose portrait he painted many times. Yet in mid-October, van Gogh welcomed to his rooms in the "Yellow House" the stockbroker-turned-artist Paul Gauguin, another strong, even rebellious, personality with whom conflict might have been foreseen. Gauguin had traveled to Arles and was to be maintained there at Theo's expense in exchange for paintings. For a time, van Gogh and Gauguin valued their artistic relationship, but the domestic situation abruptly deteriorated, culminating—by Gauguin's account—in van Gogh's attack upon him with a razor blade. Before Gauguin could effect a departure from Arles, van Gogh had cut off part of his own earlobe, delivering it to the door of a local prostitute before returning, delirious and bleeding profusely, to his room at the Yellow House.

Following his recovery in the local hospital, van Gogh returned to the Yellow House on January 7 and began painting on the following day. The next month, he suffered hallucinations and was interned in a hospital cell for ten days, then released. By early May, he had agreed with Theo that he ought to enter an asylum in Saint-Rémy, several miles northeast of Arles, where he remained under the humane but ineffectual care of the asylum staff for slightly more than one year. A diagnosis of epilepsy, easily doubted but less easily supplanted by modern speculation, was made by the director, Dr. Peyron. Throughout his year at Saint-Rémy, van Gogh's condition varied enormously; sometimes he was not only calm and productive but also optimistic, and at other times he was uncommunicative and even suicidal. Remarkably, during his period of lucidity and physical well-being, he created many of his great masterpieces, including *The Starry Night* and a *Self-Portrait* of 1889. Like many of the works painted during his stay at Saint-Rémy, these canvases are characterized by vibrant color and the use of a sinuous line that make the surface of the painting seem to pulsate with energy. *The Starry Night*, along with another Saint-Rémy picture of irises, were included in a fall exhibition in Paris, where they attracted attention.

In January, 1890, the first article on van Gogh, and the only one published in his lifetime, appeared in *Mercure de France*. Entitled "The Isolated Ones: Vincent van Gogh," the article was the work of a perceptive young critic named G.-Albert Aurier, who had seen many of van Gogh's works at Theo's home. Aurier's observations were overwhelmingly enthusiastic, yet van Gogh wrote to Theo asking him to dissuade Aurier from writing any more about him. Although there was an element of modesty in this, it was more Vincent's accelerating exhaustion of spirit that caused him to be wary of acclaim. Events that buoyed his spirit, such as Theo's marriage and the birth of a nephew—also named Vincent Willem—could also have created new strains in his fragile mind.

Van Gogh left the asylum at Saint-Rémy on May 16, 1890, and traveled alone to Paris without incident, where he stayed four days with Theo and his family before traveling to nearby Auvers-sur-Oise to live under the supervision of Paul Gachet, an art-loving doctor of sixty-two. For several weeks, van Gogh carried on with his painting and even printed an etching using Gachet's press, but on July 27 he walked several hundred yards to a farm near Auvers and shot himself in the stomach. He managed to return to his room, and in the last thirty-six hours of his life he dozed, smoked his pipe, and spoke at length with Theo, who had been summoned from Paris. He died in the early morning hours of July 29, 1890. Only weeks later, Theo suffered a breakdown that seemed clearly connected to his grief over his brother's death, and on January 25, 1891, he died in Utrecht, the Nether-lands.

Summary

Vincent van Gogh's tumultuous life is so well documented by his letters and the recollections of family, friends, and associates, that an unusual de-gree of study and speculation has been devoted to his personal circumstances and particularly to the tragedy of his illness. In this respect, van Gogh has become virtually an archetype of the modern artist—a man ill at ease with himself and society, and restless in the personal as well as the artistic sphere. Van Gogh himself was well aware of the implications of his personality and his social situation, accepting his dependence upon his brother as well as his status as an outsider in order to pursue his art without compromise.

As compelling as van Gogh's story has been for critics and public alike, it is his paintings, and to a lesser extent his drawings, that are the cornerstone of his lasting significance. From the early drawings made during his ministry in the Borinage to the final paintings made in the weeks preceding his death in Auvers-sur-Oise, van Gogh's works are characterized by passionate sin-cerity. Yet as important as their psychological authenticity is their adven-turous form. Starting in the early 1880's from a vigorous but rather insular style, he assimilated the heritage of Dutch painting, then went on to adapt the lessons of Impressionism to new and visionary purposes. Van Gogh's singular artistic triumph, differentiating him from his Postimpressionist col-leagues such as Gauguin and Georges Seurat, was his ability to communicate both his visual experience of nature and his insight into man's social and spiritual condition.

Van Gogh, whose personal relationships were often catastrophic, saw his art as an act of love for humanity, and one avenue of psychological analysis views the fervor of his career as compensation for the emotional failures of his life. While there is doubtless some truth to this view, if taken too literally it can reduce the immense complexity of his life to a formula. Van Gogh was both highly intelligent and acutely self-aware, and it seems likely that even as he descended toward a tragic suicide, he was aware of the great, though painfully forged, achievement of his life as a painter.

Bibliography

Barr, Alfred H., Jr., ed. *Vincent van Gogh: With an Introduction and Notes Selected from the Letters of the Artist*. New York: Arno Press, 1966. This reprint edition of the catalog to a 1935 exhibition of the artist's work at the Museum of Modern Art, New York, is joined to an annotated bibliography, originally published in 1942, of articles, books, and other materials on van Gogh.

Cabanne, Pierre. *Van Gogh*. London: Thames & Hudson, 1963. Both the small format of this book and its somewhat breathless text frustrate the reader's wish to meet the artist, as much as possible, at first hand. Its efficiency is matched by its superficiality.

Gogh, Vincent van. *Complete Letters, with Reproductions of All Drawings in the Correspondence*. 3 vols. Greenwich, Conn.: New York Graphic Society, 1958. Van Gogh's letters rank among the finest literary artifacts in the sphere of visual art. Books of selected letters are useful but inevitably omit even items of general interest.

_____. *Van Gogh: A Retrospective*. Edited by Susan Alyson Stein. New York: Macmillan, 1986. A magnificent collection of documentary material and excellent color plates, this large book also contains a lengthy chronology of the artist's life, which corrects a number of factual errors scattered throughout many earlier sources.

_____. *Vincent van Gogh*. Text by Meyer Schapiro. New York: Harry N. Abrams, 1950. This volume, in a uniform series of artist monographs, contains a fine essay coupled with large color plates annotated on the facing page. The text is excellent as an introduction to the artist, but the plates do not reach the quality of modern reproductions.

_____. *The Works of Vincent van Gogh: His Paintings and Drawings*. Text by J.-B. de la Faille. New York: William Morrow, 1970. A complete (so far as scholarship can ascertain) catalog of the artist's works, each one illustrated, follows an essay, "Van Gogh and the Words," by A. M. Hammacher, which provides a history of the appreciation of van Gogh's works by leading writers and critics.

Krauss, André. *Vincent van Gogh: Studies in the Social Aspects of His Work*. Göteborg: Acta Universitatis Gothoburgensis, 1983. This compact study is a doctoral dissertation investigating the issue of social messages in the painter's work. Though it is specialized, it is very readable.

Wallace, Robert. *The World of Van Gogh, 1853-1890*. New York: Time-Life, 1969. Aimed at a popular audience, the text of this well-illustrated book is reliable, though sketchy. A justifiable, and even valuable, limitation is that van Gogh is presented alongside his contemporaries Toulouse-Lautrec and Seurat.

C. S. McConnell

NIKOLAI GOGOL

Born: March 31, 1809; Sorochintsy, Ukraine, Russia
Died: March 4, 1852; Moscow, Russia
Area of Achievement: Literature
Contribution: Gogol made an important contribution to the development of
modern comic fiction, particularly short fiction. By combining such disparate narrative elements as oral folklore and literary Romanticism, Gogol
paved the way for such modernist writers as Franz Kafka.

Early Life

Nikolai Gogol was born on March 31, 1809, on his family's country estate
in the Ukraine near the small town of Sorochintsy. A sickly child, he was so
pampered and idolized by his mother when he was young that he developed
an inflated opinion of himself. At the age of twelve, Gogol entered a boarding school in the city of Nezhin, where he stayed for seven years; however,
probably because he was bored with the routine of the classroom, he was
only an average student. He was, however, enthusiastic about literature and
drama, actively taking part in school theatricals in every capacity, from
stagehand to actor and director.

By all accounts, Gogol was a skinny, unattractive child with a bad complexion and a long nose; he was often called dwarfish by his schoolmates.
Although there is no indication that he gave serious thought to a writing
career while in school, Gogol did write one long poem during his adolescence entitled "Hans Küchelgarten" (1829), which he took to St. Petersburg
with him after graduation in 1828 and published at his own expense. Yet, as
most critics agree, the poem is highly imitative and immature; the derisive
reception it received by the few reviewers who noticed it at all probably
made Gogol decide to abandon poetry forever and focus instead on drama
and prose, in which his talent for mixing traditional styles and genres could
best be exhibited.

After his father's death, Gogol's mother was unable to manage the family
estate profitably; as a result, Gogol found himself without funds and without
prospects. Securing a position in the civil service to support himself, he began writing stories in his spare time about the Ukraine and submitting them
to a St. Petersburg periodical. By gaining the attention of such influential
Russian writers as Baron Anton Delvig and Vasily Zhukovsky with these
pieces, Gogol was introduced to the great Russian poet Alexander Pushkin,
who admired Gogol's fiction. Gogol's early stories were published in two
volumes in 1831 and 1832 as *Vechera na khutore bliz Dikanki* (*Evenings on
a Farm Near Dikanka*, 1926), and they received an enthusiastic response
from critics in Moscow and St. Petersburg; Gogol had thus arrived as an
exciting new talent and was admitted to the highest literary circles.

Life's Work

The stories in *Evenings on a Farm Near Dikanka* introduce readers to Gogol's major stylistic innovation—the combining of the fanciful and earthy folklore of his native Ukraine with the literary and philosophic imagination of German Romanticism, about which he had learned in school. The hybrid generic form that resulted from the combination of fantastic events and realistic detail not only characterizes Gogol's short stories in particular but also typifies similar narrative experiments being conducted with the short prose form in the United States, Germany, and France; Gogol's experimentation with short prose fiction gives him a place in the creation of the short story equal in importance to Edgar Allan Poe, E. T. A. Hoffmann, and Prosper Mérimée.

In 1834, Gogol obtained a position as a history professor at the University of St. Petersburg and lectured there for a little more than a year; however, he was so bad at it that the administration gently compelled him to leave. Essays in art, history, and literature on which Gogol had been working while teaching appeared in 1835 under the title *Arabeski* (*Arabesques*, 1982). Although these essays were not distinguished in any way, the three new stories that appeared in the collection—"Portret" ("The Portrait"), "Nevsky Prospekti" ("Nevsky Prospect"), and "Zapiski sumasshedshego" ("Diary of a Madman")—are significant Gogol works. Along with "Nos" (1836; "The Nose") and "Shinel" (1839; "The Overcoat"), and often referred to as the Petersburg Cycle, these stories are his major contribution to the short story and the novella forms.

Of the three stories that appeared in *Arabesques*, "Diary of a Madman" is perhaps the best known. Drawing some of his ideas from the German Romantic writer Hoffmann, Gogol has his central character, a minor government official, tell his own story of his hopeless infatuation with the daughter of the chief of his department. The story is an effective combination of social criticism, psychological analysis, and grotesque comedy, for, by intertwining the "mad" perception of the narrator with the supposedly "sane" perception of the bureaucratic world that surrounds the narrator, Gogol manages to underline the relativity of madness itself.

Gogol's story "The Nose" is perhaps second only to his masterpiece "The Overcoat" in its influence on subsequent fiction. The fantastic plot of the story begins when a St. Petersburg barber finds the nose of the assessor Major Kovalev, whom he shaves regularly, in his breakfast roll one morning. On the same morning, Kovalev wakes up to find a smooth, shiny place on his face where his nose used to be. When he goes to the police to have the case of the missing nose investigated, he is astonished to see his nose on the street wearing a gold-braided uniform. After finally recovering the nose, Kovalev tries unsuccessfully to stick it back on his face; finally, he wakes up one morning to find it back where it belongs. Although, like "Diary of a

Madman," the story is filled with ironic social criticism, what makes it so influential is the integration of this fantastic plot premise with the most straightforward style of narration. Like Kafka's twentieth century masterpiece *Die Verwandlung* (1915; *The Metamorphosis*, 1936), Gogol's "The Nose" only asks that the reader accept the initial incredible premise; all the rest follows in a strictly realistic fashion.

This combination of different realms of reality reaches a powerful culmination when Gogol unites it with two different literary styles in what all critics agree is his most nearly perfect work, "The Overcoat." The story of the poverty-stricken copyist with the absurd name of Akakii Akakiievich Bashmachkin is so well known that it has been said that most modernist Russian fiction springs from under Gogol's "overcoat." Once again, Gogol combines what seems to be social realism of everyday St. Petersburg life with the fantastic style of folklore. Indeed, most of the commentary that has been written on the story focuses on either its realistic nature or its fantastic style. Irish short-story writer Frank O'Connor has said that what makes the story so magnificent is Gogol's focus on the copyist and his emphasis on Akakii's implicit call for human brotherhood. On the other hand, in what is perhaps the best-known discussion of the story, Russian formalist critic Boris Eichenbaum claims that the genius of the story depends on the role played by the author's personal tone and the story's use of the oral conventions of Russian folktales.

Although Gogol published more ambitious works, at least in terms of scope, than these three short fictions, none of his later work surpasses them in narrative and stylistic control. Among Gogol's longer works, only one drama—*Revizor* (1836; *The Inspector General*, 1890)—and one novel—*Myortvye dushi* (part 1, 1842, part 2, 1855; *Dead Souls*, 1887)—remain as influential indicators of Gogol's genius. *The Inspector General*, although comic like his short fictions "The Nose" and "The Overcoat," is not fantastic like them. In fact, it has been called his most conventionally realistic work. Because of its satirical thrusts at government bureaucracy, the play was attacked, when it was first produced, by conservative critics as a slander on Russian government. Today it is remembered as one of Gogol's most emphatic social satires.

Many critics, more impressed with the broader scope of the novel than the more limited perfection of the short story, consider Gogol's novel *Dead Souls* to be his undisputed masterpiece. Indeed, it is an ambitious work, taking Gogol six years to complete. Building on an idea given him by Pushkin—that dead souls, or serfs, are taken as live ones—Gogol creates the character Tchitchikov, who buys dead souls to bolster his own wealth. Boasting an unforgettable assembly of grotesque comic characterizations, *Dead Souls* is often called one of the great comic masterpieces of European literature.

During the last ten years of his life, after the publication of part 1 of *Dead Souls*, Gogol worked on part 2. All that remains, however, are the first four chapters and part of a final chapter. In 1845, he burned all the other manuscript pages of the novel he had been working on for four years. Before his death in March, 1852, he once again put a match to the work he had subsequently done on part 2. He died a little more than a week later.

Summary

Although Nikolai Gogol died when he was only forty-two, thus leaving a body of work that is relatively small—certainly nothing to rival the monumental output of such nineteenth century greats as Leo Tolstoy and Fyodor Dostoevski—his influence has loomed much larger than his output would suggest. Although he is generally remembered as a writer of biting social satire on Russian government bureaucracy and as a creator of comic types that rival those of Charles Dickens, it is his short fiction in particular that has had the most significant impact. Gogol is indeed a writer's writer, for short-story writers themselves are the ones who most recognize his greatness. From his countryman Ivan Turgenev to Irish short-story writer Frank O'Connor to American philosopher and fiction writer William H. Gass, Gogol has been recognized as a powerful nineteenth century innovator in the creation of that strange blend of fantasy and reality—the comic grotesque—that has come to be recognized as an essential element of modernism and postmodernism.

Bibliography

Driessen, F. C. *Gogol as a Short-Story Writer: A Study of His Technique of Composition*. Translated by Ian F. Finlay. The Hague: Mouton, 1965. A formalist study of Gogol's technique as a short-story writer. Focuses on anxiety as a major Gogol theme before analyzing selected stories, including "The Overcoat," which Driessen says represents an isolated attempt of Gogol to overcome his anxiety.

Erlich, Victor. *Gogol*. New Haven, Conn.: Yale University Press, 1969. A study of Gogol by an expert on Russian formalist criticism. Focuses on Gogol's technique and his most typical themes and images. More theoretical than practical in its approach to Gogol, the study contains numerous provocative ideas and concepts for understanding his genius.

Fanger, Donald L. *The Creation of Nikolai Gogol*. Cambridge, Mass.: Harvard University Press, 1979. An attempt to compensate for what the author calls the overabundance of eccentric views of Gogol in American criticism. Fanger outlines the Russian cultural context of Gogol's work and then examines his works to elucidate the progressive development of its basic underlying pattern.

Lindstrom, Thaïs S. *Nikolay Gogol*. Boston: Twayne, 1974. A general introduction to Gogol's life and his art in chronological order. The focus is on Gogol's essential modernity and his creation of the comic grotesque. Includes a chronology of his life as well as a brief annotated bibliography of criticism.

Maguire, Robert A., ed. *Gogol from the Twentieth Century: Eleven Essays.* Princeton, N.J.: Princeton University Press, 1974. Includes eleven essays on Gogol from the perspective of various twentieth century Russian critical approaches, including formalist, psychological, religious, sociological, and historical criticism. Includes a famous essay by Boris Eichenbaum, "How Gogol's 'Overcoat' Is Made."

Peace, Richard. *The Enigma of Gogol.* Cambridge, England: Cambridge University Press, 1981. A study of Gogol's works from the point of view of their place in the Russian literary tradition, particularly focusing on the enigma of the scope of Gogol's influence on a realistic tradition in spite of his own grotesque rhetorical style.

Setchkarev, Vsevolod. *Gogol: His Life and Works.* Translated by Robert Kramer. New York: New York University Press, 1965. A readable introduction to Gogol's life and art. This straightforward study does not pretend to break any new critical ground but rather summarizes previous criticism and analyzes Gogol's works both thematically and formally.

Charles E. May

CHARLES GOUNOD

Born: June 18, 1818; Paris, France
Died: October 18, 1893; St. Cloud, France
Area of Achievement: Music
Contribution: Because of his great popularity and stylistic influence on the next generation of composers, Gounod is often considered to be the central figure in French music in the third quarter of the nineteenth century.

Early Life

Charles-François Gounod's father, Nicolas-François Gounod, was a gifted painter and winner of a Second Prix de Rome in 1783; his mother, Victoire Lemachois, a pianist, gave her son his early musical instruction. After completing his academic studies at the Lycée Saint-Louis, Charles Gounod received private musical training from composer-theorist Antoine Reicha; in 1836, when Gounod entered the Paris Conservatoire, he studied with such professors as Jacques Halévy (counterpoint), Jean-François Le Sueur (composition), and Pierre Zimmermann (piano). The extent of his musical education before entering the Paris Conservatoire, coupled with his exceptional talent, led him to win a Second Prix de Rome in 1837 and the Grand Prix de Rome two years later.

On December 5, 1839, Gounod left Paris for Rome; it was during his years in Rome that he met several women who played a significant role in his musical development. Felix Mendelssohn's married sister, Fanny Hensel, an accomplished pianist, introduced Gounod to the music of her brother, the music of Johann Sebastian Bach and Ludwig van Beethoven, as well as to the works of Johann Wolfgang von Goethe. Pauline Garcia was the sister of Maria Felicia Garcia Malibran, a singer who had been much admired by the young French artistic world before her death in 1836 at the age of twenty-eight. Pauline, besides being an excellent singer with a unique mezzo-soprano voice, was also married to Louis Viardot, director of the Théâtre-Italien and a valuable ally for a young composer. Yet another important influence in Gounod's life was the Dominican Friar Père Lacordaire. Lacordaire's sermons, which caused a great stir in Rome between the years 1838 and 1841, also impressed the young Gounod, whose sensibilities were constantly engaged in a battle between the sacred and the profane.

In the fall of 1842, Gounod left Rome for Vienna, where he received commissions for two masses, which were performed at the Karlskirche on November 2 (a requiem) and on March 25, 1843. During his stay in Vienna, Gounod had an opportunity to hear the Gewandhaus orchestra, probably the best orchestra in Europe at the time. Fortunate among French musicians of his generation, Gounod became acquainted with music, past and present, that was neither operatic nor within the French tradition.

After his return to Paris, Gounod became organist of the Missions Étrangères. Yet he soon found himself in conflict with congregations who viewed the music of Bach and Giovanni Palestrina, music which Gounod greatly admired, as strange and unattractive. At this time in his life, Gounod's inclinations as well as his work led him to frequent ecclesiastical circles. Undoubtedly, this fact, combined with the influence of Lacordaire's sermons, inspired his decision to study for the priesthood. Although he took courses at St. Sulpice between 1846 and 1848, Gounod later referred to this interest in the priesthood as but a passing fancy.

Life's Work

The music that Gounod wrote immediately after his ecclesiastical studies was still intended for the Church. When he discontinued his studies at St. Sulpice, however, he soon turned to the field cultivated by most French composers of his day, the opera. In fact, it was Pauline Viardot who persuaded him to write his first opera, *Sapho* (1851), by promising to sing the title role. Although Hector Berlioz praised the music, and another critic detected in it the influence of Christoph Gluck, the work was generally considered a failure.

Since her performance as Fides in *Le Prophète* in 1849, Pauline Viardot had been one of the favorite artists of Giacomo Meyerbeer, whose reputation in Paris was at its zenith. It is therefore not surprising that Gounod's next opera, *La Nonne sanglante* (1854), based on Matthew Lewis' *The Monk*, should have been crafted in the Meyerbeer tradition. Yet this opera also proved to be a failure. In the meantime, however, Gounod had written music for the choruses of François Ponsard's drama *Ulysse*, performed at the Comédie Française in 1852, and these earned for him an appointment as conductor of the largest male choir in Paris, L'Orphéon de la Ville de Paris. At this time he married Anna, the daughter of Pierre Zimmermann, who from 1820 to 1848 had been chief professor of the piano at the Paris Conservatoire.

During the decade 1855-1865, Gounod was at the height of his musical powers. In the area of church music, in which he had already succeeded, the *Messe solennelle de Sainte Cécile*, first performed on November 22, 1855, was a masterpiece in an ornate style which had come to replace the austere style in which he composed his early masses.

In 1858, Gounod began his association with the Théâtre-Lyrique, a theater founded in 1851 and dedicated to the performance of musico-dramatic works. Of the seven stage works that Gounod wrote between 1855 and 1865, five were first performed at the Théâtre-Lyrique; it is these five operas for which he is remembered more than a century later. Two of these are small-scale, lighthearted works in which his refined craftsmanship and unpretentious lyrical abilities were joined to well-known stories: Molière's play adapted by Jules Barbier and Michel Carré in *Le Médecin malgré lui* (1858) and the same adapters' version of the classical myth in *Philémon et Baucis* (1860). In these, Gounod finally discarded his Meyerbeerian pretensions and cultivated his own unique brand of wit and lyricism. The same librettists wrote for him not only the comic opera *La Colombe* (1860) but also the far more important *Faust* (1859), the work by which the composer first became famous with the general public. The success of *Faust* had already opened the doors of the opera to Gounod. Yet it was only when he returned to the Théâtre-Lyrique and to the singer Marie Miolhan-Carvalho, who had sung the role of Marguerite in *Faust*, that Gounod scored two more major successes. The first was *Mireille* (1864), based on Frédéric Mistral's Provençal poem *Mirèio*, which had appeared in 1859. The second was the opera *Roméo et Juliette* (1867).

A disruption in Gounod's career as well as his private life came during the Franco-Prussian War of 1870-1871. On September 13, 1870, he and his family took refuge with English friends outside London. Although he was offered the directorship of the Conservatoire in June, 1871, it was not until June, 1874, that he returned to Paris.

While he never stopped writing occasional motets and cantatas for church use, he had written no mass since 1855; his major energies had been devoted to the opera. Even now it was an opera in which he eventually decided to incorporate for the first time his new musical ideals, which included writing music of tranquillity and feeling, music which transported the listener outside the realm of everyday life. While completing his opera *Polyeucte* (1878) in England, Gounod recognized the popularity of choral music in that country and was anxious to exploit both his own status as the composer of *Faust* and his experience as a choral conductor. Thus, when the Royal Albert Hall Choral Society was formed in 1871, Gounod became its first conductor. During this period in his life, Gounod was high in the royal favor (*Faust* was Queen Victoria's favorite opera) and was glad to indulge the demand for sentimental ballads popular in mid-Victorian England. He had already written the notorious *Bethléem* and *Jésus de Nazareth* in the mid-1850's; the *Méditation sur le prélude de S. Bach* (1852), from which come the endless arrangements of *Ave Maria*, was composed in 1852.

Gounod gave up all the advantages of his position in England, however, when, in February, 1871, he met Georgina Weldon, an amateur singer separated from her husband and well connected socially. Weldon sang the solo part in Gounod's patriotic cantata *Gallia* (1871) at the reopening of the Conservatoire and again at the Opéra-Comique that summer. When she returned to London in 1871, she took Gounod with her. He was installed in Tavistock House, Bloomsbury, which Weldon had taken for her projected National Training School of Music. Gounod was quite seriously ill at the time and responded with growing hysteria to the hectic life in which he found himself at the school. Yet, in spite of these conditions, he managed to write most of *Polyeucte*, the incidental music to Jules Barbier's *Jeanne d'Arc* (1873), a requiem, ten psalms and anthems, twelve choruses, and three songs and short pieces. Yet his social position was rapidly deteriorating. He was soon to enrage not only his own son, Jean, but also the English court as well when Weldon attempted to blackmail Queen Victoria into giving Gounod royal support for the Tavistock Academy and reinstatement in the Royal Albert Hall Choral Society after his falling out with the director.

For many reasons, then, Gounod's years in England seem to mark the end of his fruitfulness as a composer. As his ideals became loftier and his ideas more profound, his art became increasingly repetitive and platitudinous. The simplicity at which Gounod aimed in *Polyeucte* and *La Rédemption* (1882) disintegrated more and more into banality. Between 1882 and 1885, *La Rédemption* was performed all over Europe, including Vienna and Rome. Yet while it was immensely popular, it was sharply attacked by the critics. *Polyeucte* fared little better.

It was not until June, 1874, that Gounod finally returned to France after a frightening cerebral attack during which he lay unconscious for long periods of time. With failing eyes but much determination, he struggled to complete his last piece of music, a requiem for his grandson Maurice, who had died prematurely. While reading through the manuscript, Gounod lapsed into a coma and died two days later, on October 18, 1893.

Summary

In England, Charles Gounod had a strong and long-lasting influence on choral music, especially in the ecclesiastical and oratorio spheres, where *La Rédemption* occupied a prominent position in the 1880's. Like Giacomo Puccini and Richard Strauss a generation later, both Gounod and Mendelssohn expressed with skill and dignity the hopes and dreams of the contemporary bourgeoisie. The combination in *Faust* of tender sentiment and power of musical characterization with clean and imaginative craftsmanship made a deep impression on Peter Ilich Tchaikovsky, who owed almost as much to Gounod as to Georges Bizet and Léo Delibes.

Only a generation after Gounod's death, François Poulenc and Georges Auric were proclaiming as characteristically French the virtues of *Le Médecin malgré lui*, *La Colombe*, and *Philémon et Baucis* in their reaction against the music of Richard Wagner. All three works were revived by Sergei Diagilev in January, 1924. At the same time, a number of Gounod's songs were also revived; they have remained in the French repertory ever since. It was Gounod's belief that France was the country of "precision, neatness, and taste," and it is as a master of these qualities that he is best remembered.

Bibliography
Cooper, Martin. *French Music: From the Death of Berlioz to the Death of*

Fauré. New York: Oxford University Press, 1951. Provides a historical perspective on French music and includes a brief section on Gounod. Offers a succinct overview of the composer's life. Contains a bibliography and a table of events listing the major composers and other artists (and their principal works) during the years 1870-1925.

Gounod, Charles-François. *Memoirs of an Artist*. Translated by Annette E. Crocker. New York: Rand McNally, 1895. Gounod's intriguing but sentimental autobiography, spanning the years from his childhood to the writing of *Faust*.

Harding, James. *Gounod*. New York: Stein & Day, 1973. This informative biography discusses Gounod as a man of contradictions and extremes, demonstrating how the elements at war within his personality were reflected in his music. Assesses the impact of Gounod's music on later composers. Bibliography and appendix.

Hervey, Arthur. *Masters of French Music*. New York: Charles Scribner's Sons, 1894. This work contains a lengthy chapter devoted to Gounod. The author also focuses his discussion on Gounod's *Faust*, especially on the themes of love and religion in the work.

Tiersot, Julien. "Charles Gounod: A Centennial Tribute." *Musical Quarterly* 6 (July, 1918): 409-439. Tiersot examines the work and career of Gounod, as well as the man. Attempts to assess more objectively Gounod's contribution to French music.

Genevieve Slomski

FRANCISCO DE GOYA

Born: March 30, 1746; Fuendetodos, Spain
Died: April 16, 1828; Bordeaux, France
Area of Achievement: Art
Contribution: A painter and engraver, Goya was not only one of Spain's greatest artists but also one of Western art's most original practitioners. His aesthetic range was so comprehensive that he anticipated all the major artistic schools from the French Romantics to the German Expressionists.

Early Life

Francisco de Goya was born in the desolate hills of northeastern Spain, in the province of Aragon, a dry, parched, and barren land. His father was a gilder of Basque origin and was frequently unemployed. The family possessed little property and poverty forced them to work in the fields to feed themselves. Goya's lifelong terror of returning to the indigence of his early youth stimulated him to negotiate complex political maneuvers during several of Spain's stormiest changes of government in order to retain his comfortable household. When he was five years old, his father moved the family to the nearby town of Saragossa, where the boy spent the rest of his youth.

Because of his family's financial needs, the fourteen-year-old Goya was apprenticed to the highly successful church artist José Luzán. After four years of grinding colors, he began composing his own pictures, most of which were imitations of his master, Luzán, and realistic reproductions of old masters. It was also in Saragossa that Goya met and became close friends with Martin Zapater, a classmate; their mutual correspondence over many years, though far from complete, provides the basis of what is known of Goya's complex personality. The years of hard and monotonous work in Luzán's studio contributed to the characteristic rapidity and proficient technical craftsmanship that Goya was able to maintain throughout his creative life. He would become famous for his ability to complete a portrait during one long morning session. He corrected virtually nothing substantial because his hand and his eye were so practiced.

In spite of these long years of grueling apprenticeship, Goya was unable to advance his career as quickly as he wished. In 1763 and 1766, he entered contests for scholarship admittance to the Royal Academy of San Fernando in Madrid and failed both times. Frustrated and angry, he left Spain for Rome, where he assiduously studied, copied, and absorbed the influences of the Italian masters, particularly Correggio and the Venetian Giovanni Tiepolo. Indeed, many critics attribute Goya's warmer and richer colors in his work at this time to Tiepolo's influence. Another, and possibly more compelling reason for Goya's quick departure from Spain was the increasing pressure he and other free-spirited liberals were under from the reactionary pro-

ponents of the Inquisition. The Italians were considerably more appreciative
of the young artist's talents and awarded him second prize in a contest
sponsored by the Academy of Art of Parma in 1770. It seems that Goya then
left Rome suddenly because he had become involved in several exciting but
dangerous romantic escapades, a habit Goya never relinquished for the remainder of his life.

After ten years of neglect and failure, Goya's dogged tenacity prevailed,
and he managed to gain recognition outside his own country. He returned to
Saragossa and was promptly commissioned to paint frescoes in the Cathedral
of Our Lady of the Pillar. He had returned home with honor and a promising
project that lasted for the next ten years. He painted these works in the
prevailing Baroque-Rococo style of the day but was still able to lend his
personal touch to them; they were, even at this early stage, unmistakably
Goya's work.

During these years, 1770-1773, the young artist pursued further studies
with the well-known and highly influential painter Francisco Bayeu, a fellow
Aragonese. He married Bayeu's sister, Josefa, in 1773, a move that did not
hurt his steadily growing reputation. Indeed, it was through his brother-in-
law that he received an important commission to do the enormous mural
paintings of the Carthusian Charterhouse of Auli Dei in Saragossa, work that
dramatically caught the attention and respect of both the artistic and royal
communities in Madrid. Again, because of the influence of Bayeu, he was
summoned to Madrid in 1774 by the reigning artistic dictator of the court of
Charles III, the powerful German-Czech exponent of neoclassicism, Anton
Raphael Mengs. Mengs commissioned him to participate in preparing fifty
cartoons to be submitted to the royal tapestry factory of Santa Barbara, a
project that brought him into direct contact with King Charles III and the
royal household. By 1774, the twenty-eight-year-old Goya found himself at
the threshold of a career that would eventually lead him to the post of first
painter to the king.

Life's Work

The year 1775 marked two significant events in Goya's life. One was the
birth of his son, Xavier, the only child who lived beyond infancy. The other
was his first self-portrait, a strikingly optimistic one at that, and the first of
many throughout the years. His cartoons for the tapestry factory of Santa
Barbara demonstrated, in a relatively short time, the emergence of his own,
unique style once he overcame his initial timidity and stopped trying to
imitate the flaccid neoclassicism of his brother-in-law. Not only did Goya
forge a new phase of Spanish art which started with El Greco, but also he
managed to imprint his own character on everything he touched. Several of
these cartoons have become examples of Goya's earliest work, notably *The
Parasol* and *The Washerwoman*.

During these years, 1776-1780, Goya was received into the court of the intelligent and kindly Charles III and given the opportunity to examine in depth the royal collection of paintings. The first and perhaps most revolutionary influence he was to encounter was the work of Diego Velázquez. The influence was immediate and permanent. Goya's subsequent paintings displayed a deft handling of reflected light and atmospheric effects that had been absent from his earlier pictures. Goya stated on several occasions that he acknowledged only three masters: "Rembrandt, Velázquez, and Nature!" His adaptations of effects and techniques from earlier masters eventually enabled him to synthesize the neoclassical and Baroque-rococo elements in his work into his own, quasi-romantic treatment of even the most banal subjects.

After winning several competitions and important positions in the Royal Academy of San Fernando, he become painter of the royal household under Charles IV, Charles III's considerably less sensitive and frivolous son. The work that won for him these lucrative positions was a series of portraits he had begun in 1783. The first, *Portrait of the Count of Floridablanca* secured for him nationwide fame. It was also the first major portrait in which he portrayed himself, an act simultaneously imitating and paying tribute to his spiritual master Velázquez. It was also an unmistakable sign that Goya saw himself, quite consciously, as a successor in a line of Spanish painters beginning with El Greco and Velázquez.

Other portraits followed quickly, and his work was in great demand by every level of aristocracy. It is in these portraits, particularly the justly famous *Portrait of Don Manuel Orsorio* (1788) and *The Duke and Duchess of Osuna* (1789), that Goya successfully developed a quality of luminescent impressionism that become his hallmark. With this quality, he managed to avoid any suggestion of mere prettiness or sentimentality but at the same time beautified, without decorating, his sense of the world about him.

Just as Goya was concluding his work on the tapestries of Santa Barbara, he contracted a mysterious malady that manifested itself in the form of enormous noises in his head. The illness, along with the monstrous sounds, eventually disappeared but left him permanently deaf. Critics have theorized that, like Ludwig van Beethoven's deafness, Goya's terrible misfortune isolated him from much of society—he had been the darling of society up to that point—but at the same time deepened his content and forced it into areas beyond the realm of brilliant portraiture. It was shortly after his recovery from the illness that he began a series of etchings, the first of three extended studies that have come to be considered his major intellectual contributions not only to the world of eighteenth century art but also to the general history of ideas and images of Western Europe. He called them *The Caprices* (1793-1796); they consisted of eighty aquatint etchings that detail with satiric savagery man's inhumanity to man and "existence as catastrophe." They also employ techniques and procedures that would later be called surrealistic and expressionistic, modes that recalled the hallucinatory terror of Hieronymus Bosch. They express a sense of existential emptiness, but the void is actively corrosive. The etchings present man as a victim of not only all ideologies and beliefs but also the pincers of his own mind. They became major prophetic and satiric warnings of what civilization was sliding into during the eighteenth century.

Although *The Caprices* became the map of his own and Europe's fall into spiritual torpor, Goya's career as a portrait painter flourished as he produced what would later be regarded as prototypical Goyaesque works. His relationship with the royal house of Alba and specifically his love for the Duchess of Alba, who may or may not have been his lover, inspired two masterpieces of her and spilled over into two even more famous portraits that unquestionably established his reputation, the stunningly sensuous *The Clothed Maja* and *The Naked Maja*. The climax of Goya's career, however, occurred with his appointment, one for which he had been waiting and maneuvering, as first court painter in 1799, the same year in which he produced the two Maja paintings. The next year, he produced what most critics see as his greatest single painting: *Portrait of the Family of King Charles IV*. In this huge work, he accomplished the task of rendering the members of this venal, not very bright, and distinctly ugly family with pitiless accuracy. A more sensitive and intelligent patron and his family would have been highly insulted, but Goya's genius was so sure-handed that he was able to blind these people to their own ineffectual self-indulgence while demonstrating it to the world. Moreover, he vividly portrayed the disastrous effects that genetic inbreeding, both physical and spiritual, had had on the great house of Bourbon and, by implication, the equally destructive forces that were bringing all the great houses of Europe to ruin within the next fifty years. In this single magnificent portrait, Goya verified the beginning of the end of what had started as the Holy Roman Empire in A.D. 800.

With the death of the Duchess of Alba and the chaos created by the Franco-Spanish War, Goya began his second series of etchings, known as *The Disasters of War* (1810). They further deepen and certify the despair of *The Caprices* but specify the horrors in the atrocities, agonies, and starvation of actual war. By 1814, he was able to paint perhaps the greatest and most compelling images of war in all of Western art, *The Executions of May Second* and *The Executions of May Third*. Both series of etchings and these last paintings demonstrate a darkening of Goya's vision and expression, an expression that found its most despairing depictions in his final series of etchings, known as *The Proverbs* (1815-1816). Here he expresses his profound grief and dismay in eighteen viciously satiric allegories that seem to be utterly disengaged from any rational foundations. His penultimate statement on the human condition he saved for the walls of his own house, which he named *Quinta del Sordo* (house of the deaf man). He called these works *The Black Paintings*, and they could have been rendered by Salvador Dali or Pablo Picasso in their most surreal periods, since they depict apocalyptically hallucinatory visions that seem to foretell the fall of Western civilization.

In fear that the new leadership resulting from the Franco-Spanish War would punish him for his outspoken views, Goya exiled himself in France temporarily. Once he saw that it was safe to return, he was received kindly by Ferdinand VII and given a hefty pension for life. He found life under the new regime too repressive, however, and moved back to Bordeaux, where he produced his final masterpiece. He returned to the subjects of his youth, the common folk, and created *The Milkmaid of Bordeaux* (1827), a work that brings together all the styles within which he worked and created, centering them within an autumnal but hopeful serenity. He died peacefully at age eighty-two on April 16, 1828.

Summary

Francisco de Goya shared with the English poet and engraver William Blake and the great German composer Ludwig van Beethoven the unenviable position of connecting two of the stormiest centuries of the Christian era: the eighteenth and nineteenth centuries, the Age of Enlightenment and the Romantic Age. He, like the other two geniuses, was more than a mere transitional figure. His work, because of the vividly regenerative power of his imagination, created an intellectual and spiritual world in which the work of such great French artists as Eugène Delacroix, Théodore Géricault, and Honoré Daumier could draw sustenance and find validation. Goya's major achievement was, in short, the enlargement of the possibilities of the Western imagination to an almost limitless degree. Like Beethoven in his early formalistic work, Goya too moved from safe traditional forms into later projects where form and content became extensions of each other. In one dramatically vivid lifetime, Goya moved from the highly traditional Baroque-Rococo to the openness and complexity of the Romantic mode which, in turn, made possible the modern sensibility.

Goya's direct influences on later artists are varied and sometimes remarkably surprising. His work prefigures that of Delacroix by embodying the principle that the personal is always the political, certainly a controlling idea in Delacroix's and other Romantics' work. Goya's sardonic satires paved the way for the work of another French social satirist, Daumier, while his impeccable handling of light and shade and his uniquely luminescent textures undoubtedly influenced the major French Impressionists, such as Édouard Manet, Claude Monet, and Pierre-Auguste Renoir. Indeed, Manet derived from Goya's *The Executions of May Third* his own *Execution of Maximilian*, and he offered no apologies. Finally, Goya's nightmarish and hallucinatory etchings of *The Proverbs*, *The Caprices*, and *The Disasters of War* unquestionably anticipate the work of such major nineteenth and twentieth century European Expressionists as Käthe Kollwitz, Edvard Munch, Emil Nolde, and Paul Klee. Without Goya's aesthetic permission, his fellow Spanish surrealists, Picasso and Dali, could not have flourished. Goya was unquestionably one of the major revolutionary figures in the history of European art, and his rich legacy continues to resonate.

Bibliography
Chabrun, Jean-François. *Goya*. Translated by J. Maxwell Brown John. New York: Tudor Publishing, 1965. A highly readable novelistic narrative with much biographical information. Amply illustrated with both color and black-and-white prints. Excellent for beginners.
Glendinning, Nigel. *Goya and His Critics*. New Haven, Conn.: Yale University Press, 1977. The most intelligent treatment of the artist from the point of view of his place and influence within the history of art and European intellectual tradition. The author has spent much effort in tracking down every reference to Goya in the works of many other artists. Also examines and analyzes his work with the latest critical approaches.
Goya, Francisco de. *Goya*. Text by José Gudiol. New York: Harry N. Abrams, 1965. A handsome volume with vivid and exceptionally well-produced reproductions of many of Goya's major masterpieces. The introduction traces Goya's life chronologically and offers intelligent, if sometimes stuffy, analyses of the works.
Klingender, Francis D. *Goya in the Democratic Tradition*. New York: Schocken Books, 1968. An unashamedly partisan treatment of Goya in relation to his intellectual and social background. Thoroughly grounded in historical fact, highly readable, and stimulating.
Lewis, D. B. Wyndham. *The World of Goya*. London: Michael Joseph, 1968. Tends to be told in a quasi-novelistic narrative but done with much closer adherence to historical facts than Chabrun's work. Excellent cross-reference system. Densely illustrated. Highly readable and stimulating.
Licht, Fred. *Goya: The Origins of Modern Temper in Art*. New York: Universe Books, 1979. A comprehensive and scholarly book that is unfortunately marred by the fact that all the illustrations are done in black and white. Each chapter is concerned with only one group of works—cartoons, or religious paintings, and so on—thus helping the reader focus on the similarities and differences found within the groups. Extremely helpful and thoroughly grounded in historical facts.
_____, ed. *Goya in Perspective*. Englewood Cliffs, N.J.: Prentice-Hall, 1973. An intelligent and comprehensive collection of essays written by art critics and historians. The essays offer a variety of views on Goya from the poetic to the sociological.

Patrick Meanor

EL GRECO
Doménikos Theotokópoulos

Born: 1541; Candia, Crete
Died: April 7, 1614; Toledo, Spain
Area of Achievement: Art
Contribution: Adapting principles he learned in Venice and Rome, El Greco achieved a unique artistic style and became Spain's greatest religious artist and one of the world's foremost portrait painters.

Early Life

El Greco (Doménikos Theotokópoulos) was born in Candia, Crete, in 1541. Of his family, little is known, except that his father's name was Jorghi and one brother was named Manoussos. Since his knowledge of languages and his wide intellectual interests suggest a good education, El Greco's biographers have assumed that his Greek family belonged to the middle class. During his boyhood, Crete was a center of Byzantine culture and Greek Orthodox religion. Art on the island was primarily church related, depicting saints in the somber manner of orthodox iconography. Intended to inspire devotion, it often features stereotypical human forms against a dark and undeveloped background. From a surviving document, it is known that by age twenty-five El Greco was a practicing artist.

For unknown reasons, El Greco left Crete, probably in 1567, for Venice, where he continued his study of painting. There he encountered the warm, rich coloration and carefully balanced perspective of the Venetian school. Biographers have surmised that he became a member of Titian's workshop. In Venice, he adopted the nickname "Il Greco" (the Greek), later changing the article to the Spanish *El.*

In 1570, El Greco left Venice for Rome, where he came under the influence of the Florentine-Roman school, dominated by the rich artistic legacy of Raphael and Michelangelo. The mannerist influence of Roman painting, which featured elongated human forms, unusual gestures, convoluted and contorted body positions, foreshortening, and half figures, left a lasting impression on El Greco's work. In 1572, he was admitted to the Roman Academy of St. Luke, the painters' guild, a membership that entitled him to artistic patronage and contracts. Among the paintings that remain from his Roman experience are one extraordinary portrait, that of his patron Giulio Clovio, *Christ Healing the Blind* (1577-1578), and *Purification of the Temple* (c. 1570-1575), an early work that includes a large group of figures. According to anecdote, El Greco did not thrive in Rome because he made disparaging remarks about Michelangelo, and, while that cannot be confirmed, his later written comments reveal that he thought Michelangelo's work defective in coloration. Among his circle of acquaintances in Rome were two Spanish theologians who later became his patrons, Luis de Castilla and Pedro Chacón, both from Toledo. Sometime during the middle 1570's, he left Rome for Spain, where he hoped to secure patronage and to establish his reputation.

Life's Work

In 1577, the year of El Greco's arrival, Toledo reflected the culture of Spain following the Council of Trent, an event which inaugurated the Catholic Counter-Reformation. In art, its canons called for religious themes and events to be related closely to human experience and to embody strong and immediate sensory appeal. The Spanish monarch Philip II was intent on preserving Spanish power, prestige, and grandeur, and commissions for artists were readily available. Among El Greco's early Spanish paintings, *The Martyrdom of Saint Maurice* (c. 1580) was commissioned by the king for his palace, El Escorial. The painting did not please the royal patron, for he did not regard it as adequately devotional; thereafter, El Greco acquired most of his patronage from Toledo. Shortly after his arrival in the city, El Greco settled into domestic life. His Spanish mistress, Doña Jerónima de las Cuevas, bore in 1578 his son Jorge Manuel Theotokópoulos, whom he trained as an artist and collaborator. In the Villena Palace, he acquired spacious apartments (twenty-four rooms) and established a workshop employing several assistants. There is some indication that he lived an affluent if not lavish lifestyle. He accumulated a substantial library, largely of classics and Italian literature, and hired musicians to perform during his dinner. His personality was somewhat haughty and contentious, and he often found himself involved in conflicts over the remuneration for his work, which at times resulted in lawsuits.

The workshop approach and collaborators were necessitated by the exigencies of contracts available at the time. The most profitable were for altarpieces, groups of five or six large paintings arranged above and beside the altars of churches and chapels. These paintings required elaborately sculpted bases and frames, and the artist who was prepared to undertake an entire project held an advantage. Contracts were usually specific as to subject, size, and arrangement. Many of El Greco's best-known paintings resulted from such contracts; for example, his masterpiece *The Burial of the Count of Orgaz* (1586), a painting that measures ten by sixteen feet, has never been removed from the Church of Santo Tomé, Toledo.

El Greco's total output is estimated at 285 paintings, although the number attributed to him has ranged upward to 850. A firm figure is not easily ascertained for several reasons. First, he often produced several versions of the same subject, and these can easily be classified as copies or imitations. Second, his workshop produced smaller-scale copies of his better-known works for sale to clients, and these can easily be mistaken for originals.

Third, paintings by an obscure contemporary, named Doménikos, have been confused with those of El Greco. Finally, after his death, his associates continued to paint in his style, and some of their paintings have been attributed to him.

A number of paintings represent portraits of his contemporaries, usually Spanish clergy, gentry, and nobility. El Greco, however, was primarily a religious painter. His normal subjects are Christ and the Holy Family, New Testament scenes, miracles from the New Testament and from the early Christian era, saints, and significant rites. While some are epic in scale, presenting views of heaven, earth, and hell, and including divine, angelic, and human figures, others include single saints or clergymen.

El Greco considered himself a learned painter as opposed to an artisan; thus, he sought to formulate a theory of painting and to apply it. Francisco Pacheco, a lesser Spanish artist, mentions his writings on painting, sculpture, and architecture, though none exists today. Yet some evidence of El Greco's aesthetic judgment may be gleaned from extant marginalia in books he owned. In practice, he consciously attempted to combine the rich coloration of the Venetian school and the mannerist style of the Florentine-Roman school. These two cultural influences, combined with the canons of religious art of the Counter-Reformation and his iconographic background, represent the dominant influences on his artistic production. Although nothing in El Greco's art is entirely original, the combination of disparate influences creates a strong impression of originality and even of eccentricity.

In exploring the prominent features of his work, one may consider composition, color, and illumination. Except for the early paintings, incorporating architectural forms and the views of Toledo, the paintings usually have a shallow background. Distant perspective is interrupted by a wall or draperies, or by the darkened, cloudy sky so prevalent in his work. In general, dimensions are handled aesthetically, not naturalistically, creating within a single painting a combination of flatness and depth. The focus of most paintings is the human form, whether in portraits or in the epic paintings featuring numerous individuals. The body is often elongated, perhaps the most characteristic feature of El Greco's composition, as if to intimate that the character has striven to surpass human limitations. Often, the heads, with gaunt and angular faces, appear too small for the long bodies. Following the mannerist tradition, El Greco often foreshortens some figures, includes half figures that are cut by the edges, and places human forms in curved positions, contributing to a geometric pattern in the painting as a whole. In addition, arms and legs are sometimes positioned at unusual angles, creating the effects of imbalance and distortion.

Viewing El Greco's human forms, one is drawn to their faces and hands, their most expressive elements. The hands are sometimes pointing, sometimes clasped, sometimes at rest, but always refined, graceful, and expressive. The faces—usually angular, unlined, and elongated—reveal a limited range of human expression. El Greco's gaunt faces carry a serious cast, accompanied by the appropriate religious emotions. His subjects are grave, restrained, reserved, devout, and penitent. In some paintings, the eyes peer upward toward heaven with a facial expression mingling devotion, fear, and hope. In others, they look directly at the viewer, but somehow past him, as if to perceive a spiritual world that remains invisible to others. It may be that the contrast between the extravagant gestures in the paintings and the taut control of the faces represents El Greco's most compelling technique of composition. The restraint and self-control evident in the faces suggest that the individual will has been conquered, and the gestures denote a spiritual significance that transcends time.

A painter whose early experience was with the dark tones of Orthodox iconography must have found the bright colors of the Venetian school highly pleasing. El Greco sought to use a range of colors to enliven religious art, though the bright reds and blues of his early paintings darken during the course of his career. His preferred colors are blue, red, yellow, yellow-green, and slate gray, though his use of neutral tones appears to increase with time. Illumination, as critics have observed, is aesthetic rather than naturalistic. Typically, light from an undetermined source is directed toward the most significant portions of a painting. In *The Trinity* (1577-1579), for example, God the Father embraces the crucified Christ. Christ's body is illuminated from a source to the left and behind the viewer, while, at the same time, light radiates outward from heaven behind the Father's head. At times El Greco's illumination has the yellowish-green cast of early morning or of light breaking through a darkened, cloudy, windswept sky, creating heightened tones not of the familiar world.

Despite his success as a painter and his many large commissions, El Greco did not attain wealth, though numerous contemporaries praised his genius. He died in Toledo on April 7, 1614, and was interred in the Church of Santo Domingo el Antiguo, which he had decorated.

Summary

El Greco's mannered style, his unusual handling of illumination, and his intensely religious subjects proved difficult for succeeding ages to appreciate. Because his paintings were not seen outside Spain and because Spain possessed no critical tradition in art, he became a forgotten artist in the rest of Europe. Although El Greco was capable of finely detailed drawing, he was inclined to leave large portions of his paintings indistinct, producing a blurred effect. This tendency is pervasive in the later paintings, especially those dealing with miracles and mystical events. During the late nineteenth century, he was discovered by the French Impressionist Édouard Manet, who saw in El Greco an earlier practitioner of Impressionist aesthetics. Like them and like the expressionists, he freely altered reality in order to enhance aesthetic effect.

Once his artistic power became recognized and widely acclaimed, art critics sought to account for him through a number of highly speculative theories: that he was a mystic, that he elongated figures because of astigmatism, or that he was quintessentially Spanish. More systematic and careful scholarship has demonstrated that El Greco derived from his study and experience, largely of Italian painting, the characteristic elements of his art. To be sure, he combined the influences of Italy in an unusual and highly original way and adapted his painting to the Spanish Counter-Reformation. He is recognized as among some half dozen of the world's greatest portrait painters and as Spain's greatest religious artist.

Bibliography
Brown, Jonathan, ed. *Figures of Thought: El Greco as Interpreter of History, Tradition, and Ideas*. Washington, D.C.: National Gallery of Art, 1982. An illustrated collection of six essays by El Greco scholars. Centers on individual paintings and portraits. The final essay explores the artist's legal entanglements over the remuneration for his works.
Greco. *El Greco of Toledo*. Boston: Little, Brown, 1982. A catalog of the 1982-1983 international El Greco exhibit. Includes numerous color and black-and-white reproductions and three valuable scholarly essays concerning the history of Toledo, El Greco's career and life, and the altarpieces that he completed.
Guinard, Paul. *El Greco*. Translated by James Emmons. Lausanne, Switzerland: Skira, 1956. In this small book with fifty-three high-quality color reproductions, Guinard presents a biographical and critical study attempting to correlate the painter with his milieu. Back matter includes commentary on the artist by six contemporaries, biographical sketches of twenty-five contemporaries, and an annotated bibliography.
Theotocopuli, Domenico, called El Greco. *El Greco*. Edited by Léo Bronstein. New York: Harry N. Abrams, 1950. This work offers reproductions in color of approximately forty of El Greco's better-known paintings, with evaluation and analysis. The comments, written for the nonspecialist, emphasize technique and appreciation.
_____. *El Greco*. Edited by Maurice Legendre. New York: Hyperion Press, 1947. Primarily a volume of reproductions, most in black and white. Offers a brief, interesting, and highly conjectural assessment of the artist's life, work, and philosophy, plus an extended nonannotated bibliography.
Wethey, Harold E. *El Greco and His School*. 2 vols. Princeton, N.J.: Princeton University Press, 1962. Applying sound scholarly research, Wethey explores questions of authenticity in an effort to establish El Greco's

canon. He describes each painting and provides a complex classification according to subject matter. His biographical account of El Greco places heavy emphasis on the Venetian period. The work is comprehensive, reliable, and highly detailed—indispensable for serious students.

Stanley Archer

EDVARD GRIEG

Born: June 15, 1843; Bergen, Norway
Died: September 4, 1907; Bergen, Norway
Area of Achievement: Music
Contribution: Drawing on Norwegian folk culture for inspiration, Grieg created an original, distinctive music of Romantic nationalism that made him
the foremost composer in Norway and the first Scandinavian composer to
achieve world renown.

Early Life

Edvard Grieg was the fourth of five children born to Gesine Hagerup
Grieg and Alexander Grieg. Edvard's mother was musically gifted and, having been reared in a prominent and prosperous family, had received the best
musical training available in Bergen and Hamburg. She was in great demand
as a pianist and throughout her life played an important role in the musical
life of Bergen. She gave Edvard his first piano lessons when he was six. His
father, Alexander, the son of a prosperous merchant, also took an active
interest in music, playing piano duets with his wife and invariably attending
concerts on his many business trips abroad. Even when his own financial
position deteriorated, he selflessly supported Edvard's lengthy and expensive
musical education. Grieg was undoubtedly fortunate to be born into a home
where music was a part of everyday life, and to have cultivated, sympathetic, and even indulgent parents. In an autobiographical reminiscence, "My
First Success" (1903), Grieg states that his early childhood years were deeply
formative and that his later creativity would have been stifled if constraints
had been placed too early upon his sensitive and imaginative nature. Not
surprisingly, his temperament resulted in an increasing dislike of school:
"School life was to me deeply unsympathetic; its materialism, harshness,
and coldness were so contrary to my nature that I would think out the most
incredible things to be quit of it even if only for a little while."

Although Edvard was fond of composing and improvising at the piano, he
never thought of becoming an artist; he was certain that he would follow the
path of numerous ancestors and become a minister. Yet, in the summer of
1858, the famous Norwegian violinist Ole Bull visited the Griegs and after
hearing Edvard play persuaded Grieg's parents to send Edvard to the Leipzig
Conservatory. Thus began for Grieg at age fifteen an experience that he
always remembered with distaste. After overcoming his initial homesick-
ness, he found the pedantic methods at the conservatory dry and uninspiring,
even occasionally absurd, as when he was required to write a string quartet
although he had received no instruction in the form and knew nothing of the
technique of string instruments. He applied himself diligently to what he
considered sterile exercises, but he was at best a mediocre student and left

the conservatory nearly as ignorant as when he had entered it (an account of himself as a student that is curiously contradicted by the records which survive). At the bottom of Grieg's always-bitter reflections on his student days in Leipzig (1858-1862) was the conflict between his inherently lyrical-romantic nature and the German classicism which the conservatory required. He acknowledged that the quantity of music he was able to hear performed in Leipzig was important to his development, particularly the works of the Romantics Robert Schumann, Felix Mendelssohn, and Frédéric Chopin— compensation, he said, "for the instruction in the technique of composition which I did *not* get at the Conservatory." In 1862, he received his certificate and returned to Bergen, where he gave his first concert. In 1863, he took up residence in Copenhagen (then the cultural center of Denmark and Norway), where he met a number of musicians and artists: Hans Christian Andersen, some of whose poems Grieg had already set to music; author Benjamin Feddersen; singer Julius Stenberg; and Niels Gade, the leader of the Scandinavian Romantic school of music. He also met his cousin Nina Hagerup, a gifted singer who would, a few years later, become his wife. He had, however, not yet discovered his own distinctive musical personality.

Life's Work

In 1864, Grieg met the charismatic young composer and fiery champion of Norwegian nationalism Rikard Nordraak. While still a student in Berlin, Nordraak abandoned German music and literature and turned for inspiration to Norwegian sagas, folk tales, ballads, folk music, anecdotes, and history. He saw clearly what Grieg had only dimly felt: not only the sterility of German classicism but also the impossibility of using German Romanticism to create a new, distinctly Norwegian music. Prior to meeting Nordraak, Grieg had known little of Norway's folk culture. He had heard Ole Bull praise Norwegian folk music and had heard him play a few folk tunes, but Norwegian music had not been played in Grieg's home. In Copenhagen, he had met Gade, supposedly the leader of a new school of northern music, but whose compositions were actually heavily derivative of German Romanticism. Grieg's discovery of a rich native heritage was liberating and transforming. He at last felt able to link the best that was within him (his lyric-romantic nature) with the best that was in his native land—the untainted peasant culture with its long memory of an ancient past, its uninhibited expressions of both joy and sorrow, and its intense awareness of Norway's spectacular mountains, waterfalls, and fjords.

In 1865, Grieg, Nordraak, and Danish musicians C. F. E. Horneman and Gottfred Matthison-Hansen founded Euterpe, an organization to promote contemporary Scandinavian music. Although Euterpe flourished for only a short time, it was one indication of Grieg's orientation toward northern music. The early death of Nordraak from pulmonary tuberculosis in 1866 only strengthened Grieg's resolve to champion and create a truly national music, and Nordraak's death became the occasion for one of Grieg's most original and powerful compositions, *Sörgemarsch over Rikard Nordraak* (1866; funeral march in memory of Rikard Nordraak). In 1866, Grieg gave an overwhelmingly successful concert of Norwegian music in Christiania (modern Oslo), which established him as one of his country's foremost young musicians. He became a popular teacher and collaborated with critic Otto Winter-Hjelm to establish a Norwegian Academy of Music. In 1867, Grieg and Nina Hagerup were married, the same year his first book of *Lyriske smaastykker* Op. 12 (lyric pieces) for piano appeared, some of whose titles reflect a growing nationalism: *Norsk* (Norwegian), *Folkevise* (folktune), and *Faedrelandssang* (national song). In 1868, he composed his famous Piano Concerto in A Minor, the same year his only child, Alexandra, was born; she died thirteen months later. His discovery in 1869 of Ludvig Lindeman's collection of folk music was a further important impetus in his evolution toward a distinctively Norwegian style; it became a rich source of inspiration for the numerous tone poems he composed.

Partly because of the enthusiastic support he received from the famed Franz Liszt, Grieg obtained a government grant to further his musical education by travel and study abroad. In 1870, he went to Rome, where he was gratified by Liszt's appreciation of his work, particularly of the recently completed Piano Concerto in A Minor. Grieg's prestige was further enhanced by his close association in the 1870's with Norway's most prominent dramatist-poets, Henrik Ibsen and Bjørnstjerne Bjørnson. He set many of Bjørnson's poems to music and collaborated with him to produce an opera, *Olav Trygvason* (a project which was never completed and which occasioned a long period of estrangement between the two artists). In 1874, Ibsen invited Grieg to compose music for a stage production of *Peer Gynt* (1867; English translation, 1892), which resulted in some of Grieg's best-known and most-loved compositions. Additionally, some of Ibsen's poems provided the inspiration for Grieg's highest achievements in song, his *Sex digte* Op. 25 (six songs). A government pension given to Grieg in 1874 freed him from his teaching responsibilities and allowed him to devote himself to composition. Still, Grieg continued to the very end of his life to give substantial amounts of time and energy to conducting and to concert tours (both at home and abroad), possibly as an escape from periods of nonproductivity as composer but additionally to renew himself by contact with the centers of creative life abroad. Grieg's best remedy for artistic sterility, however, was to seek regeneration through contact with nature, particularly through Norway's spectacular scenery. In 1877, he moved to Lofthus in the Hardanger district, where he composed *Den bergtekne* Op. 32 (the mountain thrall), the String Quartet in G Minor Op. 27, *Albumblade* Op. 28 (album leaves), and *Improvisata over to norske folkeviser* Op. 29 (improvisations on two Norwegian folk songs). His love of "the great, melancholy Westland nature" caused him eventually to build a villa at Troldhaugen, overlooking the fjord a short distance from Bergen, even though the damp climate was not the best for the health problems that increasingly beset him in later life.

When the Griegs moved to Troldhaugen in 1885, they were moving into their first settled home, such had been the roving nature of their lives. Still, the final two decades of Grieg's life reveal the same restless life-style. As an internationally known composer-conductor-pianist, Grieg undertook numerous concert tours to England, Paris, Brussels, Germany, Sweden, Vienna, the Netherlands, and Warsaw. He met other famous musicians such as Johannes Brahms, Max Reger, Frederick Delius, and Peter Ilich Tchaikovsky. Kaiser William II invited Grieg aboard his yacht (moored in Bergen Harbor) to hear a program of Grieg's works performed by William's private orchestra. Despite increasing complaints about his failing powers and health, Grieg continued to be productive in composition, revising earlier compositions and creating new ones, including the important works for the piano, *Norske folkeviser* Op. 66 (1896; nineteen Norwegian folk tunes), and seven books of *Lyrische Stücke* (1901; lyric pieces). He also composed the last of his Norwegian songs and one of his most original works, *Haugtussa* Op. 67 (1895). *Slåtter* Op. 72 (1902-1903), published as a work for piano, was inspired by Hardanger violin tunes. His final composition was a choral work, Four Psalms Op. 74.

Many years earlier, while a student at Leipzig, Grieg had suffered an attack of pleurisy so severe that it had interrupted his studies and left him with a permanent health liability—a collapsed lung. Although his active life seemed to belie it (frequent walking trips through the mountains, exhausting concert tours, and great bursts of creativity), Grieg's health was always frail. During his last years, it deteriorated significantly. Still, in the last year of his life, he made a tour to Copenhagen, Munich, Berlin, and Kiel, sustaining himself largely through nervous energy and sheer will. Characteristically, Grieg was preparing to leave Norway for a concert tour of England when his doctor, realizing the gravity of Grieg's condition, insisted that Grieg go instead to the hospital in Bergen. He died there the next day. Grieg's funeral in Bergen, September 9, 1907, was an important national and international event, a final tribute to the eminence that Grieg attained as conductor, performer, and composer.

Summary

In assessing Edvard Grieg's contribution to music, typically two questions have been raised: How original an artist was he? and How major? Much that is attractive and uniquely expressive of the northern spirit in Grieg's mature style derives from Norwegian folk songs and dances: a bold use of dissonance reminiscent of the Hardanger fiddle; frequent use of second, seventh, and perfect as well as augmented fourth and fifth intervals; irregularities of rhythm and accent. Yet his music is far from being a transcription or adaptation of sources. Comparisons of Grieg's works with the sources of his inspiration reveal how thoroughly he assimilated their color and spirit and how he transformed them by his own romantic imagination. The result is a fresh, original music which is uniquely expressive of his country's spirit but which invariably bears the deep impress of Grieg's own musical gifts: his ability to express a wide range of emotions and ideas, and particularly his genius for idiosyncratic and impressionistic use of harmony.

The second question of Grieg's ranking among composers is more problematic. Although he attained a popularity such as few artists experience and achieved numerous distinctions (among them membership in the French Legion of Honor and honorary doctorates from Cambridge and Oxford), Grieg himself was ambivalent about his popularity and unimpressed by his many honors and awards. He was aware that his very popularity caused critics to view him with suspicion, lamenting that his "standing as an artist suffers thereby. . . . More fortunate are those artists who do not win so-called popularity while they are still living." Undoubtedly influenced by the prevailing critical standards that confounded greatness with bigness, Grieg was also dismayed by his inability to handle the so-called larger forms, such as oratorios, operas, and symphonies. Yet Wolfgang Amadeus Mozart, a great master of the larger forms, observed: "Our taste in Germany is for long things; BUT SHORT AND GOOD IS BETTER." Qualified critics today tend to view Grieg's songs and piano composition as his most substantial and distinctive achievement.

Bibliography

Abraham, Gerald, ed. *Grieg: A Symposium.* London: Lindsay Drummond, 1948. A collection of specialized critical essays that examines every aspect of Grieg's music. A bibliography (focused on the music rather than the man) contains few entries in English. Includes a chronological list of compositions and forty pages of musical examples.

Finck, Henry T. *Grieg and His Music.* New York: John Lane, 1929. Includes the author's visit with Grieg in Norway and some valuable written communications he received from Grieg a few years before his death. An ardent supporter of Grieg, he offers an uncritical appraisal of Grieg's music and a warmly sympathetic account of his life. Contains numerous photographs, a bibliography, and a catalog of Grieg's compositions.

Grieg, Edvard. "My First Success." *Contemporary Review*, July, 1905. Anecdotes and reminiscences of Grieg's childhood and three years spent at the Leipzig Conservatory. Provides insights into Grieg's character and a glimpse of the humorous and self-deprecating side of his personality.

Horton, John. *Grieg.* London: J. M. Dent & Sons, 1974. A succinct overview of Grieg's life and works. Contains an illuminating calendar of Grieg's life (correlated with the birth/death dates of contemporary musicians), an index identifying names important in any study of Grieg, a complete catalog of works, and an extensive bibliography. The survey of Grieg's life is concise and authoritative, the discussion of Grieg's music is scholarly but eminently readable.

Monrad-Johansen, David. *Edvard Grieg.* Translated by Madge Robertson. Princeton, N.J.: Princeton University Press, 1938. A full-length biography of Grieg by a well-known Norwegian composer who had access to documents and letters unavailable to other writers. A balanced and objective but enthusiastic appreciation of Grieg's work and life, especially of his significance for Norway. Contains a few photographs.

Karen A. Kildahl

HUGO GROTIUS

Born: April 10, 1583; Delft, Holland
Died: August 28, 1645; Rostock, Mecklenburg
Area of Achievement: Law
Contribution: Grotius' 1625 treatise *On the Law of War and Peace* has gained for him the reputation of the father of international law.

Early Life

Hugo Grotius (Huigh de Groot) was born into a prominent Dutch family on Easter Sunday, April 10, 1583. His father was Burgomaster of Delft before becoming curator (member of the board of trustees) of the University of Leiden; an uncle was a professor of law at that institution. A child prodigy, Hugo began his own studies there in 1594 at the age of eleven, majoring in philosophy and classical philology. He received a doctorate of laws in 1598 from the University of Orléans while he was visiting France with a Dutch diplomatic mission. He so impressed his elders with the breadth of his knowledge that the French king, Henry IV, publicly hailed him as "the miracle of Holland."

In 1599, Grotius was admitted to the bar in his native province of Holland. He was named in 1601 Latin historiographer of Holland, became in 1604 legal counsel to the commander in chief of the armed forces of the United Netherlands, Prince Maurice of Nassau (Orange), and was appointed in 1607 advocaat-fiscaal for the court of Holland, Zeeland, and West Friesland (a position combining responsibility for prosecution of criminal cases with that of looking after the state's property interests). On July 7, 1608, he married Marie van Reigersberch. The marriage produced four sons and three daughters. One of the sons and two of the daughters died in infancy.

In 1613, Grotius was sent on a special diplomatic mission to England. That same year, he was appointed pensionary (paid officer) of the city of Rotterdam, a post that included a seat in the States (or parliament) of Holland. In 1617, he became a member of the College van Gecommitteerde Raden (committee of councillors), which, with the Landsadvocaat (de facto prime minister) Johan van Oldenbarnevelt, was responsible for the day-to-day administration of provincial affairs. In these positions, Grotius became entangled in the bitter conflict between the Arminians and the Calvinists—with himself emerging as a leader of the Arminian party. The theological issue was the Arminian affirmation of man's moral freedom, in contradiction to the Calvinist doctrine of unconditional predestination. The conflict became transformed into a constitutional crisis that pitted the provincial authorities of Holland, on one side, against Prince Maurice and the central government of the United Netherlands, on the other. The result was a military coup by Prince Maurice in 1618 in which Grotius was arrested and then sentenced the following year by a special tribunal to life imprisonment for treason. In 1621, he escaped from prison, thanks to a daring plan devised by his wife, and went into exile in France with a modest pension from King Louis XIII of France.

Life's Work

Grotius was a prolific writer. While still a student, he had gained fame for his poetry in Greek and Latin. He continued his literary endeavors throughout his life. His output included two lengthy poetic dramas in Latin on religious themes, *Adamus exul* (1601; *The Adamus Exul*, 1839) and *Christus patiens* (1608; *Christ's Passion*, 1640); editions of Greek and Latin poetic and historical texts; and patriotic histories of ancient Holland. During his later years, his major preoccupation became theology and biblical commentary. Nearly eight thousand letters to and from Grotius have survived.

Grotius is remembered primarily, however, for his legal treatises. His first, *De jure praede commentarius*, upholding on the grounds of natural law the right of captors to the proceeds of property captured during war, was written around 1604-1606 for the Dutch East India Company. The work was not published, however, until 1868, after the manuscript had been rediscovered. An English translation appeared in 1950 under the title *Commentary on the Law of Prize and Booty*. A chapter from this longer work—setting forth Grotius' arguments in favor of freedom of navigation and trade—was published anonymously in 1609 as *Mare liberum* (*The Freedom of the Seas*, 1916).

In 1622, Grotius published what was simultaneously an analysis of the public law of Holland and a defense of his own official conduct to rebut the accusations for which he had been imprisoned. The work, which appeared in Latin and Dutch editions, is entitled *Apologeticus eorum qui Hollandiae Westfrisiaeque et vicinis quibusdam natioibus ex legibus praefuerunt* (defense of the lawful government of Holland and West Friesland, together with some neighboring provinces, as it was before the change occurring in 1618). Of more long-term significance was his analysis of Dutch private law—the rights that are enjoyed by individuals to and in things—in his *Inleidinge tot de Hollandsche Rechts-geleerdheyd* (1631; *Introduction to Dutch Jurisprudence*, 1845). Although written during his imprisonment, the work was not published until 1631. Modeled upon Justinian's Institutes (c. 533)—and amalgamating Roman law principles with Old Dutch customs and charters—*Introduction to Dutch Jurisprudence* would enjoy in Holland the same authority that Sir William Blackstone's *Commentaries on the Laws of England* (1765-1769) would have in the Anglo-American legal world. For more than a century, the work remained the foundation of instruction in civil law in the Dutch universities. Whereas *Apologeticus* has never been translated into English, *Introduction to Dutch Jurisprudence* has appeared in three different English translations.

Grotius' most influential work was his *De iure belli ac pacis libri tres* (1625; *On the Law of War and Peace*, 1654). He appears to have written the work after his escape from prison while living in France; the first edition, in three volumes, was published in Paris. Grotius' revisions and additions were incorporated into the second edition, published in Amsterdam in 1631; that edition is generally regarded as the definitive text. Grotius' purpose, as he explains in the preface to the work, was to elucidate the laws that should govern "the mutual relations among states or rulers of states."

His starting point is the existence of a common law governing all mankind derived from three sources: the law of nature (that is, rules discovered by the right reason implanted in men by God); the *ius gentium* ("law of nations"), or rules that have been accepted in the actual customs and usages of all or nearly all peoples; and God's direct commands expressed through revelation. As a result, states, like individuals, enjoy legal rights, are bound by legal duties, and are liable to punishment for violation of such rights and disregard of such obligations. Yet there is one crucial difference between individuals and states. Within an organized political society, civil law provides legal remedies for the protection of individual rights. States, however, in their relations with one another have no superior authority to which to turn for the redress of wrongs. Therein lies the basis for Grotius' concept of the just war—war as an instrument for enforcing a state's legal rights and securing redress for violations of those rights in the absence of any judicial remedy. As he summed up his position, "Authorities generally assign to wars three justifiable causes, defense, recovery of property, and punishment."

In this sense, Grotius legitimated war. At the same time, however, he hoped that peaceful measures short of war could be developed to resolve disputes among states. He thought that there was no practical possibility of establishing a world government. He did suggest, however, three methods by which disputes could be settled short of war: conferences, arbitration, and "single combat" by "lot." If war could not be avoided, he aspired to limit its destructiveness by laying down mitigating rules of warfare, such as those barring the killing of noncombatants. He thus emphasized that there remained in force even during war unwritten laws governing how enemies should behave "which nature dictates or the consensus of nations has established."

In 1631, Grotius returned to Holland, but he was forced to flee to Germany early the following year. In 1634, the Swedish chancellor Count Axel Oxenstierna appointed him Swedish ambassador to France—a post he would retain until the end of 1644. He played a key role while in Paris in maintaining the French subsidy to Sweden in the Thirty Years' War. He died at Rostock in what is modern East Germany on August 28, 1645. His last words were reportedly, "By undertaking many things, I have accomplished nothing."

Summary

Hugo Grotius underestimated his legacy. More than one hundred editions and translations of *On the Law of War and Peace* have appeared since its first publication. The work has had a dual significance. On one hand, Grotius accepted—and legitimated—the modern system of sovereign states that was emerging at the time out of the breakdown of the former legal unity of Christendom under the Papacy and the Holy Roman Empire. On the other, he put forth the vision of a still law-bound world to limit, or at least to mitigate, the potential anarchy of the new state system. That vision struck a responsive chord not only among many of his contemporaries but with later generations as well. The revival of Grotian ideas in the nineteenth century owed much to Henry Wheaton's *History of the Law of Nations* (1841). The influence of those ideas can be traced through The Hague Peace Conferences of 1899 and 1907, Woodrow Wilson's attempt to establish the League of Nations, the establishment of the so-called World Court, and modern-day peace-through-law activists.

Bibliography

Dumbauld, Edward. *The Life and Legal Writings of Hugo Grotius*. Norman: University of Oklahoma Press, 1969. The life part consists of a brief (under fourteen pages of text) biographical sketch. The remainder is a collection of previously published articles by the author examining Grotius' major legal treatises. Regretably, the thinnest treatment is of Grotius' most important work, *On the Law of War and Peace*.

Edwards, Charles S. *Hugo Grotius, the Miracle of Holland: A Study in Political and Legal Thought*. Chicago: Nelson-Hall, 1981. A valuable examination of the sources of the ideas in *On the Law of War and Peace* that successfully places Grotius in the larger intellectual context of his time. Edwards downplays the novelty of Grotius' ideas, demonstrating how Grotius synthesized themes found in the thought of the late Middle Ages.

Gellinek, Christian. *Hugo Grotius*. Boston: Twayne, 1983. A self-styled exercise in literary analysis. Although Gellinek has a chapter on the legal treatises, the bulk of his text deals with Grotius' poetic works, philological texts, and patriotic histories. Although the book is the fullest examination in English of the lesser known of Grotius' works, the writing is nearly unreadable.

Knight, W. S. M. *The Life and Work of Hugo Grotius*. London: Sweet and Maxwell, 1925. Reprint. Dobbs Ferry, N.Y.: Oceana, 1962. The most comprehensive, detailed, and balanced treatment of Grotius' life and work available in English. The work requires revision, however, in the light of the large body of scholarly research done since its publication, most of which remains accessible only to those with a knowledge of Dutch.

Ter Meulen, Jacob, and P. J. J. Diermanse. *Bibliographie des écrits imprimés de Hugo Grotius*. The Hague: Martinus Nijhoff, 1950. The standard bibliography listing more than twelve hundred items with accompanying annotations. The works are broken down into nine categories: poetry; philosophy and natural science; philology; international law; history; law (other than international); church-state relations; theology; and correspondence. The indispensable basis for all serious research upon Grotius.

Vollenhoven, Cornelis van. *The Framework of Grotius' Book "De Iure Bellis ac Pacis" (1625)*. Amsterdam: Moord-Hollandsche Uitgeversmaatschappij, 1931. A perceptive and detailed analysis of *On the Law of War and Peace* by the man who was probably the foremost modern Dutch expert on Grotius.

Vreeland, Hamilton, Jr. *Hugo Grotius: The Father of the Modern Science of International Law*. New York: Oxford University Press, 1917. Basically, an English-language summary of the standard but now out-of-date eighteenth century Dutch biography by Caspar Brandt and Adriaan van Cattenburgh, *Historie van het Leven des Heeren Huig de Groot* (1727). Gushingly laudatory on how Grotius rescued the ideals of justice and peace amid "the prevailing darkness."

John Braeman

MATTHIAS GRÜNEWALD
Matthias Gothardt

Born: c. 1475; Würzburg
Died: August, 1528; Halle, Magdeburg
Area of Achievement: Art
Contribution: Grünewald was the culmination of the Gothic tradition in German painting while giving evidence of the primacy of individual artistic expression within the tradition of the Italian Renaissance. He employed Gothic principles of expressiveness and Renaissance pictorial conventions, creating a unique style which transcended the limitations of the traditions out of which he worked.

Early Life

Matthias Grünewald, a figure of great stature in his own time, appears to have been quickly forgotten after his death. This neglect may be attributed in part to his preference for Gothic expressiveness in a period given over to the aesthetic concerns of the Italian Renaissance. Grünewald's preoccupation with mystical interpretations and paintings which were largely religious was out of place in an increasingly worldly age for which strong, stark religious themes had less and less impact and significance. Direct knowledge of Grünewald is scant. Besides his extant works, little was left behind by the artist himself which would give a clear picture. Instead one must rely on secondary sources and documents and letters of the time. Early knowledge of Grünewald arose from the efforts of Joachim von Sandrart, a seventeenth century German artist and historian. Even Sandrart had difficulty in finding information on Grünewald. In the early twentieth century, another German scholar, Heinrich Schmidt, uncovered some of the facts of Grünewald's life. In the 1920's yet another German scholar, W. K. Zulch, wrote the basic modern work on Grünewald, discovering Grünewald's actual surname in the process. There exists no unchallenged portrait of Grünewald, although the painting of Saint Sebastian in Grünewald's Isenheim altarpiece is thought to be a self-portrait. Grünewald is thought to have been born near Würzburg around 1475. Of his early life little is known. The exact place and source of his training is not known, although it is generally believed that Grünewald's general style and coloring reflect the predisposition of artists who worked in the Franconian region along the Main and Rhine Rivers.

Life's Work

Grünewald's first known work is the Lindenhart altarpiece, dating from 1503. Between 1504 and 1519, he was a resident in Seligenstadt, outside Würzburg. There he is listed as a master with apprentices; he executed paintings, the Basel *Crucifixion* for one, and was court painter to Archbishop

Uriel von Gemmingen from 1508 to 1514. During this same period, Grünewald supervised design and repair of various buildings, notably Schloss Aschaffenburg. In 1514, during the difficult time of the Thirty Years' War between Protestant and Catholic factions in Germany, Grünewald became the court painter for Albrecht von Brandenburg. In 1519, Grünewald is believed to have married, although the marriage may not have been a happy one. His wife brought with her a son, Andreas, whom Grünewald adopted. He apparently used his wife's surname, Niethart, occasionally. In 1525, Grünewald left the service of the archbishop under accusations related to his sympathies with the Peasants' War. He was acquitted by the archbishop but did not return to his service. Books he left behind at his death testify to his Protestant/Lutheran sympathies. These included a New Testament, a number of sermons, and pamphlets, all by Martin Luther. In 1526, Grünewald apprenticed his adopted son, Andreas Niethart, to Arnold Rucker, an organ builder, sculptor, and table maker. Grünewald died in August of 1528, while working on a commission for the cities of Magdeburg and Halle in Saxony.

Grünewald treated exclusively religious subjects when he painted. Only a small number of Grünewald's works have survived, but his total output was probably not extensive. Only two of his works bear autograph dates, and these form the basis for a chronology of all of his work. These works include the Bindlach altarpiece (1503) and his greatest work, the Isenheim altarpiece (1515). Two other works are dated on the frames, *The Mocking of Christ* (1503) and the Maria Schell altarpiece (1515). All other dates are conjecture, based on historical clues and stylistic evidence. As did his contemporaries Albrecht Dürer, Hans Burgkmair, and Lucas Cranach, the Elder, Grünewald did not conform to the fashions of the time or concede to the ideals of the Italian Renaissance which dominated in matters of taste and style. In his gruesome realism and complex iconography, Grünewald remained German and Gothic in his treatment of his subjects. He restricted himself to illustrating the fundamental themes of Christian faith, rendered with a sense of the mystical and the ecstatic.

Grünewald painted the Madonna and saints, but either by conscious intent or out of religious fervor and fascination with the subject—or both—he specialized in painting the Passion of Christ. From the beginning to the end of his career, Grünewald returned time after time to the subject of the Crucifixion, of which four versions are still preserved in galleries in Switzerland, the Netherlands, and West Germany.

Grünewald's work is subjective, the intuitive product of a personal artist who feels his work deeply. Grünewald's work substitutes force and sincerity in place of the Italian Renaissance preference for beauty and elegance. Instead of the concrete depiction of form through the use of descriptive line and chiaroscuro, Grünewald emphasizes the mystical through expressive line and color. While he understood and made use of the Italian Renaissance conventions of perspective and correct proportion, Grünewald saw them as being of lesser value than the spiritual qualities of his work. For the artists of the Italian Renaissance, the new conventions were at least as important as the old values which arguably might be said to have become means to using the new conventions as much as anything else. All the qualities the Italian Renaissance considered important—dignity, repose, symmetry, balance, serenity, perfection—were for Grünewald merely ornamentation, elements not pertinent to his interest and interpretation of his subject.

Yet Grünewald's work was not merely emotional display. For one thing, he did not portray superficial emotions. The emotive character of his work came from his use of strong dichotomies—real, temporal, and secular versus ideal, eternal, and spiritual—in his interpretation of his subject. The conditions of his figures are symbolic, with emphasis placed on their devotional and spiritual aspects rather than their merely being descriptive and narrative. His subjects were traditional, but his treatment of them is unique, often overwhelming. An excellent example is Grünewald's interpretation of the risen Christ in the Isenheim altarpiece, which makes use of all the above mentioned dichotomies.

One is prepared by one's initial encounter with the excruciating, visceral vision of the painfully crucified Christ on the outside panel of the altarpiece. Then to behold the risen Christ on the inside is to be moved ecstatically. Grünewald, moved as he had to have been by his desire to express the spirituality of his subject, transcended the limitations of the medium and conventions he employed. One's admiration is inspired not by the artist's mastery of technique, though clearly Grünewald was a superb craftsman, but by the spiritual impact of his work, which is as real and felt today as it surely had to have been when it was first viewed in the sixteenth century. His figures appear forced and affected in pose and manner, because they are meant to be larger than life—more than mere representations of a historical event. While understanding line and form in realistic representation, Grünewald gives primacy to expression of qualities rather than to accurate depiction of appearances. He did this through his extreme treatments of the human figure, creating the expressiveness of a psychic condition and presenting a spiritual reality as much as a visual image.

Summary

Matthias Grünewald was a Gothic artist with the sensibility of the spirituality of the Middle Ages. To compare Grünewald's work and style with the standards of the Italian Renaissance would be a misplaced attempt to understand and appreciate his work. Judged in terms of the Italian Renaissance, Grünewald's work appears repellent, disdainful of form, contemptuous of moderation, and lacking in grace. Judged in terms of an individual's ability to give form and expression to those images central to Western Christian spirituality, Grünewald's work appears poignant, penetrating, and transcendent. Grünewald was not so much a Gothic artist as he was an artist who recognized that the Gothic era gave best and fullest expression to spirituality. Grünewald did not imitate the Gothic style, but he adopted fully the principles of the Gothic, realizing their timeless nature. Nor did Grünewald refute the ideals of the Italian Renaissance as much as he ignored them, choosing only to use those formal elements useful to his artistic purpose.

Bibliography
Benesch, Otto. *German Painting from Dürer to Holbein*. Translated by H. S. B. Harrison. Geneva, Switzerland: Éditions d'Art Albert Skira, 1966. Based on a series of lectures given by Benesch in 1959 and 1960 at the University of Vienna. Benesch, an eminent scholar, emphasized the Germanic and Gothic aspects of his subjects' work.
Burkhard, Arthur. *Matthias Grünewald: Personality and Accomplishment*. Cambridge, Mass.: Harvard University Press, 1936. Reprint. New York: Hacker Art Books, 1976. The first comprehensive treatment in English of the life and work of Matthias Grünewald. The author's intent is to suggest the aesthetic and personal underpinnings of Grünewald while connecting him closely with his German Gothic heritage. The extensive bibliography cites only German sources.
Cuttler, Charles D. *Northern Painting from Pucelle to Brueghel: Fourteenth, Fifteenth, and Sixteenth Centuries*. New York: Holt, Rinehart and Winston, 1968. A later study of painting of Northern European artists, attempting not only to place them in context with the Italian Renaissance but also to show their own peculiar characteristics and styles. Suggests the social, philosophical, and aesthetic influences of the time.
Mellinkoff, Ruth. *The Devil at Isenheim: Reflections of Popular Belief in Grünewald's Altarpiece*. Berkeley: University of California Press, 1988. A lavishly illustrated iconographic study of the Isenheim altarpiece. Mellinkoff focuses on the panel depicting the Madonna and Child being honored by a concert of angels; in an original and persuasive interpretation, Mellinkoff argues that among the angels is Lucifer himself, shown in the moment of awareness of the folly of his rebellion.
Scheja, Georg. *The Isenheim Altarpiece*. Translated by Robert Erich Wolf. New York: Harry N. Abrams, 1969. An extensive, authoritative discussion of Grünewald's best-known work. The author cites possible visual and literary sources for the work. The extensive footnotes are an excellent second source of information.

Donald R. Kelm

GUARINO GUARINI

Born: January 17, 1624; Modena
Died: March 6, 1683; Milan
Area of Achievement: Architecture
Contribution: Guarini's fusion of medieval and Moorish architectural vaulting systems, his theologically symbolic geometric floor plans, and his dramatic use of light allowed him to create structures which are perennially fascinating and influential.

Early Life

Guarino Guarini joined the Theatine priesthood in 1639, at the age of fifteen. His decision catapulted him from the small north Italian town of Modena to Rome, the dynamic cultural center of Baroque Italy. Guarini remained in Rome studying theology, philosophy, mathematics, and architecture in the monastery of Silvestro al Quirinale until 1647. During Guarini's Roman years, Francesco Borromini and Gian Lorenzo Bernini created the buildings and sculpture which defined the Roman Baroque style. The precise conditions of Guarini's early training as an architect are unknown. Nevertheless, his biographers all agree that Borromini was Guarini's primary architectural inspiration. Borromini's Church of San Carlo alle Quatro Fontane is in the same district of Rome as the monastery where Guarini was a student. In addition to being in Rome at the same time, Borromini and Guarini have in common a youthful contact with medieval architecture. Borromini worked on the fabric of the Gothic cathedral at Milan before he came to Rome, and Guarini was reared in a town dominated by the splendid Romanesque cathedral of St. Germinian.

Guarini's membership in the Theatine Order and his training in mathematics as well as philosophy and theology set him on a path toward a theologically complex and expressive multinational style of architecture. The Theatines were one of the new orders created in the sixteenth century known as the Clerks Regular. These orders devolved out of the Roman Catholic church's Counter-Reformation program advocated in the sixteenth century by Gian Pietro Carafa, one of the founders of the Theatines. Carafa became Pope Paul IV in 1555. The Theatines, recognized by Pope Leo X in 1524, were the first of the Clerks Regular, setting the model for other sixteenth and seventeenth century Counter-Reformation orders, including the Barnabites, Somaschi, Caracciolini, and the well-known Jesuits. All these groups needed new churches, and all moved freely throughout Europe since Clerks Regular were not bound to a single parish.

Cajetan, one of the founders of the Theatines, sought to reform both clergy and laity with ideals much like those of the thirteenth century reformers Saint Dominic and Saint Francis. Therefore it is not surprising that

Guarini would feel a kinship with the architecture of the thirteenth century as well as the theology of that age. As the Gothic church functioned as a bible of the poor in the Middle Ages, so Baroque Counter-Reformation architects such as Borromini, Bernini, and Guarini created an architecture to inspire and amaze the worshiper through the use of startling visual effects designed to make the intervention of the divine in the natural world a concrete event.

The illusionistic use of light is paramount in Italian Baroque architecture, and Guarini probably learned this lesson from Bernini. He was in Rome when Bernini began his sculpture *Saint Theresa in Ecstasy* (1645-1652). For this work, Bernini designed the space of the Coronaro Chapel in Santa Maria della Vittoria so that it seems as if the worshiper has suddenly come face to face with the living saint in an intimate spiritual moment. Above and behind the figures, Bernini concealed a window so that the impression of a sudden, light-filled visionary moment is made all the more believable. Guarini would use just such dramatic illusionistic lighting in his domes in Lisbon, Sicily, Paris, and Turin, making them appear to float on slender, interlaced ribs.

From Borromini, Guarini learned the use of complex geometry as a basis for floor plans. Borromini's Church of San Carlo alle Quatro Fontane is an oval inscribed in a rectangle, an elongated version of the circle inscribed in a square which was the geometric basis for much Gothic decoration. Borromini's second Roman church, Saint Ivo della Sapienza, was a star hexagon plan created by superimposing two equilateral triangles. Guarini used such a format in the presbytery dome of San Lorenzo in Turin.

Life's Work

After completing his studies in Rome, Guarini returned to Modena in 1647, where he worked with Giovanni Castiglione on the Church of San Vincenzo and the Theatine monastery. For some reason he left Modena in 1657 and his activities are not documented again until 1660, when he appears as a teacher of mathematics and philosophy at Messina, in Sicily. It seems quite likely that during the years 1657-1660 Guarini went to Spain. Juan Antonio Ramirez's well-argued conclusion that Guarini traveled on the Iberian peninsula is based on Guarini's use of the twisted or salomóniac column in his published designs for Santa Maria della Divina Providenza in Lisbon. Unfortunately this church was lost in an earthquake in 1755.

Another frequently suggested proof that Guarini was in Spain is the similarity between the vaulting system he developed in his mature work, and the Moorish design of the vaults of the mosque at Cordova. In any case, Guarini knew the Talvera Chapel in the old Cathedral of Salamanca, for he cited it in his treatise on architecture.

Although few of his buildings remain standing, Guarini did leave major monuments in the north Italian city of Turin and records of his intellect and designs in his books. His interest in philosophy resulted in *Placita phi-*

losophica of 1665. He wrote a mathematical treatise, *Euclides adauctus et methodicus*, in 1671; his architectural drawings were published three years after his death as *Desegni d' architettura civile e ecclesiastica* in 1686; and his most well-known and influential book, *Architettura civile*, was published posthumously by Bernardo Vittone in 1737. The architectural books document Guarini's international reputation, because they contain plans for churches in Prague as well as Lisbon, Nice, and Paris. His books were never translated into English, but they found a wide readership in eighteenth century Western Europe and twentieth century editions of the architectural works were published in London and Milan in 1964 and 1968.

By 1662, Guarini was in Paris, a fully mature, well-traveled architect, uniquely suited to design the Theatine Church of St. Anne-la-Royale. He had assimilated the influences of Borromini, Bernini, and the lessons of medieval and Moorish vault construction. The Theatines, invited to Paris by Jules Mazarin, had royal protection, but David R. Coffin attributes their popularity in seventeenth century Paris to their dramatic liturgies. Guarini set the stage for those practices with a floor plan for St. Anne-la-Royale consisting of four diamond shapes which overlapped the corners of a fifth central diamond. Above the central space rose a dome laced with eight overlapping semicircular ribs pierced with kidney-shaped windows. On the exterior, this startling shape was expressed as an octagon with concave faces. While the exterior reveals the influence of Borromini, the interior was Guarini's invention. He experimented with this kind of vault in the hexagonal Church of the Somaschi in Messina before he came to Paris and presumably just after he returned to Italy from Spain. Unfortunately, all of his works in Messina were destroyed by an earthquake in 1908, and St. Anne-la-Royale was demolished by 1823.

The final phase of Guarini's development took place in northern Italy. In 1666, Guarini became the chief architect of the house of Savoy, making their capital city, Turin, the most progressive architectural center in Italy at the close of the seventeenth century. His secular commissions there consisted of additions to the Palace of Racconigi, the unfinished Collegio dei Nobili, and the main wing of the Palazzo Carignano. Guarini's contribution at Carignano was a sophisticated rippling façade of concave and convex pattern which Rudolf Wittkower notes is suggestive of Bernini's rejected plans for the Louvre. The façades of Borromini's San Carlo and St. Ivo are also recalled at Carignano. A most unique feature of this palace is Guarini's use of cast brick ornament around the windows and in dense vertical bands of eight-pointed stars on the courtyard façade. Carignano was completed in the nineteenth century and so does not as fully represent Guarini's mature style as do his ecclesiastical commissions in Turin.

San Lorenzo was the Theatine church in Turin and received the full measure of Guarini's intellectual and visual complexity. It is an octagon which at the second floor area becomes a four-sided Greek cross and then meta-morphoses into an eight-pointed star floating between the floor and a second-ary dome. Guarini intensified his illusory space by piercing the wall between the first and second domes with windows. A six-pointed star formed by two overlapping equilateral triangles crowns the adjoining dome of the presby-tery, giving visual form to the theological concept of the Trinity. Guarini's floating domes at San Lorenzo are matched only by his Chapel of the Holy Shroud, also built at Turin.

With this dome/tower, Guarini captured the illusion of a telescope focused on infinity which brings a vision of the Holy Spirit to the congregation. Using spaces and structures based on multiples of three, he raised six hex-agons of increasingly smaller dimensions toward an apparently free-floating, twelve-edged golden star upon which he depicted a white dove in flight. The hexagons are set at angles to one another, adding to the mystery of the space, while the walls between the hexagons are pierced by windows framed with segmental arches. Christian Norberg-Schulz termed the Chapel of the Holy Shroud "one of the most mysterious and deeply stirring spaces ever cre-ated."

Summary

Guarino Guarini's arguments that one could create a miraculous architec-ture with Gothic vaulting were persuasively presented in his commentary on Gothic building in his *Architettura civile* and in his buildings. His book was widely circulated in eighteenth century Austria and Germany, contributing to the development of such architects as Johann Lucas von Hildebrandt, Johann Bernhard Fischer von Erlach, and Johann Balthasar Neumann. In the twen-tieth century, his understanding of skeletal construction and window-pierced walls has appealed to architects who use steel and reinforced concrete to sup-port their curtain-walled constructions. Guarini's ability to activate a spir-itual space remains a model for all designers.

Bibliography
Blunt, Anthony, ed. *Baroque and Rococo: Architecture and Decoration.* New York: Harper & Row, 1978. A general introduction to seventeenth and eighteenth century architecture in Europe and the Americas. Includes chapters by Christopher Tadgell, Kerry Downes, and Alastair Laing. Ex-cellent for setting Guarini's work in historical context. Includes annotated bibliographical citations in the footnotes.

Cannon-Brookes, P., and C. Cannon-Brooks. *Baroque Churches.* London: Hamlyn, 1969. Contains a chapter on Guarini in Turin and specific infor-mation on Guarini's early training.

Coffin, David R. "Padre Guarino Guarini in Paris." *Journal of the Society of Architectural Historians* 15, no. 2 (1956): 3-11. Focused on the Parisian

church of St. Anne-la-Royale. Excellent coverage of contemporary estimates of the church with very full footnotes, including a foreign-language
bibliography.

Müller, Werner. "The Authenticity of Guarini's Stereotomy in His *Architettura civile.*" *Journal of the Society of Architectural Historians* 27, no. 3
(1968): 202-208. Analysis of the mathematical content of Guarini's treatise on architecture. Müller notes the errors of Guarini's publisher or editor in transcribing parts of his text on Euclidian geometry into the architectural treatise. Excellent discussion of sixteenth and seventeenth century
mathematical theory and the science of stonecutting. Annotated bibliography in footnotes as well as a bibliography of sixteenth to nineteenth century foreign-language sources.

Norberg-Schulz, Christian. *Baroque Architecture.* Reprint. New York: Rizzoli, 1986. Many very clear photographs of pages from Guarini's architectural writings as well as good photographs of most extant buildings. Interesting discussion of Guarini's concept of architecture as a union of spatial
units. Select bibliography on seventeenth century architecture in general.

Ramirez, Juan Antonio. "Guarino Guarini, Fray Juan Ricci, and the 'Complete Salomonic Order.'" *Art History* 4 (1981): 175-185. A well-argued
case for Guarini's visit to Spain in the late 1650's. Extensive annotated
foreign-language bibliography in the footnotes. Useful information about
seventeenth century Spanish architectural theory.

Wittkower, Rudolf. *Art and Architecture in Italy, 1600-1750.* Rev. ed. Baltimore: Penguin, 1980. Frequently revised, this is the most readily available general text on Italian Baroque architecture in English. Analysis of
Guarini superb for its balanced insights on his engineering innovations and
sensitivity to his theological symbolism. Footnotes contain an annotated
bibliography and additional information. Concluding bibliography is useful for general information and foreign-language citations.

Alice H. R. H. Beckwith

OTTO VON GUERICKE

Born: November 20, 1602; Magdeburg
Died: May 11, 1686; Hamburg
Areas of Achievement: Physics, invention, and technology
Contribution: His experiments with electricity and, especially, air pressure
  make Guericke an important figure in the era of the scientific revolution.

Early Life

Otto von Guericke was the only son of Hans Guericke (or Gericke) and his second wife, Anna von Zweidorff. The elder Guericke was a prominent citizen and important city official of Magdeburg, who could afford to provide tutors for the elementary education of his son. In 1617, the fifteen-year-old Otto went to Leipzig and then, in 1620, to Helmstedt for studies that would prepare him for a higher education in philosophy. The death of his father may have changed his plans, as he went to Jena to study law between 1621 and 1622. In 1623, he was in Leiden, the Netherlands, where he studied foreign languages, mathematics, geometry, mechanical arts, and the like. He completed his education with a tour through England and France before returning to Magdeburg to marry Margarethe Alemann in 1626. At about the same time, he entered city government as Director of Public Works and soon became Magdeburg's Director of Military Affairs as well.

The Thirty Years' War had begun in 1618, and Magdeburg was spared none of the evils of that particularly horrible war. Guericke warned that the city was in danger of attack by Imperial Catholic troops and that it could not withstand such an attack. In May of 1631, his predictions came true as forces under Johann Tserclaes seized Magdeburg and forced the conversion of its forty thousand inhabitants to Catholicism. During the process, many people were killed and much of the city, including Guericke's house, was sacked and burned. His youngest son was wounded and his family threatened with death. Finally, after paying a ransom of three hundred talers, he managed to leave for Erfurt, where he became an engineer for the Swedish army. In the spring of 1632, he returned to Magdeburg to help in the rebuilding of the city.

From about 1642, Guericke was diplomatic representative of Magdeburg in the negotiations for the reconstitution of Germany. In that capacity, he was successful in obtaining recognition of the former rights of the city and in completing other diplomatic missions for the next twenty years. In 1646, he began his thirty-year tenure as Mayor of Magdeburg. An Imperial patent of nobility dated January 4, 1666, allowed him to attach "von" to his name as an indication of noble status. In view of his active political life, it is remarkable that he was able to find time for the scientific experiments that are his greatest claim to fame.

Life's Work

Guericke was interested in cosmology and, consequently, in two particular subjects—magnetism and the nature of space. Experiments concerning the latter subject led to his theories and famous experiments regarding atmospheric pressure.

In the seventeenth century, there was a continuing argument between the Aristotelian and the "new" natural philosophers concerning the emptiness of space. The Aristotelians maintained that forces of nature, such as magnetism or heat, could not operate through empty space. This view was a result of Aristotle's explanation of physics, which was based on the notion that mechanical contact is necessary for an object to influence another object. The Aristotelians, therefore, believed that a true vacuum is impossible and that all space is filled with the aether—an undetectable but real substance. René Descartes had adopted the Aristotelian view and asserted that space is, in fact, matter. On the other side of the issue, the Galilean Evangelista Torricelli had shown that a vacuum could exist by inventing the barometer. He filled a glass tube open at one end with mercury and inverted it in a container of mercury. The mercury in the tube fell to an approximate height of thirty inches, leaving a space at the top of the tube that could contain nothing, since everything in the tube had been previously displaced by the mercury. Another aspect of the demonstration was the indication that the weight of the atmosphere suspended the column of mercury in the tube by acting on the surface of the liquid in the open container.

Since his student days at Leiden, Guericke had taken the side of the anti-Aristotelians. Torricelli's experiments were apparently unknown to him, but he determined to conduct experiments of his own that would demonstrate the possibility of a vacuum and that space and matter were not the same. If Descartes and Aristotle were correct, the evacuation of the air from a hollow object should lead to its collapse, as it would be impossible to create a vacuum. Pursuing this line of reasoning, Guericke first invented the vacuum pump. It resembled a modern bicycle pump except that it worked in reverse. With this pump, he tried to evacuate a sealed barrel filled with water. The seals were insufficient, however, and air could be heard whistling into the barrel as the water was removed. He then tried placing a water-filled barrel inside a larger barrel also filled with water. His hope was that the outer barrel would act as a seal, but he could not prevent the surrounding water from leaking into the inner barrel as it was evacuated.

Having failed with wooden barrels, he turned to metal spheres. His first attempt was with a copper ball, but the copper proved too weak and collapsed as the air was pumped out of it. Although this seemed to substantiate the Aristotelian view, Guericke tried again with a stronger vessel, and this time he succeeded in creating a vacuum without collapsing its container. After this success, he proceeded to perform a number of experiments that were to shed light on the nature of atmospheric pressure and the properties of air.

At first he assumed from the example of water that the air sank as it was removed from the valve in the bottom of the vessel; changing the location of the valve seemed to make no difference in any of his results, however, and he concluded that the air remained evenly distributed in the sphere regardless of how little there was of it. He showed that a candle flame is extinguished and the sound of a bell becomes muffled as the air around them is depleted. Further experiments showed that floating objects sank lower as the density of the air was reduced.

His most famous experiments showed the effect of air pressure. They became famous because of their scientific importance and, perhaps more significant, because of their dramatic appeal. Guericke's travels within Germany as a representative of Magdeburg also helped spread his reputation as he performed his experiments before several dignitaries. One of his demonstrations involved a piston closely fitted inside a tube. When an air valve at the bottom of the closed end of the tube was open, the piston could be lifted easily by means of a rope passing through a pulley and attached to a ring on top of the piston. With the valve closed, several men could lift the piston only part of the way up in the cylinder and, as the air was pumped from the bottom of the tube, they could not prevent its descent. Guericke performed this demonstration before the Imperial court in 1654.

Another of Guericke's devices was a water barometer. He constructed brass tubes, filled them with water and used them in the same way that Torricelli had used his smaller mercury-filled tubes. Guericke realized that changes in the weather produced changes in the height of the water and used his device to make weather predictions. Yet the experiment with which his name is most often associated utilized the so-called Magdeburg hemispheres. These were two copper hemispheres about twenty inches in diameter and constructed in such a way that they could be placed together to form a sphere with surfaces matching so well that a gasket between them formed an airtight seal. He first wrote of the hemispheres on July 22, 1656, when he described how "six strong men could not separate them" after he had evacuated the air from them. In 1657, he repeated the experiment with two teams of horses attempting the separation. He demonstrated the phenomenon for the Imperial court in Berlin in 1663.

Guericke's purpose in these experiments was to understand the nature of space. In this connection, he became interested in magnetism because of the argument about how forces could act across empty space. He was inspired by the work of William Gilbert to construct a variety of spheres with magnetic properties. Finally, he made a sphere of pure sulfur that could be caused to act as a magnet by rubbing it while it was spinning. He noted that objects such as feathers were attracted to it but were also repelled after they had touched it. Gilbert had denied the existence of repulsion and believed that gravity was actually magnetism with the earth acting as a huge magnet. Guericke, on the other hand, concluded that gravity is related to electricity because his sphere had to be rubbed to induce its magnetic properties. He realized that electricity was different from magnetism because he saw sparks and heard the crackling of electrical discharge. He also demonstrated that a charge could be made to travel through a linen string coming from the ball.

Guericke's cosmological conclusions from these experiments were that the universe consists of a large number of stars (suns), each with its own planetary system; these solar systems are held together by a gravitational force centered in each system; and the space in which they are contained is empty and infinite. Earlier speculations on the infinity of space had run into religious objections because only God was believed to be infinite and His creations finite. Guericke neatly solved this problem by maintaining that nothingness (space) already existed when God began filling it with creations. In 1681, Guericke retired and went to live in Hamburg with his son. He died there in 1686 at the age of eighty-three.

Summary

In his day, Otto von Guericke was an important political figure in his own small sphere of central Germany. During a long and productive life, he led his city of Magdeburg through some of the most troubled years in its history. In addition to his political activities, he was able to establish a reputation as an ingenious inventor of experiments that became famous throughout Europe. He also offered scientific theories about the nature of the universe, but his scientific theories were to prove much less important than his experiments. Many more famous scientists, such as Robert Boyle and Christiaan Huygens, were stimulated by his work with air pressure and vacuum pumps to duplicate and continue it with important results. It may be said that those who speculated about the possibility of creating an engine that worked by means of atmospheric pressure were inspired by Guericke. This line of inquiry led directly to the steam engine, without which the Industrial Revolution would have been impossible.

Although writers in the eighteenth century noted his importance, Guericke's work with electricity has not been recognized as much as it deserves because it has been maintained that he did not fully understand his observations. As with the experiments regarding atmospheric pressure, the example of his investigations of electrical phenomena is more important than his conclusions. The hints about conduction and induction, generation of electricity, transmission lines, and the construction of a crude generator led to Benjamin Franklin and later experimenters.

Bibliography

Dibner, Bern. "Ten Founding Fathers of the Electrical Science, II: Otto Von Guericke and the First Electric Machine." *Electrical Engineering*, May, 1954: 396-397. An article by an engineer who gives Guericke credit for greater than usual importance as a pioneer in understanding electricity. Dibner explicates the construction and operation of Guericke's sulfur sphere. Contains illustrations of woodcuts from the seventeenth century.

Kauffeldt, Alfons. *Otto von Guericke*. Leipzig: B. G. Teubner, 1973. This book is in German. Kauffeldt has written other works on Guericke, but this is probably the easiest one to read. Contains illustrations.

Krafft, Fritz. "Otto von Guericke." In *Dictionary of Scientific Biography*, edited by Charles Coulston Gillispie, vol. 5. New York: Charles Scribner's Sons, 1972. The entry on Guericke includes very little biographical information but provides a concise overview of his scientific work. Describes Guericke as a "convinced Copernican" and emphasizes the extent to which his Copernicanism directed his "attempt to reach a complete physical world view."

Philip Dwight Jones

FRANCESCO GUICCIARDINI

Born: March 6, 1483; Florence
Died: May 22, 1540; S. Margherita ia Montici, Florence
Area of Achievement: Historiography
Contribution: Guicciardini helped revolutionize history writing by breaking
with Humanist conventions. He was one of the first historians to present
history as a series of interrelated causes and effects and to treat the history
of Italy in the larger context of European affairs.

Early Life

The Guicciardini family was one of the aristocratic supports of the early
(circa 1430) Medici regime in Florence. Francesco Guicciardini's father had
close ties to Lorenzo de' Medici, evidenced by the many positions offered
him by Lorenzo and by the fact that Marsilio Ficino, Lorenzo's colleague in
the Platonic Academy and a member of the Medici household, was godfather
to young Francesco. At his father's urging, Guicciardini pursued a career in
law. He studied at the Universities of Pisa, Ferrara, and Padua. Upon his
return to Florence, he established himself as a lawyer and professor of law
and in 1508 married Maria Salviati, whose family was active in the affairs of
republican Florence. His earliest writings belong to this period and include
his family memoirs and the *Storie fiorentine* (1509; *The History of Florence*,
1970), which covered the years 1378 to 1509. The latter is an important
source for historians interested in the Florentine Republic.

Life's Work

In 1511, the year of Pope Julius II's formation of Holy League against
France—consisting of the Papal States, Venice, Aragon, and the Holy Roman Empire—Guicciardini was elected to his first public post, as ambassador to the court of Ferdinand II of Aragon. When he returned to Florence
three years later, he found the Medici family restored to power and Florence
a member of the league. He returned to his legal profession, and, though no
friend to the younger generation of Medici, he served the new rulers first as
a member of the *Balia*, or body of eight, in charge of internal security and in
1515 in the *Signoria*, the governing council of the city.

Guicciardini's career took a new course in 1516, when he was appointed
by Pope Leo X to a series of posts. He would serve the Papacy almost
continuously until 1534. Until 1521, he was Governor of Modena and Reggio and general of papal armies. Temporarily removed from these posts upon
the death of Leo X, Guicciardini was reappointed by Pope Adrian VI. Under
his harsh but efficient rule, these provinces were brought under control. The
war in Italy between the Valois French and the Habsburg, Charles V, Holy
Roman Emperor and King of Spain, turned Reggio into a military outpost of

the Papal States. Guicciardini's major military success was the defense of Parma against the French in December, 1521. He also successfully preserved Modena from the Duke of Ferrara, though Reggio capitulated.

Guicciardini's literary output during this time consists of numerous letters and memorandums that manifest his tireless energy in the performance of his duties. From 1521 to 1526, he wrote *Dialogo del reggimento di Firenze* (dialogue on the government of Florence). From a historical case study illustrating the defects of one-man rule and of democracy, Guicciardini deduced his ideal Florentine government: a republic in which the aristocratic element has a leading role. In 1521, too, began Guicciardini's correspondence with Niccolò Machiavelli. From 1501 until the restoration of the Medici in 1512, Machiavelli had been a leading actor in Florence under Piero Soderini, the gonfalon, or ensign, of the republic. The Guicciardini and Salviati families had been aristocratic opponents of that regime, and Guicciardini had called Machiavelli the "tool of Soderini." The two found a common bond in their distaste for Medici rule after 1512. Though younger by fourteen years, Guicciardini played the aristocratic patron to Machiavelli the commoner. About 1530, he began *Considerazioni sui "Discorsi" de Machiavelli* (*Considerations on the "Discourses" of Machiavelli*, 1965), which he never finished. He criticized Machiavelli's theories and his interpretation of Roman history as a guide to contemporary political thought.

Guicciardini's star continued to ascend under Pope Clement VII, a Medici family member with whom he was friends. In 1524, he was made president of the Romagna region, and he became a trusted adviser to the pope. The victory of Charles V over Francis I of France at Pavia in 1525 proved a turning point in the life and the historical consciousness of Guicciardini. He was catapulted into the highest echelons of European politics. From then on, he was both enabled and required to comprehend events in Italy as intricately bound up in the larger schemes of the great powers. In 1526, Guicciardini was in Rome as a papal adviser. His advice was important in the formation of the League of Cognac, the alliance of the Papacy with France and Venice against the Habsburgs; Machiavelli also supported this alliance. Guicciardini became the lieutenant-general of the league's forces. This action by the pope placed Florence in danger of Habsburg reprisal and resulted in another overthrow of Medici rule in 1527, ten days after the sack of Rome by Habsburg troops under the Duke of Bourbon. Guicciardini thus found himself out of favor with the pope and unwelcome in Florence, because of his Medici associations. He later commented that he had suddenly been thrown from the height of honor and esteem to the other extreme. He began to comprehend the power of fortune in historical events, a notion which would attain increasing prominence in his thought.

Guicciardini retired to his villa at Finocchietto, where he worked on *Cosi fiorentine* (Florentine affairs), *Ricordi* (*The Maxims*, 1845), and three personal pieces—*Consolatoria*, *Accusatoria*, and the unfinished *Defensoria*. These three personal pieces are written as speeches against himself; they contain indictments of actions which had long bothered him, including his formation of the league, the sack of Rome, and the pope's imprisonment. A major charge by his imaginary accuser was that he had used high position for personal gain. *The Maxims* is a collection of political maxims culled from his various papers and treatises. Their tone is uniformly cynical, more so, even, than Machiavelli's writings; for example, Guicciardini suggests that one should gain a reputation for sincerity in order to be able to lie successfully on an important matter. In *Cosi fiorentine*, a second history of Florence covering 1375 to 1494, Guicciardini returned to the classical Humanist style of history, but unlike previous histories, he surpassed the typical Humanist histories by using many sources, including documents. In this and in his conviction that to understand the history of Florence one must also understand events throughout all Italy, Guicciardini was taking the first steps in modern historiography. He never finished his Florentine history; in 1529, the Treaty of Cambrai dictated the return of the Medici to power in Florence, and Guicciardini returned to eminence under Alessandro de' Medici's rule.

Personally opposed to Medici rule, Guicciardini still aspired to a leadership role in Florence, but his political career lacked luster during his later years. Pope Clement appointed him Governor of Bologna in 1531; Pope Paul III removed him in 1534. In Florence, Guicciardini was legal adviser to Alessandro until his assassination in 1537. Duke Cosimo de' Medici allowed Guicciardini to remain in office but with an ever-diminishing influence over affairs.

In 1536 Guicciardini began *Storia d'Italia* (1561-1564; *The History of Italy*, 1579), the only book he wrote not for himself but for public consumption. Retiring in 1537 to his villa, he took with him the entire foreign correspondence of the Florentine Republic. *The History of Italy* was written, revised, and polished many times during the last three years of Guicciardini's life. Aside from its value as a source for the years 1494-1532, it is a great milestone in historiography. Guicciardini had come to believe that traditional Humanist history was artificial and prevented history from being useful. He thought that the Humanist view that the moral failures of individual Italian princes were responsible for conflict was inadequate; he believed that not man but uncontrollable fortune governed events. Most important, he realized that the wars of foreign powers in Italy had causes from beyond the Alps. Guicciardini viewed *The History of Italy* as a tragedy brought on Italians by themselves. Because of their rivalries, Italian rulers invited foreign powers onto Italian soil. Guicciardini frequently reiterates that all men act only from self-interest, and the interests of the foreign powers caused the Italian rulers to be initiators of events no longer, so that even their best efforts could not relieve the situation. It was Guicciardini's gift to show how human illusions are an integral part of history and how events, or fortune, and human intentions constantly act and react upon one another. Is history still useful if it teaches nothing but the arbitrariness of fortune? Guicciardini believed that the value of history was as a reminder to men to consider the effect of their every action upon their names and dignity. He died while still polishing his book on May 22, 1540.

Summary

Francesco Guicciardini's achievement was to set the writing of history on a new and intellectually sound path. Before his generation, Humanist historians had slavishly imitated the historians of classical antiquity. If the main subject was a war, then Sallust was to be imitated and attention devoted to the generals' speeches before a battle and to the battle itself. If the focus was the history of a particular city, then Livy was the preferred model. History was regarded as a branch of rhetoric whose purpose was to provide moral instruction by examples. Thus, history did not require completeness but merely those episodes which demonstrated a certain virtue or vice.

Guicciardini accepted the didactic purpose of history (he quoted Cicero's prescription for writing history), but he saw it as teaching the concrete effects of various types of government rather than the general rules of ethics. In the end, he concluded that men always act from personal interest and that fortune plays its fickle part more frequently than one might think. Throughout a lifetime as an actor at the edge of events, he came to perceive the complex networks of causation between events, so that episodic history was no longer plausible to him. Another contribution was his heightened standard of factual accuracy, possible only by comparing literary sources and documents.

Guicciardini's *The Maxims* and *The History of Italy* were published soon after his death. His other writings, ten volumes of *Opere Inedite* (unedited works), did not see print until 1857-1867.

Bibliography

De Sanctis, Francesco. *History of Italian Literature*. Translated by Joan Redfern. 2 vols. New York: Barnes & Noble, 1968. Chapter 15 compares Machiavelli and Guicciardini. Gives an unfavorable view of the career and mind of Guicciardini as advocating self-interest as the motive force of history.

Gilbert, Felix. *Machiavelli and Guicciardini: Politics and History in Sixteenth Century Florence*. New York: W. W. Norton, 1984. A survey of Guicciardini's career and literary output seen against the tradition of Renaissance historiography prevalent in his day. Contains an excellent annotated bibliography.

Guicciardini, Francesco. *The History of Florence*. Translated by Mario Domandi. New York: Harper & Row, 1970. The complete text in English with an excellent and detailed introductory biography.

_____. *The History of Italy*. Translated by Sidney Alexander. New York: Macmillan, 1969. Contains extensive and well-chosen excerpts in English from his twenty-volume history.

_____. *Maxims and Reflections of a Renaissance Statesman*. Translated by Mario Domandi. New York: Harper & Row, 1965. An English translation of *The Maxims*.

_____. *Selected Writings*. Edited by Cecil Grayson. Translated by Margaret Grayson. New York: Oxford University Press, 1965. A good sampling of Guicciardini's various writings in English translation.

Luciani, Vincent. *Francesco Guicciardini and His European Reputation*. New York: Karl Otto, 1936. Contains copious scholarly material on Guicciardini; lists editions and translations of his works up to 1936. Discusses *The History of Italy* as a historical source and summarizes the views of it held by Italian, French, Spanish, Catholic, Protestant, and nineteenth century historians.

Ridolfi, Roberto. *The Life of Francesco Guicciardini*. Translated by Cecil Grayson. New York: Alfred A. Knopf, 1968. An intimate, thoroughly footnoted, highly favorable biography by a major Guicciardini scholar.

Daniel C. Scavone

GUSTAVUS II ADOLPHUS

Born: December 9, 1594; Stockholm, Sweden
Died: November 6, 1632; Lützen, Saxony
Areas of Achievement: The military, monarchy, and statecraft
Contribution: Gustavus was one of the greatest military commanders in the history of warfare. He was responsible for brilliant military innovations in strategy and tactics, and in the development of modern weaponry. Gustavus also transformed Sweden into one of the leading nations in Europe by implementing wide-ranging domestic reforms in the fields of government administration, economic development, and education.

Early Life

Gustavus II Adolphus was born on December 9, 1594, in Stockholm, Sweden, the first son of Charles IX and Christina of Holstein. As a youthful member of the royal family, he received a traditional education; his childhood was largely uneventful. When his father died in 1611, however, Gustavus found himself King of Sweden at the age of sixteen. As the new king, Gustavus inherited what appeared to be unsurmountable problems. In 1600, his father had usurped the throne and deposed his nephew Sigismund, who was also King of Poland at the time. That resulted in a dynastic dispute between Sweden and Poland that continued for almost sixty years; for twenty years of his own reign, Gustavus always had to confront the possiblity of a legitimate invasion by Poland to restore the vanquished monarchy. As if that were not enough, Charles IX also precipitated a war in Russia to place his own candidate on the vacant Russian throne; while his troops were deeply inside foreign territory, he recklessly started a war with Denmark.

Charles's domestic policies were no less harmful. His rule of Sweden after taking the throne was harsh and arbitrary; soon afterward, he did away with the aristocratic constitutionalism which had functioned under the previous king, and he executed five leading members of the aristocracy. In addition, although Charles had replaced a Catholic sovereign who had threatened the very existence of Swedish Lutheranism, his strict religious views, most probably a form of Calvinism, put him into endless conflict with the Lutheran church. When Charles died, the country suffered from religious strife, the monarchy was unpopular, and the people themselves were tired of the incessant warfare. Gustavus was only permitted to succeed his father as king and assume control of the government by agreeing to important constitutional concessions demanded by the Swedish Estates (or assembly).

Life's Work

When Gustavus therefore assumed the throne in 1611, he was faced not only with three major foreign wars but also with a constitutional crisis in

Sweden. Since he regarded the war with Denmark as lost, he immediately decided to end it. The terms stated in the Peace of Knäred (1613) required Sweden to give its only North Sea port to Denmark to function as a guarantee for the payment of an extremely large war idemnity. The war with Poland could not be concluded as easily, and it continued intermittently for years.

The consequences of the war with Russia were much more serious for Gustavus—it was here that he learned the strategy and tactics of warfare. His father had initally invaded Russia to prevent a Polish candidate from being crowned czar, but with the election of Michael Romanov, a Russian, this threat had ended. Gustavus, however, continued the war with the intention of occupying as much Russian land as possible. He was driven by the fear that, once Russia's political situation had stabilized, the country might become a major military and naval power in the Baltic region. The Peace of Stölbova (1617) rewarded his efforts; according to the terms of the treaty, Sweden annexed Ingria and Kexholm and established a continuous strip of occupied territory from Finland to Estonia. The result—Russia was denied access to the Baltic and turned back toward Asia, thereby delaying its emergence as a major power in Europe for more than one hundred years.

In the meantime, the domestic situation in Sweden had improved markedly. The concessions demanded from Gustavus by the Estates might have resulted in the nobility dominating the monarchy. That did not happen, because the man who had actually drawn up the demands, Chancellor Axel Oxenstierna, became Gustavus' confidant and collaborator for the entire duration of his reign. These two men complemented each other's capabilities and temperaments; the result was a unique and historic partnership that led to sweeping domestic reforms.

In 1614, a new Swedish supreme court was established along with a permanent treasury and chancery four years later; both an admiralty and a war office were founded by the end of Gustavus' reign. For the first time in Sweden's history, the Council of State became a permanent fixture of the government and assumed responsibilities for the nation's affairs while the king was fighting overseas. While one reform professionalized local government and subsumed it under the control of the king, another limited the number of estates at four, including the nobles, clergy, peasants, and burghers. By 1634, Sweden had the most progressive and efficient central government administration in all Europe. Yet the most impressive of Gustavus' domestic accomplishments was in the field of education. He provided financial security to the University of Uppsala so that it could continue its development; he founded the University of Dorpat (modern Tartu State University); and, during the 1620's, he was deeply involved in the creation of the *Gymnasia* in Sweden.

Gustavus renewed the war with Sigismund in 1621 with the intention of ending the continual Polish claim to the Swedish throne; by 1626, he had concentrated his main point of attack in Prussia, where he hoped to control the Vistula River and defeat the Polish commanders. Yet his attention was gradually directed toward the danger posed to German Protestantism by the brilliant and successful Catholic generals of the Habsburg Empire, Albrecht Wallenstein and Johann Tserclaes. Thus, for Gustavus, the war in Poland became part of the Protestant resistance against the Catholic Counter-Reformation; if Sigismund were victorious, all of Scandinavia would be recatholicized. When the Protestant cause in Germany began to experience one military defeat after another, its leaders looked to Gustavus as the one man who could save Europe from complete Catholic domination.

The Polish struggle ended with the Truce of Altmark in 1629; in June of 1630, Gustavus landed with his Swedish force at Peenemünde to enter the Thirty Years' War. What had been an inconclusive war waged by traditional strategies, tactics, and weapons was now revolutionized by Gustavus' presence. In Germany, the king completed the transformation of the art of warfare started by Maurice of Nassau, Prince of Orange, and one of the greatest military commanders in the early seventeenth century. Gustavus adhered to Maurice's idea that a professional army should be paid on a regular basis; that prevented looting in time of war and desertion in time of peace. He also followed Maurice's advice on discipline: The Swedish army under Gustavus' command was instilled with a sense of corporate discipline, which meant that each soldier was thoroughly prepared for large-scale maneuvers, reorganization on the battlefield, and coordination among artillery, calvary, and infantry units. Largely as a result of Gustavus' articles of war, his army was one of the best behaved in all Europe: Swearing, blasphemy, fornication, looting, and drunkenness were strictly forbidden. In arming his men with weapons he thought necessary to fight a modern war, Gustavus decreased the weight of the musket to make it less cumbersome and made large strides in standardizing powder and caliber. These reforms and innovations gave the Swedish army extraordinary power and mobility—Europe was both amazed and frightened by the unusual quality of Gustavus' forces.

At Breitenfeld, in September of 1630, Gustavus' army routed Tserclaes' Catholic forces in a battle that forever changed the course of German history. This one battle assured the survival of Protestantism in Germany and is regarded by historians as a textbook example of the art of war. Over the next few months, Gustavus swept through central Germany rather easily, consolidating his control as he advanced. By the end of the year, he was being called the "Lion of the North," the Protestant hero of the Thirty Years' War.

At the end of 1631, with the liberation of north and central Germany complete and the plans for a campaign in southern Germany well under way, Gustavus broadened his strategy. He was now convinced that the only means whereby the German Protestant princes could guarantee their security against the Catholic forces lay in the formation of a *Corpus Evangelicorum*, or

Protestant League. This league would consist of a comprehensive and permanent association of all the German princes for their mutual defense. Most important, Gustavus would become its political leader and military director.

The formation of the league and its establishment depended to a large extent upon the result of Gustavus' campaign of 1632; the Catholic control over Bavaria was to be broken as a prelude to the conquest of Vienna in 1633. At the River Lech in Bavaria, Gustavus brilliantly managed to cross boats over a bridge while concealing his exact location by burning damp straw for a smokescreen and to rout Tserclaes' new army on the opposite bank. The road was now open to Munich.

Wallenstein, however, appeared to threaten the Swedish-controlled city of Nürnberg. In order to relieve the city, Gustavus attacked Wallenstein's forces in the Battle of the Alte Veste but failed because of the Catholic commander's prepared fortifications and the inability of the Swedish calvary and artillery to play their part. After a period of maneuvering by both armies, Gustavus finally met Wallenstein in the open field at Lützen on November 6, 1632. Mist and bad weather deprived Gustavus of the advantage of surprise, but the Swedish army fought fiercely and appeared to be gaining ground. At the very moment when victory seemed certain, Gustavus led a calvary charge against the enemy, was separated from his men, and was shot in the back. He fell from his horse and lay in the mud until one of Wallenstein's men killed him with a pistol.

Summary

The Swedish army won a tactical victory at the Battle of Lützen; Gustavus II Adolphus' innovations in strategy and tactics, logistics, and weaponry made it the most powerful armed force in Europe—and it continued to influence the course of German history even after his death. Yet, with Gustavus gone, the army lost its vital spark, and Sweden's presence in European affairs began gradually to diminish. Less than a century later, Sweden's military and political influence on the Continent was negligible. Yet Gustavus had personally guided the course of history for the few short years before his death and had transformed Sweden into one of the most modern and powerful nations of the era. Not the least of his accomplishments were the domestic reforms in the areas of government administration, education, and economic development that he bequeathed to his country.

Bibliography

Dupuy, Trevor N. *The Military Life of Gustavus Adolphus: Father of Modern War.* New York: Franklin Watts, 1969. A very good description of Gustavus' military genius and technical innovations. Focuses on his development as the first great modern commander.
Fletcher, C. R. L. *Gustavus Adolphus and the Struggle of Protestantism for*

Existence. New York: G. P. Putnam's Sons, 1890. An account of the king's participation in the Thirty Years' War; the author contends that Gustavus actually saved Protestantism in Central Europe because of his involvement.

Parker, Geoffrey, ed. *The Thirty Years' War*. London: Routledge & Kegan Paul, 1984. An excellent treatment of the Swedish influence on Europe during the Thirty Years' War. Deals with the diplomatic and economic elements of Swedish influence as well as Swedish military prowess.

Roberts, Michael. *Gustavus Adolphus: A History of Sweden, 1611-1632*. 2 vols. London: Longmans, Green, 1953-1958. The standard work in English on Gustavus' relationship to his own nation and his influence on an era. A masterfully written study, placing Gustavus' military achievements in a rich historical perspective. Contains a detailed and extensive bibliography that is still considered an important reference source.

_____. *Gustavus Adolphus and the Rise of Sweden*. London: English Universities Press, 1973. A classic study on selected aspects of Sweden's rise to power in Europe. Emphasizes the personal traits and characteristics that contributed to the king's leadership.

Wedgwood, C. V. *The Thirty Years' War*. New York: Doubleday, 1961. Includes an examination of Gustavus' motives for declining to intervene in the Thirty Years' War and a discussion of his contribution to the art of warfare up to that time.

Thomas Derdak

ERNST HAECKEL

Born: February 16, 1834; Potsdam, Prussia
Died: August 9, 1919; Jena, Germany
Areas of Achievement: Biology, natural history, zoology, and philosophy
Contribution: Haeckel studied and classified many marine organisms, especially the radiolaria and the medusae. He is most noted for his refinement of Charles Darwin's theory of evolution, its extension to mankind and the origin of life, the refinement of the biogenetic law, and the development of monism as a religion.

Early Life

Ernst Heinrich Philipp August Haeckel was born in Potsdam, Prussia, on February 16, 1834, to Karl Haeckel and Charlotte Sethe Haeckel. Both the Haeckel and Sethe families contributed prominently to German history and intermarried on several occasions. In both families there were several prominent lawyers. Karl Haeckel was a state councillor.

Shorly after Ernst was born, his family moved to Meresburg. There, he attended school until he was eighteen. As a boy he had a great love of nature, which was fostered by his mother. He collected and classified many plants as a youth; his father occasionally gave him words of encouragement. He had a strong sense of independence and individuality, and even as a youth he was a compulsive worker.

In 1852, Ernst entered the University of Jena to work with Matthias Schleiden, a codeveloper of the cell theory. Schleiden taught him how to combine his interests in botany and philosophy. Not long after entering Jena, however, he became ill and had to return to Berlin to stay with his parents. He entered the University of Würzburg in the fall of 1852 to work with the botanist Alexander Braun. His father's persistence, however, made him turn his attention to medicine. While at Würzburg, he studied under Albert Kölliker, Franz Leydig, and Rudolf Virchow. At Würzburg, he developed an interest in embryology.

The philosophy at Würzburg, where learning through research was emphasized, was well suited for the young Haeckel. Natural phenomena were explained and studied through cause-and-effect relationships and allowed little opportunity for the intrusion of mysticism and the supernatural. These philosophies laid the foundation for Haeckel's future work.

Life's Work

During the summer of 1854, Haeckel had the opportunity to study comparative anatomy under Johannes Müller. Müller gave Haeckel permission to work in the museum. During that summer, Müller took the young Haeckel to sea, where he taught him how to study living marine organisms. Haeckel stayed the winter at Berlin and wrote his first essay under the great Müller. In the spring of 1885, Haeckel returned to Würzburg, where, under Kölliker's influence, he earned a medical degree in 1857 with a zoological/ anatomical emphasis rather than a strictly medical one. Although Haeckel earned a medical degree, he seldom practiced medicine. This resulted from the fact that he spent most of his time studying marine animals and saw patients only from five to six A.M. During his first year of practice, he saw only three patients.

In the winter of 1859-1860, Haeckel studied the radiolaria collected off Messina. This project laid the foundation for his interest and future work in zoology. By the spring of 1860, he had discovered 144 new species of radiolaria. His work at Messina culminated in the publication of *Die Radiolarien* (*Report on the Radiolaria*, 1887) in 1862. This work was one of his finest and most influential, and it established his position as a zoologist. After a fifteen-year hiatus, he again pursued the study of radiolaria and published the second, third, and fourth parts of *Report on the Radiolaria* from 1887 to 1888. He eventually classified more than thirty-five hundred species of radiolaria.

In March, 1861, he was appointed private teacher at the University of Jena, and in 1862 he was appointed extraordinary professor of zoology at the Zoological Museum. In 1865, he became a professor at Jena. In August, 1862, he married his cousin, Anna Sethe. Anna died two years later at the age of twenty-nine. Stricken with grief over the loss of his beloved wife, he became a hermit and a compulsive worker, often surviving on only three to four hours of sleep each day. In 1867, he married Agnes Huschke.

In May, 1860, Haeckel read Charles Darwin's *On the Origin of Species* (1859). The book profoundly influenced Haeckel's intellectual development, and he became Germany's most devout supporter and popularizer of Darwinism. It has often been said that without Haeckel there would have been Darwin, but there would not have been Darwinism. Haeckel came to view evolution as the basis for the explanation of all nature.

Haeckel, whose faith was enfeebled by the study of comparative anatomy and physiology, was also profoundly influenced by his friend Johann Wolfgang von Goethe and became a believer in Goethe's God of Nature. Haeckel no longer believed in a Creator, since Darwin's theory permitted him to explain nature without divine influence. This enabled Haeckel to accept Darwinism better than Darwin. For Haeckel, it became possible to develop a philosophy of nature without having to interject God or a vital force. Haeckel's support of Darwinism made him the target of attack by his German colleagues, many of whom were doubters of Darwinian ideas. Haeckel first revealed his belief in Darwinism in *Report on the Radiolaria*. He acknowledges that in the radiolaria there are several transitional forms that connect the various groups and that they form "a fairly continuous chain of related forms," and he expresses his "belief in the mutability of species and the real genealogical relation of all organisms."

In an address to the Scientific Congress of 1863, eight years before Darwin published *The Descent of Man and Selection in Relation to Sex* (1871), Haeckel said that man must recognize his immediate ancestors in apelike mammals. He realized, however, that Darwin's theory may not be perfect and may need refinement. He especially realized that it explained neither the origin of the first living organism nor how man was connected to the genealogical tree. Haeckel thought that the first living organism was a single cell, a cell even more primitive than the eukaryotic cell. Not long afterward, the prokaryotic cell, a primitive cell without a nucleus, was described. After studying the brains and skulls of the primates, Haeckel produced a genealogical tree which showed the relationship of man to the other primates and to lower animals.

In the mid-1860's, Haeckel began to study the medusae, a study which culminated in the publication of *Das System der Medusen* (*Report on the Deep-Sea Medusae*, 1882) in 1879. The treatise was a detailed description of the medusae. In the later 1860's, he studied the social aspects of the medusae.

Haeckel's greatest achievement was his *Generelle Morphologie der Organismen*, published in 1866. The monograph is considered a landmark and one of the most important scientific works of the latter half of the nineteenth century. In *Generelle Morphologie der Organismen*, Haeckel clearly presented his reductionist philosophy. He reduced the cell to the laws of chemistry and physics, and through the influence of Darwin, raised the study of zoology to that of the physical sciences. He strengthened the laws of evolution, refined the biogenetic law, and presented a philosophy of life and a new story of its creation. In it, too, he described his early education as defective, perverse, and filled with errors. He lambasted the educational system that emphasized memory of dead material which interferes with normal intellectual development.

In *Generelle Morphologie der Organismen*, Haeckel presented two ideas, monism and the biogenetic law, which would occupy the rest of his life. The biogenetic law, which was originally proposed by Darwin, was refined and expanded by Haeckel. According to the biogenetic law, ontogeny recapitulates phylogeny, which means that during embryological development animals pass through developmental stages which represent adult stages from which the developing animal evolved. Haeckel viewed embryonic development of an individual animal as a brief and condensed recapitulation of its evolutionary history. Haeckel used the biogenetic law to strengthen his case for evolution. Although the law was eventually proved to be in error, it was accepted by many scientists and stimulated much discussion and research. In *Generelle Morphologie der Organismen*, he presented a genealogical tree with bacteria and single-celled organisms on the bottom. From the bacteria and single-celled organisms arose two branches: the animals and the plants.

In his search for a religion that did not rely on a vital force or a personal god, Haeckel developed monism, a scientific and philosophical doctrine which advocated nature as a substitute for religion. The basic principles of monism can be summarized as follows: Knowledge of the world is based on scientific knowledge acquired through human reason; the world is one great whole ruled by fixed laws; there is no vital force that controls the laws of nature; living organisms have developed by evolution through descent; nothing in the universe was created by a Creator; living organisms originated from nonliving matter; man and the apes are closely related and evolved from a common ancestor; God as a supreme being does not exist; and God is nature.

These outspoken and heretical ideas about God made Haeckel the target of attacks not only from the Church but also from his colleagues. Indeed, many of his colleagues called for his resignation as a professor, Yet he stayed at Jena and raised it to the level of an intellectual metropolis. His reputation as a great scientist and thinker attracted many young, bright scientists to Jena.

Not being one to walk away from the battlefield and collapse under fire, Haeckel published *Natürliche Schöpfungsgeschichte* (*The History of Creation*, 1876) in 1868. This book was a condensation and a popularization on the ideas originally presented in *Generelle Morphologie der Organismen* and was written primarily for the layperson. In the book, Haeckel approached the problems of life through Darwinism. The book was attacked by theologians and by many scientists, but it became a best-seller in its time.

The History of Creation was followed by *Anthropogenie* (1874; *The Evolution of Man*, 1879), a survey of all that was learned in the nineteenth century about the history of mankind, and *Die Weltratsel* (1899; *The Riddle of the Universe at the Close of the Nineteenth Century*, 1900), an intentionally provocative and popular study of monism that was translated into more than a dozen languages.

In his many popular writings, Haeckel unleashed a relentless attack on the Church and the clergy, which he thought preyed on the gullibility of the ignorant masses in order to further their selfish aims. He was criticized for being outspoken against established, organized religion while ignoring what his critics regarded as more serious ills of his country. He answered these charges in *Die Lebenswunder* (*The Wonders of Life*, 1904).

Haeckel founded the phyletic museum at the University of Jena and the Ernst Haeckel Haus to house his collections, books, and letters. He retired from active teaching and research in 1909 at the age of seventy-five and died at Jena in 1919.

Summary

Ernst Haeckel was one of the greatest natural historians, zoologists, and philosophers of the nineteenth century. His descriptions of many marine organisms, especially of the radiolaria and the medusae, were monumental and unparalleled in the zoological sciences. He classified several thousand new species of plants and animals.

Moreover, Haeckel's knowledge of zoology provided him with a platform from which he launched an advocacy and popularization of the ideas of Darwin. He described evolution as "the most important advance that has been made in pure and applied science." He was quick to extend and develop Darwin's theory. He refined the biogenetic law and was one of the first to extend Darwin's ideas to the origin of life and mankind.

Haeckel's staunch support of Darwinism and his monistic philosophy alienated him from the clergy and from older scientists but attracted many younger scientists as disciples. Although he had many critics, more than five hundred university professors (many his critics) around the world contributed to the making of a marble bust of Haeckel, which was unveiled at the University of Jena in 1894. Haeckel's ideas influenced a generation.

Bibliography
Bölsche, Wilhelm. *Haeckel: His Life and Work*. Translated by Joseph McCabe. London: T. Fisher, 1902. This is the most extensive biography of Haeckel, and the only one to have been translated into English. It is an excellent account of Haeckel's work as a scientist and philosopher. Bölsche was one of Haeckel's students.
De Grood, David H. *Haeckel's Theory of the Unity of Nature: A Monograph in the History of Philosophy*. Boston: Christopher, 1965. Originally written as a master's thesis, it was reprinted in 1982 by Gruner of Amsterdam. Summarizes Haeckel's monistic philosophy.
Haeckel, Ernst. *The Evolution of Man*. Translated by Joseph McCabe. New York: G. P. Putnam's Sons, 1905. The first edition to be translated into English.
_____. *The Riddle of the Universe*. Translated by Joseph McCabe. New York: Harper & Row, 1902. This book offers a popularization of Haeckel's monistic philosophy "for thoughtful readers . . . who are united in an honest search for the truth."
Slosson, Edwin. *Major Prophets of Today*. Boston: Little, Brown, 1914. Contains a chapter summarizing the life of Haeckel as a scientist.

Charles L. Vigue

FRANS HALS

Born: c. 1583; Antwerp, Spanish Netherlands
Died: September 1, 1666; Haarlem, United Provinces
Area of Achievement: Art
Contribution: Hals was the most celebrated northern painter of his era except for Rembrandt, who was a few years his junior. Hals specialized in painting group scenes and individual portraits in which his highly original use of grays provided his work with a chromatic unity that in the work of artists such as Leonardo da Vinci was achieved through chiaroscuro, the play of light and dark.

Early Life
The first record of Frans Hals's family is dated March 19, 1591, the day on which Dirck Hals, Frans's younger brother who was also a painter, was baptized in Haarlem. It is thought that Hals's parents, Franchoys and Adriaentgen van Geertenrijk Hals, came from Mechelen but settled in Antwerp before 1580. They are known to have fled Antwerp for the north during Frans's early childhood to avoid religious persecution. By 1591, they had settled in Haarlem, where Hals spent most of his life.

Hals's father was a weaver and maker of cloth; his wife probably assisted him in his work when she was able. Hals is thought to have begun studying art with Karel van Mander, cofounder of the Haarlem Academy, around 1600. By 1610, five years after van Mander's death, Hals was a member of the Guild of St. Luke, part of whose charge was to regulate the duties and privileges of Haarlem's painters.

Hals married Annetje Harmansdr in 1610. She died in 1615, leaving Hals with two children. One of them, Harmen, baptized in Haarlem on September 2, 1611, became a painter. Annetje was buried in land that Haarlem reserved for the burial of its poor, so it is clear that Hals was not prosperous at the time of his wife's death. Hals married Lysbeth Reyniers on February 12, 1617, nine days before their first child, Sara, was baptized. Their union produced eight children, of whom his sons Frans, Nicolaes, and Jan became painters. Hals's daughter Adriaentgen married Pieter Roestraten, a noted still-life painter.

Between the death of his first wife and his marriage to his second, Hals apparently visited Antwerp, where, it is speculated, he first encountered the paintings of Peter Paul Rubens. Shortly before he remarried, Hals was commissioned by members of the St. George Civic Guard Company to paint a picture of their banquet, a group portrait whose composition presented problems comparable to those Leonardo da Vinci faced in the composition of *The Last Supper* (1498) more than a century earlier. The general tone of the Hals painting, however, depicts revelry rather than the reflective contemplation of

The Last Supper. Hals, nevertheless, had to present reasonable likenesses of each of the twelve people in the picture, because each was paying for this recognition. Those who paid the most or who had important positions in the company had to be most prominently presented. Hals struck on the brilliant unifying technique of placing slightly left of the center of the picture a boy carrying the company's standard over his shoulder, so that its horizontal axis forms about a twenty-degree angle. Hals coordinates the colors in the standard with the colors in each member's sash and enhances the perspective and dimensionality by the placement of the figures and by placing immediately behind the standard a window opening onto an obscure cityscape. A vertical standard at the far right of the painting and highlighted drapery toward the top of the far left portion reinforce the dimensionality of the total work. Each figure is clad in black but wears a white ruff that ties in with the white damask tablecloth, intricately reproduced in all its detail, that covers the table at which the company has feasted.

Life's Work

Hals was essentially a portrait painter. Flourishing two centuries before even the crudest cameras existed, Hals, like his contemporaries, was called upon to preserve the memories of people by painting them as accurately as he could, either singly or in groups. Because it was generally the subjects of his paintings who paid for them, he had to make them look as good as possible, a limitation he shared with his contemporaries.

That Hals, a fun-loving man given to free spending and serious drinking, was popular among the painters of Haarlem is attested by his having been given six separate commissions to paint the officers of the Civil Guard Company in slightly more than two decades, as well as by the number of paintings he produced during his lifetime, nearly all of them painted on commission.

Hals worked rapidly and painted with a sure hand. At a time when many artists worked in pairs, Hals preferred to work alone, although on rare occasions he collaborated with such fellow artists as Nicolaes van Heussen, Willem Buytewech, and Pieter de Molyn. Hals was particularly adept at reproducing exquisitely and intricately detail in cloth and jewelry. More important, he was able to produce recognizable likenesses of his subjects while simultaneously probing their inner beings and capturing, much as Rembrandt was able, what can best be called their "inner lights."

Unlike many artists of his day, Hals seldom painted himself into his group portraits. He did, however, depict himself as a background figure in his Civic Group Company painting of 1639. He appears in the upper left of the painting and, judging from a close examination of this single self-portrait of him when he was at least fifty-five years old, he had long, dark hair, dark eyes, a mustache, and a goatee. At first glance, the picture, like that of his most celebrated portrait, *The Laughing Cavalier* (1624), seems to be of a happy-go-lucky, self-assured person. Closer examination of both pictures, however, reveals that the seemingly upturned lips are really not upturned. It is the mustache that gives the illusion that the figure in each case is laughing. In actuality, Hals's cavalier has at best a Gioconda smile, a quizzical smirk. The self-portrait reveals a melancholy figure, one whose mustache is laughing but whose eyes and lips reveal someone quite the opposite.

It is at least in part Hals's ability to paint enigmatically that has helped to assure his position among the leading painters of the world. Leonardo's *Mona Lisa*, begun in 1503, and Hals's *The Laughing Cavalier* each put a burr in the minds of those who see them, establishing them not only as unforgettable but also as intellectually provoking. It is unlikely that Hals was imitating Leonardo when he painted *The Laughing Cavalier*; rather, he was revealing the sardonic nature inherent in his own temperament.

Although one can point to pockets of prosperity in Hals's life, it can generally be said that he almost constantly lived near the edge financially. As his children, four of them artists, grew older, they could contribute little to the household. Hals and his family moved from one rented dwelling to another, often being evicted when they could not pay their rent. In 1654, a Haarlem baker to whom Hals owed two hundred guilder seized his furniture and five of his paintings to satisfy the debt. Seven years later, the Guild of St. Luke's waived the payment of Hals's annual dues because of the artist's poverty. The following year, the burgomasters of Haarlem granted Hals's request for a subvention of fifty guilders, and they followed that gift shortly with one three times as large. In 1663, they agreed to pay him two hundred guilders a year for the rest of his life. Nine years after his death, the city fathers had to grant his widow a pittance on which to live. Hals continued to paint until the year of his death, completing some of his finest work in 1664, when he undertook a commission to paint the regents of the Haarlem Almshouse. This commission brought him a modicum of prosperity, so that when he died in 1666 he was in less dire straits than he had been during much of his life.

Among Hals's greatest artistic inventions was that of controlling his work by infusing it with color values obtained by his use of grays. The chiaroscuro perfected by Leonardo and Masaccio in Italy in the early fifteenth century had been widely imitated. Hals, however, sought a new means of handling light and of bringing chromatic unity to his work. Like Rembrandt and Jan Vermeer, he experimented extensively with light and its sources, finally developing, through the use of grays, his unique way of solving the problem.

Summary

Despite his persistent penury, Frans Hals was recognized as a leading citizen of Haarlem. The two hundred guilder annual subvention the town fathers settled on him was a munificent sum in its day. In the Groot Heiligland, from which Hals and his family once had to move because they could not pay their rent, the Frans Hals Museum, a significant tourist attraction, now stands. The artist's place in the history of art is secure. He ranks only slightly below Rembrandt, and his influence has been substantial. Among those who imbibed directly of his artistic spirit are Hieronymous Bosch, Pieter Brueghel, the Elder, Pieter Brueghel, the Younger, and Jan Brueghel, all of whom painted in a popular style infused with wit. What was sardonic wit in Hals became a broader, puckish—sometimes outrageous and scatological—wit in Bosch. Paintings such as Hals's *The Lute Player* (c. 1621) or *Seated Man Holding a Branch* (1645) could easily have been incorporated into any of Bosch's or the Brueghels' busy, crowded paintings.

On September 1, 1666, Hals's body was placed in its grave in the choir of St. Bavo's Church in Haarlem, an honor accorded only to those who had brought honor to the town. Perhaps the final irony in the Hals story is that despite the poverty in which he lived, Hals's paintings, which seldom come on the market, have commanded prices in excess of ten million dollars.

Bibliography

Baard, H. P. *Frans Hals*. Translated by George Stuyck. New York: Harry N. Abrams, 1981. This oversize volume has excellent color plates of most of Hals's major paintings. The text gives valuable biographical detail that dispels the myth that Hals's work was essentially humorous. Perceptive commentary on specific paintings. Includes a chronology of Hals's life.

Beeren, Willem A. *Frans Hals*. Translated by Albert J. Fransella. London: Blanford Press, 1962. This book presents accurate information about Hals's life and the lives of his artist children but is at its best in relating Hals to the artistic milieu of his day. Presents sensitive interpretations of Hals's style and artistic method.

Gratama, Gerrit D. *Frans Hals*. 2d ed. The Hague: Oceanus, 1946. Gratama understands Hals in relation to such other artists as Jan Steen, Peter Paul Rubens, and Rembrandt. Hals's paintings are discussed from a technical viewpoint, indicating how Hals achieved the detail he did despite the boldness of his heavy textures. Gratama's Hals emerges as a highly original craftsman who solved artistic problems in singular ways.

Hals, Frans. *The Civic Guard Portrait Groups*. Text and foreword by H. P. Baard. New York: Macmillan, 1950. Discusses Hals's six paintings of the Civic Guard Company, executed between 1616 and 1639, as well as those of his contemporaries who were commissioned to paint the Civic Guard Company. The book presents interesting contrasts and comparisons, demonstrating clearly the uniqueness of Hals's work.

_____. *The Paintings of Frans Hals.* Text by Numa Trivas. New York: Oxford University Press, 1942. Despite its age, Trivas' discussions of Hals's major paintings remain pertinent. The accompanying illustrations are appropriately chosen, and, considering the difficulties of printing art books during the years of World War II, they are of acceptable quality. Trivas shows a fine grasp of Flemish art.

Valentiner, Wilhelm R. *Frans Hals Paintings in America.* Westport, Conn.: F. F. Sherman, 1936. Although badly dated, this book lists and has reproductions of Hals paintings in collections in the United States. Most of the paintings listed here remain in the same collections in the United States that held them in 1936, although some Hals acquisitions have been made since the publication of this valuable catalog. The book is not essentially interpretive.

R. Baird Shuman

KARL VON HARDENBERG

Born: May 31, 1750; Essenrode, Hanover
Died: November 26, 1822; Genoa, Kingdom of Sardinia
Areas of Achievement: Government, politics, and diplomacy
Contribution: Hardenberg played a leading role in the Prussian reform movement. He also directed the foreign policy of his country during the eventful years 1810-1822 and played a pivotal role in forming the coalition of powers that defeated Napoleon. He was the spokesman for Prussia at the Congress of Vienna in 1815, which determined the political fate of Europe for the next fifty years.

Early Life

Karl August von Hardenberg was born at Essenrode, Hanover, on May 31, 1750, to Christian and Charlotte von Hardenberg. His father, the scion of an old Hanoverian family, had a distinguished military career. Hardenberg's parents determined that he should pursue a career in government service, and they sent him to Göttingen University in 1766, to study law and political science. He also studied briefly at the University of Leipzig in 1768. He completed his studies in 1770, having returned to Göttingen. Upon graduation he entered the Hanoverian bureaucracy in the department of justice.

In 1775, Hardenberg made an unfortunate marriage to the Countess Juliana von Reventlow, after which Hardenberg was appointed as the Hanoverian minister to England. His wife became involved in a sordid affair with the Prince of Wales, which, when it became a public scandal in 1781, forced Hardenberg's recall from England and ultimately his resignation from service. Hardenberg managed to find a new post in the Brunswick bureaucracy in 1782, serving for more than a decade. His service in Brunswick was also terminated by a scandal when, after securing a divorce from Juliana, he married a divorcée. Leaving Brunswick in 1792, Hardenberg obtained a position in the Prussian bureaucracy as minister for several newly acquired provinces.

Life's Work

Hardenberg quickly displayed to his new monarch unusual ability in both internal administration and in foreign affairs. In domestic affairs, he was entrusted with the reorganization of the Prussian administrations of finance, justice, education, and transportation. In foreign affairs, Frederick William II made him plenipotentiary to conclude a territorial settlement with the revolutionary government of France in 1795. Through his adroit handling of the negotiations resulting in the Peace of Basel, Prussia actually emerged stronger than before, despite having fared poorly in the War of the First Coalition. Hardenberg continued to grow in favor, and in 1804 Frederick

William III appointed him foreign minister of Prussia.

As minister for foreign affairs, Hardenberg openly advocated a policy of territorial aggrandizement, contending that the Prussian government should seize every opportunity to acquire new territory. He pursued a policy of peace with Napoleon and territorial expansion through negotiation. In 1806, however, Hardenberg's counsel was disregarded and Prussia allied with Russia in a new war against Napoleon.

The war ended disastrously for Prussia. The Prussian army was overwhelmingly defeated at the Battles of Jena and Auerstedt in 1806, and the Prussian monarch was forced to sign the Treaty of Tilsit in 1807. The treaty not only diminished Prussia territorially but also limited her autonomy. Part of the settlement at Tilsit was that Hardenberg, whom Napoleon distrusted, should retire from government service. Before leaving office, however, Hardenberg began the restructuring of the old administrative system, the first step in what has come to be known as the Prussian reform movement.

In 1807-1808, the reform movement was expanded by Freiherr vom Stein, who oversaw the emancipation of Prussian serfs and the extension of self-government to the municipalities of Prussia before being forced from office by Napoleon. Hardenberg remained in contact with Stein; during his forced retirement he produced his famous Riga Memorandum in 1808, which became the blueprint for the further reforms of Prussian institutions. The central thesis of the memorandum was that if the monarchical form of government was to survive in Prussia, the government must adopt many of the liberal institutions produced in France by the Revolution of 1789. Hardenberg's memorandum showed that he, like Stein, recognized that the forces of nationalism and democracy unleashed by the revolution in France would ultimately destroy the old order of Europe if they were not brought under control. He proposed that the Prussian government should introduce liberal reform from above to prevent revolution.

In 1810, Napoleon allowed Frederick William to recall Hardenberg to the Prussian government, this time as prime minister. His initial reforms aimed at making the tax structure of the kingdom more equitable and at simplifying tax collection. Hardenberg imposed a property tax on all citizens (the nobility had formerly been exempted), an excise tax on all areas, and a profit tax. Concurrently, most restrictions on trade and commerce were removed, and civic equality for Jews was established.

Hardenberg then took a hesitant step toward establishing a representative assembly to permit popular participation in the making of governmental policy. By convening an assembly of notables he hoped to create widespread enthusiasm for the further changes he intended to make. Unfortunately, the *junkers* (aristocratic landowners) opposed the idea of representative government and used their influence with Frederick William to thwart the hope of a national parliament. Nevertheless, Hardenberg was able to open admission of the officer corps and of the bureaucracy (formerly the exclusive preserves of the *junkers*) to all citizens.

From 1812 until his death, most of Hardenberg's attention was focused on foreign policy. In 1812, Napoleon forced Prussia to sign a military alliance in preparation for his planned invasion of Russia. When Napoleon's Russian campaign ended in a French debacle, Hardenberg saw the possibility of escaping the domination Napoleon had exercised over Prussia since 1806. Moving cautiously, Hardenberg engineered a military alliance in 1813 between Prussia and Russia, the Treaty of Kalisz. Ironically, Stein, in his new capacity as political adviser to Alexander I, was the Russian representative at Kalisz.

During the ensuing War of Liberation, a wave of patriotic enthusiasm swept through Prussia. After Napoleon's defeat at Leipzig in 1813 led to his withdrawal from the German states, Hardenberg went to Vienna to represent Prussia at the international congress whose purpose was to restructure Europe.

At Vienna, Hardenberg immediately came into conflict with Metternich, the Austrian representative. Metternich, an archconservative intent on reestablishing the old aristocratic order in Europe, opposed German unification in particular (Hardenberg's aim) and nationalism in general, which he saw as destructive to the interests of the multiracial Austrian Empire. The clash between Austria and Prussia over this and other matters at Vienna almost led to war and was instrumental in Napoleon's decision to return from his first exile and reclaim the throne of France.

After Waterloo, Hardenberg and Frederick William seemed to become more and more dominated by Metternich. They acquiesced to the creation of the Germanic confederation, a weakly unified government of largely independent small states. Hardenberg gave up his plan to introduce a constitution and a parliament in Prussia and signed the Holy Alliance, which obligated Prussia along with the other signatories to intervene militarily whenever a legitimate monarch anywhere in Europe was threatened by revolution. Nevertheless, domestic reform continued and considerable passion for unification and parliamentary government flourished, especially in Prussian universities.

After the assassination of a conservative newspaper editor by a young nationalist in 1819, Metternich convinced Hardenberg and Frederick William to adopt the Karlsbad Decrees, which ushered in a period of total reaction in the German states. The Prussian reform movement was ended. Hardenberg, completely under the spell of Metternich, continued to direct Prussian foreign policy until his death, in Genoa on November 26, 1822.

Summary

Karl von Hardenberg enjoyed considerable successes in domestic reform and diplomacy. Under his leadership, the principle of civic equality became firmly established in Prussia. Prussian Jews began to play leading roles in government, in the arts, and in education after 1812, as a result of Hardenberg's leadership in social reform. The bureaucracy and the army became more efficient because careers in those organizations were opened to all men of talent and promotions became based on merit rather than family. Hardenberg laid the foundation for the Prussian educational system to become the model and the envy of the rest of the world. Hardenberg was responsible for the establishment of a more equitable system of taxation and for the removal of many archaic restrictions on trade and commerce in Prussia.

Through his diplomacy, Hardenberg was instrumental in the defeat of Napoleon. His leadership in foreign affairs allowed the Prussian kingdom not only to survive the dangerous times of the Napoleonic Wars but also to emerge from the era larger and more powerful than it had been in 1780. For these accomplishments, Hardenberg is often recognized as being second in importance only to Otto von Bismarck among Prussian prime ministers. Despite these impressive accomplishments, Hardenberg is sometimes criticized for missing opportunities to accomplish much more. Yet Hardenberg's goals in foreign and domestic policy were to preserve the old order insofar as possible. He could not have led a movement that would have dismantled that order when the possibility existed of preserving most of it under the Metternichian system. In the final analysis, Hardenberg was an effective diplomat and an able administrator whose tenure as Prime Minister of Prussia was a decisive step toward the transformation of his country into a modern nation-state.

Bibliography
Holborn, Hajo. *A History of Modern Germany.* Vol. 2, *1648-1840.* New York: Alfred A. Knopf, 1964. Contains several chapters on the reform movement and provides sketches of its most important leaders, including Hardenberg. Places the Prussian reform movement and the reformers in their proper perspective in German history.

Meinecke, Friedrich. *The Age of German Liberation, 1795-1815.* Translated by Peter Paret and Helmut Fischer. Berkeley: University of California Press, 1977. One of the best accounts of the period, Meinecke's book provides a good account of Hardenberg's life and work.

Schenk, H. G. *The Aftermath of the Napoleonic Wars: The Concert of Europe, an Experiment.* New York: Oxford University Press, 1947. Perhaps the best account of the congress system implemented by Metternich after 1815. Hardenberg's role in diplomatic affairs during this era is amply and sympathetically treated.

Simon, Walter M. *The Failure of the Prussian Reform Movement, 1807-1819.* New York: Simon and Schuster, 1955. Simon is very critical of both the reforms and the reformers in Prussia, particularly Hardenberg. Simon argues that the failure of the reforms to establish a unified, parliamentary German state led directly to the development of the authoritarianism of the German Empire after 1871 and ultimately to the Third Reich.

Webster, C. K. *The Congress of Vienna*. New York: Oxford University Press, 1919. This older study of the Congress of Vienna is still the standard work on the subject.

Paul Madden

FRANZ JOSEPH HAYDN

Born: March 31, 1732; Rohrau, Austria
Died: May 31, 1809; Vienna, Austrian Empire
Area of Achievement: Music
Contribution: For nearly fifty years, Haydn expressed his joy of life and love of beauty through music. He is considered the father of instrumental music (he developed the form of the string quartet). Haydn's collected works include seventeen operas, sixty-eight string quartets, sixty-two sonatas, and 107 symphonies.

Early Life

Franz Joseph Haydn was born in 1732 to Mathias and Maria Koller Haydn. His father, a wagonmaker, though not poor by the standards of the day, was nevertheless unable to provide the education or training which his son so obviously needed. Young Haydn's musical talents were noted at an early age and, when he was six years old, he was given the opportunity to study at the Church of St. Philip and St. James in Hainburg. At the age of eight, fortune smiled on him again, and he was chosen to become a member of the boys' choir at St. Stephen's Cathedral in Vienna. There his musical talents were nurtured and his love of beauty stimulated. There also his love of mischief flourished, and a combination of boyish pranks and a changing voice led to his dismissal in 1749.

On his own at the age of seventeen, Haydn found that the world of Vienna offered a variety of opportunities for an industrious and talented musician. Haydn earned his keep by giving music lessons and by playing with the strolling musicians who populated Vienna. Haydn's talent and teaching (and a certain amount of luck) brought him into contact with an ever larger and more important circle of musical patrons in Vienna, and, in 1859, he was hired as musical director for Count Ferdinand Maximillian von Morzin. Through this position, he met and married Anna Aloysia Apollonia Keller. Haydn had loved her younger sister, who became a nun, but married Anna and was thus bound into a loveless marriage.

When financial reverses led Count Morzin to give up his orchestra, Haydn moved into the service of the family with which he was associated for the fifty years of his greatest musical development. In 1761, Prince Pál Antal Esterházy hired Haydn as vice-Kapellmeister, and Haydn, with his wife, moved to the great estate of Eisenstadt, where he had his own church, opera house, choir, and orchestra. When Prince Miklós József Esterházy succeeded his brother, Haydn found the perfect patron, a man whose passion for music equaled his own. Most of his early works were composed for Prince Miklós, for whom Haydn developed the form of string quartet. It was also for Prince Miklós that Haydn wrote his *Surprise Symphony* (1791), as a subtle hint that he and his musicians needed a vacation from the isolation imposed by Miklós' sojourn at the remote, fairy-tale palace at Esterháza. Each of the performers, as he completed his part, quietly blew out his candle and left the orchestra.

Life's Work

Haydn's fortune and fame grew under the Esterházy patronage. Becoming Kapellmeister in 1766, Haydn happily lived a rather isolated existence, but one in which his musical style developed, while meeting a rigorous schedule of two concerts per week. In 1781, Haydn met the young Wolfgang Amadeus Mozart. Though vastly different in age, temperament, and musical development, these two men shared an enormous respect for each other, and each influenced the other's work. Haydn, by the 1780's, had a reputation which had spread beyond the Esterházy estates and even beyond Vienna and Austria.

In 1790, Prince Miklós died. His successor, Prince Antal, had great love neither for music nor for the enormous and remote palace of Esterháza. He paid Haydn a pension which kept him nominally in service but which, in fact, left Haydn free to move to Vienna, which he did almost at once. Scarcely had he settled himself and his wife when he was invited to visit and perform both in Italy and in England. Faced with the choice, Haydn accepted the offer to journey to London. When Mozart protested, saying that Haydn had no experience with travel and could not speak the language, Haydn replied: "But my language is understood all over the world."

At the age of fifty-eight, Haydn set forth for London, where some of his greatest music was composed and where he expanded his genius into the new musical form of oratorios. Haydn was young in spirit and in good health, and his two years in London were happy and spectacularly successful. He composed dozens of new works and gave a variety of public concerts, all of which were well received by the English. For the first time, Haydn, who had always been a servant of princes, moved in royal circles as a free and equal man. He was a house guest of the Prince of Wales and was awarded an honorary doctor of music degree from the University of Oxford. As always, he was admired by women, and his diary contains many love letters from a wealthy London widow.

Haydn was short but solidly built—his legs seemingly almost too short to support his body. His face was characterized by a strong nose, a broad forehead, and remarkably bright eyes. In spite of the smallpox scars which marred his face, his portraits show a not unattractive man of pleasant visage wearing the curled wig of his day. Far more appealing than his features were Haydn's naïve pleasure in his surroundings, his love of beauty, his zest for life, and his frank admiration of women. Especially strong were his ties to Maria Anna von Genzinger, to whom his long letters revealed both his activities and his observations on music and the world. His letters to her from

London provide an especially valuable insight into Haydn's state of mind as well as a record of his many activities in England.

Haydn was enormously successful in London. The warm adulation of the crowd nourished his creative talents. Among the triumphs of his sojourn in England were the symphonies inspired by the visit, which mark the peak of Haydn's instrumental compositions and the height of his maturity as a composer. In London, also, Haydn attended a performance of George Frideric Handel's *The Messiah* (1742) in Westminster Abbey, with a choir of more than one thousand voices. He was greatly moved by this performance and musical style and was stimulated and challenged to emulate that style. The result was that Haydn began work on his own masterpiece, *Die Schöpfung* (1798; *The Creation*).

As he returned to Austria in 1792, Haydn met the young Ludwig van Beethoven, who made plans to join Haydn and study under his direction in Vienna. Haydn returned to London again in 1794, where he was also extremely popular. Though encouraged to make his home in London, Haydn returned to Vienna in 1795 at the behest of his nominal employer, Prince Miklós II, who had succeeded to the title and who, like his more illustrious ancestor, was eager to use his world-famous Kapellmeister.

Haydn's duties upon his return were not arduous, consisting largely of the requirement that he compose masses for the prince and works for special occasions. Meanwhile, Haydn began work on his great oratorio, *The Creation*, basing the libretto on John Milton's *Paradise Lost* (1667). For three years, Haydn labored over this work. When the premier performance was given in 1798 to selected guests in Vienna, twelve policemen and eighteen mounted guards were necessary to contain the excited crowds of music lovers who thronged outside. *The Creation* was a triumph and was performed for many years, with the considerable proceeds going largely to charity.

The work on *The Creation* drained Haydn both physically and emotionally, but still the master continued to work. Another oratorio, *Die Jahreszeiten* (1801; *The Seasons*), followed, as did various orchestral works. Haydn's health, however, continued to decline, and on May 31, 1809, he died. Napoleon I (whose troops occupied much of Austria) sent members of the French army to form an honor guard around the catafalque, a tribute to a truly international man. There was a curious epilogue to Haydn's death. When his body was removed to Eisenstadt for reburial in 1814, it was discovered that his head was missing. It had been removed by two of Haydn's admirers and was eventually bequeathed to the museum of the Society of Friends of Music in Vienna. In 1954, it was finally united with the body in the mausoleum built for Haydn by Prince Esterházy.

Summary

Franz Joseph Haydn was a man who enjoyed life, and this attitude was reflected in his music. His talent matured slowly; by the age at which Mozart died, Haydn had barely begun to compose. His long life and robust health enabled him to compose many works—an accurate accounting of which is made all the more difficult by the unfortunate habit minor composers had of publishing their own works under Haydn's name in the hope of encouraging their sale. Haydn was primarily an instrumental composer, and his major works include at least thirty-seven concerti, sixty-two sonatas, 107 symphonies, sixty-eight string quartets, and forty-five piano trios, as well as other lesser works. In addition, he composed seventeen operas, two oratorios, sixty songs, and fourteen masses.

The whimsical Haydn also composed lovely small works, including a symphony for toy instruments and strings to delight children. He composed small pieces for musical clocks as well, and these were often gifts to his patron prince. A staunch patriot, Haydn was especially impressed during his sojourn in London by the stirring strains of "God Save the King," and he felt strongly the lack of a similar anthem for his own land. As the advances of Napoleon I threatened his beloved Austria, Haydn authorized the writing of a patriotic text which he set to music as the Austrian national anthem. It was first played for the emperor's birthday in 1797 and enjoyed great popularity. A variation of the familiar tune (made notorious through its use by the Nazi movement) formed the basis for one of Haydn's string quartets (Op. 76), but is most often enjoyed in the English-speaking world as the church hymn "Glorious Things of Thee Are Spoken."

Haydn was a truly remarkable individual whose musical style influenced two generations of composers. He developed and perfected the intimate form of the string quartet, more difficult to write even than symphonies. Haydn worked with the different voices of the four instruments and the ways in which they could be blended together. It was a musical form uniquely his own. Haydn's own style grew and changed as he studied and experimented with music. The tranquil years at Esterháza were especially valuable for the isolation and the time they provided him for this study. He was fundamentally interested in structure for its own sake, and this interest expressed itself in his music. His works are joyous and forthright in mood, seldom delving into the complex emotional conflicts of the Romantic composers who so often despised Haydn's singleness of style and purpose. His rare ability to use the different sounds and range of each instrument in the orchestra makes Haydn's instrumental music especially fine. Often rebuffed by musicians and critics for his style and for the supposed lack of seriousness in his adaptation of folk music to his symphonies, the twentieth century has seen a rebirth of Haydn's reputation and a new appreciation of his greatness. Haydn's life, reflected so perfectly in his music, was joyous and optimistic, and inspirational both to his era and to the future.

Bibliography

Barrett-Ayers, Reginald. *Joseph Haydn and the String Quartet*. London: Barrie & Jenkins, 1974. A specialized book for a serious student of music. Nevertheless, because of its size, simplification of approach, and manageability of subject, this is an excellent book devoted to special areas of Haydn's music.

Geiringer, Karl, with Irene Geiringer. *Haydn: A Creative Life in Music*. Rev. ed. Berkeley: University of California Press, 1968. Originally published in 1946 and revised in 1968, this book is by far the best single-volume treatment of Haydn's life. The later edition includes up-to-date scholarship and evaluation of available manuscripts. Includes a sympathetic portrayal of the composer, and almost half of the book is devoted to a brief analysis of Haydn's work and the stylistic development throughout his life. Probably the most useful source for a broad overview of Haydn.

Griesinger, G. A., and A. C. Dies. *Joseph Haydn: Eighteenth-Century Gentleman and Genius*. Translated by Gernon Gotwals. Madison: University of Wisconsin Press, 1963. A delightful firsthand report on Haydn, often in his own words, by two men who knew him and worked with him. Griesinger, a business associate of Haydn, emerged as the official biographer to whom Haydn recounted the major events of his life. Dies was an art-gallery director employed by Prince Esterházy, who counted at least thirty visits with Haydn.

Hughes, Rosemary. *Haydn*. New York: Farrar, Straus & Giroux, 1950, rev. ed. 1970. This short biography of Haydn includes an analysis of his music in its various forms. The author credits the Geiringers as the inspiration for the biography, and this book follows much the same pattern as that earlier work. A worthwhile study of both the man and his music. As part of the Master Musicians series, it may be the most readily available source for the life of Haydn.

Landon, H. C. Robbins. *Haydn*. New York: Praeger, 1972. A slim volume, easily read. A good introduction to Haydn. Provides an excellent portrait of the physical as well as the emotional man and includes brief musical bars and references to incorporate Haydn's music into a brief sketch of his life.

_____. *Haydn: Chronicle and Works*. 5 vols. Bloomington: Indiana University Press, 1980. Absolutely invaluable to the serious student of Haydn. The definitive work on Haydn, this book takes advantage of the most up-to-date publications of Haydn's music. The volumes provide a strong framework of Austrian history and culture as well as that of England during Haydn's visits. Very detailed research on Haydn's music makes these volumes difficult for a lay reader but invaluable for the trained musician.

Carlanna Hendrick

GEORG WILHELM FRIEDRICH HEGEL

Born: August 27, 1770; Stuttgart, Württemberg
Died: November 14, 1831; Berlin, Prussia
Area of Achievement: Philosophy
Contribution: Hegel developed many theories of great philosophical importance that over the past century have influenced the social sciences, anthropology, sociology, psychology, history, and political theory. He believed that the mind is the ultimate reality and that philosophy can restore
humanity to a state of harmony.

Early Life

Georg Wilhelm Friedrich Hegel was born into a Protestant middle-class
family in Stuttgart, the eldest of three children. His father was a minor civil
servant for the Duchy of Württemberg, and his family had roots in Austria.
To escape persecution by the Austrian Catholics in the sixteenth century, his
ancestors settled among the Lutheran Protestants of the German territories,
which consisted of more than three hundred free cities, duchies, and states
loosely united under the rule of Francis I of Austria. Though little is known
about his mother, all accounts describe her as having been highly intelligent
and unusually educated for a woman of that time. Hegel had the conventional schooling for his social class, entering German primary school in
1773, Latin school in 1775, and the Stuttgart *Gymnasium illustre* in 1780.
Upon graduating from the *Gymnasium* (equivalent to high school) in 1788,
he entered the famous seminary at the University of Tübingen to study philosophy and theology in preparation for the Protestant ministry. As a student,
Hegel became friends with Friedrich Hölderlin, a Romantic poet, and Friedrich Schelling. He shared the top floor of the dormitory with Schelling, who
became famous before Hegel as an Idealist philosopher. In 1790, Hegel
received a master's degree in philosophy.

After passing his theological examinations at Tübingen in 1793, Hegel
began many years of struggle to earn his living and establish himself as a
philosopher. Instead of entering the ministry, he began working as a house
tutor for a wealthy family in Bern, Switzerland. In 1797, he became a tutor
in Frankfurt, continuing throughout this time to read, think, and write about
philosophical questions, usually along radical lines. For example, he considered Jesus inferior to Socrates as a teacher of ethics, and he considered
orthodox religion, because of its reliance on external authority, an obstacle
in restoring mankind to a life of harmony. Although Hegel always retained
some of his skepticism toward orthodox religion, he later in life considered
himself a Lutheran Christian. In 1798, he began to write on the philosophy
of history and on the spirit of Christianity, major themes in his philosophical
system. Upon his father's death in 1799, Hegel received a modest inheri-

tance and was able to stop tutoring and join his friend Schelling at the University of Jena, in the state of Weimar.

Life's Work

Hegel's life's work as a teacher and philosopher began at Jena. From 1801 to 1807, Hegel taught as an unsalaried lecturer at the University of Jena, his first university position as a philosopher, for which he was paid by the students who attended class. While in Jena, Hegel cooperated with Schelling in editing the *Kritisches Journal der Philosophie*. He also published the *Differenz des Fichte'schen und Schelling'schen Systems der Philosophie* (1801; *The Difference Between Fichte's and Schelling's Philosophy*, 1977). During this time, Hegel began to lecture on metaphysics, logic, and natural law. In 1805, he was promoted to Ausserordentlicher Professor (Distinguished Professor) on the recommendation of the German Romantic poet Johann Wolfgang von Goethe. Hegel was very prolific, yet beginning in 1802 he announced each year a significant forthcoming book to his publisher without producing it.

These were momentous times. In 1789, just after Hegel's nineteenth birthday, the fall of the Bastille announced the French Revolution across Europe; in 1806, after putting an end to the thousand-year Austrian Empire, Napoleon I crushed the Prussian armies at the Battle of Jena. On October 13, 1806, Napoleon victoriously entered the walled city of Jena, an event that Hegel described to a friend as follows: "I saw the Emperor—that world-soul—riding out to reconnoiter the city; it is truly a wonderful sensation to see such an individual, concentrated here on a single point, astride a single horse, yet reaching across the world and ruling it. . . ."

October 13, 1806, was also the day that Hegel finished his book, long promised to his publisher, and sent the manuscript amid the confusion of war. The book was his early masterpiece, *Phänomenologie des Geistes* (1807; *The Phenomenology of Spirit*, 1931, also known as *The Phenomenology of Mind*). On October 20, the French army plundered Hegel's house, and his teaching position at the University of Jena came to an end. Hegel left for Bamberg in Bavaria, where he spent a year working as a newspaper editor. He then became headmaster and philosophy teacher at the *Gymnasium* in Nuremberg, where he worked successfully from 1808 until 1816.

The Phenomenology of Spirit, which exemplifies the young Hegel, was strongly influenced by German Romanticism. This movement provided a new and more complete way of perceiving the world and was developed by German philosophers and artists, such as Schelling and Hölderlin. German Romanticism stood in opposition to French rationalism and British empiricism, the two major philosophies of the seventeenth and eighteenth centuries dominated by reason and immediate sensory experience, respectively. German Romanticism had been influenced by the German philosopher Immanuel

Kant, whose theory of knowledge synthesized rational and empirical elements. Kant argued that the laws of science, rather than being the source of rationality, were dependent on the human mind and its pure concepts, or categories, such as cause and effect. Kant believed that it is the mind which gives its laws to nature, and not the reverse.

Hegel's philosophical system expands upon this philosophy, which has reality depend on the rational mind for its perception. Hegel's absolute Idealism unites the totality of all concepts in the absolute mind or spirit, which he also referred to as the ultimate reality, or God. Hegel's metaphysics thus takes from German Romanticism the "inward path" to truth; the notion of nature as spirit, or the immanence of God within the universe; the quest for the totality of experience, both empirical and rational; and the desire for infinity.

Hegel argued that reality belongs to an absolute mind or a totality of conceptual truth, and that it consists of a rational structure characterized by a unity-amid-diversity. The purpose of metaphysics is to reveal the truth of this unified diversity. To this end, Hegel developed his highly influential theory of dialectic, a process involving three concepts: the thesis, the antithesis, and the synthesis. This dialectical process provides a way of transcending oppositions to a higher level of truth. Hegel argued that the dialectical triad, as the rhythm of reality, underlies all human knowledge and experience. Moreover, he defined the absolute mind as being the totality of concepts in a dialectical process. Yet Hegel believed that contradictions are never entirely overcome. Rather, the dialectic is both the essence of reality and the method for comprehending reality, which is always a unity-amid-diversity. Hegel's notion of conceptual truth, being immanent within the world, is time-bound rather than transcendental, despite his ambiguous reference to the absolute mind as God. Hegel's dialectic thus differs from that of Plato, which gives rise to timeless forms.

On the basis of his dialectic, Hegel begins *The Phenomenology of Spirit* by introducing his theory that the history of philosophy is a biography of the human spirit in its development over the course of centuries. The relationship between successive philosophies is one not of conflict but of organic growth and development. Hegel describes philosophy as a living and growing organism like the world itself. Each philosophy corresponds to the stage of a plant: the bud, the blossom, and the fruit. In addition to organicism, Hegel developed the metaphor of historicism, which holds that the understanding of any aspect of life is derived through its history, its evolution, and not through its static condition in the present. Hegel ends *The Phenomenology of Spirit* by arguing that the age of reason and philosophy must supersede the age of religious consciousness. He also argued that history evolves toward a specific goal, a state of freedom, and that the purpose of history is the unfolding of the truth of reason. Hegel's arguments on this topic are collected in his *Sämtliche Werke* (1927; translated in *Lectures on the Philosophy of History*, 1956).

During the time Hegel taught in Nuremberg, he published *Wissenschaft der Logik* (1812-1816; *Science of Logic*, 1929) and *Encyclopädie der Philosophischen im Grundrisse* (1817; *Encyclopedia of Philosophy*, 1959). Hegel regarded the latter as having a dialectical structure, with the opposites of thought and nature united in mind and society, and ultimately in the self-referential act of philosophical self-consciousness. In 1811, Hegel married Maria von Tucher of Nuremberg, and in 1816 his nine-year-old illegitimate son, Ludwig, joined the household. Also in 1816, Hegel became a professor at the University of Heidelberg and in 1817 for the first time taught aesthetics. By this time, his reputation was so well established that the Prussian minister of education invited him to accept the prestigious chair of philosophy at the University of Berlin, where Hegel taught from 1818 until his death during a cholera epidemic in 1831.

During this final period, the climax of his career, Hegel lectured for the first time on the philosophy of religion and the philosophy of history. He published one of the great works of genius of Western culture, *Grundlinien der Philosophie des Rechts* (1821; *Philosophy of Right*, 1875), which exemplifies the mature or late Hegel in contrast to the early Hegel seen in *The Phenomenology of Spirit*. Hegel argued in his moral philosophy that ethics, like the individual, has its source, course, and ultimate fulfillment in the nation-state, particularly the state of Germany. The nation-state is a manifestation of God, which Hegel defines not as a personal God but rather as the Absolute. This totality of truth manifests itself in stages to each of the key nations of history, culminating in Germany.

During the 1820's, Hegel toured Belgium and the Netherlands and also traveled to Vienna and Prague. In 1824, he interceded with the Prussian government to free his friend Victor Cousin, a French liberal philosopher. Hegel was not an eloquent lecturer, but after his death, a group of his students collated their lecture notes and published an edition of his works in eighteen volumes (1832-1840). Hegel's writing is notoriously difficult, both stylistically and conceptually.

Summary

Georg Wilhelm Friedrich Hegel's Idealist philosophy has been criticized for elevating the reality of concepts over the material aspects of reality, such as economics, environment, technology, and natural resources. Moreover, there seems to be a contradiction in Hegel's notion of the Absolute, in his definition of God as being externalized or existing in human consciousness. Finally, Hegel's philosophy of history has been criticized for masking a hidden defense for German nationalism, an aversion for democracy and individualism, and a fear of revolutionary change.

Nevertheless, Hegel has contributed many profound concepts to Western philosophy: the dialectical nature of thought, organicism and historicism, the concept of culture, the theory of ethics, and the theory of humanity's need for wholeness, in terms of both consciousness and social unification. Hegel believed that there are three important dialectical stages in ethical life responsible for social unity: the family, its antithesis in civil society, and their synthesis in the developed national state. As the French philosopher Maurice Merleau-Ponty says, "All the great philosophical ideas of the past century, the philosophies of Marx, Nietzsche, existentialism and psycho-analysis had their beginning in Hegel."

Although he supported Christianity, Hegel placed philosophy above religion. He believed that religion and art are different ways of understanding the absolute idea, but that philosophy is a better way because it allows one to comprehend the absolute conceptually, not in religious symbols, and thereby subsumes both religion and art. For Hegel, ethical ideals, such as the ideals of freedom, originate in the spiritual life of a society.

Bibliography

Butler, Clark. *G. W. F. Hegel.* Boston: Twayne, 1977. A comprehensive study of Hegel that aims not to be merely about Hegel but to communicate the essence of Hegelian philosophy to a wider public. Presenting Hegelianism in an abstract philosophical context, Butler strives to be accessible but not oversimplistic. Approaches Hegel from the cultural standpoint of the present. Contains a selected annotated bibliography and a chronology of Hegel's life.

Christensen, Darrel E., ed. *Hegel and the Philosophy of Religion: The Wofford Symposium.* The Hague: Martinus Nijhoff, 1970. Collection from the proceedings of the first conference of the Hegel Society of America. These excellent essays analyze many aspects of Hegel's philosophy of religion in relation to his historical context, his philosophical system, and the philosophies of Immanuel Kant, Friedrich Wilhelm Nietzsche, and Karl Marx. More appropriate for the advanced student.

Findlay, J. N. *Hegel: A Re-examination.* New York: Humanities Press, 1958. Findlay is the one most responsible for reviving Hegel scholarship in the English-speaking world. Provides a close exposition of Hegel's system, paragraph-by-paragraph, and is especially good in its treatment of his logic and philosophy of nature.

Hegel, Georg Wilhelm Friedrich. *Hegel: The Essential Writings.* Edited by F. G. Weiss. New York: Harper & Row, 1974. Contains an excellent introduction to Hegel's philosophy and also concise introductions to the different selections, which include *Encyclopedia of the Philosophical Sciences in Outline, The Phenomenology of Spirit,* and *Philosophy of Right.* Weiss also provides a useful annotated bibliography of primary and secondary texts. A popular text for introductory college philosophy.

Kojève, Alexandre. *Introduction to the Reading of Hegel: Lectures on the Phenomenology*. Edited by A. Bloom. Translated by J. H. Nichols. New York: Basic Books, 1969. Although he describes Hegel's thought as historicist and atheistic, Kojève has been instrumental in reviving Hegel's philosophy. Appropriate for beginning students; makes lucid Hegel's influential theories in *The Phenomenology of Spirit*.

Lavine, T. Z. *From Socrates to Sartre: The Philosophic Quest*. New York: Bantam Books, 1984. A survey of six major Western philosophers, Hegel being the fourth and receiving a sixty-page condensed review. Lavine lucidly presents for the general public Hegel's life and work in relation to his intellectual and historical context, highlighting Hegel's influence on the theories of Marx. The book was aired as a Public Broadcasting Service television series.

Singer, Peter. *Hegel*. New York: Oxford University Press, 1983. A clearly written, ninety-page book in the Past Masters series intended for readers with no background in philosophy. Singer provides a broad overview of Hegel's ideas and a summary of his major works. He also discusses Hegel's influence on Marx and the Young Hegelians. Contains a useful index.

William S. Haney II

PIET HEIN

Born: November 15, 1577; Delfshaven, Holland
Died: June 18, 1629; at sea, near Dungeness, off the coast of Dunkirk
Areas of Achievement: The military and diplomacy
Contribution: Hein aided substantially in the Netherlands' breaking away
from Spanish control. He defeated the Spanish and Portuguese several
times in naval combat, including the most celebrated capture of treasure
ships in the history of the Spanish Main.

Early Life

Piet Hein was born on November 15, 1577, in the small port town of
Delfshaven on the Meuse River near Rotterdam. He was christened Pieter
Pieterszoon Heyn but is known to history simply as Piet Hein. His father was
an ordinary Dutch fisherman, but he secured additional income from pri-
vateering and trade and earned a modest living for his family. Piet learned
seamanship from his father, whom he accompanied on voyages into the
North Sea. The fishing boats of that period were small but were armed with
two or three cannons and sailed in fleets for mutual protection against both
Spanish and French corsairs.

The Dutch had declared their independence from Spain in 1581, but maintaining that independence took decades. Catholic Spain refused to accept the
Reformed Protestant faith of the United Provinces or their self-governing
constitutional autonomy. With valor and determination, the Dutch prevented
the most powerful nation in the world in the sixteenth century from controlling the small country of Holland. In 1609, a Twelve Years' Truce began,
but war between Spain and Holland resumed in 1621, culminating in Hein's
celebrated capture of the combined treasure fleet in 1628 off the coast of
Cuba. By then, the Spanish knew that they were not going to regain control
of the Netherlands. Nevertheless, it was not until the Peace of Westphalia in
1648 that Spain officially recognized the independence of the Netherlands.

That was the international situation that faced Hein during his entire life.
The Dutch had always been a seafaring people, but in the seventeenth century they had the largest merchant marine in the world, well in excess of the
combined merchant fleets of Spain, Portugal, France, Scotland, and Germany. Spain, however, had a large navy while the Dutch relied on privateers, armed vessels that were also involved in fishing and trade. Some
10 percent of the adult male population of Holland made their living on the
ocean.

Every time Hein ventured from shore, usually merely to catch fish to help
support his family, he risked armed confrontation with the Spanish or with
privateers authorized by the Spanish to attack Dutch ships. At the age of
twenty, he was captured at sea and spent the next four years as a Spanish

galley rower. He gained his freedom in 1601 in an exchange of Dutch and Spanish prisoners.

Life's Work

Hein became a director of the Dutch West India Company in 1621, the same year Spain renewed hostilities with the Netherlands. In 1623, he was appointed vice admiral of the fleet of the Dutch West India Company and sailed with twenty-six ships with five hundred guns, sixteen hundred sailors, and seventeen hundred soldiers to attack São Salvador on the coast of Brazil. Spain ruled Portugal at the time, so Brazil was also controlled by Spain. The Dutch objective was to secure a base there for depredations against Spanish shipping in the Caribbean.

São Salvador was the first capital of Brazil and was strongly fortified by three forts. Fifteen large Spanish ships defended the bay. Into that strong position Hein led his column of ships and fought a three-hour gun battle and then boarded the Spanish ships. Seven Spanish ships were burned, but the Dutch captured the other eight. This sudden disaster enabled the intrepid Hein and his aggressive fighters to climb to the top of the nine-foot walls and, with darkness closing in, spike the Spanish guns and blow up the ammunition depot.

Hein left behind a garrison of troops and set sail with his eight Spanish ships heavily loaded with sugar, wines, oils, and spices. Though greatly outnumbered, the Dutch had defeated a Spanish fleet and captured a Spanish stronghold. The reception at home in the Netherlands was joyful; Hein was promoted to admiral. For two years, the new admiral sailed the Caribbean, capturing whatever Spanish prizes he could find. He returned to Holland and then was given the assignment that resulted in one of the greatest losses ever inflicted on the Spanish and made Piet Hein's name known throughout the European and American worlds.

The Spanish had four main ports—Veracruz, Havana, Porto Bello, and Cartagena—in which to rendezvous the two annual treasure fleets, the one from Peru and the other from Mexico. The Dutch knew that all four ports were too strong to permit an attack in port. The best place, they judged, to waylay the fleet was outside Havana harbor. With surprising ease, Hein and his thirty ships caught nine Spanish treasure ships from Mexico running along the Cuban coast and trapped six more in Matanzas Bay. The treasure taken and sent to Holland included 177,537 pounds of silver in chests and bars, 135 pounds of gold, 37,375 hides, 2,270 chests of indigo, 7,691 pieces of logwood, 735 chests of cochineal, 235 chests of sugar, and some pearls, spices, and various tropical products. The total value of the booty was 11,509,524 Dutch florins, the greatest theft in the history of the Spanish-American Empire. The profits enabled the Dutch West India Company to pay a phenomenal dividend of 50 percent to stockholders that year. The sailors involved were given a rather small share, and Hein received only seven thousand guilders. The unfortunate Spanish admiral was imprisoned for two years by the Spanish king and then executed. Hein, however, was given a hero's welcome and wined and dined in many parts of Holland and even with the Prince of Orange and the King of Bohemia. His admirers even wrote a little song to Piet which has become part of Dutch folklore:

> Piet Heyn, Piet Heyn, Piet Heyn,
> His name is small,
> His deeds are great, his deeds are great.
> He has won the Silver Fleet.
> Hurrah, hurrah, hurrah,
> He has won the Silver Fleet.

That same year, Hein, at fifty, decided that he had had enough of action and retired from the sea to a comfortable home in Delft. His retirement ended less than a year later, when Hein was appointed admiral-in-chief and lieutenant general of Holland. His first task was to clear the English Channel of privateers who were wreaking havoc with Dutch shipping. In May of 1629, the new admiral-in-chief sailed in a single reconnaissance ship along the Channel off Dunkirk. He sighted three privateers on June 18, and, following his lifelong habit of aggressive daring, he immediately attacked the three ships and was killed by an enemy shot. His enraged men captured the privateers and threw all survivors overboard. The jubilation of the previous year was reversed as the Spanish rejoiced and the Dutch mourned.

Summary

In the seventeenth century, the Dutch could not maintain their independence, culture, and maritime economy without a strong fleet. The entire nation owed much to Piet Hein and the men who served with him in protecting Dutch trade routes worldwide. They left their mark all over the world as many of the place names in both the East Indies and West Indies were given permanent Dutch names, such as Spitsbergen, Cape Hoorn, and New Zealand. Superior seamanship and superior ships enabled the tiny nation to influence events far more than would be expected by the population figures of that small nation along the coast of Europe. That Hein played a significant role in persuading the Spanish to recognize finally the independence of the Netherlands should be obvious.

Bibliography

Geyl, Pieter. *The Netherlands in the Seventeenth Century.* Rev. ed. London: Ernest Benn, 1961. Gives details concerning the Dutch maritime system of the seventeenth century, a detailed description of Hein's maritime exploits, and his significance in that period of history.

Haley, K. H. D. *The Dutch in the Seventeenth Century.* London: Thames & Hudson, 1972. The 158 illustrations, including sketches, maps, coins, monuments, and portraits make this a particularly attractive book. Describes the Dutch civilization and economy of the seventeenth century and places Hein in his historical setting.

Israel, Jonathan I. *The Dutch Republic and the Hispanic World, 1606-1661.* Oxford, England: Clarendon Press, 1982. Describes life in both the Dutch and Spanish settings of the seventeenth century and their relationship to each other. There is a lengthy section on the war in the Caribbean between the Spanish and Dutch, including a detailed description of Hein's victory at Matanzas Bay in Cuba.

Parker, Geoffrey. *Spain and the Netherlands, 1559-1659.* Short Hills, N.J.: Enslow, 1979. An important interpretive study of the diplomatic relations of Spain and Holland. Deals with such topics as why the Dutch revolt lasted so long; the larger world of international politics to which this conflict belonged; and the economic consequences of the war.

Peterson, Mendel. *The Funnel of Gold.* Boston: Little, Brown, 1975. The best treatment in English of the protracted war for treasures in the Caribbean in the sixteenth and seventeenth centuries. Discusses in detail the ships, weaponry, and tactics of that era, including a description of Hein's fighting abilities and techniques. Also includes an account of the capture of 1628 in Hein's own words.

William H. Burnside

HEINRICH HEINE

Born: December 13, 1797; Düsseldorf
Died: February 17, 1856; Paris, France
Area of Achievement: Literature
Contribution: Through his literary and journalistic works, Heine exposed the hypocrisy and oppressiveness of feudal society as it existed in many parts of Europe during the first half of the nineteenth century.

Early Life

Chaim Harry Heine was born in Düsseldorf, the economic and cultural capital of the German Rhineland, into a respected Jewish family. His father, Samson, was a moderately successful textile merchant, who had little influence on Heinrich's upbringing. Indeed, the boy was reared almost exclusively by his well-educated, rationalist mother, Betty, who instilled in him—as well as in his siblings Charlotte, Gustav, and Maximilian—a deep sense of justice and morality, on the one hand, and an aversion for anything deemed impractical (such as art, literature, and theater), on the other.

Despite his mother's efforts, Heine was eventually introduced to the arts and humanities—and also to Christian ideology—when he, at age ten, enrolled in the Jesuit school near his home. There, encouraged by his teachers, he began to develop his innate talent for writing, a talent upon which he hoped to build one day a viable literary career. His parents envisioned an entirely different future for him, however, and sent him to Hamburg in 1817 to begin an apprenticeship in business with his uncle Salomon Heine, a wealthy and influential banker, who was to become his longtime benefactor. Salomon attempted to transform his rather reluctant nephew into a true entrepreneur and even established a textile trading firm in the boy's name, but Salomon finally succumbed to the youth's wish to study law at the University of Bonn.

Once in Bonn, Heine did not pursue jurisprudence as he had originally planned, but instead took his course work in literature and history. Most noteworthy among his courses was a metrics seminar taught by the famed German Romanticist August Wilhelm von Schlegel, from whom he received valuable advice concerning the style and form of his early poetic attempts. After a year in Bonn, Heine transferred to the University of Göttingen to begin his legal studies in earnest, but involvement in a duel—strictly prohibited by university code—soon forced him to transfer again.

In 1821, he settled in Berlin, where he continued his education by electing courses in law and by visiting a series of lectures held by the renowned philosopher Georg Wilhelm Friedrich Hegel, a major proponent of the historical dialectic, of the history of ideas, and of personal and intellectual freedom. While in Berlin, Heine was befriended by Karl and Rahel Varnhagen von Ense, a liberal aristocrat and his outspoken Jewish wife, who were the focal points of a literary salon frequented by Hegel and other intellectual luminaries of the day. At the age of twenty-seven, Heine returned to Göttingen to complete his legal studies, earning his doctorate in 1825, a year significant in that it also marks his conversion to Christianity and thus to a way of life which could, in his estimation, promote him from a Jewish outsider to an active participant in European culture.

Life's Work

Heine's career as a writer—inspired by the events of his youth, which culminated in a series of travels to Poland, England, northern Germany, and the Harz Mountains during the 1820's—formally began in 1827, when he published his immensely popular *Buch der Lieder* (*Book of Songs*, 1856), which pairs such traditionally Romantic elements as idealism, melancholy, and sentimentality with a unique brand of satire and irony. This collection, containing poems written as early as 1819, has love or, more specifically, unrequited love as its central theme. It no doubt was influenced by Heine's unsuccessful attempt at wooing his cousin Amalie during his apprenticeship in Hamburg.

The year 1827 proved to be an eventful year for Heine. In addition to his *Book of Songs*, he published two volumes of *Reisebilder* (*Pictures of Travel*, 1855), describing his aforementioned trips and containing detailed commentaries on social and political ills, especially the oppression of Jews, blacks, and other minorities in many parts of Europe. *Pictures of Travel* brought Heine instant fame and notoriety—so much so, in fact, that Johann Friedrich von Cotta, the liberal-minded publisher of the great German masters Johann Wolfgang von Goethe and Friedrich Schiller, invited him to Munich early in 1827 to become coeditor of a new journal, *Politische Annalen* (political annals). Not particularly overjoyed by this offer because he had set his sights on a university appointment, Heine allowed himself a considerable amount of time to complete the journey to Munich from the north German city of Lüneburg, his home since 1825. Indeed, he made lengthy stops while en route, visiting the famous folklorists Jakob and Wilhelm Grimm in Kassel and Ludwig Börne, one of Germany's most controversial political writers, in Frankfurt. When he finally did arrive in Munich, he was only willing to commit himself to the *Politische Annalen* for a scant six months.

In the latter half of 1828, Heine left Bavaria and, following Goethe's example, traveled to northern Italy. His sojourn in this romantic area was cut short, however, by news of his father's death, upon which followed a rather abrupt return to Germany. Heine now settled with his grieving mother at the home of his Uncle Salomon in Hamburg. There, he put forth two additional volumes of *Pictures of Travel* (1830-1831), in which he primarily recounted his Italian travels. He also used these volumes to comment on the political situation in France, a nation which had, in July, 1830, experienced a revolution, in the course of which the Bourbon Charles X was replaced by the more liberal "citizen-king," Louis-Philippe. So enthralled was Heine by this development that he proclaimed France the new "Promised Land" of the liberal cause and, in so doing, contrasted it with conservative Germany, still ruled by the oppressive proponents of the old feudal order.

In May, 1831, Heine, still subsidized by his Uncle Salomon, journeyed to Paris to experience the new wave of liberalism at first hand. There, he joined the ranks of the ultraliberal Saint-Simonians and, as a foreign correspondent for the *Allgemeine Zeitung* (city of Augsburg newspaper), attempted to acquaint Germans with the major tenets of French progressivism. Heine also attempted, in book form, to acquaint Germans with contemporary trends in French literature through the various volumes of his *Der Salon* (1834-1840; *The Salon*, 1893), which combine commentaries written in a distinctly conversational tone with a variety of original literary pieces, including the fragmentary novel *Der Rabbi von Bacherach* (1887; *The Rabbi of Bacherach*, 1891).

Heine was extremely popular in France. His extensive circle of admirers included such luminaries as Honoré de Balzac, Victor Hugo, George Sand, Hector Berlioz, and Frédéric Chopin. In his native Germany, however, where the archconservative Metternich government banned his works in 1835 because they allegedly represented an affront against "altar and throne," his circle of supporters was comparatively small. In fact, it was not until 1840, the year the ban was lifted, that it again became safe to appreciate Heine in Germany.

The year 1840 is significant in that it also marks the beginning of a very productive period in Heine's life, during which he resumed his reports for the *Allgemeine Zeitung* and began work on a wide variety of literary projects. These included the well-known mock epics *Atta Troll* (1847; English translation, 1876) and *Deutschland: Ein Wintermärchen* (1844; *Germany: A Winter's Tale*, 1892), both of which were directed against the hypocrisy and self-righteousness of the German bourgeoisie. In 1843, Heine interrupted his heavy work schedule for several months to travel to Hamburg, where he met with his mother as well as with his publishers at the firm of Hoffmann and Campe. Accompanying him on this journey was Mathilde (née Eugénie Mirat), his Belgian-born wife of nearly two years. Shortly after he returned to Paris in 1844, his Uncle Salomon died, leaving Heine's economic future uncertain. His health also began to fail drastically, and in 1848, the year of the German revolution, his health deteriorated completely, leaving him a cripple, permanently confined to his bed.

Almost miraculously, Heine managed to remain lucid throughout the entire ordeal and, on his better days, even continued his writing. Using secretaries, he was able to produce a final great collection of poems in 1851, *Romanzero*

(English translation, 1859).

After eight years of intense suffering, Heine—having readied many of his writings for publication in a collected works—died in February, 1856, at the age of fifty-eight. According to his wishes, he was buried in Paris' Montmartre Cemetery under a headstone bearing the simple yet significant inscription: "Here lies a German poet."

Summary

Heinrich Heine's fame is rooted primarily in his lyric poetry, which not only gave rise to some of the most beloved folk songs ever written in the German language but also appeared in countless foreign translations. On the basis of his early poetry, Heine is often classified as a major proponent of the Romantic tradition. In truth, however, he often criticized the Romantic movement for its idealism and its lack of social and political commitment. During the turbulent period preceding the Revolution of 1848, he called for a new German literature focusing on such pressing issues of the day as human rights, women's emancipation, and equal representation of the masses in national government. Indeed, Heine is still known as one of Germany's most outspoken champions of the liberal cause. His name is frequently associated with the progressive Saint-Simonians in France as well as with Young Germany, a prerevolutionary movement among liberal authors, of which Heine was generally regarded the spiritual leader.

Heine has often (and by no means incorrectly) been described as an anomaly, a literary outsider of sorts, who combines Judaism and Christianity, Romanticism and realism, rationality and imagination, and beautiful verses and the most biting forms of satire and irony in a single person. Yet it is Heine's uniqueness which has prompted such a lively interest in his life and works, an interest which has led to the formation of both a Heine Institute and a Heine Society in Düsseldorf and which has spawned countless scholarly publications throughout the world.

Bibliography
Atkins, H. G. *Heine*. New York: E. P. Dutton, 1929. A standard biography providing detailed information on Heine's life and work. Characterizes Heine as an unusually gifted poet but, at the same time, questions the validity of his political writings. Includes an excellent bibliography of secondary sources.
Brod, Max. *Heinrich Heine: The Artist in Revolt*. Translated by Joseph Witriol. New York: New York University Press, 1957. A standard biography which frequently utilizes excerpts from Heine's works to shed light on important facts and events. Deals at length with Jewish-Gentile relationships and their bearing on Heine's life and career. Short but useful bibliography.

Browne, Lewis. *That Man Heine*. New York: Macmillan, 1927. This well-written, highly entertaining biography focuses on Heine's outsider status in terms of both literature and society. It characterizes his existence as a constant exile from the German feudal order. Bibliography centers on biographical references.

Butler, E. M. *Heinrich Heine: A Biography*. London: Hogarth Press, 1956. This colorful account focuses on the Saint-Simonian influences on Heine, on his discovery of the Dionysian experience for German literature, and on his final years of great physical and emotional suffering spent in his "mattress grave."

Fejtö, François. *Heine: A Biography*. Translated by Mervyn Savill. London: Allan Wingate, 1946. A detailed account of Heine's life, aimed at identifying "the very essence of the man." Attempts to explain the personality capable of producing such a timeless and widely acclaimed work of art as the *Book of Songs*. Bibliography includes many sources on Heine's relationship to France.

Rose, William. *The Early Love Poetry of Heinrich Heine: An Inquiry into Poetic Inspiration*. Oxford, England: Clarendon Press, 1962. In this excellent book, the author investigates—and seriously questions—the extent to which Heine's early love poetry can be viewed as an autobiographical confession.

Sammons, Jeffrey L. *Heinrich Heine: A Modern Biography*. Princeton, N.J.: Princeton University Press, 1979. One of the most critical studies ever written on Heine's life and work. The poet emerges as a problematic individual, perpetually at odds with his surroundings. This biography is fully documented and avoids the subjectivity which pervades many early treatments of Heine's life. Contains an excellent discussion of Heine's reception in Germany as well as a useful bibliography.

Spencer, Hanna. *Heinrich Heine*. Boston: Twayne, 1982. This Twayne series book represents a brief introduction to Heine's life and works geared specifically to the beginning student of German literature. It includes a chronology of Heine's life, interpretations of his major works, and a select, annotated bibliography containing a large number of primary and secondary sources in English.

Dwight A. Klett

HERMANN VON HELMHOLTZ

Born: August 31, 1821; Potsdam, Prussia
Died: September 8, 1894; Berlin, Germany
Areas of Achievement: Physiology and physics
Contribution: Helmholtz contributed to the fields of energetics, physiological acoustics and optics, mathematics, hydrodynamics, and electrodynamics. His most important work was in establishing the principle of conservation of energy and in his experimental and theoretical studies of hearing and vision.

Early Life

Hermann Ludwig Ferdinand von Helmholtz was the eldest of four children born to Ferdinand and Caroline Penne Helmholtz. His mother was a descendant of William Penn. His father studied philology and philosophy at the University of Berlin and was a teacher at the Potsdam *Gymnasium*. He was a typical product of German Romanticism and Idealistic philosophy, with strong interests in music and art. These interests were passed on to his son, especially music, and became important aspects of his life and later work in physiological acoustics and optics.

Helmholtz was a sickly child, not entering the *Gymnasium* until the age of nine, but he advanced rapidly and was encouraged by his father to memorize the works of Johann Wolfgang von Goethe, Friedrich Schiller, and the Greek poet Homer. His interest soon turned to physics. In 1837, he received a scholarship to study medicine at the Friedrich Wilhelm Institute in Berlin, with the provision that he would serve for eight years as an army surgeon after completing his degree.

While in Berlin, Helmholtz supplemented his medical studies with many science courses at the University of Berlin and studied mathematics on his own. In 1841, he began research under the great physiologist Johannes Peter Müller, who followed the German tradition of vitalism in explaining the unique characteristics of living organisms. Helmholtz joined the circle of Müller's students, including Emil Du Bois-Reymond, Ernst Wilhelm von Brücke, and Carl Friedrich Wilhelm Ludwig, and they later became known as the Helmholtz school of physiology for their rejection of the nonphysical vital forces in favor of purely physical and chemical explanations of life processes.

Helmholtz completed his medical degree in 1842, with a dissertation showing that nerve fibers are connected to ganglion cells. After some further research on fermentation that seemed to support vitalism, he was appointed as army surgeon to the regiment at Potsdam. From that time on, he wrote at least one major paper every year except 1849, publishing more than two hundred articles and books before he died. In 1849, he was granted an early release from his military duty to accept an appointment as associate professor of physiology at Königsberg. Just before leaving Potsdam, he married Olga von Velten, the daughter of a physician, by whom he had two children.

Life's Work

Helmholtz began to make major contributions to science even during his five-year tour of duty in the army, when he had little free time or laboratory facilities. Pursuing the ideas of the chemist Justus von Liebig, he made a quantitative study with homemade apparatus of the effects produced by muscle contraction and showed that it is accompanied by chemical changes and heat production. With this experimental evidence for transformation of energy (or force, as he called it), he undertook to establish the general principle that energy remains constant in all processes, whether animate or inanimate.

Arguing from the impossibility of perpetual motion with surprising mathematical sophistication, he demonstated the principle of conservation of energy in its most general form and used it to refute vitalism. In 1847, "Über die Erhaltung der Kraft" ("On the Conservation of Force," 1853) was presented to the Physical Society in Berlin. The importance of this discovery led to fierce controversy over scientific priorities, but Helmholtz willingly shared the credit. Julius Robert von Mayer's prior announcement of this principle in 1842 was unknown to Helmholtz, whose work was much more detailed and comprehensive. James Prescott Joule is also given credit for this discovery for providing the first experimental verification.

After moving to his first academic post at Königsberg in 1849, Helmholtz began to try to measure the speed of nerve impulses, which Müller had considered too fast to be measured. This work led to the invention of the myograph for measuring short intervals from marks on a revolving drum. In 1851, he succeeded in measuring the speed along a frog's nerve by stimulating it at increasing distances from the muscle and found it to be surprisingly slow at about 30 meters per second. About the same time, he invented the ophthalmoscope, which brought him world fame in the field of medicine. This invention made it possible for the first time to view the inside of the living human eye, opening up the field of ophthalmology.

In 1855, Helmholtz became a professor of anatomy and physiology at Bonn. Continuing his work on sensory physiology, he published the first of three volumes of his massive *Handbuch der physiologischen Optik* (1856; *Treatise on Physiological Optics*, 1924). He also wrote several papers on acoustics. His interest in acoustics led to his first paper on theoretical physics in 1858, creating the mathematical foundations of hydrodynamics by finding vortex solutions. At this time he accepted a position as professor of physiology at Heidelberg.

After moving to Heidelberg in 1858, Helmholtz established the new Physiological Institute. At Bonn, his wife's health had started to deteriorate, and she died in 1859. During this stressful period, he achieved his greatest success in acoustical research, formulating his resonance theory of hearing, which explains the detection of differing pitches through variations of progressively smaller resonators in the spiral cochlea of the inner ear. He also published analyses of vibrations in open-ended pipes and of the motion of violin strings. In 1861, he wed Anna von Mohl, by whom he had three more children. In 1862, he completed the first edition of his highly influential treatise *Die Lehre von den Tonempfindungen als physiologische Grundlage für die Theorie der Musik* (1863; *On the Sensations of Tone as a Physiological Basis for the Theory of Music*, 1885).

During this time, Helmholtz also continued his optical research, amending Thomas Young's theory of color vision to distinguish between spectral primaries and physiological primaries of greater saturation. The resulting Young-Helmholtz theory could then explain all color perception by proper mixtures of three physiological primaries and could be used to explain red color blindness as well. He incorporated these results in the second volume of *Treatise on Physiological Optics* and began work on the third volume, in which binocular vision and depth judgments were treated. This included a defense of empiricism against the nativist view that some aspects of perception are innate, leading to original work in non-Euclidean geometry. After the third volume was published in 1867, he believed that the field of physiology had grown beyond the scope of any one person, and he turned his attention almost exclusively to physics.

In 1871, Helmholtz accepted the prestigious chair of physics at Berlin after Gustav Robert Kirchhoff had turned it down. A new Physical Institute was established and he became the director, with his living quarters in the institute. He began his research in Berlin with a series of papers on electrodynamics, which brought James Clerk Maxwell's electromagnetic field theory to the attention of continental physicists. In Germany, the interaction between electric charges was explained by Wilhelm Eduard Weber's law of instantaneous action at a distance rather than action mediated by a field in an intervening ether. Helmholtz developed a more general action-at-a-distance theory but included Maxwell's field theory as a limiting case, allowing for wave propagation at the speed of light. This work inspired his former student Heinrich Rudolph Hertz to do experiments leading to the discovery of radio waves in 1887.

Returning to his early interest in energetics, Helmholtz began to investigate energy processes in galvanic cells and in electrochemical reactions. This led him to the idea that electricity consists of discrete charges, or atoms of electricity, and that chemical forces are electrical in nature. Research in thermochemistry resulted in the concept of free energy that determines the direction of chemical reactions. An analysis of solar energy led to an estimate of 25 million years as the amount of time since the formation of the planets; this estimate was far too conservative, however, because of the ignorance of nuclear processes. In the late 1880's, he formulated a theory for cloud formation and storm mechanics. One of his last great efforts was an unsuccessful attempt to derive all of mechanics, thermodynamics, and electrodynamics from Sir William Rowan Hamilton's principle of least action.

Helmholtz was elected Rector of the University of Berlin for one year in 1877. He was granted hereditary nobility by Emperor William I in 1882. Helmholtz became the first president of the new Physical-Technical Institute in 1888, freeing him from teaching so he could spend more time in research. For several years, he had suffered from migraine and fits of depression, which only long vacations seemed to cure. In 1893, he traveled to the United States as a delegate of the German government to the Electrical Congress at Chicago. On his return voyage, he fell down the ship's stairs and injured his head. A year later, he suffered a cerebral hemorrhage, and, after two months of semiconsciousness, he died.

Summary

Hermann von Helmholtz was one of the leaders among German scientists who rebelled against the scientific romanticism of the first half of the nineteenth century. He successfully replaced vitalism with a rigorous physicochemical empiricism, but he also shared the goal of his predecessors in his desire to find unifying principles in nature. He succeeded in this goal with his elaboration of the principle of the conservation of energy. He demonstrated the interconnections among physiology, chemistry, medicine, and physics; he fell short, however, in his efforts to extend the principle of least action. Especially important were his three-color theory of vision, his resonance theory of hearing, and his invention of the ophthalmoscope.

Helmholtz also contributed to the transition of German universities from teaching academies to research institutions. The great laboratories he established at Heidelberg in physiology and at Berlin in physics placed Germany in the forefront of scientific research. Some of the most famous scientists at the end of the century had been his students, including Hertz, who discovered radio waves and the photoelectric effect, Max Planck, who introduced quantum theory, and the Americans Henry Augustus Rowland and Albert Abraham Michelson.

As a master and leader in biology, physics, and mathematics, he surpassed all others in the imposing theoretical and experimental treatises he produced, especially in sensory physiology. As perhaps the greatest scientist of the nineteenth century, he was the last scholar whose work embraced virtually all the sciences together with philosophy, mathematics, and the fine arts.

Bibliography

Boring, Edwin B. *Sensation and Perception in the History of Experimental Psychology.* East Norwalk, Conn.: Appleton-Century-Crofts, 1942. This volume, dedicated to Helmholtz, is a comprehensive history of sensory physiology and psychology. Describes the work of Helmholtz in physiological optics and acoustics, its historical background, and later developments from his ideas.

Elkana, Yehuda. *The Discovery of the Conservation of Energy.* Cambridge, Mass.: Harvard University Press, 1974. A history of the energy concept, including the physiological background and a chapter on the famous 1847 paper by Helmholtz on conservation of energy. Contains a bibliography and an appendix.

Helmholtz, Hermann von. *On the Sensations of Tone as a Physiological Basis for the Theory of Music.* Translated by Alexander Ellis. Mineola, N.Y.: Dover, 1954. An English translation of the fourth (and last) German edition (1877) of the great treatise on physiological acoustics. Includes a six-page introduction on the life of Helmholtz by Henry Margenau and a five-page bibliography of his major works with titles given in English translation.

Jungnickel, Christa, and Russell McCormmach. *Intellectual Mastery of Nature: Theoretical Physics from Ohm to Einstein.* Vol. 1, *The Torch of Mathematics, 1800-1870.* Chicago: University of Chicago Press, 1986. The first volume of this two-volume work on German science describes some of Helmholtz's physiological research. The second volume, *The Now Mighty Theoretical Physics, 1870-1925*, discusses his work in physics, especially in electrodynamics and energetics.

Königsberger, Leo. *Hermann von Helmholtz.* Translated by Frances Welby. Mineola, N.Y.: Dover, 1965. An abridged translation of the complete biography of Helmholtz in German published in 1906. The best source of information concerning his life and work, including discussions of his major publications.

Warren, Richard, and Roslyn Warren. *Helmholtz on Perception: Its Physiology and Development.* New York: John Wiley & Sons, 1968. Contains the English translations of six selections from lectures and articles by Helmholtz on sensory physiology. Includes a thirteen-page sketch of his life and work, a six-page evaluation of his work on sensory perceptions, and a five-page bibliography.

Joseph L. Spradley

HENRY IV

Born: December 14, 1553; castle of Pau, Basses Pyrenees
Died: May 14, 1610; Paris, France
Areas of Achievement: Monarchy, government, and politics
Contribution: Henry IV brought peace and national prestige to France within the structure of powerful monarchy after protracted strife, which had included eight civil wars. He settled the long-standing Catholic-Protestant conflict by embracing Catholicism while granting broad toleration to the French Reformed church. He is the most noteworthy of early modern rulers who made religious liberty the law of the state.

Early Life

Henry of Navarre, first of the Bourbon line, was born in the castle of Pau in the Pyrenees Mountains to Antoine de Bourbon, Duke of Vendôme, and Jeanne d'Albret, Queen of Navarre. He was a direct descendant of Louis IX, one of France's most illustrious rulers. Although he was baptized a Catholic, Henry received instruction in the Calvinist (Reformed) faith at his mother's direction, and he eventually joined the French Protestants, then known as Huguenots. In 1568, his mother placed Henry in the service of Admiral Gaspard de Coligny, the leader of the Protestant cause. As a soldier in the Huguenot army, he fought bravely and acquired a reputation as a skillful military leader. When Jeanne d'Albret died in 1572, Henry succeeded her as monarch of Navarre. That same year, he married Margaret of Valois, sister of King Charles IX of France.

Life's Work

By the time Henry joined Coligny in 1568, France had been wracked by civil war for more than eight years. The death of Henry II in 1559 initiated a power struggle in which political and religious considerations were intertwined. Francis II and Henry II had tried to crush the Protestants, but the Reformed faith had made impressive gains nevertheless, especially among the bourgeoisie and the aristocracy. Calvinism gained adherents who could exert far greater influence than their numbers would seem to indicate.

Because the sons of Henry II were feeble rulers, nobles asserted their authority and rival factions competed for power. Antoine de Bourbon and Louis I de Condé, both princes of the blood, allied with Coligny to promote the Protestant cause. The family of Guise, with Duke Francis at the head, led the Catholic faction. When Francis II succeeded to the throne as a minor in 1559, the Guises obtained control of the government. After they executed some of their opponents, Protestants responded with militant resistance. Francis II died after one year on the throne, and Charles IX became king with his mother, Catherine de Médicis, as regent. She then became the pivotal figure in French politics for the next quarter century. Catherine had no deep religious convictions, so she tried to manipulate both sides and to create a moderate party loyal to the Crown. In 1562, however, the Guises seized power and forced the regent to resume persecuting the Protestants. France became the scene of all-out civil war.

The marriage of Henry of Navarre to Margaret of Valois occurred in 1572, as Catherine de Médicis tried to placate the Huguenots by marrying her daughter to one of their most popular leaders. The nuptial festivities, however, became the occasion for the Saint Bartholomew's Eve Massacre, in which Coligny and some other Protestants were murdered. Although the assassins may have intended to kill only a few Huguenot leaders, word of the slayings soon led to the slaughter of thousands of Protestants across France. The civil war resumed with renewed fury.

The sickly Henry III became king in 1574, and soon a militant Catholic faction, now led by Duke Henry of Guise, organized the Catholic League without royal approval. The civil strife then became the War of Three Henrys, as Henry III, Henry of Guise, and Henry of Navarre fought for control of the kingdom. The eventual assassination of the king and the duke left the Protestant Henry of Navarre the legal heir to the throne. He declared himself King of France in 1589. Civil war continued, however, until the last remnants of the Catholic League abandoned resistance in 1596. The concurrent war with Spain did not end until 1598.

Although Henry IV had become king legally, he knew that his throne would never be secure so long as he remained a Protestant. His Huguenot supporters, only 10 percent of the population, were unable to cement their leader's authority. Moderate Catholics urged the king to convert, but Henry delayed because he wanted his enemies to recognize his kingship first. When he became convinced that that would not happen, he announced his decision to become a Catholic. An old but probably apocryphal account relates that he justified changing religions with the remark "Paris is well worth a Mass." Henry's embrace of Catholicism shows clearly that this king was a *politique*, that is, one without strong religious beliefs who follows the course of action he deems politically advantageous. He had done this before, when he had joined the Catholic church to marry Margaret of Valois, only to return to the Reformed faith in 1576.

In order to obtain papal approval for his succession, Henry had to seek absolution for his Protestant heresies, something the Vatican was in no hurry to grant. Pope Sixtus V had tried to block his path to the French throne and had declared him deposed as King of Navarre. The reigning pontiff, Clement VIII, chose to defer action on the royal request, even though French prelates had hailed the king's return to the Church.

Henry chose Jacques Davy Duperron as his emissary to Rome. Duperron, who had once been a Huguenot and had adopted Catholicism after reading

Thomas Aquinas' *Summa theologica* (1266-1273), supervised the religious instruction of the royal convert. Since Duperron was a learned apologist for Catholicism, he was an effective representative to the pope. As a reward for his services, the king made Duperron a royal chaplain and a councillor of state, and, in 1596, Bishop of Évreux. In order to convince the pope of his sincerity, Henry promised to rebuild monasteries destroyed in the civil wars, and he agreed to support the decrees of the Council of Trent (1563), the Counter-Reformation program to combat Protestantism. At the least, this meant that the king would maintain the Catholic religion in all areas of France that had supported the Catholic League. He promised similarly to prohibit Protestant worship in Paris, Lyons, Rouen, and other cities.

Moderate Protestants accepted Henry's conversion and his concessions to Rome as necessary for the peace and security of France. Militant Huguenots, however, protested. The king had to deal with them cautiously to prevent them from deserting him. It is a tribute to Henry's diplomacy that he was able to pay the price demanded by the pope without alienating his Protestant supporters completely. By 1598, Henry was convinced that his rule was secure, so he took a bold step to reassure the Huguenots of his goodwill. The king proclaimed the Edict of Nantes, a landmark enactment in the history of religious freedom.

The Edict of Nantes expressed the king's wish for the eventual reunion of all Christians, but its provisions show that Henry knew that that would not occur. This law ratified concessions granted to Protestants earlier, and it recognized full freedom of belief and the right to public worship in two hundred towns and in many castles of Protestant lords. Calvinists could worship in private elsewhere, and they would be eligible for most public offices. The king also granted subsidies for a number of Protestant schools and colleges, and the edict created special sections of the *parlements* (royal courts) to try cases in which Protestant interests were involved. The king allowed the Huguenots to fortify about two hundred towns under their control. The policy of toleration satisfied the Protestants, and it contributed immediately to the achievement of national union. Its provisions, however, created almost a state-within-the-state, a condition which was to cause disruption at a later time, when subsequent monarchs tried to impose their authority upon those towns.

Catholic reaction to the Edict of Nantes was predictably hostile. Pope Clement VIII denounced it, and some *parlements* tried to obstruct publication of the royal decree. Militant opponents of toleration tried to reactivate the Catholic League, and the government discovered several plots to assassinate the king. Most Frenchmen, nevertheless, were too weary of strife to support another civil war, and news about the plots against the king caused an upsurge of support for his policy. His opponents could not find a single magnetic leader. Under royal pressure the Parlement of Paris registered the edict, and the other courts followed suit. Extensive, though not complete, religious freedom became the policy of Western Europe's largest state.

Whatever satisfaction Henry derived from the success of his policy toward religion, it could not obscure the serious problems which confronted him as king. Foreign and domestic wars had brought France to a state of impoverishment approaching bankruptcy. The kingdom was almost impotent in foreign affairs. Henry faced the mammoth task of rebuilding with determination. Although he was an intelligent and energetic ruler, Henry was not a skilled administrator. He entrusted that responsibility to the Duke of Sully, a Protestant and a longtime friend. Under Sully's competent direction, the government eliminated much corruption and inefficiency, reformed taxation, and gained solvency. Financial success made it possible to improve the army and to initiate public works for building canals, roads, and harbors to promote economic growth. The government sponsored the expansion of arable lands by draining swamps, and it developed new industries, including the production of silk. Henry founded the French colonial empire by sending the first French explorers and settlers to Canada.

In foreign affairs, Henry sought to protect France from the encircling power of the Habsburgs of Austria and Spain. Because he knew that France was vulnerable to Habsburg attack, he allied with Protestant states in Germany and with the Netherlands. Just when he was ready to strike at his enemies, however, an assassin struck him. He died on May 14, 1610, at the hand of François Ravaillac. The assailant seems to have acted on his own to slay a Catholic monarch who had decided to war against the Catholic Habsburgs, which would have aided the Protestant cause internationally. Although his enemies rejoiced at the death of Henry, the French people mourned the passing of a great, humane king.

Summary

Henry IV was a popular ruler because he truly cared for the welfare of his subjects. Most Frenchmen accepted his absolutism as the only alternative to the anarchy which had prevailed for so long. His pragmatic policies brought peace and prosperity with order.

Although Henry was a hero to the Huguenots, despite his defection to Catholicism his private life must have offended their stern Calvinist moral sensibilities. In 1599, he obtained papal dissolution of his marriage to Margaret of Valois and quickly took Marie de Médicis as his next wife. He was not faithful to either wife but had several mistresses and illegitimate children. He was not above practicing ecclesiastical corruption, as when he made one of his bastards Bishop of Metz at age six. Henry often coerced *parlements* and subjected provincial and local officials to forceful supervision. He controlled the nobles effectively and left his son Louis XIII a kingdom at peace, one where royal authority was supreme and prosperity was in progress.

Bibliography
Daumgartner, Frederic. "The Catholic Opposition to the Edict of Nantes." *Bibliothèque d'Humanisme et Renaissance* 40 (1970): 525-537. This valuable study relates how Henry shrewdly overcame the criticisms of his opponents. A work of thorough research that propounds a convincing argument. The notes are rich in research data.
Dickerman, Edmund H. "The Conversion of Henry IV." *The Catholic Historical Review* 68 (1977): 1-13. While others have concluded on the basis of appearances and superficial research that the king was a *politique*, Dickerman has made a penetrating examination of the sources to show how and why Henry regarded religion pragmatically.
Gray, Janet Glenn. *The French Huguenots: The Anatomy of Courage*. Grand Rapids, Mich.: Baker Book House, 1981. This decidedly partisan survey of the religious and political climate in France is vivid in descriptions and contains many perceptive interpretations. Places Henry's career in the context of the French and European struggles for religious liberty.
Leathes, Stanley. "Henry IV of France." In *The Cambridge Modern History*, edited by A. W. Ward et al., vol. 3. Cambridge: Cambridge University Press, 1904. This substantial essay, despite its age, is indispensable to any serious study of the subject. An excellent source with which to begin one's inquiry.
Russell, Lord of Liverpool. *Henry of Navarre*. New York: Praeger, 1970. For the average reader, this is probably the most enjoyable biography of the subject. Portrays the king as a humane ruler, licentious in life and a *politique* in religion. The author is an exceptionally talented writer.
Sutherland, N. M. *The Huguenot Struggle for Recognition*. New Haven, Conn.: Yale University Press, 1980. This thorough study of the Huguenot movement and the issues which it raised for church and state in France is a model of research and writing by a truly erudite scholar. Not for beginners.
Wilkinson, Burke. *The Helmet of Navarre*. New York: Macmillan, 1965. This delightfully readable account of Henry should be of particular interest to juvenile readers. Contains nothing original in either fact or interpretation and so will be of no use to scholars.
Willert, P. F. *Henry of Navarre and the Huguenots in France*. New York: G. P. Putnam's Sons, 1893. Although more recent treatments have superseded this one and brought some of the author's judgments into question, this work remains a useful and rather full account which features lucid style and interesting coverage.

James Edward McGoldrick

JOHANN GOTTFRIED HERDER

Born: August 25, 1744; Mohrungen, East Prussia
Died: December 18, 1803; Weimar, Saxe-Weimar
Areas of Achievement: Philosophy and literature
Contribution: Herder was a major figure in the transitional period in German letters encompassing the second half of the eighteenth century. He was a universalist whose writings dealt with many areas of human thought.

Early Life

Johann Gottfried Herder was born on August 25, 1744, in the small East Prussian town of Mohrungen. He came from a family of modest financial resources; his father worked as a teacher, organist, and church warden. Both parents were pious people, and Herder grew up influenced by the moderate Pietist ideas common in the clergy at this time, which were opposed to orthodoxy and dogma in favor of a more personal, inner-directed religious life.

Herder had two sisters, who married and remained in Mohrungen. He showed his great desire to study rather early in life. While in Latin school, he became the favorite student of the stern schoolmaster, and at the age of sixteen he obtained free lodging with a vicar named Sebastian Trescho in exchange for work as a copyist. This arrangement was particularly advantageous for Herder because the vicar had an excellent library, where Herder could satisfy his avid desire to read.

Although Herder wished to attend the university, family finances might have made that impossible. Fortunately, when the Russian troops moved into the region in 1762, the regimental surgeon met Herder and generously offered to pay for his medical studies at Königsberg. In the spring of that year, Herder enrolled in medicine at the university, but he was clearly not suited to that field. Changing his field to theology, he lost his benefactor's support but was able to finance his own studies with a stipend and money earned by tutoring at the Collegium Fridericianum.

In Königsberg, Herder met Johann Georg Hamann, whose ideas greatly influenced him even though his own philosophical views differed from Hamann's, for example, on the origin of language. Hamann's thoughts on the Bible inspired some of Herder's early attempts at a better understanding of the book through its poetic medium and an understanding of its social and historical context. During those same years, Herder attended lectures by Immanuel Kant on a wide range of subjects, which offered great stimulus to his thought, as did contact with humanistic and humanitarian ideas, such as those of the "Deutsche Gesellschaft" (German society).

Life's Work

In 1764, Herder began his professional life in the *Domschule* of Riga. He stayed for five years, during which time he became a successful teacher and preacher and published his first two books, *Über die neuere deutsche Literatur: Fragmente* (1767; on recent German literature: fragments) and *Kritische Wälder* (1769; critical forests), which brought him recognition and also criticism. His ideas about language became central to many other parts of his thinking as well. In his literary criticism, Herder rejects absolute standards and argues instead that the critic must enter into the spirit of the literary work, judging it from the point of view of its intentions.

In 1769, Herder departed from Riga for France. He spent several months in Nantes, where he wrote a type of diary of his voyage, revealing important parts of his inner life (not for publication). His intended destination was Paris, which he found that he disliked, and he soon left to accompany the Prince-Bishop of Oldenburg-Eutin's son on a three-year tour. He first went to the Netherlands and then continued on to Hamburg, were he met Gotthold Ephraim Lessing and Matthias Claudius. The companion role did not suit Herder, so he soon separated from the prince; however, the tour did bring him in contact with his future wife, Karoline Flachsland, in Darmstadt. After an unsuccessful eye operation in Strasbourg, he met Johann Wolfgang von Goethe in 1770. Herder's ideas on language, the historical development of humanity, and Hebrew poetry in the Old Testament had a great influence on the young Goethe. Herder was working on *Abhandlung über den Ursprung der Sprache* (1772; *Treatise upon the Origin of Language*, 1827), which was awarded a prize from the Prussian Academy of Sciences and which was something of a nucleus for future works. Through his organic philosophy of history and his recourse to the senses, Herder became recognized as a leading figure of the *Sturm und Drang* (storm and stress) literary movement.

Also in 1771, Herder decided to accept a church position as a *Hofprediger*, or court preacher, in Bückeburg so that he could be married, and he began a period of intensive writing. Herder's views put him in conflict with the count (Wilhelm of Schaumburg-Lippe), since Herder defended the rights of the Church. At the same time, the clergy found him too liberal. When he was unable to move to Göttingen as a theology professor because of opposition from the other clergy, he took a position in Weimar, which Goethe helped him to obtain.

Herder moved to Weimar in 1776, where he remained, although he complained that his efforts—in church and school reform, for example—were not appreciated. Herder's relationship with Goethe was difficult now that they were peers, but a period of friendship and collaboration followed which lasted from 1783 to 1789. A serious rift occurred in 1794, when Goethe's friendship with Friedrich Schiller deepened. Jealousy created part of the conflict; however, another part was clearly a difference of philosophical opinion.

Herder was extremely productive in Weimar, writing some of his most important works, including *Ideen zur Philosophie der Geschichte der Mensch-*

heit (1784-1791; *Outlines of a Philosophy of the History of Man*, 1800), often considered his most important work. His plan to write a fifth part was abandoned with the outbreak of the French Revolution. Instead, he began his *Briefe zu Beförderung der Humanität* (1793-1797; *Letters for the Advancement of Humanity*, 1800), in which he included some indirect commentary on events of the time. Herder saw human history as a natural development according to universal laws. His point of view was a religious humanism based on his conviction that creation was an indivisible whole. Furthermore, although he wished to take into account advances in science, he did not accept a mechanistic view of nature. Herder believed that both history and nature reflected the working of a divine spirit and that gradual progress was taking place. The French Revolution, however, caused him to doubt his views. His most mature religious ideas, making explicit his conception of God by combining a dynamic concept of nature with the idea of a divine immanence, appeared in his work *Gott: Einige Gespräche* (1787; *God: Some Conversations*, 1940).

Herder joined Goethe and Schiller in their project of a nonpolitical journal, *Die Horen* (1795-1797), but withdrew after an argument with Schiller about the role of literature in society. Also during this time, Herder became more and more hostile to Immanuel Kant's ideas. In 1785, Kant harshly reviewed the first two parts of Herder's major work, *Outlines of a Philosophy of the History of Man*, and in 1799, Herder retaliated by criticizing several of Kant's major works.

Herder's later work includes many shorter pieces. His last collection, *Adrastea* (1801-1804), which remained unfinished, comprised a discussion of eighteenth century history, culture, and religious ideas, including New Testament studies. His criticism of his times is also evident.

Herder felt isolated in Weimar after his break with Goethe and his criticism of the classical movement, although his friendship with Jean Paul Richter lessened this feeling somewhat. Toward the end of his life, Herder was interrupted in his work by illness. He died on December 18, 1803, leaving behind an extensive body of work.

Summary

Johann Gottfried Herder was a major figure of the eighteenth century whose ideas had an impact on his age and on the nineteenth century in many areas of thought. Most commonly, he is acknowledged as a stimulus for the *Sturm und Drang* writers, including Goethe, and is counted among the critics of Kant's philosophical ideas as well as of German classicism.

In his writing, Herder attempted to achieve a type of synthesis which is associated with the universality of a Renaissance man. He wrote on religion, society, history, literary criticism, psychology, science, education, aesthetics, and the arts. He attempted to capture the totality of human experience, seeing creation as an organic whole, and rejected rationalism and any type of philosophical system, such as that proposed by Kant. Although maintaining his religious ties, he saw religion as something which should serve humanity, and he was equally opposed to orthodoxy (dogmatism) and antireligious secularization. Herder viewed the human soul as an entity where a person's powers are in harmony. The body is the mediator for the soul in its relationship with the material world, but the soul is the center of creative powers and has within it the drive toward perfection (*Humanität*).

As a thinker, Herder constantly sought to reconcile opposing currents in the intellectual community and within his own views. For example, he attempted to reconcile the early influence of Hamann's transcendental ideas with empiricism, gained in part by Kant's early influence; he synthesized religious and scientific elements; and he tried to balance some of the irrationalism of *Sturm und Drang* with more rationalist ideas. The result is an important body of writing with a rather consistent view developed from his first major works through his final essays. Herder influenced many of his important contemporaries, especially Goethe, but, unfortunately, by the 1790's his ideas were in conflict with the dominant values of classicism and the beginnings of Romanticism. Still, he was a keen observer of historical and cultural movements. His greatest importance may well be in sowing ideas which others later brought to fruition.

Bibliography
Barnard, F. M. *Herder's Social and Political Thought: From Enlightenment to Nationalism.* Oxford, England: Clarendon Press, 1965. A study of the development of Herder's concept of organism and organic politics, ending with an assessment of his impact on German political Romanticism and of his immediate influence outside Germany. The discussion also includes a separate chapter on the central concept of *Humanität* in relation to religion, ethics, and politics.
Clark, Robert T. *Herder: His Life and Thought.* Berkeley: University of California Press, 1955. The most detailed Herder biography available in English, including a characterization of his important works set against the intellectual background of his time. Contains many quotations from Herder's work in English translation as well as an extensive bibliography, with a listing of available translations.
Fugate, Joe K. *The Psychological Basis of Herder's Aesthetics.* The Hague: Mouton, 1966. A discussion of the aesthetic questions considered by Herder from the perspective of his psychological ideas and principles. Fugate's position is that in Herder's work human endeavors in the arts cannot be understood without taking into account the powers inherent in the human soul. A selected bibliography includes general works and individual studies pertaining to Herder, some in English.

Herder, Johann Gottfried. *God: Some Conversations.* Translated with an introduction and notes by Frederick H. Burkhardt. New York: Hafner Press, 1949. Ths book's introduction discusses Herder's development and places this work in the context of his times, relating it specifically to Immanuel Kant and Baruch Spinoza. Serving as a table of contents, there is a brief summary of each of the five conversations and the epilogue.

Koepke, Wulf. *Johann Gottfried Herder.* Boston: Twayne, 1987. A readable general introduction for the nonspecialist. Koepke follows the unity in Herder's ideas and concerns through his life in historical sequence and emphasizes the importance of Herder's own achievements rather than viewing him mainly as Goethe's mentor or as a figure whose ideas were incorporated and improved by his successors. Useful selected, annotated bibliography.

_____, ed. *Johann Gottfried Herder: Innovator Through the Ages.* Bonn, Germany: Bouvier, 1982. Eleven articles by different authors, reflecting some of the concerns of North American scholarship on Herder. Among the topics are the concept of *Humanität*, Herder's language model, and his theological writings. A selected bibliography of mostly German-language sources and a useful index of names and works are included.

Nisbet, H. B. *Herder and the Philosophy and History of Science.* Cambridge, England: Modern Humanities Research Association, 1970. A detailed consideration of Herder's place in the history of the social, biological, and physical sciences. Nisbet argues that far from subscribing to Johann Hamann's antiscientific irrationalism, Herder affirmed the value of science in human history. Extensive bibliography on the subject, including works in German and English.

Schick, Edgar B. *Metaphorical Organicism in Herder's Early Works: A Study of the Relation of Herder's Literary Idiom to His World-View.* The Hague: Mouton, 1971. A focused study of Herder's essays up to 1778 showing metaphors of organicism as central to an understanding of the work. Schick applies his thesis to Herder's writings on language, aesthetics, literary criticism, and historical development, concluding with an assessment of the conservative and innovative elements in Herder's organicist thought.

Susan L. Piepke

ALEKSANDR HERZEN

Born: April 6, 1812; Moscow, Russia
Died: January 21, 1870; Paris, France
Areas of Achievement: Social reform and literature
Contribution: As one of the "fathers" of the Russian intelligentsia, Herzen urged an increased pace of Westernization for Russia, yet harbored a Slavophile attraction for the village commune. From his offices in London, he edited the influential émigré newspaper *Kolokol* (the bell) from 1857 to 1866, thereby helping to shape the direction of Russian radical opinion.

Early Life

Aleksandr Herzen was the illegitimate son of Ivan Alekseyevich Yakovlev, of a distinguished aristocratic family, and of Louise Ivanovich Haag, a German daughter of a minor official from Württemberg. The name "Herzen" was given him by his father to indicate that he was the product of matters of the "heart," as was his elder and also illegitimate brother, Yegor Herzen.

In the family home on Arbat Street in Moscow, young Herzen was isolated from many children, but he developed a close friendship with Nikolay Ogaryov, with whom he developed a lifelong partnership. Attracted to the Romanticism of Friedrich Schiller, the two boys took an oath to avenge the five Decembrist rebels executed by Czar Nicholas I after the abortive uprising of 1825. Both entered the University of Moscow in 1829, and Herzen joined the department of natural sciences. At the university, he also acquired a deep interest in history, philosophy, and politics. His circle of friends included Ogaryov, Nikolai Satin, Vadim Passek, Nikolai Kh. Ketscher, and Anton Savich. These friends reflected a popular mystical bent for politics, and they avidly read the works of Friedrich Schelling and Saint-Simon, espousing the radical democracy of brotherly love, idealism, and even socialism. In 1834, following a critical remark about the czar which was reported to the police, Herzen was arrested, jailed for nearly a year, and exiled to Perm and Viatka.

Life's Work

In 1838, after three years in exile, he married Natalya Alexandrovna Zakharina in Vladimir, and the next year they had a son, Aleksandr, Herzen's only surviving male heir. The czar pardoned Herzen in 1839, and he entered state service in Novgorod, partly to qualify for noble status and partly to acquire the rights of inheritance. His work caused him to travel often to St. Petersburg, where he quarreled with Vissarion Grigoryevich Belinsky over the ideas of Georg Wilhelm Friedrich Hegel. Ironically, Belinsky abandoned Hegelian thought shortly before Herzen's own conversion to that system. Herzen won the admiration of Belinsky, however, when he published two installments of his early memoirs, *Zapiski odnogo molodogo cheloveka* (1840-1841; notebooks of a certain young man).

In 1840, Herzen again ran afoul of the authorities and was arrested, only to be released owing to his wife's illness. It was about this time that he rejected his wife's religious inspiration for Hegel's more radical thought, blaming police harassment for his wife's new illness and the subsequent death of their second child. He abandoned the Idealism of Schelling for the realism of Hegel and a materialist worldview; hence, he was regarded as a Left-Hegelian. He wrote *Diletantizm v nauke* (1843; dilettantism and science), an essay reflecting his new radicalism. His newfound hostility toward religion and all officialdom caused difficulties with his wife.

From 1842 to 1846, Herzen formed a new circle of friends in Moscow, including Ketscher, Satin, Vasily Petrovich Botkin, E. F. Korsh, Timofei Granovski, Mikhail Shchepkin, and Konstantin Kavelin. Belinsky and his St. Petersburg friends were sometimes in attendance. Although an avowed admirer of Western socialist thought, Herzen was increasingly attracted to the Russian peasant and the commune, central to the thought of the Slavophile community. The Slavophile attraction to religion and disdain for the West kept Herzen from entering their circles. In 1845-1846, Herzen published *Pisma ob izuchenii prirody* (letters on the study of nature), which combined his interest in science and philosophy.

In 1846, Herzen inherited a substantial fortune from his father, including a Moscow house and 500,000 rubles. That same year, he left Russia, never to return. His wife, his three children, his valet, and two of his friends escorted him to the West. The year of his departure, he published a novel, *Kto vinovat?* (1845-1846; *Who Is to Blame?*, 1978), in which he paid his homage to George Sand and the women's movement. In Europe, Herzen read deeply the socialist literature of Louis Blanc, Charles Fourier, and Pierre-Joseph Proudhon. There followed *Pisma iz Frantsii i Italii* (1854; letters from France and Italy), *Vom andern Ufer* (1850; *From the Other Shore*, 1956), "Lettre à M. Jules Michelet" (1851), and "Lettre d'un Russe à Mazzini" (1849). These works reflected his pessimistic reactions to the revolutions in Europe two years earlier; he concluded that western institutions were fatally ill.

His commitments to socialism and atheism made life difficult for his wife, Natalya, whose own affair with the German poet Georg Herwegh led to a crisis in the marriage. Shortly after the couple's reconciliation in 1851, their deaf-mute son, Nicholas, and Herzen's own mother died in a boating accident in the Mediterranean Sea. On May 2, 1852, his wife died after giving birth to a stillborn child.

In 1852, Herzen left for England, where he lived for the next eleven years. There he worked on his *Byloe i Dumy* (1861-1867; *My Past and Thoughts: The Memoirs of Alexander Herzen*, 1924-1927). In London, Herzen also founded a journal, *Poliarnaia zvezda* (the polar star), which was founded in the year that Nicholas died and on the exact anniversary of the rebellion of the five Decembrists, whose pictures were in the first issue. He wrote a public letter to the new czar, Alexander II, giving him advice on the need for freedom for his people.

During these years, Herzen's home in London was a haven for Russian revolutionaries. There, Herzen carried on a vigorous dispute with his boyhood friend Mikhail Bakunin. With the visiting Ogaryov, he launched his newspaper *Kolokol* (the bell). It was Ogaryov who suggested the title, reminiscent of the assembly bell of the Novgorodian republic which Grand Prince Ivan III removed, an action symbolically destroying the freedom of that community in the fifteenth century. The paper was extremely popular for eight years in Russia, where it was distributed bimonthly, despite the interference of the security police. Throughout this period, Herzen campaigned for the emancipation of the serfs, relief from government censorship, elimination of corporal punishment, and establishment of legal due process.

Despite his disappointment with the terms of the emancipation edict in 1861, Herzen's revolutionary radicalism was muted, since he began to doubt the efficacy of violence. Younger radicals were drifting to the more uncompromising positions of Nikolay Chernyshevsky, depicted often as the leader of the "sons" among the intelligentsia. Fearing loss of influence among the young radicals, Herzen was persuaded by Bakunin to support the Polish rebels in 1863, thereby risking the loss of many moderate liberals in Russia. By then Herzen seemed to have resolved his ambivalence toward revolution and to have approved the new radical party, Land and Freedom. When the expected peasant uprisings failed to occur, Herzen was left without his former supporters.

Meanwhile, complications arose in his personal life. Ogaryov's wife, Natalya, arrived in London in 1856, and she and Herzen began an affair that resulted in a daughter, born in 1858, and in twin boys two years later. Strangely enough he and Ogaryov remained close friends. Four years later, the twins died of diphtheria in Paris. In 1865, Herzen moved his paper and journal to Geneva, but publication ceased two years later. When the radicals of Sergey Gennadiyevich Nechayev attempted to enlist Herzen's support in new conspiracies, he was wise enough to resist. Ogaryov, however, used his portion of the fund from *Kolokol* to aid the new movement in 1869. That year, Herzen first began to mention to Ogaryov his desire to return home, and he wrote to Bakunin expressing new reservations about violent revolt. On January 21, 1870, however, after a short illness, Herzen died in Paris. His remains were later removed to Nice.

Summary

Through *Kolokol*, Aleksandr Herzen gave advice to czar and radical alike.

Influenced by German philosophy and French socialism, he belonged to those educated Russians who looked upon their own nation as backward. As Herzen grew older, however, he strengthened his belief in the values of the Russian peasant and his unique village commune. He viewed the Russian peasant not as a backward and embarrassing example of Russian culture but as an exemplar of moral purity. Observing the seamier side of Western industrialism and capitalism, Herzen, like the Slavophiles, saw an opportunity to build socialism in Russia with the peasantry. By avoiding industrial capitalism, Russia could catch up with and even surpass Western Europe. The village commune offered a romantic alternative to, and an escape route from, the urban degradation that marked so many European cities of his day.

Unlike his younger colleagues, Herzen saw hope in political reform. He once addressed the czar as a true populist and a benevolent father. When the emancipation came for the serfs, he was disappointed by the terms of the edict but nevertheless recognized that the government had moved in a liberal direction and that further reforms were to be expected. He reproached those who refused to see anything positive in the state reform. To Herzen, they were more interested in revolution as an end in itself than they were in bettering society. To the younger radicals, however, Herzen was a haughty nobleman offering advice to his servants.

If Herzen typified the fathers, Chernyshevsky typified the sons. This split among the intelligentsia of the 1860's was best described by the writer Ivan Turgenev in his novel *Ottsy i deti* (1862; *Fathers and Sons*, 1867). How understandable that Leo Tolstoy the famed pacifist novelist deplored the decline of Herzen's influence since his influence was the last opportunity for radicalism to avoid terror and bloodshed. Yet his ambivalent attitude toward revolution enabled liberals, radicals, and Marxists to claim his support. What was not ambivalent was his constant defense of the dignity and freedom of the individual.

Bibliography
Acton, Edward. *Alexander Herzen and the Role of the Intellectual Revolutionary.* Cambridge: Cambridge University Press, 1979. Stresses the era of 1847-1863, when Herzen struggled with the concept of revolution. The author's biographical approach shows the interaction between Herzen's personal life and his career.
Gershenzon, M. O. *A History of Young Russia.* Translated by James P. Scanlon. Irvine, Calif.: Charles Schlacks, Jr., 1986. Although not a single chapter is devoted to Herzen, this paper edition remains a brilliant mine of ideas and information about him. The chapters on Ogaryov and others reveal different sides of Herzen.
Herzen, Aleksandr. *My Past and Thoughts: The Memoirs of Alexander Herzen.* Translated by Constance Garnett. New York: Alfred A. Knopf, 1973.

Still the best source not only for Herzen but also for all members of his circle. Beautifully translated and rendered enjoyable to read in a single volume.

Malia, Martin. *Alexander Herzen and the Birth of Russian Socialism, 1812-1855.* Cambridge, Mass.: Harvard University Press, 1961. The principal study of Herzen, treating his career up to the death of Nicholas. Malia seeks to explain why the basis for Russian socialism was laid in an era without an industrial working class.

Pomper, Philip. *The Russian Revolutionary Intelligentsia.* New York: Thomas Y. Crowell, 1970. This short survey focuses on the principle that ideologies are as much traced to individual personalities as they are to ideas.

Ulam, Adam B. *In the Name of the People: Prophets and Conspirators in Prerevolutionary Russia.* New York: Viking Press, 1977. A fascinating account of nineteenth century radicals. Ulam sees the turning point in the conspiratorial caste of mind that was fashioned in the early 1860's.

Walicki, Andrzej. "Alexander Herzen's Russian Socialism." In *The Slavophile Controversy: History of the Conservative Utopia in Nineteenth Century Russian Thought.* Oxford, England: Clarendon Press, 1975. Walicki describes how Herzen merged the utopias of the Slavophiles and the Western liberals. He shows Herzen's faith in the future of Russia despite his frequent bouts with disillusionment.

John D. Windhausen

THEODOR HERZL

Born: May 2, 1860; Pest, Hungary
Died: July 3, 1904; Edlach, Austria
Areas of Achievement: Diplomacy and journalism
Contribution: Often called the "father of modern Zionism," Herzl expounded on the need for a Jewish homeland and created an effective organizational framework for this political movement. His diplomatic missions to secure a Jewish state lent worldwide credibility to early Zionism.

Early Life

Theodor Herzl was born to a Jewish family which, like so many others of the era, diplayed confused notions about its cultural heritage. His grandfather, Simon Loeb Herzl, adhered to traditional religious observance, while his two brothers converted to Christianity. A successful businessman and banker, Theodor's father, Jacob, hewed a middle line: He remained a culturally assimilated Jew. As the young Herzl approached his thirteenth year, his parents announced a "confirmation" rather than a "bar mitzvah." Thus, Theodor made the passage into Jewish manhood.

The city of Pest (which merged with Buda in 1872 to become Budapest) similarly polarized its residents into either the Hungarian or the German cultural camp. Nationalism was only beginning to stir Europe. With a respect for what she deemed the more refined and cosmopolitan culture, Jeannette Herzl inculcated in her son a love of German language and literature.

Herzl began his formal education at the age of six, attending a bilingual (German and Hungarian) parochial school, the Israelitische Normalhauptschule. In 1869, he moved to a municipal technical institute, where he could pursue his alleged proclivities for the sciences. During the course of four years, however, Herzl found himself only motivated by the humanities. He even initiated and presided over a literary society, an activity which foretold both his journalistic interests and his leadership drive. The anti-Semitic remarks of a teacher finally hastened Herzl's departure from the institute.

After these early educational experiments, the young Herzl at last entered the Evangelical Gymnasium, a nondenominational academy with a largely Jewish student body, which emphasized German culture and classical learning. He proved to be committed to his writing and, while still in secondary school, published a political article in the Viennese weekly, *Leben*, and book reviews for the *Pest Journal*. As Herzl neared graduation, his only sibling, an elder sister, Pauline, died of typhoid fever. The Herzls moved to Vienna one week later. Theodor returned to Budapest in June to complete his examinations, then entered the University of Vienna's law school.

Law school proved to be rather routine, except for one incident. Herzl joined Albia, a fraternity at the University of Vienna. When the organization endorsed a memorial rally—with strong anti-Semitic overtones—for the composer Richard Wagner, Herzl issued a vehement protest letter and offered his resignation. Albia responded by expelling him. Herzl received his law degree in 1884. He was admitted to the Vienna bar and subsequently worked for criminal and civil courts. A year after commencing his legal practice, he left law altogether, finally choosing a writer's life.

Perhaps Herzl most vigorously aspired to be a playwright. Though one of his works made it to the German-language stage in New York, critics generally judged his plays mediocre. He achieved far greater success writing *feuilletons*, observations of the various people, places, and characteristics defining late nineteenth century life. Summer travels, heavily subsidized by the elder Herzls, also yielded articles for the vaunted *Neue Freie Presse*. With his career advancing, Herzl married Julie Naschauer, an attractive young woman from a prosperous Jewish family. The union was to produce three children—and numerous difficulties. Thought to have had emotional problems, Julie probably also clashed with her domineering mother-in-law. Herzl's prolonged absences only exacerbated the situation.

Life's Work

Herzl, now married and in his thirties, received a professional assignment which, in its own way, was to change his life. October, 1891, brought a telegram from the *Neue Freie Presse*: The paper's editors wanted Herzl to serve as Paris correspondent. For the rest of his days, he remained affiliated with the journal. Herzl's locus, Paris, stood at the nucleus of late nineteenth century culture, and the writer developed from a *feuilletonist* into a journalist. With the trial of Captain Alfred Dreyfus, however, he also added a new element to his restless personality.

Dreyfus, a Jew, had been accused by the French government of treason. Perhaps the most egregious aspect of the 1894 trial was the virulent, far-flung anti-Semitism which it invoked. True to journalistic ethics, Herzl did not debate Dreyfus' guilt or innocence; rather, he reported on the less-than-humane treatment meted out to the captain in this most civilized of Western European nations. As a result of the Dreyfus trial and a resurgence of anti-Semitism across the continent, Jewish issues emerged in Herzl's writings, thoughts, and most important, actions. Mid-1895 marked the initiation of his Zionist career.

Preparing for visits with millionaire Jewish philanthropists Baron Moritz Hirsch and members of the Rothschild family, Herzl crystallized and committed to paper his developing ideas about a Jewish state. The meetings did not go well. As some scholars note, the philanthropists dwelled on charity; Herzl instead pondered nationhood as a self-help mechanism for the Jewish people. The notes which Herzl prepared for these visits, however, subsequently appeared in a revised, printed form. *Der Judenstaat* (1896; *A Jewish*

State, 1896) became both the inspiration of and the primer for a fledgling Zionist movement.

Herzl's booklet identified Jews as a people, rather than merely as a religious group. Moreover, it indicated that the absence of a homeland denied Jews the status enjoyed by other nations. Even those attracted to the more tolerant Western European countries, for example, could only assimilate and advance to a certain point before their increasing numbers and greater visibility would provoke anti-Semitism. Eastern European Jews lived in a constant state of racially based poverty and repression. Herzl concluded that statehood would "liberate the world by our freedom" and allow Jews—both individually and collectively—to realize higher goals.

These themes were not new, but Herzl added articulation and administrative structure to them. Small, loosely organized groups, *Hoveve Zion*, already had initiated isolated migrations to Palestine. Herzl argued, however, that without the existence of an autonomous state, a Jewish presence could easily kindle anti-Semitism. In order to advance nationhood, *A Jewish State* proposed a political/moral "Society of Jews" and a "Jewish Company," capable of conducting economic activities and land acquisition. Herzl suggested both Palestine and sparsely populated, fertile Argentina as possible sites for the homeland.

Reactions to *A Jewish State* varied. Comfortable Western European Jews believed that they had been granted adequate civil liberties and that Herzl's concept of nationhood might only raise anti-Semitic furor. Much to their discomfort, "Jewish unity" also linked them with their impoverished, ill-educated brethren in Russia and other countries. Yet Herzl did find an audience. His backers included intellectuals, students, and many Eastern European Jews for whom assimilation proved impossible and for whom misery was a way of life. With increasing fervor and occasional encouragement, he commenced publication of *Die Welt* (the world), the movement's premier communications vehicle. Supporters also urged their leader to organize a world conference in Basel, Switzerland. On August 29, 1897, the first Zionist Congress met, attracting 197 delegates. An organizational statement was adopted, membership goals and fees set, and a committee structure devised. A total of six Zionist conferences would convene during Herzl's lifetime. Each drew more delegates, media participation, and, sometimes, controversy.

In the interim, Herzl traveled through Europe, seeking diplomatic support for an automonous Jewish state. He financed his own trips, just as he underwrote the publication of *Die Welt*. The money came from his salary; by late 1895, the *Neue Freie Presse* had promoted him to literary editor. Journalistic renown may have opened diplomatic doors, but Herzl's demeanor won for him converts among heads of state. He was an impeccable dresser; his proud stance and trim profile added greatly to his five-foot, eight-inch frame. Yet the perfect manners and piercing, dark good looks belied ill health. Maintaining a demanding job, filling every spare minute with political activity, and balancing family finances with those of his organization slowly weakened an already ailing heart.

If Herzl was to grow weary by the failure actually to procure a Jewish homeland, his persistence lent Zionism global credibility. He eventually obtained audiences with the German kaiser Wilhelm II; Russian ministers Count Sergei Yulievich Witte and Vyacheslav Pleve; Pope Pius X; British ministers Neville Chamberlain, David Lloyd George, and Arthur James Balfour; Sultan Abdul Hamid II; and Italian king Victor Emmanuel III. His approach was pragmatic: Sometimes he presented the Jewish state as a neutral, autonomous buffer in a region which would change radically after the inevitable collapse of the Ottoman Turkish Empire; on other occasions, he suggested that Zionism might help European countries alleviate "Jewish problems," anti-Semitic hatred, and the internal discord it evoked. Diplomatic efforts, however, were directed mainly at Turkey and England. The former was a rapidly deteriorating power, with a huge territory to administer and an equally large foreign debt. Turkey also held Palestine.

The Jewish Colonial Trust had been established by the second Zionist Congress for the purpose of generating funds to purchase land. Now Herzl sought an acquisition. He told the sultan that a sale of Palestine would boost the sagging Turkish economy. Furthermore, the Jewish settlers would bring new commerce to the empire and remain faithful to the Ottomans in the face of adversaries. However appealing the financial aid, Turkey refused to grant the Zionists a fair measure of autonomy. Negotiations broke in 1902.

Great Britain, on the other hand, had internal problems. With a reputation for political tolerance, it attracted Eastern European Jews fleeing repression. British leaders became concerned about limited jobs and other domestic issues; they sought to restrict Jewish immigration. While the debate proceeded, the British offered Herzl El Arish, in the Sinai peninsula, but irrigation and other problems barred the agreement. Then, in the wake of the Kishinev pogrom, which killed forty-five Jews and precipitated an outpouring of worldwide sympathy, the British suggested a Zionist charter for Uganda.

Herzl took the proposal to the sixth Zionist Congress in 1903. He explained that East Africa merely represented an interim step to Palestine. The congress voted, narrowly, to send a delegation to Uganda, but the powerful Russian delegation—fresh from the Kishinev pogrom—refused to accept anything resembling a territorial substitute and stormed out of the session. The Russian group presented Herzl with a leadership ultimatum several months later. Tremendously hurt, he nevertheless proved somewhat successful in ending the dispute. Herzl also continued on his diplomatic missions until halted by a severe heart attack in May, 1904. Ordered to rest, he became more sedentary but constantly accepted work and visits from his supporters. Pneumonia set in, further aggravating his heart condition. Herzl died on July 3, 1904, at the resort of Edlach, Austria. His remains were moved to the new State of Israel in 1949.

Summary

Theodor Herzl came to his mission relatively unaware of contemporary Zionist philosophy or Jewish issues in general. Yet he left many astute prophecies. Following the first Zionist Congress, he wrote, ". . . I founded the Jewish State. If I were to say this today, I would be met by universal laughter. In five years, perhaps, and certainly in fifty, everyone will see it." Israel came into being fifty years and three months after Herzl committed these visions to his diary. The connection, however, is far more direct. While the Uganda episode almost divided the fledgling Zionist movement and hastened Herzl's own death, it enabled him to establish relations with Lloyd George and Balfour, two British leaders responsible for the 1917 Balfour Declaration mandating Jewish settlement in Palestine.

Herzl's novel *Altneuland* (1902; *Old-new Land*, 1941) introduces the reader to a utopian state, circa 1923. The book describes conditions which were to inspire Israel's settlers: a desolate land transformed through agricultural technology; modern, gleaming cities; and a progressive social system. Most telling, however, the title page bears an inscription: "If you will it, it is no dream."

Bibliography

Bien, Alex. *Theodore Herzl*. Translated by Maurice Samuels. Philadelphia: Jewish Publication Society of America, 1945. This sympathetic general biography views Herzl as an exemplary, independent, and selfless leader whose Zionist organization strongly advanced democratic participation while abiding by an ordered structure. Contains a good bibliography, though many additional sources subsequently have been published.

Elon, Amos. *Herzl*. New York: Holt, Rinehart and Winston, 1975. Drawing heavily on archival material made accessible since the release of Bien's work, this book presents Herzl, the sensitive journalist, sometime playwright, and driven activist, who infused a sense of drama into statecraft.

Herzl, Theodor. *Theodor Herzl: A Portrait for This Age*. Edited by Ludwig Lewisohn. Cleveland: World Publishing, 1955. The book uses Herzl's own writings to show the personal conflicts behind the Zionist leader. An interesting psychological study, employing historical analysis and assessment of the subject's literary career.

Lacquer, Walter. *A History of Zionism*. New York: Schocken Books, 1972. Perhaps the most authoritative source on Zionism. Lacquer devotes fifty pages exclusively to Herzl. Excellent chronological overview of the sub-

ject's politics, diplomatic efforts, and organizational endeavors, with a
fine summary of *A Jewish State*, his most influential work. The book
includes a concise, useful bibliography, a glossary, and six maps.

Neumann, Emanuel. *Theodor Herzl: The Birth of Jewish Statesmanship*.
New York: Herzl Press, 1960. Unfailingly sympathetic in its depiction of
Herzl, this brief work proves most valuable when discussing the philosophical differences between the practical Zionists, seeking colonization
or infiltration into Palestine, and the political Zionists, who focused their
efforts on securing an independent, autonomous homeland. Contains a
timetable.

Patai, Raphael, ed. *Herzl Year Book*. Vol. 3. New York: Herzl Press, 1960.
Twenty-one scholars address little-known aspects of Herzl's life, gather
reminiscences, argue the merits of his political and diplomatic involvements, and reflect upon his legacies. Part of a six-volume set, this collection is designed for those who want to research more specific Herzelian
issues.

Lynn C. Kronzek

JOHANN LUCAS VON HILDEBRANDT

Born: November 14, 1668; Genoa
Died: November 16, 1745; Vienna, Austria
Area of Achievement: Architecture
Contribution: One of the supreme architects of the Austrian Baroque, Hildebrandt specialized in the design and construction of palaces and pleasure gardens for the Austrian and German nobility. His finest achievement was the Belvedere Palace, built for Prince Eugene in Vienna.

Early Life

Johann Lucas von Hildebrandt was one of several Austrian artists (despite the fact that he was born in Genoa, where his parents were then living), who, in reaction to the almost universal employment of Italian architects, decorators, and painters by both secular and ecclesiastical patrons in the Habsburg Empire, developed a distinctly Austrian version of the Baroque. This has come to be known as the *Kaiserstil*, or Imperial Style, because it was associated with the Habsburg dynasty and with the rebuilding of Vienna as an imperial capital in the late seventeenth and early eighteenth centuries.

Hildebrandt was born in 1668 in Genoa to a German captain who served first in the Genoese and then in the imperial army. His mother is presumed to have been Italian. In Italy, the young Hildebrandt studied architecture, city planning, and engineering, and for a time was a student of Carlo Fontana. Besides being much influenced by Fontana, Hildebrandt was also greatly impressed by Guarino Guarini, who was associated with Turin, a city where Hildebrandt may have spent some of his early years. By the 1690's, Hildebrandt was earning his living as a military engineer with the imperial army, and it was in this capacity that he attracted the attention of Prince Eugene of Savoy, with whom he campaigned in northern Italy in 1695-1696.

It was probably with Prince Eugene's encouragement that Hildebrandt left the army to pursue the career of a professional architect. He reached Vienna in 1697, and within a year, presumably on Prince Eugene's recommendation, he was appointed an imperial councillor and, in 1700, a court architect. By that date, however, the imperial family had already bestowed their architectural favors upon Johann Fischer von Erlach, and following the latter's death in 1723 they transferred their loyalty as patrons to his son, Joseph Emanuel Fischer von Erlach. In part because of the intense rivalry between Hildebrandt and the Fischer von Erlachs, the former received few commissions from the Habsburgs, although he received a lifelong salary from the court and was ennobled in 1720.

Soon after his arrival in Vienna in 1697, Hildebrandt received his first commission, to build a garden palace in the suburbs for Count Heinrich Franz Mansfeld-Fondi. Drawing upon his extensive knowledge of both Ital-

ian and French architecture and landscaping, he developed a striking design
for a residence at the lower end of a slope, a triangular-shaped piece of
property off the Rennweg which would rise from the residence in a series of
terraces. He continued to work on this first project while other commissions
were raining upon him thick and fast, but it was not completed at the time of
the count's death in 1715. The next purchaser of the still-unfinished residence turned it over to Fischer von Erlach for completion. Thus, it is from
the original plans rather than from the present structure that Hildebrandt's
intentions can best be gauged. No doubt he must have resented having to
hand this project over to his rival, but by this time he was fully occupied
elsewhere, particularly on behalf of Prince Eugene, now the emperor's greatest subject in his various roles as commander-in-chief, governor in absentia
of the Spanish Netherlands, and a prince of the ruling house of Savoy.

It seems that Prince Eugene's first commission for his young protégé was
to enlarge his town house and official residence, built for him by Fischer von
Erlach on the Himmelpfortgasse. There is no evidence of a quarrel between
Prince Eugene and Fischer von Erlach, but from 1701 onward it was to
Hildebrandt that the prince turned for all major architectural commissions.
Meanwhile, the prince had purchased the island of Czepel on the Danube
River below Budapest and had instructed Hildebrandt to design a summer
retreat there at the village of Ráckeve. The architect drew up plans for a
single-story, three-sided structure with a cupola and proceeded with its construction, but despite the idyllic rustic setting Prince Eugene lost interest in
the project, perhaps as a result of the Hungarian uprising under Ferenc
Rákóczi between 1703 and 1709, and he is only recorded as having visited it
once, in 1717. By then, however, Hildebrandt had already embarked upon
the building of what would eventually be his masterpiece.

Life's Work

By this time, it had become the fashion for the nobles of the empire to
build, in addition to their town palaces within the cramped confines of the
old city and their country palaces on their estates, garden palaces in the
suburbs of Vienna. Such had been the Mansfeld-Fondi Palace, which had
been Hildebrandt's first commission. Since 1693, Prince Eugene had been
buying plots of land off the Rennweg, which were now consolidated into an
extended triangle of land on which he planned to build for himself a sumptuous residence. The architect was to be Hildebrandt, but, to perhaps an even
greater extent than with most patrons of this period, the prince had definite
ideas about what he wanted. The first part of the complex to be completed
(between 1714 and 1716) was the elegant Lower Belvedere, intended to
house the prince's paintings (Prince Eugene was one of the greatest collectors and connoisseurs of the age). The rooms opened directly onto the garden, which swept upward to where, between 1721 and 1725, the much more

elaborate Upper Belvedere was erected. Both prince and architect conceived of the landscaping in the grandest terms, and a French pupil of the great André Le Nôtre, Dominique Girard, was brought from Munich to assist in the work. The Upper Belvedere provided the setting for Prince Eugene's almost regal entertainments. "The Belvedere," the art critic Anthony Blunt has written, "is Hildebrandt's supreme achievement and shows him at the height of his powers, finally in possession of an idiom wholly his own." Not that Hildebrandt's work for the prince ended there. In 1725, just when the Upper Belvedere was nearing completion, Prince Eugene purchased a dilapidated property, known as Schlosshof, on the river March to serve as a country palace where he could entertain guests with hunting and *fêtes champêtres*. Between 1725 and 1732, Hildebrandt added two new wings to the old seventeenth century palace and laid out gardens of exquisite beauty and originality. Unfortunately, little remains of the palace, apart from the plans, to indicate what Schlosshof was originally like.

Throughout the years when Hildebrandt was occupied with these major undertakings for Prince Eugene, there was no lack of commissions from other members of the Viennese nobility, although frequently he handed over projects for completion to his deputy, the master mason, Franz Jänggle. Prince Eugene had never attempted to monopolize Hildebrandt's time or talent, and in addition to his friendship with the prince, the architect established a close connection with the powerful ecclesiastical dynasty of the Schönborns. In 1705, Friedrich Carl von Schönborn was appointed vice-chancellor of the empire, a post which he held until 1734, by which time he was also Prince-Bishop of Bamberg and Würzburg. The vice-chancellor had a passion for building which amounted to an obsession. He greatly admired Hildebrandt, enjoyed his company, and consulted him on matters of architecture, decoration, and furnishings for the best part of four decades, an extraordinary example of an enduring friendship between patron and artist. In 1705, Hildebrandt began building a magnificent garden palace for the vice-chancellor in the suburbs, and although neither palace nor garden survive in their original form the plans suggest that this may have been one of the most original exercises in landscaping of the period. Then, in 1710, Schönborn purchased an estate at Göllersdorf in the country to the north of Vienna, and from 1712 Hildebrandt worked intermittently on restoring the former palace, enlarging it, and laying out the gardens.

Meanwhile, during the period when Schönborn was acquiring Göllersdorf, his uncle, Lothar Franz von Schönborn, imperial chancellor, Electoral-Archbishop of Mainz, and Prince-Bishop of Bamberg, decided to build for himself a palace at Pommersfelden in the country a few miles outside Bamberg. For the overall design, he sought the services of Johann Dientzenhofer, whose work included the cathedral at Fulda, the Benedictine Abbey at Banz, and the design for the Neumünster at Würzburg. In addition, he engaged

Hildebrandt, perhaps at the urging of his nephew, and also the court architect from Mainz, Maximilian von Welsch, who had been involved with Hildebrandt at Göllersdorf and who would work with him again at the Würzburg Residenz. Johann Michael Rottmayr was summoned to paint the ceiling of the spectacular *Marmorsaal*. In the end, Hildebrandt's contribution to Pommersfelden was relatively small, but it was to be of outstanding quality: He was responsible for the central staircase, built between 1713 and 1715. In an age when the *Treppenhaus* (an entrance hall with a double staircase) often provided the focus for an entire palace, Hildebrandt's creation at Pommersfelden was without equal, including his own later staircases at Schloss Mirabell and Göttweig.

In 1719, Johann Philipp Franz von Schönborn, brother of Friedrich Carl, became Prince-Bishop of Würzburg and immediately began to plan a city residence for himself as an alternative to the former episcopal castle across the river. Characteristic of the Schönborns as patrons, he involved more than one architect in the project. Baltasar Neumann, who, like Hildebrandt, had been trained originally as a military engineer, was to have overall responsibility, but Hildebrandt, von Welsch, and Dientzenhofer were all involved at one time or another, along with several others. There seems to have been considerable friction between Hildebrandt and Neumann; in the end, Neumann's ideas prevailed, and it is uncertain how much of the Residenz is Hildebrandt's work, although certainly the Hofkapelle contains features by both men. When, in 1743, engravings of the Residenz were published, attributing the achievement to Neumann, Hildebrandt wrote bitterly to Friedrich Carl von Schönborn, "It grieves me very much, that another should parade himself in my clothes."

Although primarily associated with secular commissions, Hildebrandt also designed several ecclesiastical buildings, of which the most important were the Dominican Church of St. Laurence in Gabel (modern Czechoslovakia), built between 1699 and 1711; St. Peter's Church off the Graben in Vienna; and the Piarist Church of Maria-Treu in Vienna. He competed unsuccessfully against Fischer von Erlach to design the Karlskirche (as was to happen again with the rebuilding of the Hofburg), but in 1718 a fire damaged much of the Benedictine Abbey of Göttweig, and its abbot, Gottfried Bessel, a former protégé of Lothar Franz von Schönborn, called upon Hildebrandt for its rebuilding. Encouraged and assisted by Friedrich Carl von Schönborn, the architect immediately began drawing up plans, and although today they only exist on paper, potentially they constituted Hildebrandt's most ambitious undertaking. The immense project proved to be beyond the abbot's means, and between 1724 and 1739 only the north and east wings and a *Treppenhaus* were completed. This stairway, however, ascending to a frescoed vault by Paul Troger, is one of Hildebrandt's finest conceptions and a token of one of the great "might have beens" of architectural history.

Summary

It was Johann Lucas von Hildebrandt's achievement to be able to draw together Italian, French, and native Austrian elements into an architectural synthesis, both dynamic and fluid. As a designer, he demonstrated a tireless virtuosity; as a decorator, inventiveness on the grandest scale, combined with close attention to detail. These qualities are perhaps most conspicuously displayed in his celebrated stairways: at the Upper Belvedere, Schloss Mirabell, Pommersfelden, and Göttweig. The Belvedere is almost the only surviving monument to his extraordinary gifts for combining architecture and landscaping as a single art form. Many of his projects were left unfinished, were modified by others, or have been allowed to fall into decay. His magnificent plans and drawings, preserved in the Hofbibliothek, most of them never undertaken or abandoned before completion, are reminders of the constraints imposed upon even the most successful artists by changing circumstances or the whims of a patron.

Yet Hildebrandt was exceptionally fortunate in his patrons. Prince Eugene and the Schönborns were enlightened and discriminating men, well able to appreciate the ideas and suggestions of an employee whom they respected as an artist and, in some sense, treated as a friend. It must have helped that Hildebrandt seems to have possessed an equitable temperament and obliging, courtly manners, notwithstanding the odd flash of temper and an enthusiasm for the grandiose which led extravagant spenders into even greater extravagance. His relations with his patrons were surely very different from the dealings of the scholarly, withdrawn Fischer von Erlach with his dour Habsburg masters.

Inevitably, the two rivals invite comparison: Fischer von Erlach, Roman and academic; Hildebrandt, the creator of an architecture of fantasy and enchantment. Yet, as Victor L. Tapié has expressed it, "Fischer von Erlach and Hildebrandt are complementary, and one is inevitably reminded of Bernini and Borromini, for here again are two artists with incompatible genius both working at the same time to beautify and transform a capital city."

Bibliography

Blunt, Anthony, et al. *Baroque and Rococo Architecture and Decoration.* New York: Harper & Row, 1978. This is a sumptuously produced volume, with beautiful illustrations, which while doing full justice to the Austrian Baroque, places it clearly in a broader European perspective. Strongly recommended.

Grimschitz, Bruno. *Johann Lucas von Hildebrandt.* Vienna, Austria: Herold, 1959. This remains the definitive monograph on the architect, though it is available only in German.

Hempel, Eberhard. *Baroque Art and Architecture in Central Europe.* Translated by Elisabeth Hempel and Marguerite Kay. Baltimore: Penguin

Books, 1965. A volume in the Pelican History of Art series, this is the standard work in English on Austrian and German Baroque.

Henderson, Nicholas. *Prince Eugene of Savoy.* London: Weidenfeld & Nicolson, 1964. An excellent general biography of the prince, emphasizing his role as a patron as well as a military commander. Hildebrandt's commissions are discussed.

McKay, Derek. *Prince Eugene of Savoy.* London: Thames & Hudson, 1977. This biography places emphasis upon the prince as a statesman. Chapter 20, however, deals with him as a patron and discusses Hildebrandt.

Norberg-Schulz, Christian. *Late Baroque and Rococo Architecture.* New York: Harry N. Abrams, 1974. An outstanding survey of the subject, this book gives due weight to Hildebrandt's originality and his contribution. Excellently illustrated with photographs and ground plans.

Powell, Nicolas. *From Baroque to Rococo: An Introduction to Austrian and German Architecture from 1580 to 1790.* London: Faber & Faber, 1959. A literate and perceptive general introduction to the subject. Good for beginners.

Sitwell, Sacheverell, ed. *Great Houses of Europe.* New York: G. P. Putnam's Sons, 1961. This anthology on European palaces includes essays by Monk Gibbon on Pommersfelden and the Würzburg Residenz, both superbly illustrated.

Tapié, Victor L. *The Age of Grandeur: Baroque and Classicism in Europe.* Translated by A. Ross Williamson. London: Weidenfeld & Nicolson, 1960. Virtually an instant classic upon publication, this book provides the best general background to the art and aesthetics of Baroque Europe.

Gavin R. G. Hambly

HIROSHIGE

Born: 1797; Edo, Japan
Died: 1858; Edo, Japan
Area of Achievement: Art
Contribution: Hiroshige was one of the last masters of the *ukiyo-e* woodblock prints in Japan and was famed for his poetic landscapes.

Early Life

Andō Hiroshige was born Andō Tokutarō in 1797 in Edo (modern Tokyo). His father, Andō Gen'emon, was an official of the fire department attached to Edo Castle. Hiroshige's talent for drawing surfaced early; even as a child, he showed an interest in art. First he studied with Okajima Rinsai, a painter and also a fireman, who had been trained in the traditional Kano school of classical Chinese academic painting. Hiroshige's mother died when he was twelve years old and when his father resigned shortly thereafter, Hiroshige was obliged to assume the hereditary duties. Attempting to study with the popular Utagawa Toyokuni, he was turned down; persevering, he managed, however, when he was fourteen, to be accepted as a pupil of the less popular Utagawa Toyohiro.

The following year, he was allowed to use the name "Utagawa Hiroshige," a sign of his promise as an artist. Despite this honor, Hiroshige did not publish until 1818, when book illustrations with the signature Ichiyūsai Hiroshige appeared. When Hiroshige was thirty-one, his master died, but Hiroshige did not take over his name or his studio, as would have been customary for the best pupil to do. About this time, he called himself "Ichiyūsai," then dropped the first character and signed himself simply "Ryusai."

Art historians sometimes divide Hiroshige's artistic career into three stages. In his student days, from 1811 to 1830, he spent his time learning from his predecessors, working on the figure prints of actors and warriors, and, in his mid-twenties, on figure prints of beautiful women. Lessons with Ōoka Umpō taught Hiroshige the Chinese-influenced Nanga style of painting, with its use of calligraphy in depicting landscape. From the Shijō style of painting, Hiroshige learned the art of using ink washes in paintings for a softer effect. His master, Toyohiro, passed on the Western technique of the single-point perspective, which he himself had learned from his teacher, Toyoharu. Hiroshige's early, limited success came from his representation of flowers and birds, sometimes with his own accompanying poem. Prints of these are rarer than his landscapes and are much treasured.

Life's Work

Hiroshige's early work featured sketches of warriors, courtesans, actors, and other subjects typical of *ukiyo-e*, the art form which resulted from the political and geographical shift of power from Kyoto, the old capital, to Edo. By the time Hiroshige was born, Edo, a relatively new capital established by the Tokugawa Shogunate, had turned into a populous city with more than one million inhabitants. Because of the complexity of the caste system then prevailing, the change in the capital of the country led to a series of other complex artistic, social, and commercial changes which defined the art form Hiroshige was to master so successfully. The main patrons of the arts in the old capital of Kyoto, the wealthy merchants called *machischū*, refused to be lured by the economic possibilities offered by the new capital, leaving the path open for merchants of a lower class (*chōnin*) to profit from Edo's position as the commercial capital of Japan. Though now successful economically, the lower-class merchants still had no social clout. In search of entertainment, they would seek out the pleasure districts which sprang up outside the city limits and allowed members of different classes to mingle. This "floating world" was composed of the world of the highly trained and respected courtesans in the pleasure districts, and the art form which evolved to record their activities was the *ukiyo-e* woodblock print.

While the staple subject of the *ukiyo-e* print was the varying fashions in hair, dress, customs, and manners of the evanescent world of the pleasure districts, the landscapes of which Hiroshige became a skilled master had always been traditional in Japanese painting, if only as background for the figures in *ukiyo-e* prints.

In the second and most productive stage of his career, from about 1830 to 1844, Hiroshige left the competitive field of figure designs and concentrated on landscapes. His most famous and finest series seemed to be a result of a journey he took around 1832, directly connected to his family tenure. The shogun in Edo, the real seat of power, annually presented horses from his stables to the emperor, secluded in Kyoto. As a minor official of the Shogunate, Hiroshige joined the expedition so as to Kyoto to paint the ceremony of the presentation for the shogun. During the journey, he made several sketches of the Tōkaidō, as the main highway between Edo and Kyoto was called. These sketches were the basis of the first *Tōkaidō Gojūsantsugi* (fifty-three stations of the Tōkaidō), a collection of fifty-five scenes consisting of the fifty-three stations on the highway and one each in Kyoto and Nihonbashi, the beginning and ending of the road. Published separately at first, the complete series was issued as a set in 1834. It brought Hiroshige immediate and enduring fame and success. Over the course of the next twenty-five years, in response to popular demand, Hiroshige designed some twenty additional sets of these views of the Tōkaidō.

Hiroshige's prints were so popular that some of his designs had runs of ten thousand, and he was kept so busy producing a series of prints on Edo, the suburbs, Lake Biwa at Otsu, and Kyoto that he was seldom present to direct the reproduction of his designs. Greedy publishers were responsible for turning out very inferior copies of his designs in their haste to cash in on their popularity, and Hiroshige himself was not consistently good.

The first Tōkaidō series is considered the most original of his landscape series. What distinguished Hiroshige's vision of the highway were his personal and direct reactions to what he saw. Though inspired by the landscape, Hiroshige adapted freely; he changed the seasons or the time of day or added nonexistent features if his sense of composition required it. Unlike the famous Hokusai, Hiroshige was interested in the human drama around him, not merely in the possibility of the design. Thus, his prints are praised for their humorous point of view, their warmth and compassion, and their close observation of the changing atmospheric conditions, their poetic sensitivity to the relationship between man and nature. He is even referred to as master of rain, mist, snow, and wind.

In the third stage of his career, from around 1844 to his death in 1858, Hiroshige became more interested in depicting figures in his landscapes. He worked in collaboration with Utagawa Kunisada, a figure print designer, and Utagawa Kuniyoshi, a designer of historical prints, to produce another Tōkaidō series jointly. Kunisada added the figures to Hiroshige's landscapes; the two also produced several other series. *Meisho Edo Hyakkei* (1856-1858; one hundred views of Edo), which Hiroshige produced at the age of sixty, is particularly remarkable for the interesting points of view and the placement of the figures in the landscape.

By this time, Commodore Matthew Perry and the U.S. fleet had intruded upon the closed Japanese society. Japan's opening its market to world trade brought the end of the feudal Tokugawa era and the way of life reflected in the *ukiyo-e* prints. With the passing of Hiroshige, who probably died in the great cholera epidemic in 1858, went the world he had recorded with such wit and warmth.

Because popular artists were not deemed worthy of official records, relatively little is known of Hiroshige's personal life. Such skimpy details as are known suggest a life of personal sorrows. Not only was Hiroshige orphaned as a teenager but also his family had to be rebuilt. He was married twice, once to Tatsu, the widow of a samurai, by whom he had one son, Nakajiro; his wife died in 1840, his son in 1845. Hiroshige's second wife, Yasu, was twenty years younger. His small government pension kept Hiroshige from starving, but he was hardly ever a wealthy man.

Despite these personal setbacks, Hiroshige was a fun-loving man who was enormously productive as an artist. It is estimated, for example, that Hiroshige designed eight thousand woodcuts and that more than forty publishers were involved in publishing his designs. He was also enormously popular in his day, once receiving a commission from thirty innkeepers who wanted prints of their winehouses to present as souvenirs to their guests.

Summary

The last major figure in the development of *ukiyo-e*, Hiroshige is inextricably linked with Hokusai in historical reputation. Hiroshige was the more melancholy, romantic, and poetic artist, but like most of the great Edo masters of the woodblock print who came from middle-class artisan families, his work, intended for and appealing primarily to bourgeois circles, was not considered fine art until Western artists, particularly the Impressionists, discovered and glorified the woodblock print. The prints of Hokusai and Hiroshige, the last of the masters, were at the time still readily obtainable. The roster of great Western artists influenced by them includes James Whistler, Paul Cézanne, Henri de Toulouse-Lautrec, Paul Gauguin, and Vincent van Gogh.

James Michener, while critizing Hiroshige for his weak designs, his undistinguished drawing, and his lack of focus, accords him the rare talent of an "honest, clean eye." Though many of the Hiroshige prints available are the late copies which do not convey his subtlety, he is probably the most accessible of the *ukiyo-e* artists because, in Michener's words, Hiroshige's inspired eye "can teach an entire nation, or even a substantial segment of the world, to see."

Bibliography

Addiss, Stephen, ed. *Tōkaidō, Adventures on the Road in Old Japan*. Lawrence, Kans.: Spencer Museum of Art, 1980. A collection of essays about the Tōkaidō, including chapters on Hiroshige's humor and his Tōkaidō prints in the context of traditional Japanese painting.

Andō, Hiroshige. *The Fifty-three Stages of Tōkaidō*. Edited by Ichitaro Kondo. English adaptation by Charles S. Terry. Tokyo, Japan: Nippon Express, 1960. A brief introduction to Hiroshige's most popular series. Each print is accompanied by text in English and Japanese.

_____. *Hiroshige*. Edited by Walter Exner. London: Methuen, 1960. An oversized book, with large-print text and color plates throughout. Contains a general introduction to the life and work of Hiroshige, written by the son of the Viennese art dealer who collected Hiroshige's work.

Lane, Richard. *Images from the Floating World: The Japanese Print*. New York: G. P. Putnam's Sons, 1978. Provides historical background, tracing the rise of *ukiyo-e* through the seventeenth and eighteenth centuries. Contains color photographs, a bibliography, an index, and an illustrated dictionary of *ukiyo-e*.

Michener, James A. *The Floating World*. New York: Random House, 1954. Traces the life and death of the art known as *ukiyo-e* through the individual artists who practiced it. Contains sixty-five prints, a chronological table, brief biographies, a bibliography, and an index.

Narazaki, Muneshige. *Studies in Nature: Hokusai-Hiroshige*. Translated by

John Bester. Tokyo, Japan: Kodansha International, 1970. Focuses on the achievements of these two artists in the depiction of flowers and birds, with a brief introduction to the development of the genre.

Whitford, Frank. *Japanese Prints and Western Painters*. New York: Macmillan, 1977. Discusses the influence of Japanese woodblock prints on European painting in the nineteenth century. Contains a chronology, a glossary, a bibliography, an index, and color plates.

Shakuntala Jayaswal

HOKUSAI

Born: 1760; Edo, Japan
Died: 1849; Japan
Area of Achievement: Art
Contribution: A versatile, productive artist, Hokusai was one of the last great masters of the woodblock print.

Early Life

Katsushika Hokusai, a man who changed his name several times during his lifetime, was born Kawamura Tokitarō in Edo (modern Tokyo) in 1760. His family was probably of peasant stock and poor. When he was around four, a prestigious artisan family, the Nakajima, adopted him without, however, making him an heir. Later, Hokusai's own son was made an adopted heir; because of these two events, there is some speculation that Hokusai may have been the son of a Nakajima concubine.

The variety of occupations that characterized Hokusai's later life started early. He probably worked as a clerk in a bookshop and from age fifteen was an apprentice to a woodblock engraver for three years. Then, in 1778, he started his studies with Katsukawa Shunshō, the leading *ukiyo-e* master. The next year, his first publications under the pen name Shunrō appeared. During the twelve years of his apprenticeship with the Shunshō school, Hokusai published in the genre most associated with the school: prints of Kabuki actors, as well as prints of wrestlers, historical landscapes, and illustrations for novels. Among the most prized of his early work are the *surimono*, the delicate, high-quality prints issued in limited quantities and used as greeting cards or announcements by a small group of aesthetes.

Hokusai probably married his first wife in his twenties and had several children. His subject matter changed accordingly. Prints of historical and landscape subjects predominated, as well as prints of children. In 1793, his master, Shunshō, died, and then his young wife. Hokusai left the Shunshō school and struck out on his own. He studied the styles and techniques of more than a dozen different masters and schools: He learned about brushwork from the Kano school, based on classical Chinese painting, about ink paintings from the work of Sesshū, an ancient master, about flower and bird painting from the Chinese Ming period, and about perspective from Western paintings.

Life's Work

In 1797, Hokusai remarried and took the name by which he is known today. This time has been referred to as the start of the golden age of his work, when his delicate prints of girls, his stylish love scenes, his greeting prints, and his colored book illustrations marked the achievement of his first great style. Yet Hokusai's life never became settled or smooth. Indeed, the last of many names Hokusai took toward the end of his life, Gakyō-rōjin (the old man mad about drawing), characterizes the romantic turbulence that made him, in Richard Lane's words, "the prototype of the single-minded artist, striving only to complete a given task."

When his eldest son, the one who had been adopted by the wealthy Nakajima family, died in 1812, Hokusai no longer received a stipend. Supremely indifferent to money, Hokusai had several jobs—as an errand boy, a bookseller, and a novelist; he also sold calendars, red peppers, and painted banners to have enough money to continue painting.

Hokusai publicly exploited his talent in every conceivable way, drawing from bottom to top, right to left, painting with a finger or an egg or a bottle. The publicity sometimes worked for him, once even attracting the attention of the court. Though he charged highly for his work, he was always poor. He is said to have paid his bills in uncounted packets of money when he had it. He moved frequently, not only when he owed rent but also when his homes became too dirty. His children led equally turbulent lives, eventually leaving their spouses and returning to live with him; his irresponsible grandson was the cause of much of his financial problems.

The prodigality of his personal life matched the eclecticism in his professional life. He changed his name whenever he changed his artistic interests and is said to have used anywhere from thirty to fifty different names. He also wrote poetry, novels, and humorous works, and was widely read in Chinese and Japanese literature.

Even his crowning achievements as a woodblock print artist were marred by the vastness of his interests. Not content to work methodically and selectively, Hokusai produced more than thirty thousand designs in his restless search and eagerness to experiment. Indeed, it was his ambition, perhaps his lack of discrimination, that marred Hokusai's reputation in the view of Japanese critics.

In 1830, and for several years afterward, however, Hokusai published the series that changed the conception of *ukiyo-e* painting and established him in the first rank of artists. *Fugaku sanjūrokkei* (thirty-six views of Mount Fuji) is among the best known of Japanese woodblock prints in the West and is one of the most accomplished of Hokusai's achievements. It was so popular that ten more prints were added, making a total of forty-six in this most famous of Hokusai's work. It has been surmised that the "thirty-six" was kept in the title partly as a literary allusion, for the number thirty-six referred to all the known poets of the Heian period, and partly to make the most of a best-selling series. Three prints in particular, *Mount Fuji at Dawn*, *Mount Fuji in Storm*, and *Fuji Under the Wave at Kanagawa*, with their distinctive bright blues, are perhaps the most recognized of any Japanese prints in the West.

When the success of Hokusai's own series led to the popularity of a younger artist, Hiroshige, and his *Tōkaidō Gojūsantsugi* (fifty-three stations of the *Tōkaidō*) in 1833, Hokusai tried to surpass himself, which he did with a three-volume picture book, *Fugaku hyakkei* (1834; one hundred views of Mount Fuji). It is safe to say that Hokusai's obsession with this beautiful mountain in Japan has made it one of the most recognizable natural features in art.

Summary

Hokusai's reputation has sometimes been as checkered as his own life. Always popular among the lower classes from which he came and from whose point of view he worked, he was initially hailed in the West as the greatest of Japanese artists. Collectors were so eager for his work that anything remotely connected with him was snapped up, with the result that much of his inferior work reached European and American museums. The excessive inflation resulted, naturally, in a correspondingly steep decline in his reputation, until he was considered to be only a minor figure.

Because he was so prolific, so eager to experiment, and admittedly, so undiscriminating, Hokusai, like Hiroshige, suffers a paradoxical fate. The work of these two artists is probably the most accessible and easily recognized of all Japanese artists in the West, with endless reproductions of their most famous works appearing as postcards, calendars, and other mass reproductions—a justifiable fate for craftsmen who worked in the mode designed for the common folk. Yet the true originality of their work remains accessible only to the few who can examine original copies of their work.

Unlike Hiroshige, however, whose fondness for food, drink, and companionship made him seem more ordinary, Hokusai fits the romantic ideal of the driven artist, who sought ceaselessly with his talent to penetrate the mystery of what he saw. Though he lived a long and productive life, he is said to have shouted on his deathbed that if heaven would grant him ten more years, or only five, he might still become a great artist. In his attempts to synthesize a variety of styles, including Western techniques, Hokusai did make his unique style of Japanese art easily accessible to Western audiences, and, by so doing, he influenced European artists and opened the world of Japanese art to outsiders. Charmed by the prints of these two late masters of *ukiyo-e*, Western painters and collectors sought out the older masters. For some, Hokusai's own output is flawed by his excess; for others, the best he accomplished is still superb.

Bibliography

Bowie, Theodore R. *The Drawings of Hokusai.* Bloomington: Indiana University Press, 1964. Concentrates on a discussion of Hokusai as a draftsman, with examples drawn from the familiar as well as the little-known drawings. Includes chapters on Hokusai's stylistic shifts, his method of working, and his teaching. Contains notes, a bibliography, and an index.

Fenollosa, Ernest Francisco. Introduction to *Hokusai and His School*. Boston: Museum of Fine Arts, 1893. The author's introductory remarks in this exhibition catalog provide a brief but useful background of Japanese art and set the work of both Hokusai and the *ukiyo-e* school of art in its historical context.

Katsushika, Hokusai. *The Thirty-six Views of Mount Fuji*. Edited by Ichitaro Kondo and Charles S. Terry. Tokyo, Japan: Heibonsha, 1966. A companion volume to Hiroshige's *Tōkaidō Gojūsantsugi*. The English adaptation accompanying the reproductions provides a brief introduction to Hokusai's most famous series. Contains prints with texts in Japanese and English.

Lane, Richard. *Images from the Floating World: The Japanese Print*. New York: G. P. Putnam's Sons, 1976. Provides historical background, tracing the rise of *ukiyo-e* through the seventeenth and eighteenth centuries. Includes color photographs, a bibliography, an index, and an illustrated dictionary of *ukiyo-e*.

Michener, James A. *The Floating World*. New York: Random House, 1954. Traces the life and death of the art known as *ukiyo-e* through the individual artists who practiced it. Includes sixty-five prints, a chronological table, brief biographies, a bibliography, and an index.

Narazaki, Muneshige. *Studies in Nature: Hokusai-Hiroshige*. Translated by John Bester. Tokyo: Kodansha International, 1970. Focuses on the achievements of these two artists in the depiction of flowers and birds, with a brief introduction to the development of the genre. Includes prints.

Whitford, Frank. *Japanese Prints and Western Painters*. New York: Macmillan, 1977. Discusses the influence of Japanese woodblock prints on European painting in the nineteenth century. Includes a chronology, a glossary, a bibliography, an index, and color plates.

Shakuntala Jayaswal

HANS HOLBEIN, THE YOUNGER

Born: 1497 or 1498; Augsburg
Died: 1543; London, England
Area of Achievement: Art
Contribution: A master of portraits and an excellent draftsman, Holbein was an important transitional figure in European art. Holbein's portraits offer a revealing look at the personalities of his time.

Early Life

Hans Holbein, the Younger, was born in either 1497 or 1498 in the city of Augsburg, at that time an important commercial center of the Holy Roman Empire. The Holbein family was an artistic one: Hans Holbein, the Elder, was a widely known painter, much sought after for his skill in portraits, while his brother Sigmund was also an artist. The younger Holbein and his brother, Ambrosius, spent their early years learning the craft of painting from their father.

In 1515, Holbein moved to Basel, Switzerland, where he came to the attention of the noted printer and publisher Johann Froben, also known as Frobenius. Holbein was soon actively designing book illustrations and title-page borders for Froben and other printers in Basel. Since Froben was the publisher of Desiderius Erasmus, a noted Humanist scholar, Holbein came to know that internationally famous writer. Through Erasmus, Holbein was introduced to the circle of Humanist thinkers and leaders of the time. Holbein made other important contacts, including a 1516 commission to paint the portrait of Jacob Mayer, Burgomaster of Basel, and his wife; this work is an early indication of Holbein's mastery of the portrait genre. During this time, he also produced several conventional religious paintings, a form of art popular at the time.

From 1517 to 1519, Holbein was away from Basel, perhaps traveling with his father on commissions in Switzerland, perhaps on a brief visit to northern Italy. By the fall of 1519, he had returned to Basel, for on September 25 of that year he was admitted as a master in the Painters' Guild. The next year, Holbein became a citizen of the town and married Elsbeth Schmid, the widow of a tanner; the couple had four children.

Holbein received a considerable amount of work in Basel, primarily designs and illustrations for printers, but also a series of religious paintings influenced by his contemporary Albrecht Dürer; mural decorations for the Basel Town Hall; and more portraits, including his 1519 portrayal of the lawyer and scholar Bonifacius Amerbach. This portrait is the first showing Holbein's true genius in portraiture; fittingly, Amerbach later became the earliest collector of Holbein and preserved much of his work. In 1523, Holbein produced his first portrait of Erasmus; a second soon followed, which Erasmus sent to his friend Sir Thomas More in England. The English connection, so important in Holbein's life and career, was soon to be established.

A number of Holbein self-portraits have survived. They show him with a square, rather full face, a short, neatly trimmed beard but no mustache, and hair that was dark and worn moderately long. The most notable features are his mouth, firmly and tightly closed, and his eyes, which have a careful, wary expression. It is not the face of a man who revealed himself lightly or freely.

Life's Work

During the mid-1520's, the Protestant Reformation swept through Basel and the climate for the visual arts became much less favorable than before. In 1524, Holbein found it convenient to depart on an extended visit to France, where he was exposed to the influence of Italian painting, including the work of Leonardo da Vinci. In August of 1526, he left Basel again, this time for England. He carried with him a letter of introduction from Erasmus; once in England, he was welcomed into the household of Erasmus' good friend Sir Thomas More.

Through More, Holbein had an entry into the court of Henry VIII, then approaching the apogee of its brilliance. While Holbein did execute some decorations for court pageants, his initial relationship with the monarch was not as close as it would later become. Instead, he concentrated on portraits of prominent individuals and groups. One of his most striking works from this time, a group portrait of the More family (most likely painted in 1528) has been lost, but the preparatory drawings remain. As always, Holbein captures the character of his sitters with deft precision; equally important, this group portrait is the first known example in northern European art where the figures are shown sitting or standing in natural positions, rather than kneeling, a definite break with the religiously oriented art of the Middle Ages.

In 1528, Holbein returned to Basel, probably because of a previous agreement with the town council, since he promptly resumed his work of public commissions, devoting much time and energy to them over the next two years. The financial rewards seem to have been considerable, since he was able to purchase a new house and, in 1531, to buy the adjoining property as well. The same year as his return, Holbein was admitted into the Lutheran faith. Within two years, and certainly by late 1520, however, Holbein seems to have ceased all work in the area of religious painting, once a staple of any artist's career. Perhaps that reflected the preferences of the Reformation; it certainly allowed Holbein's talents to flow into paintings and portraits which favored his realistic and psychological technique.

Holbein's ability in portraiture reached its most profound and personal depths in his *Portrait of His Wife and Two Elder Children* (1528). In this searching, almost painful work, Holbein presents part of the family from which he was so long and so often absent. The painter's wife, Elsbeth, seems weary, perhaps sad; has this been caused by the absence of the artist who still records her features so faithfully? That is impossible to determine, but the technical mastery of the work is undoubted, as is its debt to Holbein's study of the works of Leonardo.

Leaving his wife and children in Basel, Holbein returned to England in 1532; he would remain there for the remainder of his life. His friend More had fallen from the king's favor over the matter of divorcing Queen Catherine and the marriage to Anne Boleyn, so Holbein first concentrated on a series of portraits of German merchants living in London. Called the "Steelyard portraits," after the section of town where the sitters lived, these works marked a new development in Holbein's art. His acute perceptions of character increased, his draftsmanship acquired new and fluid power, and attention was focused upon the person, because backgrounds and surroundings were greatly simplified.

Holbein also began to paint portraits of members of the court, including Thomas Cromwell, More's successor as Lord Chancellor; eventually, Holbein came to the attention of Henry himself. In 1537, Holbein executed a fresco for the royal palace of Whitehall, which brought him considerable fame (the work was destroyed in a 1698 fire). In 1538 came the first entry in the royal accounts of a salary paid to Holbein, indicating that he had officially entered the service of the king. Over the next five years, he would complete more than 150 portraits, in oils, chalk, and silverpoint, capturing some of the most influential and memorable figures from one of England's most turbulent periods. Holbein also remained active in preparing illustrations for printers, including the woodcut borders for the important English Bible of 1535, and he designed costumes, jewelry, cups, and other art objects for the court.

Holbein's portraits remain his most important and enduring work. Among his sitters were Henry VIII himself and most of the major figures of his court, including several of Henry's wives. Most of these works have survived in chalk, or pen-and-ink studies, rather than completed oils, yet all of them retain the vitality and insight which Holbein brought to his work. Some of them, such as the stunning full-length portrait *Christiana of Denmark, Duchess of Milan* (1538), rank among Holbein's supreme achievements.

The portrait of Christiana was painted for one of the frequent marriage negotiations engaged in by Henry; he often assigned Holbein to capture the likeness of a prospective bride. One of these, Holbein's study of Anne of Cleves (1539), seems to have been his downfall. Pleased by the portrait, Henry agreed to the marriage, but within six months he divorced the woman he called "the Flanders mare." After this, there were no more important royal commissions for Holbein.

Holbein continued to live in London, securing work from other patrons. His last portrait of Henry, for example, is that of the king granting a charter to the Barber-Surgeon's Company. The work was painted for that guild and was commissioned in 1541. Significantly, Holbein did not paint Henry from life but rather copied him from earlier works. Holbein did not live to complete the painting, for he died during an outbreak of the plague in London in 1543. His wife and children in Basel were attended to by his estate there and by a pension negotiated with the town council. In his last will in England, Holbein left funds for the keeping of two young children there. He was forty-six years old when he died.

Summary

Hans Holbein, the Younger, marks a turning point in the development of European art. His portraits show a decisive change from the older, religious orientation to the newer, more secular and worldly temper of the Renaissance and modern times. A number of critics have remarked on a lack of spiritual involvement by Holbein with his work, and perhaps Holbein did concentrate upon the actual, the physical, and the immediate. That was appropriate, however, for his sitters were men and women of intense individuality, and often of supreme ambition; their concerns were often not spiritual but temporal. Holbein's portraits may lack piety, but they have psychological insight, an insight that he captured not by hands clasped in prayer or holding a Bible but by hands fingering a jewel given by Henry VIII or the look of shrewd eyes calculating the latest events in the king's court. With Holbein, medieval painting departs and the art of the modern world begins.

Even in his religious paintings, Holbein took a new and sometimes disturbing stance. One of his most famous works, *The Body of the Dead Christ in the Tomb* (1521-1522), has intrigued and unsettled viewers since its creation. Some have complained that the painting dwells too closely on the material nature of Christ, slighting the spiritual side. While other religious paintings of the time used Christ's physical sufferings as an aid to devotion and meditation, Holbein's work is different and evokes different responses, because of the intense, unflinching realism in which it is rendered. There is no softening or evading the facts of brutal bodily injury and certain death.

Occupying a pivotal point in European artistic development, Holbein was not entirely a modern painter. The influence of older forms is seen most clearly in his woodcuts and illustrations, in particular the Dance of Death series, designed from 1522 through 1524, and executed by the brilliant woodblock carver Hans Lützelburger. Although not published until 1538, this series is one of the most famous variants on the "Dance macabre" theme so popular in the Middle Ages.

It is Holbein's portraits, however, which are the key to his work. His technical mastery is unmatched, and his ceaseless efforts at perfection allowed him to produce a series of masterpieces of psychological interpretation. Most famous are the portraits Holbein produced at the court of Henry VIII, which have left for later generations a true sense of the important and intriguing figures of the time, from the king himself to his friend and victim, Sir Thomas More. In these, and other drawings, portraits, and paintings, Holbein captured the essence of the northern Renaissance and the men and women who created it. Through the works of Holbein, that world comes to life in all its vibrant energy.

Bibliography

Holbein, Hans, the Younger. *Holbein*. Introduction by Roy Strong. New York: Rizzoli, 1980. This slender volume is one of the Every Painting series. Gives a rapid visual overview of Holbein's career. Especially useful in conjunction with any of the other volumes mentioned here.

Hueffer, Ford Madox. *Hans Holbein the Younger: A Critical Monograph.* New York: E. P. Dutton, 1905. A perceptive, if sometimes highly individual study of Holbein's work by the famous English novelist, better known as Ford Madox Ford. The book does well in placing Holbein within the atmosphere of the Renaissance and provides a good, if idiosyncratic, overview of his achievement.

Roberts, Jane. *Holbein*. London: Oresko Books, 1979. A good study of Holbein's art, with particular emphasis on the drawings and portraits of his two English sojourns. There is a brief, but generally informative biography.

Rowlands, John. *Holbein: The Paintings of Hans Holbein the Younger.* Oxford: Phaidon Press, 1985. Essentially a study of Holbein's works in oil, this book contains an excellent introductory biography. Very helpful in providing accessible critical commentary on the artist's work.

Strong, Roy. *Holbein and Henry VIII.* London: Routledge & Kegan Paul, 1967. A volume in the Studies in British Art series, this work provides an extensive review of Holbein's relationship with the Tudor court. In addition to the paintings and drawings, Holbein was productive in all aspects of decorations and embellishments.

Michael Witkoski

FRIEDRICH VON HOLSTEIN

Born: April 24, 1837; Schwedt an der Oder, Pomerania
Died: May 8, 1909; Berlin, Germany
Area of Achievement: Diplomacy
Contribution: Holstein was a controversial chief adviser on German foreign policy from 1890 to 1906, sometimes blamed for German diplomatic isolation before World War I.

Early Life

An only child, Friedrich von Holstein passed a sickly and lonely boyhood on his family's estate or in their Berlin town house. His adolescence was spent with his parents and private tutors at European health resorts, where he became fluent in English, French, and Italian, before attending the University of Berlin. Physically unfit to follow the example of his father's army career, Holstein was briefly and unhappily in the Prussian government's legal division. Through the influence of a neighboring family friend, Otto von Bismarck, Holstein was admitted to the diplomatic service in 1860 and sent as attaché to the legation at St. Petersburg, where Bismarck was then Prussian minister.

In 1863, Holstein passed his foreign service examination and was assigned to Rio de Janeiro but was recalled to Berlin by his patron, Bismarck, who had become Prussian minister-president. In the Danish War of 1864, Holstein served as one of Bismarck's liaison officers to Prussian army headquarters and was later sent to London for the 1864-1865 Conference on the Danish Question.

An 1865-1867 sojourn in the United States began as a travel leave with the purpose of self-discovery, as his father's accidental death in 1863 had left Holstein without family but with some inherited wealth. Photographs of the young baron depict a slender man of medium height with conventionally bearded good looks but a somewhat wary expression. He combined adventures on the Western frontier with a vague assignment at the Washington legation. His friendship with the unconventional young wife of Senator Charles Sumner was later magnified by gossip into an improbable tale of scandalous romance. More prosaically, Holstein began, in the United States, an ultimately unprofitable business enterprise, which continued after his 1867 return to Germany, caused him to leave diplomatic service in 1868, and apparently consumed most or all of his inheritance.

When the Ems Telegram in July of 1870 foreshadowed the Franco-Prussian War, Holstein put himself at Bismarck's disposal and was sent to Italy as the chancellor's private agent to organize anti-French republican activists there in case King Victor Emmanuel II supported Napoleon III. During the 1871 Prussian siege of Paris, Holstein served as Bismarck's unofficial contact with

Communard leaders in order to weaken the French government's position in the preliminary peace negotiations.

After the war, Holstein remained in France as chief secretary for Germany's Paris embassy, soon headed by the baron's new chief, Count Harry von Arnim, a political ambassador of great influence and aspirations. Arnim intrigued to overthrow the new French republic as a step toward himself replacing Bismarck as chancellor. His exposure led to sensational trials involving, among much else, purloined state documents. A courtroom charge that Holstein had taken the missing papers made headlines, and his subsequent vindication was not as widely remembered as the false but memorable accusation. Holstein entered the public mind as a man suspected.

Life's Work

In 1876, Holstein was promoted to the Berlin foreign office, where he spent the rest of his career. He became head of an information apparatus for whatever Bismarck needed to know as well as a conduit for some of what Bismarck decided to do. The baron gradually became a work-absorbed bureaucrat. Rustic in dress and slightly grotesque in the special glasses his eyes came to require, he avoided government social functions and lived simply in three small rooms in an unfashionably remote suburb, though sometimes hosting a few personal friends, generally at Borchardt's restaurant.

Occasionally rude to his superiors, jealous of his prerogatives though considerate of the clerical staff, and with no clear public role, Privy Councillor Baron Holstein seemed to be a consequential official, simply because he possessed important information. The possibilities for blackmail in the German society of the time were abundant, and speculation grew about the basis for Holstein's influence. The result was the Holstein legend, since discredited, of an intelligence chief with spies everywhere and a "poison cupboard" of secrets about those in high places—a dim-sighted but dangerous "mole." Bismarck, among many, fed the rumors, when he described "the man with the hyena eyes" as useful because "sometimes I must do evil things."

In the foreign policy field which was much, though not all, of his job, Holstein followed Bismarck's views almost entirely for about five years. By the mid-1880's, however, his own anti-Russian sentiments increasingly diverged from Bismarck's insistence on a "bridge to St. Petersburg." Like others in German politics, Holstein assumed that the 1888 accession of Kaiser William II would hasten the day of Bismarck's retirement. The baron's efforts to postpone the break while preserving his own position were at least made with the knowledge of both parties.

It is sometimes claimed that from Bismarck's dismissal by the kaiser in March of 1890 to Holstein's own resignation in April of 1906, Holstein was "the real master" of German foreign policy. This exaggerates Holstein's control and underrates the extent to which he was forced to yield to the judgment of his superiors, the impulses of the kaiser, and the pressures of the Navy League and the colonial enthusiasts. The chancellorship of Leo von Caprivi (1890-1894) was the administration most influenced by Holstein, especially in the 1890 decision to abandon the Russian reinsurance treaty in order to have a free hand for pursuing an alliance with England. Yet the generous territorial exchanges of Caprivi's treaties with England were merely seen by the British government and press as "trying to buy our friendship." England showed no interest in joining the Triple Alliance of Germany, Austria, and Italy.

Meanwhile, Russia used her diplomatic "free hand" for the Franco-Russian Alliance of 1893-1894, a blow to German security on two fronts, which caused wide criticism of the kaiser's new advisers, including Holstein. When Chlodwig von Hohenlohe succeeded Caprivi as chancellor, Holstein was often reduced to ineffective protests against the kaiser's insistence on the 1895 Triple Intervention, which alienated Japan, the needless Kruger Telegram of 1896, and the naval construction program begun by Alfred von Tirpitz in 1898.

Holstein's renewed attempts at an English alliance expired in fruitless negotiations between 1898 and 1901. The Anglo-French Entente Cordiale of 1904 was a heavy blow to Holstein's policy direction, but the Far Eastern War between Russia and Japan did give Germany some diplomatic opportunities. Holstein supported the kaiser's hope of attracting Russia and perhaps even France into an anti-British front. At the same time, Holstein pressed on Chancellor Bernhard von Bülow and the kaiser a policy of detaching England from the Entente Cordial by challenging French claims in Morocco. The kaiser's speech in Tangier escalated this move into a crisis, and a war between France and Germany seemed an imminent possibility. Holstein argued that Great Britain would not support a France whose Russian ally was temporarily helpless and that therefore France would back down. He urged going to the brink of war, but the responsibility for going over the brink was not one the kaiser wished to take. The Algeciras Conference of 1906 found Great Britain ready to support France, the United States unexpectedly pro-French, and Italy predictably neutral. That left the Austro-German alliance diplomatically isolated. Such a conspicuous failure of German diplomacy caused foreign office reverberations leading to Holstein's resignation on April 16, 1906.

Summary

Friedrich von Holstein was a career foreign officer who became an important foreign policy adviser following Bismarck's dismissal. As such, he never possessed the real authority of policy decisions because he had no political power base. On the whole, his advice was better than the inconsistent policies of his superiors. Holstein worked in the unfavorable atmosphere of an autocratic regime on the way to the scrap heap of history. The kaiser, with his frequent delusions of grandeur, was surrounded by irresponsible flatterers who isolated him from reality. Too outspoken and abrasive for such an entourage, Holstein tried to promote sensible policies by influencing the monarch's key advisers. Inevitably his efforts were gossiped about as part of the court circle intrigues, and, after the defeat of 1918, memoirs of the fallen regime often made Holstein the scapegoat for the diplomatic blunders leading to the lost war.

Holstein's papers and modern research have vindicated his character from the charges of base motives. Of the men in the kaiser's government, he was certainly above average in ability, patriotic dedication, honesty, and courage, and less given to malice or feline remarks. That comparison does not elevate him to a place among leading statesmen. His long apprenticeship under Bismarck did not qualify Holstein as a diplomatic sorcerer.

On balance, Holstein's record shows an impressive command of European and world problems; he foresaw more clearly than most the danger to Europe of the growing power of Russia. Unfortunately, he was unable to comprehend effectively "the other side of the hill." He lacked the penetration, vision, and intuitive human understanding of great statesmanship. If by that standard Holstein failed, so also did the Germany and Europe of his generation.

Bibliography

Bülow, Bernhard von. *Memoirs of Prince von Bülow*. Translated by F. A. Voigt. 2 vols. Boston: Little, Brown, 1931-1932. References to Holstein are widely scattered but plentiful, negative, and frequently malicious. Bülow presents Holstein not as a masterful gray eminence but as incompetent, disagreeable, and emotionally unstable.

Gooch, George Peabody. *Studies in Modern History*. Reprint. Freeport, N.Y.: Books for Libraries Press, 1968. This essay by a widely respected historian, revised from a 1923 article, had great influence in establishing the Holstein legend for a generation of students and presents a readable collection of anecdotes.

Haller, Johannes. *Philip Eulenburg: The Kaiser's Friend*. Translated by Ethel Colburn Mayne. 2 vols. New York: Alfred A. Knopf, 1930. Holstein's attempts to influence Wilhelm II through the kaiser's adviser are well presented. Haller's biography is a frame for Eulenburg's collection of expansive letters and recollections. An appendix gives Eulenburg's specific comments on Holstein.

Holstein, Friedrich von. *The Holstein Papers*. Edited by Norman Rich and M. H. Fisher. 4 vols. London: Cambridge University Press, 1955. These four volumes collect the relevant data on which much of Rich's biography is based. Volume 1 includes a useful introduction as well as Holstein's autobiographical sketches. Volume 2 contains Holstein's diaries and volume 3 contains his correspondence.

Hull, Isabel V. *The Entourage of Kaiser Wilhelm II, 1888-1918*. New York: Cambridge University Press, 1982. The kaiser and Eulenburg are at the center of this comprehensive account, but Holstein's relation to the group is established in this study, which includes a useful examination of some of the Holstein-Eulenburg letters from a different perspective.

Rich, Norman. *Friedrich von Holstein*. 2 vols. New York: Cambridge University Press, 1965. A long-awaited work, this is the only full-length biography of Holstein. The narrative follows Holstein's viewpoint, but objective judgment is maintained. A historical context of considerable detail makes the book especially useful to scholars of German and diplomatic history.

K. Fred Gillum

FRANÇOIS HOTMAN

Born: August 23, 1524; Paris, France
Died: February 12, 1590; Basel, Swiss Confederation
Areas of Achievement: Law and political science
Contribution: Hotman, a brilliant French legal scholar and teacher, used his considerable knowledge and writing ability for the Huguenot cause of freedom of conscience, and, in the process, developed a philosophy of limited constitutional monarchy and became one of the first modern revolutionaries.

Early Life

François Hotman was born on August 23, 1524, in Paris, France. His father, Pierre Hotman, was a successful lawyer and landowner who, in 1524, had just entered the king's service. He was to be rewarded after twenty years for his loyalty to the Crown with an appointment as Conseiller in the Parlement de Paris, which made him an important member of the feudal office-holding nobility. Little is known of François' mother, Paule, née de Marle, or of his early childhood, except that, as the eldest son who would inherit his father's fief and office, he grew up being prepared for a legal career.

In 1536, Hotman entered the University of Paris, where he was exposed to the new Humanistic learning and developed considerable enthusiasm for classical literature and languages. At fourteen, considered something of a prodigy, Hotman enrolled in the school of law at the University of Orléans. Although the teaching of law was dominated by the Scholastic method, Hotman was also exposed again to the new Humanist approach and learned the methodology of subjecting civil law to historical criticism. The curriculum was rigorous, but Hotman worked hard and received his license in civil law in only two years. Returning to Paris to begin his career, he soon made friends with several leading Humanist scholars, who increased his devotion to the historical school of interpreting the law. Within one year, he had published the first of his many books on law, and, in August of 1546, he assumed his first teaching position at the University of Bourges.

The Reformation, which in time would shake Western civilization to its foundations and profoundly affect Hotman, had begun in earnest only seven years before he was born. In 1536, the Reformation entered a new and more troubled phase with the publication of John Calvin's *Christianae religionis institutio* (*Institutes of the Christian Religion*, 1561). Little is known of when Hotman first came into contact with Reformation ideas. His conversion to Calvinism seems to have begun slowly during his years at the Universities of Paris and Orléans, quickened after his return to Paris, and culminated during his first visit to Switzerland in 1547.

Hotman returned from the University of Orléans to live at home with his parents for some months, but his father's work on a special tribunal of the Parlement de Paris, which was hearing the cases of Lutheran and Calvinist "heretics," apparently became more than he could tolerate. He fled in the spring of 1548, constantly afraid of pursuit by his father. He ended up in Geneva, where, for a short time, he was secretary to John Calvin, the man he now considered his spiritual father. Hotman's break with home and parents was complete and painful. His father disinherited him and the French government and French Catholic church began to consider him dangerous because of his writings in support of the Huguenot cause. Hotman was never again either financially secure or able to return to France and Paris for any length of time. Geneva had become and remained the spiritual, intellectual, and often physical focus of Hotman's life.

Hotman was a moderately attractive man but otherwise had no outstanding or remarkable physical characteristics. His portrait shows penetrating, wide-set eyes and a high forehead and receding hairline that left him mostly bald by middle age. In the fashion of most Huguenots, he wore a beard and mustache but kept them relatively short, unlike many of his long-bearded colleagues. Within a year of arriving in Geneva, he married Claude Aubelin, the daughter of Sieur de la Rivière, formerly of Orléans, but who now was a fellow exile in Geneva for the Huguenot faith. Eleven children were born to them, eight of whom reached adulthood. Despite the frequent moves of the household, the uncertainty, and, occasionally, the fear of French reprisals, the marriage seems to have been a happy one.

Life's Work

Calvin took a deep interest in his followers. Now that Hotman was married, he needed a position with a larger income. Calvin found it for him at the Academy of Lausanne, where Hotman was to teach dialectic and Greek and Latin literature. The Lausanne Academy was the oldest Reformed (non-Catholic) school in a French-speaking area, and Hotman's salary was adequate. During these early years, he published a series of translations and commentaries on great Greek and Latin classical works. He also produced books and tracts on law, but only one of these won for him any particular recognition. In 1551, Hotman published his *De statu primitivae ecclesiae* (1553; state of the primitive church), a Calvinist tract that attacked the Catholic church for its deviations from original Christianity. His particular achievement with this work was to take standard Calvinist doctrine and support it with a wide selection of legal and historical authorities and precedents, a style he would perfect in the years to come.

In time, Hotman grew restless in Lausanne. In 1554, he returned to Geneva, which had granted him citizenship, and was soon involved in promoting the Huguenot cause. He did not stay long, however, moving to Strasbourg in October of 1555, where he remained eight years teaching at the

academy there. Although not the oldest, it was the most famous and successful of all the Protestant schools and an important adjunct to the Calvinist
church in Geneva. The new position had special significance for Hotman
because he was taking the place of a rival legal scholar who had fallen out
with Calvin, partly because of Hotman. In Strasbourg, Hotman was able to
concentrate on teaching and studying civil law, especially the examination of
Roman law from a historical point of view. His study of Justinian's *Corpus
juris civilis* led to a number of publications over the next five years and laid
the foundations of his fame as a distinguished legal scholar of the Humanist
school. These works also earned for him the doctoral degree from the University of Basel in 1558.

During this time, Hotman's vital interests in Calvinism and in legal scholarship combined, as his consciousness of politics awakened, into a career as
a revolutionary propagandist. His central theme became the need to limit
constitutionally the power of the French government, especially in religious
matters. To this end, he built a case, based on legal and historical precedent,
that it was legitimate to resist the exercise of unjustified authority by the
French monarchy. Hotman discussed these matters with anyone who was
interested and acquired a network of contacts with Protestant leaders all over
Europe. He exchanged a large volume of letters with them over the years.
He particularly admired the English and regarded Elizabeth I as one of the
great hopes of the Protestant cause. He sent Jean, his eldest son, to study at
the University of Oxford.

His first major propaganda pamphlet was published in 1560. It was a vigorous denunciation of the noble house of Guise, especially Charles, Cardinal
of Lorraine, who led the ultra-Catholic Party in France. The cardinal and the
Guise family had pressured King Henry II and his successors to increase the
repression of Protestantism in France to counteract the increasing popularity
of Calvinism, particularly among the French nobility and burgher classes.
Following Hotman's lead, and in some cases undoubtedly with additional
contributions written but not publicly acknowledged by him, a large number
of Huguenot propaganda pamphlets were published attacking the Cardinal of
Lorraine and his faction, and presenting the Huguenot case. The Guises
countered with claims that the Huguenots had attempted to murder the Catholic party's leaders and the king, and were also guilty of heresy and sedition.
These were the opening salvos of what became a series of eight religious
civil wars in France. Hotman had become the leading ideologist of the Huguenot cause for liberty of conscience, one of the trusted diplomatic agents
and advisers of the Huguenot leadership, and a revolutionary.

By August of 1572, Hotman's reputation as a scholar and his list of texts
and essays on legal subjects had grown considerably. His work for the Huguenots had brought him many friends and admirers among the Protestant
leadership. His connections with important French nobles had made possible

a return to France and a position at the University of Bourges. The Saint Bartholomew's Day Massacre, however, caused him to leave again. In Paris on August 23, 1572, Hotman's forty-eighth birthday, the ultra-Catholics began slaughtering Huguenots. The king and the queen mother were parties to this butchery, which spread from Paris throughout France wherever there were concentrations of Huguenots. Suspicious of what could happen, Hotman walked out of town in disguise and without any of his possessions the instant he learned of the events in Paris. He and his family lost everything, although Hotman was later able to recover a few of his more important manuscripts. Once again, now in mid-life, he sought asylum in Geneva, where after a few months he accepted a faculty position at the Geneva Academy.

The Saint Bartholomew's Day Massacre resulted in the fourth of the French religious civil wars and in making Hotman an overtly declared revolutionary. In the propaganda tracts that were pouring from his pen, he no longer blamed the political tyranny and persecution of the Huguenots on the ultra-Catholic Party but took aim directly at the king. Hotman spent much of the rest of his life developing his ideas on limited constitutional monarchy and freedom of religion and conscience.

Hotman's masterwork on these themes was *Franco-Gallia*. Although he had been working on this project for at least six years, its publication in 1573 was especially timely. Hotman's fundamental proposition, supported with a wide variety of evidence, was that the ancient and medieval Gauls and Franks had a constitution that limited the monarch's authority by requiring that the making of law be shared with a national council called the Estates-General. This council also elected the king. In Hotman's description, the powers of the Estates-General were remarkably similar to those of a twentieth century legislature and not a medieval assembly. Hotman argued that the king did not rule by hereditary right but by the authority of the people as expressed in the Estates-General. After equating royal absolutism with tyranny, Hotman suggested that the people have the right to depose a tyrant king. That was probably his most radical proposition. In an obvious reference to the Guise family of Lorraine, which was not considered an integral part of France at the time, Hotman also included the use of foreign mercenaries as typical of tyrants.

In *Franco-Gallia*, Hotman was clearly attempting to prove that ancient and medieval France had known a considerable degree of political and religious freedom that more recent national leaders, specifically the Queen Mother Catherine, her sons, and the Guise family, had distorted and corrupted for their own personal gain and at the people's expense. It was an enormously popular work among Protestants—infamous among the ultra-Catholics—and was translated into several other languages and went through several editions in Hotman's lifetime. It was a propaganda work and not entirely accurate historically but so impressive in its demonstrated learning and so brilliantly done that the Calvinist king, Henry of Navarre, who in time would end the French religious civil wars and become King Henry IV of France, enlisted Hotman's aid on numerous occasions. On the other hand, the Catholic party felt obliged to put their best talent to work in trying to refute Hotman.

Hotman's remaining years were not spent in comfort. When a temporary peace came in the French religious wars in 1576 and various offers came to return to France, Hotman was too fearful of another massacre of Huguenots and rejected all offers. His financial situation in Geneva was grim, and his health was deteriorating. To make matters worse, Geneva, which had been threatened by the Duchy of Savoy periodically for years, entered a prolonged period of heightened anxiety over the possibility of being attacked and invaded. When the constant state of fear became more than he could bear, Hotman once again moved his family in August of 1578. He had had numerous offers but decided to accept a teaching position at the University of Basel, where he thought he could live and work in peace. While that proved to be true, his financial condition did not significantly improve and he found that his faith was tolerated but increasingly unpopular. Hotman's physical retreat to Basel, however, was only a semiretirement, not a full retreat from the Huguenot cause. He continued to be actively involved in the plots and schemes of his party, and in writing tracts and pamphlets. As something of a celebrity whose list of frequent correspondents contained the greatest minds of Protestant Europe, he also had many visitors, including the famous essayist Michel de Montaigne.

Basel was not immune to the ravages of the plague, which, in February of 1583, swept through the region. Hotman's wife, who had always taken extraordinary measures to get herself and her family away whenever the plague broke out, caught the disease this time and died soon afterward. Hotman was further deeply disturbed when Daniel, one of his sons, converted to Catholicism. As he had done so often before when distressed, he moved, this time back to Geneva, in late September, 1584, where he knew that a position at the academy was still available to him.

Besides the troubles in his personal life, the urging of his coreligionist Henry of Navarre to write in support of his claim to the French throne may also have influenced Hotman to return to Geneva. After Charles IX died in 1574, his brother became King Henry III. Henry III's only heir, however, had died in 1584 and the succession was between Henry of Navarre, now the most legitimate heir, and his uncle, the Cardinal of Bourbon, who had the support of the ultra-Catholics. Hotman wrote and published several works on the question, basing the case for Henry of Navarre on fundamental constitutional law. The Guises were sufficiently disturbed by Hotman's work to set several of their best writers to work answering him. Henry of Navarre was sufficiently impressed and made Hotman a councillor and member of his privy council in 1585, a position Hotman held until his death. In that same year, the ultra-Catholics virtually forced Henry III to provoke a war with Henry of Navarre and the Huguenots. This was the War of the Three Henrys, the eighth and final religious civil war in France. Apparently, the Guises hoped that the war would eliminate Henry of Navarre as a possible heir to the throne. The war, although not decisive, went more in favor of the Catholics than the Huguenots until 1589. In that year, Duke Henry of Guise seemed to be positioning himself to seize the throne and Henry III had him assassinated. The ultra-Catholics rose in rebellion, and Henry III was forced to flee. On his way to Henry of Navarre for sanctuary, he was murdered by a Catholic monk. Meanwhile, the situation in Geneva was bleak. Savoy was once again threatening and the city was in a virtual state of siege. In September of 1589, Hotman and his remaining three unmarried daughters escaped Geneva by water on Lake Lausanne to Basel. His health had been declining for some time and severe edema was added to his other health problems. On February 12, 1590, he died. In his will, he disinherited his son Daniel. To the end, his cause was the most important aspect of his life.

Summary

François Hotman was an uncompromising idealist and would have had mixed reactions to the immediate outcome of his cause. He would have been overjoyed when Henry of Navarre finally prevailed in the field of battle over the ultra-Catholics and became King Henry IV of France in 1594. He also would have applauded Henry IV's Edict of Nantes in 1598, which gave the Huguenots political and religious rights. He would have been appalled, however, by the high cost: the conversion of Henry IV to Catholicism. He would also have been disturbed by the failure of the Estates-General to develop into an institution capable of limiting and controlling royal authority. In the next century, Catholicism regained much of the ground lost to the Huguenots, sometimes by force, as in Louis XIV's Revocation of the Edict of Nantes in 1685. In 1789, during the reign of Louis XVI, the Estates-General would emerge as a limiting force, but with such suddenness and violence as to create a great revolution.

Hotman, who wanted to restore religion and law to an idealized primitive perfection and thereby establish popular sovereignty and liberty of conscience, did not succeed in his own time. He did succeed, however, in raising issues and laying foundations upon which later theorists of the seventeenth and eighteenth centuries would build a new vision of the state, which included not only concepts of popular sovereignty and religious freedom but also of social contract, individual freedom, and the rule of law.

Bibliography
Bainton, Roland H. *The Reformation of the Sixteenth Century.* Boston: Beacon Press, 1952. For those interested in the religious issues of Hotman's era, this older but still quite useful work explains the development of Protestant thought and doctrine with sympathy and precision.
Dunn, Richard S. *The Age of Religious War, 1559-1715.* New York: W. W. Norton, 1970, 2d ed. 1979. An excellent, readable, yet scholarly general history of Europe which includes the era of the wars between Protestants and Catholics that began in the latter half of the sixteenth century and lasted until the mid-seventeenth century. The Catholic-Huguenot wars of France and how they fit into the overall pattern of European history are well presented.
Kelly, Donald R. *François Hotman: A Revolutionary's Ordeal.* Princeton, N.J.: Princeton University Press, 1972. The only full-length biography of Hotman in English. A sympathetic treatment of Hotman's life, but it does not ignore his faults. Sometimes omits background that increases understanding of the significance of Hotman's work.
Myers, A. R. *Parliaments and Estates in Europe to 1789.* New York: Harcourt Brace Jovanovich, 1975. A good general discussion of the origins and evolution of representative political assemblies and legislatures in Europe from their medieval origins to the French Revolution. Mentions Hotman in the discussion of the French Estates-General and the impact of the religious wars.
Neale, J. E. *The Age of Catherine de Medici.* London: Jonathan Cape, 1943. An excellent history of France during the latter half of the sixteenth century. Concentrates on political and legal issues, the collapse of the Valois dynasty, and assumption of the French throne by Henry of Navarre.
Reynolds, Beatrice. *Proponents of Limited Monarchy in Sixteenth Century France: François Hotman and Jean Bodin.* New York: Columbia University Press, 1931. An older but still-interesting, in-depth treatment of Hotman's ideas of constitutional monarchy. Not as clear as it could be on the relationship of Hotman's political ideas to his religious beliefs.
Skinner, Quentin. *The Foundations of Modern Political Thought.* 2 vols. Cambridge: Cambridge University Press, 1978. Perhaps the best scholarly study of the political philosophy of the Renaissance and Reformation. Volume 2 has numerous references to Hotman and the Huguenot cause. Particularly valuable in explaining the connections between religious doctrine and political philosophy.

Richard L. Hillard

VICTOR HUGO

Born: February 26, 1802; Besançon, France
Died: May 22, 1885; Paris, France
Area of Achievement: Literature
Contribution: Hugo was one of the great authors of the nineteenth century, and by the force of his personality he became one of its great public figures, using his enormous popularity in the service of many political and social causes. His literary career, spanning six of the most turbulent decades in modern European history, encompassed poetry, drama, the novel, and nonfiction writing.

Early Life

Victor-Marie Hugo was born on February 26, 1802, in Besançon, France, the third son of Joseph Léopold Sigisbert Hugo and Sophie Trébuchet Hugo. At the time of their marriage in 1797, Joseph Hugo was a rising young Bonapartist soldier imbued with the ideals of the French Revolution; Sophie, the orphaned daughter of a Breton ship's captain, had been reared by an aunt of pronounced Royalist sympathies. Thus, in his earliest years, the two poles of contemporary French politics became factors in his life.

An early estrangement of Hugo's parents, the result of personal incompatibilities magnified by the dislocations of his father's military career, became permanent, and Victor and his brother Eugène went with their mother to live in Paris. Though Victor's childhood was touched by the color and the upheaval of the Napoleonic era, by the age of seven he was able to read and translate Latin, and by his tenth year his spotty education had been augmented by trips to Italy and Spain.

After 1814, Hugo's education proceeded along more orthodox lines, but it left him time to write verse and plays; at age twenty, financial and critical recognition of his talent enabled him to wed his childhood playmate, Adèle Foucher, a shy, pious young woman to whom he had pledged his love in the spring of 1819. An early novel, *Han d'Islande* (1823; *Hans of Iceland*, 1845), is the feverishly emotional product of Hugo's courtship of Adèle, but more significant for Hugo's development at this time were his contributions to the short-lived periodical *Muse française*, which shows a modification of his Royalist sympathies and a recognition that a poet should play a role in society. Hugo's ideas of literary form were evolving from a conservative classicism, which had won for him early popularity, toward a forward-looking but less well-defined Romanticism. In 1826, a small book of poems, *Odes et ballades*, signaled the poet's embrace of Romanticism by substituting the inspiration of "pictures, dreams, scenes, narratives, superstitious legends, popular traditions" for the authority of literary convention.

Though of somewhat short stature, Hugo was a strikingly attractive man in youth as well as old age. With a high forehead and penetrating eyes, he seemed both austere and engaging, and he had a reputation as an excellent conversationalist. Few nineteenth century personalities were portrayed as often as Hugo was; contemporary drawings and photographs show him as an extraordinarily intense and commanding personality. As early as the 1820's, the poet's home had become a magnet for other young authors and artists. Newly married to an attractive wife, he was often host to an informal group of Romantic personalities which included his friend Charles-Augustin Sainte-Beuve, the painter Eugène Delacroix, and the sculptor David d'Angers. Known as the *cénacle*, or brotherhood, Hugo's circle became not only a source of mutual support for its youthful members, but also a font of the new movement in art, Romanticism. Its ideals can be gauged by reference to Hugo's *La Préface de Cromwell* (1827; English translation, 1896), which was celebrated as a manifesto of Romanticism. In this preface to his long play *Cromwell* (1827; English translation, 1896), Hugo contributes to the redefinition of the three unities of time, place, and action that lie at the heart of French classical literature. He calls for greater realism and freedom in dramatic production, stating that "all that is in nature belongs to art" and arguing for the union of the grotesque and the sublime in the work of literary art. *La Préface de Cromwell* has been called Hugo's masterpiece as a literary apprentice; it marks his liberation from the vestiges of eighteenth century ideas and heralds the beginning of a productive decade that brought his work into the mainstream of French culture.

Life's Work

The publication in 1829 of a book of poems, *Les Orientales* (*Les Orientales: Or, Eastern Lyrics*, 1879), placed Hugo at the head of the Romantic movement, a role which was confirmed with the appearance of his melodramatic five-act play *Hernani* (English translation, 1830) in February, 1830. *Hernani* was a popular sensation and brought much-needed income into the Hugo household, which was strained by nearly a decade of pregnancies and shaky finances. In fact, the artistic success Hugo enjoyed in these years had been invisibly pursued by Adèle's unhappiness and a growing, secretive love between her and Sainte-Beuve, who was as much a family friend as an artistic colleague. Hugo was deeply shaken by the failure of his imagined, ideal relationship with his wife and the treachery of his friend, but he responded to his misfortune by composing the poems issued in November, 1831, as *Les Feuilles d'automne*, a collection that far surpassed his earlier verses.

Hugo had signed a contract in 1828 to produce a novel, but the project was displaced by his many other projects and by the July Revolution of 1830, which Hugo and his liberal contemporaries embraced. In September, 1830, he set to work on this novel in earnest, and completed *Notre-Dame de*

Paris (1831; *The Hunchback of Notre-Dame*, 1833) within six months. A descriptive tapestry of fifteenth century Paris, the novel embodies the author's extraordinary visual imagination and his affinity for art and architecture. Hugo had, by this time, shown a related capacity for drawing, and in the years to come his sketches often achieved a mastery of dramatic visual effect and characterization quite beyond his nominally amateur status as an artist.

The theater continued to attract Hugo's interest. In November, 1832, *Le Roi s'amuse* (1832; *The King Amuses Himself*, 1842) was banned by the government following its first performance; yet on November 8, 1838, he achieved another triumph with *Ruy Blas* (English translation, 1890), widely considered to be his best play. It was also his last success as a dramatist; after the failure of *Les Burgraves* (*The Burgraves*, 1896) in 1843, Hugo no longer wrote for the stage. By then, however, he had achieved one of his main objectives in courting public and critical acclaim in the theater: election to the Académie Française, an event which occurred on his fifth attempt, on January 7, 1841. Celebrated as a poet, dramatist, novelist, and critic, Hugo's role as a youthful, rebellious Romantic had been outgrown. Financially secure, perhaps emotionally battered but artistically more refined, he now pursued his career with determination but with no less passion than before.

Since 1833, Hugo had maintained a liaison with a beautiful actress, Juliette Drouet, who for twelve years followed a cloistered existence relieved only by six-week summer holidays with her lover. Notwithstanding the author's devotion to Juliette and his increasingly frequent love affairs with other adoring women, he was a devoted father to two sons and daughters. In 1843, Léopoldine, Hugo's favorite, perished in a boating accident with her husband of six months. His sons, Charles and François-Victor, died prematurely in their middle years, after sharing in many of their father's trials and successes; his daughter Adèle died in 1915, after a life darkened by madness.

In the 1840's, Hugo was something of an establishment figure in French letters. In April, 1845, he was raised to the peerage, becoming Viscount Hugo—a circumstance which in July saved him from almost certain prosecution on the complaint of the husband of one of his mistresses. After this perilous event, Hugo remained prudently quiet for several years, but in 1848, with France again in political turmoil, he sought to renew his political influence. Initially supporting France's "bourgeois king," Prince Louis-Napoleon, through the newspaper that he had founded with his sons, Hugo soon came to oppose his rule. His sons were imprisoned, and Hugo himself skirted arrest until it seemed absolutely necessary to leave France. He departed for Brussels on December 11, 1851, probably with the unstated tolerance of the authorities.

Hugo's nineteen-year absence from France, at first a necessity, later became a matter of principle, which conferred upon him the distinction of an exile of conscience. In comfortable circumstances, first in Jersey and, from 1855, in Guernsey, Hugo wrote great quantities of verse and prose, much of it concerned with social and political problems. His popularity as a writer continued to grow. Among the notable volumes of poetry in these years are *Les Châtiments* (1853), which includes satiric poems aimed at Louis-Napoleon, *La Légende des siècles* (1859-1883; *The Legend of the Centuries*, 1894), and a collection of earlier work, *Les Contemplations*, which earned for him enough money within months of its publication in April, 1856, to buy Hauteville House, where he surrounded himself with his family and admirers. Drouet lived within sight of the house, and by 1867 her relationship with Hugo was acknowledged even by Hugo's wife. Madame Hugo was to die in her husband's arms in Brussels the following year, during a family holiday.

Hugo's prodigious and best-known novel, *Les Misérables* (English translation, 1862), was published in 1861. It weaves together many of the themes of earlier books and manuscripts as well as historical and autobiographical elements from the author's youth. It is a singular novel both in Hugo's career and in the whole of European literature—a sprawling, twelve-hundred-page narrative that overcomes its liabilities by sheer energy. Hugo seeks to show no less than ". . . the advance from evil to good, from injustice to justice, from falsity to truth, from darkness to daylight, from blind appetite to conscience, from decay to life, from bestiality to duty, from Hell to Heaven, from limbo to God," and thus the book is in some fashion a religious book. *Les Misérables* is centered upon an account of the pursuit of a convict, Jean Valjean, by the detective Javert. Valjean, released on parole after nineteen years of imprisonment for a trivial crime, experiences a transformation of character that is repeatedly challenged both by his conscience and by Javert's detection. Within a vast framework of historical events and human affairs, the two principal characters are shown locked in a social and existential combat that remains compelling even for modern readers who are not conversant with the novel's political context.

Hugo's attention never wandered far from the political scene, and in 1870, as a prosperous Germany threatened war with a weakened France, Hugo determined to return to his homeland to aid it in its crisis. He arrived on September 5 to a tumultuous welcome, but by then the military situation was desperate. Paris was soon under full siege and the population was approaching starvation—Hugo himself was said to have been sent bear, deer, and antelope meat from the zoo at the Jardin des Plantes. In late January, 1871, an armistice was concluded and elections called for a National Assembly to make peace with the Germans and to debate the terms of defeat. Hugo ran successfully for the Assembly and traveled to Bordeaux to participate in it, but the rancorous events of the following months soon outpaced the capacities of a seventy-year-old man, and he returned first to Paris and then to Brussels, where, amid much public controversy, the Belgian government expelled him. After a few months in Luxembourg, he returned to Paris, where he was defeated in the elections of January, 1872.

From 1872 until his death in 1885, Hugo lived alternately in Guernsey and in Paris. His last years saw the completion of a major novel of the French Revolution, *Quatre-vingt-treize* (1874; *Ninety-three*, 1874), and the revival of several of his major theatrical works. *L'Art d'être grand-père* (1877), a book about Hugo's experiences with his two grandchildren, became a sentimental classic with the French public. During the Third Republic—the more liberal political regime which followed the turmoil of 1869-1872—Hugo came to be regarded as a patriarch, and the nation gave him almost limitless affection.

The beginning of Hugo's eightieth year was celebrated as a national holiday on February 26, 1881, with 600,000 admirers filing past the windows of his apartment on the Avenue Eylau, which was soon renamed Avenue Victor-Hugo. In late summer, he made up his will, in which he stated:

> God. The Soul. Responsibility. This threefold idea is sufficient for mankind. It has been sufficient for me. It is the true religion. I have lived in it. Truth, light, justice, conscience: it is God. . . . I leave forty thousand francs to the poor. And I wish to be taken to the cemetery in a pauper's hearse.

Hugo had suffered a very slight stroke three years earlier, but otherwise his health was remarkably good for a man of seventy-nine. During the next two years, he supervised the publication of the little of his work that remained unpublished, but his creative activity was at an end. Juliette Drouet, who for fifty years had been his devoted friend, died in May, 1883. Hugo lived on until May 22, 1885, when an attack of pneumonia claimed him at the age of eighty-three. His last words were "I see black light."

Summary

Victor Hugo had one of the broadest-ranging, most celebrated public careers of his time. He was a poet, dramatist, novelist, literary and social critic, journalist, politician, and social activist, and often pursued more than one of these roles at a time. Above all a man of feeling, Hugo turned from the ardent Royalism of his childhood and adolescence to an equally passionate Romanticism, in which his natural literary gifts reached their full potential. As a poet, he was a great musician of words, who brought increasingly refined ideas to his work. His legacy as a dramatist is not as great as in other literary forms, but he helped effect a transition from classicism to Romanticism, and he held contemporary audiences spellbound on more than one occasion.

The contributions made by Hugo to fiction were diverse and influential.

Some novels, such as *The Hunchback of Notre-Dame*, are notable for their descriptive power; others, such as the early *Le Dernier jour d'un condamné* (1829; *The Last Day of a Condemned*, 1840), combine adventurous narrative devices with a profound concern for social justice. *Les Misérables*, despite its unwieldy length, combines much of what is best in Hugo's craft and his philosophy, and after a century is still read as a living masterpiece. Other books, suffering perhaps from the miscalculation that can attend unbounded productivity, embody his poetic craft more than his sense of narrative substance.

In his life as well as in his work, Hugo was a spokesman for the common man against the power of the state; his long association with the political Left, however, was more a matter of human compassion than of social theory. He had experienced a range of political regimes, which made him a shrewd political observer, but increasingly he applied his genius to projects which transcended the affairs of his own historical epoch, creating an imaginative world of mythic dimensions.

Bibliography

Brombert, Victor. *Victor Hugo and the Visionary Novel*. Cambridge, Mass.: Harvard University Press, 1984. The author of this sophisticated, scholarly study of Hugo's novels became a dedicated "Hugolian" in 1940 as a teenager, during the German Occupation. His method of analysis is to combine the resources of modernist formal criticism with an "intricate network of aesthetic, social, political, psychological, and ethical preoccupations." Twenty-seven remarkable drawings by Hugo are reproduced.

Grant, Elliott M. *The Career of Victor Hugo*. Cambridge, Mass.: Harvard University Press, 1945. This scholarly but very readable book is principally a survey of Hugo's literary production, although it deals of necessity with the circumstances of his life.

Grant, Richard B. *The Perilous Quest: Image, Myth, and Prophecy in the Narratives of Victor Hugo*. Durham, N.C.: Duke University Press, 1968. The author, who is the son of Hugo scholar Elliott Grant, defines the essential motif of Hugo's narrative works as the myth of the heroic quest toward an ideal. Isolating his discussion as much as possible from biographical detail, he argues the view that the novels, the main plays, and narrative poems can be viewed as self-contained artistic unities.

Ionesco, Eugène. *Hugoliad: Or, The Grotesque and Tragic Life of Victor Hugo*. New York: Grove Press, 1987. This uncompleted work of Ionesco's youth—written in the 1930's in Romanian—is a sort of polemical antibiography, intended to dethrone its subject. The reader must take responsibility for separating fact from fiction, to say nothing of judging the aptness of the playwright's cheerless embellishments of anecdotal material. Postscript by Gelu Ionescu.

Maurois, André. *Olympio: The Life of Victor Hugo*. Translated by Gerard Hopkins. New York: Harper & Row, 1956. Originally published in French in 1954. This is probably as close an approach as possible to an ideal one-volume biography dealing with both the life and the work of a monumental figure such as Hugo. Of the sparse illustrations, several are superb; the bibliography, principally of sources in French, provides a sense of Hugo's celebrity and influence, which persisted well into the twentieth century.

_____. *Victor Hugo and His World*. London: Thames and Hudson, 1966. The 1956 English translation of Maurois' text noted above was edited to conform to the format of a series of illustrated books. The result is interesting and intelligible, but rather schematic. In compensation for the vast cuts in text, a chronology and dozens of well-annotated illustrations have been added.

Richardson, Joanna. *Victor Hugo*. London: Weidenfeld & Nicolson, 1976. Richardson's aim was to produce a comprehensive account of Hugo's life and work in the context of her specialty, the study of nineteenth century European culture. Her book is complementary to Maurois' account of Hugo and is somewhat more efficient as well as being agreeably less literary in style. There is an excellent biography and reproductions of several classic Hugo family photographs.

C. S. McConnell

ALEXANDER VON HUMBOLDT

Born: September 14, 1769; Schloss Tegel, near Berlin, Prussia
Died: May 6, 1859; Berlin, Prussia
Areas of Achievement: Geography, meteorology, and plant geography
Contribution: Humboldt, a native of Germany, undertook a famous four-year
  expedition to the Americas. The outcome of this expedition was the new
  sciences of geography, plant geography, and meteorology. Humboldt insisted on seeing a geographical site as a whole including climate, elevation, and distribution of plants, animals, and natural resources. He was
  one of the founders of modern science and scientific methods.

Early Life

The Humboldt family was, at the time of Alexander von Humboldt's birth,
not part of the ancient Prussian nobility. The title had only been in the family
a few generations. Alexander's father, Major Alexander George von Humboldt, had fought in the Seven Years' War in the Prussian army and later
became adjutant to the Duke of Braunschweig. Because he was not of the
ancient Prussian elite, Major Humboldt decided that his sons would not
become military men, but scientists and politicians.

Alexander was the younger of two brothers, both destined to become
famous scholars—albeit in different fields. His other brother, Wilhelm, was
early perceived to be the one with scholastic aptitude, whereas Alexander
did not seem very interested in academic pursuits. He liked nature and spent
much of his childhood in the parks surrounding his childhood home, Schloss
Tegel, near Berlin. He also showed early talent for map drawing and reading, and for drawing nature.

The two brothers were, from the earliest years, inseparable and would
remain so throughout their lives. They were only two years apart, and at
least one biographer claims that the strong bonding between them compensated for some degree of parental neglect—especially of Alexander because
of his perceived lack of talent.

Alexander read one of Georg Forster's works on the South Sea Islands
while he was still quite young, and a desire to see the tropics was born in
him. He fell in love with the dragon tree and dreamed of seeing one in real
life. He collected plants, insects, birds' eggs, and rocks.

The two brothers were initially taught at home by tutors, but eventually
Wilhelm went to university, and Alexander followed. The brothers studied at
the University of Frankfurt an der Oder and later at the University of Göttingen. While Wilhelm studied philology and philosophy, Alexander focused
his studies on mineralogy.

From his earliest years, Alexander had planned to undertake a major scientific journey. His studies and pursuits were all focused on this goal. In

1792, however, he was employed by the Prussian government as superintendent of mines. He worked in this capacity until 1797, gaining valuable experience. From 1797 to 1799, he prepared himself for his great journey.

Life's Work

While still a child, Humboldt met the towering spirit of his time, Johann Wolfgang von Goethe. Later, in 1797, he spent three full months in the company of the great poet and scientific theoretician. The exposure to Goethe and his ideas about nature and science became central to Humboldt. His life's work became the practical application of some of the key aspects of Goethe's theories: He saw the world as a *Naturganzes*, or natural whole. To the Romantic theory he added an emphasis on stringent empirical observation.

His theoretical and scientific baggage securely packed in his fine mind, Humboldt embarked from La Coruña in Spain on June 5, 1799, on his expedition to the Americas. His companion on the trip was the French botanist Aimé Bonpland. The two scientists had strong mutual respect and divided the work between them, Bonpland being primarily responsible for collecting and studying plants.

The expedition was to last four years, from 1799 to 1803. The first part was focused on the Orinoco River in Venezuela, where Humboldt first tested his holistic theory, or his "idea of the physical nature of the world." He was interested in correlating facts and observations rather than in individual facts. He studied the biology, geology, geophysics, archaeology, and meteorology of the areas through which he passed. The two companions traveled the entire length of the seventeen-hundred-mile-long Orinoco River on foot and by canoe. Interestingly, the hardships of this travel restored Humboldt's health. For his entire youth, he had been frail and sickly, and he emerged from his trip along the Orinoco River the very image of good health. Contemporaries describe him as a short, healthy-looking, robust, and powerfully built man.

The work describing the trip and Humboldt's findings did not appear until many years later. It was published in French, because the bulk of Humboldt's life after the trip was spent in Paris. The work was published in thirty-three volumes under the title *Voyage aux régions équinoctales du Nouveau Continent, fait en 1799, 1800, 1801, 1802, 1803, et 1804, par Al de Humboldt et A. Bonpland* (1805-1834; a historical description of the voyage to the tropical regions of the new continent made in 1799, 1800, 1801, 1802, 1803, and 1804, by Al. de Humboldt and A. Bonpland).

The eighteenth century was an age of grand voyages and explorations. Humboldt's expedition fits the pattern, but there was a difference: His voyage had infinitely more repercussions for the future of science than probably any other until Charles Darwin's famous voyage on the *Beagle* a half-

century later. Humboldt had a program. He firmly believed that nature embodied an overarching idea and that studying nature as a whole and overlooking no aspect, however apparently insignificant, would bring him closer
to an understanding of the idea. Humboldt believed that there is a unity to
the cosmos and to the world. He saw this not as a phylogenetic unity of evolution but as a Platonic, idealistic unity: He thought that for each type of
animal or plant there was a prototype. Another aspect of this unity is the so-
called compensation principle (also known as metamorphosis or transformation), which states that if an animal or plant is strongly developed in one
aspect, it will be lacking in some other aspect. Thus, if the giraffe has a long
neck, it must be less developed somewhere else. This type of thinking was
typical for Goethe and his followers. While the static, idealistic aspects of
Humboldt's theorizing have since been abandoned in favor of evolutionary
ones, the idea of studying environments as integrated wholes and the emphasis on empirical observation are central to modern geography and ecol-
ogy. Exactly those aspects of his work have earned for him the reputation as
a founder of modern geography.

Humboldt and Bonpland proceeded to Mexico, Peru, and Cuba to conduct
further studies. They not only continued their meticulous studies of eco-
systems wherever they went but also took the time to study indigenous
cultures, dabble in archaeology, and take a fresh look at the Spanish-
speaking societies of the New World. One witness who encountered them in
Quito, Ecuador, recounts that Humboldt, after a long day's work of studying
plants, minerals, and soil types, would spend most of the night gazing at the
stars.

Many rivers, mountains, and counties in the New World bear Humboldt's
name, and the entire expedition was a great success. He returned to Europe
in 1804, sailing from Philadelphia to Bordeaux. Humboldt lived in Paris,
working on his life's project. When the work was complete and his inheritance spent, he accepted a job as chamberlain of the Prussian court and lived
the rest of his life in Berlin. Yet he made one more substantial trip. At the
request of the Russian czar, he visited the Urals, the Altai, and parts of
China. The purpose of the trip was to give advice regarding the economic
exploitation of the areas covered on the trip. The scientific outcome of Humboldt's last major trip was meager compared to his trip to the Americas, but
it was a success in terms of its stated goals. Humboldt could indeed give
lucrative advice and make predictions with regard to the mineralogical composition of the Urals. Humboldt lived to the age of eighty-nine and worked
until the very end. He died on May 6, 1859, in Berlin.

Summary

Alexander von Humboldt represents the emergence of modern empirical
science. He was a child of his times in that his theoretical ideas about the

world were rooted in German Romanticism and in that he joined many of his contemporaries in exploring parts of the world that were comparatively new to Europeans. Yet he also broke the mold by combining his Romantic idealism with a hard-nosed empiricism that helped usher in the new age of technology and science.

Humboldt was amazingly eclectic. He studied plants, rocks, volcanoes, fauna, archaeology, and comparative religions, and he studied everything in minute detail. The thirty-three volumes that constitute Humboldt's testimony to future scientists contain not only a catalog of his physiognomic-typological primary forms of plants but also the painstakingly accurate descriptions of ecological systems that have made his scientific heirs name him the founder of not only geography but also the specialized field of plant geography and modern, systematic, and scientific meteorology.

Bibliography
Gendron, Val. *The Dragon Tree: A Life of Alexander, Baron von Humboldt.* New York: Longmans, Green, 1961. More than anything else a psychological portrait of Humboldt. The approach is Freudian and verges, from time to time, on hero-worship. Written entertainingly, with bits of dialogue between the protagonist and his friends and colleagues. Especially good description of Humboldt's early life and relationships to parents and brother.
Kellner, L. *Alexander von Humboldt.* New York: Oxford University Press, 1963. A solid, scholarly biography. Relates Humboldt's early life as it emerges from the record without Freudian or other interpretations. Excellent account of the two major expeditions and of their scientific import.
Klencke, W. *Alexander von Humboldt: A Biographical Monument.* London: Ingram, Cooke, 1852. Focuses on the role of the Humboldt brothers in the emergence of modern Germany. A political monument that contains a good description of Humboldt's early life and his education.
Meyer-Abich, Adolph. "Alexander von Humboldt and the Science of the Nineteenth Century." In *Biological Contributions: A Collection of Essays and Research Articles Dedicated to John Thomas Patterson on the Occasion of His Fiftieth Birthday.* Austin: University of Texas Press, 1959. A good exposition of eighteenth century scientific ideas and beliefs. Sets the intellectual stage for Humboldt's achievements, primarily by explaining Goethe's scientific views: the holism, the types, and the compensation principle. Explains Humboldt's law of plant geography, which states, among other things, that the same type of climate will foster the same types of flora and fauna. Gives a list of the nineteen plant types Humboldt established. Compares Humboldt's scientific theories to such later developments as mechanism and evolutionary theory.
_____. "Humboldt's Exploration in the American Tropics." *The*

Texas Quarterly 1 (1958). Brief but very full description of Humboldt's life and major expeditions. The focus is on exploring the nature of Humboldt's achievement. Outlines Humboldt's education and gives a good picture of the intellectual community to which he belonged.

Per Schelde

HUNG HSIU-CH'ÜAN

Born: January 1, 1814; Hua-hsien, Kwangtung, China
Died: June, 1864; Nanking, China
Areas of Achievement: Government, politics, and religion
Contribution: Hung created and led the first revolutionary movement to shake
the traditional Chinese political system. His movement, the T'ai-p'ing
Heavenly Kingdom, was a cataclysmic upheaval that greatly influenced
both Sun Yat-sen and Mao Tse-tung.

Early Life

Hung Hsiu-ch'üan was born in a small village thirty miles from Canton,
the great port of south China. He was the third son of a Hakka family,
clannish, hard-working peasants who spoke a distinct dialect and were often
discriminated against by the Han Chinese majority. He was later described as
tall with a fair complexion and large, bright eyes. For young Chinese men,
there was one sure way to climb in the ancient society: to pass the civil
service examinations used to assign positions in the bureaucracy. The examinations were based upon the Confucian classic texts and demanded profi-
ciency in the Chinese language with its tens of thousands of characters.
Students often had wealthy families who could support them, since study had
to begin early and usually did not culminate before a man's late twenties or
early thirties. Although poor, Hung had unusual intelligence; many of his
relatives, therefore, sacrificed to enable him to study. At the age of sixteen,
he had to quit studying and work on his father's farm. The villagers thought
so much of his talents that they hired him to teach their children, giving him
an opportunity for part-time study.

Despite Hung's intelligence and ambition, part-time study was not enough.
He repeatedly failed the first level of the examinations. In 1837, he collapsed
in nervous exhaustion and was bedridden for some time. In this state, he
had a series of religious visions combining traditional Chinese notions with
themes derived from Western Christianity.

Earlier, China had been strong and self-reliant and had repelled the repeated attempts of Western diplomats, businessmen, and missionaries to
gain entrance. Yet problems, above all overpopulation, mounted. China's
last dynasty, the Ch'ing (1644-1912), were Manchus, formerly a fierce warrior people. They had grown corrupt and incompetent and were unable to
stem China's accelerating decline. By the time Hung was born, many West-
erners were in China though their activities were closely regulated. Western
businessmen, primarily British, were selling increasing amounts of opium.
Great Britain hoped both to defray the costs of controlling India, where the
opium was grown, and to use opium profits to pay for British purchases of
Chinese teas and silks. The numbers of Western missionaries also increased

rapidly, and their access to Chinese society expanded.

The missionaries meant well and made a lasting contribution to Chinese society by improving education and social welfare; China, however, had never known a monotheistic religion, and the impact of Christian ideas upon the Chinese was unpredictable. Hung had cursorily examined some translations of missionary texts the year before his collapse. In his illness, Hung had visions that continued over some months. He believed that God was calling upon him to drive evil spirits and demons, represented by the Manchus, out of China.

Life's Work

Hung recovered and began to preach ideas that struck most listeners as very strange. It was a time of great turmoil, however, and friends and relatives began to listen to Hung; soon he was making converts. In 1844, he damaged local temples and drew the attention of the authorities, who strictly prohibited teachings outside the three religions of Taoism, Buddhism, and Confucianism. Hung and one of his first converts, Feng Yün-shan, left for the neighboring province, Kwangsi. Kwangsi was very poor and many of its inhabitants were racial minorities such as the Yao, Miao, and Chuang peoples. The Chuang were the most numerous Chinese minority and had often served as mercenaries in Chinese armies in the past. That winter, Hung went back to Kwangtung, leaving Feng, who had relatives among the numerous Hakka in Kwangsi, to stay and preach. In Kwangtung, Hung continued to preach and write, studying briefly in Canton with a noted American missionary, Issachar J. Roberts. In 1847, Hung returned to Kwangsi. Feng was a spellbinding speaker and had been very successful in winning converts, particularly among the Chuang and the Hakka.

China was in increasing turmoil. The Manchus had fought and decisively lost a war with Great Britain in 1840-1842. The ostensible cause of the war was the Chinese attempt to control the opium trade, but the real issue was foreign demands for greater freedom of action in China. The Opium War, as it was called, caused immense dislocation in south China. Kwangsi, already very poor, suffered from recurrent drought; banditry became widespread. Many peasants joined secret societies, traditional organizations that frequently became violently antigovernment. The authorities created local militia, which easily became tools of local despots.

Hung's congregations, known as the Society of God Worshipers, became embroiled in local conflicts, and the authorities attempted to suppress them. Yet the combination of Hung's messianic fervor and of Feng's mystical appeals was irresistible in troubled Kwangsi. In 1850, the Society of God Worshipers won a battle at Chin-t'ien village, attracting new converts as well as the cooperation of the secret societies and pirate bands eager for plunder. In 1851, his forces swollen with tens of thousands of new followers, Hung declared the "T'ai-p'ing T'ien-kuo" (the T'ai-p'ing Heavenly Kingdom) as both a new Chinese dynasty and a new holy order on earth. The group repelled government counterattacks and moved north, into the Yangtze River valley, China's populous economic center. Disaffected peasants flocked to Hung's banner. From 1851 to 1853, victory followed victory, and the T'ai-p'ing established their capital at Nanking, a major city on the Yangtze River. Yet the government in Peking rallied, led by a new generation of Han Chinese more willing to adopt Western weapons and techniques than the traditional Manchu leadership had been.

A major question was the attitude of the Western powers, who had won many privileges following the Opium War. They now had access to many Chinese ports and were gaining control of import and customs duties, making trade much easier. They were dubious of Hung's religious ideas, which were based upon only a small portion of the Bible, particularly upon the mystical Book of Revelation. Some thought him insane. A decisive issue in the minds of many foreigners was that Hung absolutely prohibited the opium trade. After considerable debate, the Western powers decided to maintain a public posture of neutrality, but they encouraged private assistance to the Manchu regime and gave necessary financial support. Foreign adventurers, such as the American Frederick Townsend Ward and the Englishman Major Charles George "Chinese" Gordon, formed units of Filipino and Western mercenaries, who fought for the government and trained Chinese soldiers.

Fighting was widespread and savage. Armies of hundreds of thousands marched and countermarched across central China. Prolonged sieges of large cities resulted in mass starvation. Enormous fleets clashed on China's many lakes and rivers. The peasants often found it impossible to farm, and famines resulted. It has been estimated that from 20 to 40 million Chinese died in these upheavals.

Feng died in battle in 1852, but Hung had many talented soldiers, some of whom were made "kings" in the T'ai-p'ing Heavenly Kingdom. The T'ai-p'ing could not, however, win over the Confucian bureaucracy, who were instrumental in governing local communities in China. The Confucians preferred the Manchus, who were a known quantity and themselves highly Confucian, to the alien ideas of the T'ai-p'ing, who held land in common and preached social leveling and the equality of the sexes.

In August of 1856, the T'ai-p'ing were split by a series of internal struggles in which several of the kings died. Other able generals arose, and the war seesawed; however, the T'ai-p'ing failed to deal with their internal problems. Without the help of the local Confucian gentry, they could not produce the necessary revenues to fight an increasingly modern war. The foreigners openly supported the government. In the late years of the T'ai-p'ing kingdom, Hung grew increasingly isolated and less and less realistic. He believed that God would ultimately protect the T'ai-p'ing Heavenly Kingdom, but the capital at Nanking fell on July 19, 1864. Hung had died in June, reportedly by his own hand.

Summary

Despite his ultimate failure, Hung Hsiu-ch'üan had great impact for a Chinese peasant. The odds against him were very great. In Chinese history, only one peasant had founded a new dynasty, and that had been more than five hundred years earlier. Hung's religious ideas inevitably were unconventional. He necessarily perceived Western Christianity through the veil of his own Chinese culture, which alienated contemporary Western observers. Some scholars have questioned his sanity.

As well as dreaming of a China divinely purified of the Manchus, Hung also dreamed of a China that would be a better place for common men and women, a strong China free of foreign influence, without opium, slavery, prostitution, and marked social inequality. His example influenced a later generation of revolutionaries, such as Sun Yat-sen, another Hakka peasant from Kwangtung, who helped to overthrow the Manchus, becoming the first President of Republican China in 1913. Hung also influenced the Communists led by Mao Tse-tung, who founded the People's Republic of China in 1949. The Chinese government and people revered Hung as the first Chinese revolutionary, a visionary who fought for a new and more equitable Chinese government.

Bibliography

Boardman, Eugene. *Christian Influence upon the Ideology of the Taiping Rebellion, 1851-1864*. Madison: University of Wisconsin Press, 1952. Many works on the T'ai-p'ing rebellion largely ignore Hung as an individual, but not Boardman's. This work brings together everything that is known about Hung and examines his beliefs in both the Chinese and Western Christian context of the period.

Hamberg, Theodore. *The Visions of Hung-Siu-tshuen, and Origin of the Kwangsi Insurrection*. San Francisco: Chinese Materials Center, 1975. This book was written during the T'ai-p'ing rebellion by a Western missionary who investigated Hung's background, particularly his exposure to Christian ideas, and his resulting religious beliefs.

Jen, Yu-wen. *The Taiping Revolutionary Movement*. New Haven, Conn.: Yale University Press, 1973. Most scholarly works on the T'ai-p'ing rebellion are primarily interested in the contemporary Chinese social scene or in the war or in T'ai-p'ing institutions. This work treats in detail the issue of Christian influences upon Hung's values and beliefs.

Kuhn, Philip A. "The Taiping Rebellion." In *The Cambridge History of China Late Ch'ing, 1800-1911*, edited by John K. Fairbank. Vol. 10, Cambridge: Cambridge University Press, 1978. Kuhn is one of the foremost historians of the rebellion, and this is an excellent introductory essay to it and to China during that period. Several other essays in the volume also relate to the rebellion. Contains a bibliographic guide to sources in Asian and Western languages.

Michael, Franz, and Chung-li Chang. *The Taiping Rebellion: History and Documents*. 3 vols. Seattle: University of Washington Press, 1966-1971. The first volume of this massive work is a narrative history of the rebellion. The final two volumes are translations of important documents. The work is considered a standard history for research purposes.

Teng, Ssu-yü. *The Taiping Rebellion and the Western Powers*. London: Oxford University Press, 1971. Teng is a leading historian in the field. This is an excellent study of the diplomatic context of the rebellion, particularly of the relations between the foreign powers and the Chinese court.

Jeffrey G. Barlow

CHRISTIAAN HUYGENS

Born: April 14, 1629; The Hague, the Netherlands
Died: July 8, 1695; The Hague, the Netherlands
Areas of Achievement: Physics, astronomy, invention, and technology
Contribution: Huygens was one of the greatest minds of the scientific revolution. His wave theory of light became highly influential in the nineteenth century. He invented the pendulum clock and discovered through his improved telescope the rings of Saturn.

Early Life

Christiaan Huygens was born in The Hague, in 1629. His father was Constantijn Huygens, a diplomat in Dutch government service and a poet who even today is better known in the Netherlands than his son. Constantijn was a Renaissance man who attracted many notables to his house, among them the philosopher René Descartes. Christiaan and his brother were, until the age of sixteen, tutored at home in Latin, Greek, and the classics. In fact, all the learning available at that time was offered to them.

Christiaan studied for two years (1645-1647) at the nearby University of Leiden, where the supporters of the Aristotelian view of science were battling with the followers of the new Cartesian approach. Young Huygens joined the discussions before transferring to the new University of Breda, where Cartesianism was unopposed and the views of the Scholastics were not to be found. Huygens, after two years of study at Breda, had absorbed all the mathematical and scientific learning then available. He then went home and devoted himself for several years to advancing the frontiers of mathematics. He proved, for example, that the catenary formed by a chain hanging from two points was not a parabola, as Galileo had asserted.

In 1655, Huygens made his first extended visit to Paris. France and England were the countries where the scientific revolution was centered. Huygens' greatest periods of achievement were to be spent in France, where his precocious publications on mathematics and his family connections afforded him entrée into the highest intellectual circles.

Huygens was good-looking, affable, well dressed, slightly effeminate, and, although he never married, he enjoyed the company of women. His health seems to have been delicate, and he had several periods of serious illness.

Life's Work

Huygens' first plunge into scientific research took place in 1655 and after, when he and his brother built improved telescopes, grinding their own lenses. With these instruments, the best made up to that time, Huygens found a satellite of Saturn, Titan, and discovered that Mars has a varied surface. He gradually discerned a ring around Saturn that nowhere touched the planet, thus improving on Galileo's more primitive observation. In order to protect the priority of this discovery while continuing his viewing, he announced by the publication of a coded message that he had found the ring.

Huygens continued his work in mathematics, which he had begun in the early 1650's with publications on hyperbolas, ellipses, and circles, and he published in 1657 the world's first formal treatise on probability.

Seeking greater scientific precision by the more accurate measurement of time, Huygens in 1656 built a pendulum clock, his greatest original invention, and with it he inaugurated modern, accurate timekeeping. Galileo had experimented with pendulums and with escapement mechanisms but had not actually constructed a clock. Huygens described the clock in his *Horologium* (1658), not to be confused with his later and greater *Horologium oscillatorium* (1673).

Huygens was preoccupied after 1660 with attempting to use his clock to solve the problem of determination of longitude at sea, as the Dutch, with the world's largest merchant fleet, were intensely interested in navigational advances. Latitude could easily be ascertained by quadrant or sextant, but calculating longitude required an extremely accurate time measurement. Huygens had great hopes for his pendulum mechanism, and his marine clocks were given extensive sea trials but proved an ultimate failure in determining longitude. Not until well into the eighteenth century was the problem actually solved by the invention of a superbly accurate spring-driven chronometer. In an attempt to subject space as well as time to greater quantitative precision, Huygens built a micrometer in 1658. With it he could establish, within a few seconds of arc, the position of a heavenly body.

In 1661, the year he joined the Royal Society, Huygens returned to Paris, where Louis XIV's chief minister, Jean-Baptiste Colbert, anxious to retain Huygens' services for the French, procured for the Dutchman a significant government grant for scientific work.

Scholars interested in science had been meeting in Paris for years in the salons, or drawing rooms, of wealthy and intellectual people. Finally the Crown wished to formalize such gatherings by founding the Académie Royale des Sciences in 1666. Huygens' scientific reputation was so formidable that he was made a charter member of the academy, given a regular salary larger than that of any other member, and handed the keys to an apartment in the Bibliothèque Royale. Thus, he commenced, in 1666, a period of residence in Paris lasting until 1681. Except for two extended visits home to The Hague, Huygens remained in Paris. Still, when Huygens left Paris in 1681 for a third trip to the Netherlands, he never returned. His patron Colbert died in 1683, and anti-Protestant sentiment was growing in France, making Huygens' position difficult, as he was nominally a Calvinist.

Huygens' philosophy of science was intermediate between those of the two giants of his day: René Descartes in France and Sir Isaac Newton in

England. Huygens grew up a Cartesian but broke with his mentor over the latter's extreme devotion to the mathematical, or deductive, approach to science. Descartes attempted to explain all phenomena by use of deductive logic alone. Newton, on the contrary, relied on observations and experiments as the bases for his laws.

Huygens' basic approach to the universe was mechanistic, an impact or billiard ball physics, in which he denied all action at a distance. He preferred Descartes' supposedly more tangible "vortices" of "subtle matter" to Newton's "gravity" in explaining the movements of heavenly bodies. Gravity worked unseen and over distance, moving bodies without apparently touching them. In the matter of relativity, however, Huygens was in advance of Newton. For Huygens, all motion in the universe was relative. Huygens in this regard was closer to the later work of Albert Einstein.

Huygens and Newton also differed over what constituted the nature of light. Newton considered light to be composed of particles or corpuscles emitted in steady streams from a light source; Huygens regarded the transmission of such particles through empty space to be mere Newtonian "action at a distance" again and incompatible with a mechanistic view of nature. Huygens propounded a wave theory of light, maintaining that a medium, an ether, must exist in space and that light is transmitted with a rapid but finite speed as shock waves in this medium. The ether, he believed, was composed of tiny, closely spaced, elastic particles, which vibrate and pass on the waves of light. Thus he did not view light itself as a substance as did Newton, nor did he consider it to be instantaneously transmitted as did Descartes.

Huygens remained in communication with Newton, although his relations with the Royal Society dwindled after 1678. Huygens visited England again in 1689, conversing with Newton and addressing the Royal Society on his non-Newtonian theory of gravity, a theory published the following year as *Discours de la cause de la pesanteur* (1690; discourse on the cause of gravity). Huygens' last years were spent in The Hague, where he died in 1695.

Summary

Christiaan Huygens would have been a great intellect in any age, but the magnitude of his brilliance was not as apparent as it might have been had he not been so close in space and time to such luminaries as Newton and Descartes. Nevertheless, his achievements were considerable.

As an astronomer he not only discovered the rings and a satellite of Saturn but also was the first to notice the nebula in the constellation Orion. In his work on centrifugal force, he was the first to theorize that Earth must be an oblate spheroid. He worked with microscopes as well as telescopes and translated some of the letters of the great pioneer microscopist Antoni von Leeuwenhoek. His work in mechanics of systems led him to invent the pendulum clock, the world's first truly accurate timepiece.

Huygens originated the wave theory of light and thereby established the science of physical optics, although the wave theory was not accepted in his own century or the next one as the fundamental explanation of the nature of light. In the seventeenth and eighteenth centuries, Newton's theory of the corpuscular or particulate nature of light held sway, but nineteenth century scientists focused on the diffraction of light, which can only be explained by wavelength. Thus the ether enjoyed a renewed popularity, and in the nineteenth century Huygens' theory was the prevailing view.

In the early twentieth century, the work of Albert Einstein and Max Planck led to a synthesizing of Newton's and Huygens' views into the quantum theory, in which both concepts were correct. Light today is considered indeed to have various wavelength properties, but it is also seen as moving in packets of energy called photons. A mathematical genius, Huygens improved on the work of Galileo in mechanics as well as astronomy, and he conferred and contested with the giants of his own generation. Always the pure scientist, he never dabbled in the metaphysical and was uninfluenced by religion—either the Calvinism of the Netherlands or the Catholicism of France. He died as he had lived, sure of only one thing: that there is in this universe no ultimate certainty.

Bibliography
Bell, Arthur E. *Christian Huygens and the Development of Science in the Seventeenth Century.* New York: Longmans, Green, 1947. This scholarly but quite readable volume has long been the standard biography of Huygens in the English language. Bell gives a thorough and interesting account of Huygens' life, his theoretical approach to science, and his actual scientific work.

Elzinga, Aant. *On a Research Program in Early Modern Physics.* New York: Humanities Press, 1972. This book was originally a doctoral dissertation, and it contains a lengthy chapter devoted to Huygens' theory of research and how Huygens broke with the system of his mentor, Descartes.

Huygens, Christiaan. *The Celestial Worlds Discovered: Or, Conjectures Concerning the Inhabitants, Plants, and Productions of the Worlds in the Planets.* London: Childe, 1698. Reprint. London: Cass, 1968. Short, nontechnical, and readable, this continually popular book gives excellent insight into Huygens' thinking. He was one of the first scientists to conjecture about life on other planets.

Struik, Dirk J. *The Land of Stevin and Huygens: A Sketch of Science and Technology in the Dutch Republic During the Golden Century.* Boston: D. Reidel, 1981. A short and illustrated volume, this book centers on Huygens as the Netherlands' chief claim to fame in the scientific revolution of the seventeenth century. Struik not only describes Huygens' scientific work but also shows how Huygens was influenced by technological demands and commercial pressures.

Yoder, Joella G. *Unrolling Time: Huygens and the Mathematization of Nature*. Cambridge, England: Cambridge University Press, 1988. This book describes how Huygens used mathematics to substantiate his mechanistic view of the universe. Huygens' discoveries, including his invention of the pendulum clock, are detailed, and their links to his mathematical universe are described.

Allan D. Charles